Medical Law and Ethics

Medical Law and Ethics

Seventh Edition

JONATHAN HERRING

Professor of Law

Exeter College, University of Oxford

OXFORD

UNIVERSITY PRESS

OXFORD

UNIVERSITY PRESS

Great Clarendon Street, Oxford, OX2 6DP,
United Kingdom

Oxford University Press is a department of the University of Oxford.
It furthers the University's objective of excellence in research, scholarship,
and education by publishing worldwide. Oxford is a registered trade mark of
Oxford University Press in the UK and in certain other countries

Fourth edition 2012
Fifth edition 2014
Sixth edition 2016

Impression: 2

Public sector information reproduced under Open Government Licence v3.0
(http://www.nationalarchives.gov.uk/doc/open-government-licence/open-government-licence.htm)

Published in the United States of America by Oxford University Press
198 Madison Avenue, New York, NY 10016, United States of America

British Library Cataloguing in Publication Data
Data available

Library of Congress Control Number: 2018936018

ISBN 978-0-19-881060-5

Printed in Great Britain by
Bell & Bain Ltd., Glasgow

To Mog

Preface

This book is designed to provide readers with coverage not only of medical law, but also of the context, philosophical, social, and political, within which the law operates. It attempts to take the 'ethics' part of a Medical Law and Ethics course as seriously as the 'law' part. Although there is therefore extensive reference to legal material, there is also substantial reference to writings from non-legal perspectives. In this regard, I am all too aware that I have been able to present, in some cases, only the merest outline of a rich vein of material from non-legal disciplines. It would be absurd in a book of this length to suggest that the reader can be provided with an in-depth guide to all that philosophers, sociologists, or theologians, for example, might have to say about medicine. I hope, however, that I have provided enough to excite the interest of the reader and at least to indicate the variety of perspectives from which it is possible to view the subject. There is ample further reading listed, both at the end of chapters and in the bibliography, for readers to undertake their own studies.

With the use of various boxes in some chapters, I have sought to highlight feminist and theological perspectives on particular questions. Readers of the book have complained that this either gives undue prominence to these perspectives or sidelines them. I intend neither, but merely to break up the text and to provide space in which readers can think about what might, or might not, be an interesting viewpoint. It need hardly be said that feminist perspectives are represented throughout the text and are not limited to points made in these boxes.

I have been fortunate to have the support of many colleagues and friends during the writing of this book: Cressida Auckland, Alan Bogg, Shazia Choudhry, Charles Foster, Stephen Gilmore, Kate Greasley, Imogen Goold, George P. Smith, Rachel Taylor, and Jesse Wall, to mention just a few. John Carroll at Oxford University Press has been an encouraging and supportive editor, and Paul Nash has done a wonderful job on the copy-editing. I am grateful to Jacky Cheng for comments on the book. Above all, I am thankful to my family: to my children, Laurel, Joanna, and Darcy, who entertained me greatly when I was not writing, and who forcefully encouraged me to get to my computer and not bother them whenever there was something more fun to do; and to my wife Kirsten, whose love and care are boundless.

Jonathan Herring
Oxford
October 2017

Guide to the Book

Medical law is a highly topical and often contentious aspect of the law with many interest groups voicing differing opinions on the legal provisions and regulation. Use the following features which appear throughout this book to get to grips with the broad spectrum of opinion and understand some of the key debates and tensions.

Key case features provide the key facts of the most important cases providing relevant case extracts from the judgment so that you can understand how the laws translate into judgments and understand the development of the law.

KEY CASE *R v Cambridge Health Authorit*

B was a 10-year-old girl with leukaemia. A bone was unsuccessful. Doctors in London and Cambri to live and that any further treatment would be i this assessment, and found a professor in London offered the girl further treatment. The professor a possible second transplant was experimental an

European angles outline the EU legislation, regulations, and perspectives on key topics which are so important in light of the significant weighting of Europe on UK medical law policies.

EUROPEAN ANGLES

Article 5

Article 5 ECHR states that:

Everyone has the right to liberty and security of person. No liberty save in the following cases and in accordance with a p

But this is subject to a number of exceptions. The relevant one

Feminist perspectives highlight some of the many opinions within the umbrella term of 'feminists', particularly in the area of reproductive medicines and technology which evoke great debate and interest. Look out for these boxes to gain an understanding of the concerns and opinions from feminist viewpoints.

FEMINIST PERSPECTIVES

Consent

Feminist writers on consent have tended to fall into one of thre nists see strengths in all three positions.[408]

(i)   There are those who greatly welcome the emphasis on a past, women were too easily seen as subject to the pate Women were regarded as incapable of making decisions f were needed to make decisions for them. Autonomy

A view from above boxes reflect the beliefs from some of the different religious groups on the contentious aspects, particularly on topics such as euthanasia and abortion.

A VIEW FROM ABOVE

Religious views on contraception

Many religions have no objection to contraception. The mos from the Roman Catholic Church, which has consistently opp of contraception. Pope Paul VI explained:

God has wisely disposed natural laws and rhythms of fecundit a separation in the succession of births . . . [This teaching] i

Reality check boxes provide the most up-to-date official statistics alerting you to the reality and context of the situations law seeks to regulate. Use these to add weight to your arguments!

REALITY CHECK

Confidentiality in practice

As we have seen, in theory, the law takes breaches of confident confidentiality protected in real life?

According to David Stone, 'many observers would say that, duties arising from patient confidentiality are honoured more vance'.[67] As he points out, such a large number of people will they cannot realistically be described as private. One write

Public opinion boxes present survey and opinion poll results to illustrate the differing opinions of the public. Don't forget it isn't only established interest groups which have opinions on medical law, medical law is a topic which can evoke strong beliefs in the general public too.

PUBLIC OPINION

In a later poll, MORI (2011) 70 per cent of people questioned to choose about abortion free from government interference cent disagreed and 23 per cent agreed with the suggestion th to obtain an abortion; 53 per cent agreed that 'a woman shou pregnancy if she wants an abortion'. A poll in 2013 found th began at conception and 17 per cent believed it began at b 8 per cent said they did not know when life began. Althou

A shock to the system features expose some interesting aspects of medical law and the provision of health care, many of which you may not know about. Look out for these boxes to discover an eye-opening account of issues in medical law.

A SHOCK TO THE SYSTEM

It is easy, in discussions of healthcare policy, to forget the indi following quote from Valerie Tugwell, aged 72, who was largely that the number of baths given to her on social care had to be r

I feel unclean half the time. I felt deprived when social serv to one bath a week in 2004—deprived of feeling like a norn I had to stop having the one bath a week I have now becau

To ponder boxes pose interesting topics for debate allowing you to consider your opinions and reflect upon the existing legal provisions.

TO PONDER

There are three patients in your care. There is only enough them. Which will you fund?

(i) Alf is a newborn. He has a serious disability and needs in likelihood of him surviving into his 20s is moderate, and iously disabled. Without the treatment, he will die.

(ii) Steve is a student who is suffering serious liver failure many years. A liver transplant and further treatment

Online Resources

Remember to use the accompanying online resources at **www.oup.com/uk/ herringmedical7e/** where the following resources can be found.

- A complete bibliography

- An introductory video from the author

- Useful web links

- Links to key cases

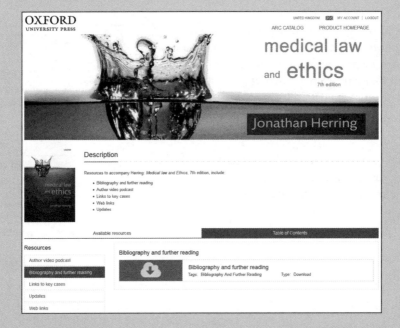

Outline Contents

Detailed Contents

Table of Cases

Key Case entries are identified with **bold** page references. Definite (The) or indefinite (A or An) articles at the start of case names are ignored in the alphabetical ordering e.g. A Local Authority *see* Local Authority (A).

Table of Statutes

Provisions cited in whole or in part are identified with **bold** page references.

Table of Statutory Instruments

Table of European and International Legislation

Provisions cited in whole or in part are identified with **bold** page references.

1   Ethics and Medical Law

INTRODUCTION

Medical law is being transformed. Rapid scientific advances mean that lawyers and ethicists are constantly required to face new issues. More significantly, our attitude towards our health, health services, and the medical professions is changing dramatically.[1] There was a time when doctors were given a 'godlike' status and were held in the highest of esteem, and patients were intended to be—well—patient: passive and submissive. The following exchange exemplifies this well:

> DOCTOR: [reading case notes] Ah, I see you've a boy and a girl.
> PATIENT: No, two girls.
> DOCTOR: Really, are you sure? Thought it said. . . [checks in case notes] Oh no, you're quite right, two girls.[2]

Nowadays doctors are not regarded as infallible and beyond questioning. Medical professionals understand their job to be working *with* patients to find out what is the best treatment for them. Hence it is common to see talk of 'shared decision making' between doctors and patients.[3] The doctor–patient relationship has, according to some, become closer to that between consumer and supplier. As Lords Kerr and Reid put it *Montgomery v Lanarkshire Health Board*:[4]

> patients are now widely regarded as persons holding rights, rather than as the passive recipients of the care of the medical profession. They are also widely treated as consumers exercising choices.

A rather different challenge to the status of doctors is that patients have ready access to healthcare information, via the Internet especially.[5] Kits to test yourself for illnesses at home, and even to discover information about your genetics, are readily available.[6] I am sure I am not alone in checking what my doctor says against information available online. All of these changes have, as we shall see, had a significant impact on legal and ethical approaches to medicine.

1   What is medical law?

A Secretary of State for Health once said: 'The only place for a lawyer in the NHS [National Health Service] is on the operating table.'[7] This is wishful thinking. If medicine was practised without any legal regulation, history suggests that many wrongs would

---

[1] Chadwick (2016).   [2] Oakley (1980: 41).   [3] Health Foundation (2013).
[4] [2015] UKSC 11, para. 75.   [5] Glover-Thomas and Fanning (2010).
[6] See Tamir (2010), for a discussion of the ethical issues raised by such self-diagnostic kits.
[7] Frank Dobson, quoted in Brazier and Glover (2000: 17).

be committed.[8] Medical law is at worst a necessary evil. However, the definition of medical law as an academic discipline has proved controversial. One view is that medical law is 'essentially concerned with the relationship between health care professionals (particularly doctors and to a lesser extent hospitals or other institutions) and patients'.[9]

Others have regarded this definition as too narrow: first, it places doctors at the fore, neglecting the role of other healthcare professionals; second, by focusing on the doctor–patient relationship, it does not attach sufficient weight to issues surrounding the provision of healthcare services, such as rationing, structural issues within the NHS, or issues concerning public health.[10] And what about the crucial role played by those caring for relatives and friends at home?[11] As these examples show, there is no natural point at which to draw the boundaries between what is, and what is not, medical law. Those sympathetic to these points sometimes prefer to talk of 'healthcare law', rather than medical law. Using that label indicates that the subject under discussion is broader than the doctor–patient relationship, and covers all areas in which law and health intersect. Although this book does look at these broader issues, it uses the term 'medical law' because that is still what the subject is most popularly called.

Medical law is made up of bits from a large number of different branches of law: criminal law; human rights law; tort law; contract law; property law; family law; and public law. One commentator has suggested that a medical lawyer needs to be a 'Jacqui of all trades'.[12] Another commentator has called medical law 'an academic version of the cuckoo'.[13] Indeed, until fairly recently, medical law was not really studied as a subject in its own right. However, it is now widely acknowledged as its own area of legal study, with an extensive range of journals, textbooks, and conferences. Despite its acceptance, there is still some unease amongst medical lawyers over what the subject includes and how medical law is distinct from other areas of law. Kenneth Veitch has claimed that academic medical lawyers have struggled to find a niche for medical law and to grant it expertise over the resolution of issues within the subject.[14] It's not just medical lawyers who are feeling insecure. There seems to be a 'crisis' among medical ethicists, with one leading commentator writing of the 'the death of bioethics'.[15] Julian Savulescu,[16] one of the world's leading bioethicists, has a damning critique of the current state of the field:

> Now medical ethics is more like a religion, with positions based on faith not argument, and imperiously imposed in a simple-minded way, often by committees or groups of people with no training in ethics, or even an understanding of the nature of ethics ... the field has in many ways dried up or become dominated by moralists bent on protecting privacy and confidentiality at great cost and 'getting consent', and in other ways 'protecting basic human rights and dignity'. Medical ethics isn't sufficiently philosophical, and when it is philosophical, it's the bad arguments or a narrow range of arguments that often seem to make a difference.

Perhaps you can understand why Ruth Macklin has expressed concern that bioethicists are becoming increasingly rude to each other![17]

---

[8] Consider, for example, the Harold Shipman case, discussed in Chapter 9.
[9] Kennedy and Grubb (2000: 5).   [10] Coggon (2012b).   [11] Herring (2007a).
[12] Sheldon and Thomson (1998: 5).   [13] Wicks (2007: 1).   [14] Veitch (2007: 3).
[15] Macklin (2010). See Wilson (2014) for a fascinating study of the history of bioethics in Britain.
[16] Savulescu (2015a).   [17] Macklin (2010).

Perhaps one problem is that with competing strongly held views it can be difficult for parties to understand each other's perspective. There is a particular difficulty in communication between those coming from a religious perspective and those not. Is there a danger that because people are coming from such different starting points that dialogue is impossible? Another concern is that commercialization is infecting ethical discussions.[18] The idea that people might be bought off when expressing their ethical beliefs is somewhat ironic!

The relationship between law and medicine is interesting. In the past, it was characterized as one of mutual deference. Medical decisions were regarded as clinical matters best reached by the medically trained experts and anyone seeking to challenge a doctor's decision in the courts faced an uphill struggle. However, more recently, the relationship has changed. Courts, it seems, are a little more willing to accept challenges to medical expertise. No longer will courts uphold a practice as lawful, simply because something is accepted medical practice.[19]

Scandals, such as those involving the Mid-Staffordshire Hospital (where there were between 400 and 1,200 excess deaths between 2005 and 2008)[20] and countless reports of abuse of older people in healthcare settings,[21] have further damaged the profession's reputation. All of this has meant that doctors are no longer on the pedestal that once they were. Patients now have rights. This is reflected in the jargon used within the NHS, where services are to be 'patient-led', and in the NHS Constitution, which lists the rights patients have.[22]

2 The link between law and ethics

The connection between medical law and medical ethics is revealing.[23] It might be thought that the two would be closely connected. After all, the courts would be unlikely to make an order that required a healthcare professional to act in a way that was unethical. But that is to overlook several points. One is that something may be unethical, but not illegal. To be discourteous to a patient may be unethical, but it would not necessarily be illegal. The law sets down minimally acceptable standards, while ethical approaches may include deciding what would be the ideal way for a person to behave. Similarly, something may give rise to a legal sanction, but not be unethical. For example, according to section 44(1) of the Modern Slavery Act 2015 a doctor is required to report to the relevant authorities any incidents of people trafficking. In rare cases it may be that a doctor believes that to do so would be contrary to the best interests of a patient and so unethical, but the legal obligation would still arise.[24]

Nevertheless, the courts have been willing to accept that ethical issues can play an important role in deciding how the court will reach a decision. Hoffmann LJ, in a case concerning the treatment of a patient suffering from persistent vegetative state, stated:

> This is not an area [in] which any difference can be allowed to exist between what is legal and what is morally right. The decision of the court should be able to carry conviction with the ordinary person as being based not merely on legal precedent but also upon acceptable ethical values.[25]

---

[18] Sherwin (2011).   [19] Foster and Miola (2015).   [20] Dyer (2011).   [21] Herring (2012a).
[22] NHS (2010b).   [23] See the stimulating discussions in Miola (2007) and Brownsword (2008a).
[24] Jackson (2015).   [25] *Airedale NHS Trust v Bland* [1993] 1 All ER 821, 850.

However, this has proved difficult for the courts. In that same case in the House of Lords, Lord Browne-Wilkinson questioned whether complex moral issues would be better resolved in Parliament rather than in the courts.[26] In *Re A (Children) (Conjoined Twins: Surgical Separation)*,[27] a case concerning the separation of conjoined twins, Ward LJ stated:

> In this case the right answer is not at all as easy to find. I freely confess to having found it exceptionally difficult to decide—difficult because of the scale of the tragedy for the parents and the twins, difficult for the seemingly irreconcilable conflicts of moral and ethical values and difficult because the search for settled legal principle has been especially arduous and conducted under real pressure of time.

It is interesting to note the way in which, in some cases, the ethical issues have come to dominate the courts' reasoning;[28] in others (while potentially raising moral issues), the issues have been dealt with on a more traditional legal basis using principles of statutory interpretation or precedent.[29] It is also interesting to note the way that the courts attach weight not only to views of Parliament but also professional bodies and governing agencies (such as the Human Fertilisation and Embryology Authority and NHS Trusts) in their decision making.[30]

There is another point to emphasize: the law must be based on rules that are sufficiently clear that they can provide guidance to medical professionals and are capable of being susceptible to proof.[31] That means that the law sometimes needs to be somewhat cruder than a sophisticated ethical analysis might be able to provide. A twenty-page treatise might provide a careful consideration of all of the appropriate ethical values; it cannot guide a doctor needing to deal with an emergency.

3 The nature of illness

It is surprisingly difficult to define 'illness' or 'disease'.[32] Perhaps the most insightful comment comes from Anthelme Brillat-Savarin, a French writer, who, when asked 'What is health?', replied: 'It is chocolate!'[33] More seriously, many definitions of ill-health care are too broad. Consider the following suggestion in one medical textbook: 'Disease is any disturbance of the structure or function of the body or any of its parts; an imbalance between the individual and his environment; a lack of perfect health.'[34] The problem with this is that it would include as a disease clipping toenails or being tied to a chair.

The difficulty is in finding a definition that is not overly broad, or too narrow, or too vague. Perhaps the problem lies in society itself. We ourselves do not agree about what disease is. Are baldness or infertility or hypochondria diseases? Is penile dysfunction or

---

[26] [1993] 1 All ER 821, 878.   [27] [2001] Fam 147, 151.

[28] See, e.g., *Gillick v West Norfolk and Wisbech Area Health Authority* [1985] 3 All ER 402.

[29] See, e.g., *R (Quintavalle on behalf of Pro-Life Alliance) v Secretary of State for Health* [2003] UKHL 13. See Dawson (2010) and Montgomery (2006) for a further discussion of this.

[30] Montgomery, Jones, and Biggs (2014).   [31] Foster, Herring, Melham, and Hope (2013).

[32] De Campos (2017).

[33] To be more accurate, he was asked, 'Qu'est-ce que la santé?' and he replied 'C'est du chocolat!' (quoted in Lang and Delpierre 2009: 212).

[34] Peery and Miller (1971: 18).

premature ejaculation medical conditions for which drugs should be made available?[35] Is cosmetic surgery a medical treatment or a lifestyle decision? If a person eats very little and becomes thin, he or she is labelled anorexic and presumed to lack mental capacity; if a person eats a lot and becomes obese, many people regard that as a moral failing.[36] Someone who is considered unattractive may suffer disadvantages as a result of their body, does that make ugliness an illness?[37] As these examples show, the interplay between societal expectations, moral values, and illness is complex.[38]

A common view is that ill-health is a departure from what is 'normal' for a human being.[39] But such an approach is based on an assumption of what is normal. Biology does not give us a clear answer to what is normal.[40] Robin Mackenzie has argued that:

> Medical conceptions of normal health have shifted from a statistical mean of characteristics and capacities to an elevated, more ideal level of health, attainable for most of us only through taxing regimens of discipline and self-denial. Anything lesser, although statistically more representative, becomes pathologised as ill health.[41]

It is clear, then, that social factors change what is perceived as an illness. Homosexuality was regarded as a psychological illness by the American Psychiatric Association until 1973,[42] and only in recent times have dyslexia and myalgic encephalomyelitis (ME) been widely accepted as medical conditions.

Anyone seeking to come up with a definition of disease or ill-health would need to consider the following issues.

3.1 Does the notion of a disease carry a judgement that the condition is undesirable?

When we use the word 'disease', do we include within it an assessment that the condition is one that people would rather not have, or is it a neutral condition?[43] For example, would it be wrong to refer to double-jointedness as a disease because it is not normally regarded as a bad thing to be double-jointed? Or is 'disease' to be used as simply a word to indicate that someone has a condition that is not 'normal' for humans, without any connotation that the condition is undesirable? But, if this were the case, would we be committed to saying that the body of a well-trained athlete is diseased because it is abnormal? Although most people would think that the natural meaning of 'disease' is that the condition is undesirable, to take that view renders defining disease much more problematic because there is little agreement within society about what conditions are undesirable.

3.2 The 'disability debate'

Traditionally, a disability has been seen in terms of a physical disadvantage that a person has—but that definition has come under challenge. The Union of Physically Impaired People against Segregation has stated: 'In our view it is society which disables physically

---

[35] Söderfeldt et al. (2017). [36] Giordano (2008). [37] Minerva (2017).
[38] Rogers and Walker (2017) [39] Daniels (2007). [40] Matthewson and Griffiths (2017).
[41] Mackenzie (2008: 131). [42] Hart and Wellings (2002).
[43] The issue is considered in depth in Fulford (2001).

impaired people. Disability is something imposed on top of our impairments by the way we are unnecessarily isolated and excluded from full participation in society.'[44] Under this 'social model' of disability, it is the social environment, rather than the individual, which causes the disability. If only society were differently ordered and made appropriate provision, then things that we currently call 'disabilities' would cease to be so. Therefore, a wheelchair user is disadvantaged only if society fails to provide appropriate facilities to enable his or her access to anywhere.

The social model of disability has been subject to a challenge from Tom Shakespeare, who himself has restricted growth.[45] He argues that, for disabled people, the fact of impairment is an important aspect of their lives. The social model shifts the focus of attention away from the disabled person and onto the provision of services that a society can offer. The disadvantage of this is that the experience of disabled people and of their bodies is ignored. Further, he argues, the social model ignores the fact that there are some disabilities that cannot be entirely explained by social barriers, such as severe learning disabilities. Also, the focus on social barriers downplays the importance of medical interventions on the body of the disabled person that can provide significant practical benefit. The social model may even mean that less weight is placed on seeking a cure for the disability. He certainly does not discount the social model altogether, but sees the need to emphasize both the role of the body and society in disability. Hence he defines disability 'as the outcome of the interaction between individual and contextual factors'.[46]

The concept of disability may also be challenged by questioning whether the 'able-bodied' are as 'able' as they like to think. I have argued that:

> It is recognising that we in our nature vulnerable; that caring relationships are core to our being human; and that we need each other; that we might begin to find true health. We must never seek to hide from or be embarrassed by our precarious, leaky, interdependent bodies. True health is found not in the scalpel of the surgeon or the pill of the pharmacist; but in the touch of a lover; the smile of a child; and the wind in the hair.[47]

The World Health Organization has suggested that we see 'disability as a continuum rather than categorizing people with disabilities as a separate group: disability is a matter of more or less, not yes or no'.[48] While this approach has the advantage of not stigmatizing certain people as 'disabled' it might be thought to hinder political and social programmers which are designed to help people who are particularly disabled. Particular disabled people report discrimination, disadvantage, and mistreatment. Saying 'we are all disabled' might not assist in remedying the lived reality for disabled people.[49]

Another issue in the disability debate is whether being disabled should be seen as a disadvantage or whether it is simply being different. Being on the autism spectrum might be a good example.[50] It is highly debatable whether being on the spectrum is a disadvantage as such, or whether it is simply a difference.[51] While the argument seems plausible with that example, you might think some disability which severely impairs

---

[44] Quoted in Fulcher and Scott (2003: 288).
[45] Shakespeare (2006). For a critique of his views, see Thomas (2008).
[46] Shakespeare (2006: 58). See further Scully (2017); Mackenzie (2008) and Silvers (2009) for an excellent discussion of feminist approaches to disability.
[47] Herring (2017).   [48] WHO (2011).   [49] Martiny (2015).   [50] Ripamonti (2017).
[51] Bognar (2016).

functioning and causes high levels of pain, cannot be described as a mere difference. The issue is particularly important when it comes to asking whether medicine should seek to 'cure' the disability. That seems questionable if we are merely talking about a difference, but if it is seen as a disadvantage then it is appropriate. Even if a bodily state causes a disadvantage does not mean it should be remedied. Being of a certain race or gender in many societies will result in disadvantage. That does not mean medicine should seek to change someone's race or gender.[52]

3.3 The mind/body debate

The cause of some illness and treatments is unknown. Some people claim that certain illnesses are 'all in the head'.[53] Although this is often a comment made by those ignorant about a particular condition (for example ME, also known as 'chronic fatigue syndrome'), there can be an element of truth to it. As Kay Toombs has pointed out, when a person is diagnosed with a terminal condition, his or her life is changed forever.[54] Even if there are no noticeable symptoms present, the person's body comes to be regarded by them as diseased, meaning that the person's attitude to his or her body completely changes. Indeed, it is becoming increasingly controversial to separate out the mind and the body.

3.4 Is health a negative or positive concept?

The World Health Organization (WHO) has described health as 'a state of complete physical, mental and social well-being and not merely the absence of disease and infirmity'.[55] Crucially, this defines health in a way that is more than the absence of illness, but in a positive way that involves well-being.[56] To many, this is too broad a definition. To expect medicine to limit pain is a tall order; to expect it to make people happy is an unattainable goal. To others, being healthy involves an acknowledgement that it is natural that our bodies change and are dependent on others. Charles Foster and I have written:

> The top five NHS tips for health are: sleep more; drink milk; eat more fruit and vegetables; try new activities and eat a hearty breakfast (ideally porridge). How sad. You cannot hug yourself. A lithe body can encase a dreary, sad soul. Health involves accepting our vulnerability and our changing bodies—bodies that are exhilaratingly different from other bodies, yet interact meaningfully with them.[57]

4 The scope of medicine

Thana de Campos[58] has expressed concern that the concept of health has merged into the concept of well-being. She is concerned that if health is defined as having a contented, happy, fulfilled life, then a claim to a right to health becomes meaningless. If we want to separate out claims that relate to basic health needs (e.g. treatment for serious illness)

---

[52] Akhtar (2016).   [53] For a useful discussion of this, see Cooper (2002).   [54] Toombs (1999).
[55] Scully (2004: 31).   [56] Scambler (2009c).   [57] Foster and Herring (2013: 241).
[58] De Campos (2016 and 2017).

from claims that relate to pleasures (e.g. free Wi-Fi), we need to find a way of separating health claims from welfare needs. But this raises the question of whether our 'health needs' are special and that governments have a stronger obligation to meet health care needs, than other needs we might have.[59]

This leads us to a wider debate on what health care should be aiming to do.[60] Indeed, it is unclear what ultimate ideal medicine is striving to achieve.[61] Is it a life without illness or death? Would that be a life that we would want? Philosophers have debated long and hard whether life without death would make us happier or not.[62]

If the promotion of health is the main goal of medicine, it is clear that it has a fairly small role in achieving that goal:

> The best estimates are that health services affect about 10 per cent of the usual indices for measuring health . . . the remaining 90 per cent are determined by factors over which doctors have little or no control: individual life-style, social conditions and physical environment.[63]

Alan Cribb has written of the 'diffusion of the health agenda', with notions of the proper scope of 'medicine' expanding and becoming complex.[64] Issues such as obesity, stress, or behaviour problems in children are now regarded as medical issues, while in the past they would not have been seen as something with which doctors or the NHS should be concerned.[65] Defining the scope of medicine raises a number of issues:

4.1 **Prevention**

One issue is whether medicine should be regarded as simply about dealing with illness, or whether it should extend to preventing illness. From the point of view of the NHS, vast sums of money could be saved if the public were to take greater care of its health, and of course most patients would rather take steps to avoid falling ill than deal with illness once it has arisen. Indeed, it might be thought difficult to object to health promotion.[66] However, concern has been expressed at the way in which matters that might normally be regarded as private (for example individuals' diets, amount of exercise, and alcohol consumption) are regarded as 'health issues', and can then become transformed into public issues.[67] Is it any of a doctor's business what a patient's eating or sexual habits are? Or does the fact that, in England, health care is paid for through general taxation mean that an individual's health is not a matter of concern only to that individual?[68] This leads to an ever larger question: do we have a responsibility as citizens to do what we can to keep in good health?[69] The difficulty is that good health depends on the quality of access to good healthcare, income, housing, and the environment.[70]

4.2 **Non-diseases**

One concern that is expressed by the medical profession and its critics is that an ever-increasing range of problems are being regarded as requiring medical treatment. General

---

[59] Rumbold (2016).   [60] Gostin (2008).   [61] Greaves (2002)   [62] See, e.g., Denier (2008).
[63] Hunter (1997: 18).   [64] Cribb (2005: ch. 1).   [65] Evve, Nielsen Martin, and Anderson (2014).
[66] Daniels (2007), although see Schramme (2009) for a critical discussion of the significance of opportunities for health.
[67] Miles (1991: 183).   [68] Brazier (2006a).   [69] Ahola-Launonen (2015).   [70] Wilson (2009).

practitioners (GPs) complain that their assistance is being sought by patients for a range of non-diseases. The *British Medical Journal* carried out a survey to find which were the most common 'non-diseases', which resulted in the following 'top twenty':

(1) Ageing

(2) Work

(3) Boredom

(4) Bags under eyes

(5) Ignorance

(6) Baldness

(7) Freckles

(8) Big ears

(9) Grey or white hair

(10) Ugliness

(11) Childbirth

(12) Allergy to the twenty-first century

(13) Jet lag

(14) Unhappiness

(15) Cellulite

(16) Hangover

(17) Anxiety about penis size/penis envy

(18) Pregnancy

(19) Road rage

(20) Loneliness

Another recent report found that GPs had been asked for advice on issues including how to deal with sore feet after dancing in high shoes; what to do if your nipple is too hairy; and how to overcome an addiction to crisps.[71]

But perhaps we are wrong to be critical about those who see their doctors about these 'non-diseases'. One way of looking at these instances is to argue that doctors are failing to deal with the kinds of issues that are really troubling people and are focusing on too narrow an understanding of medicine. Perhaps disease is understood and experienced differently by the medical profession and by a patient?[72] Or does our society need to create a new profession to deal with these 'non-medical worries'?[73] Or do people simply need to pull themselves together?

Claims of 'over-medicalization' are also made against the pharmaceutical industry.[74] An argument is sometimes made that drugs firms are particularly keen to promote the recognition of certain conditions as diseases because this will lead to a greater market for

---

[71] Cooper (2015).   [72] Toombs (1999).

[73] Of course, alternative medicine would seek to deal with patients 'in the round', although its effectiveness is disputed: see, e.g., the discussion of homeopathy in Smith (2010).

[74] Welch, Schwartz, and Woloshin (2011).

their products.[75] One example might be the use of the drug Paxil, which is said to 'cure shyness'. Supporters may reply that if medicine can improve the lives of the shy, those with anxiety about penis size, and so forth, why should it not do so? Whether or not these are diseases is an interesting intellectual question, but if 'treatment' is available, why should doctors not provide it?

Indeed it might be argued that we are seeing an increase in what William Davies has called 'The Happiness Industry'.[76] People no longer expect simply to be free from illness but to be happy and there are a wide range of professional and non-professional services designed to make people happy. Cederström and Spicer[77] argue people nowadays suffer from a 'wellness syndrome', which causes people to become obsessed with their health and fitness and this is making them unwell. They cite Fitbits as an example of how people are becoming paranoid about their health.

4.3 Anti-medicine

Although, at first sight, a campaign to oppose medicine might seem to have as much chance of success as a campaign to ban banoffee pie, there is more to the argument than first appears. The leading anti-medic is Ivan Illich.[78]

Central to his argument is that part of being human is coping with illness, pain, and death. In the past, societies and individuals found a way of coping with and understanding these issues. Now that we have lost those coping strategies, we seek medical treatment for every pain and illness, and death is regarded as the ultimate evil to be avoided at all costs. Illich argues that the loss of these coping mechanisms has diminished our humanity and impoverished our society. In addition, Illich makes the point, alluded to already, that medicine is ever encroaching in treating normal aspects of life as illness. Indeed Amartya Sen provides evidence that the more a society spends on health care, the more its citizens are likely to regard themselves as sick.[79] The special place that health care has in our society means that there are pressures to present issues as health issues, which might not naturally be understood in these terms. Others have pointed out that increasing medicalization enables moral judgements to be made on people. Attacks on individuals' ways of life that would normally be regarded as inappropriate are legitimated by being labelled as 'health promotion'. The so-called 'war on obesity' might be one example. These are perhaps modern-day examples of what Foucault called 'biopolitics' in his study of the way in which, over history, medicine has been used by the state to justify exercising power over people and keeping surveillance over them.[80] Of course, many others argue that educating people about the dangers of obesity and unsafe sexual behaviour, and informing them of ways of living healthier lifestyles, is not only proper, but also morally required.

All of these points are important, but Illich's critics argue that, at most, they point to the dangers of over-medicalization rather than provide a case against all medicine. Not to provide someone in severe pain with medical treatment and telling him or her to rely on his or her own, and society's, coping mechanisms is not likely to prove a popular suggestion. Indeed, it is notable that although Illich is eloquent on the flaws in current medicine, he has written less on what its alternatives are.[81]

---

[75] Moynihan, Heath, and Henry (2002) provide some fascinating examples of how the drugs industry has helped to create a market for some of its products.
[76] Davies (2015).   [77] Cederström and Spicer (2015).   [78] Illich (1975).   [79] Sen (2002).
[80] Armstrong (2004).   [81] Moynihan (2002).

4.4 **The changing doctor–patient relationship**

There have been some significant changes in the doctor–patient relationship in recent years.[82] In the past, the doctor was very much the dominant party, with the patient's role being to answer the doctor's questions and then do what the doctor ordered. Nowadays, doctors talk about mutual decision making. Patients are encouraged to ask questions; doctors are encouraged to see patients as having expertise. Indeed, access to the Internet may mean that patients rapidly acquire a greater knowledge about a particularly unusual condition than a GP.[83] It would not, however, be correct to suggest that all of the movements in modern times are towards a more equal relationship. The days when you had 'your GP' whom you could consult whenever you felt ill are long gone. It is common now for a surgery to have quite a number of GPs who might see a patient. This means that building up a long-term relationship with a GP is less common. In *Montgomery v Lanarkshire Health Board*[84] the Supreme Court examined the changing doctor–patient relationships and stated:

> The social and legal developments which we have mentioned point away from a model of the relationship between the doctor and the patient based upon medical paternalism. They also point away from a model based upon a view of the patient as being entirely dependent on information provided by the doctor. What they point towards is an approach to the law which, instead of treating patients as placing themselves in the hands of their doctors (and then being prone to sue their doctors in the event of a disappointing outcome), treats them so far as possible as adults who are capable of understanding that medical treatment is uncertain of success and may involve risks, accepting responsibility for the taking of risks affecting their own lives, and living with the consequences of their choices.

4.5 **The sociological impact of being ill**

Sociologists have done much work on the concept of illness and the consequences for a person of being declared 'ill' by a doctor. This, it is said, permits a person to adopt the 'sick role'.[85] He or she becomes exempt from some of the normal responsibilities of life: work; domestic chores; even politeness. But the person also takes on responsibilities: he or she must follow the advice of doctors and try to get better. Much opprobrium falls on those who do not fall into this model, for example those who go to work and do not seek medical advice, even though they are sick, or those who act as if they are sick when they are not (taking a 'sickie'—that is, claiming a day off work, claiming untruthfully to be ill). This said, the 'sick role' may be culturally specific and different communities take a different approach to what is appropriate for a sick person to do.[86]

This analysis is particularly useful in relation to conditions about which there is scepticism over whether they are 'real' illnesses or not. For example, although widely accepted as a recognized condition, some experts still dispute the diagnosis of dyslexia; only fairly recently has evidence emerged concerning the biological causes of ME that may assist in that condition having wider acceptance as a 'proper' illness.[87]

---

[82] Morgan (2009).
[83] The Supreme Court in *Montgomery v Lanarkshire Health Board* [2015] UKSC 11 at para. 76 acknowledged that it is now common for the public to use the Internet to seek medical advice.
[84] [2015] UKSC 11, para. 81.   [85] Scambler (2009a).   [86] Quah (2001).   [87] Action for ME (2005).

4.6 Personalized medicine

There is increased interest in the idea of personalized medicine. Sebastian Schleidgen et al.[88] explain:

> Personalised medicine seeks to improve tailoring and timing of preventative and therapeutic measures by utilising biological, information and biomarkers on the level of molecular disease pathways, genetics, proteomics as well as metabolomics.

This means that increasingly medicines are used that are designed for a particular individual, rather than generally at a disease. This may be most useful where someone has a range of conditions and the medicine can target the particular combination affecting an individual. This may be seen in a broader context with doctors seeking to find treatments which will work with the particular values, interests, and lifestyle of a patient, rather than assuming all patients with disease X need treatment Y. The concept is, however, not without concerns. It might be seen as downplaying the importance of public health initiatives and encouraging an image of health as a private personal matter.[89]

5 Health statistics

Of course, to provide a complete picture of health in the UK would require a lengthy document, but the following are some statistics to offer a flavour.

- In the 2011 Census, 81.2 per cent of people in England and Wales reported their general health as either 'Very good' or 'Good'.[90]
- In 2015, 17.2 per cent of adults reported that they were currently smokers.[91]
- In a survey of adults in England in 2015, 15 per cent of people said they had drank more than 8/6[92] units of alcohol on their heaviest day in the previous week. Interestingly, 43 per cent of people said they had not drunk alcohol at all in the previous week. 20.9 per cent of adults say they never drink alcohol. The Office for National Statistics states: 'Young people aged 16 to 24 years in Great Britain are less likely to drink than any other age group.'[93] Who said students were a drunken lot?!
- The NHS found that in 2017 68 per cent of men and 58 per cent of women were either overweight or obese. Looking only at those who were technically obese, 27 per cent fell into this category.[94]

6 General ethical principles

6.1 What is medical ethics?

The British Medical Association (BMA) has defined medical ethics as 'the application of ethical reasoning to medical decision making'.[95] This leaves unanswered the question:

---

88 Sebastian Schleidgen et al. (2015: 20).   89 Vollman (2015).
90 Office for National Statistics (2013).   91 Office for National Statistics (2017a).
92 Six units for women and eight units for men.   93 Office for National Statistics (2017b).
94 Office for National Statistics (2017c).   95 BMA (2009a: 3).

'What are ethics?' As might be imagined, this could be the topic of several books. It might be thought that ethics is all about finding principles that can govern a good life. Of course, even that will not be agreed on by everyone. Should ethics be concerned with principles for a 'good life' or 'not a bad life'? After all, there are many different views of what makes a life 'good'.

Bioethics has received contributions from a variety of disciplines: philosophers, sociologists, lawyers, theologians, economists, and anthropologists have all contributed to the writings on the topic. The wide range of disciplines writing in this field leads to a rich variety of material; the relationship between the disciplines can be problematic, especially where there are differences in terminology and uncertainty over the role that different disciplines should play within bioethics.[96] This led José Miola to describe contemporary medical ethics as 'an amorphous, incoherent and fragmented collection of discourse rather than a "structured conscience" for the medical profession'.[97] Of course, that may be a good thing. There might be something concerning if everyone were to agree on the right answers and approach to medical ethics. This has led to some difficult issues over the extent to which a healthcare professional can refuse to participate in certain activities due to their conscience.[98]

It is important to realize that in ethics, in respect of some questions at least, there is not a 'right' answer which is waiting to be discovered. Julian Savulescu[99] is keen to emphasize the difference between ethics and science:

> Ethics is concerned with norms and values. Its subject matter is the way the world ought to be or should be. It is about good and bad, right and wrong. Science is about the way the world is, was, will be, could be, would be. Ethics is about values; science is about facts.

6.2 Consequentialism and deontology

An important divide among those approaching medical ethics is between those who support consequentialism and those who support deontology. We shall look at what these terms mean in a moment, but before doing so it is important to realize that many writers reject both of these schools of thought and seek to develop a 'third way', combining the two approaches.

The basic difference between the two approaches is as follows.

- *Consequentialism* judges whether an action is ethically right or wrong by the consequences it produces. A consequentialist will say that an action is right if, all things considered, the consequences are good, but wrong if they are bad.

- *Deontological absolutism* holds that certain things are right or wrong regardless of the consequences.

An example that shows the difference between the two approaches might be a man who is asked by a friend whether he likes an outfit that she has just bought. He does not. A consequentialist would weigh up the benefits of telling the truth (she will be upset; she may lose self-confidence) with the disadvantages of not telling the truth (if she finds out

---

[96] DeVries (2004).   [97] Miola (2007: 54). See also Smith (2015).
[98] Favargue and Neale (2015); Miola (2015).   [99] Savulescu (2015a).

that he lied, she may not trust him in the future). Such a balance might well lead the man to conclude that he should untruthfully say he likes the dress. A deontological approach might take the line that telling the truth is an important moral principle and that, even if the consequences will be bad, the man should be honest.

Let us have a look at these two approaches in a little more detail.

6.2.1 *Consequentialism*

Consequentialism stresses that, in assessing the morality of an action, one must judge its consequences. You must weigh up all of the good and all of the bad consequences of each alternative course of action. Quite simply, if you are faced with two alternative courses of action, you should choose the one that has the best overall consequences. You should consider each person who may be affected and be sure not to count one person's interests as more important than those of another.

The attraction of this approach is that it is 'common sense' and how most of us make decisions in day-to-day life. When faced with alternatives, we naturally look at the consequences. In choosing between two flavours of yoghurt, you will ask yourself: 'Which will give me greater pleasure?' Or, in choosing a present for a friend: 'What will they enjoy most?' There are, however, problems with consequentialism.

One such problem is that consequentialism is based on deciding which result will produce the most 'good'. But what is 'good'? A popular consequentialist theory is utilitarianism. This argues that the most important good is that people be happy or have pleasure. Therefore, in making ethical judgements, we should ask which act will most increase the sum of human happiness. We see this approach used in some medical cases in which courts have to consider whether to permit the non-treatment of a seriously ill baby. The courts have held that it is better that the baby die than carry on living with a painful existence. But is pleasure all there is to life? What about other goods? Would we really enjoy a life that was nothing but pleasure? Would we regard a good life as one full only of pleasure?[100] Utilitarianism is not the only version of consequentialism on offer. Other forms are willing to include values such as friendship, trust, and health in their calculation of what makes a consequence good or bad. The difficulty, though, is finding agreement over what is 'good' once you leave out happiness. We might, for example, take the view that what is good for a person is what that person thinks is good for him or her.[101] But that robs utilitarianism of some of its practical usefulness: how can I judge how to act if I do not know whether those affected will regard themselves as benefited or harmed by my actions?

Consequentialism also faces the problem of unpredictability: we often do not know what the consequences of our acts are. In such a case, can they be used as a guide as to the morality of our actions?

Another problem is: 'good' for whom? Earlier, I suggested that, in choosing a flavour of yoghurt, I should decide which I will enjoy more, but is the utilitarian calculation that straightforward? Should a consequentialist consider factors such as fair trade issues? Or the fact this is the last yoghurt of that flavour in the supermarket and there may be others who have even stronger views than me on yoghurt flavour? More seriously, when deciding about medical treatment for a patient, is it only a question of what is best for this patient, or one of what is best for all patients in the NHS? Or, indeed, all patients

---

[100] Smart (1993).   [101] Singer (1994).

in the world? Once we start to consider every conceivable consequence of our actions, decision making becomes very complex.

Another problem is motivation: should utilitarians be concerned by motivations? Consider a gynaecologist who finds sexual pleasure in carrying out intimate examinations, although he does his job well. If we focus only on the consequences of his actions, we may describe them as good. But many people would feel that his motivations are relevant in assessing the ethics of his behaviour. Under a traditional consequentialist model, his motivation would be irrelevant.

A major problem for consequentialism is that it can produce a result that many feel instinctively is wrong. Let us imagine a doctor who has four patients all in desperate need of transplant organs without which they will die. Could a doctor kill a nurse and use his organs to save the lives of the patients, and then argue, under a consequentialist approach, that she had done more good than harm in killing one person to save four and hence that her actions were justified? Some utilitarians feel that this is an acceptable result. To deal with concerns of this kind, however, some utilitarians have developed a version of utilitarianism known as 'rule utilitarianism'.

Rule utilitarianism suggests that we should adopt the set of rules that govern how we act which will, if followed, produce the best outcome. Rule consequentialism asks: 'Which general rules will promote the best consequences in the long term, assuming that everyone accepts and complies with them?'[102] So even if, in the particular case, following the rule will not produce the best outcome, if having the strict rule produces overall the best for society, we should adopt it. For example, it might be said that doctors should keep confidential all information given to them by patients. Even though there may be individual cases in which it would produce a better outcome to make that information public, the rule of medical confidentiality produces generally good outcomes, in enabling people to be frank with their medical advisers.

As can be seen from this discussion, although rule utilitarianism is popular, it has difficulties. It is problematic for an individual seeking guidance on what to do in his or her particular situation. Working out the consequences of alternative courses of action as required for 'act utilitarianism' is difficult enough; attempting to work out what general rule to apply in cases of this kind would be very complex. Further, there is the issue of whether, within 'rule utilitarianism', the rules have exceptions, and if so, how these exceptions are to be calculated.

6.2.2 Deontology

A deontological theory holds that certain kinds of actions are good not because of the consequences they produce, but because they are good and right in themselves. We should tell the truth not because that makes people happy or gives them pleasure, but because truth-telling is the right thing to do. We have a duty to tell the truth. Immanuel Kant is widely regarded as a leading exponent of this thinking. He regarded as a key maxim that no one should be treated merely as a means to an end. A person should not be used merely to help others. We should not therefore use someone in a human research project without his or her consent, even if using that person will produce all kinds of good (for example finding a cure for a terrible illness). Deontologists are keen to point out that some of the atrocities carried out in the name of medicine (such as research

---

[102] Glennon (2005: 10).

by Nazi doctors on non-consenting people) have been justified in the name of utilitarianism. Deontology could never justify such actions.

Key to deontological theories is the principle that you cannot justify the breach of a deontological principle only by referring to the consequences. It is not permissible to kill an innocent person even if, by doing so, you save four lives. Some deontologists will say that all, or some, deontological principles are absolute: that there are no circumstances under which a deontological principle can be breached. For example, under Article 3 of the European Convention on Human Rights (ECHR), torture can never be justified. Others will accept that if there are overwhelmingly good consequences, a breach may be justified. So although you should not normally torture someone, if they have placed a bomb in central London, it might be appropriate to torture them to find out where it was and thereby save many lives. Deontologists can also claim to have the benefit of clarity. However complex the issue may appear, if there is a clear deontological principle (for example 'you must not treat a patient without her or his consent'), then this provides the guidance without the need to look further.[103]

Deontologists often place much weight on duties. They emphasize that the duties parents owe to their children, or physicians to their patients, are overlooked in utilitarian approaches. When making a decision about your children, you must take into account the duties that you owe them, not only the consequences for all children. If three people are in danger in a fire, parents are expected to rescue their own child first even if that means that the other two are likely to perish.

The difficulty deontologists face is explaining what the principles are and where they come from. To those with religious beliefs, the principles of good or bad behaviour come from God. Others claim that there are things that are naturally right or wrong and which require no justification as such. They may point out, for example, that in most modern societies incest is regarded as wrong. Even though there may be no consequentialist justification for this, it seems to be part of human nature to recognize the wrongness of incest. Some claim that there are goods that are 'self-evident': truth, knowledge, and friendship, for example. Others have sought to appeal to some form of 'social contract' under which every member of society can be taken to have agreed to abide by certain principles.

The difficulties facing deontologists particularly relate to how we define the most important obligation. If two moral people profoundly disagree about what the rights or obligations require, how can they resolve this debate? Consequentialists can debate with each other about the benefits and disadvantages of acting in a certain way, but there seems no way forward for disputing deontologists. Further, as already indicated above, there is dispute over whether deontological principles are absolute and, if they are not, in what circumstances they may be infringed. One solution to this dilemma is to try to locate within society an acceptance of how moral principles should be ranked. But in an increasingly multi-religious, multicultural society, this becomes increasingly difficult.

6.2.3 *Mixing consequentialism and deontology*

The distinction between consequentialism and deontology, although important and useful, is not as clear-cut as it may at first appear. Deontologists often accept that consequentialism is an appropriate approach where there is no absolute principle to apply.

---

[103] For an argument that there are circumstances under which it is appropriate for a doctor to lie to a patient, see Helgesson and Lynöe (2008).

Further, there is much debate over how we decide which principles should be deontological absolutes. One possibility is to adopt those that will produce the best society. For example, we might decide that people should always keep their promises because a truthful society is better than one in which lies are told. But this uses consequentialist reasoning to decide what the deontological absolutes are. Deontological theories may also face difficulties where two principles clash, in which case some will turn to consequentialist reasoning to decide which principle to follow.

Consequentialists are not immune from seeking to use deontological approaches too. They may hold on to a principle such as the sanctity of life and claim that even if it appears that there would be more good than harm from killing this individual, the impact on society as a whole, over time, of not respecting the sanctity of life will be to society's detriment. Peter Singer, a leading consequentialist, has argued that we should start with 'utilitarianism' as a 'first base'.[104] Only if there are good reasons should we be persuaded to accept any 'non-utilitarian moral rules or ideals'.

Doug Morrison has complained that, in the context of medical ethics, neither consequentialism nor deontology appears appropriate.[105] Consequentialism appears to place too little weight on the right of autonomy and would permit a doctor to carry out treatment on a patient without the patient's consent if the overall consequences of the treatment were beneficial. On the other hand, deontology, by regarding the consequences of actions as irrelevant, ignores the importance that medical practice inevitably places on the consequences of alternative forms of medical treatment. Morrison promotes a hybrid approach that involves looking at both the consequence of the action and the rights and duties of those involved, and striking an appropriate balance between them.

To many, especially those of a philosophical bent, this attempt to 'have one's cake and eat it' is unacceptable. Consequentialism and deontology are two very different approaches to a problem, which, in difficult cases, lead to dramatically different outcomes. Taking both perspectives into account will do nothing to assist the medical professional in the most complex cases in which clear guidance is needed.

6.3 The role of intuition in medical ethics

What role should intuition play in medical ethics?[106] As we shall see in Chapter 6, a respectable philosophical case can be made for arguing that someone only becomes a person and therefore entitled to human rights when they are several months old. This argument is used to justify abortion, but it would also justify the killing of newborn babies. To many, this consequence is so revolting that intuitively it must be rejected. However logical and clear the argument, 'our hearts' tell us that 'our heads' have got something wrong. Many react in this way to human cloning or to the creation of human–animal hybrids; even though it is not possible to explain why, it just feels wrong. Some call this the 'yuck factor'. But is it legitimate to rely on this kind of intuitive reasoning? Or should medical ethicists be considering only rational arguments?

The BMA has suggested that conscience and intuition can be useful components of ethical guidance, even if dangerous when used alone.[107] In practice, a doctor required to make an urgent ethical decision is likely to rule based on her or his intuition and it may

---

[104] Singer (1993: 32).   [105] Morrison (2005).   [106] Kaebnick (2008); Niemela (2011).
[107] Sommerville (2003). See also Smith (2015).

be argued that this is right. Indeed, ethical guidance issued to medical professionals that goes against the dictates of their consciences is unlikely to be respected or effective.[108] As one of the BMA's ethical advisers, put it:

> Doctors also want guidance that seems to them to be intuitively correct and consistent with what they understand to be the core purposes of medicine. Moral justifications for various actions are rehearsed but practical solutions sometimes arise quite unexpectedly from intuition or a doctor's hunch that an improbable solution could work, rather than solely from rational analysis.[109]

Others are more sceptical about encouraging doctors to rely on intuition. Ruth Macklin claims: ' "Yuck" ' is a conversation stopper, not an argument.'[110] Imagine you are discussing human cloning with a friend and you say: 'The idea of human cloning is disgusting. I oppose it.' And your friend says: 'The idea of human cloning sounds cool. I like it.' It is hard to see how your discussion can proceed. Unless you start to discuss reasons and arguments relying on emotional reactions does not get you very far.[111]

6.4 What can we expect from medical ethics?

There is some debate among medical ethicists about what we can expect from medical ethics. Some are highly sceptical of any claim that someone is an expert in medical ethics.[112] What makes a person an expert on whether an embryo has a right to life? Or whether the sale of organs is ethical? While many of us would be willing to accept that a professor of physics would have a better chance than us of calculating the speed of light, would we agree that a professor in bioethics is more likely than those of us who are not to know whether euthanasia is morally acceptable or not? Anne Maclean, critical of philosophers claiming to provide the 'correct answer' to morally controversial issues, writes:

> [P]hilosophy as such delivers no verdict upon moral issues; there is no unique set of moral principles which philosophy as such underwrites and no question, therefore, of using that set to uncover the answers which philosophy gives to moral questions. When bioethicists deliver a verdict upon the moral issues raised by medical practice, it is their own verdict they deliver and not the verdict of philosophy itself; it is their voice we hear and not the voice of reason or rationality.[113]

This scepticism may reveal a misunderstanding of how many medical ethicists would understand their role. They would argue that it is not to provide the right answer, but to assist in clear thinking: to set out arguments that are logically coherent and consistent with the facts, and to point out logical or philosophical flaws in the arguments of others.[114] So although the ethicist may not have greater claim to producing the right answer, he or she might claim to have a better chance of producing a logically and morally coherent one.[115]

Ruth Macklin[116] gives examples of what would not be good reasons for holding a view: 'The decision appeared to me in a dream'; 'I flipped a coin to decide'; 'I followed

---

[108] Fulford (2005).   [109] Sommerville (2003: 282).   [110] Macklin (2015).
[111] Sheehan (2016).   [112] Archard (2011).   [113] Maclean (1995: 5).
[114] Chan (2015).   [115] Gordon (2013); Gesang (2010).   [116] Macklin (2015).

what my (mother, father, teacher, mentor) always did'. Medical ethicists should be able to do better than that.

While it might therefore be unreasonable to turn to medical ethicists to produce the 'correct' answer, it may be reasonable to expect assistance in thinking through the issues with sensitivity, logic, and clear-headedness. John Harris has, for example, been sceptical of relying on polls of members of the public to ascertain the correct response to controversial issues.[117] He argues that most people are ignorant of the facts and do not think through their arguments coherently. A good ethicist is therefore more likely to reach the correct answer than the person in the street. But is that simply intellectual snobbery?[118]

6.5 Bioethics 'as entertainment'

An uncomfortable claim that can be legitimately levelled against Western bioethics is that, in focusing on the intellectually interesting issues surrounding abortion, euthanasia, and human enhancement, the really important issues concerning health have received no coverage. As Leigh Turner puts it:

> Many of the questions that bioethicists address only make sense within the context of wealthy developed nations. Some of the favourite topics of bioethicists seem trivial compared with the important health issues facing people in the world's poor countries and in impoverished regions in rich countries.[119]

One response is that the issues concerning world poverty are simply too large to be discussed in the context of a course on medical law or ethics. But even looking within the UK, it is arguable that bioethicists' focus has been narrow: much is written on how to ration limited medical resources appropriately, but little on why there are only limited resources available; much on the importance of autonomy, but little on the illiteracy and lack of education that makes autonomy a problematic concept on the ground.[120]

Another issue is the extent to which bioethics research is driven by academics seeking to obtain research grants or academic promotion. This might mean that research is focused on 'sexy' topics that are more likely to attract funding or publication.[121] Hence it has been claimed that bioethics is becoming like a business: driven by market concerns rather than the moral significance of issues involved.[122]

7 The notion of rights

Much of the legal thinking and writing in medical law is now put in terms of 'rights'.[123] This is partly because of the impact of the Human Rights Act 1998, but also reflects the power of patients to challenge the paternalism of the medical profession that has been so prevalent until fairly recently.[124] A rights-based approach focuses on the interests of the

---

[117] Harris (1984).   [118] Gesang (2010) suggests that a good ethicist might be a semi-expert.
[119] Turner (2004: 175).   [120] Koch (2003).   [121] Biller-Andorno (2009).
[122] Biller-Andorno (2009).
[123] Wicks (2007); Ashcroft (2008). Although see Sperling (2008), who discusses the dangers of seeing all medical issues in terms of rights and duties.
[124] Garwood-Gowers and Tingle (2001).

individual and is designed to protect the individual from improper claims that harming him or her is justified in the interests of society or the interests of others. As we have seen, utilitarianism can be criticized for permitting one person to be seriously harmed if it can be said that the benefits outweigh the costs. A rights-based approach seeks to prevent this from happening, or at least to put limits on when it can happen. The use of human rights talk is, however, not without difficulty. A number of general points about the nature of rights need to be made first.

7.1 Absolute versus conditional rights

An absolute right is one that cannot be infringed, whatever the circumstances. As already mentioned, the ECHR states in Article 3 that an individual has an absolute right not to suffer torture. Other rights in the ECHR are conditional in that there are circumstances under which the right can be infringed. Under Article 8, for example, there is a right to respect for one's private life, but that can be interfered with if necessary, under paragraph 2, in the interests of others.

7.2 Rights and obligations

A hotly disputed issue in jurisprudence is whether it is possible to have a right without an obligation—in other words, whether one can claim a right to X, without someone else being under an obligation to supply X. If the two are inevitably linked, then any 'right to health care' must be matched by a clear statement as to who has the obligation to supply that health care.

7.3 Positive and negative rights

Traditionally, human rights have focused more on negative rights (prohibiting people acting in a certain way towards you) than on positive rights (requiring people to act in certain ways towards you). So although the negative right not to have treatment given to you that you do not want is a strongly protected right, the positive right to receive treatment that you do want is protected to a far lesser extent, if at all. Derek Morgan has argued that, in the context of a socialized medical system, positive rights must be treated with much caution because respecting the positive rights of one person is likely to interfere with the rights of another.[125] As Lord Walker has put it: 'There is no general human right to good physical and mental health any more than there is a human right to expect (rather than to pursue) happiness.'[126]

7.4 What rights are relevant in medical law?

As we go through the book, various rights will be explained, but we will mention a few of the most important here.

(i) *The right of autonomy* The right of autonomy plays a huge role in medical law writing, and indeed in court judgments. In essence the right of autonomy is the right

---

[125] Morgan (2001: ch. 1).
[126] *R (Razgar) v Secretary of State for the Home Department* [2004] UKHL 27, [34].

to decide what medical treatment you receive. In truth, talk of the 'right to autonomy' is misleading. As already indicated, whilst your decision about not receiving treatment is strongly protected in the law, your decision as to what treatment you would like need not be followed. It may therefore be more accurate to describe this as 'the right to refuse treatment', or 'the right to bodily integrity', rather than 'the right to autonomy'.[127]

(ii) *The right to dignity* As Roger Brownsword has usefully noted, the notion of 'dignity' is used by different people writing in this area in disparate ways.[128] He distinguishes the use of human dignity as empowerment and its use as a constraint. Dignity as empowerment sees human dignity as a powerful source of rights. It requires the respecting of individuals' choices and empowering them to live an autonomous life. Dignity as constraint is less straightforward. Brownsword suggests that the notion appeals to a coalition of Kantians, Catholics, and communitarians. This view rejects the argument that respecting an individual's autonomy is necessary to respect his or her dignity.

Respecting a person's dignity requires more than respecting his or her choices.[129] Holders of the view of dignity as constraint might therefore argue that an individual should not be able to sell his or her own organs because to do so is to demean the individual's dignity as a human. Similarly, allowing couples and researchers to clone humans would contradict human dignity. 'Dignity' here is used to refer to what a community or society regards as special about individuals. Brownsword uses an example of a French case,[130] which concerned a police order prohibiting a 'dwarf-throwing' competition that involved, as the title suggests, a 'game' involving participants throwing people of restricted growth. Although all involved were consenting to the game, and it might therefore be said to be an infringement of their autonomy and therefore dignity not to allow them to perform, it could also be argued that the 'game' dehumanized the participants, and did not respect their humanity and their dignity. Suzy Killmister argues that dignity can be distinguished from autonomy because autonomy concerns self-government, while dignity concerns self-worth.[131] Allowing those of restricted growth to be thrown might have respected their self-governance; it might not have respected their self-worth.

In an important contribution to the debate, Charles Foster has argued that dignity is the essential principle in bioethics. He sees dignity as 'objective human flourishing'.[132] It is about thriving as a human.[133] Foster argues that an ethical analysis requires a concept of dignity. He gives some examples to explain why:

> It is wrong to use the head of a dead person as a football, for medical students to practise vaginal examinations on a woman in permanent vegetative state or to let youths at a Casualty Department gaze lustfully at the undraped body of a seriously brain-damaged girl—even though she enjoys their attention. The wrongness can only properly be described in the language of dignity.[134]

The point of these examples is that the wrongfulness cannot be explained in terms of pain or distress to the 'victim'. The only wrong, he claims, is to their dignity.

---

[127] Herring and Wall (2017).

[128] Brownsword (2003a). See also Duwell (2017); Rosen (2012) and Waldron (2012) for a range of views on dignity.

[129] For further discussion, see Melo-Martín (2011).

[130] Ville d'Aix-en-Provence, 1996 Dalloz 177 (Conseil d'État), req. nos 143–578.

[131] Killmister (2011).   [132] Foster (2011: 6).   [133] Foster (2011: 4).   [134] Foster (2015c).

Mary Neal argues that at the heart of dignity is the notion that all humans have intrinsic worth.[135] Connected to this is a range of ideas, including that we should respect people's moral agency, that humans are beyond price and so should not be commercialized, and that we should not use people as a means to end. In response to those who say that the concept of dignity is too vague, she argues that we need accept that there is not 'one single concept of dignity', but rather 'different conceptions' that are used in different contexts. They overlap and might be vague at the edges, but that should not be problematic. Interestingly, Neal, in a novel insight, suggests that we consider dignity to:

> ... reflect a valuing of the sense in which human existence (perhaps uniquely) embodies a union between the fragile/material/finite and the transcendent/sublime/immortal. In valuing us because of, and not in spite of/regardless of our vulnerability.[136]

Not everyone is convinced that dignity is a useful concept.[137] Critics argue that its meaning is so vague that the term may be abandoned. What to one person might be undignified is life-affirming to others. Mattson and Clarke write:

> Human dignity is in such disarray that it does not provide even a minimally stable frame for global discourse and action. Much about this idea remains implicit or even contradictory, in the service of diverse and sometimes contra-dignity ends . . .[138]

Cynics might argue that dignity is a term used by those who want to stop people who they believe are behaving immorally.[139] History teaches us of the dangers of allowing those in power to prevent others from living as they wish because they find their behaviour 'undignified'.[140]

(iii) *The right to life* The right to life for many people is the key human right that must trump all others. However, there is great debate over the meaning of life and what it means to respect the right to life. These issues particularly come to a head in the context of euthanasia and abortion, and we will be considering them in Chapters 6 and 9.

7.5 Critiques of rights

Not all commentators are convinced that talk of rights is helpful.[141] Jesse Wall argues that in difficult cases rights clash and then do not provide a helpful way of looking at a case. It would be more profitable to 'look straight through' these rights to the values and principles behind them. Only then can we hope to resolve difficult cases. A rather different concern is that rights encourage an individualistic approach which focuses on the interests of particular people, rather than the good of society or the relational values between them.[142] While these concerns have merits, rights are so commonly referred to in public debates and legal cases it is difficult to avoid the language of rights.

---

[135] Neal (2011).   [136] Neal (2011: 71).   [137] Macklin (2003).
[138] Mattson and Clark (2011: 304).   [139] Cochrane (2010).
[140] Huxtable (2015); Waldron (2015).
[141] Wall (2015). Murphy (2013) seems rather agnostic on the benefits of rights talk.
[142] Herring (2013a) explores this argument and the extent to which rights talk can overcome it.

8 Patients' obligations

Much has been written on patients' rights; rather less, on patients' duties.[143] Concern that the 'rights of patients' have become too dominant can even be found among the judiciary. In *R v Collins and Ashworth Hospital Authority, ex p Brady*,[144] Kay J stated: '[I]t would seem to me a matter of deep regret if the law has developed to a point in this area where the rights of patients count for everything and other ethical values and institutional integrity count for nothing.' Of course, there will be many who are convinced that we still have a long way to go if we are to protect patients' rights properly.

Considering the issue of responsibilities, an important issue that has not received the attention it deserves is the extent to which patients should be held responsible for their own health.[145] The NHS Constitution produces a formidable list of the responsibilities that patients have:

- Please recognise that you can make a significant contribution to your own, and your family's, good health and wellbeing, and take personal responsibility for it.
- Please register with a GP practice—the main point of access to NHS care as commissioned by NHS bodies.
- Please treat NHS staff and other patients with respect and recognise that violence, or the causing of nuisance or disturbance on NHS premises, could result in prosecution. You should recognise that abusive and violent behaviour could result in you being refused access to NHS services.
- Please provide accurate information about your health, condition and status.
- Please keep appointments, or cancel within reasonable time. Receiving treatment within the maximum waiting times may be compromised unless you do.
- Please follow the course of treatment which you have agreed, and talk to your clinician if you find this difficult.
- Please participate in important public health programmes such as vaccination.
- Please ensure that those closest to you are aware of your wishes about organ donation.
- Please give feedback—both positive and negative—about your experiences and the treatment and care you have received, including any adverse reactions you may have had.[146]

These obligations are not legally enforceable, but are a marked recognition that patients may have health responsibilities of moral significance.[147]

If one is persuaded that the law ought to take patients' responsibilities more seriously, a number of issues arise. The first is what notion of responsibility we are talking about. Is it simply a causal question: did the patient cause his or her own illness? Or are we looking at blame as well: is the patient to be held responsible only if he or she caused the illness in a blameworthy way?[148] Also, to what extent may a person hold responsibilities if his or her refusal to receive health care (such as a vaccine) leads others to become ill?[149]

---

[143] Coggon (2013); Brazier (2006); Iltis and Rasmussen (2005); Buetow and Elwyn (2006).
[144] [2000] Lloyd's Rep Med 355, 361.   [145] Schmidt (2009); Buyx (2008).
[146] NHS (2013a: 10).   [147] See also Schmidt (2009); Buyx (2008).
[148] Schmidt (2009).   [149] Caplan, Hoke, Diamond, and Karshenboyem (2012).

The second issue is whether it is possible to treat all those who cause their own ill-nesses equally. The temptation may be to pick out 'obvious cases', such as those who smoke, but if we do that and do not attach responsibility when people harm themselves in other ways, smokers may be unfairly treated.[150]

A third issue is whether, even if one accepts that one should be responsible for one's health, other factors may mean that it is not appropriate to hold people responsible.[151] Daniels argues:

> [T]oo much emphasis on [personal responsibility] ignores egalitarian considerations central to democratic equality. Our health needs, however they arise, interfere with our ability to function as free and equal citizens. [We] must meet the[se] needs however they have arisen, since capabilities can be undermined by both bad brute and bad option luck.[152]

Holding people responsible for healthcare decisions could interfere with other values that we hold dear, such as autonomy and freedom.

A final point, as hinted at by Daniels, is that it can be difficult to know to what extent a person is responsible for his or her own health. Consider obesity, for example: it is far from clear what the causes of obesity are. To say that it is simply the result of a person's choice to eat too much is hugely over-simplistic. The causes of most ill-health are a complex mixture of public and private matters.

9 Principlism

One of the most influential approaches to bioethics is known as 'principlism'. It is so-called because it is based on a set of principles that can be applied to any bioethical issue. The most influential book advocating this approach is *Principles of Biomedical Ethics* by Tom Beauchamp and James Childress.[153] This book has formed the basis of much teaching on medical ethics, and is widely respected and used within the medical profession. A leading ethicist has even suggested that Beauchamp and Childress be given a Nobel prize for their work![154]

They advocate an approach that is based on four principles:

- respect for autonomy;
- non-maleficence;
- beneficence; and
- justice.

We shall be examining the exact meaning of these terms shortly.

Beauchamp and Childress argue that these four principles represent a 'common morality'—that is, principles that are respected within societies generally around the world.[155] They argue that the best way in which to approach ethical problems is to apply each of these principles to it and, if they recommend different courses of action,

[150] Brown (2013).   [151] For further discussion, see Herring and Foster (2009).
[152] Daniels (2007: 69).   [153] Beauchamp and Childress (2013).   [154] Gillon (2003).
[155] Beauchamp and Childress (2013: 6).

to weigh up the different principles. Although the authors regard all four principles as of equal value, it is clear that a special place is held for autonomy. Indeed, Raamon Gillon, a leading supporter in the UK of Beauchamp and Childress's work, has argued that autonomy is the 'first among equals'.[156] It might be considered that, in many cases, these principles will conflict, but Beauchamp and Childress believe that once the principles are precisely defined and specified, then the degree of conflict is far less than may be thought. But where there is a conflict, principlism offers no ready solution to how it should be resolved. As Beauchamp and Childress emphasize, they are presenting a framework for identifying the moral issues, rather than providing the answer.[157]

Principlism is regarded as having a number of benefits.

(i) It provides an accessible and usable approach. Medical professionals can use it in a practical context. It provides a coherent way of addressing problems in which most of the important issues are likely to be raised. Indeed, supporters claim that all of the relevant ethical issues will be raised by a proper consideration of the four principles.[158]

(ii) It is claimed that these principles are culturally neutral and could be accepted worldwide because they are not based on a particular religious faith or cultural norm. Gillon[159] argues that principlism 'provides a universalisable set of prima facie moral commitments to which all doctors can subscribe, whatever their culture, religion (or lack of religion), philosophy or life stance; in addition it provides a basic moral language and a basic moral analytic framework that all interested in biomedical ethics can share'.

(iii) The use of the four principles ensures a degree of consistency, in that all cases will be approached in the same way when it comes to balancing the different principles.

(iv) Its supporters see it as a strong counter to moral relativism, a view that there are no right or wrong answers to ethical issues.

(v) The approach is flexible enough to enable ethicists coming from a wide range of perspectives to use it. Even if they might disagree about how to balance the different principles, they are able to agree on the basic approach to these issues.

It is time to look in more detail at the four principles promoted by Beauchamp and Childress.

9.1 **Autonomy**

We shall be looking at the principle of autonomy in depth in Chapter 4. Here, we will consider some of the main issues concerning it.

Autonomy has become the premier principle in medical ethics.[160] To many commentators, it should be regarded as *the* primary medical principle. At the heart of autonomy is the right to decide how we wish to live our lives. To respect autonomy is to accept a person who has a right to hold views, make choices, and take actions based on personal values

---

[156] Gillon (2003). For a strong rejection of this view, see Dawson and Garrard (2006); Lee (2010).
[157] Beauchamp and Childress (2013: ch. 1).   [158] Gillon (2003).   [159] Gillon (2015).
[160] Although see Foster (2009) and Dawson (2010) for a challenge to its pre-eminence.

and beliefs. To override a person's wishes is to treat that person as a means to reach other people's ends and to fail to respect their humanity. The decision of a Jehovah's Witness to refuse a blood transfusion should be respected, even though without it he or she will die. An individual doctor may believe the patient's decision to be utter folly, but the decision is for the patient and for him or her alone. Of course, in many cases, following a patient's wishes will be promoting his or her welfare. Indeed, given the harm that a person will suffer if treatment is forced on him or her against his or her wishes, it would be rare that it would be beneficial for a patient to be treated contrary to his or her wishes. Nevertheless, supporters of autonomy insist that the reason why we respect autonomy is *not* just because it promotes people's welfare, but also because it respects their human rights.[161]

Beauchamp and Childress explain the principle in this way:

> To respect autonomous agents is to acknowledge their right to hold views, to make choices, and to take actions based on personal values and beliefs. Such respect involves respectful action, not merely a respectful attitude . . . Respect, in this account, involves acknowledging the value and decision-making rights of persons and enabling them to act autonomously, whereas disrespect for autonomy involves attitudes and actions that ignore, insult, demean, or are inattentive to others' rights of autonomous action.[162]

In fact, the so-called 'right to autonomy' is perhaps mislabelled in the medical context. A patient does not have a right to decide which medical treatment he or she will be given. A patient has no right to demand that she or he be given cosmetic surgery, for example. A healthcare professional may refuse because he or she does not want to provide the treatment or because rationing of healthcare resources means that it is not available. What is really being claimed here is a right of 'bodily integrity': a right not to have something done to your body without your consent.[163]

Autonomy does not require the respect of every choice, but only of choices that are competent. A young child's refusal to receive an injection can therefore be overridden if he or she is not able to understand the issues. Similarly, the refusal to consent to treatment of a person suffering from such severe mental impairment that he or she lacks mental capacity can be overridden.

The importance attached to autonomy has grown in recent years. In part, this reflects the growth of rights. We no longer regard ourselves as subjects of a higher authority, but as individuals with rights. In the medical sphere, doctors are no longer held in unquestioning respect and reverence.[164] Trust that 'doctor knows best' has weakened.[165] The scandals affecting the medical professions already mentioned and the increase in knowledge about medical matters that the lay person has, or can acquire, have also led to rejection of the view that a patient should simply lie back and accept whatever the doctor recommends.

As we shall see in Chapter 4, not everyone approves of the weight that has become attached to autonomy and others have proposed alternatives to the traditional understanding of autonomy.

---

[161] See further the discussion in Molyneux (2009).
[162] Beauchamp and Childress (2009: 103).   [163] Herring and Wall (2017).
[164] Although see McCulloch (2011) for a questioning of this presentation of history.
[165] O'Neill (2002).

9.2 Non-maleficence

At its core, the principle of non-maleficence asserts that one person should not cause harm to others. For medical professionals, there is the well-established principle *primum non nocere* ('above all do no harm'). The Hippocratic Oath states: 'I will use treatment to help the sick according to my ability and judgment, but I will never use it to injure or wrong them.'[166] As Beauchamp and Childress put it: 'The principle of non-malfeasance imposes an obligation not to inflict harm on others.'[167]

What, however, does it mean to be harmed? That is a far from straightforward question. Shlomit Harrosh has suggested four aspects of humanity that can lead to harm:

(1) We are conscious beings and can have harmful negative experiences such as pain, discomfort, sadness, and a sense of worthlessness.

(2) We are beings with a physical and psychological integrity which can be harmed through disease or improper functioning of the body.

(3) We are rational beings who set goals and form values. We can be harmed if our plans for our life or values are hindered.

(4) We are creatures of meaning and can be harmed if we cannot engage with the basic goods of life, such as relationships.[168]

This is a wide-ranging understanding of harms. It shows that it is possible to have a definition of harm that goes well beyond pain.

The importance of the non-maleficence principle is that it urges against harming one patient to help another. This point can be demonstrated by the American case of *McFall v Shimp*.[169] McFall needed a bone marrow transplant to improve his chances of surviving a serious medical condition. McFall's cousin, Shimp, was found to be compatible for donation. Shimp, having initially indicated that he would be willing to donate bone marrow, changed his mind and decided against it. McFall sought an order that Shimp had to donate. The court refused. The decision could be seen as support for the principle of non-maleficence: it would be wrong to harm Shimp by taking the bone marrow without his consent, even though it would be being done for a good motive—saving McFall's life.

Notice, however, that this principle would not be infringed if Shimp had consented to the bone marrow transplant. Although he would have suffered a harm in a sense (there would be physical pain involved in the donation), because he consented to it, it would not be seen as a wrong against him. So what counts as harm is determined to a significant extent by the individual concerned. This, then, forms a strong link to the idea of autonomy:[170] where the patient consents to the treatment and the doctor provides it, the non-maleficence principle may not be infringed.

But it must be questioned whether this last point is always true. If a patient asks a doctor to provide treatment that is manifestly harmful to the patient (for example to remove a limb when there is no medical reason for doing so), can a doctor rely on the

---

[166] Beauchamp and Childress (2013: 149).   [167] Beauchamp and Childress (2013: 149).
[168] Harrosh (2011: 13).   [169] 10 Pa D & C 3d 90 (1978).
[170] For an argument that autonomy and well-being should be regarded as 'friends', see Dunn and Foster (2010).

principle of non-maleficence to refuse to perform the treatment?[171] Some commentators believe that, under the principle, 'harm' must not always be given the meaning that the patient would give it, particularly where the patient's views as to harm are out of line with generally accepted norms in society. A good example of the kinds of debate this approach can generate are whether it is harmful for a boy born to a Jewish family to be circumcised.[172]

The principle of non-maleficence, if taken too literally, is absurd.[173] Most significant medical treatments involve the causing of some harm, even be it just the prick of a needle. So to tell a doctor to 'do no harm' would be counter-productive. The principle is best understood as saying that, seen as a whole, the medical intervention should not cause harm,[174] but in that case it appears to mirror the beneficence principle, which we discuss next.

9.3 Beneficence

Beneficence is the principle that medical professionals must do good for their patients. They must cure any disease or injury where possible and avoid the infliction of pain where possible. As the Hippocratic Oath puts it, the physician promises to 'follow that system of regimen which, according to my ability and judgment, I consider for the benefit of my patients'.

It may be that doctors are under a special duty to put the interests of patients above even their own interests, and that is a duty of a higher level than that imposed on individuals in other professions. Others, however, point out that, in many professions, professionals are expected to put their clients' interests first, even if that involves self-sacrifice.[175] Why, even lawyers have been known to leave their beds to attend clients detained in police cells in the middle of the night! So whether the principle of beneficence here is a special obligation for doctors or one that is found in many other situations is a matter for debate.

The principle of beneficence is not unproblematic. Simply stated, it might suggest a paternalistic approach: the doctor decides what is best and provides that for the patient. However, many commentators argue that, in deciding what is best for the patient, the healthcare professional should take the competent patient's views as to what is best for him or her. So a doctor who does not impose treatment on a Jehovah's Witness who is refusing to consent to a life-saving blood transfusion can be said to be complying with the principle, because she or he is acting in the best way for the patient, as the patient understands that to be. That way of explaining beneficence sounds a lot like autonomy. This principle focuses on the positive ethical obligations owed in the medical context. We have already discussed the principle of non-maleficence, which requires us not to harm others. The principle of beneficence deals with when we are required positively to help others. It must be stated straight away that, in general, the law rarely requires one person to do something to assist another.[176] There is much in the general law that prohibits one person harming another and provides sanctions where such harm is caused,

---

[171] See Elliott (2009) for further discussion.   [172] Manzor (2017).   [173] Szasz (1977: 1).
[174] On this basis Sullivan (2017) suggests it may be appropriate for a medical professional to allow a patient to self-harm if that is psychologically the best option.
[175] Downie (1988).   [176] Foot (1976).

but rarely is one person compelled to provide benefits to another. Society may want, and even encourage, people to assist others, but generally it does not compel them to do so. But in ethics, the principle of seeking to benefit others, or at least doing an act that causes greater good than harm, is one that is central to many people's ethical thinking. In short, then, the principle of beneficence is an important one in ethical thought, but is rarely a legally enforced one.

9.4 Justice

The meaning of 'justice' is contested. It is often expressed in terms of what is fair, equitable, or reasonable. In the context of health care, justice becomes particularly significant in the area of allocation of resources.[177] Where there are not enough funds to be able to provide everyone with the health care that they would like, we need a just way of deciding who should be treated and how. We shall be looking at this issue in Chapter 2.

At the heart of most theories of justice is the principle of formal equality: all equals should be treated equally and unequals should be treated unequally. The principle, so baldly stated, is perhaps uncontroversial. Its application causes the difficulties: how do we know if two people are equal? How do we know if treatment is equal?

Another aspect of justice that is relevant to health care is whether there is equal access to medical treatment. There are concerns that certain sections of the community find it difficult to access certain forms of treatment.[178] Also, when considering issues of public health, it is apparent that those in lower socio-economic groups and certain ethnic groups suffer worse health than those in higher ones.[179] This raises important questions about the justice of health.

9.5 Critics of principlism

It may be fair to say that the most vehement criticism against principlism is not levelled at the approach as it is developed to a high degree of sophistication by Beauchamp and Childress in their book, but at the way in which it has been used and developed in practice. A simplistic understanding of the principles and applying them in a naive way can lead to unsophisticated lines of thought.[180] The approach is also open to misuse because, stated baldly, the principles are open to a wide variety of meanings. It might be claimed that almost anything could be justified under one or other of the principles. Although, in their book, Beauchamp and Childress provide much guidance as to the meaning of the terms involved, it is arguable that, in a summary form, the notion of beneficence, for example, can mean pretty much whatever you want it to.[181]

To some, the principles are simply liable to lead to contradiction. The principles of doing one's best for one's patient (beneficence and non-maleficence) are simply antithetical to autonomy and justice. Autonomy only means something when the wishes of the patient are not in line with what the doctor wishes to do, but then the clash between the principles is set up. As we have seen, this need not be so. If beneficence is understood in terms of how the patient regards his or her best treatment, the potential conflict is

---

[177] Fox and Thompson (2013) provide a helpful discussion of the role of justice in health care.
[178] Higgs (2009).   [179] Bartley and Blane (2009).   [180] Campbell (2005).
[181] Clouser and Gert (1990).

lessened. However, that approach leads to a danger that maleficence and beneficence lose any meaning. If harm or benefit to a patient is to be determined by the patient, then the concepts become the same as autonomy. Although Sullivan[182] has suggested that a patient may have deeply held goals, but be mistaken as to how to reach those goals. For example, a patient may very much want to be cured of their illness, but believe that eating herbs is a better treatment, than that offered by the doctor. It might be argued that beneficence, giving the treatment, can be justified as it best helps the patient in reaching their goal (being cured) even if it overrides their decision about how to reach the goal.

Another objection is the lack of a clearer way of balancing the principles when they do clash. The difficulty for Beauchamp and Childress is that if they do indicate that, in the event of a clash, one particular principle trumps the others, this would undermine their claim that the four principles are of equal value. But critics argue that there is a need for a unifying moral theory to justify these four principles, which would then provide a way of reconciling them in the event of a clash. This leads some critics to argue that autonomy should be recognized as the primary principle. In fact, Beauchamp and Childress do give some guidance for cases in which it is necessary to infringe one principle in order to abide by another. They argue that this is justifiable only where the moral objective sought is realistic, no morally preferable alternative is available, the infringement is the least possible, and the healthcare professional must act to minimize the effects of the infringement. Further, we should remember that Beauchamp and Childress do not claim that principlism provides answers; rather, it provides an effective way of approaching an issue.[183] But this then leads some commentators to argue that there is simply not enough in the Beauchamp and Childress approach to deal with genuinely difficult cases.[184] Callahan, however, has argued that, given the way in which principlism is used in fact, autonomy ends up winning in any conflict between the principles—and that renders it objectionable to those who are concerned by an overemphasis on autonomy.[185]

A final objection is that using the four principles is simply too narrow. John Harris suggests that it causes 'sterility and uniformity of approach of a quite mind-bogglingly boring kind'.[186] Although he accepts that reference to the four principles would be a useful 'checklist' in ethical discussion, they must not be regarded as the final word, and there are a host of other issues and arguments that must be considered, even though they do not fit within the four principles approach.[187]

Tom Walker has also suggested that principlism fails to capture other moral values that people might want to consider.[188] He mentions the principles of respect and purity. He argues that principlism cannot explain why urinating on a grave or bestiality is wrong. In reply, Daniel Sokol defends principlism, arguing that the urination example can be explained as being contrary to the principle of non-maleficence to the deceased person (or surviving relatives and friends), and that bestiality can be explained as infringing the non-maleficence or autonomy principles in relation to the animal.[189] Such a debate, to defenders of principlism, demonstrates its flexibility, while to opponents it

---

[182] Sullivan (2016).
[183] Beauchamp (1995). See Gordon, Rauprich, and Vollmann (2011) for an attempt to use 'common morality' to deal with conflicts between the principles.
[184] Holm (1995).   [185] Callahan (2003).   [186] Harris (2003c: 303).
[187] See Baines (2008), who argues the principles do not operate well in cases involving children, in which the views of parents should carry some weight.
[188] Walker (2009).   [189] Sokol (2009).

demonstrates that the concepts of harm and autonomy are so flexible as to be meaningless.[190] For Charles Foster, principlism fails to provide an explanation for why these values are important.[191] Until we have a developed theory of human dignity from which the values used in principlism flow, he argues it will be hard to move ethical debates on.

10 Hermeneutics

The hermeneutic process is based on listening.[192] Where there is disagreement between a patient and a medical professional about a course of treatment, it encourages those involved to talk to each other and to listen to the 'stories' each have to tell.[193] The aim is that, by listening to each other, the parties can begin to work out for themselves the ethical problems and produce a shared understanding of the situation. In colloquial terms, each party can find out where the other is 'coming from'. This is not, then, an approach to ethics that suggests there are right answers or even general principles to apply, but rather one that suggests that the solution is that which is right for the people involved.

To many, this is idealistic. Not only is there rarely enough time to engage in this kind of dialogue, but it is also effective only where all parties are willing to engage in the process. If there is a belligerent patient, then the approach has nothing to offer. Further, where no solution can be found, the approach offers no resolution.[194] It may be that, in a few cases, it will enable the parties to develop a solution that is nuanced to respond to the special features of the problems as perceived by the parties.

11 Casuistry

Casuistry emphasizes that each case has its own unique circumstances and facts. Rather than starting with grand principles and applying them to the case at hand (as principlism does), casuists argue that we should start with the facts of the particular case and seek to find a resolution by comparing or contrasting other cases.[195] Lawyers will have some familiarity with this approach, because this is similar to the doctrine of precedent used in the common law. Lawyers tend to argue about whether the case at hand is similar to or distinct from earlier cases in which the law has been set down, rather than work from broad principles. The building blocks of the casuist approach are cases on which there would be a high degree of agreement among people as to the correct approach. Casuists emphasize that principles cannot be found or established outside the context of a particular factual situation.

12 Feminist medical ethics

No account of medical ethics would be complete without a consideration of feminist approaches to the question.[196] It would be wrong to think that there is 'one' feminist approach to medical ethics, and indeed there is fierce debate among feminists on some of

---

[190] See further Downie and Macnaughton (2007: ch. 1).   [191] Foster (2011).   [192] Boyd (2005).
[193] Boyd (2005); Hudson Jones (1999).   [194] Beauchamp (2004).
[195] Jones (1986). See also the dispute between Lawlor (2007) and Benatar (2007) over whether studying general ethical theories is useful in teaching medical ethics.
[196] Wolf (1996); Lindemann Nelson (2007).

the issues.[197] For example, while the vast majority of feminists regard increasing access to abortion as a major achievement for feminists, not all do. Frederica Mathewes-Green[198] argues that abortion is about promoting men's interests:

> For women, the condition of living in a man's world, on men's terms, was to be willing to never be pregnant. Why do feminists march in the streets to demand access to abortion? Because it has become a necessity. If women are going to fit men's demands in the bedroom and in the boardroom, they have to have a quick and easy way to get rid of their children.

So what makes an approach feminist? Susan Wolf suggests that 'feminist work takes gender and sex as centrally important analytic categories, seeks to understand their operation in the world, and strives to change the distribution and use of power to stop the oppression of women'.[199] Much work has been done to argue that medicine has become a way of controlling and exercising power over women.[200] For example, the 'medicalization of childbirth', it has been claimed, has led to a loss in control for women over the birthing process.[201] Similarly, the characterization of abortion as a medical issue has meant that it has been seen as one about which doctors should make decisions, rather than a social issue for the women concerned.

Feminists are keen to point out the inequalities in healthcare provision.[202] Feminist work has shown the lack of research into diseases that affect women particularly and how women's medical conditions are belittled or regarded as non-medical. Medics too often overlook the different impact that a particular condition has on men and women. By contrast, other normal aspects of women's lives (such as menstruation) are treated as illnesses.[203]

Feminist ethics has also been keen to emphasize how male norms can be used in a medical context to deprive women of power.[204] Women who are regarded as acting 'emotionally' are improperly treated as incompetent and therefore can be subjected to medical treatment against their will.[205] For example, there have been several cases in which women in labour have been regarded as incompetent to make decisions about the treatment of their pregnancy. There is also a persistent concern that traditional medical ethics rely on abstract principles which are applied to the case, rather than seeking to understand the realities of the individuals and their relationships in the particular context of the case.[206]

Cosmetic surgery is a good example of an issue over which feminists have disagreed. To some, cosmetic surgery represents the pressures that men place on women to accord to a certain kind of appearance.[207] The significance that is attached to women's appearance, and the extent to which they are judged by it, is revealed by the fact that women are willing to resort to surgery. The fact that some women do have surgery increases pressure felt by other women also to undertake the surgery. It may be argued that:

> In contemporary patriarchal culture, a panoptical male connoisseur resides within the consciousness of most women: they stand perpetually before his gaze and under his

---

[197] Marway and Widdows (2015); Wolf (1996: 5).   [198] Mathewes-Green (2013).
[199] Wolf (1996: 8).   [200] Foster (1995); Davis (1988).   [201] Hoffman (2005); Nettleton (2001).
[202] Rogers (2006); Mahowald (2006); Scambler (2009d).   [203] Purdy (1996).
[204] Sherwin (1996).   [205] Lupton (1994).   [206] Marway and Widdows (2015).
[207] And men too, with 'Moob surgery' being an option for some: BBC News online (28 January 2013).

judgment. Woman lives her body as seen by another, by an anonymous patriarchal Other.[208]

Such concerns have led some feminists to call for cosmetic surgery to be rendered illegal owing to the harm that it causes women.[209] Other feminists complain that these arguments fail to acknowledge the agency that women have. There may be some pressure on women to have a certain appearance, but to assume that the pressure is enough to mean that women are not free to make their own decisions is to assume that women are weak and easily swayed. Latham argues for a third approach emphasizing:

> . . . the importance of fully informed consent, counselling, a two-way constructive dialogue between a cosmetic surgeon and his patient, self-awareness by professionals of the impact of cultural ideals of beauty and, ultimately, an institutional recognition of a responsibility to combat negative social and cultural expectations.[210]

This would permit cosmetic surgery, but seek to combat the pressures to accord to stereotyped ideals of beauty.

Feminists have also worked on developing different ethical approaches to medical issues. Particularly influential has been the 'ethic of care', which will be described next.

13　Care ethics

Considerable attention in recent years has been paid to the 'ethics of care'.[211] Care ethics is critical of traditional bioethics, with its focus on rights and individual autonomy; instead, it focuses on relationships and care. Rather than valuing individual freedom, it values the interdependency and mutuality in relationships. Susan Wolf has argued:

> By depicting the moral community as a set of atomistic and self-serving individuals, it [liberal individualism] strips away relationships that are morally central. This not only is impoverished, but may also be harmful, because it encourages disregard of those bonds. It is also inaccurate; developing children as well as full-grown adults are profoundly interdependent. Indeed, we are so interdependent that we cannot even understand the terms of moral debate without some community process and shared understanding.[212]

Approaches based on ethics of care therefore tend to avoid using abstract principles as the primary tool of ethical analysis, and rather seek to find an approach that fits in with the needs and relationships of the individual case.[213] Hence the focus is less on questions such as 'What do I owe others?', and rather on questions such as 'How can I best express my caring responsibilities?' and 'How can I best deal with vulnerability, suffering, and dependence?'[214]

The following are some of the key themes that are found in much writing on care ethics.[215]

---

[208] Latham (2008: 12).　　[209] Bordo (1989).　　[210] Latham (2008).
[211] See Rogers (2015); Harding et al. (2017); Herring (2013b); Lõhmus (2015), McSherry, and Freckleton (2013); Held (2006); Herring (2007a); Bridgeman (2008).
[212] Wolf (1996: 17–18).　　[213] Tronto (1993).
[214] Gremmen, Widdershoven, Beekman, et al. (2008).
[215] Herring (2007a).

(i) ***The inevitability of interdependence*** Caring is the essence of life. From the very start of life, we are in relationships of dependency with others. The law should therefore see caring relationships as of crucial social significance.

(ii) ***The value of care*** Care is not only an inevitable part of life, but also a good part of life. The law should therefore value and encourage it.

(iii) ***Relational approaches*** The law should not treat us as atomistic individuals with individual rights and interests that clash with those of others.[216] Rather, the focus should be on the responsibilities that flow from our relationships with others. Virginia Held makes the point by contrasting ethics of care and an ethic of justice:

> An ethic of justice focuses on questions of fairness, equality, individual rights, abstract principles, and the consistent application of them. An ethic of care focuses on attentiveness, trust, responsiveness to need, narrative nuance, and cultivating caring relations. Whereas an ethic of justice seeks a fair solution between competing individual interests and rights, an ethic of care sees the interest of carers and cared-for as importantly intertwined rather than as simply competing.[217]

The ethics-of-care approach has, inevitably, received its fair share of criticism. First, it has been argued by feminists that its glorification of caring and dependency is likely to be harmful to women. The role of women as carers and dependants has been one that has led to their oppression and subordination.[218] To elevate and promote that role is harmful. Supporters of ethics of care would reply that the way ahead for women is not to seek to live the lives of independent, autonomous, unobliged individuals that some men appear to live, but rather to promote those values of care and dependency.

A second concern is that the notion of care is too vague.[219] It might be pointed out that not all caring relationships are good ones: they may involve manipulation and oppression. Without a far clearer concept of what 'good care' is, it cannot form the basis of an ethical approach. Many supporters of an ethic of care would accept that more work needs to be done to 'flesh out' the concept and that it is in relatively early days of development.[220]

A third concern is that elevating the role of care can be seen to denigrate the 'cared for'. Disability scholars are concerned that focusing on care leaves the person receiving care as simply the recipient of care. Richard Woods[221] argues:

> Disabled people have never demanded or asked for care! We have sought independent living, which means being able to achieve maximum independence and control over our own lives. The concept of care seems to many disabled people a tool through which others are able to dominate and manage our lives.

Care can be seen as an exercise of power. Julia Twigg's recent qualitative research on older people's experiences of being bathed highlights this quite clearly:

> One person, strong and able, stands above and over another who is frail and physically vulnerable, forced to rely on their strength and goodwill. Being naked in the face of

---

[216] Herring (2013a).   [217] Held (2006: 94).   [218] Wolf (1996: 9).   [219] Allmark (2002).
[220] Smart and Neale (1999).   [221] Quoted in Shakespeare (2000).

someone who is not, contains a powerful dynamic of domination and vulnerability, and it is often used in situations of interrogation and torture as a means of subjugating the individual.[222]

In response to such concerns I have emphasized the importance for care ethicists to explain care in relational terms:

> They require us to emphasise that we should seek to promote caring relationships, not just carers. We should emphasise that respect is central to good care, and that, most importantly, in the caring relationships we are all in there is a merging of interests and selves. Vulnerabilities, care and identities become mutual and interdependent. We need to break down the division between the 'carer' and the 'cared for', between the 'disabled' and the 'able-bodied'. Instead, we need to recognise our mutual vulnerability and need for care and ensure that there is a fair division of the burden and costs attached to caring relationships.[223]

14 Vulnerability

Closely connected to care ethics is the universal vulnerability thesis.[224] This argues that traditionally the law has assumed people are autonomous, self-sufficient, and independent. Individuals who do not fit this mould are labelled as vulnerable and in need of protection. The universal vulnerability thesis argues that everyone is vulnerable. As Rogers, Mackenzie, and Dodds put it:

> . . . all human life is conditioned by vulnerability, as a result of our embodied, finite, and socially contingent existence. Vulnerability is thus an ontological condition of our humanity.[225]

The claim is that we all need each other for physical, emotional, and practical support. Some vulnerability thesis supporters argue that society helps meet the needs of some better than others and so although we all share a vulnerability, the precariousness of some is more evident than it is to others. As Martha Fineman argues:

> Throughout our lives we may be subject to external and internal negative, potentially devastating, events over which we have little control—disease, pandemics, environmental and climate deterioration, terrorism and crime, crumbling infrastructure, failing institutions, recession, corruption, decay, and decline. We are situated beings who live with the ever-present possibility of changing needs and circumstances in our individual and collective lives. We are also accumulative beings and have different qualities and quantities of resources with which to meet these needs of circumstances, both over the course of our lifetime and as measured at the time of crisis or opportunity.[226]

The significance of this approach is that it recognizes that our health and well-being relies on the support and care of others.[227] The law should, therefore, do less to emphasize self-sufficiency and independence and more to recognize our mutual interdependence.[228]

---

[222] Twigg (2000).   [223] Herring (2014a).   [224] Herring (2016a); ten Have (2016).
[225] Rogers, Mackenzie, and Dodds (2015).   [226] Fineman (2013).   [227] Herring (2016).
[228] Wrigley (2015) expresses concerns about the use of vulnerability.

15 Virtue ethics

Virtue ethics goes back to the writings of Socrates and Aristotle. It emphasizes that, in assessing what is the morally correct thing to do, it is not the consequences of your actions that matter, but rather the attitudes (virtues) motivating your actions.[229] It is the character of an individual, not the consequences of his or her actions, which is more important. Virtues are good habits that will direct human nature towards good actions. Rachels suggests that a virtue is 'a trait of character, manifested in habitual action, that it is good for a person to have'.[230] We therefore require that our healthcare professionals act compassionately, honestly, fairly, and with diligence. Some professionals might find this attractive. In the heat of the hospital faced with an appalling ethical dilemma, they may not be confident of choosing the right course of action, but they may be confident that their decision was based on compassion and kindness.[231]

Stephen Holland summarizes virtue ethics in this way:

> Virtues are character traits, or dispositions of character, such as courage and benevolence, acquired during upbringing; one ought to develop and practise the exercise of the virtues and inculcate them in children. The fully virtuous agent possesses and is adept at exercising the virtues. Actions can be evaluated by asking whether the virtuous agent would endorse them.[232]

Virtue ethicists disagree over the extent to which consequences can be used to assess the appropriateness of an act. Some argue that consequences are irrelevant, so that a well-motivated act cannot be wrong regardless of the consequences.[233] Others argue that the bad consequence can render an act wrongful. Similarly, there is a dispute over whether an ill-motivated act that produces a good result can be regarded as right. What all virtue ethicists do agree on is that the motivation is a crucial element in any moral assessment. Philippa Foot explains:

> Men and women need to be industrious and tenacious of purpose not only so as to be able to house, clothe and feed themselves, but also to pursue human ends having to do with love and friendship. They need the ability to form family ties, friendships and special relations with neighbours. They also need codes of conduct. And how could they have all these things without virtues such as loyalty, fairness, kindness and in certain circumstances obedience?[234]

One concern with virtue ethics is how we should decide what are 'good virtues'. In such a diverse society, there is no agreement on what a 'good person' is like; there are many different ideas of what makes a 'good life'. It may be that, in Western society, keeping fit or eating moderately would be regarded as a virtue, but it is unclear whether in other societies this would be so. But virtue ethicists often argue that there are moral values that are essential for any decent society: love, friendship, truth-telling, faithfulness, and wisdom would be accepted around the world as virtues.[235]

---

[229] Pellegino (1995); Gardiner (2003).   [230] Rachels (1999: 35).
[231] See Holland (2011) and Jackson (2006) for a developed account of medical ethics using a virtues-based approach.
[232] Holland (2011: 112).   [233] Macintyre (1984).   [234] Foot (2001: 41).
[235] Nussbaum (1988); Olkin (1998).

Some critics complain that focusing on virtues could uphold unacceptable activities as moral. The suicide bomber may be said to show great courage and steadfastness of purpose, yet the consequences of his or her action reveal it clearly to be immoral. This has led many to recommend an approach that considers both virtues *and* Beauchamp and Childress's four principles.[236] Indeed, Beauchamp and Childress list five focal virtues—compassion, discernment, trustworthiness, integrity, and conscientiousness—but argue that those would be displayed by any doctor following their four principles.[237] Another concern is that although virtue ethics might provide good guidance in relation to whether a particular medical professional has acted appropriately, it does not provide adequate guidance over other public issues that trouble medical ethicists, such as whether or not human cloning should be permitted or how health care should be rationed.[238]

There are particular difficulties in applying virtue ethics to law. Consider, for example, a law which required medical professionals to act compassionately.[239] This would be problematic because it would be very difficult to know what was motivating a professional when they acted. It would also fail to give professionals clear guidance as to how they behave.

16 Communitarian ethics

Communitarian ethicists are critical of the overemphasis on individualism within much current bioethics.[240] Too much weight has been placed on the rights of individuals, and too little on individuals' responsibilities and the interests of the wider community.[241] As members of society, we have an obligation to make some sacrifices in order to promote it, and we should have no objection because it is only as a member of society that we can flourish as an individual. Communitarians are therefore more willing to allow acts to be done without the consent of an individual, if necessary, to further the interests of society. Some communitarians therefore support the use of organs from the deceased for transplant purposes, regardless of the views of the deceased.

Communitarians emphasize that living in a decent community and society is key to a good life. When we consider an issue such as whether a person should be allowed to sell his or her kidneys, therefore, seeing the issue in terms of the rights of the different people involved is to ignore what communitarians suggest is a key question: is selling kidneys compatible with a decent society?[242]

Critics might pick up on this last point and argue that a decent society is one that respects individuals' rights.[243] If this is correct, we may be back with the individualist approach to rights that communitarianism seeks to oppose. Critics also point to the dangers of being willing to interfere with individuals' rights 'for the greater good'. While this might sound attractive, this kind of reasoning has been used by all kinds of oppressive regimes. In particular, there is a danger that promoting the interests of the community will work against the interests of those on the edges of society, who may

---

[236] Campbell (2003); Gillon (2003).   [237] Beauchamp and Childress (2009: ch. 2).
[238] Although see Holland (2011), who promotes 'virtue politics', which could be used to deal with such questions.
[239] Herring (2017)   [240] Etzioni (2011); Callahan (2003).
[241] See English, Mussell, Sheather, et al. (2006).   [242] Callahan (2003).
[243] Childress and Bernheim (2003).

be its most vulnerable members.[244] Critics also argue that the notion that determines 'the interests of the community' has become impossible given the wide range of groups within society.

17 Theology

It might be thought inappropriate to discuss theology in a book on medical law and ethics.[245] True, some individuals might be influenced by their religious beliefs in deciding what treatment they wish to receive, but should theology have any role to play when deciding what the law should be or what ethical standards should govern the behaviour of doctors generally?[246]

The justifications put forward by those who promote theological ideas in medical law and ethics include the following. First, it is argued that, in the UK, even though the percentage of people attending religious services may not be great, there is still a high percentage of people who regard themselves as religious. The 2017 Social Attitudes Survey census found that 50 per cent of people said they were religious.[247] Interestingly, around half of those who said they belonged to a religion did not attend any religious meetings regularly. However vaguely they may understand the concept, it seems that many people have some appreciation of the spiritual. If medical law and ethics are to reflect the attitudes of society, then arguably something spiritual needs to be part of that. Critics would respond by arguing that even if there is a bare majority of people who have some kind of religious belief, these are so diverse and so vague as to be of little relevance. Mark Sheehan has noted that the diversity of beliefs even among one branch of one religion indicates that socio-economic factors or personal experience are as significant, if not more so, than a person's religion.[248]

Second, it might be argued that some theological points of view, although supportable by theological arguments, can also be supported rationally.[249] These arguments should then be considered alongside other 'rational' arguments.[250]

A third point is that religious ideas do play a very important role in many people's lives and, even if that is so for only a small minority of individuals, medical professionals will be faced with religious patients, meaning that an awareness and discussion of the approaches is useful.[251]

A fourth point is that a religious perspective can offer a challenging alternative to orthodox approaches to medical ethics and that, in considering and replying to it, the secular view can be clarified and strengthened. There is, however, a difficulty here: many religious arguments are based on precepts that may not be readily open to challenge and negotiation. A person who believes that euthanasia is immoral because

---

[244] Parker (2002).
[245] See Keown and Jones (2008) on the dangers of lawyers dabbling in theology and vice versa.
[246] For a discussion of the interaction of Christianity and English medical law, see Wicks (2009).
[247] National Centre for Social Research (2017). 44 per cent of people questioned said they were Christian and 6 per cent other religions.
[248] Sheehan (2013).
[249] For example, Ramsey (1970), which, although written from a religious perspective, has proved highly influential on secular bioethics.
[250] Bishop (2014); Messer (2002; 2009).   [251] See further McHale (2008); Biggar and Hogan (2010).

it is prohibited in a holy text is not going to receive much from, or be able to negotiate with, secular ethicists unless the validity of the holy text is open to debate.[252]
For some commentators such as Tristram Engelhardt, there is a huge divide between
secular and religious perspectives, which is not based on a particular reading of
scripture:

> On the one hand, there is a perspective rooted in traditional Christian views of repro-
> duction, sexuality, living, suffering, dying, and death, which bear on health care and the
> biomedical sciences. On the other hand, there is a secular ideology that is increasingly
> dominant in the West and across the world, which affirms personal autonomy, equality,
> and a sense of human dignity and social justice rooted in Enlightenment commitments,
> all of which sustain a quite different bioethics. This laicist moral vision seeks to deflate
> the moral significance of choices regarding sexuality, reproduction, health care choices
> in general, and choices at the end of life in particular, so that these areas of 'moral con-
> cern' become largely matters of personal choice, rather than being considered to be
> governed by generally binding moral norms.[253]

The difficulty is that a full appreciation of most religious views requires an in-depth
understanding of the theology underpinning that religion, which in the case of many
religions has been developed to a high degree of sophistication. Nevertheless, there
are themes that appear to unite the world's religions.[254] There is a strong line taken
on the sanctity of life. Life is seen as a precious gift from God, which should not be
readily taken away. All human life has an intrinsic value.[255] This leads to a strong line
often being taken against abortion and euthanasia. There is also a strong emphasis on
the values of love and compassion, which can resonate with virtue ethics. The notion
of humans being stewards of the world, placed by God to look after it, is a theme that
is found in many religions. However, how this works out in bioethics is hotly debated.
Some religious people are very wary of new medical techniques that are regarded as
'playing God'; others argue that God has given humans the talents and abilities to develop new technologies, and therefore that they should be applied where they would
prevent suffering and promote good.[256]

In *Re A (Children) (Conjoined Twins: Surgical Separation)*,[257] the Court of Appeal
took the unusual step of allowing the Roman Catholic Archbishop of Westminster to
make written submissions to the Court. This has proved controversial. On the one
hand, there are those who argue that the Church, just like anyone else, has the right
to participate in a court case. As long as religious groups are not seeking to 'insinuate
doctrine under the guise of legal argument', there is no objection.[258] Harris and Holm
accept that religious groups can be involved in court cases and public debates, although
their arguments must be based on rational argument supported by evidence rather than
prejudice.[259] Supporters of religious involvement might argue that religious groups, just
as anyone else, can make arguments about what makes a good society and about the
moral values that underpin our community. Such contributions, they argue, may be

[252] See, e.g., Padela (2007), making this point from an Islamic perspective.
[253] Engelhardt (2011: 2).
[254] Although see Sarma (2008) on the difficulties in developing a Hindu approach to bioethics.
[255] Saunders (2015).   [256] Shahzad (2007); Daar and Khitamy (2001).   [257] [2000] 4 All ER 961.
[258] Skene and Parker (2002).   [259] Harris and Holm (2002).

useful to courts and policymakers.[260] Smith,[261] however, believes that the differences between secular and religious scholars is too great to allow fruitful discussion:

> The distinction between secular philosophical schools and religion is fundamental. With the former, ethical discourse is based on sets of principles that are open to rational analysis and dissection. . . . By contrast, religiously inspired ethical claims are posited upon belief in God(s). Accordingly, many of the resulting ethical claims derive from God's authority, not reason.

Nigel Biggar[262] does not accept the assumption that only non-religious views are based on reason and argues that religious voices should be permitted at the table of debate. He rejects an argument that religious views cannot be proved and so should not be considered:

> It is true that religious believers believe in things that they cannot put under a microscope or demonstrate mathematically—God's existence, for example, or cosmic teleology or the afterlife. But, then, many unbelievers have faith in human dignity and in the unstoppable progress of human history, neither of which can be proven empirically or logically, and both of which attract rational doubts.[263]

He argues, however, that believers must join the conversation with 'good manners'. That means they cannot simply assert the authority of a religious text or leader, but must put their arguments in terms that can appeal to non-religious parties to the debate.[264] By contrast, some writing from a religious perspective have argued that religions should not seek actively to influence legal or political decisions for fear of being seen as imposing their beliefs on others.[265]

18 Relativism

Moral relativism, or pluralism, argues that there are many different answers to complex moral issues and that it would be wrong to suggest that one view is necessarily superior to another. In short, there are no 'right answers'. Basically, you choose the option that seems to work best for the particular case with which you are dealing.[266] In fact, there are few absolute moral relativists. To say that whether rape is wrong is a matter of opinion appears a rather extreme view. Opponents (moral objectivists) reject such approaches, arguing that there *are* moral absolutes. Although the men charged with child abuse on the island of Pitcairn might have tried to claim that, within their culture, sexual relations with children were widespread, that did not and should not have rendered their actions morally permissible.[267] The growth of international conventions on bioethical issues indicates that consensus can be reached over fundamental principles.

There is a further point here: are the medical ethics developed in the West also based on a 'Western mindset'? We tend to focus on individual rights, and concepts of

---

[260] Gormally (2002).   [261] Smith (2017).   [262] Biggar (2015a and b).
[263] Cherry (2017) argues without a belief in God it is not possible to determine moral truth.
[264] Earp (2015)   [265] Coady (2002).
[266] As Pattinson (2011a: 4) points out, a true moral relativist would not even accept that you must respect other people's points of view, because that would be stating a moral absolute.
[267] BBC News online (29 September 2004).

community, tradition, and relationships may be neglected. Are these ethical principles no more than a reflection of certain Western norms, based on an assumption that the individualist lifestyles of the West are best?[268]

Complex issues also arise in relation to 'medical' practices that are acceptable in some cultures, but not particularly dominant in the UK. The government has, for example, through the Female Genital Mutilation Act 2003, rendered female circumcision illegal even though it is regarded as acceptable in some cultures. No doubt there are medical practices that take place in the UK that would be unacceptable elsewhere. This raises issues surrounding the right to 'impose' a dominant cultural view on a minority group and further issues surrounding moral pluralism.[269] This issue can be exaggerated—there are, in reality, few issues on which, in the field of bioethics, there are significant cultural differences of an ethical kind, even if the way of reasoning may not be the same.

19 Personhood

19.1 The concept of personhood

A major theme in many debates in medical law involve a dispute over the concept of personhood. This, somewhat unhelpful, term, refers to a moral claim: that the being is entitled to have the highest moral status. Those things which are 'persons' have a higher moral status than non-persons. It means, for example, if you are in a burning building and you can only save a person or a non-person you should prefer to save a person. It is, therefore, not necessarily the same as the idea of a human being: that is a description of a biological category, rather than a moral claim. However, it is generally assumed that human beings, or at least most of them, are persons. In other words, there is nothing it would be better to save than a human being from the fire.

Thinking about personhood requires us to determine what is morally significant or special about humans. Why do human beings have a higher moral status than dogs, Picassos, or computers? Why does the law give persons human rights, but other entities lesser protections? Three main views can be found in the literature, although even among the views there is diversity in how they are expressed.[270]

19.2 Mental capabilities

This is a very popular school of thought and argues that mental capabilities, such as cognition, self-consciousness, and practical rationality are key to personhood. The precise formulations of the key criteria differ and might include self-awareness, being an entity who can value its own existence, or being an entity who can experience itself as a being whose life can go better or worse.[271] Wasserman proposes the following list:

> self-consciousness, awareness of and concern for oneself as a temporally-extended subject; practical rationality, rational agency, or autonomy; moral responsibility; a capacity

---

[268] Bowman (2004).   [269] The issue is discussed well in Charlesworth (2004).
[270] For example, whether it is sufficient to show capacity for these criteria or whether they must be currently demonstrated.
[271] Baker (2005); McMahan (2002); Singer (1993); Harris (1985).

to recognize other selves and to be motivated to justify one's actions to them; the capacity to be held, and hold others, morally accountable.

For some writers the ability to act autonomously is key. A table cannot be wronged as it is not possible to act against its wishes. Indeed, a table cannot have wishes. The ability to decide how to live and to make morally good choices, rather than be driven by brute desires, is what separates out humans as being of the highest moral value.

There are a number of problems with this approach. One is that it might mean intelligent non-human animals, dolphins, and gorillas, for example, might fulfil these requirements. That is not really a problem because they can be included within the definition of persons. More problematic is that some human beings will lack the listed abilities, especially those with profound mental impairments and young children.[272] Indeed, the logic of the approach could be that personhood is granted to a high-functioning chimpanzee, but not an adult human being with severe cognitive impairment. You can begin to see why the argument has proved so controversial. Some philosophers are happy to bite the bullet and say that this is correct. A non-human animal with higher mental capabilities may be of greater moral status than a human without them. Peter Singer[273] has argued that those who reject that conclusion are guilty of speciesism: giving an irrational preference to members of one's own species. He sees that as analogous to racism.

There might also be a challenge to the assumption that all persons are of equal moral value. Most people would reject a claim that one category of humans is more morally valuable than another, that being the argument used by racists and the like. However, if what makes us valuable is certain mental capabilities then that appears to imply that people with more of those capabilities are of more value.

A final challenge is simply to question whether it is mental capabilities that generate moral value. Ideas about intelligence change over time and it is a notoriously difficult concept to measure. Nor does it seem to follow that those with mental capabilities are more moral than those without. Vehmas,[274] however, points out that virtue need not be connected to intelligence:

> positive and virtuous traits of character are often characteristic of individuals with intellectual disabilities as well: honesty, courage, persistence, love, a lack of pretence and other similar virtues which individuals with intellectual disabilities are often more able to embrace than normal individuals due to the lack of intellectual reflection; we normal individuals often prevent our moral virtues from becoming actualised by the practice of our intellectual skills.

Although the reply to this is that there is something particularly moral about a person who after weighing up the options decides to do good. That is only possible for a person with a degree of mental capability.

19.3 Personhood and membership of the human community

A second view is that personhood flows from being a member of the human species. Bernard Williams[275] imagines a scenario in which aliens conquer the planet and claim to be superior to humans and so entitled to dominate them. Williams suggests that if any human accepted the aliens' argument we would ask legitimately, 'Whose side are

---

[272] Vukov (2017).   [273] Singer (1985 and 2016); McMahan (2016).   [274] Vahmas (1993).
[275] Williams (1996).

you on?' He claims we are entitled to say: 'We're humans here, we're the ones doing the judging; you can't really expect anything else but a bias or prejudice in favor of human beings.' As Scanlon[276] asserts:

> the mere fact that a being is 'of human born' provides a strong reason for according it the same status as other humans. This has sometimes been characterized as prejudice, called speciesism. But it is not prejudice to hold that our own relation to these beings gives us reason to accept the requirement that our actions be justifiable to them.

This argument has its attractions. It has no difficulty in explaining why human beings with profound mental impairments or babies can still be persons. However, its difficulty is explaining why the human species deserves a higher moral status. As Singer argues, unless you can point to some morally relevant characteristic you are just relying on an irrational preference.

Linked to this difficulty is the question of what defines a member of the human species. Is it having a particular kind of DNA?[277] That is problematic as chimpanzee DNA is very similar to human DNA. Is it simply being recognized by other human beings as human?[278] But that may be problematic because some of the darkest times in history have been when one group of humans claims another group is 'second class'. The temptation is to refer to the characteristics of what a typical human can do, but that might too easily collapse into an argument that some humans lack those capabilities.[279]

19.4 Relational personhood

This view, which has fewer supporters,[280] is that we should attach moral status not to individuals but to human relationships. It is relationships of love and care which are of moral value. As Feder Kittay puts it:

> We human beings are the sorts of beings we are because we are cared for by other human beings, and the human being's ontological status and corresponding moral status needs to be acknowledged by the larger society that makes possible the work of those who do the caring required to sustain us. That is what we each require if we are some mother's child, and we are all some mother's child.[281]

Under this view human beings or other animals on their own do not have a particular moral status. However, it is the relationships which generate moral care. As Foster and I put it:

> In isolation our lives have no great value. In isolation they lack meaning. As the Obuntu people put it 'I am, because we are; and since we are, therefore I am'. Our greatest claim to moral value lies not in ourselves, but in relationships of care. Am I a person? By myself, no. Are we people? Yes, if we care. Together we are so much more than we are alone.

There are three primary difficulties with this view. The first is that there may be people who have relationships with no one: a hermit or an abandoned baby, for example. Do they therefore lack any moral status?[282] The second is that the term 'relationships of love and care' is very vague and may therefore not provide a coherent guide as to personhood.

---

[276] Scanlon (1998: 185). See also McGee (2016).   [277] DeGrazia (2016).
[278] Curtis, Vehmans, and Vehmas (2016); Vehmas and Curtis (2017); Häyry (2017).
[279] See the discussion in Wilkins (2016).   [280] Foster and Herring (2017).
[281] Feder Kittay (2009).   [282] Jones (2017).

Third, it does not explain why all people are seen as equal. If someone has more caring relationships are they more valuable?

20 Conclusion

It is an exciting time to study medical law. Technological advances are raising new issues; sociological changes are challenging the established power relationships; and new ways of thinking about ethics are emerging. This chapter has set out some of the ways of approaching ethical questions. Some of these more easily translate into traditional legal thought: especially those such as deontology which are based on following rules. Others, such as care ethics, are harder because they insist on a careful working through of the issue within the context of the particular set of relationships. That, if adopted by the law, would require a very different kind of legal intervention. What is certainly true is that as medical law and ethics progress there are exciting times ahead.

QUESTIONS

1. Do you think that medical lawyers need medical ethics?

2. Is cosmetic surgery a proper use of medicine? Should it be outlawed? What about surgery that would make a black person appear more 'white'?[283]

3. Consider how the different ethical approaches would deal with a case in which a father wanted to donate his heart to his daughter, who needed a heart transplant, even though the result would be that the father would die.

4. Should religious reasoning ever be relevant to those developing medical law or ethics?

5. Some 3.7 million people care for sick relatives or friends, with 1.7 million spending more than twenty hours a week caring—all unpaid. These figures exceed the workforce of the NHS. Should medical law and ethics pay far more attention to the work of carers than that of the 'professionals'?[284]

6. Some commentators have complained that medical ethics focuses exclusively on issues concerning the permissibility of certain medical activities, but that this leaves out a consideration of emotions such as regret or guilt.[285] Some things are permissible, but regrettable. Do you agree that permissibility should be only one issue for ethicists to consider?

7. Many commentators have noted the increased commercialization of medicine.[286] Do commercial pressures pose a greater threat to good medical practice than ignorance of ethical matters? Donna Dickenson, in a powerful book, has argued that we are seeing increased personalization of medicine, with rich people buying for themselves what they need and a shift away from the idea of health being a communal matter.[287]

8. José Miola suggests that the volume of writing on medical ethics has 'not made medical ethics more effective but, rather, has allowed the various discourses to cancel

---

[283] Lamkin (2011).   [284] See Dodds (2009); Herring (2008b).
[285] See, e.g., MacKenzie (2007).   [286] See, e.g., Reiman (2007).   [287] Dickenson (2013).

each other out, leaving a regulatory vacuum to be filled by the conscience of the individual medical practitioner'.[288] Is there a danger that there are so many different ethical theories that medical ethics are of no use to the practitioner? If so, what should be done about it?

FURTHER READING

A comprehensive bibliography, including all references used throughout the book, is available online at www.oup.com/uk/herringmedical7e/.

For general books on medical law and ethics, see:

Beauchamp, T. and Childress, J. (2013) *Principles of Biomedical Ethics* (Oxford University Press).

Campos de, T. (2017) *The Global Health Crisis* (Cambridge University Press).

Dickenson, D. (2013) *Me Medicine v We Medicine* (Columbia University Press).

Foster, C. (2011) *Human Dignity in Bioethics and Law* (Hart).

Foster, C. (2013) *A Very Short Introduction to Medical Law* (Oxford University Press).

Fulford, K., Dickenson, D., and Murray, T. (2002) *Health Care Ethics and Human Values* (Blackwell).

Goold, I. and Herring, J. (2014) *Great Debates in Medical Law and Ethics* (Palgrave).

Herring, J. and Wall, J. (2015) *Landmark Cases in Medical Law* (Hart).

Hope, T. (2005) *A Very Short Introduction to Medical Ethics* (Oxford University Press).

Hursthouse, R. (1999) *On Virtue Ethics* (Oxford University Press).

Lõhmus, K. (2015) *Caring Autonomy: European Human Rights Law and the Challenge of Individualism* (Cambridge University Press).

Miola, J. (2007) *Medical Ethics and Medical Law* (Hart).

Murphy, T. (2013) *Health and Human Rights* (Hart).

Rogers, C. (2016) *Intellectual Disability and Being Human* (Routledge).

Seay, G. and Nuccetelli, S. (2016) *Engaging Bioethics* (Routledge).

Veitch, K. (2007) *The Jurisdiction of Medical Law* (Ashgate).

Wilson, D. (2014) *The Making of British Bioethics* (Manchester University Press).

For feminist approaches to medical ethics, see:

Harding, R., Fletcher, R., and Beasley, C. (eds) *Revaluing Care in Theory, Law and Policy* (Routledge).

Herring, J. (2013) *Caring and the Law* (Hart).

Herring, J. (2016) *Vulnerable Adults and the Law* (Oxford University Press).

Mahowald, M. (2006) *Bioethics and Women* (Oxford University Press).

---

[288] Miola (2007: 1).

Marway, H. and Widdows, H. (2015) 'Philosophical feminist bioethics', *Cambridge Quarterly of Healthcare Ethics* 24: 165.

Rogers, W., Mackenzie, C., and Dodds, S. (2015) 'Why bioethics needs a concept of vulnerability', *International Journal of Feminist Approaches to Bioethics* 5: 11.

For religious perspectives, see:

Biggar, N. (2015) 'Why religion deserves a place in secular medicine', *Journal of Medical Ethics* 41: 229.

Biggar, N. and Hogan, L. (2010) *Religious Voices in Public Places* (Oxford University Press).

Cromwell, S. (2003) *Hindu Bioethics in the Twenty-First Century* (New York University Press).

Engelhardt, H. (2011) 'The culture wars in bioethics revisited', *Christian Bioethics* 17: 1.

Keown, D. (1995) *Buddhism and Bioethics* (Macmillan).

Messer, N. (2002) *Theological Issues in Bioethics* (Darton, Longman and Todd).

Mustafa, Y. (2014) 'Islam and the four principles of medical ethics', *Journal of Medical Ethics* 40: 479.

Sachedina, A. (2009) *Islamic Biomedical Ethics* (Oxford University Press).

Sinclair, D. (2005) *Jewish Medical Ethics* (Oxford University Press).

Smith II, G. (2005) *The Christian Religion and Biotechnology* (Springer).

Tsai, D. (2005) 'The bioethical principles and Confucius' moral philosophy', *Journal of Medical Ethics* 31: 159.

On personhood

Curtis, B., Vehmans, S., and Vehmas, S. (2016) 'A Moorean argument for the full moral status of those with profound intellectual disability', *Journal of Medical Ethics* 42: 41.

Feder Kittay, E. (2009) 'The personal is philosophical is political', *Metaphilosophy* 40: 606.

Foster, C. and Herring, J. (2017) *Identity, Personhood and the Law* (Springer).

McMahan, J. (2002) *The Ethics of Killing* (Oxford University Press).

Vukov, J. (2017) 'Personhood and Natural Kinds: Why Cognitive Status Need Not Affect Moral Status', *Journal of Medicine and Philosophy* 42: 261.

The Structure of the National Health Service and the Rationing of Healthcare Resources

INTRODUCTION

Politicians on all sides of the political spectrum claim to be committed to the NHS. It is not only of great national importance, but it is also the scene of huge political controversy and regularly appears at election times as one of the issues about which voters feel most strongly.

This chapter will be looking at the structure of the NHS and some of the key issues facing those dealing with its management. Although the structure of the NHS, and the way in which the money allocated to it is distributed and spent, may not at first sight appear the most fascinating of topics, in fact it raises a large number of important and interesting issues. To discuss properly the structures of the NHS and all of the surrounding issues would take, at least, a substantial book in itself.

This chapter will briefly summarize the structure of this vast institution and then select some of the most topical issues facing it. The first point to emphasize is that the NHS is, quite simply, enormous. Consider the following statistics:[1]

- NHS net expenditure was £78.881 bn in 2006/07 and rose to £120.512 bn in 2016/17. Planned expenditure for 2017/18 is £123.817 bn and for 2018/19 is £126.269 bn.

- Health expenditure (medical services, health research, central, and other health services) per capita in England was £2,106 in 2015/16.

- In March 2017, across Hospital and Community Healthcare Services (HCHS), the NHS employed (full-time equivalent): 106,430 doctors; 285,893 nurses and health visitors; 21,597 midwives; 132,673 scientific, therapeutic, and technical staff; 19,772 ambulance staff; 21,139 managers; and 9,974 senior managers.

- The NHS deals with over 1 m patients every thirty-six hours.

- In 2015/16 there were 10.119 m operations.

- In 2016/17 there were 23.372 m attendances at accident and emergency departments.

---

[1] Taken from NHS (2017b).

1 What are the principles underpinning the NHS?

The NHS has a Constitution.[2] This opens with a statement about what the NHS is for:

> It is there to improve our health and wellbeing, supporting us to keep mentally and physically well, to get better when we are ill and, when we cannot fully recover, to stay as well as we can to the end of our lives. It works at the limits of science—bringing the highest levels of human knowledge and skill to save lives and improve health. It touches our lives at times of basic human need, when care and compassion are what matter most.[3]

It then sets out seven core principles:

1. **The NHS provides a comprehensive service, available to all** irrespective of gender, race, disability, age, sexual orientation, religion, belief, gender reassignment, pregnancy and maternity or marital or civil partnership status. The service is designed to diagnose, treat and improve both physical and mental health. It has a duty to each and every individual that it serves and must respect their human rights. At the same time, it has a wider social duty to promote equality through the services it provides and to pay particular attention to groups or sections of society where improvements in health and life expectancy are not keeping pace with the rest of the population.

2. **Access to NHS services is based on clinical need, not an individual's ability to pay.** NHS services are free of charge, except in limited circumstances sanctioned by Parliament.

3. **The NHS aspires to the highest standards of excellence and professionalism**— in the provision of high quality care that is safe, effective and focused on patient experience; in the people it employs, and in the support, education, training and development they receive; in the leadership and management of its organisations; and through its commitment to innovation and to the promotion, conduct and use of research to improve the current and future health and care of the population. Respect, dignity, compassion and care should be at the core of how patients and staff are treated not only because that is the right thing to do but because patient safety, experience and outcomes are all improved when staff are valued, empowered and supported.

4. **The NHS aspires to put patients at the heart of everything it does.** It should support individuals to promote and manage their own health. NHS services must reflect, and should be coordinated around and tailored to, the needs and preferences of patients, their families and their carers. Patients, with their families and carers, where appropriate, will be involved in and consulted on all decisions about their care and treatment. The NHS will actively encourage feedback from the public, patients and staff, welcome it and use it to improve its services.

5. **The NHS works across organisational boundaries and in partnership with other organisations in the interest of patients, local communities and the wider population.** The NHS is an integrated system of organisations and services bound together by the principles and values reflected in the Constitution. The NHS is committed to working jointly with other local authority services, other public sector

---

[2] NHS (2013a).   [3] NHS (2013a: 3).

organisations and a wide range of private and voluntary sector organisations to provide and deliver improvements in health and well-being.

6. **The NHS is committed to providing best value for taxpayers' money and the
   most effective, fair and sustainable use of finite resources.** Public funds for
   healthcare will be devoted solely to the benefit of the people that the NHS serves.

7. **The NHS is accountable to the public, communities and patients that it serves.**
   The NHS is a national service funded through national taxation, and it is the
   Government which sets the framework for the NHS and which is accountable to
   Parliament for its operation. However, most decisions in the NHS, especially those
   about the treatment of individuals and the detailed organisation of services, are
   rightly taken by the local NHS and by patients with their clinicians. The system of
   responsibility and accountability for taking decisions in the NHS should be transparent and clear to the public, patients and staff. The Government will ensure that
   there is always a clear and up-to-date statement of NHS accountability for this
   purpose.[4]

The NHS Constitution informs patients of the rights to which they are entitled, under
a range of headings:

Access to health services:

- You have the right to receive NHS services free of charge, apart from certain limited
  exceptions sanctioned by Parliament.

- You have the right to access NHS services. You will not be refused access on unreasonable grounds.

- You have the right to expect your NHS to assess the health requirements of your
  community and to commission and put in place the services to meet those needs as
  considered necessary, and in the case of public health services commissioned by local
  authorities, to take steps to improve the health of the local community.

- You have the right, in certain circumstances, to go to other European Economic Area
  countries or Switzerland for treatment which would be available to you through your
  NHS commissioner.

- You have the right not to be unlawfully discriminated against in the provision of
  NHS services including on grounds of gender, race, disability, age, sexual orientation, religion, belief, gender reassignment, pregnancy and maternity or marital or civil
  partnership status.

- You have the right to access certain services commissioned by NHS bodies within
  maximum waiting times, or for the NHS to take all reasonable steps to offer you a
  range of suitable alternative providers if this is not possible. The waiting times are
  described in the Handbook to the NHS Constitution.

The NHS also commits:

- to provide convenient, easy access to services within the waiting times set out in the
  Handbook to the NHS Constitution (pledge);

---

[4] NHS (2013a: 6). The Constitution was referred to by the court in *R (Booker) v NHS Oldham* [2010]
EWHC 2593 (Admin) in ruling unlawful the actions of a trust in denying a patient treatment on the basis
that the patient had been awarded damages in a court case to pay for private treatment.

- to make decisions in a clear and transparent way, so that patients and the public can understand how services are planned and delivered (pledge); and
- to make the transition as smooth as possible when you are referred between services, and to put you, your family and carers at the centre of decisions that affect you or them (pledge).

Quality of care and environment:

- **You have the right** to be treated with a professional standard of care, by appropriately qualified and experienced staff, in a properly approved or registered organisation that meets required levels of safety and quality.
- **You have the right** to expect NHS bodies to monitor, and make efforts to improve continuously, the quality of healthcare they commission or provide. This includes improvements to the safety, effectiveness and experience of services.

The NHS also commits:

- to ensure that services are provided in a clean and safe environment that is fit for purpose, based on national best practice (pledge);
- to identify and share best practice in quality of care and treatments (pledge); and
- that if you are admitted to hospital, you will not have to share sleeping accommodation with patients of the opposite sex, except where appropriate, in line with details set out in the Handbook to the NHS Constitution (pledge).

Nationally approved treatments, drugs and programmes:

- **You have the right** to drugs and treatments that have been recommended by NICE [the National Institute for Health and Care Excellence] for use in the NHS, if your doctor says they are clinically appropriate for you.
- **You have the right** to expect local decisions on funding of other drugs and treatments to be made rationally following a proper consideration of the evidence. If the local NHS decides not to fund a drug or treatment you and your doctor feel would be right for you, they will explain that decision to you.
- **You have the right** to receive the vaccinations that the Joint Committee on Vaccination and Immunisation recommends that you should receive under an NHS-provided national immunisation programme.

The NHS also commits:

- to provide screening programmes as recommended by the UK National Screening Committee (pledge).

Respect, consent and confidentiality:

- **You have the right** to be treated with dignity and respect, in accordance with your human rights.
- **You have the right** to accept or refuse treatment that is offered to you, and not to be given any physical examination or treatment unless you have given valid consent. If you do not have the capacity to do so, consent must be obtained from a person legally able to act on your behalf, or the treatment must be in your best interests.
- **You have the right** to be given information about the test and treatment options available to you, what they involve and their risks and benefits.

- **You have the right** of access to your own health records and to have any factual inaccuracies corrected.
- **You have the right** to privacy and confidentiality and to expect the NHS to keep your confidential information safe and secure.
- **You have the right** to be informed about how your information is used.
- **You have the right** to request that your confidential information is not used beyond your own care and treatment and to have your objections considered, and where your wishes cannot be followed, to be told the reasons including the legal basis.

The NHS also commits:

- to ensure those involved in your care and treatment have access to your health information so they can care for you safely and effectively (pledge);
- to anonymise the information collected during the course of your treatment and use it to support research and improve care for others (pledge);
- where identifiable information has to be used, to give you the chance to object wherever possible (pledge);
- to inform you of research studies in which you may be eligible to participate (pledge); and
- to share with you any correspondence sent between clinicians about your care (pledge).

Informed choice

- **You have the right** to choose your GP [general practitioner] practice, and to be accepted by that practice unless there are reasonable grounds to refuse, in which case you will be informed of those reasons.
- **You have the right** to express a preference for using a particular doctor within your GP practice, and for the practice to try to comply.
- **You have the right** to make choices about the services commissioned by NHS bodies and to information to support these choices. The options available to you will develop over time and depend on your individual needs. Details are set out in the Handbook to the NHS Constitution.

The NHS also commits:

- to inform you about the healthcare services available to you, locally and nationally (pledge); and
- to offer you easily accessible, reliable and relevant information in a form you can understand, and support to use it. This will enable you to participate fully in your own healthcare decisions and to support you in making choices. This will include information on the range and quality of clinical services where there is robust and accurate information available (pledge).

Involvement in your healthcare and in the NHS:

- **You have the right** to be involved in discussions and decisions about your health and care, including your end of life care, and to be given information to enable you to do this. Where appropriate this right includes your family and carers.

- **You have the right** to be involved, directly or through representatives, in the planning of healthcare services commissioned by NHS bodies, the development and consideration of proposals for changes in the way those services are provided, and in decisions to be made affecting the operation of those services.

The NHS also commits:

- to provide you with the information and support you need to influence and scrutinise the planning and delivery of NHS services (pledge);
- to work in partnership with you, your family, carers and representatives (pledge);
- to involve you in discussions about planning your care and to offer you a written record of what is agreed if you want one (pledge); and
- to encourage and welcome feedback on your health and care experiences and use this to improve services (pledge).

Complaint and redress:

- **You have the right** to have any complaint you make about NHS services acknowledged within three working days and to have it properly investigated.
- **You have the right** to discuss the manner in which the complaint is to be handled, and to know the period within which the investigation is likely to be completed and the response sent.
- **You have the right** to be kept informed of progress and to know the outcome of any investigation into your complaint, including an explanation of the conclusions and confirmation that any action needed in consequence of the complaint has been taken or is proposed to be taken.
- **You have the right** to take your complaint to the independent Parliamentary and Health Service Ombudsman or Local Government Ombudsman, if you are not satisfied with the way your complaint has been dealt with by the NHS.
- **You have the right** to make a claim for judicial review if you think you have been directly affected by an unlawful act or decision of an NHS body or local authority.
- **You have the right** to compensation where you have been harmed by negligent treatment.

The NHS also commits:

- to ensure that you are treated with courtesy and you receive appropriate support throughout the handling of a complaint; and that the fact that you have complained will not adversely affect your future treatment (pledge);
- to ensure that when mistakes happen or if you are harmed while receiving health care you receive an appropriate explanation and apology, delivered with sensitivity and recognition of the trauma you have experienced, and know that lessons will be learned to help avoid a similar incident occurring again (pledge); and
- to ensure that the organisation learns lessons from complaints and claims and uses these to improve NHS services (pledge).

The exact nature of these rights is unclear. Some are clearly enforceable, while it seems others are less obviously so. Some are well established in the law (for example the right to compensation following medical treatment); others are not. They may be taken into account by courts when considering claims that a patient may bring against the NHS.

Section 2 of the Health Act 2009 requires NHS bodies to have regard to the NHS Constitution.[5] If an NHS body were to ignore a right under the Constitution, it might open itself up to a successful claim in negligence or judicial review.

The Constitution is not only about the rights of patients, but also lists their responsibilities, as we saw in Chapter 1.

2 The structure of the NHS

The structure of the NHS differs between England, Wales, Scotland, and Northern Ireland. This chapter will look only at England. To describe the structure of the NHS is not an easy task. This is partly because it is labyrinthine and partly because the NHS has been, and still is, undergoing enormous structural changes, with bodies being created, merged, and destroyed at an astonishing rate.

At a basic level, it is possible to examine the structure as consisting of four levels, as follows.

(i)   *Policymaking and centralized planning* This task is carried out primarily by the Department of Health.

(ii) *Supervision, inspection, and regulation* This task is now often carried out by 'arm's-length bodies' (ALBs). These bodies are created by and are responsible to the Department of Health, but are independent of it.

(iii) *Service commissioners* These bodies decide which health services are 'purchased' and from whom. This is carried out by, for example, clinical commissioning groups (CCGs). They have the responsibility for assessing the health needs of people in their areas and ensuring that those needs are appropriately met.

(iv) *Healthcare providers* These are those on the front line who directly provide the health care to patients, and include, for example, doctors and nurses.

We will now look at these different groups of bodies in more detail.

3 Policymaking and central planning in the NHS

3.1 Parliament

It is, of course, Parliament that approves the allocation of funds to the NHS via the taxation system. The Secretary of Health is accountable to Parliament for the performance of the NHS in England. There are also three Parliamentary Select Committees that can make enquiries and produce reports in relation to the NHS:

- the *Health Committee*, which examines the Department of Health's expenditure, administration, and policymaking;
- the *Public Accounts Committee*, which ensures that the NHS is running economically, effectively, and efficiently; and
- the *Public Administration Committee*, which scrutinizes the Health Service Commissioner's reports.

---

[5] As must the Secretary of Health: National Health Service Act 2006, s. 1A.

3.2 The Department of Health

Under the National Health Service Act 2006, section 1A:[6]

(1) The Secretary of State must continue the promotion in England of a comprehensive health service designed to secure improvement—

(a) in the physical and mental health of the people of England, and

(b) in the prevention, diagnosis and treatment of physical and mental illness.

(2) For that purpose, the Secretary of State must exercise the functions conferred by this Act so as to secure that services are provided in accordance with this Act.

(3) The Secretary of State retains ministerial responsibility to Parliament for the provision of the health service in England.

(4) The services provided as part of the health service in England must be free of charge except in so far as the making and recovery of charges is expressly provided for by or under any enactment, whenever passed.

Section 3(1) states:

The Secretary of State must provide throughout England, to such extent as he considers necessary to meet all reasonable requirements—

(a) hospital accommodation,

(b) other accommodation for the purpose of any service provided under this Act,

(c) medical, dental, ophthalmic, nursing and ambulance services,

(d) such other services or facilities for the care of pregnant women, women who are breastfeeding and young children as he considers are appropriate as part of the health service,

(e) such other services or facilities for the prevention of illness, the care of persons suffering from illness and the after-care of persons who have suffered from illness as he considers are appropriate as part of the health service,

(f) such other services or facilities as are required for the diagnosis and treatment of illness.

The Department of Health fulfils these obligations through the NHS. Note that section 3 requires the Secretary of State to provide the services only 'to such extent as he considers necessary'.[7] That limits the enforceability of the provision. Notice also the presumption in section 1(3) that services will be free of charge.[8] The Health and Social Care Act 2012 has added to the duties on the Secretary of State to act with a view to securing continuing improvement in the quality of service,[9] to have regard to the NHS Constitution,[10] to reduce health inequalities,[11] and to promote autonomy, education,

---

[6] As amended by the Health and Social Care Act 2012.

[7] They do not require the Secretary of State to ensure services are provided in England to people resident in other countries, including Northern Ireland: *R (A) v Secretary of State for Health (Alliance for Choice)* [2017] UKSC 41 (concerning abortion services).

[8] For a discussion on the scope of s. 1(3), see *North Dorset NHS Primary Care Trust v Coombs* [2013] EWCA Civ 471; *R (A) v Secretary of State for Health (Alliance for Choice)* [2017] UKSC 41.

[9] National Health Service Act 2006, s. 1A.

[10] National Health Service Act 2006, s. 1B.   [11] National Health Service Act 2006, s. 1C.

training, and research.[12] The wording of these duties is so vague that it is hard to imagine a legal action being successfully brought for a breach of them. In *R (National Aids Trust) v National Health Service Commissioning Board*[13] the Court of Appeal rejected an argument that preventative treatments (in this case a drug designed to prevent the development of AIDS) did not fall into the remit of the NHS, but rather was a matter for local authorities.

The 2012 Act has sought to limit the direct management of the NHS by the Department of Health. Hence the NHS explains: 'The Department of Health (DH) will be responsible for strategic leadership of both the health and social care systems, but will no longer be the headquarters of the NHS, nor will it directly manage any NHS organisations.'[14]

3.3 NHS England

NHS England is a body that is independent of the government. Its primary role is to improve the health outcomes in England. Its roles include:

* providing national leadership for improving outcomes and driving up the quality of care;
* overseeing the operation of clinical commissioning groups;
* allocating resources to clinical commissioning groups; and
* commissioning primary care and specialist services.[15]

3.4 Public Health England

Public Health England was created in 2013 to provide national oversight and leadership on public health issues. It will offer services and support to the NHS and to local government. In particular, it will:

* coordinate a national public health service and deliver some elements of this;
* build an evidence base to support local public health services;
* support the public to make healthier choices;
* provide leadership to the public health delivery system; and
* support the development of the public health workforce.[16]

4 Quality control: regulation and inspection

4.1 The Care Quality Commission

The Care Quality Commission (CQC) oversees what might broadly be called 'quality control' within the NHS, and indeed the provision of all health and adult social care

---

[12] National Health Service Act 2006, ss 1D–F.   [13] [2016] EWCA Civ 1100.
[14] NHS (2013b: 15).   [15] NHS (2013b).   [16] NHS (2013b).

services, whoever they are provided by. It is independent of government. It issues regulations and guidance on particular areas. These may be backed up by inspections or looser forms of enforcement. The Care Act 2014 gives the Commission a wide range of powers to carry out its task.[17] Its primary role is to ensure the provision of health services of a consistently high standard.

4.2 NHS Improvement

NHS Improvement works with NHS Trusts and providers of NHS care and supports them 'to give patients consistently safe, high quality, compassionate care within local health systems that are financially sustainable'.[18] It has a broad remit to promote good practice within the NHS and ensure that budgets are controlled.

4.3 Healthwatch

Healthwatch is a newly created body that is intended to operate as 'an independent consumer champion, gathering and representing the views of the public about health and social care services in England'.[19] It seeks to ensure that the views of the public are taken into account in the provision of NHS services.

5 Commissioning and planning services

5.1 Clinical commissioning groups

Clinical commissioning groups (CCGs) are now in charge of commissioning NHS services. They took over this role from primary care trusts (PCTs) on 1 April 2013. So now, when a patient visits a general practitioner (GP) and needs further treatment, this will be commissioned by a CCG. The CCG may turn to an NHS hospital, charity, or private body to supply this. The CCGs will have control of the vast majority of NHS expenditure.

All GP practices belong to a CCG, and each group will also contain GPs, a nursing director, a registered nurse, a specialist clinician in secondary care, and two lay people (one with financial expertise and the other with knowledge of the local area).

5.2 Health and well-being boards

Health and well-being boards will be set up by local authorities, and are designed to help CCGs in commissioning services and to provide general oversight of care and social services. In particular, they are intended:

- to increase democratic input into strategic decisions about health and well-being services;
- to strengthen working relationships between health and social care; and
- to encourage integrated commissioning of health and social care services.[20]

---

[17] Health and Social Care Act 2008, ss 62–65.   [18] NHS Improvement (2017).
[19] NHS (2013b: 15).   [20] NHS (2013b).

5.3 Social services departments

The provision of social services (as opposed to health care) is the responsibility of the local authority. It can either provide the services itself or purchase them from other providers. The distinction between social services and health care is a problematic one, as we shall see. 'Social services' cover assistance in living independently and will include provision of 'meals on wheels', help with hygiene, and sheltered accommodation, for example. These are not regarded as 'health care'.

6 Charging: community versus health care

As mentioned at the start of this chapter, one of the precepts of the NHS is that it should be free at the point of delivery.[21] Services must be free of charge unless there is express legal provision saying that charges may be made.[22] There is, for example, provision to require payment for wigs, drugs, and optical and dental appliances. This makes the definition of what is a service that can be expected of the NHS crucial, because if a service does not fall under the purview of the NHS, it may be subject to charging. The reinforcement of the distinction between health and social care in recent years has meant that services previously offered free under the NHS are now classified as personal care and need to be paid for.[23] This issue emerged in the 2017 general election with the Conservative Party's so-called 'dementia tax' proposal (that people pay for their social care out of a payment from their estate) proving a major point of debate.

The point is powerfully made that those who are unable to provide their own personal care are in that position because they are suffering some kind of health problem. Their problems are therefore symptoms, at least, of their ill-health. Indeed, without the personal care, they are likely to develop further health problems. So whether the inability to care is seen as an aspect of health promotion or dealing with the consequence of ill-health, the distinction is hard to justify. Indeed, it is hard to avoid the perception that the division has more to do with attempts to cut costs to the state, while holding on to the claim that health services are provided free at the point of delivery, than being one based on a sound policy.[24]

As mentioned, the local authority can require the client to pay as much of the cost of personal services as is reasonable.[25] The distinction thus created between healthcare services, which are free at the point of delivery, and community care, which is not, is one that is hotly debated. Section 22 of the Care Act 2014 provides that nursing or health care cannot be charged for by a local authority.

In 2011, the Dilnot Report on Social Care bluntly opened with the following points:[26]

- The current adult social care funding system in England is not fit for purpose, and needs urgent and lasting reform.
- The current system is confusing, unfair, and unsustainable. People are unable to plan ahead to meet their future care needs. Assessment processes are complex and opaque.

[21] See DoH (2009a) on patients who wish to combine NHS and private treatment.
[22] National Health Service Act 2006, s. 1.   [23] See Herring (2013: ch. 3).
[24] National Health Service Act 2006, s. 1(3).
[25] Health and Social Services and Social Security Adjudications Act 1983, s. 17.
[26] Commission on Funding of Care and Support (2011: 1).

Eligibility varies depending on where you live and there is no portability if you move between local authorities. Provision of information and advice is poor, and services often fail to join up. All of this means that, in many cases, people do not have good experiences.

A SHOCK TO THE SYSTEM

It is easy, in discussions of healthcare policy, to forget the individuals involved. Consider the following quote from Valerie Tugwell, aged 72, who was largely immobile. Her council decided that the number of baths given to her on social care had to be reduced:

> I feel unclean half the time. I felt deprived when social services cut me down from two to one bath a week in 2004—deprived of feeling like a normal adult. Then they told me I had to stop having the one bath a week I have now because my care was taking longer than the one hour I was allocated. I told them I was doubly incontinent and why on earth couldn't I have a bath? Wasn't I entitled to be properly cleaned? They told me that time and money would not allow it. But we're talking about 15 minutes.[27]

7 The provision of services

The providers of services are those who provide the hands-on care of patients within the NHS. 'Primary care' is the term used for the services provided by those people who are the normal first port of call in the case of a medical problem. They include GPs (general practitioner doctors), opticians, dentists, pharmacists, and NHS Direct (a phone service). 'Secondary care' is the care to which a patient may be sent by a primary carer. It involves acute and specialist services. Clinical commissioning groups are responsible for planning secondary care. They must decide which services should be commissioned to meet people's needs.

The main bodies providing care include the following.

7.1 NHS trusts

NHS trusts were created by the NHS and Community Care Act 1990, although their precise role has undergone substantial revision. Their primary function is the provision of healthcare services in their area.

NHS trusts are allowed to offer private health care or to offer extra amenities for NHS patients for a charge.[28] They may also borrow money within annually agreed limits. Any income generated must, however, be spent within the trust's statutory powers; this means that the trust cannot make a profit as such.

7.2 Foundation trusts

Foundation trusts are 'independent public benefit corporations', although they are not permitted to make a profit.[29] They are run by a board of governors made up of local

---

[27] Revill, Campbell, and Hill (2007: 12).   [28] Health and Social Care Act 2001, Sch. 2.
[29] DoH (2005b: para. 5.16).

managers, staff, and members of the public. Foundation trusts have far more financial and organizational freedom than other NHS trusts. This freedom is intended to mean that they can best meet the particular needs of people in their area. Such trusts are, of course, still within the NHS and are subject to performance inspections. The Health and Social Care Act 2012 puts in place a process to turn all NHS trusts into foundation trusts.

7.3 GPs

General practitioners are doctors who look after the health of those who are listed with them. As well as providing general health advice and prescribing medicines, they can also carry out simple surgical operations and give vaccinations. A GP will often work with a team of healthcare professionals, including nurses, midwives, and physiotherapists. If the GP is not able to deal with a patient's problem, he or she will refer the patient to a hospital for tests or treatment, which may involve a meeting with a specialist consultant.

8 Structural issues

We will now briefly look at some of the structural issues facing the NHS.

8.1 The provider/commissioning distinction

An important distinction is drawn between the commissioning of services and the provision of services. The concept was introduced under the Conservative governments of the 1990s, with the creation of the 'internal market'.[30] It is reinforced by the Health and Social Care Act 2012. The idea behind it is that, by giving a CCG the power to decide from whom to purchase the health services needed, the healthcare providers will strive to offer an excellent service to ensure that they are selected. In short, it creates a form of competition between healthcare providers seeking to provide better services than each other. This, it was hoped, would drive up the standards within the NHS. It is important to note, however, that there is no market in price. The price for services is fixed by NHS Improvement and the Department of Health. So the market exists simply in terms of the quality (and speed) of the service.[31] NHS Improvement has been given the specific job of ensuring that there is an effective market in health services.

Critics of the system argue that competition inevitably means that there will be winners and losers. They suggest that encouraging consortia to develop mutually beneficial relationships with CCGs will be more effective than encouraging competition between them.[32]

Certainly, following the 2012 Act, CCGs find themselves faced with an onerous task. Time will tell the extent to which GP-led CCGs will succeed. It is not surprising to learn that many GPs are seeking to bring in firms of management consultants and accountants to help them to organize the commissioning. While that might improve the efficiency of

---

[30] See Harrington (2009) for an excellent discussion.   [31] Davies (2013).   [32] BMA (2011a).

commissioning, it might introduce into the NHS market-based thinking, which some will find an anathema to the principles underpinning it. The sight of NHS funds being given to London-based city firms will undoubtedly prove politically controversial.

A different concern is that the 2012 Act has made the use of private firms a legal, rather than political, issue. As Anne Davies explains:

> Under the 2012 Act . . . there are legal obligations on NHS bodies to operate a 'level playing field' between public and private sector providers. This means that when a private provider wins a contract, this can be presented as a result of 'legal technicalities'. While this is, in a literal sense, true, it has the potential to undermine political accountability for what goes on in the NHS.[33]

8.2 The use of arm's-length bodies

As can be seen from the list of bodies involved in the structure of the NHS, arm's-length bodies (ALBs) play a significant role. These are commissions, institutes, and authorities who are separate from government, yet answerable to it, and which are in charge of regulating particular areas.

Supporters of ALBs emphasize that they enable the regulation of sensitive areas of health care to be provided free from political interference. Consider, for example, the Human Fertilisation and Embryology Authority, which must issue guidance on sensitive issues relating to embryo research and advances in reproductive technology. If the issue were to be decided by the government, this would create concerns that the regulation would reflect what the government thinks is acceptable to the general public, rather than what is scientifically and ethically appropriate.

But opponents of ALBs may claim that this is precisely the problem with them: that these bodies are not accountable, and are made up of professionals working in the area who are out of touch with the feelings and thoughts of ordinary people.

8.3 Decentralization

One of the key themes in the current NHS is to devolve power to local CCGs and front-line staff. The argument is that front-line staff are in the best position to know what patients in their area of the country need and how best to meet those needs. The independence given to CCGs is seen as key to enabling local NHS bodies to meet needs in their areas.

In introducing the 2012 Act, the Health Secretary stated that it would 'put clinicians in the driving seat on decisions about services'—that the government would 'liberate the NHS from the old command and control regime' and 'phase out the top-down management hierarchy'.[34] Anne Davies notes that:

> The reforms seek to offer NHS purchasers and providers greater autonomy through the regulatory model they adopt. Purchasers are insulated from ministerial interference by the NHS Commissioning Board, and providers are insulated from ministerial interference by [NHS Improvement].[35]

---

[33] Davies (2013: 566).   [34] Quoted in BMA (2011b: 2).   [35] Davies (2013: 577).

However, some are concerned that the Secretary of State will still be able to put pressure on these bodies, by means of regulations and control of members.[36] The concern is that although power will formally have been delegated to local organizations, behind the scenes central government will still control what is done.

8.4 Improving quality: targets

One of the main ways in which the government has sought to improve the services provided by the NHS has been through the use of targets. A huge range of issues, from reducing suicide rates to cutting waiting times, has been subject to targets.[37] Great pressure is placed upon NHS bodies to meet these. One of the primary roles of the Care Quality Commission is to ensure that NHS bodies comply with the National Service Frameworks, which set out standards expected of the NHS.[38] Where standards are met, the government naturally seeks to claim credit for the very tangible benefit of the extra funding it has put into the NHS. We will not consider in detail here what these targets are or the extent to which they have or have not been met;[39] rather, we shall look briefly at whether targets are a useful way of improving the quality of NHS performance.[40]

The use of targets does provide a very concrete measure of improvement. Without them, politicians may fear that the money given to the NHS will go into a 'black hole', and there will be no measure of improvement to which politicians can point and say: 'That outcome has resulted from the improvements that we've made.' Of course, where patients have received treatment more quickly because of waiting list targets, for example, the patients benefit.

There are, however, concerns over the use of targets. The Audit Commission emphasizes that targets must be 'the means not the end'.[41] The danger with targets is that an obsession develops with filling in the form at the end of the day saying that the target has been reached, rather than actually improving the service offered. Indeed, it has been found that some trusts have found ways of technically meeting waiting list targets (for example by cancelling operation appointments on the day in question) that have ended up harming patients, even if appearing to meet the targets.[42]

8.5 Choice

'Choice' has become one of the 'buzz words' of the modern NHS.[43] The emphasis on choice has been seen by many as an emphasis on consumerism within the NHS.[44] It reflects what might be seen as a shift from seeing the patient as the 'recipient' of care, to treating him or her as a consumer who chooses what services he or she wants. Supporters argue that increased choice will lead to increased satisfaction, as individuals get the treatment that they really want, and improved quality of services, as healthcare providers vie to be the providers of choice for patients.

[36] BMA (2011a).   [37] DoH (2000d).
[38] Health and Social Care Act 2008, ss 62–5. See NHS (2009c).
[39] See King's Fund (2005).   [40] Leatherman and Sutherland (2005).
[41] Audit Commission (2003).   [42] Audit Commission (2003).
[43] Barr, Fenton, and Blane (2008).   [44] Harrison and Ahmad (2000).

Since 2008, patients referred by a GP for a first non-urgent outpatient appointment can choose to be seen at a hospital or clinic anywhere in England.[45] The significance of this is increased because, under the new system whereby trusts are paid by 'results' (that is, are paid for the work that they do with each patient), there is an incentive for trusts to make themselves attractive to patients outside their immediate geographical area.[46] We are moving towards a 'patient-led NHS',[47] which it is hoped will lead to an improvement in the quality of care offered.

Some of this may frighten some patients. They want to go to the doctor and be told what treatment is best for them, and they want the doctor to make the necessary arrangements. To be involved in 'shared decision making' may not be what they want at all. Others—perhaps those with access to the Internet and other healthcare resources—will have strong views on how they want their health problems to be dealt with and will find the new approach liberating.

At first, giving patients choice may appear to be an inevitable good, but this is not beyond dispute.[48] Providing a choice will cost money and that raises the question about its cost-effectiveness. Also, offering a choice means that we must accept that, on occasion, the wrong choice will be made. It might also be argued that it is a little misleading to talk about choice when, given rationing within the NHS, the choices of an individual patient must be weighed against the interests of the general public. Can we really allow patients to choose treatments under the NHS that are not cost-effective? Will that not amount to a waste of precious NHS resources? Surely we cannot let one patient's choice mean that another is denied the treatment he or she needs? There are also concerns that choice empowers the educated middle class, who are in a better position to make 'choices' and to insist that their wishes are met; conversely, it is seen to disadvantage weaker members of society, who are not in a position to make a choice, nor have the voice to insist upon it. Exercising choice may require having the means to travel to a hospital far from home and this may not be possible for those with low incomes. Indeed, if a majority of people in an area with a struggling hospital were to choose to go elsewhere for treatment, this may lead to the closing of the hospital and the restriction of choice for those less able to travel. There is some evidence already that choice within the NHS is used by better-off, privileged groups and may work against goals of equal access to services.[49] These arguments may not mean that choice should not be a relevant goal for the NHS, but rather are a warning that respecting choice can carry expenses and dangers, and that steps may need to be taken to limit those costs.

8.6 Change

The pace of change in the structures and workings of the NHS is astonishing. Bodies are created and removed with remarkable speed. One leading commentator has stated that, since 1982, there has been some kind of 'organisational upheaval' almost every year.[50] To some, this may indicate how seriously governments have been taking the need to improve the quality of service offered by the NHS. Others have claimed that institutional reform has been a smokescreen for hiding really important changes—in particular, that the supply of NHS services now depends increasingly on private providers, rather than public bodies.

---

[45] DoH (2008b).   [46] King's Fund (2008a).   [47] DoH (2005a).   [48] King's Fund (2003b).
[49] Den Exeter and Guy (2014); King's Fund (2008c).   [50] Newdick (2005: 67).

9 Rationing

It would be wonderful if everyone who needed medical treatment could receive it. However, there appears to be a widespread consensus that this ideal is simply not feasible. There are not enough medical professionals and not enough money to provide a comprehensive service.[51] It would simply bankrupt the NHS to give every person the treatment that he or she wanted. No one would want to see the NHS providing 'wasteful care' that provided no real benefit.[52] As a result, some means had to be found of restricting access and deciding, given the limited funds available, who should receive which treatment. This is generally known as 'rationing'.

Some commentators have challenged the language of rationing. Yvonne Denier has argued that the language of rationing assumes a lack of money to fund appropriate care.[53] It might be preferable to talk in terms of selecting the best treatments to purchase, rather than which treatments we need to deny.[54] Denier argues that we need to challenge the view that medicine can or should extend life and improve normal functioning. Instead, we need to accept the finality of life as something of value. The fact that our lives are finite gives them a focus and intensity. According to such a view, the 'problem' of rationing is not the lack of money, but the excessive availability of medical interventions. This is a useful and important challenge to the way in which the problem of rationing is commonly presented. Although the argument has power at a theoretical level, however, it applies less straightforwardly when we need to decide which drugs to provide to which patients.

The question of rationing, from a legal perspective, can be looked at in two ways. One is to focus on healthcare authorities, and to ask in what ways it is lawful for them to restrict access to health care and how they should make rationing decisions. The other is to focus on patients and to ask whether we have a right to healthcare treatment, and if so, of what kind. This is not asking the same question in a different way. Consider a cash-strapped health authority that fails to provide urgent healthcare treatment to a patient on economic grounds: it may be found that the individual's right to health care was infringed, but that the health authority acted reasonably in allocating its resources in the way that it did. In such a case, the claim may be better made against the government for failing to provide sufficient funding for trusts to be able to provide the care required. There could also be a case in which a patient was denied health care and, although it did not think that there was a right to the kind of care in question, the court nonetheless decided that the health authority had acted improperly in allocating resources as it did.

9.1 What does rationing mean?

Rationing is said to occur where there is only a limited resource of health care and the decision is made to offer it to some people, but not to others. Rationing does not therefore arise where a patient is not offered treatment because it is not clinically effective.

A central issue in rationing is the definition of a 'healthcare need'. If a person has no healthcare need, denying him or her 'treatment' does not really involve rationing.

---

[51] See Light (1997) for an argument that this assumption should be challenged.
[52] Tilbut and Cassel (2013); Fleck (2016).   [53] Denier (2008).   [54] Menzel (2014).

However, the notion of 'need' is unclear. Andreas Hasman, Tony Hope, and Lars Østerdal[55] have suggested three possible meanings of 'need' in this context:

- that the patient is below an accepted state of well-being and there is a treatment that can improve his or her condition;

- that there is a need if a treatment will raise the patient's well-being from below a certain threshold to above it; and/or

- that a treatment will offer a patient a significant increase in well-being.

9.2 How does the NHS ration at present?

The National Health Service Act 2006 obliges the Secretary of State, in section 1, to promote 'a comprehensive health service'. In *R v Secretary of State for Social Services, ex p Hincks*,[56] the Court of Appeal emphasized that even where the Secretary of State for Health had a duty under the NHS Act 1977 (the predecessor to the 2006 Act), the duty was to provide the services 'to such an extent as he considers necessary to meet all reasonable requirements such as can be provided within the resources available'. It is therefore clear that it is permissible to take into account financial considerations when deciding whether to offer treatment to a particular patient or group of patients.[57] However, treatment cannot be denied to a patient on the basis that he or she can afford to pay for private treatment.[58]

Throughout the 2006 Act, the following phrase appears: '. . . to such extent as he [the Secretary of State] considers necessary to meet all reasonable requirements.' This applies, inter alia, to duties to provide hospital accommodation and medical, dental, nursing, and ambulance services. This makes the enforcement of the Secretary of State's obligations difficult, because the applicant would need to show that the Secretary of State believed it would be reasonable to supply a service, but decline to provide it.[59]

Under regulation 11 of the National Health Service Commissioning Board and Clinical Commissioning Groups (Responsibilities and Standing Rules) Regulations 2012, NHS England is responsible for arranging 'to such extent as it considers necessary to meet all reasonable requirements' for the provision of a long list of health needs. The legal obligation on NHS England created by the regulations is, however, limited. They have a wide discretion 'not only as to the scope of the reasonable requirements and as to the services that it considers necessary to meet them, but as to how it goes about its task'.[60]

Claims under European law were considered in *R (Watts) v Bedford Primary Care Trust and Secretary of State for Health*,[61] which discusses whether a patient who is refused treatment, or who faces a lengthy delay in obtaining treatment, can seek to have the operation conducted in another European country and require payment for it from the NHS.[62] If Brexit occurs it is extremely unlikely such claims will be able to be made.

---

[55] Hasman, Hope, and Østerdal (2006); Hope, Østerdal, and Hasman (2010).
[56] (1980) 1 BMLR 93, 95.   [57] *R v Sheffield Health Authority, ex p Seale* (1994) 25 BMLR 1.
[58] *R (Booker) v NHS Oldham* [2010] EWHC 2593 (Admin).
[59] *Re HIV Haemophiliac Litigation* (1990) 41 BMLR 171.
[60] *R(SB) v NHS England* [2017] EWHC 2000 (Admin), para. 18.
[61] Case C-372/04 [2006] ECR I-04325.   [62] Veitch (2012).

Successive governments have been adamant that there is no such thing as rationing within the NHS. However, as the Bristol Inquiry said:

> Governments of the day have made claims for the NHS which were not capable of being met on the resources available. The public has been led to believe that the NHS could meet their legitimate needs, whereas it is patently clear that it could not. Health care professionals, doctors, nurses, managers, and others, have been caught between the growing disillusion of the public on the one hand and the tendency of governments to point to them as a scapegoat for a failing service on the other . . . The NHS was represented as a comprehensive service which met all the needs of the public. Patently it did not do so.[63]

Whatever politicians may say, it is clear that, when deciding what treatment a patient should be given, NHS trusts and doctors themselves are influenced by the monetary restrictions facing the NHS. Even if not rationed explicitly, the limits on resources mean that some patients are denied treatment that might be clinically desirable. So where and how does rationing occur?[64]

(i) *The government* At one level, the amount of money allocated by HM Treasury to the Department of Health and the taxation levels set by the government play an important role in determining the amount of money that the NHS can use to fund treatments to patients.

(ii) *The National Institute for Health and Clinical Excellence (NICE)* The most overt way in which rationing decisions are made is through the guidance issued by NICE. This guidance can recommend that treatments are not made available or are made available only to certain categories of patient within the NHS. We will look further at the work of this body next.

(iii) *The NHS Commissioning Groups* They consider the funding of treatments generally and where an individual claims their case is exceptional and makes an 'individual funding request'. The decisions of the board are governed by the *Ethical Framework for Priority Setting and Resource Allocation*.[65] A key principle is as follows:

> If funding for a treatment cannot be justified as an investment for all patients in a particular cohort, the treatment should not be offered to only some of the patients, unless it is possible to differentiate between groups of patients on clinical grounds. This is because a decision to treat some patients but not others has the potential to be unfair, arbitrary, and possibly discriminatory. A treatment policy approved by the NHS CB should therefore not be approved unless the NHS CB has made funds available to allow all patients within the clinical group identified in the policy to have equal access to treatment. Individual patients may be considered for funding through the individual funding request process if their clinician can demonstrate that the patient is clinically exceptional.

---

[63] Bristol Royal Infirmary Inquiry (2001: para. 31).
[64] Carter, Gordon, and Watt (2016).
[65] NHS (2013b).

(iv) **Waiting lists** Another significant means of restricting access to treatment is the waiting list: a patient is not denied treatment outright, but must wait. Many trusts have systems under which urgent cases can be speeded to the top of the list. Further, it is not uncommon for patients to be told of the delay under the NHS and then, if they are able to afford it, to seek speedier treatment under a private health scheme.

(v) **Clinicians** Medical professionals themselves ration. Perhaps unconsciously, the decision may be made that the treatment is not 'worthwhile' for this patient, or that he or she is not considered an urgent case. In fact, there is very little evidence about the way in which 'clinical' decisions can, in reality, be rationing. It has been said that 'deterrence, delay, deflection, denial and dilution' of care all play their part.[66] The benefit to politicians of clinical judgement is that it:

> . . . renders the process of rationing as if it were politically invisible, by fragmenting it across space and time into individualised and private transactions between doctors and patients. The result was that the NHS was able to maintain the fiction of meeting everyone's needs.[67]

In a survey of healthcare professionals who make rationing decisions, it was clear that four factors played a major role in rationing: cost-effectiveness; clinical effectiveness; equality; and gross cost.[68] Those interviewed did not agree on how these should be prioritized.

9.3 Judicial review of rationing decisions

The most common way of using the courts to challenge a rationing decision is judicial review.[69] Such attempts have rarely succeeded. There are three main bases on which judicial review can be sought, as follows.

(i) The decision was illegal. For example, it may have been a decision that the PCT had no power to make.

(ii) The decision was irrational or unreasonable. 'Unreasonable', in the context of judicial review, has a special meaning: it must be shown that the decision was so unreasonable that no reasonable person would have made it.

(iii) There was procedural impropriety in the making of the decision.

The following are some of the key points that emerge from the case law:

9.3.1 There is no general duty to provide medical treatment

Although there is a statutory duty to provide medical treatment, that is not an absolute duty, because resources are finite.[70] In R v North and East Devon Health Authority, ex p Coughlan,[71] the Court of Appeal said that, in exercising judgements about resource

---

[66] Newdick (2005: 50).   [67] Harrison (1998: 18).   [68] Hasman, McIntosh, and Hope (2008).
[69] In R (Cavanagh) v Health Service Commissioner (2005) 91 BMLR 40, it was held that the Health Service Commissioner could not hear a complaint about a rationing decision.
[70] In R v Secretary of State for Social Services, ex p Hincks (1980) 1 BMLR 93.
[71] [2000] 3 All ER 850, 861.

allocation, the Secretary of State for Health (and therefore all bodies that took their powers from him) had:

> . . . to bear in mind the comprehensive service which he is under a duty to promote. However, as long as he pays due regard to that duty, the fact that the service will not be comprehensive does not mean that he is necessarily contravening [his statutory duty]. The truth is that, while he has the duty to continue to promote a comprehensive free health service and he must never . . . disregard that duty, a comprehensive health service may never, for human, financial and other resource reasons, be achievable . . . In exercising his judgment the Secretary of State is entitled to take into account the resources available to him and the demands on those services.

Financial considerations can, therefore, be taken into account in deciding whether to offer treatment.[72] The courts have, therefore, been reluctant to declare a patient has a right to certain treatment. As Hickinbottom J stated in *R (Dyer) v The Welsh Ministers and others*.[73]

> There is no enforceable individual entitlement to a particular level or location of care from the NHS . . . That is consistent with article 8 of the European Convention on Human Rights (ECHR), which does not give a patient a right to any particular type of medical treatment from the State, given the fair balance that has to be struck between the competing interests of the individual and society as a whole and the wide margin of appreciation enjoyed by States especially in the assessment of the priorities in the context of allocation of limited state resources.

9.3.2 A fixed policy is likely to be unlawful

A fixed policy that is not responsive to the needs of particular individuals may well be unlawful. In *R v NW Lancashire Health Authority, ex p A, D and G*,[74] a rigid policy against funding gender reassignment surgery was found to be unlawful, because it fettered the discretion of the authority and failed to enable it to consider the individual facts of each case. Of course, a policy that stated that generally a certain kind of treatment would not be available would be permissible, as long as each case was considered individually. If the court determined that, although a trust said that it did not have a rigid policy, in fact a rule was automatically applied in every case, a legal challenge would succeed.[75] Collins J in *S (A child) v NHS England*[76] seemed to go further and suggest that if the concept of exceptionality was interpreted so narrowly that it could only apply in very unusual cases that would be unlawful too. He explained:

> it must be borne in mind that exceptional is not the same as unique and that there should not be an approach that denies that any but an extreme case is regarded as exceptional. In its ordinary meaning, exceptional can mean no more than a case which does not meet what is normal.

---

[72] *R v Secretary of State for Social Services, ex p Hincks* (1980) 1 BMLR 93; *R v Sheffield Health Authority, ex p Seale* (1994) 25 BMLR 1.
[73] [2015] EWHC 3712 (Admin), para. 17.   [74] [2000] 2 FCR 525.
[75] *R (Ross) v West Sussex Primary Care Trust* [2008] EWHC 2252 (Admin).
[76] [2016] EWHC 1395.

In *R (Rose) v Thanet Clinical Commissioning Group*,[77] a Clinical Commissioning Group developed a policy which did not fund the freezing of eggs for fertility, save in exceptional circumstances. The basis of the policy was that freezing of eggs had a low chance of success and so was not clinically effective. Jay J queried the policy: 'If the general policy is justified on the basis that the evidence for clinical effectiveness is lacking, why should someone asserting exceptionality have to do more than demonstrate that in her or his case there is—contrary to the general run of the mill of cases—evidence of clinical effectiveness?' There was no need to show any other 'exceptional' basis. This case shows that the courts will look carefully at the reasons why the treatment is rationed to see if an exceptionality test is appropriate.

9.3.3 *Patients should be given reasons and a chance to make representations*

Patients should have a chance to explain why they should be given treatment and to hear why they are being denied it.[78] This does not mean that the patient should be able to address the decision maker directly, but that the patient's views must be properly considered.[79]

9.3.4 *Irrelevant considerations should not be taken into account*

A successful judicial review challenge could be brought if, in reaching its decision, the NHS body had taken into account irrelevant considerations or had failed to take into account relevant considerations. It is clear that the likelihood of success of the treatment[80] and National Institute for Health and Care Excellence (NICE) guidelines would be relevant factors. So, in *R v Derbyshire Health Authority, ex p Fisher*,[81] it was found to be improper to fail to follow an NHS circular without explanation. In *R (Ross) v West Sussex Primary Care Trust*,[82] the Trust's committee had failed to consider relevant medical evidence properly and so was successfully challenged. Section 2(a) of the NHS Constitution states:

> NICE (the National Institute for Health and Clinical Excellence) is an independent NHS organization producing guidance on drugs and treatments. 'Recommended' means recommended by a NICE technology appraisal. Primary care trusts are normally obliged to fund NICE technology appraisals from a date no later than three months from the publication of the appraisal.

So a failure to follow NICE guidance without a good reason is likely to lead to a successful judicial review challenge. Obviously, a decision that was based on sex or race would also be unlawful. It is less clear whether age would be an impermissible factor. We shall consider this issue in more detail later in this chapter. Further, a committee that failed to consider relevant medical evidence properly could be open to challenge.

---

[77] [2014] EWHC 1182 (Admin).
[78] *R v Ethical Committee of St Mary's Hospital, ex p Harriott* [1988] 1 FLR 512.
[79] *R v Cambridge District Health Authority, ex p B* [1995] 2 All ER 129.
[80] *R v Sheffield Health Authority, ex p Seale* (1994) 25 BMLR 1.   [81] [1997] 8 Med LR 327.
[82] [2008] EWHC 2252 (Admin).

9.3.5 *Legitimate expectations should be met*

If a public body has created a legitimate expectation that a certain form of treatment will be provided and unfairly alters its policies to the disadvantage of those who have relied on the expectation, then a successful claim could be sought. In *R v North and East Devon Health Authority, ex p Coughlan*,[83] it was found that the applicant had been assured by the health authority that she would have a home for life in a residential facility that it managed. Her legitimate expectation rendered the later decision to close the facility unlawful.

9.3.6 *Challenging clinical assessments are unlikely to succeed*

It is unlikely that a clinical assessment concerning treatment will be found unreasonable. In *R v Secretary of State for Social Services, ex p Walker*,[84] the applicant was the mother of a child who needed an operation to rectify a congenital heart defect. The difficulty was that there was a shortage of beds on a neonatal unit. Other children were continually being assessed to be in greater need than the applicant's child and she sought to challenge the health authority's decisions. The Court of Appeal accepted that the local authority had acted properly in preferring to give cots to the most urgent cases. This was, in effect, a clinical decision and not open to challenge in the courts. Similarly, courts will not force doctors to provide care that, in their clinical judgement, they think inappropriate.[85] However, if the court is persuaded that the trust has overlooked an important piece of clinical evidence, the policy could be susceptible to judicial review. A good example is *R (Otley) v Barking & Dagenham NHS Primary Care Trust*,[86] in which Victoria Otley's PCT refused to fund a treatment using an anti-cancer drug (Avastin). She sought a judicial review of that decision. The decision not to fund her treatment was made by a panel of the Trust. The panel had received a report that recommended the drug in Ms Otley's case. However, a member of the panel noted that, in research studies, Avastin had not been used as part of a cocktail of drugs. On appeal, it was held that the panel had failed to give sufficient weight to the fact that this regime of drugs was the only set of drugs available. Although the chance that Avastin could lengthen her life by more than a few months was slim, this was an important chance that Ms Otley should be allowed to have. The Court emphasized that this was not a decision that had been made on the basis of scarce resources. Similarly in *R(SB) v NHS England*[87] a decision not to fund treatment for a child with a rare metabolic condition with a particular drug on the basis that the drug was clinically ineffective was held to be irrational as all the studies before the committee indicated the drug was effective. Again, the willingness of the court to intervene may reflect the fact the refusal to fund was not said to be a resource-based decision.

We will now look at some of the key cases that have applied these principles.

---

[83] [2000] 3 All ER 850.   [84] (1987) 3 BMLR 32.
[85] *R v Ealing District Health Authority, ex p Fox* [1993] 3 All ER 170.
[86] [2007] EWHC 1927 (Admin).   [87] [2017] EWHC 2000 (Admin).

KEY CASE   *R v Cambridge Health Authority, ex p B* [1995] 2 All ER 129[88]

B was a 10-year-old girl with leukaemia. A bone marrow transplant had been attempted, but it was unsuccessful. Doctors in London and Cambridge believed that B had only six to eight weeks to live and that any further treatment would be inappropriate. However, B's father did not accept this assessment, and found a professor in London and doctors in the United States who would have offered the girl further treatment. The professor admitted that his proposal of chemotherapy and a possible second transplant was experimental and not standard. The health authority supported the decision not to offer further treatment. It explained that 'the substantial expenditure on treatment with such a small prospect of success would not be an effective use of resources'. The father sought judicial review of the decision.

   At first instance before Laws J, he succeeded. Laws J emphasized the girl's right to life under Article 2 of the European Convention on Human Rights (ECHR). This meant that compelling reasons had to be provided to justify preferring the needs of other patients over her. Simply stating that resources were limited was not sufficient; the health authority had to state explicitly which other calls on its funds meant that it was not able to offer her treatment.

   The health authority was, however, successful in its appeal to the Court of Appeal. The Court emphasized that it was not for the courts to look at the merits of the local authority's decision. It was not the courts' job to assess whether the local authority's distribution of resources was appropriate. Sir Thomas Bingham held: 'Difficult and agonizing judgements have to be made as to how a limited budget is best allocated to the maximum advantage of the maximum of patients. That is not a judgement which the court can make.'[89]

9.4 Application of the principles

The case is fascinating for its contrast between the approaches of Laws J at first instance and the Court of Appeal.[90] The Court of Appeal used the standard 'unreasonableness' test. It found that sensitive decisions on resource allocations can be said to be unreasonable only in exceptional cases. This was not such an exceptional case. The main point for the Court of Appeal was that the courts should, in cases of judicial review, not be considering the merits of the decision, but rather the process by which it was reached. Laws J, by contrast, regarded the unreasonableness test as inappropriate in cases like this in which there are fundamental human rights at stake—here, the right to life.

   The progress of the case following the Court of Appeal's judgment is revealing. B's father took her to the United States and she received treatment, which was paid for by an anonymous donor. The early signs were promising—B's leukaemia went into remission[91]—but several months later, she fell ill again; she died in May 1996. Whether this vindicated the health authority's view that the treatment was not clinically appropriate or B's father's views that the treatment enabled her to have several more happy months of life, something on which no value can be placed, is a matter of debate.

   The approach taken by Laws J in *Re B* still has some weight. In *R (Ross) v West Sussex Primary Care Trust*,[92] Grenfell J noted that 'where life and death decisions are involved,

---

[88] See Wall (2015c) for a helpful analysis of this decision.   [89] At 141.
[90] Mullender (1996); O'Sullivan (1998).   [91] BMA (2004: 156).
[92] [2008] EWHC 2252 (Admin), [18].

the courts must submit the decision making process to rigorous scrutiny'. He went on to hold that

> [T]he more substantial the interference with human rights, the more the court will require by way of justification before it is satisfied that the decision is reasonable; the Courts must subject their decision to anxious scrutiny because the Claimant's life is at stake.[93]

These comments might indicate an increased willingness to examine carefully the reasoning process and reasons behind trusts denying life-saving treatment. However, as the following case indicates, the focus will be on the nature of the decision-making process, rather than a consideration of whether the actual decision reached was correct.

KEY CASE   *R (Rogers) v Swindon NHS Primary Care Trust [2006] EWCA Civ 392*

Anne-Marie Rogers sought a judicial review of the decision of her PCT to refuse to fund her treatment with Herceptin (an unlicensed drug). She had breast cancer. Her consultant had advised her that she had a 25 per cent chance of remaining free from cancer in the next ten years, but a 57 per cent chance of dying. Initial trials of Herceptin had suggested considerable benefit in the kind of cancer from which Ms Rogers suffered. Initially, she paid for the drug herself, but when she lacked funds she asked her PCT to fund it. The Trust's policy was to fund the treatment only where there were exceptional personal or clinical circumstances. It determined that there were none in her case.

The Court of Appeal held that the policy of funding the drug only in exceptional circumstances was legal only if the policymaker had envisaged what kind of cases would be exceptional. If, in fact, it was not possible to imagine such exceptional circumstances, the policy was one of complete refusal and this would be irrational, because it failed to take into account each individual case (following *R v NW Lancashire Health Authority, ex p A, D and G*[94]). The Court found that the reality here was that there was no rational basis for distinguishing among those patients for whom the drug would be appropriate on the basis of personal or clinical grounds. Ms Rogers could not be said to be any less exceptional than anyone else in her medical condition. The policy had made no mention of costs being a factor to be taken into account. Therefore the policy was irrational and unlawful. The Court added that because there were comparatively few patients for whom the drug would be appropriate, there was no danger that the PCT would be flooded with claims.

It is important to appreciate that it was central to the Court's reasoning that the Trust had declared that costs were not a relevant factor.[95] The Court of Appeal appeared to conclude that if the PCT had openly said that budgetary considerations would be a factor in deciding whether the drug could be granted, then it would be permissible for it to deny a patient the drug on the grounds of cost. The decision is not, then, a decision saying that cancer patients have a right to drugs that will help them; rather, it is a decision that rationing decisions must be made openly. If the truth is that the PCT cannot afford to give the drug to

[93] At [35].   [94] [2000] 2 FCR 525.
[95] According to Newdick (2007), this was because they had misunderstood statements made by the Secretary of State for Health, who had stated that women should not be denied access to breast cancer treatment owing to cost.

a patient, it must be open about the relevance of the cost issue. Interestingly, Sir Anthony Clarke suggested that it might be appropriate in such a case to decide that a drug could be funded for a mother caring for a disabled son, but not a woman with no dependants.[96]

What is clear is that the courts are unlikely to find a particular rationing policy unlawful on the basis of it being substantively unreasonable. An application is more likely to succeed where the complaint is essentially procedural: the proper reasons for the decision are not given, the policy was misapplied, or the applicant's individual circumstances were not taken into account. Ironically, this may mean that it is far harder to challenge the decision of a trust that boldly states 'We cannot afford your treatment—there are other needier patients' than a trust that tries to hide behind a formula based on exceptional cases.[97] Christopher Newdick thinks it is not difficult for a court to find a procedural flaw if it wants to allow an application.[98] By contrast, Charles Foster thinks it is now easy for a trust to ensure that it complies with the law.[99] One way of reading the decisions of the courts in this area is that they want trusts to be completely honest and open about the rationing decisions that they make.[100] If it cannot afford the treatment, the trust should say so and not hide behind clever rhetoric.

9.5 The Human Rights Act 1998

A patient could seek to bring in aid her or his rights under the ECHR.[101] This could either be as an aspect of a claim for judicial review, or a free-standing application under the Human Rights Act 1998, sections 6 and 7.[102] There are four main Convention Articles that might be relied upon, although, as we will see, only rarely will they provide the basis of a right to treatment.[103]

- *Article 2 (the right to life)* A person seeking life-saving treatment under the NHS might claim that not to provide it would infringe his or her right to life. The difficulty with such an argument is that although Article 2 does protect the right to life, this has not been interpreted to mean that a person is entitled to every form of medical treatment that he or she needs to stay alive.[104] After all, in most cases, it is likely that life-saving treatment is not being offered to person A so that it is possible to provide life-saving treatment to person B. In such a case, it cannot be that both A and B's Article 2 rights entitle them to the treatment.

- *Article 3 (protection from torture or inhuman or degrading treatment)* It might be argued by an applicant that not being provided treatment leaves him or her in such a state of health that he or she is suffering inhuman or degrading treatment. Such an argument also faces difficulties. Like Article 2, Article 3 does not entitle a person to all forms

---

[96] *R (Rogers) v Swindon NHS Primary Care Trust* [2006] EWCA Civ 392, [77]. See also *R (Gordon) v Bromley Primary Care Trust* [2006] EWHC 2462, [41], in which care for young children was mentioned as a possible exceptional circumstance.

[97] See Ford (2011) for an insightful analysis of the use of 'exceptionality'.

[98] Newdick (2007: 244).   [99] Foster (2007).

[100] See also *R (Linda Gordon) v Bromley NHS Primary Care Trust* [2006] EWHC 2462 (Admin), in which Ousley J complained that the trust had failed to make it clear why it was refusing treatment.

[101] Maclean (2001).

[102] There is no right under common law to receive treatment: *Re J (A Minor) (Wardship: Medical Treatment)* [1990] 3 All ER 930.

[103] Foster (2007).   [104] Maclean (2000).

of treatment that might avoid his or her degradation.[105] However, if a patient in hospital were to be inadequately fed or washed and this caused the patient to suffer, for example, malnutrition or serious bed sores, this might infringe Article 3. It might be argued that although Article 3 does not give an automatic right to treatment, it at least gives a right to basic care. Of course, Article 3 applies only where the state of health of the individual is of sufficient seriousness as to amount to inhuman or degrading treatment.[106]

- *Article 8 (right to private life)* It might be argued that the right to respect for one's private life could include a right to receive the treatment that one wants.[107] However, in *R v NW Lancashire Health Authority, ex p A, D and G*,[108] it was held that Article 8 could not be relied upon to found a right to receive treatment. That was confirmed in the following decision.

KEY CASE   *R (Condliff) v North Staffordshire Primary Care Trust* [2011] EWHC 872 (Admin)

Mr Condliff was morbidly obese and wished to have bariatric surgery. He did not qualify for this under the Trust's policy on when such treatment would be provided. However, he made an 'individual funding request' (IFR) on the basis that his case was exceptional—in particular, the impact of his obesity on his lifestyle and general happiness. The Trust's policy on IFR stated that non-clinical, social factors could not be taken into account in determining exceptionality. The Trust refused his IFR. Mr Condliff claimed that the failure to take into account social factors breached his rights under Article 8 ECHR and that the failure to provide reasons for the refusal breached his rights under Article 6 ECHR.

The Court of Appeal held that, in excluding all social factors, the Trust would be excluding some factors that could come within the notion of private life under Article 8. When general decisions were being made about allocating medical resources, however, the public body had a wide discretion and Article 8 could not be used to challenge them. This principle meant that Article 8 should not be engaged when individual cases were considered. The Trust's policy of excluding social factors in IFR was a fair balancing exercise between individuals seeking IFR and the medical needs of the community as a whole. Article 8 could not therefore be used to challenge the IFR policy. Because there was no underlying right to any treatment, Article 6 was not involved, because that Article was relevant only in cases in which legal rights were involved.

- *Article 14 (protection from discrimination)* This is perhaps potentially the most promising line of argument for an applicant, who can claim that the allocation of resources has been discriminatory on the basis of grounds such as race, sex, or religious belief. It would, of course, be surprising if a health authority were to allocate on such grounds. But there are two categories of case that deserve greater attention.

  - The first is age: Article 14 does not list age as an unacceptable ground of discrimination, but the list of factors is seen only as a list of examples. The courts have been

---

[105] *R v NW Lancashire Health Authority, ex p A, D and G* [2000] 1 WLR 977, 1000G, per Buxton LJ.
[106] *R (Yvonne Watts) v Bedford Primary Care Trust and Secretary of State for Health* [2003] EWHC 2228.
[107] *Pentiacova v Moldova* (2005) 40 EHRR SE23.
[108] [2000] 2 FCR 525. See also *R (Yvonne Watts) v Bedford Primary Care Trust and Secretary of State for Health* [2003] EWHC 2228.

willing to add, for example, sexual orientation. If age were added, then a claim could be brought if a patient were to feel that he or she had been denied treatment that a younger person in his or her shoes would have been given.

– The second is disability. Again, this is not a factor mentioned in Article 14, but the courts may be willing to add it in. Could it be said that a decision not to give a donated kidney to a child suffering from Down's syndrome who needed a kidney transplant, but to give it instead to a 'healthy' child, amounted to discriminatory conduct?

Key case *R (C) v Berkshire Primary Care Trust* [2011] EWCA Civ 247

The applicant (C) had been diagnosed with gender identity disorder and had started a gender reassignment process, with hormone treatment. C was unhappy with the size of her breasts and sought breast augmentation surgery. The Trust determined that this did not fall under its funding policy for gender identity dysphoria, which covered 'core' surgical procedures, but did not cover 'non-core' (including breast augmentation), unless there were exceptional circumstances. The Trust claimed that its policy was based on the fact that there was limited evidence of the clinical effectiveness of non-core procedures. The Trust also argued that allowing C the surgery would discriminate against other woman who wished to have the surgery. The Trust also considered C's application under its general policy on cosmetic surgery, but under that policy breast augmentation was considered low priority. C challenged the Trust's approach to her case.

The Court of Appeal held that the Trust was entitled to place weight on the fact that there was no evidence that trans women had a clinical benefit from breast augmentation surgery. C argued that there was a similar lack of evidence of a clinical benefit for core surgery for trans women. However, that was an example of the Trust having to make difficult decisions in deciding what surgeries to fund, in an attempt to break even in each financial year. It could not be said that its policy was irrational.

All choices in this context involved discrimination. The key issue in this case was whether the choice was unacceptable. That could include treating differently people who shared the same relevant characteristic and also treating the same way people whose characteristics were different in a relevant way. The key issue became what was a 'relevant characteristic'. That involved considering whether the characteristic was logically related to the purpose that the decision maker was seeking to achieve or the effect of the distinction being made. The purpose of the Trust's policies was to regulate eligibility for breast augmentation. Hopper LJ put it this way:

> [T]he court is not appropriately placed to make either clinical or budgetary judgments about publicly funded healthcare: its role is in general limited to keeping decision-making within the law. The claimant's point of view—that she is different from and more needy than a natal woman with a similar problem—matters; but it is a point of view which has to take its place within both legal and clinical criteria. The material legal criteria are that gender and clinical needs are both relevant characteristics. Their aetiology is relevant diagnostically, but what are more critically relevant are the ethical and clinical judgment of the PCT, provided these do not transgress the law.[109]

As a result, the Trust's approach could not be said to be discriminatory. C's challenge failed.

---

[109] At [56].

What is particularly interesting about this case is the approach to discrimination. In essence, Hopper LJ was arguing that although, from C's point of view, there was discrimination, the Trust, not irrationally, took the view that there was no discrimination. Because the question for the Court was the legality of the Trust's reasoning, the challenge failed. This is a somewhat surprising approach because normally, in cases involving discrimination, it is the court that decides whether there is discrimination or not and whether it is justified, rather than the question being whether it was rational for the decision maker to take the view that there is no discrimination. That reflects the fact that, in judicial review cases of medical rationing, the courts are reluctant to interfere in the decision made unless it is manifestly wrong.

If age and disability discrimination were held to fall under Article 14, then the key issue would be whether or not the decision was 'objectively justifiable', because if it was, then the decision could not be challenged. A strong case for justification may be if the disability or age meant that the likely success of the treatment was less. If, for example, a donated organ was not given to a 70-year-old, but given to a young man on the basis that the 70-year-old was less likely to survive the transplantation procedure than the young man, then that would provide a justification.

We will consider issues surrounding age discrimination later in this chapter.

9.6 Negligence

An action in negligence could be brought against a local authority if it were to be claimed that harm had been caused to a patient as a result of a negligently made rationing decision. One issue in such a claim would be whether, in making resource allocation decisions, the health authority owes a duty of care to patients. This will depend on whether it is just and reasonable to impose a duty of care on the public authority in question. The key case on this is *DHSS v Kinnear*,[110] in which the claimant claimed to have suffered brain damage as a result of vaccinations. Stuart-Smith J drew a distinction between operational issues, which could be the subject of a tortious claim, and a policy decision, which could not be challenged by the law of tort. So, in this case, the policy of encouraging vaccinations could not be challenged. However, an allegation that misleading advice had been given about the manner and circumstances in which vaccinations should be provided *could* be challenged in the courts. This makes it extremely unlikely that an action in negligence could successfully challenge a decision about resource allocation. A greater chance of success might meet a claim that, having decided to allocate resources in a particular way, it implemented that decision ineffectively. Even then, the courts might take the view that it would not be just and reasonable to impose a duty of care on local authorities, given the availability of alternative complaint mechanisms available and given the impact on the NHS of having to deal with a large number of claims.[111]

A claim of negligence could be brought against the individual healthcare professional based on the fact that he or she improperly rationed healthcare resources. A court, when considering whether an individual professional is negligent, is likely to take into account that rationing decisions are normally taken at a higher level than that of an individual

---

[110] (1984) 134 NLJ 886.   [111] *X v Bedfordshire* [1995] 3 All ER 353.

doctor.[112] However, a professional who decided not to offer a patient treatment based on a rationing ground that was in defiance of his or her NHS trust's guidelines might face a challenge on the basis of negligence.

9.7 The Equality Act 2010

The Equality Act 2010 makes it illegal for service providers to discriminate on the basis of age, disability, gender reassignment, marriage and civil partnership, pregnancy and maternity, race, religion or belief, sex, or sexual orientation. This would mean, for example, that it would be unlawful for a health authority not to allocate resources to someone to deal with a physical problem simply on the grounds that they suffered from a mental illness or because of their age. The Act prohibits not only direct discrimination (for example where those over a certain age are not allowed access to a particular medication), but also indirect discrimination. That covers regulations or practices that do not on their face disadvantage people on the basis of their age, or sex, or race, and so on, but do so in effect.[113] So if only people of a certain height were allowed access to medication, this would be indirect discrimination, if it could be shown that, on average, women were shorter than men. However, as always with discrimination, it is possible to justify it. So if the healthcare body could show that there was a good clinical reason for the height requirement in relation to the medicine, any discrimination would be justified and not unlawful.

9.8 Should the courts be more interventionist?

Supporters of a conservative role for the courts will emphasize how the courts are ill-equipped to make rationing decisions not only because, arguably, they lack the skills, but also, more importantly, because they lack the information. They will be aware of the situation of the applicant, but they will not know about the other patients needing treatment. As Christopher Newdick asks:

> [D]uring litigation on behalf of an individual patient, who will speak for the large numbers of patients who are not party to the dispute but who may be affected by its outcome, and for those particular patients whose operations will have to be cancelled if someone else is treated first?[114]

Opponents will emphasize the rights of individuals to treatment, especially where it is life-saving treatment. Where life-saving treatment is being denied, simply to say 'It's too expensive' is too easy. The courts are entitled to know exactly *why* it is too expensive and exactly what would be the opportunity cost (what would be lost) if the treatment were provided. Only then can the courts offer an effective protection of patients' human rights.

9.9 The National Institute for Health and Clinical Excellence (NICE)

In the past, rationing was done informally and often in a hidden way. Individual doctors and health authorities would make decisions about what treatments were 'appropriate'

---

[112] Witting (2000).   [113] Equality Act 2010, s. 19.   [114] Newdick (2005: 99).

2 THE STRUCTURE OF THE NHS

for patients. These were often presented as clinical decisions about what was best for a patient, even if in fact the decision was solely, or partly, influenced by economic considerations.[115] One of the consequences of this was that the availability of treatment differed widely in various parts of the country.[116] This became known as the 'postcode lottery'. It led to a growing sense of unease, with important decisions about the allocation of healthcare resources being made in private, without full information and with little or no accountability.

It was partly as a result of these concerns that the NICE was created. The then Health Secretary stated that it would 'help to bring order and rationality to a system that all too often has appeared arbitrary and unfair'.[117] This body now plays an important role in the rationing of health care within the NHS.

The official role of NICE is to establish and set uniform standards regarding treatment across the NHS. It is to determine the effectiveness and appropriateness of treatments being offered on the NHS. For example, if it is believed that a new drug will provide an effective treatment for a particular condition, NICE will examine that drug, considering its effectiveness and cost in deciding whether to recommend that it be made available on the NHS, not made available at all, or made available only to a certain class of patients. When NICE's advice is not to prescribe a particular drug on the grounds of its cost, in effect, this is rationing. Of course, it is not quite this straightforward because NICE will be looking at all kinds of factors when considering whether to recommend a drug.

A decision not to recommend a drug or treatment will not be based on the straightforward argument 'It's too expensive', but rather on a complex combination of clinical and economic factors. In theory, a drug company or individual could seek judicial review of a decision of NICE, but it is difficult to imagine the decision of such an august body concerning such a delicate and complex issue being found unreasonable.[118] There have, however, been successful challenges based on the procedures that NICE has used.[119]

NICE has explained that its clinical guidelines:

- aim to improve the quality of care for patients;

- assess how well different treatments and ways of managing a specific condition work;

- assess whether treatments and ways of managing a condition are good value for money for the NHS;

- set out the clinical care that is suitable for most patients with a specific condition using the NHS in England and Wales;

- take account of the views of those who might be affected by the guideline (including healthcare and other professionals, patients and carers, health service managers, NHS trusts, the public, government bodies and the healthcare industry);

- are based on the best available research evidence and expert consensus;

- are developed using a standard process and standard ways of analysing the evidence, which are respected by the NHS and other stakeholders, including patients;

[115] Schmidt (2004).   [116] House of Commons Health Committee (1995).
[117] Milburn (1999: 11).
[118] In *R v Secretary of State for Health, ex p Pfizer* [1999] Lloyd's Rep Med 289, a successful challenge was made to the means by which the Secretary of State sought to ration the use of Viagra within the NHS. See also *R (Fraser) v National Institute for Health and Clinical Excellence* [2009] EWHC 452 (Admin).
[119] *R (Servier) v National Institute for Health and Clinical Excellence* [2009] EWHC 281 (Admin).

- make it clear how each recommendation was decided on;
- are advisory rather than compulsory, but should be taken into account by healthcare and other professionals when planning care for individual patients.[120]

NICE's role in assessing new treatments involves a number of factors. The first is in determining the effectiveness of the new treatments. It appears to be generally accepted that NICE carries out this technical side of its job well, using experts in relevant fields to assess proposed treatments and emphasizing the importance of evidence-based medicine. The second is in calculating the cost-effectiveness of the products. NICE states:

> In order to make sure our standards represent good value for money, we use the best evidence to weigh up benefits and costs. By using our guidance the NHS and local authorities can be sure they are getting good value for money.[121]

It is in this regard that greater concerns have arisen.

It is perhaps misleading to emphasize the role of NICE as rationing treatment. In fact, there are far more instances of NICE recommending treatment than of it suggesting that a drug should not be available. Indeed, as one commentator has pointed out, although NICE has received plaudits, these have not come from NHS trusts grateful for the amount of money saved as a result of NICE's work.[122] Indeed, this point highlights a real difficulty for NICE: it considers whether or not to approve a particular drug or treatment in isolation. It has no way of knowing which treatments a trust will have to stop providing in order to follow NICE guidance. The difficulty therefore is that NICE cannot know whether the treatments that trusts might forgo are more efficient or effective than the ones that it is promoting.[123]

The exact status and effect of guidance issued by NICE is unclear. A number of questions arise, which are explored next.

9.9.1 Are NICE guidelines meant to be binding on trusts or clinicians?

The Department of Health has issued directions, under section 8 of the National Health Service Act 2006, that CCGs should provide any treatment recommended by NICE after a technological appraisal.[124] In the NHS Constitution, one of the rights of patients is listed as: 'You have the right to drugs and treatments that have been recommended by NICE for use in the NHS, if your doctor says they are clinically appropriate for you.'[125]

Key case R (Rose) v Thanet Clinical Commissioning Group [2014] EWHC 1182 (Admin)

A 25-year-old woman suffered from Crohn's Disease and wanted to have her eggs frozen before undergoing chemotherapy and other treatments, which carried a risk of rendering her infertile. She was on benefits and so could not afford private treatment. The Clinical Commissioning Group (CCG) applied its policy which only allowed egg freezing in exceptional circumstances and determined her case was not exceptional. However, the NICE Guidance had said that egg freezing should

---

[120] NICE (2013: 15).   [121] NICE (2008: 9).   [122] Campbell (2003).   [123] Harris (2007).
[124] NICE (2009c).   [125] NHS (2013a: 17).

be offered to women undergoing the kind of treatment Ms Rose was undergoing, but the CCG disagreed with that policy, given its low success rate. Ms Rose sought judicial review on the basis that the commissioning group should have followed the NICE guidance.

Jay J held that a CCG did not have to follow NICE guidelines, but it had a public law obligation to have regard to them and provide clear reasons why they could not provide the approved treatment. While CCGs could determine they could not afford the treatment, they could not legitimately disagree with NICE on matters concerning the current state of medical science. In this case the CCG's only given reason was the effectiveness of egg freezing, whereas NICE has determined egg freezing was effective. The judicial review was therefore successful.

9.9.2 *Are trusts in fact following NICE guidelines?*

In the early days, there were varying levels of compliance with NICE guidance among NHS trusts. When the Audit Commission looked into compliance with NICE guidance in 2005, it found that 33 per cent of responding NHS bodies said that they had not been able to fund full compliance with NICE guidance.[126] A more recent study by the NHS Information Centre found evidence of increased use of drugs recommended by NICE.[127] It compared the expected use of approved drugs within PCTs with actual use and found that, of twelve drugs considered, use was higher than expected for eight drugs surveyed and lower for three drugs. It seems that, now, approval of a drug by NICE will lead to its general availability on the NHS.

9.9.3 *To what extent is NICE meant to look at economics?*

One of the complaints about the work of NICE is that it focuses on the cost-effectiveness of the drug or proposed treatment in the abstract and decides whether it provides good value for money.[128] But, being one step apart from the NHS trusts, it does not consider how the trusts are to afford the implementation of the guidance. To be blunt, if a new drug is approved by NICE and a trust adopts that drug, the money to pay for it must come from somewhere. NICE might reassure us that the drug is cost-effective, but it does not (of course) tell a trust what it should cut from its expenditure to allow it to adopt the drug. This has led some to claim that the work of NICE has skewed priorities for trusts. They are keen to follow NICE guidance, but in so doing they may be cutting back on other equally valuable treatments that NICE is yet to consider. Of course, NICE does consider the question of overall resource implication in the abstract. As Professor Rawlins, chair of NICE, put it:

> The Institute will have to take into account the NHS's broad clinical priorities and the broad balance between benefits and costs. The Institute will have to take into account guidance from Ministers on the resources likely to be available; and the Institute will have to ensure that the technology represents an effective use of available resources.[129]

---

[126] National Audit Office (2005b).   [127] NHS (2013a).   [128] WHO (2003: 6).
[129] Rawlins (2004: 225).

NICE has also emphasized that it makes decisions about whether or not a treatment is cost-effective. It does not determine whether or not the treatment is affordable. That, it seems, is regarded as primarily an issue for the government. Not surprisingly, there have been concerns that attempts to comply with NICE guidance are putting financial strains on trusts.[130]

9.9.4 *What is the relationship between NICE and the government?*

The exact relationship between the government and NICE is delicate. On the one hand, NICE can be convenient for the government: when NICE decides not to approve a new expensive drug for a particular illness, the 'flak' is directed towards NICE, rather than the government. Indeed, it has been suggested that the creation of NICE is part of a strategy of blame avoidance and blame diffusion within the NHS.[131] However, on occasion, the government will want to appear to be taking an active approach to a health problem. Hence we saw, in August 2005, NICE being ordered by a government minister to fast-track an assessment of Herceptin, a drug designed to treat breast cancer,[132] and in 2002 the government's announcement that it would provide a form of funding for a drug to treat multiple sclerosis, despite NICE's original decision that it was not cost-effective.[133] In 2011, a special fund was created to provide funding for cancer treatment that would not be available under the normal NICE assessment.[134]

NICE insists that it is free from government intervention and pressure from industry.[135] However, the success of campaigns by manufacturers (such as Glaxo-Wellcome on zanamivir) and pressure groups (the Multiple Sclerosis Society on beta-interferon and glatiramer acetate), causing a reversal of an initial decision by NICE, has indicated to some commentators that NICE is not immune from outside pressure.[136]

9.9.5 *How transparent is NICE?*

There have been concerns expressed that the process by which NICE makes guidance lacks transparency.[137] In particular, there are concerns from patient groups that it is unclear how their representations are taken into account and precisely what factors NICE is using to make its decisions.[138] That said, the NICE website is replete with policies, procedures, and decisions, and it features a 'communication strategy' to ensure it communicates effectively with stakeholders.[139]

In *R (Eisai Ltd) v National Institute for Health and Clinical Excellence*,[140] the appellant, a pharmaceutical company, challenged the decision of NICE not to approve the use of its drug for mild to moderate cases of Alzheimer's disease. In particular, the company claimed that it had not been provided with a full version of the economic model that NICE had used to assess the cost-effectiveness of the drug. The Court of Appeal found

---

[130] BBC News online (22 July 2004).   [131] Klein (2001).   [132] BBC News online (21 July 2005).
[133] Mayor (2001).   [134] BBC News online (28 September 2013).   [135] NICE (2002b: 1).
[136] Rodwin (2001: 442).
[137] NICE judgements can be subject to judicial review: *R (Eisai Ltd) v NICE* [2008] EWCA Civ 438; *Servier v NICE* [2010] EWCA Civ 346; *R (Bristol-Myers Squibb Pharmaceuticals Ltd) v National Institute for Health and Clinical Excellence* [2009] EWHC 2722 (Admin).
[138] Smith (2000: 1364).   [139] Online at www.nice.org.uk   [140] [2008] EWCA Civ 438.

in favour of the applicant. The Court rejected the arguments of NICE that providing a full version of the economic model would have caused delay. Because NICE operated a policy of openness and transparency generally, this should apply to all of the relevant information used to make its decision. The refusal to provide the economic model used put those consulted over this drug at a significant disadvantage. NICE's refusal to disclose the model had been unfair and unlawful.[141]

One way in which NICE has sought to respond to such concerns is to make greater use of the 'citizens' councils' that seek to represent the views of the general public. The difficulty is that the more weight that is given to the views of the general public, the less weight NICE's guidance will carry as an in-depth independent scientific assessment on the effectiveness of medicine. Nevertheless, NICE has faced legal challenge on the basis that its committee was biased. The challenge was unsuccessful,[142] but it shows how difficult it can be in controversial areas to maintain an appearance of fairness.

9.9.6 How does NICE decide whether a treatment is cost-effective?

In assessing cost-effectiveness, NICE places much weight on quality-adjusted life years (QALYs). This is a very popular way of deciding how medical treatments should be rationed. We will consider this concept in more detail shortly, when we consider how healthcare services should be rationed.

9.9.7 Critics of NICE

It is not surprising, given the delicate nature of the issues with which it is dealing, that NICE has been criticized. At the heart of the criticisms are the moral issues that we will be considering in detail next. But, in addition, NICE has faced other complaints. These were considered by the House of Commons Select Committee on Health, which acknowledged there were concerns that NICE focused on which treatments to approve, rather than considering which treatments could be dropped; that publication of guidance could be slow; and that the interests of carers were not sufficiently taken into account. However, their report also contained a ringing endorsement of the organization:[143]

> NICE is well regarded internationally. An external review of NICE by the World Health Organization commended the appraisal processes used by the Institute. Many countries look to NICE decisions when determining the cost-effectiveness of treatments for their own populations. Some of its clinical guidelines are regarded as the international gold standard of medical practice.[144]

9.10 How should health care be rationed?

Ethicists interested in this area enjoy conundrums of the following kind.

---

[141] See also *R (Servier) v National Institute for Health and Clinical Excellence* [2009] EWHC 281 (Admin).
[142] *R (Fraser) v National Institute for Health and Clinical Excellence* [2009] EWHC 452 (Admin).
[143] House of Commons Health Committee (2008).
[144] House of Commons Health Committee (2008), 74.

TO PONDER

There are three patients in your care. There is only enough money available to fund one of them. Which will you fund?

(i) Alf is a newborn. He has a serious disability and needs intensive care to be kept alive. The likelihood of him surviving into his 20s is moderate, and even if he does, he will be seriously disabled. Without the treatment, he will die.

(ii) Steve is a student who is suffering serious liver failure following excessive drinking for many years. A liver transplant and further treatment is required. If successful, and if he gives up drinking, there is no reason why he should not expect to have a normal life expectancy. Without the treatment, he will die.

(iii) Wendy is a young mother caring for two toddlers. She has developed a form of cancer. With the treatment, it is estimated that she will live another ten years; without the treatment, she will die a painful death within the next few months.

Of course, it is rare that choices facing medical professionals are so stark, but the discussion of such hypothetical situations helps to bring out some of the key issues.

The following are some possible responses to this conundrum.

9.10.1 'Treat all of them'

To most people, the initial response to a hypothetical scenario such as that outlined above is that we should fund *all* of their treatment. What sort of a society do we live in if we cannot provide treatment to all of these people? Those tempted by such a response might suggest that we need to determine what kind of health service is the minimally decent that we would want and to set taxation accordingly. If people were to realize that, without higher taxation, people would die, they would pay. It is, of course, not that straightforward. What this point emphasizes, however, is that, at the end of the day, if rationing decisions produce unacceptable results, then the answer may be to increase funding for the NHS, rather than to try to tweak the rationing system even further.

9.10.2 'There is no answer'

An acceptable answer to these dilemmas is that there is no correct answer. A perfectly legitimate case can be made for Alf, Steve, and Wendy. All that we can ask of the health service is that the way in which these decisions are made should be open and accessible, and that there should be a means of challenging any decision made.[145] But although these values are important, many people would not find it acceptable if the NHS were to fund cosmetic surgery, but not cancer treatment, however open, accessible, and open to review the system was. It may be correct that there is no 'right' answer, but that does not mean that there are no 'wrong' answers.

---

[145] Smith II (2002 and 2009).

9.10.3 *A rights perspective*

To some, we have a human right to a minimally decent standard of health care and that would include providing life-saving treatment. Alf, Steve, and Wendy all have a right to receive treatment. Of course, where the treatment is not life-saving, there may either be no right to it at all or the rights of individuals will need to be pitted against each other. This perspective has resonance in a legal age focused on rights. However, it does not really provide an answer to the difficult questions. If, in our scenario, there simply is not enough money, how are these rights to life to be weighed? And in the case of non-life-threatening conditions, a rights approach, without more, does little to indicate how the rights in question are to be balanced. So we need something more to assist us in balancing rights.

9.10.4 *Need*

One alternative is to follow the 'worse off' principle. This states that resources should be directed to the person who is worse off than the other(s).[146] There are clearly some situations in which that principle works well. An ambulance team arriving at the scene of a car crash will focus on those who are worse off, before turning to those with less serious injuries. It also meshes with the intuition that ensuring life-saving treatment should be a priority. One objection to it is that it does not leave much scope for preventative medicine. Further, it may be questioned whether keeping the seriously sick alive for a few more days is worthwhile.

9.10.5 *QALY*

Quality-adjusted life years is probably the most popular way of analysing the cost-effectiveness of treatments and is widely used in decision making in rationing. It is used by NICE,[147] and therefore we shall pay particular attention to this concept. As used in rationing decisions, QALY requires an assessment of three factors.

- How many years of extra life will the treatment provide this patient?
- What will the quality of those extra years be?
- How expensive is the treatment?

A treatment that provides a year of perfect health scores as one; a year of less than perfect health will score less than one. Death is equivalent to zero. In some schemes, it is possible to have a state of health worse than death, and this may achieve a negative score. Under QALY, therefore, a treatment that provided a patient with an extra year of perfect health would be preferred to a treatment that provided a patient with an extra year of pain and low life quality. A treatment that offered a large number of QALY for a small amount of money would be highly cost-effective, while one that produced a low number of QALY for a large amount of money would not be. Someone required to ration health services can therefore examine a range of different services and consider how many QALY for how much money is offered.

The main benefit of QALY is its ability to provide a way of considering not only the length of time that a patient gains, but also the quality of that time. It provides a unit

---

[146] Ottersen (2013).   [147] NICE (2008b).

that enables those at the policy level to compare contrasting treatments for a particular medical condition. Clearly, in considering alternative treatments for, say, back pain, a trust will be attracted to using that treatment which offers the lowest cost for each QALY. It also provides a way of comparing different treatments for different conditions where a health service has to choose between funding them.

How do NICE use QALYs? In 2010, NICE stated: 'Generally, we consider that interventions costing the NHS less than £20,000 per QALY gained are cost effective. Those costing between £20,000 and £30,000 per QALY gained may also be deemed cost effective, if certain conditions are satisfied'.[148] A study of public opinion suggests that a figure of up to £70,000 would match public expectations.[149] On the other hand, a survey of CCGs found that, in their rationing decisions, they used a maximum of £20,000.[150]

The question of cost can be made even more complicated. In respect of one cancer drug, NICE approved its use after the manufacturer said that the NHS would be refunded in cases in which the drug did not benefit a patient.[151] Such deals will increase the cost-effectiveness of some drugs. Further, there may be patients who are willing to contribute towards the cost of their drugs. Although currently that cannot be used as a factor in deciding whether the drug is available on the NHS,[152] it raises further issues about calculating the QALY cost of a drug.

9.10.6 Problems with QALY

The use of QALY has not proved uncontroversial. The following are some of the objections that are made:

(i) One objection to the use of QALY is the difficulty in the calculation. How is it possible to assess the quality of a person's life?[153] How can you compare being confined to a wheelchair to being blind? Is it really possible to put a figure on such things? The difficulty is that what gives our lives quality differs greatly from person to person.[154] For some people, the loss of use of a finger will matter very little; to another—a musician for example—it might hugely affect quality of life. An attempt could be made to assess an average improvement in quality of life, but this could be complex.[155] How are we to assess the improvement in quality of life produced by cosmetic surgery? In one quality-of-life study, a group of persons who won the National Lottery had similar quality-of-life ratings one year after winning as did a group of persons who had become paraplegic.[156] Can anyone really know how bad certain conditions are if they do not suffer from them?[157]

(ii) The QALY approach can produce unacceptable results. In particular, it places no weight on concepts such as dignity. A severely mentally ill person with no real awareness of what is happening to him or her, for example, could be left in appalling circumstances on the basis that to offer basic care would not improve quality of life because he or she lacks awareness of their condition.

Schlander asks:

Assuming the cost per QALY gained (incremental cost-effectiveness ratio, ICER) is, for example, £3600 for sildenafil in erectile dysfunction, £7000 for pharmacotherapy of

---

[148] NICE (2013c).   [149] Mason, Jones-Lee, and Donaldson (2009).   [150] DoH (2009).
[151] DoH (2009).   [152] Martin, Rice, and Smith (2007).   [153] Malek (2003).
[154] See Hausman (2008); Dolan (2008); Cookson (2005).   [155] Hausman (2006).
[156] Brickman and Coates (1978).   [157] Goold (1996).

children with attention deficit hyperactivity disorder, and £120 000 for beta-interferons and glatiramer in multiple sclerosis, would this ranking reflect the comparative social desirability of these interventions?[158]

His argument is that, on the basis of these figures, we would rate medication for erectile dysfunction a much better use of money than intervention in multiple sclerosis. Is that an acceptable conclusion? If not, does that cast doubt on the appropriateness of relying on QALY?

(iii) A particular concern is that QALY works harshly against older people.[159] An older person who has a low life expectancy will find it much harder, if not impossible, to show a higher number of QALY than a younger person facing a similar illness. Indeed, the older person is unlikely to be able to compete with a child with a much less serious illness.

These points have led some to argue that relying on QALYs amounts to age or disability discrimination.[160]

That seems hard to deny, certainly if QALYs are used to decide between which patient should receive treatment. However, in its use of QALYs, NICE deny any ageism, because it does not look at a particular individual, but rather at treatments, and considers how they impact on the average patient. If treatments are effective, they are recommended for anyone, young or older.[161] Nevertheless, it might be said that if NICE considers a medicine that treats a condition associated with old age, when considering its impact on an average patient with that condition, a low QALY will be produced. NICE has responded to such concerns by saying that QALYs are only one factor that it uses in its assessment and that it is committed to ensuring that its guidance will not result in age discrimination. This will not satisfy those who believe that QALYs are inherently ageist and that even if NICE ensures that they are not used in a discriminatory way, NICE's support of the system demonstrates institutional ageism.[162]

It may be argued that even if the use of QALYs amounts to age discrimination, that is perfectly acceptable. Surely most people would agree that, if we had no choice but to save the life of ten 8-year-olds or ten 80-year-olds, we should prefer the former?[163] There must be few grandparents who, faced with the awful alternative of either dying themselves or their grandchild dying, would not think it preferable that they be the ones to go.[164] Any age discrimination might be justified on the basis of an argument that the loss to the 80-year-old of a short period of life is less than the loss of many years for the young person.[165] This is not discrimination on grounds of age, but based on an assessment of the loss for the individual.

A second response might be to deny that there is age discrimination here at all. In a QALY approach, the distinction is not based on age as such, but rather on the number of future years for which a person is predicted to live. QALY draws no distinction between a 20-year-old with a terminal illness and short life expectancy and an 80-year-old with the same illness and life expectancy. Indeed, this has even led one commentator to suggest that QALY is 'not ageist enough', because we should, in the example given, prefer giving the few extra months to a 20-year-old rather than the 80-year-old.[166]

Third, it might be argued that the final months or years of life should be regarded as especially valuable in that they enable a person to reflect on and complete his or her life

[158] Schlander (2008: 534).   [159] Walker (2016).   [160] Keown (2002).
[161] Stevens, Doyle, Littlejohns, and Docherty (2012).   [162] Harris and Regmi (2012).
[163] Nord (1999).   [164] Shaw (1994).   [165] Sunstein (2004).   [166] Lockwood (1988).

story.[167] Christopher Cowley argues that adding a few extra months so that a person can reflect on and close his or her life can give that whole life extra meaning and thereby score very highly in terms of a QALY assessment.[168]

Opponents of age as a relevant factor argue that it is simply unjust to value the life of an older person as being less than that of the life of a younger person: both lives are equally precious. The use of age reinforces the all-too-common perception in our society that the elderly are a 'waste of space'. We must respect and value old age, and this means offering the same treatment that we would to a younger person. John Harris has argued that age offers an utterly arbitrary criterion: as he points out, if there is a fire in a lecture theatre, do we really think that we should try to get the 19-year-olds out before the 20-year-olds?[169] It is interesting that a survey found that people were willing to use age when making end-of-life decisions for other people, but not when making such decisions for themselves.[170]

(iv) It has been argued that QALY will work against the interests of the disabled.[171] If two people who suffer from a condition are being considered, one of whom has a disability and the other of whom has not, it is arguable that the impact of the treatment on the non-disabled person will be greater, because it will restore him or her to full health and therefore his or her QALY will be higher. For example, it has been claimed that, in deciding who should receive donated hearts, Down's syndrome children have been overlooked in favour of 'normal' children.[172] There are many to whom that is unacceptable, but it could be said to be justified on a QALY basis if Down's syndrome children are thought to have a lower quality of life than other children. In response NICE would use the same argument it did with the arguments over age. It assesses treatment, rather than individuals, and so if a treatment is cost-effective it is available to all, disabled or not.[173] That response will not get round the disability discrimination argument if a treatment is designed to deal with a side effect of a particular disability.

(v) It might be argued that QALY is too individualistic in focusing only on the impact of the treatment on the individual patient.[174] When considering a patient, the improvement in the patient's quality of life alone is considered and the impact on his or her carers counts for nothing. It may be that, for example, a drug that prevents incontinence might not hugely improve the quality of life for the patient, but may have a dramatic impact on the quality of life for their carer. Others strongly object to arguments of this kind. If we start to take into account not only the individual patient, but also all those for whom they care and who care for them, the task of comparing treatments would become highly complex.

(vi) It has been claimed that QALY inevitably causes us to weigh up the worth of different people, something that is ethically inappropriate. Muireann Quigley argues:

> If I need to decide whether to give a treatment to either patient A or patient B and I utilise the QALY, then I am effectively balancing the improvement (or deterioration) in the quality of A's life multiplied by the number of life-years he gains (or loses) against the same calculation for B. The best score will determine which person will be the most cost effective to treat from my limited resources. Unfortunately, what we are doing when we

---

[167] Sinclair (2012).   [168] Cowley (2010).   [169] Harris (1992: 87).
[170] Zikmund-Fisher, Lacey, and Fagerlin (2008).   [171] Harris (1987; 2001).
[172] Savulescu (2001b).   [173] Cookson (2015).
[174] Herring (2008a). See Camosy (2010) and Du Toit and Millum (2016) for a detailed development of such an approach.

engage in this type of calculation, in particular, is making value judgements about the lives of those two patients (identifiable or not), because the result is that their lives and health are given lower priority.[175]

Others disagree and insist that QALY is contrasting treatments, rather than people.[176] Even if Quigley is correct, it may be that the weighing up of the value of the lives of patients is an inevitable part of rationing, rather than a unique aspect of QALY.[177]

9.10.7 Daniel Callahan

Daniel Callahan has recommended an approach that suggests that we need to provide for all people a fair rationing of health care across their lives. He argues:

> It is the obligation of a good society to help the young to become old but not to help the old people become indefinitely older. The young and the old have reciprocal responsibilities: the young should support the old, and the old should not be an undue burden on the young.[178]

He suggests that our society has become obsessed with avoiding death and that we need to find again the notion of an 'acceptable death'. There comes a point in people's lives at which death should be regarded as an acceptable event. At that point, healthcare resources should not be used to assist such a person to keep on living. This might be in a person's late 70s or early 80s.[179] If people were to choose whether they would rather have money spent on them if they fell ill when young or when old, they would prefer to have the treatment that they needed when young. Another author with a similar approach has suggested that there comes a point at which a person has had a 'fair innings', and that it is right to focus healthcare resources on those who have been unlucky enough to face the possibility of not having a normal life span, rather than those who have already had such a life.[180]

Callahan's proposal has proved highly controversial.[181] Although he appears to believe that it would solve the funding crises facing health care, it should be pointed out that even if only very limited health care were to be offered to those over the age of 80, it is unlikely that this would resolve our rationing problems: the savings made by doing that would not be sufficient.[182] Further, it might be thought that the 'natural' life span that a person is entitled to expect depends on the amount of healthcare services available.[183] The notion of a 'natural life span' is not very helpful in determining the amount of health care that should be available in old age.

One objection to Callahan's approach is that it proposes one particular view of life: an active youth and middle age, followed by an old age of little worth. Many people may regard life as being like that, but many do not. Many look forward to old age as a time of rest and respect. In other words, Callahan imposes on everyone one particular vision of how to live a life—and it is one that many people feel does not show a sufficient respect

[175] Quigley (2007b: 465). For a response to that article, see Claxton and Culyer (2008).
[176] Claxton and Culyer (2006). [177] Heale (2016). [178] Callahan (2012: 11).
[179] Callahan (1990a). [180] Williams (1997). See Bognar (2015) for a critique.
[181] Cohen-Almagor (2002b). [182] Beauchamp and Childress (2003: 262). [183] Farrant (2009).

for old age.[184] It has also been pointed out that the proposal is likely to work against the interests of women, because a far higher percentage of women than men reach the age of 80.[185]

9.10.8 *Equality of treatment*

John Harris argues that each citizen has an equal claim to having her or his individual health needs met.[186] Those who are old or disabled, or who have a poor prognosis of health, have no less a right to health services than anyone else. The primary goal, Harris argues, must be to save lives. He thinks it utterly wrong that the life of an ill and expensive-to-treat person could be sacrificed under a QALY scheme to improve, by a small amount, the health of a large number of young healthy people. He argues:

> The principal objective of the NHS should be to protect the life and health of each citizen impartially and to offer beneficial health care on the basis of individual need, so that each has an equal chance of flourishing to the extent that their personal health status permits.[187]

Where it is not possible to save everyone's life with the resources available, Harris recommends that allocation should be decided by lottery and that, in that way, there will be no suggestion that one person's life is regarded as more valuable than that of another.

This approach, based on equality of access, appears to reject even placing weight on the likelihood of success of treatment. That appears counter-intuitive. To allocate a scarce organ to a person for whom it is likely to fail when there are others needing the organ with a good chance of thriving with it seems difficult to justify. Critics argue that this could lead simply to a squandering of resources.[188] To provide treatments to those with only a few months to live and to deny the same treatment to a person with many years of life ahead of him or her is likely to increase social costs and costs for the NHS.

9.10.9 *A Rawlsian approach*

John Rawls's 'original position' approach has been advocated by some as a solution to the rationing dilemma. His approach involves a 'thought experiment' in which free and equal citizens negotiate about the world in which they are to live. They have a 'veil of ignorance', meaning that they do not know what kind of life they will have or what position they will be in. How would they decide how healthcare resources should be allocated? Would they agree that young people should have a primary call on resources, fearing that they may appear in the world as a young person with a serious medical condition?[189]

This is an attractive way of considering the problem. However, there are difficulties with it. As already mentioned, it is extremely difficult for such a negotiation to take place without a full knowledge of what suffering from various conditions would be like. How can this hypothetical group decide whether money is better spent providing treatments

---

[184] Schefczyk (2009).   [185] Dixon (1994).
[186] Harris (1997; 2005c). See Claxton and Culyer (2006) for a powerful rejoinder to Harris's views. See also Upton (2011).
[187] Harris (1997: 670).   [188] McKie, Kuhse, Richardson et al. (2002).
[189] Daniels (1985) thinks it would.

for arthritis or depression without having experienced the conditions? In any event, predicting how people in the thought experiment would decide to ration treatment is problematic.

9.10.10 *Asking the general public*

One solution to the difficulties facing rationing would be to fall back on democracy.[190] Should we simply obtain the views of the general public and follow their assessments as to how priorities in the NHS should be ranked? Notably, NICE seeks the views of the general public through its citizens' councils when setting its guidance.[191] The rather limited surveys that have been carried out do provide some clear messages: the young should be given priority over the old; those with dependants (such as children) should be preferred over those without; and those who have looked after their own health should be given higher priority than those who have not.[192] Indeed, it is not clear that the public puts as much weight on cost-effectiveness as NICE does.[193]

There are, however, grave concerns about putting too much weight on public surveys of this kind. Can members of the public really understand what it is like to suffer from multiple sclerosis, infertility, or gender identity dysphoria, for example, without personal experience? There is a concern that prejudice, rather than reason, will dominate some of the decisions.[194]

9.10.11 *Patient choice*

One interesting option is to seek to develop a range of schemes of rationing and to allow patients to select the scheme that they prefer.[195] So the arrangement may be that, at the age of 18, you must choose from a variety of options.[196] If you are not concerned about being denied treatment in old age, you may opt to be part of a scheme in which rationing decisions do take account of age. If, on the other hand, you were to want a scheme under which every effort was made to postpone death even in old age, you may prefer to opt for a scheme that is willing to invest money in treatments at the end of life. The difficulties with such a proposal are that people will need to make the choice without sufficient information available to them.[197] There would also be difficulties with the treatment of children, but they could be exempt from the scheme.

9.11 **Controversies over rationing**

9.11.1 *Drawing a distinction between treatment for ill-health and lifestyle enhancement*

To some, rationing in the NHS would be easier if a clear distinction were drawn between treatment for ill-health and 'lifestyle enhancement'.[198] It is argued that it is not

---

[190] Nord (1999); Cookson and Dolan (1999).   [191] Davies (2005) examines their work.

[192] Charny and Lewis (1989); Williams (1997; 2001).   [193] Richardson and McKie (2007).

[194] Price (2000b). See the system of rationing in Oregon, which, for a time, placed weight on public opinion surveys in setting priorities: Oregon Health Services Commission (2007).

[195] A useful discussion of these can be found in Attell-Thompson (2005).

[196] The scheme could apply to younger people if parents were permitted to make choices for them.

[197] Rai (1997).   [198] See Chapter 1 for a further discussion on what 'health' or 'sickness' means.

the job of the NHS to make people happier, but only to treat ill-health.[199] Hence even if cosmetic surgery makes people happier, it should not be available on the NHS because it is not curing an illness. More controversial examples may be not providing cosmetic surgery, obesity treatment, or treatment for erectile problems on the NHS. However, as these examples demonstrate, the line between treatment and enhancement is not easy to draw.

9.11.2 *Rationing and 'clinical judgement'*

One of the objections that has been made about NICE is that it attacks medical professionals' clinical judgement. By telling them when a treatment is appropriate, NICE challenges the assessment of the professional as to the best treatment available to the patient. As we have seen, NICE insists that its guidance is not meant to restrict the freedom of doctors in individual cases, although it would be a brave doctor who departed from the guidance without a 'reasonable justification'.[200] Christopher Newdick has argued that we need to be wary about the term 'clinical judgement'.[201] He looks at the rates of hysterectomies per 100,000 population in various countries all of which provide funding for that surgery and finds the following: United States, 700; Canada, 600; UK, 250; and Norway, 110. He argues that the difference in these rates cannot be put down to 'clinical judgement' in particular cases. The figures 'call out for an explanation'. They certainly suggest that either, in some countries, some women are receiving unnecessary hysterectomies or, in others, they are not receiving them when they are required. Saying that something is clinically required may therefore reflect as much a social judgement as a medical one.

9.11.3 *Fault of the patient?*

It has been estimated that, in the developed world, a third of all diseases can be attributed to a 'lifestyle choice' involving tobacco, alcohol, blood pressure, cholesterol, and obesity. In making a rationing decision, should we draw any distinction based on whether patients have brought the condition upon themselves?[202] Should we be less willing to give treatment for heart disease to patients who have caused their condition by smoking than to those who bear no responsibility?[203] If a doctor arrives at the scene of a car crash and there are two patients, both of whom urgently need the doctor's attention, should he or she focus on the innocent pedestrian rather than the drunk driver? Many people instinctively feel that an 'innocent' patient deserves preferential treatment over the 'blameworthy' in rationing decisions.[204]

The difficulty is in deciding the extent to which someone can be blamed for their condition.[205] Is a lawyer who suffers a cardiac disorder owing to overwork and stress to be blamed for not having a more sensible work–life balance? Is a fire-fighter who suffers an injury while putting out a blaze to be blamed for taking on such a risky occupation?

---

[199] Gilbert, Walley, and New (2000).
[200] See Bristol Infirmary Inquiry (2001: 30), which suggested that retraining may be needed for professionals who regularly breach NICE guidance without a reasonable justification.
[201] Newdick (2007: 245).
[202] For discussions of this issue, see Ahola-Launonen (2015); Cappelen and Norheim (2005); Underwood and Bailey (1993).
[203] Underwood and Bailey (1993).   [204] Sandman et al. (2016).   [205] Friesen (2017).

The difficulties in making these kinds of assessments have caused the General Medical Council (GMC) to argue: 'You must not refuse or delay treatment because you believe that patients' actions have contributed to their condition.'[206] NICE states that an injury or illness being self-inflicted should not be a reason for denying treatment, but allows it to be taken into account in deciding whether treatment will be effective.[207] But others argue that if we acknowledge a right to health care, with that should come responsibilities to take care of our health. It is possible, through our irresponsible actions, to forfeit our right to health care.[208] Even if you are attracted to the argument that those who cause their own illnesses should have less of a claim on limited health resources, it can be difficult to know to what extent a person is to blame for those lifestyle choices—and indeed the extent to which a lifestyle choice causes a condition. It may be that most illnesses are, in some sense, self-inflicted.[209] An alternative response to someone sympathetic to these arguments is to say that we should tax 'dangerous' activities such as smoking or drinking and use the revenue to treat the illnesses caused. In that case, the cost incurred by the dangerous activity is shared among all those who engage in it and not only those who are 'unlucky' enough to fall ill.[210] Alan Cribb argues that we need to develop a network of health obligations that are connected to entitlements.[211]

It is generally accepted that there is a legitimate way in which prior fault can be relevant in a rationing decision and that is where it might affect the effectiveness of a treatment. A heavy drinker who requires liver treatment, but is unwilling to cease drinking, may be denied treatment on the basis that the treatment is unlikely to be effective. This is the line NICE has taken: that 'prior fault' should not be relevant unless it affects the future effectiveness of the treatment.[212]

9.11.4 *Is the contribution that a patient can or will make to society relevant?*

In allocating healthcare resources, is it appropriate to consider the contribution that a person has made or will make to society? If the choice is between offering treatment to a middle-aged leading scientist who has made a major breakthrough in research into the treatment of cancer or a person who is long-term unemployed, should those factors be taken into account? Or what about the fact that one patient has young children to care for, who will be devastated by her death, and another is a single person with no dependants? The general view seems to be that these are not factors that can legitimately be taken into account. NICE has made it clear that social class or position in life should not be a relevant factor in deciding what treatment should be offered.[213] To start to consider whether a patient is more worthy than another is to open a Pandora's box of complex issues and will inevitably lead to claims of improper discrimination. On the other hand, simply to consider the cost–benefit analysis of treatment in terms of the individuals, without a consideration of the wider interests of the community and those with whom they are in relationships, might be said to take an improperly individualistic view of the world.

---

[206] GMC (2007: 6).
[207] NICE (2005a: Principle 10). For criticism of this approach, see Holm (2006), who asks if sportspeople should not be allowed to have surgery because they are likely to continue playing sport and impede their recovery.
[208] See Sharkey and Gillam (2010) for an interesting discussion.   [209] Golan (2010).
[210] Cappelen and Norheim (2005) and Andersen and Nielsen (2017).   [211] Cribb (2005: ch. 6).
[212] NICE (2005a).   [213] NICE (2005a).

9.11.5 *Gender*

Of course, there is near universal agreement that it would be improper, in the allocation of healthcare resources, if sex were to be a relevant categorization. However, as has been pointed out, using age as a category is in effect a form of sex discrimination, because there are far more women than men among the very elderly.[214]

It has also been argued that the individualist approach of QALY, focusing on the impact of treatment on the patient without considering the effect of a rationing decision on a carer, works against the interests of women, who undertake the majority of caring work.[215]

9.11.6 *The many or the few?*

Imagine that we have a patient who is in urgent need of medical treatment without which she or he will die. The treatment will cost £500,000. The same money could be used to institute a screening process for cholesterol problems, which, it is predicted, will save ten lives. If the choice must be made between the two, which is to be preferred?[216] A QALY approach would prefer the screening programme because, for the same amount of money, a large number of lives would be saved. Yet in fact, within the NHS, large sums of money are spent to save an individual's life, at the expense of preventative health campaigns. It is not only in the NHS where this occurs. Large sums are willingly spent in a bid to rescue a sailor lost at sea or a miner trapped in a mine, whereas similar sums are not available to institute road safety measures that might save a larger number of lives. To some, this is illogical. These decisions are based on emotion: we see the face of the person who needs the treatment, or the lost sailor, but we do not know the identity of those whose lives will be saved by the screening campaign or the road safety campaign. We feel compelled to rescue those whose identity we know, yet feel no compassion for the unidentified others who will die without the preventative steps. Many argue that this is wrong and that we should feel just as strongly about those unknown number of people whose lives are lost because we fail to fund a preventative illness campaign as we do about those we see in desperate need.[217]

10 Health inequalities

Another major concern is inequalities in the level of health across the UK[218]—indeed, the world.[219] There are notable disparities in the general quality of people's health in different parts of the country, and among different social, ethnic, and economic groups.[220] There are also differences in the quality of NHS service offered.[221] The following figures demonstrate this.

- In 2006 a girl born in Kensington and Chelsea has a life expectancy of 87.8 years, more than ten years higher than Glasgow City, the area in the UK with the lowest.[222]

---

[214] Lindemann Nelson (2007).   [215] Whitty (1998).   [216] Hope (2005: ch. 3).
[217] Cookson (2015).   [218] Cribb (2005); Leatherman and Sutherland (2005).
[219] Daniels (2007).   [220] Graham (2002).   [221] Davey Smith, Chaturvedi, Harding et al. (2002).
[222] House of Commons Health Committee (2009: 9).

- For babies registered by both parents, the infant mortality rate is highest for babies with fathers in semi-routine and routine occupations—5.4/1000 compared to the national average of 4.9/1000.[223]

The House of Commons Health Committee, in a report on the issue, found:

> Health inequalities are not only apparent between people of different socio-economic groups—they exist between different genders, different ethnic groups, and the elderly and people suffering from mental health problems or learning disabilities also have worse health than the rest of the population. The causes of health inequalities are complex, and include lifestyle factors—smoking, nutrition, exercise to name only a few—and also wider determinants such as poverty, housing and education. Access to health care may play a role, and there are particular concerns about 'institutional ageism', but this appears to be less significant than other determinants.[224]

The Health and Social Care Act 2012, in section 4, places a duty on the Secretary of State, designed to tackle health inequalities:

> In exercising functions in relation to the health service, the Secretary of State must have regard to the need to reduce inequalities between the people of England with respect to the benefits that they can obtain from the health service.

11 The General Medical Council

Although we shall look at the General Medical Council (GMC), this is only by way of an example; there are similar bodies with similar powers over a range of medical professionals.[225] The Health and Social Care Act 2008, sections 98–110, provided for the creation of the Office of the Health Professions Adjudicator (OHPA), which was to take over the regulatory role of the GMC. However, the government has announced that it will not proceed with the new scheme involving the OHPA and that the GMC will continue its supervisory role. The OHPA will be abolished.

Section 1A of the Medical Act 1983 states the primary role of the GMC: 'The main objective of the General Council in exercising their functions is to protect, promote and maintain the safety of the public.' As we shall see, there have been claims that it is the interests of doctors rather than the public that have dominated the concerns of the GMC. The GMC has the job of keeping a register of medical practitioners.[226] In fact, the law on this is rather lax. It is not an offence to practise medicine if you are not registered; indeed, you do not even have to be qualified.[227] However, if you falsely represent yourself as being a qualified or registered doctor, then you commit an offence under the Medical Act 1983.[228] It is likely that the courts will find that someone who sets

---

[223] House of Commons Health Committee (2009: 15).
[224] House of Commons Health Committee (2009: 2).
[225] For example, the Nursing and Midwifery Council (NMC) and the General Dental Council (GDC). All such bodies are supervised by the Council for Healthcare Regulatory Excellence (CHRE).
[226] Medical Act 1983.   [227] Brazier and Cave (2007: 6).
[228] The deception may be sufficient to negate consent to any procedure and therefore render it an assault: *R v Tabassum* [2000] Lloyd's Rep Med 404.

themselves up as a doctor is impliedly representing themselves to be qualified. However, if someone is open about being unqualified (for example claims to be an alternative health practitioner), then people are free to trust their care to that person and no offence is committed.

12 Public health: infectious diseases

The main legislation controlling the behaviour of infectious diseases is surprisingly old, being the National Assistance Acts of 1948 and 1951 and the Public Health (Control of Disease) Act 1984.[229] It is notable how much of the responsibility for control of infectious diseases rests with local authorities, rather than central government, and that the emphasis is on protection of the public rather than upon individual human rights. The legislation must be construed with the Human Rights Act 1998 very much in mind, and so any public authority exercising the powers must act in a way that is compatible with an individual's human rights, if possible.

The Public Health Act 1984 gives local authorities powers to control the spread of diseases. The powers to control diseases include the following.

12.1 Notification

Under the 1984 Act, a doctor must notify the local authority of anyone whom she or he suspects of having a notifiable disease.[230] If the doctor does not notify 'forthwith', then, in theory, a criminal prosecution could follow. The local authority is required to notify the health authority within forty-eight hours. For some diseases (such as rabies), the government's Chief Medical Officer must be notified immediately.

12.2 Detention and treatment powers

There is a power under section 47 of the National Assistance Act 1948 for the court to remove to a place of safety a person who is no longer able to care for himself or herself. Section 45G of the Public Health (Control of Disease) Act 1984[231] gives extensive powers to detain and treat patients who are infectious or contaminated and pose a risk to others:

(1) A justice of the peace may make an order under subsection (2) in relation to a person ('P') if the justice is satisfied that—

(a) P is or may be infected or contaminated,

(b) the infection or contamination is one which presents or could present significant harm to human health,

(c) there is a risk that P might infect or contaminate others, and

(d) it is necessary to make the order in order to remove or reduce that risk.

---

[229] See DoH (2007a) for proposals for reform of the law.
[230] Health Protection (Notification) Regulations 2010, SI 2010/659.
[231] As amended by the Health and Social Care Act 2008.

(2) The order may impose on or in relation to P one or more of the following restrictions or requirements—

   (a) that P submit to medical examination;

   (b) that P be removed to a hospital or other suitable establishment;

   (c) that P be detained in a hospital or other suitable establishment;

   (d) that P be kept in isolation or quarantine;

   (e) that P be disinfected or decontaminated;

   (f) that P wear protective clothing;

   (g) that P provide information or answer questions about P's health or other circumstances;

   (h) that P's health be monitored and the results reported;

   (i) that P attend training or advice sessions on how to reduce the risk of infecting or contaminating others;

   (j) that P be subject to restrictions on where P goes or with whom P has contact;

   (k) that P abstain from working or trading.

These are extensive powers and it is possible that some of these provisions may fail to protect the rights adequately under Article 5 ECHR.[232]

12.3 Vaccination

Immunization programmes are now a widely accepted part of the medical treatment of children.[233] Such programmes have been a highly effective response to smallpox and other illnesses. However, in the UK, concerns over the measles, mumps, and rubella (MMR) vaccine in particular have seen a drop in the number of children being vaccinated. As that controversy has highlighted, vaccinations are not compulsory and parents are free to decide not to have their children vaccinated. In *Re B (A Child) (Immunisation)*,[234] the children's parents (who had separated) could not decide whether or not to have their children vaccinated and the issue was brought to court. The Court of Appeal decided that the question was simply one of what was in the child's welfare. Having heard expert evidence, the Court concluded that it would be in the child's interests to be vaccinated.

12.4 Compulsory care

There are very few circumstances in which people are forced to receive treatment against their wishes. There is a special regime for those with mental health problems, which will be discussed in Chapter 10. Here, we will focus on the compulsory treatment of people for public health concerns. The following appear to be the only circumstances in which a person can be forced to receive treatment in order to protect the public health.

---

[232] *Enhorn v Sweden* (2005) 41 EHRR 633, discussed in Martin (2006).   [233] Case (2017).
[234] [2003] 3 FCR 156.

(i) *Infectious diseases* The Public Health (Control of Disease) Act 1984, section 45C, permits the Secretary of State to make regulations 'for the purpose of preventing, protecting against, controlling or providing a public health response to the incidence or spread of infection or contamination in England and Wales'.

(ii) *Cleansing of vermin* Under the Public Health Act 1936, section 85, a person may be cleansed of vermin under a court order, compulsorily, as long as the court is satisfied that it is necessary to cleanse the person.

(iii) *National Assistance Act 1948* Section 47 allows people who are suffering from 'grave chronic disease', or who are 'aged, infirm or physically incapacitated', and are living in 'insanitary conditions' to be removed if they are not able to provide proper care and attention for themselves, and are not receiving that from others. However, the section authorizes the person only to be removed to a hospital. There is no explicit power to permit compulsory treatment.

(iv) *Fluoridation* Fluoride can be added to water, especially to assist in the dental health of children. This is widely seen as the most effective way of promoting children's dental health. However, this is controversial, because it means fluoride is added to the water supply for the whole community. The complaint is that fluoridation makes it very difficult for someone who does not want to drink fluoride to avoid it. The Water Industry Act 1991, sections 87–91, permit water suppliers to add fluoride when asked to do so by a health authority. However, water suppliers are not required to do so. Since 1985, there have been no new fluoridation schemes.[235] This is in part the result of privatization. Private companies do not want the 'hassle' of fluoridation and the aggravation that they may receive from customers who object.[236] Further, any proposal to fluoridate must go through a public consultation process. Those groups opposed to fluoridation can dominate any consultation process.

The issue of the non-consensual treatment and detention of patients raises important human rights issues. Article 5(1)(c) ECHR specifically permits the lawful detention of a person to prevent the spread of infectious diseases. However, the infringement of human rights must be justified in the name of public health, necessary in a democratic society, and be proportionate.[237] If any of the powers mentioned above are to be used, it will therefore need to be shown that there are no less coercive means of preserving the public health and that the danger to the public is sufficiently serious as to justify the interference with human rights.

The spread of HIV has given the issue of controlling infectious diseases a particular contemporary resonance. In the debate, a number of issues have been raised. It is not possible here to canvass all of the issues that this important debate raises. The further reading will direct you to where to look for an in-depth discussion. One issue, however, is whether or not there should be compulsory testing among everyone or certain groups of people. To test someone against his or her wishes appears to be contrary to fundamental principles of medical law and ethics. However, compulsory testing may be seen by some to be essential if the government is to have a clear picture of the extent of HIV infection and

---

[235] DoH (1999a: para. 9.19).
[236] See *R v Northumbrian Water Ltd, ex p Newcastle and North Tyneside Health Authority* [1999] Env LR 715 for an example of a legal challenge to proposed fluoridation.
[237] *Acmanne v Belgium* (1984) 40 DR 251.

even to ensure the safe treatment of a patient. So far, the government has not permitted widespread non-consensual testing for HIV, although it has authorized the anonymous non-consensual testing of blood of those attending antenatal and sexually transmitted disease (STD) clinics. Further, some of the powers under the Public Health Act 1984 now apply to AIDS, and compulsory examination and removal to hospital are theoretically possible. Given that, with responsible behaviour, it is possible for an HIV positive person to be non-contagious, these are controversial provisions, which have been described as permitting 'drastic interventions into the liberty of those who have or are suspected to have HIV'.[238] There is no reported case in which these powers have been used.

Another issue is that developments in criminal law mean that if X, knowing that she or he is HIV positive, has sexual relations with Y, without Y consenting to sexual relations aware of X's condition, then X can be guilty of inflicting grievous bodily harm (GBH) if Y becomes infected as a result.[239] In effect, this requires a person who is aware that he or she is infectious to inform his or her sexual partners of that condition before sexual activity. To some, this is an effective means of promoting public health, and protects the sexual and bodily autonomy rights of individuals.[240] To others, this is an improper interference with the sexual freedom of those who are HIV positive and may discourage people from taking tests to discover whether they are positive.[241]

13 **Public health: prevention**

The traditional approach to medicine has been reactive: to diagnose the sick and offer them treatment. Increasingly, the importance of preventative measures has been emphasized. Hence the NHS sees itself not only as offering treatment to the ill, but also as seeking to promote good health for the general public.[242] In economic terms, this makes sense. If the government can reduce the incidence of illness or accident, there will be less call on the NHS's resources. Obesity, smoking, increasing drug and alcohol misuse, and STDs all add to the pressure on the NHS.[243] Indeed, under Article 11 of the European Social Charter, the government is required to remove the causes of ill-health, to prevent disease, and to advise individuals on how to look after their own health.

It is also interesting that the notion of public health has been developing. In 2010, the government produced a report looking not only at health, but also at general well-being.[244] It interpreted 'well-being' in a broad way to include:

> . . . a positive physical, social and mental state; it is not just the absence of pain, discomfort and incapacity. It requires that basic needs are met, that individuals have a sense of purpose, that they feel able to achieve important personal goals and participate in society. It is enhanced by conditions that include supportive personal relationships, strong and inclusive communities, good health, financial and personal security, rewarding employment, and a healthy and attractive environment.[245]

The key issue in public health is the role that the government should play in some of the major public health issues: smoking, obesity, and alcohol misuse, for example. Should

---

[238] Montgomery (2003: 35).
[239] The offence is under the Offences against the Person Act 1861, s. 20: *R v Dica* [2004] 3 All ER 593.
[240] Herring (2005). See also the discussion in Pattinson (2009).   [241] Weait (2005).
[242] NHS (2009a).   [243] Foresight (2007).   [244] NHS (2013a).   [245] DoH (2010f).

the government be actively seeking to prevent unhealthy lifestyle choices, or is that too interventionist? Rather, should the government's role be to encourage and enable people to live more healthily? There are some areas in which it appears less controversial for the government to intervene in the name of public health. Environmental issues are one. Clean air[246] and water[247] are, of course, essential to the nation's good health. But in areas such as diet, in which the government is seen as too interventionist, it is said by some that we are suffering under a 'nanny state'.

 TO PONDER

Obesity

There is widespread acceptance that obesity is a problem. Most adults in England are over-weight and one in five (around 8 million individuals) are obese. It has been estimated that, by 2050, 60 per cent of men and 50 per cent of women will be obese.[248] At a simple level, the cause is seen to be an increasingly sedentary lifestyle and poor eating patterns. However, in fact, a host of more complex factors are behind these statistics. Obesity, it has been said, causes 30,000 deaths a year and shortens life expectancy by nine years. It has been estimated that the annual cost to the NHS of obesity is half a billion pounds.[249] Of course, not everyone accepts that there is an 'epidemic' of obesity.[250] So what is the government to do?

In its White Paper on public health, *Making Healthy Choices Easier*, the government iden-tified three core principles:

- **informed choice:** government providing support through credible information to allow people to make their own decisions about choices that impact on their health;
- **personalization:** supporting people to make healthy choices, especially for deprived groups and communities; and
- **working together:** through effective partnerships across communities.[251]

This is a delicate balance between encouraging people to adopt healthier lifestyles and being seen to be bossy. Some of the tensions between these aims can be seen in the White Paper's proposals designed to combat obesity:

- a new health advice service called Health Direct to be available by phone, Internet, and digital TV;
- a personal health guide and NHS health trainer for everybody;
- working with the food and drink industry to develop voluntary codes on food and drink pro-motion to children (and if these are not satisfactory, the government will introduce legislation);
- traffic light labelling for supermarket foods indicating how healthy they are;
- giving pregnant women vouchers enabling them to buy fresh fruit and vegetables, milk, and infant formula;
- encouraging children to cycle to school; and
- monitoring the nutritional value of school meals through the school inspection regime.

Note how it seems more acceptable to be 'nannying' to children than adults.[252]

---

[246] Clean Air Act 1993; Environment Act 1995.   [247] Water Industry Act 1991.
[248] Dawson (2014).   [249] Foresight (2007).   [250] Committee of Public Accounts (2005).
[251] Social Issues Research Centre (2005).   [252] DoH (2010f: para. 5.101).

Angus Dawson[253] argues that public health raises distinct ethical issues:

> In developing such a substantive public health ethics we can look to more social values, values that are visible and emerge from the fact that as human creatures we are social beings. Such values will not only include the kinds of values that have dominated discussions in medical ethics such as respect for autonomy, beneficence, and non-maleficence, but will also include such things as solidarity, reciprocity, common goods, trust, and social justice. Many of these can be linked to the necessary conditions for a flourishing life.

14 Conclusion

In this chapter we have explored the ever-changing structure of the NHS. Successive governments have sought to find ways to improve the quality of service, at a low cost. Controversially, markets play an increasingly important part in the provision of health care. This chapter has explored the issue of rationing. The courts have been willing to intervene when they feel that procedures have not been followed properly or the guidelines are opaque or meaningless. They have been reluctant to judge the merits of a particular rationing decision on clinical grounds. The chapter has explored the ethics of rationing decisions and particularly the difficulty in finding a method of allocating limited resources in a way which respects the value of each patient.

QUESTIONS

1. Consider the following quotation.

   > To the seventy-six-year-old woman with liver failure, we must say: 'For all your children and grandchildren, we can't spend this much on you.' To the patient with one heart transplant: 'I'm sorry but we can't afford to give you more than one heart because it costs too much and because another person awaits the next heart.' To life-long smokers: 'Sorry, no lung transplants. You could have stopped smoking.'[254]

   Do you think that we need to be more blunt about rationing? If we do, do you agree with these comments?

2. Having read this chapter, do you think we need to spend more on the NHS? What do you think of the suggestion that '[h]ardly anyone thinks that we should put all our money into the health service, and none at all into pizzas, or holidays, or schools'?[255] A 2008 survey suggested that 17,157 people died a year in the UK as a result of a lack of healthcare provision.[256] How much more tax would you be willing to pay to avoid these deaths?

3. In an ICM poll carried out for NICE, people were asked to answer, on a scale of one to ten, the question: 'How important do you think the age of the patient should be when

---

[253] Dawson (2012).   [254] Pence (2002: 110).   [255] Belshaw (2005: 48).
[256] Taxpayer's Alliance (2008).

deciding what treatments can be given on the NHS?' There was no consensus. But when asked, 'If extra money became available for the NHS, how would you prioritise where the money should go? Young children? People of working age? People over the age of 65?', the responses were 45 per cent for children, 19 per cent for those of working age, and 12 per cent for people over 65.[257]

What role do you think age should take in rationing decisions?

4. Do you think that it can never be right to give someone a multiple organ donation (that is, a donation of two organs at the same time)? The argument is that these two organs could have saved the lives of two people and so should never be used to save only one.[258]

5. If you were allowed to create your own rationing system for your own health care, for what things would you want and not want to receive treatment?

6. Consider the following statement.

    It is endemic to a system in which an expanding medical establishment faced with a healthier population, is driven to medicalizing normal events like menopause, converting risks into diseases, and treating trivial complaints with fancy procedures. Doctors and 'consumers' are becoming locked within a fantasy that everyone has something wrong with them, everyone and everything can be cured.[259]

    Do you agree?

7. Chris Newdick (2014) distinguishes three models for the NHS: '(A) clinical, in which the medical profession retains authority with respect to clinical decision-making, (B) managerial, in which independent, often non-clinical managers acquire influence over the process with the ability to impose targets and objectives of their own, and (C) commercial, where the driver for change is market forces and the incentive to generate revenue by "commoditising" health care.' Which do you think describes the current NHS?

FURTHER READING

A comprehensive bibliography, including all references used throughout the book, is available online at www.oup.com/uk/herringmedical7e/.

On rationing generally, see:

Bærøe, K. and Bringedal, B. (2011) 'Just health: on the conditions for acceptable and unacceptable priority settings with respect to patients' socioeconomic status', *Journal of Medical Ethics* 37: 526.

Bognar, G. (2015) 'Fair innings', *Bioethics* 29: 251

Cookson, R. and Dolan, P. (2000) 'Principles of justice in health care rationing', *Journal of Medical Ethics* 26: 323.

---

[257] NICE (2010b).   [258] Menzel (1994).   [259] Porter (1997: 718).

Danis, M., Hurst, S., Fleck, L., Forde, R., and Slowther, A. (eds) (2014) *Fair Resource Allocation and Rationing at the Bedside* (Oxford University Press).

Denier, Y. (2008) 'Mind the gap! Three approaches to scarcity in health care', *Medicine, Health Care and Philosophy* 11: 73.

Ford, A. (2012) 'The concept of exceptionality: a legal farce?', *Medical Law Review* 20: 304.

Golan, O. (2010) 'The right to treatment for self-inflicted conditions', *Journal of Medical Ethics* 36: 683.

Heale, W. (2016) 'Individualised and personalised QALYs in exceptional treatment decisions', *Journal of Medical Ethics* 42: 665.

McLachlan, H. (2005) 'Justice and the NHS: a comment on Culyer', *Journal of Medical Ethics* 31: 379.

Newdick, C. (2005) *Who Should We Treat?* (Oxford University Press).

Smith II, G. (2008) *Distributive Justice and the New Medicine* (Elgar Press).

On the work of NICE, see:

Claxton, K. and Culyer, A. (2006) 'Wickedness or folly? The ethics of NICE's decisions', *Journal of Medical Ethics* 32: 375.

Claxton, K and Culyer, A. (2007) 'Rights, responsibilities and NICE: a rejoinder to Harris', *Journal of Medical Ethics* 33: 462.

Harris, J. (2005) 'It's not NICE to discriminate', *Journal of Medical Ethics* 31: 373.

Harris, J. (2006) 'NICE is not cost effective', *Journal of Medical Ethics* 32: 378.

Herring, J. (2017) 'Finite care and clinical care: rationing' in I. Freckelton and K. Petersen (eds), *Tensions and Traumas in Health Law* (Federation Press).

King, J. (2007) 'The justifiability of resource allocation', *Modern Law Review* 70: 197.

Rawlins, M. (2004) 'National Institute for Clinical Excellence and its value judgments', *British Medical Journal* 329: 224.

Syrett, K. (2007) *Law, Legitimacy and the Rationing of Health Care: A Contextual and Comparative Perspective* (Cambridge University Press).

Syrett, K. (2008) 'NICE and judicial review: enforcing "accountability for reasonableness" through the courts?', *Medical Law Review* 16: 127.

On public health, see:

Ahola-Launonen, J. (2015) The evolving idea of social responsibility in bioethics, *Cambridge Quarterly of Healthcare Ethics* 24: 204.

Coggon, J. (2012a) *What Makes Health Public? A Critical Evaluation of Moral, Legal, and Political Claims in Public Health* (Cambridge University Press).

Dawson, A. (2014) 'What is public health ethics?', in A. Akabayashi (ed.) *The Future of Bioethics* (Oxford University Press).

Green, J. (2009) 'Public health and health promotion', in G. Scambler (ed.) *Sociology as Applied to Medicine* (Saunders).

On rights under EU law, see:

Veitch, K. (2012) 'Juridification, medicalisation, and the impact of EU law: patient mobility and the allocation of scarce NHS resources', *Medical Law Review* 20: 362.

On the NHS structure and regulation, see:

Davies, A. (2013) 'This time, it's for real: the Health and Social Care Act 2012', *Modern Law Review* 76: 564.

DoH (2015c) *Culture change in the NHS* (DoH).

Frith, L. (2013) 'The NHS and market forces in healthcare: the need for organisational ethics', *Journal of Medical Ethics* 39: 17.

Harrington, J. (2009) 'Visions of Utopia: markets, medicine and the National Health Service', *Legal Studies* 29: 376.

Meadowcroft, J. (2008) 'Patients, politics and power: government, failure and the politicization of UK health care', *Journal of Medicine and Philosophy* 33: 427.

Montgomery, J. (1998) 'Professional regulation: a gendered phenomenon?', in S. Sheldon and P. Thomson (eds) *Feminist Perspectives on Health Care Law* (Cavendish).

Mulcahy, L. (2015) The market for precedent: shifting visions of the role of clinical negligence claims and trials, *Medical Law Review* 22: 274.

Newdick, C. (2014) 'From Hippocrates to commodities: three models of NHS governance', *Medical Law Review* 22: 162.

Quick, O. (2017) *Regulating Patient Safety: The End of Professional Dominance?* (CUP).

Stirton, L. (2014) 'Back to the future? On the pro-competitive regulation of health services', *Medical Law Review* 22: 180.

3   Medical Negligence

INTRODUCTION

Although this chapter is going to discuss medical negligence and mishaps, it should be emphasized at the outset that, for most people, their experience of medicine is positive.[1] In a survey of patients published in 2016, 63 per cent of those questioned were satisfied with the service offered by the NHS.[2] Only 22 per cent of people questioned said they were dissatisfied with the NHS. Inevitably, the cases in which things go wrong are those that grab the attention and lead to the involvement of lawyers. But even where they do go wrong, only exceptionally is this the result of maliciousness. In a report on inadequate treatment at Bristol Royal Infirmary, it was said: 'A tragedy took place. But it was a tragedy born of high hopes and ambitions, and peopled by dedicated, hard-working people. The hopes were too high; the ambitions too ambitious.'[3]

There are few things that a patient awaiting treatment fears more than that the intervention, far from improving the condition, will make it worse. Similarly, there are few things that medical professionals fear more than that something will go wrong in their dealings with their patients, leaving a patient harmed. When something goes wrong in the medical context, it seems natural in our society that legal consequences will follow. If there is a very serious lapse of standards, it is possible that criminal proceedings can be brought against a healthcare professional.[4] More often, there is the possibility of an action in tort or contract. Such legal proceedings perform a variety of functions: they ensure that the person injured as a result of negligence receives compensation for any losses; they (where successful) provide a public statement of the wrongdoing of the professional, thereby providing a way of holding professionals accountable for their actions; and they provide a deterrent against bad medical practice. The problem is that these different functions are not always compatible. There may be a case in which, although the professional behaved wrongly and deserves censure, it is not possible (or desirable) to identify a loss to the claimant and so compensation is inappropriate. There may be other cases in which it would be desirable to compensate a patient for his or her loss, but blame cannot fairly be attributed to a particular individual. There is, further, the difficulty that requiring a National Health Service (NHS) trust to pay compensation to one patient may mean that NHS resources are taken away from other patients.

Even if the wisdom of paying damages in cases of negligence is accepted, we have the issue of where to set the standard of acceptable medical practice. Set it too high

---

[1] This chapter will not consider the regulation of medicines. For an excellent coverage see Jackson (2012).

[2] The King's Fund (2017).

[3] Bristol Royal Infirmary Inquiry (2001: 2).

[4] See Alghrani, Brazier, Farrell, Griffiths, and Allen (2011), and Erin and Ost (2007), for a useful discussion of the interaction of medical law and criminal law.

and the NHS may be flooded with claims and doctors may resort to 'defensive medicine' out of fear of potential litigation.[5] Set it too low and patients will find it impossible to get compensation for their injuries.

It is difficult to find an accurate picture of the number of 'adverse' incidents involving the medical professions in England and Wales.[6] Only a tiny proportion of these actually reach the court and so reading court reports will not provide an accurate picture.

In 2016, 1,879,822 adverse incidents in the NHS were reported in England. Of these in the July–September quarter, 73.5 per cent caused no harm and 23.1 per cent a low harm; 2.9 per cent caused moderate harm, which required increased treatment, but did not cause harm; less than 1 per cent involved death or severe harm.[7]

1 The law and medical malpractice: an overview

Imagine that a medical professional has clearly harmed a patient through negligent conduct. What legal consequences may follow?

(i) *A criminal prosecution* In the event of a patient dying as a result of the negligent conduct, the most likely criminal charge would be for gross negligence manslaughter.[8] A doctor who operated on a patient without that patient's consent could also face a charge of battery. In a case of sexual misconduct, an offence under the Sexual Offences Act 2003 could be made out.[9] Remember that criminal prosecutions (unlike civil actions) do not require the consent of the victim to be brought. It is, of course, very rare for doctors to face criminal prosecutions for actions performed in their professional capacity.[10]

(ii) *A civil action* The claimant could sue for damages relying on the tort of negligence or (in the case of private medical treatment) breach of contract.

(iii) *Professional disciplinary proceedings or the NHS complaints procedure* A complaint about a medical professional could be investigated by the relevant professional body and/or by the NHS itself. These procedures may result in a variety of punishments of the professional, but will not provide compensation to the individual victim.

A SHOCK TO THE SYSTEM

In 2009, an outcry greeted reports of unacceptable care at the Mid-Staffordshire NHS Foundation Trust. In a three-year period, between 400 and 1,200 more people died than would have been expected. The Francis Report[11] which investigated the neglect concluded that 'For many patients the most basic elements of care were neglected'. It found that 'The standards of hygiene were at times awful, with families forced to remove used bandages and dressings from public areas and clean toilets themselves for fear of catching infections'. The

---

[5] See the excellent discussion on defensive medicine in Karen-Paz (2010).
[6] See Quick (2006a) for further discussion of the statistics.
[7] NHS Improvement (2017).   [8] *R v Adomako* [1995] 1 AC 171.   [9] Ost and Biggs (2013).
[10] An NHS trust could also face criminal proceedings under, e.g., health and safety legislation: *R v Southampton University Hospital NHS Trust* [2006] EWCA Crim 2971.
[11] Francis (2010 and 2013).

first inquiry heard harrowing personal stories from patients and patients' families about the appalling care received at the Trust. On many occasions, the accounts received related to basic elements of care and the quality of the patient experience. What was particularly concerning was the length of time for which the bad treatment had gone on.

The Secretary of Health said to the House of Commons:

> The report details astonishing failures at every level, and shows that for patients admitted for emergency care at Stafford, there were deficiencies at every stage. The Health Care Commission found disorganisation, delays in assessment and pain relief, poor recording of important information, symptoms and requests for help ignored, poor communication with families and patients, and severe failings in the way the trust board conducted its business. While the management was obsessed with achieving foundation trust status, the wards were understaffed and patient care seriously compromised.
>
> The report cites incidents of patients left without food or drink for days because operations were delayed, of nurses who had not been properly trained to use basic, lifesaving equipment, and of patients admitted to A and E being triaged by receptionists. It notes that there was a dangerous lack of experienced staff, observation and monitoring of patients was poor, essential equipment often was not working, and there were no systems in place to spot where things were going wrong in order to make improvements. In short, it is a catalogue of individual and systemic failings that have no place in any NHS hospital, but which were allowed to happen by a board that steadfastly refused to acknowledge the serious concerns about the poor standard of care raised by patients and staff.[12]

The government has put in place procedures that it hopes will mean there is no repeat.[13] In particular the inspection regime for hospitals has been subject to an overhaul.

2 Criminal law

A doctor can be guilty of a criminal offence against a patient in the same way as anyone else. For example, if a doctor were intentionally to cut a patient without his or her consent, this could amount to an assault. Of course, it is rare for a doctor to harm a patient deliberately in this way.

Perhaps of greater concern to most doctors is the possibility of gross negligence manslaughter. This offence is discussed in Chapter 9.[14] Notably, a medical professional can be convicted of gross negligence manslaughter without proof that he or she intended or foresaw the harm.[15] But it needs to be shown not only that the professional was negligent, but also that he or she was so badly negligent that a criminal conviction is appropriate. It is rare for there to be a manslaughter case involving medical professionals, although such prosecutions do appear to be very slightly on the increase.[16] Since the Corporate Manslaughter and Corporate Homicide Act 2007, an NHS trust could be convicted of manslaughter if the way in which the trust was run were negligently to cause a death.

The use of the criminal law in the medical context has been questioned. Oliver Quick has argued that carelessness is an insufficient basis for criminal liability: only if a doctor

---

[12] Francis (2010 and 2013); Johnson (2009: 1).   [13] DoH (2015c).
[14] See under the heading '2.2 Manslaughter'.   [15] Quick (2010 and 2017).   [16] Quick (2006b).

has actually foreseen harm should he or she face criminal liability.[17] Yet the vast majority of criminal offences deal with carelessness and error. Should those who hurt others while carelessly driving their cars be treated differently from those who carelessly hurt others while wielding their scalpels? Perhaps there is a difference if we believe that medical professionals (unlike car drivers) are performing a valuable social activity and deserve especial shielding from the criminal law. On the other hand, some may feel that doctors have a special position in society and are highly rewarded, and that we are entitled to expect of them the highest of standards.

Section 20 of the Criminal Justice and Courts Act 2015 has created a new offence of ill-treatment or wilful neglect. It is a crime for 'an individual who has the care of another individual by virtue of being a care worker to ill-treat or wilfully to neglect that individual'. The offence covers all care workers, defined as:

an individual who, as paid work, provides—

(a)   health care for an adult or child, other than excluded health care, or

(b)   social care for an adult, including an individual who, as paid work, supervises or manages individuals providing such care or is a director or similar officer of an organisation which provides such care.

The offence covers doctors, nurses, and healthcare assistants. However, it would not cover unpaid carers, such as someone looking after a relative at home. The ill treatment or neglect must be done wilfully. That indicates that a nurse who overlooks the care of a patient because she is too busy looking after another patient or is unaware a patient is in need of help will not be guilty of this offence.

3 The law of negligence

The majority of litigation following medical malpractice is brought under the tort of negligence. In order to succeed, the claimant will need to prove three things:

(i)   that the professional who is being sued owed the claimant a duty of care;

(ii)   that the professional breached the duty of care; and

(iii) that the breach of the duty of care caused the claimant loss.

We will need to look at each of these requirements separately.

3.1 The duty of care

The duty of care is normally easily established. The basic approach in the law of tort is that you owe a duty of care to anyone whom you may reasonably foreseeably injure. There is little difficulty in finding that all staff in a hospital owe a duty of care to patients in the hospital. More difficult is whether a doctor owes a duty of care to a person who falls ill in a public place in the presence of the doctor, or whether a duty of care is owed by a medical professional to the relatives of a patient. Such cases would be dealt with using the general principles of negligence, which would focus on the following questions.

---

[17] Quick (2010). See also Brazier and Allen (2007).

(i) *Was it reasonably foreseeable that the defendant's actions would cause the victim harm?* If not, then there is no duty of care. So a doctor who prescribes medicine to a patient would not be found to owe a duty of care to the patient's grand-niece who subsequently found the medicine bottle and ate the tablets. Harm to the grand-niece would not be a reasonably foreseeable consequence of the doctor's actions.

(ii) *Is there a sufficiently close relationship between the defendant and the patient?* This is a rather vague concept, but the discussion of four scenarios may clarify the concept. First, in *Goodwill v British Pregnancy Advisory Service*,[18] it was held that a doctor did not owe a duty of care, in giving contraceptive advice to a patient, towards people with whom the patient may in the future engage in sexual relations. The doctor in such a case may, however, owe a duty of care to the patient's spouse. The difference is that doctors giving contraceptive advice to patients who they know are married will clearly have the spouse in their contemplation when giving the advice.[19] But doctors will have no awareness at all of potential future sexual partners of a single patient.

Second, in *West Bromwich Albion v El-Safty*,[20] it was held that a surgeon treating a football player did not owe a duty of care to his club, so as to be liable for financial losses suffered by the club when the player was treated negligently. The Court of Appeal emphasized that at no point had the surgeon assumed responsibility for the financial well-being of the club. It might have been different if the club had employed the surgeon, warning him of the financial consequences if the treatment was ineffective.

Third, in *Farraj v King's Healthcare NHS Trust*,[21] it was held that a private laboratory that conducted some tests on a patient's material on behalf of an NHS hospital owed the patient a duty of care. The laboratory had not communicated with the patient, but knew that the results passed on to the hospital would be used to make decisions about treatment.

Fourth, if a medical professional walks past a road traffic accident and fails to offer assistance, this will not amount to breach of a duty of care,[22] although it might infringe professional good practice.[23]

(iii) *Is there a public policy reason which argues against a duty of care being found?* It is well established in tort law that a duty of care exists only where it is 'just and reasonable' to impose one. If a hospital were to release an outpatient who had a history of violence and who then harmed a member of the public, it is unlikely that the court would find a duty of care owed by the hospital to the general public.[24] It would not be just and reasonable to require every NHS trust to detain any outpatient who could pose a risk to others. Although most cases have involved a claim that a particular medical professional was negligent, it may be possible to claim that the NHS trust or the primary care trust (PCT) was negligent. This might be appropriate where the negligence lies in the way in which the hospital was managed or staffing issues were addressed, rather than the conduct of a particular person. This was acknowledged in *A (A Child) v Ministry of Defence*,[25] in which it was recognized that an NHS trust owed a duty of care to provide a safe and satisfactory medical service to a patient.[26]

---

[18] [1996] 2 All ER 161.
[19] Although see *Less v Hussain* [2012] EWHC 3513 (QB), in which, in terms of the contract law claim, it was held that only the woman could sue because the contract was advice on conception sought for her benefit.
[20] [2006] EWCA Civ 1299.   [21] [2009] EWCA 1203.
[22] *F v West Berkshire Health Authority* [1989] 2 All ER 545, 567.   [23] GMC (2007: para. 11).
[24] *Palmer v Tees Health Authority* [1999] Lloyd's Rep Med 351.
[25] [2004] EWCA 641. See also *Garcia v St Mary's NHS Trust* [2006] EWHC 2314 (QB).   [26] Beswick (2007).

3.2 **The breach of the duty**

Having established that the defendant owed the victim a duty of care, the next question is whether the professional breached that duty. Normally, in the law of negligence, the question is whether it is shown on the balance of probabilities that the defendant acted as a reasonable person would. In the medical context, it is more complicated. In some situations the law uses what has become known as '*Bolam*' negligence and in others the normal negligence standard. In short 'clinical decisions' (what treatment to give and how to treat the patient) use the *Bolam* test, non-clinical decisions (what information to give a patient about treatment and other advice to patients) will use the standard negligence test. We will start by explaining the '*Bolam*' test.

3.2.1 *The* Bolam *test in outline*

In *Bolam v Friern Hospital Management Committee*,[27] it was held that '[a] doctor is not guilty of negligence if he has acted in accordance with a practice accepted as proper by a responsible body of medical men skilled in that particular art'. The test applies not only to doctors, but also to any healthcare professional. Although controversial, the test has been approved by the House of Lords in several cases—*Maynard v West Midlands Regional Health Authority*;[28] *Whitehouse v Jordan*;[29] *Sidaway v Bethlem Royal Hospital Governors*;[30] *Bolitho v City & Hackney Health Authority*[31]—so there is no doubt that it represents the present law.

The effect of the *Bolam* decision is that it is difficult to show a doctor breached the duty of care. It will not be enough to introduce evidence from an expert witness that he or she would not have carried out the procedure in the way that the defendant did.[32] It would be necessary to show that there is no responsible body of medical opinion that would have approved of acting in that way. All that the defendant need do to win the case would be to find an acknowledged expert to agree that the way in which the defendant dealt with the patient was within the range of acceptable practice.[33] It should be emphasized that the question is not whether the defendant was acting in the ideal way, but that his or her actions were above the minimal acceptable practice. The logic behind the *Bolam* test was explained by the House of Lords in *Maynard v West Midlands Regional Health Authority*.[34] In that case, the House of Lords held that a judge is not in a position to choose between the views of competing medical expert opinions. So as long as there is a competent school of thought that supports the belief that the defendant's actions were reasonable, the judge will find the defendant not to have been negligent.

3.2.2 *When does* Bolam *apply?*

The *Bolam* test applies to clinical decisions. Those are decisions which involve medical skill: for example, diagnosis of a condition; consideration of about what treatments are appropriate for a particular condition; and how those treatments should be provided. *Bolam* does not apply to the following:

---

[27] [1957] 2 All ER 118, 121. See Miola (2015b) for a helpful retrospective.   [28] [1985] 1 All ER 635.
[29] [1981] 1 All ER 267.   [30] [1985] 1 All ER 643.   [31] [1997] 4 All ER 771.
[32] *Newman v Maurice* [2010] EWHC 171 (QB).
[33] *Bellarby v Worthing & Southlands Hospitals NHS Trust* [2005] EWHC 2089.   [34] [1985] 1 All ER 635.

(i)   Informing a patient of what reasonable treatment options are available.

(ii)   Informing a patient of risks associated with treatment.

(iii) Some basic diagnosis decisions.

(iv)   Non-medical advice.

The first two categories are about what information a patient should be given. These have been seen as not issues of 'medical expertise', but rather legal matters about what information a patient needs to make an effective decision about treatment. We shall discuss those further later.

The third and fourth are less straightforward. In relation to diagnosis in *Muller v Kings College Hospital*,[35] Kerr J held it was important to distinguish between two categories of case:

> The first type is . . ., where the patient's condition is unknown, and what is alleged to be negligent is a doctor's diagnosis of the condition, in the form of a report, with no decision made or advice given about treatment or further diagnostic procedures. The diagnosis is either right or wrong and, if wrong, either negligently so or not. Such a case could be called a 'pure diagnosis' case.
>
> At the other end of the spectrum is the second type of case: a 'pure treatment' case, where the nature of the patient's condition is known, and the alleged negligence consists in a decision to treat (or advise treatment of) a condition in a particular manner.

The *Bolam* test applied to the second 'pure treatment' case but not to the 'pure diagnosis'. In the case before the court the claimant had a wound on his foot and a biopsy was taken. A histopathologist examined the biopsy and diagnosed a non-malignant ulcer. In fact it turned out to be a malignant melanoma. Kerr J held in such a 'pure diagnosis' case the question was not whether some doctors would have made the same mis-diagnosis, but whether 'the error was one which would be made by a professional exercising reasonable skill and care'.[36] In other words, the normal negligence test. In this case the pure diagnosis was not performed with reasonable care and skill and so was negligent. However, ultimately the claim failed as it was not shown that had the proper diagnosis been made effective treatment could have been provided. Kerr J justified the distinction between the two kinds of cases on the basis that in treatment cases 'opposed expert opinions may in a sense both be "right", in that each represents a respectable body of professional opinion'. However, that was not so in a diagnosis case where the diagnosis is either correct or not.

We will need further case law to confirm whether this approach is to be taken. In *Muller* Kerr J muddied the waters somewhat by saying that as a matter of precedent he could justify his conclusion in terms of the *Bolam* test, as interpreted in *Bolitho* (see 3.2.4): that a misdiagnosis that is made below the standard expected of a doctor using reasonable care and skill would inevitably be 'untenable in logic or otherwise flawed in some manner rendering its conclusion indefensible and impermissible'.

The fourth category of cases where the *Bolam* test would not apply would be any issue or advice outside medical expertise. Obviously if a patient slipped on a step in a doctor's office the normal rules of negligence would apply. Less obviously, advice by a receptionist at an accident and emergency department as to how long a patient may have to wait was held not to be clinical advice and so the *Bolam* test did not apply.[37]

---

[35] [2017] EWHC 128 (QB).   [36] Para. 74.
[37] *Darnley v Croydon NHS Trust* [2015] EWHC 2301 (QB).

Having grasped the basic idea of the *Bolam* test, we need to make a few more detailed points about its operation.

3.2.3 *Current state of knowledge*

A doctor is to be judged on the state of knowledge at the time of the incident. So if, by the time of the hearing, it was generally accepted that treatment of the type given by the defendant was improper, but at the time when he or she acted there was a respectable body of opinion that the treatment was acceptable, the defendant will not be negligent.[38] Further, a doctor will not be expected to have read and digested research that has only just become available. So a doctor was not negligent because she failed to read an article in a medical journal published six months earlier,[39] or did not use a piece of equipment that was not widely available.[40] It is arguable that the existence of the Internet, making research more readily available, will mean that doctors will be expected to be more up to date than they were in the past.

The courts must also be wary of acting with hindsight. In *Ministry of Justice v Carter*,[41] a case in which a doctor had failed to diagnose a cancerous tumour, the Court of Appeal warned against relying on the knowledge that we now had that the tumour was cancerous to assume the doctor was negligent in failing to spot it. The doctor's decision had to be assessed based on the evidence that was before him.

3.2.4 *Respected body of opinion*

To have a defence, all that a defendant need show is that his or her conduct would be thought acceptable by a respected body of opinion. It does not need to be a substantial body of opinion.[42] Therefore if a respectable medical expert gives evidence that what the defendant doctor did was an appropriate way of dealing with the case, it is unlikely that the claimant will succeed. In *Maynard v West Midlands Regional Health Authority*,[43] the House of Lords criticized a judge at first instance who had heard two competing experts on what course of action was appropriate and had attempted to decide whose evidence was preferable. It was emphasized that it was not for the judge to weigh up competing bodies of professional opinion. Under the *Bolam* test, once it is found that the defendant's course of action was approved of by a responsible body of medical opinion, this is enough to show that there was no negligence. The point was dramatically demonstrated in *Defreitas v O'Brien*,[44] in which the evidence was that just four or five specialist neuroscientists would endorse the defendant's way of dealing with the case. Still that was sufficient to amount to a body of responsible opinion and so there was no negligence.

The law's approach, however, is less clear-cut after the House of Lords' decision in *Bolitho v City & Hackney Health Authority*,[45] and in particular the following dictum of Lord Browne-Wilkinson:

[T]he court has to be satisfied that the exponents of the body of opinion relied on can demonstrate that such opinion has a logical basis. In particular, in cases involving, as

[38] *Roe v Minister of Health* [1954] 2 All ER 131.
[39] *Crawford v Board of Governors of Charing Cross Hospital*, The Times, 8 December 1953.
[40] *Whiteford v Hunter* (1950) 94 SJ 758.   [41] [2010] EWCA Civ 694.
[42] *Defreitas v O'Brien* [1995] 6 Med LR 108, CA.   [43] [1984] 1 WLR 634.
[44] [1993] 4 Med LR 281.   [45] [1998] AC 232.

they so often do, the weighing up of risks against benefits, the judge before accepting a body of opinion as being reasonable, responsible or respectable will need to be satisfied that, in forming their views, the experts have directed their minds to the questions of comparative risks and benefits and have reached a defensible conclusion on the matter.[46]

This led one leading academic critic of the *Bolam* test to exclaim: 'Eureka!'[47] What excited this response is that Lord Browne-Wilkinson's dictum suggests that simply because a medical expert declares that what the defendant did was acceptable, it does not mean that the judge must accept that the defendant was not negligent. Judges must satisfy themselves that the evidence had a 'logical basis'. To some, this has marked a radical change in the courts' approach. Now, judges will seriously examine a claim that the defendant acted in accordance with a responsible body of medical opinion and will not simply accept the say-so of a fellow doctor. Indeed, it might be said that the phrase 'defensible' position requires the judge to give careful scrutiny to the evidence supporting the competing views on the legitimacy of the defendant's conduct.[48]

However, other commentators do not believe that Lord Browne-Wilkinson's dictum had a dramatic impact on the law, because any judicial scrutiny of medical expert opinion will be minimal. It would be a bizarre case if a medical specialist held an illogical view and had not considered the benefits and disadvantages of his or her approach. Indeed, Lord Browne-Wilkinson accepted that 'in the vast majority of cases the fact that distinguished experts in the field are of a particular opinion will demonstrate the reasonableness of that opinion'.[49] So it is argued that even if the judge is to take a slightly harder look at claims of the defendant's expert witnesses, it is highly unlikely that the judge will declare them illogical or 'unrespectable'.

So what of the cases following *Bolitho*: how have they interpreted Lord Browne-Wilkinson's comments?[50] One notable point is that many of the cases after *Bolitho* do not cite the case and simply refer to the *Bolam* test. This in itself indicates that the courts might not regard *Bolitho* as having made a change of any great significance. But of those cases that do cite *Bolitho*, it is possible to find some that suggest it has had a significant impact on the degree of scrutiny with which judges will examine the views of the experts. Contrast the following cases.

- In *Marriott v West Midlands Health Authority*,[51] a GP called on the claimant, who had suffered a fall. The GP prescribed painkillers. He did not suggest a full neurological examination. Expert evidence was given that, because the risk that the patient had a blood clot on the brain following the fall was so small, it was not negligent not to seek further tests. However, the trial judge (supported by the Court of Appeal), in considering this evidence, held that although the risk of a clot was small, the consequences for the patient if there were a clot would be so serious that the only reasonable course of action was to require tests. In other words, although there was evidence that some experts regarded it as unnecessary to carry out the tests, such an approach was held to be irresponsible by the courts. This indicates that *Bolitho* does authorize a judge to consider carefully the views of medical experts and, where appropriate, deem them irresponsible.[52]

---

[46] At 242.   [47] Grubb (1998a: 38).
[48] See the discussion in Lord Woolf (2001) and Lord Irvine (1999).   [49] [1998] AC 232, 239.
[50] A useful analysis of the post-*Bolitho* case law can be found in Mulheron (2010).
[51] [1999] Ll Med Rep 23.
[52] *Townsend v Worcester District Health Authority* (1995) 23 BMLR 31; *Bouchta v Swindon* [1996] Med LR 62.

- In *Wisniewski v Central Manchester Health Authority*,[53] it was claimed that there was medical negligence in the management of the claimant mother's pregnancy. In particular, it was argued that there should have been further investigations of abnormalities in the foetal heartbeat. Further investigations would have resulted in an earlier Caesarean section intervention, which would have avoided the injuries that the claimant suffered. There was conflicting evidence as to whether there was a responsible body of skilled medical opinion that would not have sought further investigations. The trial judge held that there is no such body of opinion. One argument on appeal was that the judge had wrongly substituted his own assessment of what was the appropriate course of action, rather than correctly applied the *Bolam* test. That argument succeeded. It was held that the judge had heard eminent and impressive experts stating that there was a responsible body of opinion that would not have undertaken further investigations. Only rarely could a judge declare that the views of experts could not be supported logically.[54] Brook LJ stated: 'It is quite impossible for a court to hold that the views sincerely held by doctors of such eminence cannot logically be supported at all.'[55]

- In *Burne v A*,[56] a mother telephoned a doctor, concerned about her child. The alleged negligence was that the GP had failed to ask the mother about symptoms, which would have revealed a blockage in a shunt that had been inserted into his head to help to drain fluid from the brain (something that the GP knew about). Instead, the doctor simply listened to the symptoms the mother listed. The experts before the trial judge said that the doctor did not act improperly in simply taking into account what he had been told by the mother and was not required to ask about specific symptoms. The judge hearing the case found that, despite what the experts said about accepted practice, there was no reason or logic behind not asking specific questions that might reveal symptoms when it was known that the child had a shunt, which if it was blocked would produce serious medical problems.[57] On appeal, Sedley LJ thought that it understandable that the judge had considered it unacceptable that the medical profession thought it unnecessary to ask specific questions of this kind. However, he ordered a retrial because the judge had not given the experts an adequate opportunity to explain and defend common practice. Ward LJ added that a judge was not free to ignore the views of experts on what was acceptable practice and to rely on 'common sense' without giving the experts the chance to explain themselves. This case is notable for its acceptance that a judge could reject the views of the experts on what is a responsible course of conduct, but stating that, before doing so, the experts must be given the chance of justifying the practice.

- In *Ecclestone v Medway NHS Foundation Trust*,[58] a doctor followed a procedure as recommended in a current edition of a textbook. Although accepting that the procedures might not have been the best available, Reddihough HHJ stated:

---

[53] [1998] Lloyd's Rep Med 223.

[54] See also *Briody v St Helen's & Knowsley Area Health Authority* [1999] Lloyd's Rep Med 185.

[55] *Wisniewski v Central Manchester Health Authority* [1998] Lloyd's Rep Med 223, 237. See *Zarb v Odetoyinbo* [2006] EWHC 2880 (QB), in which reference was made to the qualifications and writings of an expert in concluding that his view could not be said to be irresponsible.

[56] [2006] EWCA Civ 24.

[57] In this particular case, the mother had not specifically mentioned that the child was irritable and drowsy, which would have indicated a shunt problem.   [58] [2013] EWHC 790.

It would be a very bold and inappropriate step for a court to take to find in effect that the authors of two leading world textbooks on orthopaedic surgery had described a surgical technique which could not be logically supported.[59]

- In *Border v Lewisham and Greenwich NHS Trust*[60] a doctor inserted an IV into a woman's left arm, despite her clear refusal to consent. She had mental capacity to refuse and so although other doctors gave evidence that they believed the doctor had acted appropriately the Court of Appeal, citing *Bolitho*, found that treating a competent patient against their wishes would inevitably be negligent.

At present, therefore, there is conflicting case law on the correct reading of *Bolitho*. Silber J has suggested that it would 'very seldom be right' for a judge to regard a competent medical expert's views as unreasonable.[61] Cranston J has said that it would be rare.[62] The Court of Appeal, in applying *Bolitho* to a case involving vets, said that to call an expert's view unreasonable or illogical was 'extreme'.[63] If a judge does decide to reject an expert's view on a responsible body of medical opinion, a careful explanation is required.[64] Where the expert is found logical, judges tend to see no need to justify that conclusion.[65] In *Smith v Southampton University Hospital NHS Trust*,[66] the Court of Appeal said that if there is a conflict between experts on whether the conduct of the defendant was in accordance with a respectable body of opinion, the judge must explain which expert is preferred and why. It is not enough only to say that the expert arguing that the defendant was not negligent was a responsible expert.[67] It has been suggested that courts will be more willing to find an expert's view not to represent a responsible school of thought where the medical issue is not complex or technical, but is an issue that an ordinary person can consider.[68] Cranston J has, however, suggested a more conservative approach. He has argued that 'it would be folly for a judge with no training in medicine to conclude that one body of medical opinion should be preferred over another, when both are professionally sanctioned and both withstand logical attack'.[69] Green J in *Mulholland v Medway NHS Foundation Trust*[70] suggested the following could be considered in determining whether an expert's opinion is logical:

A Judge should not simply accept an expert opinion; it should be tested both against the other evidence tendered during the course of a trial, and, against its internal consistency. For example, a judge will consider whether the expert opinion accords with the inferences properly to be drawn from the Clinical Notes or the CTG. A judge will ask whether the expert has addressed all the relevant considerations which applied at the time of the alleged negligent act or omission. If there are manufacturer's or clinical guidelines, a court will consider whether the expert has addressed these and placed the Defendant's conduct in their context.

---

[59] At [24].   [60] [2015] EWCA Civ 8.

[61] *M (A Child by his Mother) v Blackpool Victoria Hospital NHS Trust* [2003] EWHC 1744.

[62] *Birch v University College London Hospital* [2008] EWHC 2237 (QB), [54].

[63] *Calver v Westwood Veterinary Group* (2001) 58 BMLR 194, [34]. See also *Cowley v Cheshire and Merseyside Strategic Health Authority* [2007] EWHC 48 (QB), in which Forbes J held that it would be rare for an expert's views not to be found to represent a responsible body of opinion.

[64] *Elaine Ruth Glicksman v Redbridge NHS Trust* [2001] EWCA Civ 1097.

[65] *Norman v Peterborough and Stamford Hospital* [2008] EWHC 3266 (QB).   [66] [2007] EWCA Civ 387.

[67] *Hanson v Airedale Hospital NHS Trust* [2003] CLY 2989 (QB).

[68] *French v Thames Valley Strategic Health Authority* [2005] EWHC 459, [112].

[69] *Birch v University College London Hospital* [2008] EWHC 2237 (QB), [55].   [70] [2015] EWHC 268 (QB).

In a very helpful analysis of the case law since *Bolitho*, Rachael Mulheron summarizes her analysis of the case law in this way:

> In short, the court must consider whether the doctor's expert testimony:
>
> - took account of a clear and simple precaution which was not followed but which, more probably than not, would have avoided the adverse outcome;
>
> - considered conflicts of duties among patients, and resource limitations governing the medical practice;
>
> - weighed the comparative risks/benefits of the medical practice, as opposed to other course(s) of conduct;
>
> - took account of public/community expectations of acceptable medical practice;
>
> - was correct in light of the factual context as a whole;
>
> - was internally consistent;
>
> - adhered to the correct legal test governing the requisite standard of care.
>
> If the answers to any of these is 'no', then a 'red flag' should arise, because it then constitutes a ground upon which English courts, over the past decade, have been prepared to reject peer medical opinion as being indefensible.[71]

3.2.5 *Standard of skill and specialism*

The standard of care that a professional is expected to exercise is that of those in the speciality or profession involved. A GP is to be assessed by the skills expected of a GP, not a specialist consultant.[72] Similarly, a practitioner in traditional Chinese herbal medicine was not expected to meet the standard of a practitioner in orthodox medicine.[73] So a GP or an alternative medicine specialist would not be negligent in failing to diagnose a condition that would be apparent only to a specialist in the field. However, a GP in such a case may be found negligent in not referring a patient with unusual symptoms for a consultation, or at least a follow-up appointment.[74] This would be especially likely to be so if the patient were vulnerable (for example a premature baby).[75] Further, it would be negligent for a GP to attempt a medical procedure that should be attempted only by a specialist in a particular field.[76]

This also means that if a person is acting in a particular capacity, then he or she must exercise the skill expected of such a person. The fact that he or she is inexperienced,[77] or a student,[78] or aged is irrelevant. In *FB v Princess Alexandra Hospital NHS Trust*[79] it was held that there was no difference in the standard expected of a consultant or a junior doctor in taking a case history of a patient, because the task was relatively straightforward and one could expect any medical professional to do such a task to the same standard.

---

[71] Mulheron (2010: 602–3).   [72] *Stockdale v Nicholls* [1993] 4 Med LR 190.

[73] *Shakoor v Situ (t/a Eternal Health Co)* [2000] 4 All ER 181.

[74] *Judge v Huntingdon Health Authority* [1995] 6 Med LR 223.

[75] *Fallon v Wilson* [2010] EWHC 2978 (QB).   [76] *Defreitas v O'Brien* [1993] 4 Med LR 281.

[77] *Jones v Manchester Corporation* [1952] 2 All ER 125.

[78] This is assumed to be the law because it is in line with the general approach in the law on tort: see *Nettleship v Weston* [1971] 3 All ER 581 on learner drivers.   [79] [2017] EWCA Civ 334.

However, an inexperienced member of staff might not be negligent if he or she is following the advice of a more experienced colleague. In *Wilsher v Essex Area Health Authority*,[80] a house officer inserted a catheter into a vein, rather than an artery. He asked his senior registrar to check what he had done and the registrar approved it. The registrar was found to be negligent, but the house officer was not. It should not be thought, however, that it is automatically a defence for a healthcare professional to say that he or she was 'only following orders' from a more senior practitioner. First, the court may find that there was a duty on the junior professional to check that he or she has correctly understood the instructions. This might be particularly so where the instruction appears unusual. Second, there may come a point at which the instruction is so blatantly wrong that the healthcare professional should not follow it.[81] So a pharmacist who failed to seek confirmation of a prescription that was patently wrong was found to be negligent.[82] It is also interesting to note that, in *Antoniades v East Sussex Hospitals NHS Trust*,[83] the court found that the way in which a team of doctors worked together had produced a negligent level of care. The team leader was found to have been negligent in having inadequately trained his team in how to deal with the kind of case with which they had to deal.

It seems that the law will not be willing to raise the standard expected beyond that of a standard practitioner in the professional's position. In *Meiklejohn v St George's NHS Trust*[84] the claimant argued that the defendant, a highly eminent specialist, should be assessed by the standard of a leader in the field of international renown. That was rejected and it was held that they only had to comply with the standard of a consultant in their specialty.

3.2.6 Emergencies

The court will take into account the situation in which professionals find themselves. So in *Mulholland v Medway NHS Foundation Trust*[85] a doctor in a pressurized accident and emergency department was faced with an urgent case and the court accepted that he could not necessarily be able to demonstrate the same level of skill as if faced with a case with plenty of time in which to decide what to do and time to consult with colleagues.

A doctor's liability will depend on the information provided by a patient. So if a patient does not give a doctor the necessary information, it is unlikely that a negligence action will lie. Thus, if a doctor is not told about a crucial symptom, then the patient will have an uphill task establishing a negligence action. However, a doctor in an emergency room who failed to diagnose the broken ribs of a drunken man who had been involved in an accident involving a car was found to be negligent. Although the man had not mentioned any pain, his drunkenness would have dulled any pain and the doctor should have appreciated that.[86] It may similarly be that, if there is an embarrassing symptom that could be relevant, a medical professional should specifically ask about it rather than assume that a patient will mention it.

[80] [1986] 3 All ER 801.
[81] Montgomery (2003: 179), although there seems little case law to support this.
[82] *Horton v Evans* [2006] EWHC 2808 (QB); *Dwyer v Roderick* (1983) 127 SJ 806.
[83] [2007] EWHC 517 (QB).   [84] [2014] EWCA Civ 120.   [85] [2015] EWHC 268 (QB).
[86] *Wood v Thurston*, The Times, 25 May 1951.

3.2.7 Resources

It is unclear the extent to which lack of resources will be a defence to a claim of negligence.[87] In *Garcia v St Mary's NHS Trust*,[88] it was claimed that the Trust had been negligent in setting staffing levels and arranging work practices. Its failures in those areas, it was alleged, had caused the patient to receive an inadequate level of care. This claim failed. In deciding that the level of provision was not negligent under the *Bolam* standard, the point was made that budget restrictions inevitably affected staffing levels and work practices. The issue of the rationing of medical resources is considered further in Chapter 2.

3.2.8 Protocols and policies

If a hospital has an official protocol or policy from which a healthcare professional has departed, this will assist in demonstrating that the professional has been negligent. The courts appear to have taken the approach that, in such a case, unless the professional can provide good reasons for departing from the standard practice, then he or she will be found negligent.[89] On the other hand, it should not be thought that following an official protocol or policy will necessarily provide a full defence. This is particularly the case where to do so would clearly harm the patient.[90] Further, a failure to follow National Institute for Health and Care Excellence (NICE) guidelines, especially where the deviation is significant, may be taken as good evidence of a breach of a duty of care.[91] Similarly, failure to follow guidelines issued by professional bodies may also be taken as evidence that there was a breach of a *Bolam* duty.[92]

3.2.9 Res ipsa loquitur

The doctrine of *res ipsa loquitur* ('the thing speaks for itself') may be relied upon in some cases. Essentially, this doctrine is used where, although the claimant cannot directly prove medical negligence, he or she claims that it is obvious from the fact of the injury and its circumstances that there was negligence. Lord Denning, in *Cassidy v Ministry of Health*,[93] considered a case in which a patient went in for an operation with two stiff fingers and came out with four stiff fingers. Although the plaintiff could not prove that there had been negligence, Lord Denning thought that the plaintiff was entitled to say to the defendant 'explain my injuries, if you can'. In effect, then, this was because the circumstances clearly indicated that something went wrong (even though it was not clear exactly what). Where it is unclear whether an injury was caused by an act of negligence rather than a non-negligent cause, the doctrine cannot help.[94] Hobhouse LJ has stated that:

> [T]he expression *res ipsa loquitur* should be dropped from the litigator's vocabulary and replaced by the phrase 'a prima facie case'. *Res ipsa loquitur* is not a principle of law: it does not relate to or raise any presumption. It is merely a guide to help to identify when a

[87] Witting (2001).   [88] [2006] EWHC 2314 (QB).
[89] *DF Health Care v St George's Healthcare NHS Trust* [2005] EWHC 1327.
[90] *Barnet v Chelsea and Kensington Hospital Management Committee* [1968] 1 All ER 1068.
[91] *West Bromwich Albion v El-Safty* [2006] EWCA 1299.
[92] Samanta, Mello, Foster, et al. (2006); Marsh and Reynard (2009).   [93] [1954] 2 KB 343.
[94] *Howard v Wessex Regional Health Authority* [1994] 5 Med LR 57 (QB).

prima facie case is being made out. Where expert and factual evidence has been called on both sides at a trial its usefulness will normally have long since been exhausted.[95]

In *Lillywhite v University College London Hospitals' NHS Trust*,[96] Latham LJ held that the doctrine of *res ipsa loquitur* would only rarely be useful where a court had heard full evidence from all sides.[97]

3.3 The standard of care in non-*Bolam* cases

Where the *Bolam* test does not apply the general test applies: did the defendant act as a reasonable person in their position? It will not be a defence to show that there was a body of medical opinion who would have acted in the same way as the defendant, if the court determines this was below the standard expected. Hence, as discussed in Chapter 4, the Supreme Court in *Montgomery v Lanarkshire*[98] has held that in cases where a doctor fails to disclose a material risk of a treatment to a patient this will generally be seen as negligent, even if other doctors would have done the same thing.

There is lively debate over whether the *Montgomery* decision will herald a more significant retreat from the *Bolam* test. This depends on whether or not the distinction between clinical decision and non-clinical decisions will hold. As the *Muller* decision on diagnosis (discussed above) shows it is possible that an increasing range of decisions will be said to be non-specialist and therefore outside the scope of *Bolam*. That could even lead to the Supreme Court deciding to abandon the *Bolam* test altogether.

3.4 Causation

Simply showing that a healthcare professional has been negligent does not mean that the claimant has won his or her case; it must also be shown that the negligence caused the victim's injuries.[99] The basic test for causation is known as the 'but for' test.[100] This simply asks whether, 'but for' the defendant's negligence, the patient would have suffered an injury. In some cases, this is straightforward. If, in error, a doctor removes the healthy rather than the diseased kidney, it is obvious that the doctor's negligence caused the loss of the kidney. In *Less v Hussain*,[101] a doctor gave negligent advice about the risks to a woman of becoming pregnant. She became pregnant and suffered loss. However, it was found that she would have chosen to become pregnant even if correct advice had been given. She could not show that the negligence had caused her a loss.

Where the claim is that the defendant's negligence meant that the patient's disease was not diagnosed or treated properly, it is necessary to show that, had the professional acted properly, then:

(i)   the disease would have been diagnosed; and

(ii) it would have been possible to treat the patient so that his or her condition would have improved.

[95] *Ratcliffe v Plymouth and Torbay Health Authority* [1998] 4 Med LR 162, 190. Although see *Richards v Swansea NHS Trust* [2007] EWHC 487 (QB), in which the doctrine was referred to uncritically.
[96] [2005] EWCA Civ 1466.   [97] *Thomas v Curley* [2011] EWHC 2103 (QB).   [98] [2015] UKSC 11.
[99] See *Thomson v Bradford* [2005] EWCA Civ 1439, in which, although there was fault in the advice given by the doctor, that fault did not cause the loss.
[100] For discussions of the law of causation in tort generally see Green (2015); Turton (2016) and Steel (2015).
[101] [2012] EWHC 3513 (QB).

These principles were applied in *Davies v Countess of Chester Hospital NHS Foundation Trust*[102] where a doctor was dealing with a very sick man who was suffering heart failure. He injected him with magnesium, but at four times the appropriate amount. That killed the patient. Although there was clear negligence, there was no liability because the court found that the patient was so ill he would have died at about the same time even with the best treatment. Therefore, although there had been negligence, the patient was no worse off as a result.

In *Barnett v Chelsea and Kensington Hospital Management Committee*,[103] a doctor refused to see a man who turned up at casualty complaining of stomach pains. The man died shortly afterwards. It was clear that the doctor was negligent in refusing to see the patient. However, the evidence suggested that even if the doctor had seen the man, there was nothing that the doctor would have been able to do to save the man's life. Therefore, although there was negligence, it could not be said to have caused the injury. That case was, in a way, an easy one. In other cases, it will be far more difficult to show whether the patient's condition would have been apparent from a proper examination or whether any treatment would have improved the patient's condition.[104] There are some complex issues that can arise where the defendant is not shown definitely to have caused the harm, but to have been a possible cause, or to have exposed the claimant to a risk. A number of different situations need to be distinguished.

3.4.1 *Where it is unclear whether the injury suffered was caused by the defendant or some other cause*

In *Wilsher v Essex*,[105] it was unclear whether the blindness suffered by a child was caused by the negligent care given to him or by his premature birth. The House of Lords confirmed that it had to be shown on the balance of probabilities that the harm was caused by the negligence of the defendant. This could not be demonstrated on the facts and so the action failed.[106] However, it is not clear that this approach represents the current law.

In *Bailey v Ministry of Defence*,[107] partly as a result of pancreatitis and partly as a result of the hospital's negligence, the defendant was in a weakened state, which meant that when she subsequently vomited, while in hospital, she could not evacuate the vomit and this caused her serious harm. It was enough that the negligence was a material cause of the later harm, even if not the only cause of the harm.[108] The Court of Appeal emphasized that the test of material cause in cases of this kind was not the same as the 'but for' cause. An earlier negligent act might be a 'but for' cause of a later injury, but not be regarded as a material cause. An example might be a patient who, as a result of a negligent act, had to stay in hospital two days longer than he or she would otherwise have had to, but during those two extra days developed a hospital-acquired infection. Arguably,

---

[102] [2014] EWHC 4294 (QB).

[103] See also *Kay v Ayrshire and Arran Health Board* [1987] 1 All ER 417.

[104] *Wilsher v Essex Area Health Authority* [1988] 1 All ER 871.

[105] In *Wootton v J Docter Ltd* [2008] EWCA Civ 1361, the negligence simply did not increase the risk of harm resulting, and so the action failed.

[106] [2002] Lloyd's Rep Med 361.

[107] At [42].

[108] This was the test approved by the House of Lords in *Fairchild v Glenhaven Funeral Services* [2002] Lloyd's Rep Med 361, [69] for tort claims not involving clinical negligence.

in such a case, the earlier negligence would be a 'but for' cause, but not a material cause. Waller LJ stated:

> If the evidence demonstrates on a balance of probabilities that the injury would have occurred as a result of the non-tortious cause or causes in any event, the Claimant will have failed to establish that the tortious cause contributed ... If the evidence demonstrates that 'but for' the contribution of the tortious cause the injury would probably not have occurred, the Claimant will (obviously) have discharged the burden. In a case where medical science cannot establish the probability that 'but for' an act of negligence the injury would not have happened but can establish that the contribution of the negligent cause was more than negligible, the 'but for' test is modified, and the Claimant will succeed.[109]

Bailey was recently approved by the Privy Council in *Williams v The Bermuda Hospitals Board*.[110]

KEY CASE   *Williams v The Bermuda Hospitals Board* [2016] UKPC 4

A patient attended hospital with a ruptured appendix. As a result of negligence there was a delay in treating him, during which the sepsis caused by the rupture worsened, and the patient developed myocardial ischaemia. Lord Toulson explained that the disease was caused in part by 'innocent' sepsis (which had been present before he was diagnosed) and partly by 'guilty sepsis' (which developed during the negligent delay). It could not be said that if there was no delay the myocardia ischaemia would have occurred anyway. Therefore, applying *Bailey*, the 'guilty sepsis' was a material contribution and the defendant hospital was liable in negligence.

So the current position is that if the negligence is a material contribution to the harm the defendant can be liable, even though it was not the sole cause of harm.[111] Where, however, the court finds that the same harm would have occurred even if the negligent act would not have occurred, causation will not be shown and the claim must fail.

In the following case, the court had to determine whether subsequent negligence of a hospital negated the liability of a doctor, who had failed to refer a child to the hospital.

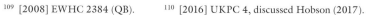

KEY CASE   *Wright v Cambridge Medical Group* [2011] EWCA Civ 669

Clarice Wright, aged 11 months, picked up a bacterial infection. Her mother took her to the defendant GP. Negligently, he failed to refer her to the hospital until two days later. There was further negligence at the hospital, which failed to diagnose her until three further days later. As a result, her hip became infected, with permanent restrictions on her movement. Proceedings were brought in Clarice's name against the defendant GPs.

---

[109] [2008] EWHC 2384 (QB).   [110] [2016] UKPC 4, discussed Hobson (2017).
[111] *John v Central Manchester and Manchester Children's University Hospitals NHS Foundation Trust* [2016] EWHC 407 (QB).

The judge held that the defendant was not liable, because even if it had not been negligent and Clarice had been referred two days earlier to the hospital, the hospital would still have been negligent and treatment would have been delayed, and she would have received the same injuries.

The Court of Appeal, by a two-to-one majority, overturned the first-instance decision. Once it had been shown that the GP was negligent and that negligence caused an injury, the GP could not rely by way of defence on the fact that the hospital would have been negligent too. Only if the GP could show that the hospital's negligence robbed his negligence of all 'causal potency' might he be able to argue that it had not been shown that his negligence caused the injury. That had not been shown here. In any event, it had not been established that, had the GP not been negligent and referred Clarice to the hospital immediately, the hospital would have negligent.[112] Further, even if the hospital had been equally negligent, the treatment would have been given two days earlier and the evidence suggested that doing so would have significantly improved her outcome.

The Court of Appeal acknowledged that where there are two negligent parties, the case law is unclear. Where A was being sued, but B had also been negligent, much turned on whether B's negligence had reduced the 'causal potency' of A's negligence to such a degree that A's negligence should be regarded as no longer sufficient to attach liability. On the facts of the *Wright* case, the Court held that the hospital's negligence was 'not such an egregious event, in terms of the degree or unusualness of the negligence, or the period of time for which it lasted, to defeat or destroy the causative link between the defendants' negligence and the claimant's injury'.[113] That led the Court to produce a more general principle:

> It appears to be a generally accepted proposition that a doctor cannot escape liability for damage caused to a patient by his breach of duty by establishing that, if he had not committed that breach, the damage would have been suffered anyway because he would have committed a subsequent breach of duty.[114]

This was justified in this way:

> By committing the breach of duty, the doctor has prevented the patient from the opportunity of being treated appropriately, and had the patient had that opportunity, she would have had a claim for the same damage against the doctor for the very negligence upon which the doctor is relying to avoid liability.[115]

3.4.2 *Cases in which the alleged negligence is that the defendant failed to examine the claimant*

The facts of *Bolitho v City & Hackney Health Authority*[116] demonstrate another difficulty with causation. In that case, a child had breathing difficulties. Although the paediatric registrar was called, she failed to attend until too late. The evidence was that, had she examined the boy within a reasonable time and intubated him, he would not have suffered the serious injuries that he did. However, one argument put before the House of Lords was that it had not been shown that the negligence caused the death, because if

---

[112] At [37].   [113] At [56].   [114] At [58].   [115] [1997] 4 All ER 771.
[116] [2007] EWCA Civ 397.

the registrar had attended, she might have decided not to intubate. The House of Lords held that it was necessary to ask two questions. First, what would the registrar have recommended had she attended on the boy? This was a factual question, which required the courts to predict only how the registrar would have acted. If the answer was that she would have decided to intubate, then it was shown that negligence caused the injuries. If the answer was that she would not, then the second question was whether it would have been negligent for her to do so (using the *Bolam* test). If it would have been negligent, then again the injuries would be caused by her negligence. For the registrar to have a defence on the causation ground, it would be necessary to show that, had she attended on the child, she would have taken the decision not to intubate and that it would not have been negligent for her to make that decision. On the facts of the case, the House of Lords held causation not to be established, because there was evidence that intubating as young a child as the claimant carried serious risks, and that therefore the registrar would not have used intubation and it would not have been negligent for her to make that decision.

By contrast, in *Gouldsmith v Mid-Staffordshire General Hospitals NHS Trust*,[117] a doctor failed to refer a patient to a specialist unit for treatment on her finger. It was not known who at the unit would have seen the patient, but it was found to be more likely than not that, if she had been referred, she would have received treatment because that was normal practice. If she had received treatment, the injuries to her finger would not have occurred. That being the case, there was no need to ask whether it would be negligent for the specialists not to offer treatment.[118] In a dissenting judgment, Kay LJ thought that it was wrong to distinguish a case in which you knew exactly who would have treated the patient (such as *Bolitho*) and a case (such as *Gouldsmith*) in which it was not known who would have seen the patient. He thought it inappropriate that, in *Gouldsmith*, a claimant needed to show only that it was more likely than not that a surgeon would provide the treatment; he thought that a claimant should show that it was more likely than not that the actual physician who would have seen him would have provided the treatment. However, as Kay LJ acknowledged, that would prove very difficult for a patient, because he or she could not know which doctor he or she would see. The majority in *Gouldsmith*, then, held that where the alleged negligence is a failure to refer a patient and it is not known to whom the patient would be referred, you imagine a hypothetical expert in the field and consider whether it was more likely than not that he or she would treat the patient.

3.4.3 *Depriving the claimant of a chance of treatment*

What if the evidence shows that, if properly cared for, the claimant's illness would have been diagnosed and he or she would have been offered treatment that might have cured his or her condition, but the defendant failed to diagnose the claimant's condition and so deprived him or her of the chance of treatment?[119]

The following three cases are crucial to the understanding of this complex area of the law.

---

[117] See also *Carter v Basildon & Thurrock University Hospitals NHS Foundation Trust* [2007] EWHC 1882 (QB).
[118] For a sophisticated analysis of the law and the issues raised in such cases, see Khoury (2006).
[119] At [56].

KEY CASE   *Hotson v East Berkshire Area Health Authority* [1987] AC 750

A boy, aged 13, fell out of a tree, injured his hip, and was taken to hospital. He argued that if his condition had been properly diagnosed when he arrived at the hospital, he would have been offered treatment. That treatment would have had a 25 per cent chance of providing a recovery. Because his condition was not properly diagnosed, he was not given the treatment and lost his chance of recovery. He suffered a vascular necrosis of the epiphysis, involving disability of the hip joint, with the virtual certainty that osteoarthritis would later develop. The trial judge granted him 25 per cent of the damages that he would have received if the health authority were fully responsible for the hip condition. The House of Lords held this approach to be wrong. As a general rule, damages could be awarded only if it could be shown that, had the patient been properly diagnosed, there was available treatment that would probably have worked (that is, treatment that had a greater than 50 per cent chance of success). Quite simply, the plaintiff had failed to show on the balance of probabilities that, had the health authority not been negligent, he would not have suffered the injury. In fact, because there was only a 25 per cent chance of success, if the boy had been given the correct treatment, he may still have suffered the injuries from which he was presently suffering.

Lord Mackay and Lord Bridge, however, refused to rule that the loss of a less than 50 per cent chance of a full recovery was never recoverable. They did not indicate in what kinds of cases they thought it might be.

KEY CASE   *Chester v Afshar* [2004] UKHL 41

Ms Chester suffered severe pain in her back. She was referred to Mr Afshar, an eminent consultant neurosurgeon. Mr Afshar recommended surgery, but failed to warn Ms Chester of the 1–2 per cent risk of significant nerve damage that was an inevitable risk of the surgery. Ms Chester agreed to the operation and, although it was performed properly, the risk of nerve damage materialized and she was left partially paralysed. The trial judge found that, had Mr Afshar informed Ms Chester of the risk, she would not have consented to the operation at that time, but would have sought a further opinion. However, on receiving the further opinion, she would have consented to the treatment, probably with Mr Afshar, at a later date. The trial judge held that it had therefore been shown that there was a causal link between the surgeon's advice and the loss to the patient. The case went up to the House of Lords.

By a majority of three to two, their Lordships found in favour of Ms Chester. It was held that where a patient had not been warned about a risk of injury and as a result of that failure underwent the operation that she would not have undertaken *at that time* if she had been properly informed, a patient was entitled to compensation. It was not necessary for Ms Chester to show that she would never have consented to the kind of operation at any time in the future; only that she would not have consented to the operation that took place. The majority accepted that, on conventional causation principles, the decision could not be supported. This was because it was found that, had she been properly informed of the risks, Ms Chester would have agreed to the operation, although at a later date. She would therefore have been undertaking an operation with exactly the same chance of causing her an injury as the operation that she undertook. Lord Steyn emphasized that, even if the risk of the injury occurring was the same whenever she undertook the operation, she would not have suffered exactly the same injury at the same time as she did had the proper information been given. In any event, whatever the arguments over causation, Lord Steyn believed that justice required a modification of the normal approach to causation. The duty of doctors to warn patients of risks was important because it protected the rights of patients to make informed choices about whether, and when and by whom, to be operated upon. To leave the patient uninformed about the risk when he or she would not have immediately consented to the operation had he or she been informed of the risk would render the duty meaningless. As Lord Hope put it:

> The function of the law is to protect the patient's right to choose. If it is to fulfil that function it must ensure that the duty to inform is respected by the doctor. It will fail to do this if an appropriate remedy cannot be given if the duty is breached and the very risk that the patient should have been told about occurs and she suffers injury.[120]

Lord Walker, for the majority, accepted that the conclusion of the majority was more about policy than the principles of causation. But the majority were not ignoring causation altogether:

> [I]f a taxi-driver drives too fast and the cab is hit by a falling tree, injuring the passenger, it is sheer coincidence. The driver might equally well have avoided the tree by driving too fast, and the passenger might have been injured if the driver was observing the speed limit. But to my mind the present case does not fall into that category. Bare 'but for' causation is powerfully reinforced by the fact that the misfortune which befell the claimant was the very misfortune which was the focus of the surgeon's duty to warn.[121]

The point of Lord Walker's analogy is that 'but for' causation is not sufficient, because otherwise the taxi driver would be liable. But, in *Chester*, the risk was within the scope of the duty and it was fair to hold the surgeon responsible for it.

The views of the dissenting judges were summarized by Lord Bingham in the following passage:

> A defendant is bound to compensate the claimant for the damage which his or her negligence has caused the claimant. But the corollaries are also true: a claimant is not entitled to be compensated, and a defendant is not bound to compensate the claimant, for damage not caused by the negligence complained of. The patient's right to be appropriately warned is an important right, which few doctors in the current legal and social climate would consciously or deliberately violate. I do not for my part think that the law should seek to reinforce that right by providing for the payment of potentially very large damages by a defendant whose violation of that right is not shown to have worsened the physical condition of the claimant.[122]

In such a case, he argued, one could not claim to have been caused a loss because one has not been given the correct odds.

[120] At [94].   [121] At [9].   [122] At [10].

KEY CASE   *Gregg v Scott* [2005] UKHL 2

Mr Gregg visited Dr Scott because he had a lump under his arm. Dr Scott negligently misdiagnosed the lump as benign. One year later, it was discovered that Gregg was suffering from cancer of the lymph gland. As a result, he had to undergo chemotherapy and was left with a poor prognosis. Gregg alleged that, had Dr Scott properly diagnosed his condition when he saw him, there would have been a much greater chance of being cured. At trial, the judge held that his chances of surviving for more than ten years were now 25 per cent, but would have been 42 per cent had he been properly diagnosed early on and treatment begun then. However, the judge held that even if properly diagnosed, it would have been more likely than not that there would not have been a cure. It had not therefore been shown that the negligence caused a loss. The Court of Appeal dismissed Gregg's appeal and the case went to the House of Lords. Their Lordships divided three to two and took eight months to produce their judgments after hearing the arguments. As that suggests, the judgment was controversial.

The majority dismissed Gregg's appeal. It had not been shown that, on the balance of probabilities, the delay in the treatment had caused a loss. Even if there had been no negligence, the most likely outcome would have been that the claimant would suffer the loss that he did. The loss of a chance of a more favourable outcome could not be sued for in tort. The minority, by contrast, regarded the significant reduction in the possibility of survival to be a loss for which the claimant should be compensated.

It is worth summarizing the judgments of each of their Lordships.

Lord Hoffmann (majority)

Lord Hoffmann argued that the most likely future for Gregg was that he would die within ten years. This would have been true even if the correct diagnosis had been made early on. The likelihood was therefore that the negligence had not affected the outcome for him. To allow people to claim for the loss of a chance would be a radical change in tort law and should be made by legislation, not judicial decision. The impact of such a change of the law on the NHS and insurers would be enormous. It would be improper for the House of Lords to make such a potentially significant change.

Lord Phillips (majority)

Lord Phillips noted that, whatever the statistics, Gregg had, by the time their Lordships heard the case, survived nine years and his chances of survival were 'climbing daily'. It therefore seemed that the lack of early intervention had not caused a premature demise. In other words, the chances of survival, given that he had lived to read the House of Lords' judgments, were higher than they had been at trial. He suggested that the issue should be seen simply as one of causation and that percentages became relevant only in deciding the effect of the negligence. As a matter of causation, what mattered was whether or not, on the balance of probabilities, it had been shown that negligence had caused loss. Here, on the balance of probabilities, the negligence had not caused loss. Lord Phillips accepted that this might be seen as unfair, but noted that '[a] robust test which produces rough justice may be preferable to a test that on occasion will be difficult, if not impossible, to apply in practice'.[123] Using this robust test, which produced rough justice, was justifiable on policy grounds and because of the need to retain coherence in the common law. Lord Phillips appeared to leave open a case in which the defendant's negligence had meant the loss of a possible cure and the claimant had in fact gone on to suffer the illness.

---

[123] At [3].

Baroness Hale of Richmond (majority)

Tort law was not about the punishment of wrongdoing, but rather the compensation of injury. Baroness Hale was concerned that a 'loss of a chance' approach would enable a claim to be made even where no harm had in fact occurred. She thought that 'almost any claim' could be reformulated to be the loss of a chance. It had not here been shown in this case that, on the balance of probabilities, the delay in treatment caused the spread of cancer. She pointed out that, under a 'loss of a chance' approach, some claimants would win, but others would lose. The winners would be those who could show only a less than 50 per cent chance of succeeding, but the losers would be those who could show an 80 per cent chance of recovery. They would be losers because, under the present system, they would recover 100 per cent of their presumed loss, whereas under the 'loss of a chance' scheme, they would recover only 80 per cent of their loss. To move to a 'loss of a chance' scheme would mean that trials and negotiations would become far more complex.

Lord Hope (dissenting)

Lord Hope argued that this case was significantly different from *Hotson*. In that case, the boy had already been injured and there was no doubt that the cause of the injury was the fall. In Gregg's case, the injury was in the future. Treatment would be preventing the injury from arising, rather than seeking to cure or mitigate it. He referred to a number of cases in which the loss of a chance (for example the loss of the prospect of promotion) was recoverable in tort law. He argued that where there was a significant reduction of the prospects of a successful outcome, then there should be compensation. This should be calculated on the assumption of the certainty of complete recovery when the negligence took place and a discount to reflect the actual prospects of recovery at the time of the case. He also argued that there could be no doubt that negligence had caused the growth in the tumour. If the growth in the tumour had increased the chances of suffering cancer, Gregg should recover for that.

Lord Nicholls (dissenting)

Lord Nicholls was highly critical of the view of the majority that if it could be shown that, on the balance of probabilities, the negligence did cause the injury, then damages are recoverable, but if not, there would be no damages. He said:

> This surely cannot be the state of the law today. It would be irrational and indefensible. The loss of a 45 per cent prospect of recovery is just as much a real loss for a patient as the loss of a 55 per cent prospect of recovery. In both cases the doctor was in breach of his duty to his patient. In both cases the patient was worse off. He lost something of importance and value. But, it is said, in one case the patient has a remedy, in the other he does not.[124]

He also voiced the concern that if a doctor could show that the correct treatment provided only a less than 50 per cent chance of recovery, then there was no recovery. This would leave a doctor's duty of care to his or her patient 'hollow'.[125] He argued that a claimant who lost a 40 per cent chance of recovery should receive 40 per cent of the damages that would be awarded had the claimant been able to show that the defendant was 100 per cent responsible for the injuries, although he thought that damages should be awarded where a patient had a 'reasonable prospect' of recovery and then negligence had reduced these by a 'significant extent'. As to concerns about the financial burdens that this might impose on the NHS, Lord Nicholls described these as speculative and argued that it was for Parliament to amend the law if the burden proved to be too great, not for the courts to deny a valid claim owing to financial concerns.

---

[124] At [4].   [125] *Marcus v Medway Primary Care Trust* [2010] EWHC 1888 (QB).

The current law after these cases appears to be as follows.

- If the claimant has suffered a harm that the defendant negligently fails to diagnose or for which the defendant negligently fails to offer treatment, it needs to be shown that it would be more likely than not that, if the treatment had been offered, the claimant would not have suffered the harm.[126] So if the claimant would have had a 40 per cent chance of recovery had the doctor given the treatment, the claim will fail, because even if the treatment had been given, the most likely outcome is that the claimant would not have recovered. However, if it was shown there was a 60 per cent chance of recovery if the treatment had been given the claim will succeed, because if offered, the most likely outcome would have been that the claimant would have recovered.

- In exceptional cases, such as *Chester*, even if it cannot be shown that the outcome was caused by the defendant's negligence, damages can be awarded.[127] If it can be shown that a medical professional negligently failed to warn of a risk and that, as a result, the claimant agreed to undergo an operation when, if properly advised, he or she would not have agreed to undergo that particular operation at that time, then a claim can be established[128]—although it seems from *Meiklejohn v St George's NHS Trust*[129] that this is true only where, if the procedure were to have been undertaken at a different time, there may have been an different outcome. Rafferty LJ said of *Chester* that he could not 'identify within it any decision of principle' and that the case was based on 'policy in relation to the particular facts of the case'. That suggests that the basis of the award in *Chester* will only be used in rare cases. In *Crossman v St George's Healthcare NHS Trust*[130] it was said the change in *Chester* to the normal causation rules were 'exceptional and limited' and limited to cases where the patient was not told about a material risk or where a patient is not told that a different surgeon is to perform the surgery from the one expected. In these kinds of cases a departure from the normal causation rules was appropriate as the failures to inform infringe the patient's right to make decisions about medical treatment.

There are a number of issues raised by these cases, including the following.[131]

(i) *Is the law of medical negligence about punishing the wrongdoing of the defendant or compensating the harm to the victim?* In *Chester v Afshar*,[132] the House of Lords emphasized the importance of the patient's bodily integrity and the importance of using tort law to uphold patients' rights of information.[133] One way of reading the case is to suggest that the courts wanted to punish the wrongdoing of the doctor, even though it was hard to show the loss to the claimant was caused by the defendant.[134] Notably,

---

[126] Hoffman (2005); *Fairchild v Glenhaven Funeral Services Ltd* [2003] 1 AC 32. See further Compensation Act 2006, s. 3; *Barker v Corus (UK) Plc* [2006] UKHL 20; *Sienkiewicz v Greif* [2011] UKSC 10.
[127] *Chester v Afshar* [2004] UKHL 41. See Green (2015) for a helpful discussion.
[128] [2014] EWCA Civ 120.
[129] Stapleton (2005; 2006); Hoffman (2005); Peel (2005); Spencer (2005); Porat and Stein (2001).
[130] [2016] EWHC 2878 (QB).　　　[131] [2004] UKHL 41.
[132] In *Beary v Pall Mall Investments* [2005] EWCA Civ 415, *Chester* was said not to be a case of general application in negligence cases. This suggests that it represents a special rule of medical negligence cases.
[133] In *Clough v First Choice Holidays and Flights Ltd* [2006] EWCA Civ 15, *Chester* was described as a 'policy decision' and not of relevance to personal injury cases generally (although see *Mountford v Newlands School* [2007] EWCA Civ 21, in which it was held to apply outside the medical context).
[134] [2005] UKHL 2.

in *Gregg v Scott*,[135] talk of patients' rights played a far less prominent role in the courts' reasoning than it had in *Chester*.[136]

The right of a patient to be fully informed of risks was seen as of sufficient importance to justify a departure from the traditional approach to causation in *Chester*, but the right of the patient to receive non-negligent diagnosis was not in *Gregg*.[137] It is not clear that the right to be fully informed is more important than the right to be given non-negligent treatment: would most patients not prefer to receive non-negligent treatment, but without full information, rather than fully informed negligent treatment? Indeed, Sarah Green argues that the claim in *Gregg* could have been characterized as one in which he was not informed of the risks of treatment/non-treatment and that there is no justifiable way of distinguishing the kinds of claims in the cases.[138]

(ii) *The problems of over-/under-compensation* In a case such as *Gregg v Scott*,[139] involving loss of a chance, their Lordships were aware that, whatever conclusion they reached, it could be seen as a case of over- or under-compensation. It may be that Mr Gregg would go on to live into his 90s, in which case any award would have to compensate him for a loss that he did not suffer. On the other hand, if he were to deteriorate shortly after the House of Lords' judgment and die, and if the early diagnosis would have led to a course of treatment that would have cured his condition (something that we will never know), then he clearly did suffer a loss, for which he would have been given no compensation. Either way, it was very unlikely that the correct level of compensation could be given.

(iii) The law after *Gregg v Scott* draws an important distinction between a case in which the defendant's negligent misdiagnosis reduces the claimant's chance of recovery from 60 per cent to 40 per cent and a case in which it causes a reduction from 30 per cent to 10 per cent. In the former case, damages can be recovered, but not in the latter. In both cases, there is a reduction of 20 per cent in the chance of recovery. Should there be any difference between them? Nor has there been a very convincing justification offered by the courts between cases where there is a failure to disclose risk (*Chester*), where causation rules are treated very laxly, and loss of chance cases (e.g. *Gregg*) where the causation rules are treated strictly.[140] The area is ripe for reconsideration by the Supreme Court.

3.5 Damages

If the defendant has succeeded on all of the issues discussed above, he or she is entitled to damages. In tort, the basic principle is that the claimant should be put back in the position in which he or she was before the negligent act was committed. The aim of damages, then, is not to punish the defendant or to reflect the gravity of his or her wrongdoing, but to compensate the claimant for his or her losses. In the case of a financial loss, this is straightforward, but where the injuries are physical, it is far more difficult.

Medical cases will use the same principles in relation to damages that are used generally in tort. Books on tort law should be consulted to give the details on this. The

---

[135] See further *Johnston v NEI International Combustion Ltd* [2007] UKHL 39, in which *Gregg* was applied and no mention was made of *Chester*.
[136] [2002] Lloyd's Rep Med 361, [11].
[137] Green (2006).   [138] [2005] UKHL 2.   [139] [2011] EWCA Civ 669.   [140] Turton (2016).

following is a very brief summary of the law of damages. A claim can include the following elements:

(i) *'Fair and reasonable' compensation for the injury suffered* It is not really possible to put a figure on the financial sum to compensate for, say, the loss of a finger. The law has dealt with this by developing a tariff that sets out sums of money for particular kinds of injury. Although arbitrary, such a tariff does at least create consistency.

(ii) *Damages can be granted for pain and suffering* The sums awarded are relatively small.

(iii) *Loss of amenity* This covers the inability of the claimant to engage in activities in which he or she had been previously able to engage.

(iv) *Expenses incurred as a result of the injuries* Any extra costs that have been incurred can be recovered. This can include a claim for private medical costs, even if the same treatment was available for free on the NHS.[141]

(v) *Loss of earnings suffered as a result of the harm up to the date of the hearing*

(vi) *Future losses* This will involve an element of guesswork, because it requires the court to calculate what expenses and loss of earnings the claimant will suffer in the future. This may also involve an estimate as to how long the claimant will live.

Having calculated this total, there may be a reduction in two cases. First is the case in which the claimant was contributorily negligent.[142] This would arise where it was found that the negligence of both the patient and the doctor contributed to the injury.[143] For example, if a patient failed to disclose an important medical fact to his or her doctor, the doctor failed to check it, and, as a result of the ignorance of the fact, prescribed medication that harmed the patient, then possibly both the patient and doctor could be regarded as negligent. In such a case, the level of damages paid by the doctor will be reduced by the percentage that it is thought the patient contributed through his or her negligence. So if the patient and doctor were equally blameworthy, the damages would be halved. However, in *Loraine v Wirral University Teaching Hospital*,[144] a hospital that asked a pregnant woman for information about earlier pregnancies, but did not actually check her records, was held to be negligent when it was shown that, had it checked the records, there would have been evidence that she was at risk of suffering serious complications.[145] By contrast, in *Ingram v Williams*,[146] a patient failed to reveal that she was suffering incontinence and, as a result, the doctor made a wrong diagnosis. It was held that the doctor had made the correct diagnosis based on the evidence that he had been given by the patient and so was not negligent. It would have been different if the doctor had failed to ask a relevant question or should have spotted that the patient had not disclosed the incontinence.

The second way in which the damages payable may be reduced is where the patient has failed to mitigate his or her loss. This means that the patient has failed to undertake reasonable steps that would reduce or limit the harm he or she is suffering. This would

---

[141] See, e.g., *Appleton v El Safty* [2007] EWHC 631 (QB), in which it was necessary to predict how a professional footballer's career might develop.

[142] For a discussion of the use of contributory negligence in this context, see Herring and Foster (2009).

[143] [2008] EWHC 1565 (QB).   [144] See also *P v Sedar* [2011] EWHC 1266 (QB).

[145] [2010] EWHC 758 (QB).   [146] *Geest Plc v Monica Lansiquot* [2002] 1 WLR 3111.

arise, for example, where the patient has failed to undertake subsequent treatment that would have ameliorated his or her condition.[147]

3.6 Damages for secondary victims

The law is generally reluctant to allow a claim in tort to be brought by someone who is not directly injured by the negligence, but is affected by the injuries of others.[148] The general position is that a 'secondary' victim (that is, someone who did not themselves suffer a physical injury) cannot sue for the psychological distress that he or she suffers because of what has happened to another. However, this is subject to two important exceptions.

(i)   Where the claimant has witnessed what has happened to his or her relative, then he or she may be able to claim damages, but only when what it witnessed is exceptionally horrifying.[149] Margaret Brazier and Emma Cave suggest that a husband who is present and watches his wife screaming in agony because she is awake during a Caesarean section owing to a failure in anaesthetic may succeed in a claim for negligence.[150] A man who witnesses medical professionals determine that his pregnant partner's foetus was dead had had 'a growing and acute anxiety' and could not claim damages for psychological distress.[151] He had not witnessed a horrific event, but rather gradually come to realize what had happened.

(ii) If the relative is told in a negligent way about what has happened and this causes a psychological injury, a claim may succeed. If a parent is told in a callous way that his or her child has unexpectedly died on the operating table and as a result the parent suffers a psychological illness, then damages may be available. In a way, this is a case in which the relative is a 'direct' victim of the negligence of the medical professional.[152] The same may be true if the trust handles the complaint about the treatment in an inappropriate way.[153] However, falling ill after simply learning that a relative has died or been harmed as a result of medical negligence will not create liability.[154]

3.7 The controversial nature of damages awarded

There is no doubt that the way in which damages are awarded can produce astonishingly unfair results. A parent losing a child is given £10,000 bereavement damages.[155] This cannot be adequate compensation for the loss. But then again, can *any* sum truly

---

[147] Extensive discussion of this issue can be found in Ahuja (2015); Mulheron (2010), Fray (2012), and Case (2004).
[148] *Ward v Leeds Teaching Hospitals NHS Trust* [2004] EWHC 2106.
[149] Brazier and Cave (2007: 158). The court was generous in *Frogatt v Chesterfield NHS Trust* [2002] All ER (D) 218, in which a husband obtained damages after he was shocked on seeing his wife naked following an unnecessary mastectomy (following a negligent and false diagnosis of breast cancer).
[150] *Wild v Southend University NHS Trust* [2014] EWHC 4053 (QB).
[151] See Mulheron (2007) for further discussion.
[152] *Jones v Royal Devon NHS Trust* [2008] EWHC 558 (QB).
[153] *Shorter v Surrey and Sussex Healthcare NHS Trust* [2015] EWHC 614 (QB).
[154] Brazier and Cave (2007: 201).   [155] Brazier and Cave (2007: 201).

represent such a loss? Are £150,000 damages adequate for a patient paralysed from the waist down by negligence? Also, one's job can profoundly affect the level of damages awarded: two people may suffer the same injury, but if one loses his or her employment as a result, he or she will receive significantly more than the other who does not. Even when the claimant is a seriously injured child, the court will attempt to calculate how much income the child would be likely to make when grown up. The high-achieving child of two barristers who is seriously injured could expect to receive significantly more than the child with learning difficulties of an unemployed single parent. The levels of award in horrific cases can be very high: they regularly exceed £3 million.[156] Should one's income or socio-economic background really be relevant in assessing the amount of damages? Or is this an appropriate way of assessing the genuine loss of a party?

Consider also the case of Hollie Calladine,[157] in which a child suffered brain damage and was awarded £700,000. Tragically, days later, she unexpectedly died. The hospital was unable to recover the damages paid. Although the money had been ordered on the basis that it was required to meet the costs of raising Hollie as a seriously disabled child, the parents could keep it. On the other hand, had the award been much lower based on the assumption that she had only a year to live, but in fact she lived much longer, she would not have been able to seek to return to court to ask for more. It is common for it to become apparent over time that the level of damages that appeared reasonable at the time of the trial was, in retrospect, too little or too much.

One solution to that difficulty is to use structured settlements.[158] These involve an initial capital sum, which covers the losses that have already occurred and are quantifiable. For future costs, a sum is paid to purchase an annuity; this will produce flexible sums of money to cover the losses as they transpire. The amounts paid out could therefore increase or decrease with those expected if the claimant's condition improves or worsens over time. There is no power yet for courts to order structured settlements, but they can be entered into if both parties consent. They are not popular with some claimants because claimants lose control over their awards and are constantly having their medical progress checked. Another option is to order an interim payment,[159] which can be increased if the applicant is later able to show losses higher than those originally envisaged.[160]

3.8 The limitation period

The law of limitation may bar a claim in some cases. If the case involves personal injury, then the action must be commenced within three years of the date of the negligence or the date on which the defendant realized that an action could be brought (note that special rules apply to minors).[161] If the loss claimed was purely financial—that is, contractual—then the limitation period is six years, rather than three.[162] Under section 33

[156] Hopwood (2001: 191–2).
[157] See *A v B Hospitals NHS Trust* [2006] EWHC 2833 (Admin) for a case in which a lump sum was seen as preferable to periodic payments. Periodic payments can be ordered under the Damages Act 1996, s. 2.
[158] *Kirby v Ashford and St Peter's Hospital* [2008] EWHC 1320 (QB).
[159] *H v Thomson Holidays* [2007] EWHC 850 (QB).   [160] Limitation Act 1980, s. 11.
[161] Limitation Act 1980, s. 2.
[162] See *A v Hoare* [2008] UKHL 6, in which this also includes intentional trespass to the person.

of the Limitation Act 1980, there is discretion in the court to extend the limitation limit in actions for 'negligence, nuisance or breach of duty of care'.[163]

The reasoning behind the limitation restrictions is that a medical professional should not have a potential claim hanging over him or her for years ahead. Of course, the disadvantage is that a claimant may have a serious injury for which he or she deserves compensation, but for which no action is brought. There is, however, a discretion of the court to extend the limitation period.[164] This can be used to permit a claim to be brought out of time if there is a good reason why the claim is being brought late and if neither party will be prejudiced by the lateness of the claim.

3.9 Who should be sued?

If a patient has suffered harm as a result of medical malpractice, he or she has a number of people whom he or she could sue:

(i)   the medical professional individually;

(ii) the employer of the professional (for example the NHS trust or hospital), relying on the doctrine of vicarious liability;[165] or

(iii) the provider unit directly for its own negligence.

Options (ii) and (iii) may not be obvious. Under the doctrine of vicarious liability, an employer is liable for the negligence of its employees who are acting in the course of their employment. In theory, if an NHS trust or health authority is sued on the basis of vicarious liability, the body could recover the damages paid out from the negligent professional concerned.[166] However, the NHS has declared that it will not do this.[167] Further, the NHS has agreed to meet the costs of litigation against medical staff. So, rather than staff having to arrange their own insurance, the NHS takes on that responsibility. However, GPs remain responsible for meeting their own costs and must maintain insurance cover.[168] This has led to a growing effort in the NHS to avoid the risk of accidents and to avoid litigation. 'Risk management' has become a buzzword.

The doctrine of vicarious liability need not involve any evidence that the employer was itself negligent. Under direct liability—option (iii)—the claim is that the provider itself was negligent (for example in failing to ensure that there were sufficient numbers of adequately trained staff).[169] In such a case, it may be that none of the staff were negligent (they all did the best that they could) and yet the trust was. Other examples of direct liability might be if there were no proper procedures to check that equipment was working properly, or that staff were not properly kept up to date with medical developments.[170] Although the courts are yet to give full consideration to the question, it seems that, when considering whether an NHS trust is negligent, the *Bolam* test will not apply. In other words, a hospital will not necessarily have a defence simply because it

---

[163] Limitation Act 1980, s. 33.

[164] An action would not lie against the Crown: *Morgan v Ministry of Justice* [2010] EWHC 2248 (QB).

[165] See Brazier and Beswick (2006).   [166] NHS Executive (1996).

[167] NHS Executive (1996).

[168] *Godden v Kent and Medway Strategic Health Authority* [2004] EWHC 1629.

[169] *Blyth v Bloomsbury Health Authority* [1993] 4 Med LR 151.

[170] *Bull v Devon Area Health Authority* [1993] 4 Med LR 117.

was acting at a level at which other hospitals act, if the judge decides that those standards are unreasonable.[171]

If a court has decided that both an individual doctor and his or her hospital are negligent, who is to pay the damages? It seems that the court will focus on the extent to which the doctor was able to avoid the harm to the patient in the context of his or her working environment. So if a junior doctor is negligent, but it is found that he or she was receiving an inadequate level of support and supervision, then the hospital may be required to pay the bulk of the damages.[172]

A primary care trust (PCT) could be sued. There is an argument that a PCT owes a duty of care to ensure that there is reasonable provision for all of the patients in its area. If, through negligence, a PCT were to fail to ensure that a patient received a reasonable level of care, then a tortious action could be brought against the PCT.[173]

An NHS patient who is referred to a private hospital for treatment within the NHS will still be able to sue the NHS for any negligence that takes place in the private hospital.[174] A patient of the NHS should not lose a legal remedy because of how the NHS decided to deliver its services. In such a case, the NHS will often seek an indemnity for the money that it has paid out from the private institution.

In *Farraj v Kings Healthcare Trust*,[175] a couple carried a gene for an inheritable condition. When the woman became pregnant, the hospital arranged tests to see if the embryo had the condition. The sample was sent by the hospital to a company, which negligently failed to detect that the embryo did carry the condition. The child was born with a serious illness. The question arose whether the hospital could delegate its duty to the company. The Court of Appeal held not. Dyson LJ explained:

> [A] hospital generally owes a non-delegable duty to its patients to ensure that they are treated with skill and care regardless of the employment status of the person who is treating them ... the rationale for this is that the hospital undertakes the care, supervision and control of its patients who are in special need of care. Patients are a vulnerable class of persons who place themselves in the care and under the control of a hospital and, as a result, the hospital assumes a particular responsibility for their well-being and safety. To use the language of *Caparo Industries plc v Dickman* [1990] 2 AC 605, 618A it is therefore fair just and reasonable that a hospital should owe such a duty of care to its patients in these circumstances.[176]

With increased use of private companies within the NHS, this decision may become increasingly significant.

3.10 Apportionment

If two medical professionals' negligence has caused the injury to the patient, then the principle of apportionment may come into play. The claimant can receive the whole of the damages from either of the defendants. It is up to that defendant to sue the other

---

[171] *Jones v Manchester Corporation* [1952] 2 All ER 125.
[172] *A (A Child) v Ministry of Defence* [2004] EWCA 641; *FB v Princess Alexandra Hospital NHS Trust* [2017] EWCA Civ 334. See also the discussion in Beswick (2007).
[173] *M v Calderdale Health Authority* [1998] Lloyd's Rep Med 157; *Farraj v King's Healthcare NHS Trust* [2006] EWHC 1228 (QB).
[174] [2009] EWCA 1203.   [175] At [12].   [176] Civil Liability (Contribution) Act 1978.

for reimbursement of its share. The damages will be divided according to the degree of responsibility for the accident.[177] In fact, the NHS indemnity scheme means that NHS staff will not be individually liable and so apportionment is rarely an issue, except in general practice, or where the patient has been treated by the NHS and another medical provider.

4 The law of contract

There is no contract between an NHS patient and the NHS or its staff.[178] Therefore NHS patients cannot sue for breach of contract if their doctor mistreats them. However, a private patient can sue his or her medical professionals for breach of contract. That said, normally, whenever a breach of contract could be established, so could a negligence claim. It is not impossible that a contract between a doctor and private patient will require the doctor to exercise a higher standard of care than that imposed by negligence, but it would be unusual. Certainly, the courts have been very reluctant to interpret a contract as a guarantee that the procedure will be a success.[179]

5 Why do people sue?

There is much talk in the media of a 'compensation culture'. The House of Commons Constitutional Affairs Committee investigated these claims that people will use the slightest opportunity to sue in the hope of making a 'fast buck';[180] the Committee found that the compensation culture was a myth. That was the same conclusion Lord Dyson reached in a public lecture, in suggesting it was a media creation, rather than the reality.[181] However, the belief that it exists created inappropriate risk aversion, which had harmful effects. The Committee stated:

> Risk aversion has a number of complex causes, including advertising by claims management companies, selective media reporting, a lack of information about how the law works and, on occasion, a lack of common sense amongst those who implement health and safety guidelines.[182]

Research suggests that those bringing actions for medical negligence are not simply trying to obtain money; their motivations are far more complicated.[183] In a leading survey, it was found that a majority of those suing were more concerned with getting an acceptance of fault, an assurance that the errors would not be repeated in the future, or a fuller investigation of what had happened.[184] Just under half were concerned with receiving an explanation, an apology, and ensuring that the professionals understood what had happened to them. Only about a third said that they were concerned with money.[185] In a study for the Department of Health, it was found that only 11 per cent of those

---

[177] *Reynolds v The Health First Medical Group* [2000] Lloyd's Rep Med 240.
[178] *Thake v Maurice* [1986] 1 All ER 497.
[179] House of Commons Constitutional Affairs Committee (2006).   [180] Hyde (2013).
[181] House of Commons Constitutional Affairs Committee (2006: 1).   [182] Morris (2007).
[183] Mulcahy, Selwood, and Nettern (1999: Fig. 2.1); Mulcahy (2003).
[184] For similar findings, see Woolf (2001).   [185] Chief Medical Officer (2003: 75).

making complaints were seeking money, although that rose to 35 per cent where serious injuries were involved.[186] That said, it may be that these points cannot be separated from money. Will an apology that is not backed up by a payment of money be regarded as a 'cheap and easy' apology and not genuine? Will patients believe that lessons have been learned only if payment is required to provide a financial incentive not to repeat the mistake?

There is also the difficulty that, for medical professionals, having a complaint made against them can be seen as an attack on their professional integrity. This leads to a defensive response to such complaints, which in turn can exacerbate the patients' feelings that they are not being listened to or are not being shown respect.[187]

6 Medical malpractice litigation in practice

The number of cases of alleged medical malpractice that actually reach the courts is, of course, small. Of cases handled by the NHS Resolution (formerly NHS Litigation Authority), in 2016/17, just over 99 per cent were settled without going to trial.[188]

Therefore, most cases end before they reach the courts: at the negotiation stage. In 2016/17 67.8 per cent of cases handled by NHS Resolution were resolved without even legal proceedings being started; 31.5 per cent of cases were settled after proceedings were started but before the case reached trial. Practically, therefore, what happens at the negotiation stage is more important than what happens in the courtroom, although some lawyers argue that the two cannot be easily separated: lawyers bargain 'in the shadow of the law'.[189] What order the lawyers believe a court will make plays an important role in deciding whether to accept or reject an offer made by the other side.

7 Costs

The payment of legal costs is a crucial aspect of litigation. Legal costs can be a large proportion of the overall costs of litigation. In 2016/17, of cases dealt with by NHS Resolution, just under £625 million was spent on paying the costs of lawyers. Over £500 million of this was for claimant lawyers. For every £2 paid in damages to a claimant, at least £1 is paid for lawyer costs.[190]

A person who has suffered an injury as a result of medical malpractice may well be deterred from suing because he or she is unable to pay for the legal costs in bringing the action. Indeed, a defendant may prefer to settle the case rather than to take the issue to court for fear of the lawyers' costs involved. Certainly, it would be a brave person on an average income who brought a medical negligence case.[191]

Legal aid is no longer available for clinical negligence cases. The alternative is likely to be a conditional fee arrangement (CFA).[192] This introduced the possibility of lawyers taking on a case on a 'no win, no fee' basis—that is, if the case is lost, then the client

---

[186] Mulcahy (2003).   [187] Mulcahy (2015).   [188] NHS Resolution (2017).
[189] NHS (2015a).   [190] NHS Resolution (2107).   [191] Newdick (2005: 130).
[192] This became possible after the Courts and Legal Services Act 1990. The House of Commons Constitutional Affairs Committee (2006) found no evidence that the advent of conditional fees increased rates of litigation.

will face no charge, while if the case is won, the lawyer will charge more than he or she would have had the client been paying fees in the normal way. From the lawyer's point of view, this is a kind of gamble: he or she could do very well if the case is won, but lose out significantly if the case fails. From the client's point of view, the option is risk-free in the sense that he or she cannot be financially out of pocket, at least as regards his or her own lawyer's fees, but the client could still face an order to pay the legal costs of the other side. However, the client must realize that if litigation is successful, he or she will see less of the damages than had he or she paid the lawyer on the traditional hourly rate basis. Although it was feared by some that CFAs would mean that there would be a flood of litigation in the medical context, in fact lawyers have been reluctant to take on risky cases for fear of having to do an enormous amount of work for no pay.[193]

8 Criticisms of the current legal position

There is a widespread perception that medical negligence litigation is unsatisfactory.[194] There seems widespread agreement that it appears to demoralize medical professionals, provides patients with stress rather than compensation, and constitutes an enormous expense for limited NHS resources.

8.1 Criticisms of the *Bolam* test

The *Bolam* test has generated much criticism. The following are some of the objections to it.

(i)   The test means that the medical profession, rather than the courts, set the legal standard required of doctors. In all other professions, it is no defence for an individual to show that others would have acted in the same way. A driver sued for negligence will have no defence if he or she can show that many other respectable drivers drive as badly as he or she did. It is the law, not drivers, that sets the standard expected of them. In other words, negligence here appears not to be setting standards that health-care professionals should strive to meet, but rather is describing the standards that are in fact practised. The need for the law, rather than the medical profession, to set standards of good practice is highlighted by the scandals at Bristol and Alder Hey.[195]

(ii) *Bolam* has put an almost impossible burden on claimants. They can be confident that they have a strong case only if they interview every expert in the relevant field and are told by each one that the alleged conduct is negligent. The defendant, by contrast, need find only one respected expert to have a good chance of success. Critics claim that the law appears to be more concerned with protecting the reputation of the professional than ensuring that the patient receives compensation if he or she has been badly treated.[196] Even where causation is demonstrated, the restrictive approach to 'loss of a chance' claims means that still no damages may be available.

(iii) Being a doctor is a well-paid and highly respected profession. Society is therefore entitled to expect high standards of those working in the field. The *Bolam* test does

---

[193] Peynser (1995).   [194] Simanowitz (1995); Lord Woolf (2001).
[195] Brazier and Miola (2000).   [196] Sheldon (1998); Montgomery (1989).

not reflect the justifiable expectations of the general public. The *Bolam* test is not used in respect of other professionals, such as solicitors.[197]

(iv) To be found negligent under the *Bolam* test is a serious indictment of a medical professional. Any expert giving evidence for the claimant is going to have to state not only that he or she would not have done as the defendant did, but also that none of his or her colleagues would have done so either. It is not surprising that, at one time, it was difficult to find expert witnesses who would give such evidence. Apparently, this has become less difficult,[198] although there are concerns that this is because of the increasing number of 'professional expert witnesses'.

Of course, *Bolam* has its supporters too. The following are some of the points that they might make.

8.2 Arguments in favour of the *Bolam* test

(i) If a judge is faced with two groups of expert medical opinion that disagree on the correct approach in dealing with a particular kind of case, it is impossible for the judge to choose between them. *Bolam* relieves the judge of such a task, because as long as the defendant was acting in line with a responsible body of medical opinion, he or she has a defence. This is preferable to a judge making an 'amateur' assessment of the two views.

(ii) The decision discourages excessive litigation. If we were to depart from the *Bolam* test, we would face an avalanche of litigation. It would be far too easy to bring a negligence claim if all that was required was to find a doctor who disagreed with the way in which a colleague dealt with a case. The potential extra costs to the NHS if it were even easier to sue than at present would lead to a negative impact on the resources available to the NHS.

(iii) *Bolam* enables innovative and exciting medical practice. Without it, all doctors, fearing litigation, will follow the officially approved line and will no longer be willing to try innovative medicine.[199] Under *Bolam*, if they can show that there were other respected colleagues who thought the innovative treatment worth trying, they will have no fear of a successful negligence claim.

(iv) The case of Wendy Savage could be used to support the *Bolam* test.[200] In that case, Dr Savage sought to develop a women-centred approach to gynaecology. In various ways, this was contrary to the traditional approach (which nowadays would be regarded as highly paternalistic). Complaints about her were unfounded; although her 'women-centred approach' was a minority view, it could be said to represent a responsible body of medical opinion.

8.3 Is there a litigation crisis?

There are certainly many who claim that the NHS is facing a litigation crisis. The NHS, it is suggested, is being crippled by the increasing cost of litigation. Something has to be

---

[197] *Edward Wong v Johnson Stokes and Master* [1984] AC 296.   [198] Brazier and Cave (2007: 197).
[199] Brazier and Miola (2000).   [200] Sheldon (1998).

done to stem the tide. But others feel that such claims are greatly exaggerated.[201] It is even suggested that the 'litigation crisis' is a myth relied upon by the medical profession to avoid proper legal scrutiny.[202]

Litigation against the NHS is handled by the NHS Resolution (formerly the NHS Litigation Authority). In 2016–17, the Authority received 10,686 claims of clinical negligence against NHS bodies. That is a fall from the figure of 11,945 in 2013/14, but a rise from 8,655 in 2010/11. Some £1,707 million was paid in connection with clinical negligence claims during 2016/17, an increase from £633 million in 2007–8 and from £432 million in 2003–4.[203]

Despite the alleged growth in litigation, it should not be forgotten that, as Margot Brazier has pointed out: 'Even today patients leaving NHS hospitals are more likely to return with a box of chocolates for the staff than with a claim form!'[204]

8.4 The impact of medical negligence litigation on doctors

There is evidence of the powerful negative impact on doctors of complaints.[205] Perhaps not surprisingly, studies have shown that doctors tend to regard complaints as challenges to their competence, rather than as revealing an issue that is troubling the complainant.[206] Thirty-eight per cent of doctors facing a medical negligence complaint are said to suffer clinical depression.[207] Fear of litigation and media vilification of doctors are cited as reasons for low job satisfaction among many doctors.[208] All NHS trusts have now joined the Clinical Negligence Scheme for Trusts, which is a pooling arrangement between NHS trusts designed to spread the cost of any especially large negligence awards.[209]

A separate point is that damages awarded against an NHS doctor will come out of the NHS budget, rather than the doctor's own pocket. This fact deters some from suing because well-minded individuals may not want to be seen to be taking money from the cash-strapped NHS. It also means that, as a means of publicly blaming the negligent professional, the legal system works poorly. The negligent doctor suffers no financial loss. A further point is that those cases that go to court and make the headlines tend to be those in which the negligence is more borderline. In cases of blatant negligence, the NHS is likely to settle. Indeed, in cases of the most serious negligence in which the patient is killed, the damages are likely to be much less than those in which the negligence may be less gross, but causes a permanent disability.

In a more general way, it has been said that the existence of negligence litigation harms the doctor–patient relationship. For example, if something has gone wrong with the patient's treatment, doctors may avoid explaining why the patient has suffered, or why or how an injury has occurred, for fear that anything that they say will lead to litigation if seen as an admission of blame. The Kennedy Report recommended that there should be a duty of candour to inform a patient if a harmful event had occurred.[210]

---

[201] Kennedy (1987).   [202] Simanowitz (1998).   [203] NHS Litigation Authority (2017).
[204] Brazier (2003b: 171).   [205] Kaplan and Hepworth (2004); Karen-Paz (2010).
[206] Allsop and Mulcahy (1998).   [207] Chief Medical Officer (2003: 43).
[208] Chief Medical Officer (2003: 44).
[209] Brazier and Cave (2007: 187). Members of the scheme must agree to comply with risk management procedures.
[210] Bristol Royal Infirmary Inquiry (2001: Recommendation 33).

Indeed, there is some old authority for the view that failure to inform a patient of an accident is negligent. In *Gerber v Pines*,[211] a doctor failed to tell a patient that the needle had broken off in the course of an injection. Although the fact that the needle broke was not the result of negligence, the failure of the doctor to tell the patient what had happened was held to be negligent.[212]

NHS Resolution has taken control of large claims and those that raise novel or contentious cases. One consequence of this might be that the organization is more concerned with dealing with the complaint in a cost-effective way than with 'clearing the name' of the doctor against whom a complaint has been made. Although settling a claim early may be efficient, for the doctor wrongly complained against, settlement can be regarded as an acknowledgement that he or she was at fault.

8.5 Defensive medicine

It is often claimed that the fear of malpractice litigation leads to defensive medicine.[213] Although this is a common complaint, it is not quite clear what 'defensive medicine' actually is. It is commonly taken to refer to treatments provided that are not needed, but which are undertaken by doctors to avoid any potential litigation, or treatments not offered for fear that they will give rise to a legal action.[214] The difficulty is in determining when this happens inappropriately. Fear of litigation can lead to some good practices: better record keeping; politeness in dealing with patients; clearer communication; and double checking. On the other hand, there is a concern that doctors are overcautious, ordering tests that are not necessary or asking for second opinions where that is inappropriate.[215] What cannot be known is whether changing practices are the result of a fear of litigation or of an improving safety culture. Research by Dingwall has shown that although the rise in rates of Caesarean section operations has been blamed on defensive medicine, similar rises have been found in countries with very little malpractice litigation.[216]

9 Learning lessons

One concern about the current approach to clinical negligence litigation is that the focus is so much on deciding who is to blame and whether there was negligence that the learning of lessons is forgotten. As Alan Merry argues:

> The fact that medical error often involves little or no moral culpability is an argument against a punitive legal response to it, but it is not an argument for tolerating medical errors or suggesting errors do not matter ... The fact that terrible harm has occurred to a patient may not, in itself, be a reason to punish someone, but it is, absolutely, a reason to take all reasonable steps to prevent such errors happening again. It is perverse in the extreme that few limits seem to be placed on the resources expended in the legal response to medical accidents once the courts are involved, but strict limits are applied to

---

[211] (1933) 79 SJ 13.
[212] There is *obiter* support for this, perhaps, in *Naylor v Preston* [1987] 2 All ER 353, 360.
[213] Jones and Morris (1989). Indeed, this led to the passing of the Compensation Act 2006.
[214] Kessler, Summerton, and Graham (2006).   [215] Kessler, Summerton, and Graham (2006).
[216] Dingwall (1995).

proactive investment into safety in health care. It is therefore critically important that the legal response to accidents in health care should promote safer practice.[217]

The NHS has sought to address this in a document entitled *An Organisation with a Memory*.[218] This report, in line with much current thinking on accident prevention, contends that steps can be taken to reduce the possibility of mistakes being made in the treatment that a patient receives.[219] Part of accident prevention is seeking to identify individuals, units, processes, or equipment whose performance is below that which the public is entitled to expect. Another part is to identify the circumstances and pressures that lead someone to make a mistake. This is based on the view that 'accidents' are more often caused by mistakes in the system than the fault of individuals.[220]

There is a concern that negligence-based compensation discourages openness.[221] A doctor who has made an error is likely to want to avoid the stigma of a finding of negligence and the harm that will result to his or her professional reputation. This may be particularly so where a junior employee has concerns about a more senior employee.[222] This secrecy is likely to mean that it is more difficult for claimants who should be entitled to damages to be awarded them. In response, Parliament created a legal duty of candour in Regulation 20 of the Health and Social Care Act 2008 (Regulated Activities) Regulations 2014.

Regulation 20 requires 'registered persons' to act 'in an open and transparent way' with patients. In particular if there is a 'notifiable safety incident' they must notify the patient and inform them of 'all the facts the registered person knows about the incident as at the date of the notification' and 'include an apology'. The patient must be informed as soon as possible after a notifiable safety incident has occurred. The NHS Standard Contract requires that to be within twenty working days. That notification must be given in person and explain to the best of the health service body's knowledge all the facts. It must advise what further enquiries are appropriate; issue an apology; and keep a written record. Regulation 20 defines a notifiable safety incident as including incidents that in the reasonable opinion of a health care professional could result in death, moderate harm, severe harm, or prolonged psychological harm. To be clear this means the regulations do not apply to a 'near miss' if that has not resulted in harm, or only a lower level of harm. As the primary purpose of disclosure is to prevent future harms it is surprising that the duty does not apply to the potential for harm, rather than the actual harm suffered.

10 The NHS Redress Act 2006

In the light of the complaints about the current system, it is not surprising that the government has sought reform. It has identified the following as the major flaws in the current system:[223]

(i)   the current system is perceived to be complex and slow;

---

[217] Merry (2009: 266).
[218] DoH (2000c). See DoH (2010d) and Care Quality Commission (2016) for developments in this project.
[219] Runciman, Merry, and McCall Smith (2001).
[220] IOM Committee (1999). For further discussion of this, see Quick (2006a).
[221] Bristol Royal Infirmary Report (2001).   [222] Burrows (2001).
[223] See Parliamentary and Health Services Ombudsman (2007); NHS Ombudsman (2005); Healthcare Commission (2004a).

(ii)   the current system is costly, both in terms of legal fees and diverting clinical staff from clinical care, and there is a negative effect on NHS staff morale and on public confidence;

(iii) patients are dissatisfied with the lack of explanations and apologies or reassurance that action has been taken to prevent the same incident happening to another patient; and

(iv)   the system encourages defensiveness and secrecy in the NHS, which stands in the way of learning and improvement in the health service.

Here, we will consider the option favoured by the government set out in the NHS Redress Act 2006.[224] We will later be considering a more radical option: a 'no fault' system.

The NHS Redress (Wales) Act 2011 has introduced the scheme to Wales. There is no clear sign when, if at all, it will be implemented in England. That is likely to depend on its perceived success in Wales. The NHS Redress Act 2006 deals particularly with claims valued at less than £20,000 and gives patients an alternative to litigation. The scheme will require the providers and commissioners of hospital services to put in place a 'consistent, speedy and appropriate response to clinical negligence'.[225] The scheme will be funded by the NHS Resolution, which will have responsibility for overseeing the financial compensation. All members of the scheme must report to the NHS Resolution cases that fall within the scheme, and the Authority will determine whether there is liability and the appropriate remedy, be that payment of compensation, an investigation, an apology, or remedial care. Interestingly, the government has indicated that it expects the scheme initially to attract higher costs because more patients will receive compensation. However, it believes that, over time, these costs will be offset by the saving in legal costs, because there will be fewer cases resorting to litigation. The government also argues that the scheme will attempt to move away from focusing on attributing blame and instead focus on preventing harm, reducing risks, and learning from mistakes. This will, in the long term, reduce the number of incidents and therefore the cost of claims for the NHS. The government has indicated that the annual cost of the scheme would be between £3.2 million and £11.2 million.[226]

One important point is that the government explains that the NHS redress scheme is meant to be additional to court procedures and not meant to replace them,[227] so a patient who is harmed in hospital can still use the court system, rather than the redress scheme. However, if an offer were to be accepted under the redress scheme, legal proceedings could not be brought in connection with the same incident. It may be only a matter of time before the redress scheme replaces the court procedure, at least in cases of smaller financial value. Indeed, it appears that the government expects that people who use the scheme will not need the assistance of a solicitor, although an applicant will be entitled to have an offer independently evaluated by a solicitor, without charge to the applicant. This will mean that, if successful, the scheme will provide redress for people who otherwise would not have been able to bring a legal action.[228]

It is hard to predict how well the scheme will work. There are certainly concerns that people who currently use the courts will continue to do so and that the scheme will attract only those who otherwise could not afford litigation. If this fear proves founded, it will certainly not be saving costs. A rather different concern is that the scheme will be

---

[224] The Act builds on Chief Medical Officer (2003).   [225] DoH (2005g: 12).
[226] House of Commons Constitutional Affairs Committee (2006).   [227] DoH (2005g: 3).
[228] See Farrell and Devaney (2007) for further discussion.

administered by the NHS Resolution and therefore may not appear impartial.[229] Brazier and Cave have also suggested that the scheme may do little more than 'formalise what already happens'.[230]

11 No fault

A more radical alternative is to move towards a 'no fault' scheme.[231] Imagine two patients left paralysed after an operation. In one case, it is shown that the paralysis was caused by a surgeon's negligence; in the other, there was no negligence and the patient was just unlucky—it was one of those rare cases in which paralysis just happens. Is it correct that one patient should receive substantial compensation and the other nothing? In other words, should compensation following injuries suffered in the course of medical treatment be due regardless of the question of whether there was negligence? The line between negligence and no negligence is difficult to draw. In many cases, to classify the case as negligent would be unfair to the doctor. But to classify the case as not negligent, and therefore attracting no compensation, also seems unfair.

This leads some to argue that we need a system in which compensation is paid to those who suffer as the result of mishaps during medical treatment, regardless of whether these are a result of negligence or not.[232] A patient who suffers an 'adverse event' while receiving medical care should receive compensation even if there was no negligence. This would mean that, for example, if the patient were one of the unlucky few to suffer an adverse reaction to a drug that was properly prescribed, compensation would be available, even if the doctor could not be blamed for prescribing it.

11.1 The 'no fault' scheme in New Zealand

Any country considering moving to a 'no fault' scheme for clinical negligence is likely to turn to New Zealand.[233] The scheme is administered by the Accident and Compensation Corporation (ACC). It is designed to compensate anyone who has suffered a personal injury as the result of an accident. The scheme is not designed to compensate for disease, infection, or ageing. In the clinical context, the Injury Prevention, Rehabilitation and Compensation Amendment Act (No. 2) 2005[234] permits compensation to be paid for 'treatment injury'.[235] This covers injuries caused by medical treatment where they are:

... not a necessary part, or ordinary consequence, of the treatment, taking into account all the circumstances of the treatment, including—

(i)   the person's underlying health condition at the time of the treatment; and

(ii) the clinical knowledge at the time of the treatment.[236]

[229] Brazier and Cave (2007: 236).   [230] Brazier and Cave (2007: 238).
[231] Note that the Vaccine Damage Payments Act 1979 creates a 'no fault' compensation scheme in respect of injuries caused by vaccinations performed by the NHS.
[232] See the discussion in Douglas (2008).
[233] 'No fault' schemes can also be found in Denmark, Finland, Sweden, and France.
[234] See Oliphant (2007) for a useful analysis of the law.
[235] This phrase replaced the term 'medical misadventure', which had been used under the previous legislation.
[236] Injury Prevention, Rehabilitation and Compensation Amendment Act (No. 2) 2005, s. 32.

This does not cover the normal consequences of a treatment (such as a scar left after surgery), but rather unexpected consequences of surgery. Notably, unlike English law, there is no need to show that the doctor behaved negligently. But the notion of 'treatment injury' is not as broad as might at first appear. Section 32(2) explains:

> (2) 'Treatment injury' does not include the following kinds of personal injury:
>
>> (a) personal injury that is wholly or substantially caused by a person's underlying health condition;
>>
>> (b) personal injury that is solely attributable to a resource allocation decision;
>>
>> (c) personal injury that is a result of a person unreasonably withholding or delaying their consent to undergo treatment.

Ken Oliphant states that the 2005 Act has simplified the scheme, meaning that more claims are made, fewer are rejected, and claims are dealt with more speedily.[237] Critics complain that the system fails to bring those medical professionals who have behaved badly to account. No distinction is drawn in the scheme between cases in which the professional behaved badly and those in which there was simply an unfortunate misadventure.[238] It is also noticeable that less than 3 per cent of those who could claim under the scheme do so.[239] The scheme is therefore affordable only because most entitled do not claim. It is of concern that there are particularly high rates of non-claiming among older people and those in low socio-economic groups.[240]

The New Zealand scheme records high rates of consumer satisfaction of 84 per cent.[241] The ACC not only works to compensate injuries, but also works to prevent accidents.

11.2 Arguments in favour of no fault

Many of the advantages of a 'no fault' scheme appear obvious. The proposal has the great attraction of simplicity: gone would be the difficulties in proving that a professional breached the duty of care; gone would be the feeling of animosity created by the adversarial nature of legal proceedings; and we could expect cases to be dealt with significantly more quickly. The following passage from the Bristol Inquiry Report sets out the case for moving away from clinical negligence and putting in its place a 'no fault' scheme:

> The system of clinical negligence litigation is now ripe for review … [W]e take the view that it will not be possible to achieve an environment of full, open reporting within the NHS when, outside it, there exists a litigation system the incentives of which press in the opposite direction. We believe that the way forward lies in the abolition of clinical negligence litigation, taking clinical error out of the courts and the tort system. It should be replaced by effective systems for identifying, analysing, learning from and preventing errors.[242]

---

[237] Oliphant (2007).

[238] Critical comments about the scheme can be found in Merry and McCall Smith (2001: 244).

[239] Bismark, Brennan, Davis, et al. (2006).

[240] Bismark, Brennan, Davis, et al. (2006).   [241] ACC (2004).

[242] Bristol Royal Infirmary Inquiry (2001: 4).

A further concern with the current system is that it may allocate blame unfairly.[243] Isolating the individual professional and considering whether he or she is to blame overlooks the institutional failures that are regarded by some experts on accidents to be more often the true cause.[244] As Merry and McCall Smith argue, '[e]ven removing the individual without correcting the system simply creates a situation where his or her replacement will be vulnerable to a recurrence of the same problem'.[245]

11.3 **Arguments against no fault**

The following are some of the main objections to a 'no fault' system.

- If the scheme is not going to compensate people simply because they are ill, it would need to draw a distinction between people who were ill and those who were suffering as a result of medical treatment going wrong in some sense. However, that would create disputes and complexity. Whether a particular harm is a natural progression of the illness, a justifiable side effect of successful treatment, or a result of a mishap may be contested. Indeed, in many cases, it may bring back to the fore the question of whether or not the doctor was at fault. The claim that a 'no fault' system is easier and cheaper may therefore prove to be unfounded.

- A 'no fault' system would be extremely expensive. The Chief Medical Officer estimated that:

  ... even with a 25 per cent reduction in the current level of compensation the cost of a true no-fault compensation scheme would vary between £1.6 billion per year ... to almost £28 billion ... This compares with £400 million spent on clinical negligence in 2000–01.[246]

- There is a concern that a 'no fault' scheme will lead to less accountability. If one of the aims of tort law is to identify wrongdoers, then a 'no fault' scheme would lose that. Should the NHS be held liable in respect of a loss even if it was not preventable?[247] Do we not need to hold medical professionals accountable for their bad behaviour and create a deterrent against negligence?

11.4 **'No compensation' scheme**

Most of the discussion surrounding the present law has concerned debates over whether we should move towards a 'no fault' system of compensation. But there is an argument for moving in a different direction and moving towards abolishing compensation payments. Imagine that a patient is harmed as a result of negligent treatment by a doctor. Certainly that patient should receive treatment for his or her current condition—but should he or she receive money from NHS funds? Might not that money be better spent treating another patient in a worse medical condition than the claimant? Is it right that money needed to develop treatment for life-saving illnesses should be taken from NHS

---

[243] Merry and McCall Smith (2001: ch. 1).   [244] Merry and McCall Smith (2001: 11).
[245] Merry and McCall Smith (2001: 15).   [246] Chief Medical Officer (2003: 112).
[247] Towse, Fenn, Grey, et al. (2004).

funds and given to one person to make up for his or her 'pain and suffering' as a result of a botched operation? John Harris, for one, thinks not necessarily.[248] At the very least, he proposes a cap on the level of damages that may be awarded, because otherwise a single person can receive a larger portion of NHS funds than other equally needy and deserving patients. He suggests that payment of compensation should be made only where there is no more urgent call on those NHS resources. One might think that that will rarely, if ever, be the case.

12 Matters other than compensation

NHS Resolution has emphasized the importance of candour, empathy, and being willing to make an apology. As they say, this can avoid claims being made. In that spirit it has set up a new mediation pilot project. They suggest this 'provides injured patients and their families with an opportunity for face-to-face explanations and apologies when things go wrong'.[249] It is too early to know how successful this will be.

In *Making Amends*, the Chief Medical Officer points out that, too often, issues of apology are lost in the heat of the litigation battle:

> Legal proceedings for medical injury frequently progress in an atmosphere of confrontation, acrimony, misunderstanding and bitterness. The emphasis is on revealing as little as possible about what went wrong, defining clinical decisions that were taken and only reluctantly releasing information. In the past, cases have taken too long to settle. In smaller value claims the legal costs have been disproportionate to the damages awarded. In larger value claims there can be lengthy and expensive disputes about the component parts of any lump sum payment and the anticipated life span of the victim.[250]

The NHS has undertaken a major review of the way in which it deals with complaints. The Parliamentary and Health Service Ombudsman's review of NHS complaints handling, published in 2010, concluded that there was 'inadequate information about how to complain or a loss of confidence in NHS complaint procedures'.[251] To be fair, this report was prepared before the new complaints system had become fully operational. Now, each trust is meant to have a Patient Advice and Liaison Service (PALS), which can listen to patients' concerns and offer information, advice, and support. It can refer people to the Independent Complaints Advocacy Service (ICAS), which assists people with the complaints system.

The NHS complaints system is now covered by the Local Authority Social Services and National Health Service Complaints (England) Regulations 2009.[252] Under the Regulations, the patient can complain to the provider or to the commissioning body (normally the PCT). NHS bodies are to have a complaints manager, who will handle the complaint. The complaint must be made within a year of the incident or when the patient becomes aware of the incident. The NHS body must investigate 'in a manner appropriate to resolve it speedily and efficiently'.[253] Within six months of the receipt of the complaint, a written response must be provided, giving an explanation of how the complaint has arisen, the conclusions reached about it, and any remedial action.[254]

---

[248] Harris (1997).   [249] NHS Resolution (2017).   [250] Chief Medical Officer (2003: 7).
[251] Parliamentary and Health Service Ombudsman (2010: 65).   [252] SI 2009/309.
[253] Regulation 14.   [254] Regulation 14.

Complaints can also be made to the Ombudsman. She acts independently from government and reports on complaints. She can deal only with complaints made within a year, unless there is good reason to consider a late complaint. Only complaints that involve 'injustice or hardship' owing to a 'failure in the service' of an NHS body or maladministration can be considered.[255] Also, she can investigate complaints only when the NHS complaints procedure has been exhausted. This means that matters such as rudeness of staff or poor food are unlikely to be considered by the Ombudsman. In considering cases of complaints about a clinical judgement, the *Bolam* test will be applied.[256] This is significant because the Ombudsman should not investigate if the patient has a remedy in the courts, unless it is not reasonable to expect the patient to pursue it. Indeed, patients are required to agree not to sue if their complaint is investigated. That said, if a patient has taken a complaint to the Ombudsman, there is nothing to stop a patient then taking the matter to the courts. The Ombudsman can, at most, order an ex gratia payment of out-of-pocket expenses. Her powers are therefore likely to be used only by patients who are more interested in having the wrong done to them recognized and learned from, rather than those interested in compensation. The Ombudsman accepted 31,444 complaints in 2016–17.[257] Most led to the Ombudsman giving advice on alternative routes through which to pursue the complaint. In only 3,767 cases was a full enquiry undertaken and report produced. In 36 per cent of investigations the complaint was wholly or partially upheld and in 52 per cent of cases the complaint was not upheld.[258] As a result there were: 1,270 apologies; 801 compensation payments; 879 recommendations for management action; and 346 other actions to put things right.

13 Professional regulation

A medical professional who has misbehaved may face disciplinary proceedings at the hands of their professional body. The best known is the General Medical Council (GMC) which deals with complaints about doctors, although there are a wide range of bodies governing different health care professionals. Here we will focus on the GMC, although similar issues are raised with different bodies. For a doctor to practise medicine in the NHS they must be registered with the GMC.[259]

The GMC organizes fitness to practise panels (also called medical practitioner tribunals). Their primary role is to investigate complaints of wrong-doing to see if as a result a doctor should be barred from practice, undertake training, face restrictions on how they practise, or other responses. An important difference from civil proceedings is that the panel is less concerned with whether the malpractice of the doctor caused the patient harm, but whether their malpractice indicates they are not fit to practise as a doctor. It is, therefore, perfectly possible for a civil claim to fail, but the GMC to intervene to strike a doctor off. Further, there is no need for the panel to be persuaded a doctor acted illegally before upholding a complaint. A doctor who is rude to patients may not be behaving contrary to the law, but the panel may still want to uphold a complaint.

---

[255] Health Service Commissioners Act 1993, s. 3.
[256] *R (Atwood) v Health Service Commissioner* [2008] EWHC 2315.
[257] Parliamentary and Health Service Ombudsman (2017).
[258] In 12 per cent of cases the investigation was stopped due to resolution or other reasons.
[259] Medical Act 1983.

Their procedures have recently been changed following growing concerns that they were not effective in protecting the public.[260] These have led to extensive reforms, including in particular that the civil standard of proof is used, rather than the criminal standard.[261]

It is notable that there has been an increase in the number of complaints made to the GMC from 1,503 in 1995 to 9,642 in 2014, an increase of some 640 per cent.[262] Remarkably, in 2014, 4 per cent of all doctors on the register had been complained about. Seventy-five per cent of complaints are not taken forward by the GMC, indicating that alternative ways of resolving complaints do not seem to be successful at responding to concerns by patients and perhaps a degree of confusion among the public as to whom complaints should be addressed. It should be noted that 26 per cent of doctors reported to the GMC have moderate to severe depression, although it cannot be assumed that necessarily results from the complaints.[263]

14 Conclusion

This chapter has considered the legal consequences that can flow when a patient suffers harm in the course of medical treatment. There is widespread dissatisfaction with the current approach, because it appears to be a cumbersome and costly process—costly in both financial and emotional terms for all involved. There are tragic cases in which compensation is not recoverable, despite the extensive burden on the claimant and his or her family.[264] However, there are difficulties with the alternatives. Finding a system that holds people who have behaved wrongly responsible for their actions, but which also encourages openness and drives the NHS to learn from past mistakes has so far proved elusive. Perhaps it is an impossibility?

QUESTIONS

1. Should it be assumed that the increasing level of litigation is bad for the NHS? Could it not be that this will lead to increasing safety standards and a lower number of mishaps?

2. Should we take a positive view of mistakes? Merry and McCall Smith argue: 'The inevitability of human error should be seen not so much as evidence of a primary human weakness, but rather as an inevitable concomitant of our impressive cognitive ability and evolutionary success.'[265]

3. Is there a problem with labelling a professional 'negligent' on the basis of a single incident and not considering the individual's whole career?

4. Studies have suggested that overwork and lack of sleep are a major cause of errors in the NHS.[266] Would we rather medical professionals worked less and saw fewer

[260] Smith (2005).   [261] Health and Social Care Act 2008.   [262] Chamberlain (2017).
[263] Chamberlain (2017). See Law Commission (2015) for further proposals for reform.
[264] *Evans v Birmingham and The Black Country Strategic Health Authority* [2007] EWCA Civ 1300.
[265] Merry and McCall Smith (2001: 71).   [266] Merry and McCall Smith (2001: 115).

patients, leading to longer delays, but made fewer mistakes? Or should we require surgeons to take medical enhancers to improve their performance? Would it be negligent for medical professionals not to take substances which could enhance their performance?[267]

5. The Healthcare Commission tells us that 6 per cent of admissions to NHS hospitals result from adverse drug reactions.[268] Do we too readily accept that drugs are the solutions to medical problems? Should a drug known to have such an adverse reaction that it requires treatment in a hospital ever be authorized?

6. Consider whether a 'no fault' scheme would, in the long term, be beneficial for (a) those injured in the course of receiving medical treatment, and (b) medical professionals.

7. What do you think of the proposal that there should be routine video recording of risky medical procedures?[269] It might ease the difficulties of proof, but might it raise other ethical concerns?

FURTHER READING

A comprehensive bibliography, including all references used throughout the book, is available online at www.oup.com/uk/herringmedical7e/.

Ahuja, J. (2015) 'Liability for psychological and psychiatric harm: the road to recovery', *Medical Law Review* 23: 27.

Brazier, M. and Miola, J. (2000) 'Bye-bye *Bolam*: a medical litigation revolution', *Medical Law Review* 8: 85.

Cane, P. (2006) *Atiyah's Accidents, Compensation and the Law* (Butterworths).

Chamberlain, J. (2017) 'Malpractice, Criminality, and Medical Regulation: Reforming the Role of the GMC in Fitness to Practise Panels', *Medical Law Review* 25: 1.

Douglas, T. (2009) 'Medical compensation: beyond "no fault" ', *Medical Law Review* 17: 30.

Green, S. (2006) 'Coherence of medical negligence cases: a game of doctors and purses', *Medical Law Review* 14: 1.

Herring, J. (2017) 'The Health Law, Ethics and Patient Safety Interface' in J. Tingle *New Directions in Patient Safety Law and Practice* (Routledge).

Jackson, E. (2012) *Law and the Regulation of Medicines* (Hart).

Karen-Paz, T. (2010) 'Liability regimes, reputation loss, and defensive medicine', *Medical Law Review* 18: 363.

Khoury, L. (2006) *Uncertain Causation in Medical Liability* (Hart).

Merry, A. and McCall Smith, A. (2001) *Errors, Medicare and the Law* (Cambridge University Press).

---

[267] See Goold and Maslen (2015a and b) for a discussion.
[268] Healthcare Commission (2005).
[269] Discussed in Gilbart, Barfield, and Watkins (2009).

Miola, J. (2007) *Medical Ethics and Medical Law* (Hart), Ch. 4.

Mulcahy, L. (2015) 'The market for precedent: shifting visions of the role of clinical negligence claims and trials', *Medical Law Review* 22: 274.

Mulheron, R. (2010) *Medical Negligence: Non-Patient and Third Party Claim* (Ashgate).

Mulheron, R. (2010) 'Trumping *Bolam*: a critical legal analysis of *Bolitho*'s "gloss" ', *Cambridge Law Journal* 69: 609.

Quick, O. (2010) 'Medicine, mistakes and manslaughter: a criminal combination', *Cambridge Law Journal* 69: 186.

Samanta, A.Mello, M., Foster, C., et al. (2006) 'The role of clinical guidelines in medical negligence litigation: a shift from the *Bolam* standard?', *Medical Law Review* 14: 321.

Lord Woolf (2001) 'Are the courts excessively deferential to the medical profession?', *Medical Law Review* 9: 1.

4 | **Consent to Treatment**

INTRODUCTION

It is a fundamental principle of medical law and ethics that, before treating a competent patient, a medical professional should get the patient's consent.[1] Gone are the days when a 'Trust me, I'm a doctor' approach justified imposing treatment on a patient. Now, it is the patient, rather than the doctor, who has the final say on whether a proposed treatment can go ahead. As Peter Jackson J in *Heart of England NHS Trust v JB* stated:[2]

> anyone capable of making decisions has an absolute right to accept or refuse medical treatment, regardless of the wisdom or consequences of the decision. The decision does not have to be justified to anyone. In the absence of consent any invasion of the body will be a criminal assault. The fact that the intervention is well-meaning or therapeutic makes no difference.

This 'principle of autonomy' involves complex issues: what does 'consent' mean? Does the consent need to be 'informed'? Are there any circumstances in which it is permissible to treat patients without their consent? Of course, consent is not only a legal requirement; in many cases, it will also be a clinical one. Forcing a treatment on an unwilling patient is likely to be counter-productive.

Consent is required, even if there is strong evidence that the procedure is in the best interests of the patient.[3] This point was dramatically made in *St George's Healthcare NHS Trust v S*,[4] in which a woman in labour was told that she needed a Caesarean section and that, without such an operation, she and the foetus she was carrying would die. Despite her refusal to consent, the operation was carried out. The Court of Appeal held this to be unlawful. Great weight was placed on the importance of the right to bodily integrity. Not even the fact that she and the foetus would die without the operation provided a good enough reason to justify carrying out the Caesarean without her consent.[5] Despite these points, as we shall see, many academics have criticized the law for prioritizing the wish to protect healthcare professionals from legal actions over protecting the right of patients not to be given treatment to which they have not consented.[6]

---

[1] See, e.g., the extensive discussion in *Re B (Consent to Treatment: Capacity)* [2002] EWHC 429, [2002] 1 FLR 1090.

[2] [2014] EWHC 342 (COP).

[3] *Williamson v East London and City Health Authority* (1998) 41 BMLR 85.

[4] [1998] 3 All ER 673.

[5] See also *R (Jenkins) v HM Coroner for Portsmouth* [2009] EWHC 3229 (Admin), in which it was held that friends of the deceased were not under a duty to summon help when he was ill because he had made it clear that he did not want medical assistance.

[6] Montgomery (1988); Harrington (1996).

Although the law takes seriously the right to be able to refuse treatment, it does not follow that if a patient wishes to receive treatment, he or she must be given it.[7] As the Court of Appeal put it in *R (Burke) v GMC*:[8]

Autonomy and the right of self-determination do not entitle the patient to insist on receiving a particular medical treatment regardless of the nature of the treatment.

This chapter will start by considering the legal consequences of treating a patient without consent and will consider the meaning of 'consent'. It will then look at the position of patients who lack the capacity to consent.

1 The consequences of treatment without consent

The basic starting point is that a healthcare professional who intentionally or recklessly touches a patient without his or her consent is committing a crime (a battery) and a tort (trespass to the person and/or negligence).[9] To be acting lawfully in touching a patient, the professional needs a defence—or what the Court of Appeal has called a legal 'flak jacket'.[10] There are three such flak jackets available:

- the consent of the patient;
- the consent of another person who is authorized to consent on the patient's behalf (for example, the consent of a parent for treatment of a child); and
- a specific defence in common law or statute.

We will be looking at the meaning of these and when they can be relied upon later in this chapter.[11]

2 Criminal law and the non-consenting patient

Technically, a medical professional who intentionally or recklessly touches a patient without consent could be charged with the criminal offence of battery. However, that is very rare, and only occurs where the professional was acting maliciously; for example, where the act involved a sexual assault.[12] Technically under criminal law anything that causes a patient actual bodily harm is a criminal offence, even if the 'victim' consents, unless it can be shown that the act falls into one of the exceptional circumstances in which consent can provide a defence. One of those, according to the infamous decision in *R v Brown*,[13] is that there is 'proper medical treatment'. This means that a doctor can undertake standard medical procedures if they have the consent of the patient without fear of prosecution. More debatable would be a case where a doctor was doing something that was not standard medical treatment (e.g., cutting off part of a person's body

---

[7] Herring and Wall (2017); *AVS v NHS Foundation Trust* [2011] EWCA 7.
[8] [2005] 3 FCR 169, [31].
[9] *Sidaway v Bethlem Royal Hospital Governors* [1985] 1 All ER 643.
[10] *Re W* [1992] 4 All ER 627, 633. For a helpful discussion, see Maclean (2008b).
[11] For two excellent discussions on the law on consent, see Maclean (2009) and McLean (2009).
[12] *R v Healy* [2003] 2 Cr App R (S) 87. See further Ost (2016).   [13] [1994] AC 212.

with their consent for fun).[14] It might even be open to question whether something like cosmetic surgery is 'treatment'.[15]

In *Potts v North West Regional Health Authority*,[16] a woman consented to the giving of what was described as a routine postnatal vaccination. In fact, it was a long-acting contraceptive. There was no difficulty in deciding that the treatment was not consented to and so amounted to a battery. Less straightforward was *R v Tabaussum*,[17] in which it was said that a deception either as to the nature or quality of the act could negate consent. In that case, women agreed to breast examinations on the understanding that they were being performed for educational purposes, whereas, in fact, they were being carried out for the defendant's own purposes (presumably sexual). Although the nature of the touching (that is, where he touched her) was consented to by the defendant, the quality of the acts was different. Touching motivated by sexual purposes has a different quality from touching for non-sexual purposes. The defendant was therefore convicted of criminal offences of battery.

A deception as to the identity of the person providing the treatment can negate the apparent consent, but a deception as to the qualities of the person does not. The distinction was revealed in the case of *R v Richardson*,[18] in which Diane Richardson had been removed from the list of the dental register, but continued to provide treatment to the patients. The patients had not been deceived either as to the nature of the treatment or as to the identity of the person (she was the very same Diane Richardson who they thought she was). Their mistake was as to one of her attributes, not her identity. However, the case has been criticized on the basis that a person receiving medical treatment may be far more concerned about whether or not the individual is medically qualified, than whether it is Dr X or Dr Y.[19]

A SHOCK TO THE SYSTEM

In August 2017, the Court of Appeal heard a case of a doctor who had performed completely unnecessary operations on patients after telling them they had cancer.[20] Hallett LJ stated:

> How any doctor, let alone one who had earned an enviable reputation, could have engaged in this level of offending we will never know. Greed, self-aggrandisement, power—however, they do not come close to explaining how a doctor can falsely tell a patient he or she has cancer when they have not, with all that such a diagnosis entails for a patient and members of their family. Nor how a doctor can then insist that he or she undergo unnecessary operations, including mastectomies, with all the physical and psychological pain such operations cause. Patients trusted him implicitly. They could never have imagined that he would put them through the agony of a diagnosis of cancer and mutilation of their breasts when there was no justification for it.

It has been suggested that hundreds of patients could have been subjected to unnecessary operations at his hands.

---

[14] Fovargue and Mullock (2016).   [15] Griffiths and Mullock (2016).
[16] *The Guardian*, 23 July 1983.   [17] [2000] Lloyd's Rep Med 404.   [18] (1998) 43 BMLR 21.
[19] Herring (2005).   [20] Bowcott (2017).

3 The law of tort and the non-consenting patient

Far more likely is litigation in the law of tort. The proceedings could be brought under the tort of battery or the tort of negligence. It appears from the reported cases that negligence is used by far the most often.[21] Indeed, it has been suggested that the tort of battery should play only a very limited role in these cases.[22] In *Border v Lewisham and Greenwich NHS Trust*[23] a doctor inserted an IV tube against the wishes of the patient. This was dealt with as a negligence case, although it could have been seen as a battery case.

Alasdair Maclean suggests two reasons for the preference for negligence.[24] First, the tort of battery has strong overtones of a criminal offence. Where it has been found that the tort of battery has been committed, it is very likely that a crime has been too. Second, the use of negligence gives the judges greater control over the scope of the tortious liability because, through the *Bolam* test, they can determine whether or not the doctor was acting reasonably. Under the tort of battery, if the patient was not consenting, liability arises even though the doctor may have been acting responsibly.

There are some important legal differences between the tort of battery and the tort of negligence. These include the following.

(i)   Negligence focuses on the question of whether the medical professional acted in accordance with an accepted body of medical opinion, whereas battery focuses on the question of whether the patient consented. So, in a case in which a patient agreed to an operation after being given only very limited information about it, if the case were considered under battery, the key issue would be 'Did the patient consent in broad terms to the nature of the procedure, given his or her limited understanding of what was entailed?',[25] whereas under negligence, it would be 'Was the information provided by the professional the amount of information considered appropriate by a respectable body of medical opinion?' It would also need to be shown that if the correct information had been given, the patient would not have gone ahead with that operation.[26] As can be seen, the battery approach is more focused on the protection of the patient's rights to make decisions about his or her treatment, while the negligence approach is focused on ensuring that doctors follow an established body of medical opinion.

(ii) To succeed in a claim of negligence, it must be shown that the patient suffered some harm. Therefore, if a doctor operates on a patient without his or her consent and can show that the operation benefited the patient, then only nominal damages will be awarded if the claim is brought in negligence. By contrast, in a case of battery, there is no need to show that a patient suffered loss because the battery will be in itself a legal wrong. But even then the damages may be very low. In *Ms B v An NHS Trust*,[27] in which a woman was given life-supporting treatment against her wishes, only £100 was awarded for the battery.

(iii) It will be a defence to a negligence claim based on non-disclosure of information to show that, had the doctor fully informed the patient, the patient would have

---

[21] For example, *Chatterton v Gerson* [1981] 1 All ER 257; *Freeman v Home Office* [1984] 1 All ER 1036; *Sidaway v Bethlem Royal Hospital Governors* [1985] 1 All ER 643; *Williamson v East London and City Health Authority* (1998) 41 BMLR 85; *Blyth v Bloomsbury Area Health Authority* [1993] 4 Med LR 151.
[22] The case law is discussed in Feng (1987) and Brazier (1987).   [23] [2015] EWCA Civ 8.
[24] Maclean (2009: 192).   [25] *Chatterton v Gerson* [1981] 1 All ER 257.
[26] *Chester v Afshar* [2004] UKHL 41.   [27] [2002] 2 FCR 1.

consented to the operation that he or she received. This is because it could not be shown that the negligence (the failure to inform the patient properly about the operation) caused any harm. This would not provide a defence in a battery claim if it were to be established that the victim had not consented.

(iv) Punitive damages can be awarded in a battery case, but not in a negligence case.[28] If punitive damages are awarded, the professional will not only have to pay for the losses suffered by the claimant, but a judge can also award a further sum by way of punishment of the defendant.

(v) In a battery case, all of the loss flowing from the operation performed without consent can be recovered in a damages award, but in a negligence case, only the foreseeable losses can be claimed.

(vi) A battery is committed only if there is a touching. So giving a patient a pill to take might not amount to a battery, but it could involve negligence.

(vii) Contributory negligence is not a defence to a battery, although it is to a claim for negligence.[29]

4 Who must provide the consent?

To answer this question, it is necessary to distinguish cases of adults with capacity, adults lacking capacity, children with capacity, and children lacking capacity.

4.1 Adults with capacity

Where the patient is a competent adult, only that person can consent. There is no doctrine of consent by proxy in English medical law. So, for example, it is not possible for a wife to consent on behalf of her husband—although it may well be possible for a man to say: 'I am willing to let my wife decide whether I should have the surgery.' In that case, he has given consent via his wife. More commonly, a patient may say: 'Doctor, you give me whatever treatment you think is best.' That form of delegated consent is presumably permissible, although there is little legal authority on it.[30] It is now accepted that a competent patient can provide an advance directive—that is, a document (normally) that sets out to what treatment a patient would or would not consent in the event that he or she lacks capacity.[31] Jehovah's Witnesses might, for example, want to sign an advance directive stating that if they are brought into a hospital unconscious, they do not wish to receive blood transfusions, even if that is necessary to save their lives.

4.2 Adults lacking capacity

If a patient lacks mental capacity, then he or she can be provided with treatment that is in his or her best interests under the Mental Capacity Act (MCA) 2005. If a woman

[28] *Appleton v Garrett* (1997) 34 BMLR 23.
[29] *Co-Operative Group v Pritchard* [2011] EWCA Civ 329.
[30] For an argument that such delegated consent should be sufficient, see Herring and Foster (2011).
[31] *R (Burke) v GMC* [2004] EWHC (Admin) 1879, [44].

collapses unconscious after a stroke, her husband cannot consent to treatment on her behalf. However, that is not a problem, because the medical professionals can provide the treatment under the MCA 2005, if that is in her best interests. Of course, the medical professionals will often want to discuss a person's medical treatment with relatives, but at the end of the day it is the medical team that decides what medical treatment is appropriate. A relative who is unhappy with the way in which a patient is being cared for can seek a court declaration as to the legality of the treatment.

There are ways in which someone, fearing that they are about to lose capacity, can arrange for a friend or relative to have decision-making power for them. The MCA 2005 enables a competent adult (P) to create a lasting power of attorney (LPA), which enables its donee (that is, the person appointed to act under the LPA) to make decisions on P's behalf when P loses capacity.[32] The 2005 Act also enables the court to appoint a deputy to make certain decisions on behalf of a person who has lost capacity.[33] Perhaps most significantly, the Act allows competent people to create advance decisions rejecting treatment in the event that they lose capacity.[34] If the patient then loses capacity, the advance decision must be respected. We shall be discussing these provisions of the MCA 2005 in much more detail later in this chapter.

4.3 Children lacking capacity

The MCA 2005 does not apply to children.[35] If a child lacks capacity to consent, then consent for treatment can be provided by anyone with parental responsibility for the child. All mothers have parental responsibility for their children, but not all fathers. Fathers who are married to the mother or are registered on the child's birth certificate do, but otherwise a father will need to enter into a parental responsibility agreement with the child's mother, or apply to the court for a parental responsibility order or residence order. It is also possible for someone who is not a parent to acquire parental responsibility if he or she is granted a child arrangements order that the child live with them.[36] If those with parental responsibility do not consent to the medical procedure, a doctor may still be authorized to treat the child by an order of the court or, in an emergency, under the doctrine of necessity.[37] If the issue comes to court, it will make an order based on what will promote the welfare of the child. The wishes of a parent will be taken into account,[38] but ultimately it will be the best interests of the child that will determine the outcome.[39]

4.4 Children with capacity

If a child is mature enough to be able to consent, then he or she can provide effective consent to treatment. We will examine later how the court decides whether a child has sufficient maturity. It should also be noted that simply because the child is sufficiently mature to consent, this does not mean that those with parental responsibility cannot make

---

[32] MCA 2005, s. 9.   [33] MCA 2005, s. 19.   [34] MCA 2005, s. 24.
[35] *B Local Authority v RM* [2010] EWHC 3802 (Fam).
[36] Children Act 1989, s. 4. The law is discussed in detail in Herring (2017d: ch. 5).
[37] *Glass v UK* [2004] 1 FCR 553.
[38] Even where they lack capacity: *An NHS Trust v Mrs H* [2012] EWHC B18.
[39] *An NHS Trust v Child B* [2014] EWHC 3486 (Fam).

decisions for the child. As we shall see, a doctor can treat a child with capacity who is objecting if the doctor has the consent of someone with parental responsibility for the child.

5 What is consent?

In order for there to be an effective consent to treatment, it is not enough simply to show that the patient said the word 'yes'; there must be a genuine agreement to receive the treatment.[40] To show a patient consented to treatment the following must be shown:

(i) the patient had capacity to consent to the treatment;

(ii) the patient exercised their capacity to consent to the treatment.

We will explore these themes in more detail.

6 The capacity test

6.1 The presumption in favour of capacity

A patient must have capacity in order to be able to provide legally effective consent.[41] The MCA 2005, section 1(2), makes it clear that a medical professional should presume that a patient has capacity unless there is evidence that he or she does not.[42] If the case comes to court, the burden is on the doctor to demonstrate that the patient lacks capacity on the balance of probabilities.[43] Understandably, when the court is determining whether a patient has capacity, the views of the medical experts carry 'very considerable importance'.[44] But, ultimately, it is for the court not the doctors to determine the issue. Difficulties can arise if a patient refuses to participate in an assessment of capacity. In such a case that refusal could itself be seen as evidence of a lack of capacity, although it may be insufficient on its own.[45]

6.2 The general test of capacity

The general test for capacity is set out in section 2(1) of the MCA 2005:

> [A] person lacks capacity in relation to a matter if at the material time he is unable to make a decision for himself in relation to the matter because of an impairment of, or a disturbance in the functioning of, the mind or brain.

Section 3(1) explains what is meant by a person being unable to make a decision for themselves:

> [A] person is unable to make a decision for himself if he is unable—
>
> (a) to understand the information relevant to the decision,

---

[40] It is generally accepted that what counts as consent for the purposes of the law does not necessarily reflect how consent would be understood by philosophers and others. For further discussion, see Epstein (2006).

[41] Donnelly (2009b), Gunn (1994), and Devereux (2006) provide a useful discussion of the meaning of incapacity.

[42] *R v Sullivan* [1984] AC 156, 170–1. See Herring (2016a) for further discussion.

[43] *Wandsworth CGC v IA* [2014] EWHC 990 (COP).

[44] *A NHS Trust v Dr A* [2013] EWHC 2442 (COP).   [45] *W NHS Trust v P* [2014] EWHC 119 (COP).

(b) to retain that information,

(c) to use or weigh that information as part of the process of making the decision, or

(d) to communicate his decision (whether by talking, using sign language or any other means).

As this indicates, there are a number of ways in which a person may be said to be unable to make a decision. They can range from not understanding a key piece of information to not being able to weigh up the different factors. Before exploring that further it is worth emphasizing that the courts take a 'generous' approach to capacity.

6.3 The 'generous' approach to capacity

Baker J warned against taking too strict an approach to capacity in *PH and A Local Authority v Z Limited & R*:[46]

> [the] courts must guard against imposing too high a test of capacity to decide issues such as residence because to do so would run the risk of discriminating against persons suffering from a mental disability.

Although this is problematic. As Jesse Wall and I have written:

> It is a terrible thing to be assessed as lacking capacity when you do not—to have others make decisions on your behalf and set aside your own wishes based on what they think is in your best interests. You lose control over your life. You are no longer in charge of your destiny.
>
> It is a terrible thing to be said to have capacity when you do not—to be left to cause yourself and those you love great harm on the basis that you know what you are doing and you are making your own choices, when in fact your decisions are not really yours. To have others harm you and to be told no protection is offered because you have chosen this harm, even though it is against your deepest values, is horrific.

As we argue, it is not obvious that the wrong done to a person who is incorrectly assessed as not having capacity is worse than the wrong to a person who is incorrectly assessed as having capacity. That is especially so when what is proposed is medical treatment.[47]

6.4 Who has the burden of proving consent?

If a criminal charge is brought, the prosecution will need to prove beyond reasonable doubt that the victim did not consent. Remarkably, the legal position on who has the burden of proving consent in civil proceedings is unclear. The limited judicial discussion to date suggests that consent is a defence that a medical professional may raise to what will otherwise be a tort, and that therefore it is for the medical professional to prove that there was consent.[48] Certainly, a medical professional is well advised to have evidence of consent before embarking on risky or controversial treatment.

---

[46] [2011] EWHC 1704 (Fam) at para. 16 (xi).

[47] See Herring (2017e) for an argument that there is a contrast been consent to sex and consent to medical treatment, where the thing proposed is objectively beneficial in the case of medical treatment, but not sex.

[48] *R (N) v Dr M, A Health Authority Trust* [2002] EWHC 1911.

6.5 Issue-specific capacity

Capacity under the MCA 2005 is assessed in an 'issue specific' way. So the question is always whether a person has capacity to decide a particular question. Someone may have the capacity to decide some issues, but not others. A patient may be found to have sufficient understanding to be able to consent to a minor, straightforward course of medical treatment, but not have sufficient understanding to be able to consent to a far more complex procedure.[49] In *A NHS Trust v X*,[50] X was found to lack capacity to make decisions about treatment for her anorexia nervosa, but to have capacity to make decisions about drinking alcohol. So, a person should not be dismissed as 'simply incompetent'. Except in the most extreme cases, there are likely to be at least some issues that someone is able to decide for themselves.

6.6 The diagnostic test and the functional test

As was explained in *A Local Authority v TZ*,[51] the test of capacity in section 2(1) MCA 2005 involves a 'diagnostic test' and a 'functional test'. Under the diagnostic test, it must be found that a person has impairment or a disturbance in the functioning of the brain. The MCA 2005 Code of Practice lists the following as examples of conditions that might involve an impairment or disturbance of the functioning of the brain:

- conditions associated with some forms of mental illness;
- dementia;
- significant learning disabilities;
- the long-term effects of brain damage;
- physical or medical conditions that cause confusion, drowsiness or loss of consciousness;
- delirium;
- concussion following a head injury; and
- the symptoms of alcohol or drug use.[52]

Under the 'functional test', it must be determined whether, as a result of the disturbance, a person must be unable to make the decision. Importantly, it must be shown that the inability to make the decision results from the impairment.[53] So, patients with no mental impairment who refuse all treatment because of their religious belief that God will cure them will not lack capacity, even if the doctors try to argue that the patients do not properly understand the reality of their situation. They do not have a mental impairment and so cannot lack capacity to make a decision. Peter Bartlett has made a powerful case that this breaches the United Nations Convention on the Rights of Persons with Disabilities.[54] Article 12(2) of the Convention provides that people with disabilities may

---

[49] A point emphasized in *Re W* [2002] EWHC 901 and *Gillick v West Norfolk and Wisbech Area Health Authority* [1986] AC 112, 169 and 186.
[50] [2014] EWCOP 35. See Wang (2015) for a discussion.
[51] [2013] EWHC 2322 (COP). See also *PC v City of York Council* [2013] EWCA Civ 478.
[52] Department for Constitutional Affairs (DCA) (2007: para. 4.12).
[53] *An NHS Trust v CS* [2016] EWCOP 10; *Wandsworth CGC v IA* [2014] EWHC 990 (COP).
[54] Bartlett (2012). See also Clough (2014) for an excellent analysis.

enjoy legal capacity 'on an equal basis with others in all aspects of life'. Yet here, if we have two people with delusions, the one whose delusion is as a result of a mental disorder is treated differently from the one whose is not.[55]

6.7 Enabling someone to have capacity

The MCA 2005 emphasizes that a patient should not be treated as lacking capacity 'unless all practical steps to help him' to reach capacity 'have been taken without success'.[56] Further, under section 2(2):

> A person is not to be regarded as unable to understand the information relevant to a decision if he is able to understand an explanation of it given to him in a way that is appropriate to his circumstances (using simple language, visual aids or any other means).

6.8 Ensuring capacity assessments are not prejudicial

A further point on competence is that the MCA 2005 makes special provision to ensure that patients are not assessed as lacking capacity in a prejudicial way. Section 2(3) states:

> A lack of capacity cannot be established merely by reference to—
>
> (a) a person's age or appearance, or
> (b) a condition of his, or an aspect of his behaviour, which might lead others to make unjustified assumptions about him.

This is designed to ensure that a patient who appears unkempt or disordered is not assessed as lacking capacity purely on that basis.[57] In *WBC Local Authority v Z*[58] part of the evidence to support a claim that a young woman lacked capacity was that her bedroom was 'in complete disarray, with numerous items strewn on the floor and every surface'. The judge placed no weight on this adding the state of the bedroom was 'a familiar sight to a parent of an adolescent or young adult'!

The use of the word 'merely' in section 2(3) is perhaps surprising, because it suggests that prejudicial attitudes can be a factor taken into account in assessing capacity.[59]

6.9 Capacity: understanding the relevant information

The law in England and Wales does not recognize the so-called 'doctrine of informed consent', which states that a patient can provide effective consent only if given the relevant and necessary information to make a proper decision. All that is required is that the patient must understand 'in broad terms the nature of the procedure which is intended'.[60] Before exploring that further it is necessary to make two distinctions.

---

[55] Although it is arguable that the person with the disability is treated more favourably in that he or she can be protected by the MCA 2005.
[56] See DCA (2007: para. 2.6) for a further discussion of what might be involved.
[57] DCA (2007: para. 4.8) also warns against assuming incapacity where someone has an appearance that includes features of Down's syndrome.
[58] [2016] EWCOP 4.   [59] Bartlett (2005: 28).
[60] *Chatterton v Gerson* [1981] 1 All ER 257, 265. For further discussion, see E. Jackson (2006).

First, it is important to distinguish two claims that patients may make in relation to a case in which it is alleged that he or she was not given the appropriate amount of information.

(i)   The patient could claim that he or she did not consent to a procedure because he or she did so only on the basis of false or inadequate information. This could be a claim in tort for battery or negligence. It can also result in criminal proceedings.

(ii)   The patient could claim that he or she *did* consent to the procedure, but that the medical professional was negligent in not informing the patient of all of the risks. This would be a claim in the tort of negligence.

We will examine cases of type (ii) later, because they are not claims of non-consent as such, but rather complaints that the doctor failed to provide the amount of information required. We will also note, when exploring that issue, that the distinction between these two kinds of claims is becoming blurred. However, it seems at the moment it is necessary to distinguish between them.

Second, we need to distinguish between cases where the patient's lack of understanding means they lack mental capacity, and (rare) cases where a patient has mental capacity, but has been deceived by a doctor about the procedure. An example of the latter is *Appleton v Garrett*,[61] in which a dentist was found to have deliberately misinformed his patients in order to persuade them to agree to unnecessary treatment for financial gain. Such a case would not fall under the MCA, because the lack of understanding was not as a result of mental disorder. However, under the general common law, the patient would not have consented to the procedure.

To lack capacity under the MCA a patient must fail to understand the 'nature, purpose and effects of the proposed treatment'.[62] This does not mean that to have capacity a patient needs to understand everything about the treatment. Macur J in *LBL v RYJ*,[63] explained that 'it is not necessary for the person to comprehend every detail of the issue … it is not always necessary for a person to comprehend all peripheral details'. So the court needs to determine whether the patient understands enough to make the decision. An easy example of this is *A NHS Trust v K*,[64] in which K needed to have an operation because she suffered from cancer. She suffered a mental disorder and refused to consent, because she did not accept that she had cancer, a key piece of information.[65] A more controversial decision was the following.

KEY CASE   *Re C (Adult: Refusal of Treatment)* [1994] 1 WLR 290 (FD)

C was a patient at Broadmoor, who had been diagnosed as suffering from paranoid schizophrenia. One of his delusional beliefs was that he was a great doctor who had a 100 per cent success rate with patients with damaged limbs. He suffered an injury to his foot, which became gangrenous. He was told that there was an 85 per cent chance that he would die without an amputation. C opposed the treatment, believing that God did not want him to have his foot amputated. Although he accepted that the doctors believed he was going to die, he did not agree with them.

---

[61] (1995) 34 BMLR 23.   [62] *Heart of England NHS Trust v JB* [2014] EWHC 342 (COP).
[63] [2010] EWHC 2664 (Fam), [24].   [64] [2012] EWHC 2922 (COP).
[65] See also *A Hospital NHS Trust v CD* [2015] EWCOP 74.

Thorpe J held that there were three aspects to competence: '… first, comprehending and retaining treatment information, second believing it and, third, weighing it in the balance to arrive at a choice.'[66] Applying that to this case, he held: 'I am satisfied that he has understood and retained the relevant treatment information, that in his own way he believes it, and that in the same fashion he has arrived at a clear choice.'[67] The doctors were therefore not permitted to operate on C's foot without his consent, even if that would lead to his death.

No operation was performed, but C managed to live and his foot largely recovered.[68]

It was crucial in this case that C understood the doctors' diagnosis and their proposed treatment.[69] It was simply that he believed that he (and God) knew better. The case can, on that basis, be contrasted with *R (N) v Dr M, A Health Authority Trust and Dr O*,[70] in which a patient believed that doctors wanted to give her drugs in order to induce her to believe she was a man. In fact, they wished to give her anti-psychotic medicine. She was found to lack capacity because she did not understand the nature of the proposed treatment. A similar result would be found under the MCA 2005 because her lack of understanding would mean that she could not make a decision for herself and this would be owing to her mental impairment.

Another controversial case and what needs to be understood to have capacity was the following.[71]

KEY CASE *PC v City of York Council* [2013] EWCA Civ 478

PC was a 48-year-old woman with significant learning disabilities, who married NC whilst he was imprisoned for serious sexual offences. He was due for release and they intended to cohabit. It was accepted that NC posed a risk to PC if they were to live together, given his history of violence against women. The local authority sought an order that PC lacked capacity to agree to cohabit with NC.

The Court of Appeal held that it had to be shown she understood what cohabitation with NC (rather than cohabitation in general) would be like. In this case, PC refused to believe that NC had been violent in the past and that he posed a risk to her. She therefore lacked understanding of a crucial piece of evidence in making the decision. However, the Court of Appeal concluded that she did not lack capacity under the 2005 Act because it had not been shown that she did not accept his violent past because of her mental disorder.[72] The Court of Appeal was also critical of the expert witness who gave evidence that PC lacked capacity, because it felt that he had focused on the decision reached, rather than the decision-making process. The fact that the decision she had made would be seen by some as foolish was not a reason for finding a lack of capacity. Because it could not be shown that she lacked capacity, the Court could not interfere.

---

[66] At 293.   [67] At 294.   [68] Stauch and Wheat (2011: 101).
[69] Van Staden and Krüger (2003) state that a person cannot be competent if he or she is unable to appreciate the need for treatment.
[70] [2002] EWHC 1911.   [71] For differing views, see Skowron (2014) and Herring and Wall (2014).
[72] The Court was not explicit about this, but the point was presumably that her lack of belief in his violent past may have been the result of her being besotted with him.

As that case demonstrates, one difficulty facing the courts is determining what information it is that the person must understand if he or she is to be shown to 'understand the information relevant to the decision'. In *PC v York* it was held that DC's violent disposition was information that was relevant to the decision to cohabit, although it had not been so held in relation to a decision to marry. The Court drew a distinction between 'person-specific' decisions and 'act-specific' decisions. Sometimes, the courts have taken an 'act-specific approach', as they did in relation to the decision to marry in this case. Then, the court determines that the person understands the nature of the act in general, even though he or she does not need to understand the nature of the person with whom he or she is doing it. This is the approach that the courts have taken in relation to marriage: the question is 'does P understand what marriage is like?', not 'does P understand what marriage to X is like?' Interestingly, in *York*, the Court thought that capacity to cohabit had to be person specific, so PC had to understand what living with X was like.

The courts have struggled in dealing with a series of cases in relation to sex.[73] The lower courts have taken the approach that capacity to have sex is act specific.[74] Parker J in London Borough of *Southwark v KA*[75] listed what information needed to be understood to have capacity to consent to sex in general:

(i)   The mechanics of the act.

(ii) That sexual relations can lead to pregnancy.[76]

(iii) That there are health risks caused by sexual relations.

(iv) The ability to understand the concept of and the necessity of one's own consent is fundamental to having capacity: in other words that P 'knows that she/he has a choice and can refuse'.

Controversially, Parker J held that understanding that one's partner should consent is not part of the capacity to consent. This reflects the general approach of the courts that there is no need for P to understand moral issues in relation to sex.[77]

The justification for the court's approach was explained in *A Local Authority v TZ*: 'To require the issue of capacity to be considered in respect of every person with whom TZ contemplated sexual relations would not only be impracticable but would also constitute a great intrusion.'[78]

The 'act specific' nature of the approach, however, sits uneasily with Baroness Hale's views in *R v C*:[79]

> My Lords, it is difficult to think of an activity which is more person- and situation-specific than sexual relations. One does not consent to sex in general. One consents to this act of sex with this person at this time and in this place. Autonomy entails the freedom and the capacity to make a choice of whether or not to do so. This is entirely consistent with

[73] See Sandland (2013) and Herring and Wall (2014) for discussions of the broader issues.
[74] *A Local Authority v TZ* [2013] EWHC 2322 (COP); *D Borough Council v AB*, [2011] EWHC 101, [32].
[75] [2016] EWCOP 20.
[76] In the case P thought that only sex between married couples would lead to pregnancy, but this was held sufficient to show P appreciated that sex could lead to pregnancy.
[77] *D Borough Council v AB*, [2011] EWHC 101. In *Luton BC v SB and RS* [2015] EWHC 3534 (Fam) reference was made to the fact P did not understand the idea of fidelity in a finding of a lack of capacity to consent to sex, but that was not the determinative issue.
[78] [2013] EWHC 2322 (COP).   [79] [2009] UKHL 42, [64].

the respect for autonomy in matters of private life which is guaranteed by article 8 of the European Convention for the Protection of Human Rights and Fundamental Freedoms. The object of the 2003 Act was to get away from the previous 'status'-based approach which assumed that all 'defectives' lacked capacity, and thus denied them the possibility of making autonomous choices, while failing to protect those whose mental disorder deprived them of autonomy in other ways.

The Court of Appeal in *IL v LM*[80] has sought to clarify the apparent conflict. It explained that Baroness Hale was looking at the issue from the criminal law perspective, while the other cases were considering the issue in advance; whether a person could, in theory, consent to have sex:

> Baroness Hale is plainly right that: 'One does not consent to sex in general. One consents to this act of sex with this person at this time and in this place'. The focus of the criminal law, in the context of sexual offences, will always be upon a particular specific past event with any issue relating to consent being evaluated in retrospect with respect to that singular event. But the fact that a person either does or does not consent to sexual activity with a particular person at a fixed point in time, or does or does not have capacity to give such consent, does not mean that it is impossible, or legally impermissible, for a court assessing capacity to make a general evaluation which is not tied down to a particular partner, time and place.[81]

It seems therefore we need to separate out two questions:

(i)   Does P have the capacity to consent to sex, in general?

(ii) Did P consent to have sex with this person at this particular time?

Question (i) will arise if the local authority are asking the court whether they need to stop P having sex with anyone. Question (ii) will generally arise if criminal proceedings are brought against someone who it is said had sex with P without their consent.

Even with this explanation, it must be questioned whether question (i) makes much sense. The court trying to foresee whether a person hypothetically has capacity to consent to sex in the abstract can say anything of such meaning.[82]

6.10 Capacity and the ability to use the information to make a decision

To have capacity, the patient must not only understand the information, but also be able to use the information, weigh it, and be able to make a decision.[83] This means that even though a patient may fully understand the issues involved, if he or she is in such a panic that he or she is unable to process the knowledge to reach a decision, then the patient will lack capacity to make the decision.[84] In *Mental Health Trust v DD*[85] a pregnant woman refusing to consent to a Caesarean section was able to understand the information relevant to the decision but due to her learning difficulties and autism spectrum disorder was found to be unable to weigh the information. Cobb J found she had

[80] [2014] EWCA 37.   [81] Para. 67.   [82] Herring and Wall (2014).
[83] See Donnelly (2009b) for an excellent discussion on how capacity is assessed.
[84] *Bolton Hospitals NHS Trust v O* [2003] 1 FLR 824.   [85] [2014] EWCOP 11.

'rigid and unshakeable thinking'. In *PCT v P, AH and The Local Authority*[86] Hedley J described the ability to use and weigh information as 'the capacity actually to engage in the decision making process itself and to be able to see the various parts of the argument and to relate one to another'.

MacDonald J in *Kings College Hospital NHS Foundation Trust v C and V*[87] emphasized that: '… the question for the court is not whether the person's ability to take the decision is impaired by the impairment of, or disturbance in the functioning of, the mind or brain but rather whether the person is rendered unable to make the decision by reason thereof'. As he notes, the MCA 2005 states that a person only lacks capacity if they are unable to make a decision. It is not enough simply to show there is an impairment in their decision-making process.[88]

The following case is a controversial example of a patient who was found not to be able to weigh the information.

KEY CASE   *A Local Authority v E* [2012] EWHC 1639 (COP)

The case concerned a 32-year-old woman who suffered from anorexia nervosa and other health conditions, including alcohol dependence and a personality disorder. In May 2012, E was severely malnourished, but refused to eat. She was willing to accept only palliative care. There had previously been many unsuccessful attempts to treat her conditions. She refused further treatment and her parents, although not wanting her to die, supported her choice. E's doctors were doubtful whether coercive treatment would be effective or desirable. The Official Solicitor instructed an expert, who advised that highly specialized treatment was available.

Jackson J concluded that E lacked capacity to refuse treatment in relation to forcible feeding:

[T]here is strong evidence that E's obsessive fear of weight gain makes her incapable of weighing the advantages and disadvantages of eating in any meaningful way. For E, the compulsion to prevent calories entering her system has become the card that trumps all others. The need not to gain weight overpowers all other thoughts.[89]

On what was in her best interests, a balance had to be struck between the value of E's life and the value of her independence. There was a presumption in favour of life that was not displaced in this case. Forced feeding, if necessary, would be in her best interests.

From one point of view, the decision in *E* is readily justifiable. As a result of her condition, she was so obsessed with avoiding calorific intake that she was unable to weigh up different factors to make a decision. A similar point was made in assessing the capacity of a vegan 15-year-old girl who refused the measles, mumps, and rubella (MMR) vaccine because it contained animal products.[90] There it was said her rigid adherence to veganism and refusal to weigh up competing factors indicated a lack of capacity. The problem is that perfectly competent people have absolute moral principles, which they apply regardless of the consequences. For example, some people believe that abortion

---

[86] [2009] COPLR 956 at [35].   [87] [2015] EWCOP 80, para. 15.   [89] At [2].
[88] Confirmed in *WBC Local Authority v Z* [2016] EWCOP 4.
[90] *F v F* [2013] EWHC 2783 (Fam).

is always wrong; there is no weighing up of competing arguments to be done, because they simply follow that rule.

When considering this case it should be noted, as we shall explore later, that simply because a patient is found to lack capacity does not meant that treatment will be forced upon them. The decision in *E* can be contrasted with *A NHS Trust v X*[91] where the medical evidence established that although X lacked capacity to make decisions about her anorexia nervosa it would not be in her best interests to continue treatment because if she was force fed there was still a 95–98 per cent chance she would die. X had been provided all available treatments previously and none had proved successful.

One way of analysing *E* is to say that the disease of anorexia had changed her reasoning process.[92] The 'real' E would want to live and we should take that into account.[93] Similar issues arise when dealing with people with severe depression.[94] Should we say the depression is impacting on their ability to make a decision and that if they were well ('the real them') they would not be making the decision? The issue is particularly acute if the person is suicidal.[95] These issues also arose in the following controversial decision.

KEY CASE   *Re SB* [2013] EWHC 1417 (COP)

A married woman with bipolar disorder became pregnant. She was initially keen to have the child. However, she was concerned that her medication would affect her child. She therefore stopped taking the medication. She became convinced that her marriage was failing and that her husband did not want the child. She was 'sectioned' under the Mental Health Act 1983. She decided that she wanted an abortion. The experts assessed her as lacking capacity to consent to a termination.

Holman J disagreed with the professional assessment. He accepted that it was rare for a judge to disagree with the expert witnesses. He emphasized that SB had made a decision and made one strongly. He was willing to accept that some of the reasons for her decision (that her husband and family were not supporting her) resulted from delusion or paranoia. However, other reasons were rational: she felt that she would be suicidal if she did not have a termination and she did not want to give birth while detained under the 1983 Act. The judge made it clear that he was not saying that she was making a good decision, but that she had made a decision and used reasons not based on delusions to do so.

Critics of the decision in *Re SB* might question whether the court should have placed more weight on her wishes when she was well than on a decision based in part on delusions. Supporters will see this as a welcome attempt to let people make decisions for themselves unless they are undoubtedly incompetent.

6.11 Capacity and the wisdom of the decision

Section 1(4) of the MCA 2005 states that: 'A person is not to be treated as unable to make a decision merely because he makes an unwise decision.'[96] However, the word

---

[91] [2014] EWCOP 35.   [92] See Clough (2016) for a very helpful discussion of the anorexia cases.
[93] Hope, Tan, Stewart, and McMillan (2013).   [94] Donnelley (2017).   [95] Huxtable (2017).
[96] Despite the clear statement of this principle, commentators have claimed that the judges have done exactly this to ensure that patients receive the treatment they need: Montgomery (2000); Harrington (1996).

merely is important here. It is legitimate to use the fact that the decision is unwise as part of a finding of incapacity, it just cannot be used as the sole factor. There is a careful line to be trod between not allowing the reasoning—'This decision is irrational, therefore the patient lacks capacity'—but permitting the reasoning—'This decision is irrational because the individual is not able to properly weigh up the different issues'.[97] Peter Jackson J in *Heart of England NHS Foundation Trust v JB*[98] emphasized:

> The temptation to base a judgment of a persons capacity upon whether they seem to have made a good or bad decision, and in particular on whether they have accepted or rejected medical advice, is absolutely to be avoided. That would be to put the cart before the horse or, expressed another way, to allow the tail of welfare to wag the dog of capacity. Any tendency in this direction risks infringing the rights of that group of persons who, though vulnerable, are capable of making their own decisions. Many who suffer from mental illness are well able to make decisions about their medical treatment, and it is important not to make unjustified assumptions to the contrary.

It is important to remember that a decision that appears irrational to a healthcare professional may make perfect sense in the context of the patient's religious and personal beliefs.[99] However, as the MCA 2005 Code of Practice indicates, there will inevitably be concerns that a person lacks capacity if he or she repeatedly makes 'unwise decisions that put [him or her] at significant risk of harm or exploitation', or makes 'a particular unwise decision that is obviously irrational or out of character'.[100] Where an apparently irrational decision is made, therefore, the court will seek to understand whether the decision is an understandable one, given the way in which P understands the world. If, however, there seems no way of making sense of P's decision, given her starting point, it may be assumed that the reasoning process was impaired.

These issues are well raised in the following case.

KEY CASE   *King's College Hospital NHS Foundation Trust v C and V* [2015] EWCOP 80

C, aged 50, had lived what MacDonald J described as a 'sparkly' lifestyle. She enjoyed looking fantastic, a lively social life, and material possessions. Following serious financial troubles and ending of a long-term relationship she attempted suicide, which caused kidney failure. Dialysis treatment was offered, which C's medical team believed had a high degree of success. Without the treatment she was likely to die in ten days. She refused treatment, saying she did not want to become old, ugly, and poor. Two psychiatrists reported she lacked capacity because she did not believe the treatment would be effective. Another expert disagreed and believed she had capacity.

McDonald J found she had capacity. Although many people would disagree with her decision, and may find it unreasonable or even immoral, it did not follow she lacked capacity. She did understand the key facts and had weighed them up, even though she had attached weight to facts many people would not have done. She had applied her own values to the facts, in particular her attachment to youth, glamour, beauty, and the good life, and so she had capacity.

---

[97] See Savulescu and Momeyer (1997), who insist that a patient's decision must be based on rational belief if it is to be respected.
[98] [2014] EWHC 342 (COP) at [7].   [99] Cave (2017).   [100] DCA (2007: para. 2.11).

6.12 **Capacity and the absence of coercion**

Even if a patient has capacity and he or she is aware of the crucial issues, if his or her consent is not given freely it will not be legally valid consent.[101] It is rare for this issue to arise and it is difficult to demonstrate that an apparent consent was given only under coercion or undue influence. In *Freeman v Home Office*,[102] it was held that the fact that a prisoner felt that he had no option but to submit to the prison medical officer's proposed treatment did not mean that he was not validly consenting. The court pointed out that he had not in any way been threatened or physically restrained. In *Mrs U v Centre for Reproductive Medicine*,[103] a man amended a form dealing with the infertility treatment that he was receiving with his wife to read that his sperm could not be used after his death. When he died, his wife sought to claim that her husband had amended the form only because he was under pressure from a nurse. It was held by the Court of Appeal that this was not a case in which it was believable that he had signed the form under undue influence. He may have felt under pressure to sign the amendment, but he did not lack the ability to make his own decision. The following comment of Butler Sloss P was approved:

> [W]hen one stands back and looks at the facts of this case, it seems to me that it is difficult to say that an able, intelligent, educated man of 47, with a responsible job and in good health, could have his will overborne so that the act of altering the form and initialling the alterations was done in circumstances in which Mr U no longer thought and decided for himself.[104]

That case might be contrasted with the following.[105]

KEY CASE   *A Local Authority v Mrs A and Mr A* [2010] EWHC 1549 (Fam)

Mrs A was aged 29 and had low intellectual functioning. Her two children had been taken into care because there were concerns that she was not able to look after them. Since then, she had married Mr A, who also had learning difficulties. Prior to the marriage, Mrs A had been receiving contraception, via a monthly depot injection. However, shortly after her marriage, she had refused to have the injection, saying that Mr A did not want her to have it. Her social services support team were concerned about her because there were reports that Mr A was assaulting Mrs A. They sought an order that Mrs A be given the contraception without her consent.

Bodey J concluded that Mrs A lacked capacity to make the decision about contraception. He rejected an argument that she did not sufficiently understand the issues surrounding contraception. Although she did not really understand what raising a child would involve, she did understand the key proximate issues around contraception (for example what contraception did) and that was sufficient to have capacity. However, she lacked capacity because, looking at the evidence as a whole, there was a 'completely unequal dynamic' in the relationship between Mr and Mrs A, and her decision about contraception had not been taken of her own free will.

Having decided that she lacked capacity to make the decision about contraception, Bodey J was required to determine what was in her best interests. Although he believed that receiving contraception was in her best interests, he did not think that compelling her to have contraception against her wishes would be. He encouraged the social services team to engage with her and seek to persuade her to consent to receiving it.

---

[101] Pattinson (2002a).   [102] [1984] 1 All ER 1036.   [103] [2002] Lloyd's Rep Med 259.
[104] At 261.   [105] See also *MCC v WMA* [2013] EWHC 2580 (COP).

7 **The form of the consent**

Consent does not need to be in any particular form. There is no legal distinction between written or oral consent. Although, in the case of major surgery, it is common to ask a patient to sign a consent form, this is not, strictly speaking, necessary. The precise nature of the consent has been described as 'pure window dressing'.[106] The benefit of having a signed form is that it can specify precisely what the patient has been told and to what he or she has consented. It should also be noted that consent is not an ongoing concept and that a professional should obtain consent for each medical procedure, rather than rely on the fact that the patient has consented to similar procedures in the past.[107]

Consent can also be express or implied. An example of implied consent would be where a doctor proposes giving an injection and the patient says nothing, but rolls up the sleeve of his shirt and presents his arm to the doctor. Although the patient has not actually said 'yes', his actions indicate that he is consenting. Of course, express written consent is the most undisputable form of consent and so the safest course of action is to ask a patient to sign a consent form.[108] However, it should be emphasized that even if a patient has signed the form, if there is no true consent, the form itself will not provide a defence.[109] It is still open, for example, for a patient to argue that he or she had been misled as to the nature of the proposed treatment when signing, or that he or she lacked the capacity to consent. Where a patient has not signed a consent form, or the form is amended without his or her signed authorization, the doctor is left open to claims that the procedures were not consented to.[110]

One important point is that consent is a 'positive' notion. The legal issue is whether or not the patient consented to the procedure, not whether the patient failed to oppose the treatment.[111] So, using the example above, if the doctor proposes an injection and the patient sits in the surgery impassively, and the doctor then injects the patient, it is not clear that there is consent. It is true that the patient did not object to the proposal, but that is insufficient to amount to consent. The doctor would have to argue that the patient's failure to get out of the way as he or she approached with a needle amounted to implied consent. Whether a court would be willing to accept implied consent from an omission is highly debatable.

We do not have clear guidance from the courts on how precise consent must be. This issue tends to arise where it has not been possible to diagnose the patient's problem precisely. Then, a physician may decide that an operation is required to investigate and diagnose the problem. Only once the patient is opened up in the operating theatre will it be clear what operation needs to be done. Of course, if the patient consents to a range of alternative operations and the surgeon performs one of these, there is no difficulty in finding consent. More difficult is consent of the most general kind: 'Operate on me and do whatever is necessary.' It is not clear whether such a broad consent would be effective; there may need to be at least some reference to the kinds of surgery that are envisioned.[112]

---

[106] *Taylor v Shropshire Health Authority* [1998] Lloyd's Rep Med 395.
[107] *Bartley v Studd*, Daily Telegraph, 12 July 1995 (QB).   [108] DoH (2001a).
[109] DoH (2001b: 11); *Chatterton v Gerson* [1981] 1 All ER 257.
[110] See, e.g., *Williamson v East London and City Health Authority* [1998] Lloyd's Rep Med 6.
[111] *St George's Healthcare NHS Trust v S* [1998] 3 All ER 673.   [112] Montgomery (2003: 236).

One scenario that can arise is if, while carrying out one operation, it becomes apparent to the physician that another operation is required. Should the physician wait until the patient recovers from the anaesthetic and get his or her consent, or can the physician assume that the patient would want the surgeon to operate? One controversial area is where a surgeon is performing an operation on a woman and discovers that there are good medical reasons for performing a hysterectomy. Although there is no clear ruling on this kind of case, it would appear that the physician must obtain consent for each procedure that he or she carries out. Consent to operation A is not consent to operation B. For example, there is an old case that makes it clear that consent to an abortion does not include consent to a sterilization.[113] However, if all that the physician does is a minor deviation from the consented-to procedure, then implied consent may be found. In *Davis v Barking, Havering and Brentwood Health Authority*,[114] a claimant failed in her action for damages based on her claim that she had not consented to a specific form of anaesthetic known as a 'caudal block'. Her claim failed because she had signed a form agreeing to the performance of an operation and 'such further or alternative operative measures as may be found necessary during the course of the above-mentioned operation and to the administration of general, local or other anaesthetics for any of these purposes'. The anaesthetic was administered as a part of the operation to which she had consented.

It should be noted that if, in the course of one operation, there is a medical emergency requiring a medical procedure, the doctor can operate on the patient without his or her consent and is protected by the defence of medical necessity.

A patient is free to withdraw his or her consent at any time. It would then be unlawful for a medical professional to continue treatment, unless he or she were to believe that, at the time of withdrawal, the patient lacked capacity.[115]

8 The patient with capacity who does not consent

8.1 Patients who do not consent

As we have seen already, it is a fundamental legal principle that a doctor cannot provide treatment without the consent of a competent patient. However, there are some very limited circumstances in which it is permissible to infringe that right.

(i) It is not an offence to touch someone without their consent if that touching is 'physical contact which is generally acceptable in the ordinary conduct of daily life'.[116] Therefore a doctor who gave her patient a welcoming handshake, or a nurse who gave a nervous patient a reassuring pat on the arm, would not be committing an offence even if the patient had not consented. However, this would be a limited exception and could not be used to provide a justification for medical treatment. It has been suggested that it could justify some basic nursing care, such as dressing and feeding.[117] However, it is hard to see how these touchings could be described as an aspect of the ordinary conduct of daily life.

(ii) If there is a medical emergency and there is not time to seek court approval, a medical professional may be able to rely on the defence of necessity. However, this is

[113] *Cull v Royal Surrey County Hospital* (1932) 1 BMLJ 1195.   [114] [1993] 4 Med LR 85.
[115] DoH (2001c: para. 45).   [116] *Collins v Wilcock* [1984] 3 All ER 374, 376.
[117] DoH (2001a: para. 19.2) suggests that 'basic care' falls within this exception and that it is not possible to refuse to consent to this.

possible only where the treatment provided is in the best interests of the patient and the patient lacks capacity.[118]

(iii) If a patient has capacity, but is deemed a 'vulnerable adult', it may be permissible to give them treatment without their consent. We will discuss this category shortly.

(iv) There has been some debate over whether it is possible to force treatment on a non-consenting patient on the grounds of public policy. If there is such a power, it would require the most unusual of circumstances. In *Robb v Home Office*,[119] a prisoner went on hunger strike. The case raised the question of whether it was lawful to force-feed the prisoner. Lord Justice Thorpe accepted that there was a clash between the right of self-determination and four state interests: (1) preserving life; (2) preventing suicide; (3) maintaining the integrity of the medical profession; and (4) protecting innocent third parties. But all of the state interests yielded to the right of self-determination. It will be recalled that, in *St George's Healthcare NHS Trust v S*,[120] the preservation of the life of the woman and her foetus were insufficient grounds to justify operating on her without her consent. However, the courts have generally stood back from saying it is never permissible to provide medical treatment against the wishes of a competent person. If a terrible disease were to take a grip on the population, threatening to kill thousands of people, it is not difficult to believe that the court would permit the taking of blood from a person who appeared to have an antibody.[121] Also, perhaps, if, in order to a save another person's life, a very minor invasion of another person were required (such as the taking of a hair), a court might be tempted to authorize it. We have little case law on such scenarios, but what can be said is that if there can be a public policy justification to justify non-consensual treatment, it will arise only in unusual situations.

(v) If a patient is suffering from a contamination or infection, he or she can be ordered to be detained by a magistrate under the Public Health (Control of Disease) Act 1984.[122]

(vi) If a person is trying to commit suicide, it is generally thought to be lawful to seek to prevent that happening. In *Savage v South Essex Partnership NHS Foundation Trust*,[123] the House of Lords held that there was a legal obligation on medical authorities to prevent a patient detained under the Mental Health Act 1983 from committing suicide. This issue is discussed in Chapter 9.

(vii) The most significant exception to the principle is that under the Mental Health Act 1983, even if a patient has capacity they can be detained and treated for a mental disorder if the requirements of that legislation are met. We shall discuss this legislation in detail in Chapter 10, but it is worth noting here that the courts have given 'treatment of mental disorder' a fairly wide meaning. It has, for example, been held to cover forced feeding,[124] although whether such an interpretation withstands challenge under the Human Rights Act 1998 remains to be seen. The Mental Health Act 1983 cannot be

---

[118] *Re F* [1990] 2 AC 1.   [119] *Secretary of State v Robb* [1995] 1 All ER 677.

[120] [1998] 3 All ER 673.

[121] See Brennan (2016); Bernstein (2016) and Cave (2017) on arguments around mandatory vaccination.

[122] That Act was amended by the Health and Social Care Act 2008 so that all infections and contaminations are now covered, whereas previously only 'notifiable diseases' were.

[123] [2008] UKHL 74.   [124] *B v Croydon Health Authority* [1995] 1 All ER 683.

used to authorize treatment for conditions that are not mental disorders. So it could not be used to authorize an abortion on a person with a mental disorder under the MHA.[125]

If a carer or medical professional incorrectly believes a person (P) lacks capacity then section 5(1) of the MCA 2005 becomes relevant. It states that the MCA applies where a person has reasonable grounds for deciding that P lacks capacity, even if in fact that person does not.[126] Presumably, in deciding whether or not there are reasonable grounds, the court will take into account whether the person making the decision is an expert or not.[127] However, section 5(1) applies only where the decision relates to care or treatment.[128] That would very probably not include financial decisions.

8.2 Vulnerable adults

The orthodox view is that if a patient is deemed to have capacity, but only just, he or she must be treated in the same way as those who undoubtedly have capacity.[129] However, in the last few years the courts have been developing the inherent jurisdiction to deal with 'vulnerable adults'—that is, adults who are found officially to have capacity, but are nevertheless thought to need protection.[130] The Court of Appeal has confirmed the existence of the jurisdiction in *DL v A Local Authority*.[131] Munby J has defined this group in the following way:

> [T]he inherent jurisdiction can be exercised in relation to a vulnerable adult who, even if not incapacitated by mental disorder or mental illness, is, or is reasonably believed to be, either: (i) under constraint; or (ii) subject to coercion or undue influence; or (iii) for some other reason deprived of the capacity to make the relevant decision, or disabled from making a free choice, or incapacitated or disabled from giving or expressing a real and genuine consent.[132]

Note that orders dealing with 'vulnerable adults' have to be made under the inherent jurisdiction, because the MCA 2005 applies only to those without capacity. In *A NHS Trust v Dr A*,[133] it was held that it could be used to authorize forced feeding on a competent, but deluded, man. The courts will make the decision based on what is in the best interests of the individual. However, the courts will prefer to make an order which is designed to enable the person to more fully exercise autonomy for themselves. Hence in *DL v A Local Authority*,[134] an elderly couple were removed from the care of their son. They had capacity and wanted to stay with him, but he was abusive and dominated their thinking. Removing them from his care was justified as enabling them to make a more autonomous decision about where to live. In *Re D (Vulnerable Adult)*[135] an 18-year-old girl with learning difficulties and emotional disorders was befriended by an older man who gave her drugs and was abusive to her. Injunctions were made under the inherent jurisdiction to stop him having contact with her. The orders could be made, even though she had not sought them.

---

[125] An abortion might be permissible under the MCA 2005 if the patient is lacking capacity.
[126] It should be remembered that without the protection of section 5 a person could be guilty of a criminal offence.
[127] *R v Adomako* [2004] UKHL 6.   [128] This is clear from the wording of section 5(1) itself.
[129] See Herring (2016).   [130] See Herring (2016 and 2009a) for a discussion of the case law.
[131] [2012] EWCA Civ 253.
[132] *Re SA (Vulnerable Adult With Capacity: Marriage)* [2005] EWHC 2942 (Fam), [77].
[133] [2013] EWHC 2442 (COP).   [134] [2012] EWCA Civ 253.   [135] [2016] EWHC 2358 (Fam).

9 The treatment of patients lacking capacity

The treatment of a patient lacking capacity is now governed by the MCA 2005. The Act applies only to those over the age of 16.[136] If a person lacks capacity, then generally a decision can be made on his or her behalf, as we shall discuss shortly. But first it should be noted that there are some things for which it is not possible to provide consent on behalf of a person lacking capacity. These are listed in section 27 as:

- consenting to marriage or a civil partnership;
- consenting to have sexual relations;
- consenting to a decree of divorce on the basis of two years' separation;
- consenting to the dissolution of a civil partnership;
- consenting to a child being placed for adoption or the making of an adoption order;
- discharging parental responsibility for a child in matters not relating to the child's property; or
- giving consent under the Human Fertilisation and Embryology Act 1990.[137]

The Court of Protection is not able to order a local authority to provide services to a person who lacks capacity.[138]

If the issue concerns something else and the patient lacks capacity, then the following questions must be considered.

(i)   Has the patient created an effective advance decision (sometimes called a 'living will'), which refuses the treatment in question? If so, the advance decision must be respected.

(ii) Has the patient effectively created a lasting power of attorney (LPA)? If so, the donee of the LPA (that is, the person named in the LPA) may be able to make the decision.

(iii) Has the court appointed a deputy? If so, the deputy in some cases can make the decision.

(iv) If there is no effective advance decision and no LPA, nor a deputy who can make the decision, then the question is whether the treatment is in the best interests of the patient.

We need therefore to consider the four scenarios separately.

9.1 Advance decisions

An advance decision is defined in section 24 of the MCA 2005 thus:

'Advance Decision' means a decision made by a person ('P'), after he has reached 18 and when he has capacity to do so, that if—

---

[136] Although the offence of ill-treatment or wilful neglect of a person lacking capacity in s. 44 has no age limit. Also, in s. 18(3), there is power for the court to deal with the property of an incapable minor.
[137] See also s. 29 preventing voting on behalf of a person lacking capacity and s. 28 preventing consent to mental disorder treatment for a person detained under the Mental Health Act 1983.
[138] *N v ACCG* [2017] UKSC 22.

(a) at a later time and in such circumstances as he may specify, a specified treatment is proposed to be carried out or continued by a person providing health care for him, and

(b) at that time he lacks capacity to consent to the carrying out or continuation of the treatment,

the specified treatment is not to be carried out or continued.

A number of points should be noted about this definition. First, the advance decision is effective only if P (the patient) was over the age of 18 and competent when he or she made it. The GMC states that doctors should start with the presumption that adults do have capacity.[139] There is to be no statutory requirement that when P makes the advance decision they have received advice from a doctor or a lawyer.[140]

Second, the advance decision is to be relevant only if the patient lacks capacity to consent to the treatment. So if a patient has signed an advance decision refusing to consent to a blood transfusion, but at the time is competent and consents, then the advance decision should be ignored.[141]

Third, the definition of advance decisions allows only 'negative' decisions: decisions to refuse treatment. An advance decision cannot be used to compel a medical professional to provide treatment. The definition of advance decision covers both treatment and the continuation of treatment. An advance decision could therefore indicate that P is willing to receive treatment, but only for a certain period of time.

Fourth, if the advance decision does reject life-saving treatment, that rejection must be in writing, and signed by P and witnessed by a third party.[142] Otherwise, the decision does not need to be in writing and can be oral.

Finally, the MCA 2005 Code of Practice states that an advance decision cannot refuse consent to basic care:

> An advance decision cannot refuse actions that are needed to keep a person comfortable (sometimes called basic or essential care). Examples include warmth, shelter, actions to keep a person clean and the offer of food and water by mouth.[143]

Section 25 explains the three ways in which an advance decision may be invalid:

- P, with capacity, has withdrawn the advance decision—which withdrawal does not need to be in writing;

- P has created an LPA after making the advance decision and has given the donee the power to make the decision in question; or

- P has done anything else that is clearly inconsistent with the directive in the advance decision.

The third way, set out in section 25(2), needs some more discussion. In *HE v A Hospital NHS Trust*,[144] a case decided before the MCA 2005 came into force, a patient had signed an advance decision indicating that she did not want to be given a blood transfusion, even if she would die without it. At the time that she signed the decision, she was

---

[139] GMC (2010a: para. 72).   [140] *Briggs v Briggs* [2016] EWCOP 53. See Auckland (2017).
[141] MCA 2005, s. 25(3). See also BMA (2007c).
[142] MCA 2005, s. 25(6), applied in *A NHS Trust v Dr A* [2013] EWHC 2442 (COP).
[143] DCA (2007: para. 9.28).   [144] [2003] EWHC 1017 (Fam).

a Jehovah's Witness. She later needed a blood transfusion, but the court heard evidence that she was no longer an active Jehovah's Witness and had indeed become engaged to be married to a Muslim. It was held that this, along with other evidence, indicated that the advance decision should be ignored. It is likely that a similar result would have been reached had the case been heard under the 2005 Act.

In *A Local Authority v E*,[145] a patient signed an advance directive that stated that it should be followed even if the patient's subsequent actions appeared inconsistent with it. It was held, *obiter*, that such a clause was ineffective.

Section 25, it must be admitted, is vague. Is a marriage, birth of a child, or a change in a religious behaviour inconsistent with a prior advance decision to refuse life-saving treatment? Another issue that is not clearly resolved is whether the behaviour of P after losing capacity can be behaviour inconsistent with an earlier advance decision.[146] In *Briggs v Briggs*[147] Charles J argued that in interpreting these provisions the court should remember that the intention of sections 24–26 was to enable people to make advance decisions. This implies that courts should be reluctant to find an advance decision ineffective.

It is also important to emphasize that the advance decision is relevant only if it specifies the treatment in question. This means that advance decisions will have to be drafted with sufficient precision to cover the treatment in question.

The directive will not apply if 'there are reasonable grounds for believing that circumstances exist which P did not anticipate at the time of the advance decision, and which would have affected his decision had he anticipated them'.[148] For example, it may be argued that, at the time that P made the decision, she did not realize what treatment options medical advances have since made available. It might even be claimed that, in making the advance directive, P did not appreciate the effectiveness of pain relief. There is certainly much scope in the MCA 2005 for a person who wishes to challenge the validity of an advance decision. In one of the few cases to uphold an advance decision, *X Primary Care Trust v XB*,[149] it was notable that the patient had drafted it in careful consultation with his doctor.

There is an extra requirement that needs to be satisfied where the advance decision is rejecting a life-saving treatment: P must state that the decision is to be respected even if his or her life is at risk as a result.[150]

The MCA 2005, section 26(1), explains:

If P has made an advance decision which is—

(a) valid, and

(b) applicable to the treatment,

the decision has the effect as if he had made it, and had had capacity to make it, at the time when the question arises whether the treatment should be carried out or continued.

This means that if P has made a valid and applicable advance decision that rejects treatment, the medical professional should not provide it. If he or she does, then there is the potential for a criminal or tortious action. However, under section 26(2): 'A person does not incur liability for carrying out or continuing the treatment unless, at the time, he is

---

[145] [2012] EWHC 1639 (COP).   [146] Accepted as an open question in *Briggs v Briggs* [2016] EWCOP 53.
[147] [2016] EWCOP 53.   [148] MCA 2005, s. 25(4).
[149] [2012] EWHC 1390 (Fam).   [150] MCA 2005, s. 25(5).

satisfied that an advance decision exists which is valid and applicable to the treatment.' In similar terms, section 26(3) provides a defence to someone who withdraws or withholds treatment believing (incorrectly) that there is a valid advance decision requiring this. Notably, both these defences appear to be in subjective terms. In other words, if the professional provides treatment believing there to be no advance decision, then he or she would not face legal consequences, even though it would have been easy for the professional to find out about the decision.[151] It might be argued that doctors should be required to take reasonable steps to find out whether there was an effective advance decision. Parliament clearly decided that this could be too onerous an obligation on medical staff. If there are doubts over the validity or applicability of an advance decision, an application to court can be made for a declaration.[152]

Alasdair Maclean has noted the numerous ways in which an advance decision may not bind a healthcare professional under the MCA 2005: the advance decision may not be validly made; it may be held not to be effective as a result of subsequent changes; and it may be held not to apply to the question at hand.[153] Even if the advance decision is technically valid, a medical professional can argue that he or she did not believe it to be valid or applicable. Maclean argues:

> The Act is arguably most successful in facilitating the provision of healthcare by supporting clinical discretion and protecting the physician who acts in good faith. Thus, the Act provides patients with a trump that only works when healthcare professionals and/or the courts are comfortable with the patient's decision.[154]

It should be emphasized again that an advance decision cannot permit a medical professional to do an act that would hasten the death of P; nor can it refuse 'basic care', such as washing;[155] nor can the advance decision prevent a medical professional giving treatment that is permitted under Part IV of the Mental Health Act 1983, even without the consent of the patient. We will consider this in Chapter 10, but, in very broad terms, this covers treatment for a mental disorder that is necessary for the protection of the patient or other people.

9.2 Lasting powers of attorney

If someone (P) wants someone else (D) to make decisions on their behalf when they lose capacity, they can make a lasting power of attorney (LPA) under the MCA 2005, section 9.[156] Then D can make decisions for general matters relating to P's welfare, including some medical decisions. In order to execute an LPA, P must be over 18 years old and have capacity to do so.[157] There are strict regulations as to the formalities surrounding the LPA and its registration. These are set out in the MCA 2005, Schedule 1. If they are not complied with, the LPA will be ineffective. However, Nugee J stated in *Miles and Beattie v the Public Guardian*:[158]

---

[151] Michalowski (2005) is concerned that this provision gives inadequate protection to the right to refuse treatment by means of an advance directive.

[152] MCA 2005, s. 26(5).

[153] Maclean (2008a). For a judicial finding of an effective advance directive see *A NHS Trust v X* [2014] EWCOP 35.

[154] Maclean (2008a: 17). See also Johnston (2014).   [155] DCA (2007: para. 9.28).

[156] See Samanta (2009); DCA (2007: ch. 7).   [157] MCA 2005, s. 9.   [158] [2015] EWHC 2960 (Ch), para 18

... it does seem to me that it is right that the Act should be construed in a way which gives as much flexibility to donors to set out how they wish their affairs to be dealt with as possible, the Act being intended to give autonomy to those who are in a position where they can foresee that they may in the future lack capacity to specify who it is that they wish to act for their affairs.

This indicates that courts may be reluctant to strike down an LPA unless it clearly breaches the statutory requirements.

It is possible to appoint more than one donee under an LPA. Unless the LPA says so, where more than one donee is appointed, they are to act jointly.[159] In other words, all of them must agree on the decision in question before using the LPA. An LPA can be revoked at any time if P has the capacity to do so.[160]

Where an LPA has been validly appointed and D has the power to make decisions about P's personal welfare, then this can extend to giving or refusing the carrying out of health care. However, this is subject to an important restriction in that D must make the decision based on what would be in P's best interests, as described in section 4 (which will be discussed later in the chapter). This means that D may not make a decision that is contrary to P's best interests, even if the donee believes that is the decision that P would have made.[161] D may be reassured that if they reasonably believe that their decision will promote P's best interests, but a court subsequently concludes that it did not, they will not face legal actions in tort or the criminal law.[162] Under section 11(8), the LPA has no power to 'authorise the giving or refusal of consent to the carrying out or continuation of life-sustaining treatment, unless the instrument contains specific provision to that effect'. So if P wants D to be able to refuse to consent to life-sustaining treatment, the LPA must specifically state this.

The concept of an LPA is not without difficulty. First, there is substantial evidence to indicate that people are very bad at predicting what decisions another person would make.[163] This is so even where the people know each other very well. So people may be mistaken if they think that appointing a good friend or partner will mean that the decisions they would have taken will be repeated.

Second, it is important to note that D does not have the role that he or she might think he or she has. D cannot simply ask himself or herself 'what decision would X have made'; rather, D must make the decision that is in P's best interests. It is not clear that P and D will appreciate that this distinction could be significant in a case in which what P would have decided would be something against his or her best interests.

9.3 Deputies

Under section 16, if P lacks capacity in relation to a matter concerning his or her personal welfare (such as a health issue), then the court can make the decision on P's behalf, or decide to appoint a deputy to make decisions on P's behalf. In deciding whether to appoint a deputy, the court should consider whether to do so would be in P's best interests (considering the factors in section 4, at which we shall be looking shortly) and also the following principles:

(i) a decision by the court is to be preferred to the appointment of a deputy to make a decision; and

---

[159] MCA 2005, s. 9(5).   [160] MCA 2005, s. 13(2).   [161] See Samanta (2009) for criticism of this.
[162] MCA 2005, s. 4(9).   [163] The evidence is discussed and summarized in Wrigley (2007).

(ii) the powers conferred on a deputy should be as limited in scope and duration as is reasonably practicable in the circumstances.

This suggests that, where there is a 'one-off' decision to be made about P, it is unlikely to be appropriate to appoint a deputy. Where decisions need to be made about P on a regular basis, then a deputy may be more suitable. However, in *G v E*,[164] Baker J held that those involved in looking after people lacking capacity should not routinely be made deputies. That was necessary only if there were particular problems or concerns. In most cases, a carer or family member could make decisions without having a formal status. A deputy must be over the age of 18 and must have consented to take on the role.[165] The court can appoint more than one deputy. The court can revoke the appointment of a deputy.[166] In considering who to appoint as deputy, P's views, if any, should be taken into account.[167]

A deputy has the power to give or refuse consent to medical treatment.[168] However, the deputy has no authority to act if 'he knows or has reasonable grounds for believing that P has capacity in relation to the matter'.[169] A further important restriction is that 'a deputy may not refuse to consent to the carrying out or continuation of life-sustaining treatment in relation to P'.[170] The deputy is required to act in accordance with the best interests of the patient, as set out in section 4.[171] The deputy will often be a member of P's family, although that may not be appropriate if there are deep divisions among family members.[172]

9.4 A court decision based on best interests

An application can be made to court in respect of any person who lacks capacity. The court can make a declaration as to the lawfulness of any act concerning the individual. The decision will be made based on what is in the best interests of the patient, as that is understood under section 4.

10 The best interests of the person

If an advance decision is valid and applicable, it must be respected; the issue of what is in P's best interests does not arise. However, where a court, or donee of an LPA, or deputy, or a person caring for or providing treatment to P is making a decision concerning P, the decision must be made based on what is in P's best interests.[173]

Section 1(6) emphasizes that:

Before the act is done, or decision is made, regard must be had to whether the purpose for which it is needed can be effectively achieved in a way that is less restrictive of the person's rights and freedom of action.

---

[164] [2010] EWHC 2512 (Fam).　　[165] MCA 2005, s. 19.　　[166] MCA 2005, s. 16(8).

[167] *Re S and S (Protected Persons)* Case Nos 11475121 and 11475138 (COP), 25 November 2008.

[168] MCA 2005, s. 16.　　[169] MCA 2005, s. 20(1).　　[170] MCA 2005, s. 20(5).

[171] MCA 2005, s. 4(9), offers the deputy protection from legal consequences if he or she reasonably, but wrongly, makes a decision that he or she believes is in the patient's best interests.

[172] *Re S and S (Protected Persons)* Case Nos 11475121 and 11475138 (COP), 25 November 2008.

[173] MCA 2005, s. 1(5).

So whenever a decision is being made about a patient who has lost capacity, it is not enough only to show that the action is in P's best interests; it also must be shown that there is not an equally good way of promoting P's interests that is less invasive of his or her rights or freedom.

The MCA 2005, section 4, states that, in deciding what is in a patient's best interests, the court or deputy must consider all of the relevant circumstances. The MCA 2005 Code of Practice states:

> When working out what is in the best interests of the person who lacks capacity to make a decision or act for themselves, decision makers must take into account all relevant factors that it would be reasonable to consider, not just those that they think are important. They must not act or make a decision based on what they would want to do if they were the person who lacked capacity.[174]

Section 4 of the MCA 2005 states that included within the factors to be taken into account in determining best interests are the following. Although the legislation does not list these in priority, in recent decisions the values of the individual have become a key feature.

10.1 A person's potential capacity

Section 4(3) states that the decision maker must consider:

(a) whether it is likely that the person will at some time have capacity in relation to the matter in question, and

(b) if it appears likely that he will, when that is likely to be.

Clearly, if the person is soon to regain capacity, it may be better, if possible, to postpone making a decision so that he or she can make it for him or herself. This is particularly significant if the impact of P's mental disorder varies from day to day.

10.2 A person's current views and feelings

While people with capacity have the right to make medical decisions for themselves, people without capacity do not. However, this does not mean that their views and feelings count for nothing. Indeed, there is a recognition in section 4 that even if it is not possible for the person to make a decision for himself or herself, he or she should still be involved to a reasonable extent in the decision-making process and his or her views listened to. The decision maker must 'so far as reasonably practicable, permit and encourage the person to participate, or to improve his ability to participate, as fully as possible in any act done for him and any decision affecting him'.[175] Further, the decision maker must consider, so far as is reasonably ascertainable, 'the person's ... present wishes and feelings ...' in deciding what is in P's best interests.[176] Of course, in the case of those who have lost capacity, it may be difficult to ascertain their views. In one case involving an elderly woman with dementia, there was considerable discussion over whether, when

[174] DCA (2007: para. 5.7).   [175] MCA 2005, s. 4(4).
[176] MCA 2005, s. 4(6)(a). See Munro (2015) for an excellent discussion of the failures of the court to listen to the views of those lacking capacity and the difficulties in doing so.

she said that she wanted to 'go home', that meant that she wanted to return to her child-hood home or to live with her daughter.[177]

In recent years the courts have been placing increasing weight on the current views and interests of the individual.[178] A range of different reasons for this can be detected in the case law and it is worth separating these out.

10.2.1 *Current views and personalized decision making*

The courts emphasize that when deciding what is in P's interests it is important to consider P as an individual and not use general comments about what an average person would want. Inevitably, therefore their current views are an important factor. In *Aintree University Hospitals NHS Foundation Trust v James* Lady Hale stated:[179]

> The purpose of the best interests test is to consider matters from the patient's point of view. That is not to say that his wishes must prevail, any more than those of a fully capable patient must prevail. We cannot always have what we want. Nor will it always be possible to ascertain what an incapable patient's wishes are… . But in so far as it is possible to ascertain the patient's wishes and feelings, his beliefs and values or the things which were important to him, it is those which should be taken into account because they are a component in making the choice which is right for him as an individual human being.

As that quote indicates it is part of respecting P and treating them in a humane way that we attach weight to their views, even though P lacks capacity.

10.2.2 *Current views and the efficacy of treatment*

If P opposes the treatment and is liable to resist it, this is particularly relevant for assessing best interests. Even if there is no physical resistance against treatment, P may suffer emotional distress at being given treatment against his or her wishes.[180] Therefore, when considering whether giving treatment against P's wishes is in his or her best interests, the medical benefits of the treatment must be weighed against the emotional distress and need for force that may be required.[181] That may be a particularly significant factor where the patient is on the borderline of incapacity. Munby J asserts that:

> The nearer to the borderline the particular adult, even if she falls on the wrong side of the line, the more weight must in principle be attached to her wishes and feelings, because the greater the distress, the humiliation and indeed it may even be the anger she is likely to feel.[182]

In *A Local Authority v Mrs A and Mr A*[183] although it was found to be in Mrs A's best interests to have a contraceptive injection, it was held to be against her interests to force her to have one.[184] That case shows that it is one question to ask whether P should be given a treatment, it is another to ask whether P should be forced to get the treatment.

---

[177] *IIBCC v LG* [2010] EWHC 1527 (Fam).

[178] *Aintree University Hospitals NHS Foundation Trust v James* [2013] UKSC 67.

[179] [2013] UKSC 67.   [180] Herring (2009d).

[181] In *Re W (Medical Treatment: Anorexia)* [2016] EWCOP 13 it was found to be ineffective to force treatment on a woman with anorexia.

[182] *Re MM (An Adult)* [2007] EWHC 2003 (Fam), [121].   [183] [2010] EWHC 1549 (Fam).

[184] Contrast *Mental Health Trust v DD* [2014] EWCOP 44, where use of force to give a contraceptive injection was approved.

Mary Donnelly argues that where a patient is actively resisting the course of action, it should be performed only if there is evidence that the procedure is very much in that patient's best interests.[185]

10.2.3 *Current views and human rights*

Forcing treatment on a patient may invade their human rights.[186] In *A NHS Trust v X*,[187] in refusing to order a hospital to feed a woman with anorexia nervosa nutrition against her wishes, it was said:

> *Articles 3* and *8* of the *ECHR* are particularly prominently engaged; repeated forcible feeding over a long period of time against her clearly expressed wishes, most especially with the use of physical restraint, is likely in my judgment to amount to inhuman or degrading treatment, certainly it would amount to a severe interference with her private life and personal autonomy. (Emphasis in original.)

As Norman Cantor has argued: 'It would be dehumanizing to ignore the will and feelings of a profoundly disabled person and to simply impose a surrogate's will. This would treat the prospective patient as if he or she were an inanimate object.'[188] I have also argued that, in the light of these points, we should follow the wishes of the person lacking capacity unless there is significant harm.[189]

10.2.4 *Equality*

Increasing weight is being attached to the UN Convention on the Rights of Persons with Disabilities. We will be exploring that in detail later (see 15.1) but it emphasizes that people with mental impairment should be treated equally to those who are not impaired. Part of that is respecting the views of those who lack capacity and not being overly protective. In a public lecture, Munby LJ stated, in a passage quoted with approval in *CC v KK*,[190] that:

> The fact is that all life involves risk, and the elderly and the vulnerable are exposed to additional risks and to risks they are less equipped than others to cope with. But just as wise parents resist the temptation to keep their children metaphorically wrapped up in cotton wool, so too we must avoid the temptation always to put the physical health and safety of the elderly and the vulnerable before everything else.

10.2.5 *Current views and other factors*

In *Re M*,[191] Munby J warned against having a precise formula for the weight to attach to a person's wishes and feelings, saying that it was 'case-specific and fact-specific'. Helpfully, he listed factors to be considered when determining the weight that should be attached to them:

- the degree of the person's incapacity;
- the strength and consistency of the views being expressed by the person;

---

[185] Donnelly (2009a).   [186] Herring (2008c).
[187] [2014] EWCOP 35. See Coggon (2015) for a helpful discussion.   [188] Cantor (2005: 206).
[189] Herring (2008c).   [190] [2012] EWHC 2136 (COP), [18].   [191] [2009] EWHC 2525 (Fam).

- the possible impact on the person of knowledge that his or her wishes and feelings are not being given effect;
- the extent to which the person's wishes and feelings are, or are not, 'rational, sensible, responsible and pragmatically capable of sensible implementation in the particular circumstances'; and
- crucially, the extent to which P's wishes and feelings, if given effect to, can properly be accommodated within the court's overall assessment of what is in her best interests.[192]

This is a particularly helpful observation because it indicates that we should not have a single view on what weight to attach to the current views of a person lacking capacity. There are good reasons why we might treat differently the views of a person who lacks capacity as a result of hallucinations from the views of someone living in an abusive relationship or someone in the throws of an addiction.[193] We should not seek a 'one size fits all' approach to determining the weight attached to the views of those who lack capacity. The following case is an excellent example.[194]

> **KEY CASE** *Wye Valley NHS Trust v B* [2015] EWCOP 60
>
> A 73-year-old man had a severely infected leg. He had a long-standing mental illness, including bi-polar affective disorder and psychotic symptoms. For most of his adult life he had heard voices from angels and heavenly beings which told him what medicine to take. He did not follow an organized religion, but regarded himself as spiritual. His medical team strongly advised amputation of the leg, but he refused to consent.
>
> Jackson J confirmed, uncontroversially, he lacked capacity to make a decision about his treatment. Applying the best interests test, Jackson J confirmed:
>
> > once incapacity is established so that a best interests decision must be made, there is no theoretical limit to the weight or lack of weight that should be given to the person's wishes and feelings, beliefs and values. In some cases, the conclusion will be that little weight or no weight can be given; in others, very significant weight will be due.
>
> He went on to say:
>
> > To state the obvious, the wishes and feelings, beliefs and values of people with a mental disability are as important to them as they are to anyone else, and may even be more important. It would therefore be wrong in principle to apply any automatic discount to their point of view.
>
> In this case the current wishes and views were crucial because they were:
>
> > such long standing that they are an inextricable part of the person that he is. In this situation, I do not find it helpful to see the person as if he were a person in good health who has been afflicted by illness. It is more real and more respectful to recognise him for who he is: a person with his own intrinsic beliefs and values. It is no more meaningful to think of Mr B without his illnesses and idiosyncratic beliefs than it is to speak of an unmusical Mozart.

[192] At [35].   [193] Van der Eijk (2016).
[194] Discussed in Series (2016); Johnson (2017) and Taylor (2016).

It is important to note that the case might have been decided very differently if B had recently developed a mental condition causing him to hear voices.[195] Then it would make sense to consider what he would have wanted had he not been afflicted by his condition. However, in this case his current views were those he had always held and were part of who he was and his religious beliefs.

It would be wrong to read the decision in *Wye* as saying that now a person's current wishes should be respected, even if they lack capacity. It makes it clear their current views can be a very important consideration, but they will not always determine an assessment of best interests.[196] In *Newcastle Upon Tyne CC v TP*[197] a young woman wanted to live with her boyfriend, but he was constantly controlling and undermining her. It was not in her best interests to live with him. Indeed, arguably in that case she was not expressing her views, but those of her partner.

10.3 **A person's past views**

The decision maker, in determining a person's best interests, must consider, so far as is reasonably ascertainable:

(a) the person's past and present wishes and feelings (and, in particular, any relevant written statement made by him when he had capacity),

(b) the beliefs and values that would be likely to influence his decision if he had capacity, and

(c) the other factors that he would be likely to consider if he were able to do so.[198]

P's past views are only one factor to consider. The MCA 2005 does not adopt a substituted judgement test (considered later in this chapter).[199] In other words, it does not require decision makers to make a decision based on what they guess the P would have decided if they had capacity.[200] However, an assessment of what P would have wanted had they been able to make the decision is an important factor in deciding what are in his or her best interests.[201] In *Ahsan v University Hospitals Leicester*,[202] a dispute arose in the context of a tort case over the care of a Muslim woman who had been seriously injured and was unaware of what was happening to her. Her family wanted her to be cared for in accordance with the Muslim tradition, but this would be more expensive than other care. The defendant argued that, because she had no awareness of what was happening to her, it was not in her best interests to receive Muslim care. This argument was firmly rejected by Hegarty J.[203] It was in her best interests to receive the Muslim care as that reflected the values she had always lived by. That case may be contrasted with *Re IH (Observance of Muslim Practice)*[204] where IH had always suffered from a profound learning disability. Although raised in a Muslim family it was held it was not required

---

[195] *NHS Trust v QZ* [2017] EWCOP 11; *Cambridge University Hospitals NHS v BF* [2016] EWCOP 26.
[196] See *A Hospital NHS Trust v CD* [2015] EWCOP 74.   [197] [2016] EWCOP 61
[198] MCA 2005, s. 4(6).
[199] See under the heading '12.3 Substituted judgement'. See also *M v A NHS Trust* [2011] EWHC 2443 (Fam).
[200] A point emphasized in *Re P* [2009] EWHC 163 (Ch).
[201] For discussions on how the courts should interpret the MCA 2005, when there is a clash between the wishes of the patient and best interests, see Herring (2009) and Donnelly (2009).
[202] *Ahsan v University Hospitals Leicester NHS Trust* [2006] EWHC 2624 (QB).   [203] At [21].
[204] [2017] EWCOP 9.

that his carer ensure he undertook a fast during Ramadan, although they should enable him to attend religious customs and services. The fast would only cause IH stress; he did not understand its significance; and the judge heard that Islam did not generally require fasts of those in IH's position. It might also be noted that IH had never had capacity and so been in a position to adopt his own religion.

In *Briggs v Briggs*[205] the assessment of what Mr Briggs would have wanted had he been able to express his views was described as 'determinative' of his best interests, trumping all other factors, even the presumption in favour of life. However, McDonald J confirmed that this assessment would depend on the facts of the case and there would be cases where it would not be in someone's best interests to follow the assessment of what they would have wanted to happen.

It is not always easy to ascertain a person's past views. In *M v A NHS Trust*,[206] Baker J refused to place substantial weight on general remarks that P made about not wanting to be dependent on others several years before she became ill. These were seen as too vague to guide the court in making a decision about a particular situation that later arose. It seems that only clear expressions of opinion on issues that directly relate to P's condition will carry significant weight.

In some cases, there may be a clash between P's current wishes and P's past wishes. Both must be considered under section 4(6). Mary Donnelly argues that where there is a clash between these preferences, current preferences should carry greater weight and prevail where there is no clear assessment of best interests.[207] This is a controversial approach to take, however. P's past views were the views that she had when competent and it might be argued that they should carry greater weight than the views that she now has when lacking capacity. Daniel Brudney argues that a decision should be made that is authentic to the life that P has led.[208] That would involve considering the values that have underpinned P's life generally.

In *A Local Authority v Mrs A and Mr A*,[209] part of the reason why it was decided that it would have been in Mrs A's best interests to receive contraception was that, before she fell under Mr A's influence, she had been keen to use it. However, the case shows the need to balance current and past needs. Although it would have been in her best interests to receive contraception had she consented, it was not in her best interests to be forced to receive it. The decision has proved controversial. I have criticized it for downplaying the dangers of not receiving contraception.[210] Should not more weight have been placed on Mrs A's free views before she met Mr A than on her compelled views once she was under his influence? Although compelling her to receive the contraceptive injection would have interfered with her bodily integrity, would it have done so any less than an unwanted pregnancy?

10.4 The view of P's relatives and carers

Yet further factors to consider in the best interests analysis are the views of:

(a) anyone named by the person as someone to be consulted on the matter in question or on matters of that kind,

---

[205] [2016] EWCOP 53.   [206] [2011] EWHC 2443 (Fam).
[207] Donnelly (2009a). See also Herring (2009d).   [208] Brudney (2009).
[209] [2010] EWHC 1549 (Fam).   [210] Herring (2010b).

(b) anyone engaged in caring for the person or interested in his welfare,

(c) any donee of a lasting power of attorney granted by the person, and

(d) any deputy appointed for the person by the court, as to what would be in the patient's best interests.[211]

The decision maker may choose to consult a wider group of people than this, but is not required to do so.[212] It is unclear how much weight should be placed on the views of a family. If P's family are all Jehovah's Witnesses and oppose the required blood transfusion, should their views carry the day? Probably not: the views of family members are only one factor and, in such a case, it would be hard to see P's death as in P's best interests, as that term is generally understood in society.[213] The views of family members are to be taken into account only in so far as they assist in determining P's best interests.[214] They can never be used to justify making an order that would be against P's best interests.[215] Where a family member has abused P, the family member's views are likely to carry little weight.[216] In *Re Aidiniantz*[217] the views of an older woman's children were said to carry no weight. They had no insight into her well-being and seemed more concerned to get the better of each other, than assess their mother's well-being. However, in *A Local Authority v E*,[218] it was held that although there is no presumption that a person lacking capacity is better off cared for by his or her family than in an institution, 'nevertheless the normal assumption [is] that mentally incapacitated adults who have been looked after within their family will be better off if they continue to be looked after within the family rather than by the state'.[219]

The focus of the best interests assessment must be on what is best for P, not on what is best for P's family or carers. However, there is not always a clear distinction between the two. In *A NHS Trust v DE*,[220] the court, in ordering DE, who lacked capacity to make the decision, to have a vasectomy took into account that, without it, his parents would be worried. That was something that DE would not want. Further, without it, he could not maintain a long-term relationship with his girlfriend. Here, the relational values played a major part in justifying the procedure. A more controversial example of that kind of thinking is the following:

KEY CASE   *Re Y (Adult Patient) Transplant: Bone Marrow* [1997] Fam 110

Y, aged 25, was severely mentally and physically disabled. She lived in a community home, but was regularly visited by her mother. Y's sister suffered from a bone disorder and her only real prospect of recovery was a bone marrow donation. Y was, in medical terms, a suitable donor, but owing to her disabilities was unable to consent. The sister sought a declaration authorizing the harvesting of bone marrow.

[211] MCA 2005, s. 4(7).   [212] DCA (2007: para. 4.23).
[213] For a case where the views of parents who refused a blood transfusion for their child were overridden, see *An NHS Trust v Child B* [2014] EWHC 3486 (Fam).
[214] *Re MM (An Adult)* [2007] EWHC 2003 (Fam), [108].
[215] *A Primary Care Trust v P, AH, A Local Authority* [2008] EWHC 1403 (Fam). See also *MCC v WMA* [2013] EWHC 2580 (COP).   [216] *IIBCC v LG* [2010] EWHC 1527 (Fam).   [217] [2015] EWCOP 65.
[218] [2007] EWHC 2396 (Fam), [66].   [219] See further Herring (2009a) for discussion of this.
[220] [2013] EWHC 2562 (Fam).

Connell J granted the declaration. The basis of the reasoning was that, by making the donation to her sister, this would benefit Y's mother, who was very important to Y's well-being. Y's mother was in ill-health, partly owing to anxiety concerning the sister's state of health. There was some evidence that if the sister were to die, this would be fatal to the mother. If the mother were to die, this would severely distress Y. Also, it was held that Y would receive an emotional, psychological, and social benefit from the operation. Connell J indicated that the fact that the operation required Y to suffer only a 'minimal detriment' was an important aspect of the decision to authorize the harvesting.

Indeed, it has been argued that it is not in P's interest to live in a relationship in which no account is taken of the interests of his or her carer, especially where that carer is a member of the patient's family.[221] Few people would be happy with the idea that, if they were to lose capacity, a decision would be made that benefited them only a little bit even at the cost of causing grave harm to the person caring for them.[222] Indeed, no carer could take every decision for a person who had lost capacity based solely on what is in that person's best interests.[223]

In *Re G (TJ)*,[224] a woman had lost capacity. The question arose whether payments that she had been making to her adult daughter, of whom she was fond and who was in financial need, should continue. Morgan J held:

> [T]he word 'interest' in the best interests test does not confine the court to considering the self-interest of P. The actual wishes of P, which are altruistic and not in any way, directly or indirectly self-interested, can be a relevant factor. Further, the wishes which P would have formed, if P had capacity, which may be altruistic wishes, can be a relevant factor.[225]

As this case demonstrates, 'best interests' need not be interpreted in a selfish way. It can include acting altruistically towards one's friends and family. This case was particularly strong because there was good evidence that the woman, when she had capacity, had wanted to support her daughter. Less straightforwardly, in *Re N (Deprivation of Liberty Challenge)*[226] the court was faced with a man with learning difficulties who had paedophilic tendencies.[227] The question arose whether he should be allowed to go out into the community alone. His lack of understanding of his tendencies meant he lacked capacity to make the decision. It was held that it was in his best interests that he not go outside his house unaccompanied. Critics of the case might claim his deprivation of liberty was for the benefit of others (children nearby) rather than for his own benefit. However, it might be argued that broadly understood it would be contrary to his well-being if he were to commit child abuse.

10.5 The use of restraint or force

There are special rules that apply where force or restraint is to be used against P. The Deprivation of Liberty Code of Practice has indicated the kind of people for whom these special rules apply:

---

[221] Herring and Foster (2012).   [222] Herring (2008a). See also the discussion in DCA (2007: ch. 5).
[223] See further Herring (2008b).   [224] [2010] EWHC 3005 (COP).   [225] At [56].
[226] [2016] EWCOP 47.   [227] He had a history of attempting to contact children for sexual purposes.

The safeguards apply to people in England and Wales who have a mental disorder and lack capacity to consent to the arrangements made for their care or treatment, but for whom receiving care or treatment in circumstances that amount to a deprivation of liberty may be necessary to protect them from harm and appears to be in their best interests. A large number of these people will be those with significant learning disabilities, or older people who have dementia or some similar disability, but they can also include those who have certain other neurological conditions (for example as a result of a brain injury).[228]

The Code produced the following non-exhaustive list of factors that would indicate whether someone is deprived of their liberty:

- Restraint is used, including sedation, to admit a person to an institution where that person is resisting admission.

- Staff exercise complete and effective control over the care and movement of a person for a significant period.

- Staff exercise control over assessments, treatment, contacts, and residence.

- A decision has been taken by the institution that the person will not be released into the care of others, or permitted to live elsewhere, unless the staff in the institution consider it appropriate.

- A request by carers for a person to be discharged to their care is refused.

- The person is unable to maintain social contacts because of restrictions placed on their access to other people.

- The person loses autonomy because they are under continuous supervision and control.[229]

Then, not only must the person doing the restraining reasonably believe that P lacks capacity in relation to the issue and that it will be in P's best interests for the act to be done,[230] but two further conditions must also be satisfied. These are set out in section 6 of the MCA 2005:

(2)   The first condition is that D reasonably believes that it is necessary to do the act in order to prevent harm to P.

(3)   The second is that the act is a proportionate response to—

(a)   the likelihood of P's suffering harm, and

(b)   the seriousness of that harm.

(4)   For the purposes of this section D restrains P if he—

(a)   uses, or threatens to use, force to secure the doing of an act which P resists, or

(b)   restricts P's liberty of movement, whether or not P resists.

(5)   But D does more than merely restrain P if he deprives P of his liberty within the meaning of Article 5(1) of the Human Rights Convention (whether or not D is a public authority).

---

[228] Ministry of Justice (2009: para. 1.7).   [229] Ministry of Justice (2009: para. 2.5).
[230] MCA 2005, s. 5.

Where P is to be deprived of his or her liberty, section 4A[231] of the MCA 2005 applies:

(1)   This Act does not authorise any person ('D') to deprive any other person ('P') of his liberty.

(2)   But that is subject to—

    (a)   the following provisions of this section, and

    (b)   section 4B.

(3)   D may deprive P of his liberty if, by doing so, D is giving effect to a relevant decision of the court.

(4)   A relevant decision of the court is a decision made by an order under section 16(2)(a) in relation to a matter concerning P's personal welfare.

(5)   D may deprive P of his liberty if the deprivation is authorised by Schedule A1 (hospital and care home residents: deprivation of liberty).

The Deprivation of Liberty Code of Practice adds:

Depriving someone who lacks the capacity to consent to the arrangements made for their care or treatment of their liberty is a serious matter, and the decision to do so should not be taken lightly. The deprivation of liberty safeguards make it clear that a person may only be deprived of their liberty:

- in their own best interests to protect them from harm,

- if it is a proportionate response to the likelihood and seriousness of the harm, and

- if there is no less restrictive alternative.[232]

It is clear that any restraint of liberty must be approved by a court order or under the Deprivation of Liberty Safeguards (DOLS) procedures in Schedule A1 of the 2005 Act.[233] The court can issue a declaration in advance authorizing an act of restraint or removal,[234] although notably some judges appear reluctant to do this unless it has proved impossible to remove the individual without force.[235] The detention could involve sedation, if necessary.[236]

Schedule A1 of the 2005 Act sets out the DOLS procedures—that is, the circumstances in which a supervisory body[237] can authorize the deprivation of a resident's liberty.[238] The supervisory body can authorize the detention only if it is in the best interests of the individual concerned[239] and the detention is a proportionate response to any harm, given its likelihood and severity.[240] An interesting further requirement is

---

[231] Inserted by the Mental Health Act 2007.   [232] Ministry of Justice (2009: para. 1.13).

[233] *W Primary Care Trust v TB* [2009] EWHC 1737 (Fam); *City of Sunderland v PS* [2007] EWHC 623 (Fam), [23].

[234] *A Primary Care Trust v P, AH, A Local Authority* [2008] EWHC 1403 (Fam).

[235] *Dorset CC v EH* [2009] EWHC 784 (Fam).   [236] *DH NHS v PS* [2010] EWHC 1217 (Fam).

[237] A local authority or healthcare trust.

[238] In MCA 2005, Sch. A1, para. 22, the circumstances in which a supervisory body has a duty to apply for a deprivation of liberty authorization are set out. The operation of these provisions can become highly complex: see *W Primary Care Trust v TB* [2009] EWHC 1737 (Fam).

[239] MCA 2005, Sch. A1, para. 39 sets out some detailed issues that should be taken into account when making an assessment of best interests.

[240] MCA 2005, Sch. A1, para. 16.

that there must be no refusal of detention in an effective advance directive, or by a donee or deputy. An important limitation on the use of the provisions is that they cannot be used to deprive a person of his or her liberty if that person could be detained under the Mental Health Act 1983 (at which we will look in Chapter 10).[241] That prevents the DOLS procedures from being used to bypass the protections offered in the 1983 Act.[242]

Where the deprivation of liberty is justified under the MCA 2005, then the Court of Appeal has held that it can be taken that the requirements of Article 5 ECHR will also have been satisfied.[243]

10.6 Independent mental capacity advocates

The MCA 2005, section 35, creates the post of 'independent mental health advocate' (IMHA). An IMHA will be created by health authorities. The IMHA's role is set out in section 36. An IMHA is to be used where there is no person other than a professional carer whom it would be appropriate to consult concerning P's interests. It involves providing support to the person lacking capacity, and ascertaining his or her wishes and feelings. The IMHA can ask for further medical opinions relating to the person and obtain other information. The regulations provide that the advocate can challenge any medical decision made concerning a person lacking capacity. Under section 37, if it is proposed to provide 'serious medical treatment',[244] then an IMHA must be appointed to represent P, unless the treatment is required urgently.

11 Consent of children

11.1 Who can consent for the medical treatment of a child?

A child is any person under the age of 18.[245] As indicated earlier in the chapter, it could be both a tort or a criminal offence for a doctor to treat a child without the 'flak jacket' of consent. Such as 'flak jacket' can be provided by any of the following.

11.1.1 A child aged 16 or 17

The Family Law Reform Act 1969, section 8, states that a child aged 16 or 17 can consent to 'treatment' and that such consent is to be treated in the same way as would be an adult's consent. Treatment includes diagnosis and procedures ancillary to treatment (such as the administration of anaesthetics).[246] However, it may not cover every 'medical procedure'. Cosmetic surgery, tissue donation, or research are very unlikely to be classified as 'treatment'. If the procedure is not treatment, 16- and 17-year-olds can consent if they can show that they are '*Gillick* competent', a concept that we shall discuss next.[247]

---

[241] MCA 2005, Sch. 1A, para. 2; *BB v MA* [2010] EWHC 1916 (Fam).
[242] This can lead to complex disputes over whether the patient is being detained for treatment for physical problems or his mental disorder: *GJ v Foundation Trust* [2009] EWHC 2972 (Fam), discussed in Allen (2010).
[243] *G v E* [2010] EWCA 822. See Fanning (2016) for further discussion.
[244] The phrase will be defined in the regulations.   [245] Family Law Reform Act 1969, s. 1.
[246] Family Law Reform Act 1969, s. 8(2).
[247] Family Law Reform Act 1969, s. 8(3), explicitly preserves the common law on the consent of children.

11.1.2 A 'Gillick competent child'

If the child can show that he or she has sufficient maturity to make the decision in question, then the child can provide legal consent for the medical procedure.[248] Such a child is known as a '*Gillick* competent child', after the decision in *Gillick v West Norfolk Area Health Authority*,[249] which first acknowledged the notion of a competent child. To be *Gillick* competent, the child must:

(a) understand the nature and implications of the treatment, which would include the likely effects and potential side effects;

(b) understand the implications of not pursuing the treatment, including the nature, likely progress and consequences of any illness that would result from not receiving the treatment;

(c) retain the above information long enough for the decision making process to take place; and

(d) be of sufficient intelligence and maturity to weigh up the information and arrive at a decision.[250]

If doctors or courts are deciding whether a child is competent, they will consider the following points.

(i) The child must understand the medical issues. As with adults, the child must understand the proposed treatment, the consequences of not having treatment, and the effect of treatment. This means that the more complex the medical procedure, the harder it will be for a child to show that he or she is competent.[251] In *Re E*,[252] a Jehovah's Witness child refused a blood transfusion. He was held to lack capacity because he did not understand the slow and painful process of his death were he not to receive the blood transfusion. A similar point has been made in several cases involving children refusing life-saving treatment.[253] These cases have been criticized on the basis that the children have not known of the nature of their death because the doctors have decided they would be too distressed to be told. To find a child not competent because he or she does not know information that doctors have decided not to provide is difficult to defend. As Montgomery puts it: '[I]t is the refusal of the adults to allow her to be informed that rendered her incompetent, not her ability to comprehend.'[254]

(ii) The child must understand the 'moral and family' issues involved.[255] Although the courts have emphasized this, the Department of Health and British Medical Association (BMA) guidance do not mention the need for the child to be morally mature.[256] Perhaps it is assumed that if the child has the mental capacity to understand the medical issues involved, he or she will also be aware of the key moral issues.

(iii) The child needs only to have the maturity needed to consent to the particular issue in question. In other words, a child may be mature enough to consent to a

---

[248] *Re JS (A Child) (Disposal of body)* [2016] EWHC 2859 (Fam).   [249] [1985] 3 All ER 402.

[250] *An NHS Trust v Mr and Mrs A* [2014] EWHC 1135 (Fam), para. 68.

[251] See the discussion in Gilmore and Herring (2011).   [252] [1993] 1 FLR 386.

[253] *Re S* [1994] 2 FLR 1065.   [254] Montgomery (2003: 292).

[255] [1985] 3 All ER 402, 424, *per* Lord Scarman. But see Montgomery (2003: 290), who is not persuaded that this is required.

[256] DoH (2001c); BMA (2001).

straightforward procedure, but not to consent to a far more complex one. Note there is no minimum age for being *Gillick* competent. In *An NHS Trust v A, B and C*[257] a girl who had just turned 13 was found to have capacity to make a decision about an abortion.

(iv) If the child is fluctuating between competence and incompetence, he or she should be treated as incompetent.[258] The primary concern here is to ensure that the law is workable. A hospital caring for a teenager who is competent to consent one moment, but incompetent the next, would be in a difficult position if it had to assess the child continually every time there were a need to treat him or her.

(v) The court will need to be persuaded that the child is sufficiently mature to reach his or her own decision and not merely be repeating the views of his or her parents. This consideration has been particularly pertinent where the courts have felt that a child with a strict religious upbringing has not been made sufficiently aware of a variety of ways of understanding the world and so is not sufficiently competent.[259] In *Re S*,[260] for example, a 15-year-old Jehovah's Witness refused a blood transfusion. She was not, however, able to explain clearly why she objected to the transfusion. The court was not confident that she was sufficiently competent to make the decision for herself. In *Re L*,[261] an expert felt able to say that the religious views of a 14-year-old Jehovah Witness were merely a reflection of those of her parents and the local church, even though he had not actually seen the girl.

(vi) In assessing whether a child is competent or not, the court should not reason that, because the decision is 'wrong', the child must lack capacity.[262]

It is not yet clear what the position would be if a doctor were to assess a child as competent and perform treatment on him or her, but the court subsequently assessed the child as lacking capacity. Kennedy has suggested that if a medical professional were to assess a child as competent in good faith, then the court would not hold the doctor to have committed a criminal offence.[263] It is less clear whether the doctor's wrong assessment would provide a defence in civil law. In cases involving adults, a court has been willing to award damages where the professionals were found to have wrongly assessed a patient as lacking capacity.[264]

11.1.3 *The consent of a person with parental responsibility for the child*

A person with parental responsibility can consent to treatment for his or her child. We have already considered who has parental responsibility.[265]

11.1.4 *An order of the court*

A court can make an order authorizing medical treatment either under the Children Act 1989, section 8, or under its inherent jurisdiction. It would also be possible for the court to order that a certain kind of treatment not be given to a child. If an application is brought under either jurisdiction, the court will make the order that best promotes the welfare of the child.[266]

[257] [2014] EWHC 1445.   [258] *Re R* [1991] 4 All ER 177.
[259] *Re L* [1998] 2 FLR 810.   [260] [1993] 1 FLR 376.   [261] [1998] 2 FLR 810.
[262] *South Glamorgan CC v B* [1993] 1 FLR 574.   [263] Kennedy (1991a: 107).
[264] *St George's Healthcare NHS Trust v S* [1998] 3 All ER 673.
[265] See earlier in this chapter, under the heading '2.3 Children lacking capacity'.
[266] Children Act 1989, s. 1.

11.1.5 *The defence of necessity*

Where a child needs urgent medical treatment to avoid death or serious harm, the doctor may perform that treatment even without the protection of a court order or parental consent. This is so in the case of life-saving treatment even if the parent objects.[267] However, the defence may be available only if there was not sufficient time to enable the doctor to get the consent of a parent or the court. It must be admitted that the doctrine of necessity is of uncertain scope. Whether it can be used to justify medical treatment for non-serious conditions is open to debate. For example, if a child in hospital were to cut a finger and a nurse want to put a plaster on the small cut, would he or she first have to obtain the consent of the parents? And if the parents cannot be contacted, must an application to court be made? Lavery has suggested that necessity can be used to justify routine medical treatment.[268] This would seem a sensible suggestion, although there is no clear judicial support for it.

11.1.6 *The Children Act 1989, section 3(5)*

The Children Act 1989, section 3(5), states that a person with care of a child may do 'what is reasonable in all the circumstances of the case for the purpose of safeguarding or promoting the child's welfare'. In *B v B*,[269] it was suggested that this could include the power to consent to medical treatment. But the extent to which this is true is unclear. It may well cover someone putting a plaster on a minor cut, but most commentators take the view that the section cannot be used to authorize treatment to which a parent objects, or major irreversible surgery.

11.2 Disagreements between the decision makers

11.2.1 *Doctors and parents or children*

It is important to appreciate that simply because a parent or competent child has consented to a treatment does not mean that the doctor must provide the treatment. So even though a doctor may decide that a child seeking cosmetic surgery is competent, this does not mean that the doctor must provide that treatment.[270] This is true for children, just as it is for adults. Not only that, but a court cannot require a doctor to treat a child in a way that the doctor believes is inappropriate. However, if a medical team wish to perform an operation, they need the consent of either the person with parental responsibility *or* a *Gillick* competent child. Failing either of these, they need to apply for court authorization to perform the operation, unless there is a medical emergency requiring the operation on the child and there is no time to apply to court.[271] It should be borne in mind that, in an emergency, it is normally possible to find a judge to hear a case within an hour. The court will make the order that will best promote the welfare of the child.

There is also an issue about whether or not there are procedures which should not be performed on children, or at least delayed until the child is an adult. A good example

---

[267] For example, *Re O* [1993] 2 FLR 149.   [268] Lavery (1990).   [269] [1992] 2 FLR 327.
[270] See, e.g., *Re R* [1991] 4 All ER 177, 184; *Re C (Detention: Medical Treatment)* [1997] 2 FLR 180.
[271] *Glass v UK* [2004] 1 FCR 553; *Royal Wolverhampton Hospitals NHS Trust v B* [2000] 1 FLR 953.

is surgery on children born with intersex bodies, where it may well be best to delay any surgery designed to ensure the child appears male or female as traditionally understood until the child is old enough to make their own decision.[272] Of course, they may decide they do not want any such surgery.

11.2.2 If the child and parents disagree

The approach taken by the Court of Appeal in *Re R*[273] and *Re W*[274] is that a doctor needs only one 'flak jacket' as protection from potential legal protection. This means that a doctor can provide treatment in any of the following situations:

- the *Gillick* competent child consents, but the parents object;
- a parent with parental responsibility consents, but the *Gillick* competent child objects;[275] or
- the court authorizes the treatment, despite the objections of parent and child.

If necessary, a reasonable level of force can be used to ensure that the treatment is given to a child who is objecting.[276]

In the decision in *R (Axon) v Secretary of State for Health*,[277] Silber J suggested that, once a child becomes *Gillick* competent, the parent loses any right under the Human Rights Act 1998 to respect for family life and to make any decisions for the child. It would be reading too much into this to conclude that the courts will not follow *Re R* and *Re W*, but it suggests that the courts are becoming more open to arguments based on the rights of children.[278] In *An NHS Trust v A, M and P*[279] Hayden J stated:

> A competent young person under the age of 16 years, who is able to understand all the relevant advice and the consequences of that advice, is to be treated as an autonomous individual and respected as such. That of course would not mean her views would be determinative, but they would be given great weight.[280]

That could be contrasted with *An NHS Trust v A, B and C*[281] in which Mostyn J concluded that a 13-year-old girl had capacity to make a decision about an abortion and therefore it would 'now be for A to decide what she wishes to do'. It may be in that context the competent girl's views decided the issue because there was no clear consensus on whether an abortion would be in her best interests or not.[282]

The law as set out in *Re R* and *Re W* is highly contentious. It appears to fly in the face of children's rights. To take an extreme example, it would mean that if a competent pregnant 15-year-old did not want an abortion, but her parents did, the doctor could lawfully carry out the termination of the pregnancy. We shall return to these

---

[272] Newbould (2016); Herring and Chau (2002).   [273] [1991] 4 All ER 177.
[274] [1992] 4 All ER 627.
[275] The Court of Appeal makes it so clear that this is the law that, in *Northamptonshire Health Authority v Official Solicitor and Governors of St Andrew's Hospital* [1994] 1 FLR 162, it awarded costs against a local authority that sought court approval for treating a child who objected to treatment, but whose parents consented. It was so clear that the local authority could rely on the parental consent that the application for a court order was unnecessary.
[276] *Re C (Detention: Medical Treatment)* [1997] 2 FLR 180.   [277] [2006] EWHC 37 (Admin).
[278] Taylor (2007).   [279] [2014] EWHC 920 (Fam).   [280] Para. 12.
[281] [2014] EWHC 1445.   [282] For a helpful discussion of this case see Moreton (2015).

issues later in this chapter. But it should be noted that what the law is saying is that a doctor may, *not*, must treat a child if a parent objects. In the abortion scenario, it is extremely unlikely that a doctor would be willing to perform an operation on a non-consenting teenager. So, in practice, it may be that the concerns that children's rights will be readily overridden are overstated. Indeed, if a parent can be said to be exercising parental responsibility in a way that positively harms the child, then arguably it is ineffective.

In a novel interpretation of the case law, Stephen Gilmore and I have suggested that the *Re R* and *Re W* cases were dealing with children who were seen by the court as having capacity to consent to treatment, but lacking capacity to refuse *all* treatment.[283] We argue that this is not as strange as it sounds because, to be able to consent to treatment, you need to understand only in broad terms the treatment proposed, while to refuse all treatment, you need to understand the consequences of refusing. So a child who has cut his or her knee might be able to understand what putting a plaster on the knee involves and so be able to consent. However, he or she may not understand the potential consequences, such as septicaemia, of not treating the cut and so may be unable to refuse. If this is the correct interpretation of the case law, then we are yet to have an authoritative decision on whether a child who is competent to refuse all treatment can have that refusal overridden by his or her parents.[284]

11.2.3 *If the parents disagree*

The Children Act 1989, section 2(7), implies that one parent with parental responsibility can act alone and consent to treatment, without consulting or having to reach an agreement with the other parent. However, the courts have stated that, in relation to important issues, parents must consult. It is not clear precisely what issues might · be regarded as 'important' issues. In *Re J*,[285] it was held that circumcision was one such issue, as was the decision not to give a child the MMR vaccine in *Re B*.[286] No doubt, abortion and cosmetic surgery would also be included. What these cases indicate is that parents with parental responsibility should consult; if they are unable to reach an agreement, an application should be made to the court to determine the issue.[287]

11.2.4 *Where the courts and parents disagree*

If there is a dispute over the correct medical treatment for the child, then the court must simply decide what is in the best interests of the child.[288] The court can override the views of the child and/or parent if they do not accord with the welfare of the child.[289] As Ward J has put it: 'Parents may be free to become martyrs themselves, but it does not follow that they are free in identical circumstances to make martyrs of their children.'[290]

---

[283] Gilmore and Herring (2011). See also Tucker (2016).

[284] See Cave and Wallbank (2012), who strongly disagree. See further Gilmore and Herring (2012).

[285] [2000] 1 FLR 571.   [286] [2003] EWCA Civ 1148.

[287] The application would be under Children Act 1989, s. 8.

[288] Children Act 1989, s. 1. *Great Ormond Street v Yates* [2017] EWHC 1909 (Fam).

[289] See, e.g., *Re C (A Child) (HIV Testing)* [2000] Fam 48.   [290] *Re E* [1993] 1 FLR 386, 391.

In cases in which the welfare decision is very finely balanced, the court may decide that the parental views tip the balance in favour of making the order that the parents are seeking.[291] However, a court will not compel a doctor to act in a way that is against his or her clinical judgement.[292] In *The NHS Trust v A*,[293] Holman J summarized the law's approach to taking into account the views of parents:

> The views and opinions of both the doctors and the parents must be carefully considered. Where, as in this case, the parents spend a great deal of time with their child, their views may have particular value because they know the patient and how he reacts so well; although the court needs to be mindful that the views of any parents may, very understandably, be coloured by their own emotion or sentiment. It is important to stress that the reference is to the views and opinions of the parents. Their own wishes, however understandable in human terms, are wholly irrelevant to consideration of the objective best interests of the child save to the extent in any given case that they may illuminate the quality and value to the child of the child/parent relationship.

11.3 Limits on parental consent

Are there some medical procedures that cannot be consented to by a parent? It appears that there are some procedures that cannot be performed on children without court approval. Unfortunately, there is very little guidance on the issue. It has been suggested that the following may be operations that require the consent of the court:

- sterilizations carried out for non-therapeutic reasons;[294]

- refusal of life-saving treatment (if a parent refuses to consent to life-saving treatment, it has been argued that the doctor should obtain court approval before following the parent's views);[295]

- abortion;[296] and

- donation of non-regenerative tissue.[297]

In the absence of a clear legal ruling, if a doctor is unsure about the advisability of an operation, court approval should be sought. This might be so in a case in which controversial cosmetic surgery is sought.

There has been dispute over the extent to which parents should be allowed to consent to 'harmful' procedures involving children, such as bone marrow donation or research.[298] The argument against this is that adults with mental capacity cannot be involved in such activities without their consent and the same principle should apply to children. The arguments in favour include the argument that being involved in altruistic activities can promote a child's welfare.

---

[291] This may be the explanation for *Re T (A Minor) (Wardship: Medical Treatment)* [1997] 1 WLR 242.

[292] *R (Burke) v GMC* [2005] 3 FCR 169. *St George's Healthcare NHS Trust v P* [2015] EWCOP 42 appeared to be a case where doctors were required to provide treatment, but see Keene (2016) who explains that properly interpreted the final order did not do that.

[293] [2007] EWHC 1696 (Fam), [40].   [294] *Re B* [1987] 2 All ER 206, 214 (Lord Templeman).

[295] Bevan (1989: 25–6).   [296] *Re P (A Minor)* (1982) 8 LGR 301.

[297] *Re F* [1989] 2 FLR 376, 390, *per* Lord Donaldson MR, and 440, *per* Neill LJ.   [298] Lyons (2011).

12 Treatment that cannot be consented to

There are two important points to make here. First, it is often emphasized that simply because a competent patient wants treatment does not mean that he or she has a right to it.[299] A doctor is at liberty to refuse to provide a treatment however keenly the patient wants it.[300] It has been said that courts will not force medical professionals to provide treatment that they do not want to provide.[301]

Second, even though a patient and a doctor agree on a form of surgery, the law may prohibit the operation. There may be some public policy objection to a proposed procedure that would render it illegal. The leading case on this is *R v Brown*,[302] in which the House of Lords held that it was unlawful to cause someone actual bodily harm, or more serious injury, unless there was a public policy argument in favour of the conduct, even if the 'victim' was consenting. In that case, a group of men were convicted of criminal offences of violence even though their 'victims' had willingly consented to the actions as part of a sadomasochistic encounter. Clearly, in most cases of orthodox medical treatment, there will be no difficulty in showing that a particular treatment was in the public interest.[303] However, if a modern artist were to ask a doctor to cut off the artist's leg so that she could use it in a new exhibit, it would probably be illegal for a doctor to perform the amputation. The issue very much turns on current social attitudes. There is now little doubt that sterilization operations,[304] gender reassignment surgery,[305] organ transplants,[306] and circumcision of males are lawful.[307] Less clear is the following.

TO PONDER

Consider the following case.[308] If the doctors had operated, would they have committed an offence?

In 2000, 55-year-old Gregg Furth, a psychoanalyst from New York, travelled to the UK to see psychiatrists and the surgeon who had previously amputated the healthy legs of two men with body integrity identity disorder (BIID). Since before he was 10 years old, Mr Furth could recall feeling that the lower part of his right leg was not part of his body. Since then, he constantly thought about being without that part of his leg and had searched for many years to find a surgeon willing to amputate it. Mr Furth had undergone many years of therapy, but had not been able to repress the feelings he had about his leg. He was assessed by two psychiatrists in the UK, both of whom confirmed that he was competent to make the decision and was suffering from body dysmorphic disorder. Both psychiatrists recommended him for amputation and the surgeon agreed to carry out the procedure. Shortly before the operation was due to take place, however, the hospital withdrew its permission for any more operations of this type to be undertaken on its premises.[309]

---

[299] Maclean (2001).   [300] *Re J (A Minor) (Wardship: Medical Treatment)* [1990] 3 All ER 930.
[301] *An NHS Trust v L* [2013] EWHC 4313 (Fam); *Re C (A Minor)* [1998] Lloyd's Rep Med 1.
[302] [1993] 2 All ER 75.   [303] *R v Brown* [1993] 2 All ER 75, 109–10.
[304] *Gold v Haringey Health Authority* [1987] 2 All ER 888.   [305] Gender Recognition Act 2004.
[306] Human Organ Transplants Act 1989.
[307] *Re J* [2000] 1 FCR 307. Circumcision of females is prohibited by the Female Genital Mutilation Act 2003. Circumcision of males is debated in Davis (2013) and Mazor (2013).
[308] BMA and Law Society (2004: 94).
[309] See further Schramme (2007), who discusses the legality of 'extreme bodily modification'.

Tracey Elliott, in her review of cases of body dysmorphic disorder (BDD) concludes that removal of healthy limbs should be permitted in some cases. She writes:

> If the criminal law has no place in controlling cosmetic surgery performed by qualified surgeons upon competent adults with their consent, why should it have any place in controlling other forms of surgery performed in similar circumstances? I suggest that provided that surgery is conducted by appropriately qualified medical practitioners upon adults who have capacity, and who have consented to the procedure, the matter could be regulated by the civil law, and by the medical profession.[310]

Her view is that as long as there is consent and the medical professional is not negligent in the *Bolam* sense, the procedure should be permitted.[311] As Mackenzie notes, some of those with BDD argue that, far from amputation rendering them disabled, they will be disabled without the operation by having too many limbs.[312] Thomas Schramme appears to go further and would permit body modification even where there is no medical need.[313] He sees it as a basic aspect of a person's liberty. Critics will respond that Elliott's approach regards such cases as private matters involving simply the patient and the doctor. It fails to place sufficient weight on the public interest in such cases. In Chapter 1, the issue of cosmetic surgery was discussed and arguments about the impact on wider society of allowing cosmetic surgery were considered. Whether allowing those who wish to have limbs removed is harming society may be a matter of debate, but the issue is certainly not simply one of autonomy. An alternative criticism is to question whether those seeking amputation are genuinely acting autonomously.[314] Similar issues are likely to be increasingly debatable, for example the practice of inserting large cosmetic subdermal implants, which give the impression of horns and the like.[315]

13 Actions in negligence based on a failure to provide sufficient information

Even though a patient may have been provided with sufficient information to consent to a procedure, he or she may claim that the doctor was negligent in failing to provide the appropriate level of information. Note this is, technically, a different argument from a claim that there was no consent. A patient may accept they did consent to the operation, but still claim they were not told all of the information they should have been. In such a case, the claim should be brought in negligence. Such claims raise a number of issues.

13.1 How much information must be provided? The general approach

A delicate balance needs to be drawn when deciding how much information needs to be given to a patient. Too much information may simply overwhelm a patient, but too little means they do not understand the key risks. The approach of English law is found in the following leading case.

---

[310] Elliott (2009: 182).   [311] See also Travis (2014).   [312] Mackenzie (2008).
[313] Schramme (2008).   [314] Patrone (2009).   [315] Oultram (2009).

KEY CASE *Montgomery v Lanarkshire Health Board* [2015] UKSC 11

Nadine Montgomery was in the late stage of pregnancy and complications arose. She was not told about the possibility of a Caesarean section nor was she told that because she had diabetes there was a 9–10 per cent risk of shoulder dystocia if she proceeded with a vaginal birth. She went ahead with a 'natural delivery'. Sadly the risk of shoulder dystocia materialized and her son was born with complex disabilities. Ms Montgomery stated that if she had been told of this risk and the option of a Caesarean section she would have opted for that and claimed damages in negligence.

The Supreme Court found in favour of Ms Montgomery. She should have been told of the risk and alternative forms of birth. Lords Kerr and Reed, writing on behalf of the Court, held that a doctor had a duty to take reasonable care to ensure the patient was aware of any material risks involved in any recommended treatment. The doctor must also inform the patient of reasonable alternative treatments or variations on treatments. By a material risk they meant either (a) risks that a reasonable person in the position of patient would be likely to attach significance to, or (b) risks the doctor should reasonably be aware that the particular patient would be likely to attach significance to. Applying this approach to the facts of the case a 9–10 per cent chance of a serious disability was a risk a reasonable woman in labour would attach significance to. She should also have been told of the alternative of a Caesarean section which carried a smaller risk to the mother and almost no risk to the baby.

There were two exceptions to this duty. The first was 'therapeutic privilege'. That meant that if the doctor believes informing the patient of the risk would be 'seriously detrimental to the patient's health' it should be disclosed. The second exception was if there was an emergency situation and no time to inform the patient of the risks.

This decision marks a clear departure from the previous law. In *Sidaway v Bethlem Royal Hospital Governors*[316] the House of Lords held a doctor was required to disclose the amount of information that a responsible body of medical opinion thought appropriate. That approach has been rejected and following *Montgomery* it is the patient, not the doctors, who determine how much information should be given. The shift here is away from ensuring the doctor follows standard professional practice to requiring the doctor to enable the patient to exercise their autonomy.

Following *Montgomery* a doctor must disclose a material risk, unless the therapeutic privilege exception applies or it is an emergency situation. Their Lordships explained two ways in which a risk might be material.[317] First, if the reasonable person would be likely to attach significance to a risk. The Supreme Court explained it was not appropriate to put a percentage at which a risk became material, because whether a risk was material depended on a range of factors including:

> the nature of the risk, the effect which its occurrence would have upon the life of the patient, the importance to the patient of the benefits sought to be achieved by the treatment, the alternatives available, and the risks involved in those alternatives.[318]

---

[316] [1985] 1 All ER 643.
[317] In *Webster v Burton Hospitals NHS Foundation Trust* [2017] EWCA 62 Simon LJ stated that the word 'material' could not be reduced to a percentage.
[318] Para. 89.

In *A v East Kent Hospitals University NHS Foundation Trust*[319] a risk of 1 in 1,000 was said by Dingemans J to be 'theoretical, negligible, or background' and not material. There is room for some debate here over what is meant by the 'reasonable patient' when considering what risks the reasonable patient would wish to have disclosed. Does that refer to the average patient? Or a patient who is governed by rational thought? Those two might not be the same thing.

Second, the risk would be material if it was one the particular patient would attach significance to, even if the reasonable person would not. Then if the doctor ought to have been aware the particular patient would attach a risk to it, they would be negligent in not disclosing it. So, for example, a risk of a very minor blemish to the skin on the hand might be ignored by most patients, but for a patient who was a hand model, this might be a serious matter and so material for them. Note that under this ground it is necessary to show the doctor ought reasonably to know the patient would think this was important. So, in our imagined scenario, the court would consider whether the doctor should have known the patient was a model. This limb of materiality would also cover cases where a patient asks about a particular risk. Clearly in asking about the risk the patient makes it clear to the doctor that it is something that concerns them and the doctor must give a full answer to such questions.

The doctor must not only disclose the risks attached to treatments, but also their chances of success.[320] This will enable the patient to weight up the pros and cons of the different options and decide which is best for them.

Having explained the general approach, some tricky issues flowing from *Montgomery* will be explored.

13.2 Difficult issues about how much information must be provided.

13.2.1 *The obsessive patient*

The example of the hand model, just discussed, is relatively straightforward. But what if the doctor knows the patient is obsessive about risks or attaches absurd significance to things that most people would think are irrelevant? It seems that in such a case, the doctor needs to disclose all possible risks. At first that seems to put an impossible burden on doctors. Perhaps in such a case referring a patient to a website or providing written information would be sufficient.

13.2.2 *The confused patient*

A major concern with the decision is that doctors may decide that the safest way to comply with *Montgomery* is to tell patients of every single risk. But if that happens a patient may simply become confused or overwhelmed. Rather than enhancing autonomy, *Montgomery* would have undermined it. As anyone who has looked at the long list of possible side effects that are listed in the leaflet that is given with medication realizes, soon one loses attention, not to mention the will to live! It seems not implausible to claim that a patient will be able to better placed to make a decision if they are told the three major risks, rather than being told every one of sixty risks, however unlikely.

---

[319] [2015] EWHC 1038 (QB).   [320] *Thefaut v Johnston* [2017] EWHC 497 (QB).

Their Lordships in *Montgomery* were aware of this danger and emphasized the information had to be provided in a comprehensive way. Lords Reed and Kerr held that:

> the doctor's advisory role involves dialogue, the aim of which is to ensure that the patient understands the seriousness of her condition, and the anticipated benefits and risks of the proposed treatment and any reasonable alternatives, so that she is then in a position to make an informed decision. This role will only be performed effectively if the information provided is comprehensible. The doctor's duty is not therefore fulfilled by bombarding the patient with technical information which she cannot reasonably be expected to grasp, let alone by routinely demanding her signature on a consent form.

It may be that the way the information is presented will depend from patient to patient and their abilities to deal with large amounts of information. Giving extensive information in written form, while highlighting the key risks verbally, is one possible way ahead.

13.2.3 *The worried patient*

Another issue of controversy is the therapeutic privilege exception. This is likely to apply to cases where if a patient is informed of a risk their health will be seriously harmed. It is clearly not sufficient simply to show that informing the patient about the risk will cause them to worry or be upset. Nor can it be used on the basis that if the patient is informed of the risk they will refuse to consent and that will be harmful to them. Rather, it would need to be shown that if the patient were told of a risk they would suffer a clear harm, such as a panic attack or depression.

But some might argue that puts the bar too high. If a patient will simply get very nervous if told of risks should it not be their choice to decide not to hear about them? The Supreme Court explained:

> A person can of course decide that she does not wish to be informed of risks of injury (just as a person may choose to ignore the information leaflet enclosed with her medicine); and a doctor is not obliged to discuss the risks inherent in treatment with a person who makes it clear that she would prefer not to discuss the matter.

This protects the right of a patient not to know information, as well as the patient who wants to know it. It is not difficult to imagine a squeamish patient, really not wanting to know the details of what will happen to them while under anaesthetic. Their right to decide what information they want to know can be protected as much as the patient who wants to know every last detail.[321] Although it is not clear what kind of claim could be brought by a patient who was informed of risks they did not want to hear about.

13.2.4 *The ill-informed patient*

What liability does a doctor face if they are dealing with a patient who has done their own research, or has made assumptions, which are incorrect? Does *Montgomery* require a doctor to not only disclose all the risks, but also correct any misperceptions a patient has after trawling the Internet? In *Worrall v Antoniadou*[322] the Court of Appeal held:

> A defendant medical professional ought not to be liable in such circumstances unless either he/she is responsible for the patient getting hold of the wrong end of the stick or,

---

[321] See for further discussion Herring and Foster (2011).   [322] [2016] EWCA Civ 1219, para. 22.

having realised that the patient has or is in danger of getting hold of the wrong end of the stick, or in circumstances where the medical professional ought so to have realised, he/she takes no step to dispel the misapprehension.

This does seem to indicate that the role of the doctor is not simply to provide correct information, but also dispel any myths.[323] Fears of medical professionals that *Montgomery* is going to increase the length of time needed for consultations are likely to prove correct. Supporters will claim if it ensures that patients are in charge of making decisions about their treatment that is time well spent.

13.2.5 *Alternative treatments*

Although the requirement to disclose material risks has received most attention in the discussion of *Montgomery*, there is another aspect which is potentially even more important. That is that it requires doctors to discuss reasonable alternative treatment options with patients. In the *Montgomery* case that meant the doctor should have discussed the alternatives of vaginal delivery and Caesarean section birth with Mrs Montgomery and explained the risks attached to both. It may seem surprising that in *Montgomery* the doctors had not told their patient of the risks. Lady Hale had an important insight into what had gone wrong in this case. She noted:

> that for too long the focus was on the risks to the baby, without also taking into account what the mother might face in the process of giving birth.

She then remarked:

> Gone are the days when it was thought that, on becoming pregnant, a woman lost, not only her capacity, but also her right to act as a genuinely autonomous human being.[324]

Indeed, she goes on to imply that the views of the medical team that a vaginal delivery was morally better than a Caesarean section had dominated their thinking. That approach had been misguided because it was for the patient to decide which treatment she wanted. Hence, *Montgomery* can be seen as a decision which rejects a paternalistic model of medical practice where decisions are made about patients to one where patients are the ones who make the decision.[325]

What counts as a reasonable alternative is open to debate. Clearly, a doctor cannot be expected to discuss every option, including, for example, alternative medicine remedies or prayer. Simon LJ in *Webster v Burton Hospitals NHS Foundation Trust*[326] referred to the patient needing know enough 'to make decisions that will affect their health and well-being on proper information'. That does not give very clear guidance. Maybe the doctor is required to disclose every remedy that a reasonable doctor might offer, even if it is not the preferred option of the particular doctor.

A difficult issue in this regard is whether a doctor has to inform a patient about treatments which are not funded by the NHS but might be available privately or overseas. In terms of maximizing patient autonomy it might be thought there is a legal duty to do this. However, it might be cruel to inform a patient that the best treatment is one they cannot afford.

---

[323] See also *Connolly v Croydon Health Services NHS Trust* [2015] EWHC 1339 (QB).
[324] Para. 116.   [325] Heywood (2014).   [326] [2017] EWCA 62.

13.2.6 *When does Montgomery apply?*

Clearly, *Montgomery* applies when a doctor is recommending a course of treatment, but what if a doctor is recommending doing nothing? In *Tasmin v Barts Health NHS Trust*[327] it was held that *Montgomery* did apply to a recommendation to continue with labour, rather than try an intervention. It was said the risk of continuing with labour should have been set out, as well as the alternatives. There may be concerns if *Montgomery* applies to cases where a doctor is recommending awaiting further tests before performing treatment or simply letting time pass. If in such a case the doctor must set out the risks for waiting and the alternatives of performing surgery before waiting, this may raise concerns that worried patients will prefer to have surgery now and suffer unnecessary interventions.

13.3 Bringing a successful legal claim where the patient has not been sufficiently warned of risks

Even if the patient is able to prove that the information given by the doctor was inadequate, he or she will still face an uphill task in claiming damages. This is because the patient must show that, as a result of the negligence, he or she suffered a loss. Therefore, if a patient is not told about the risks of an operation, and the operation is performed and fortunately the risk does not materialize, there is no possibility of obtaining substantial damages against the surgeon. The patient has not suffered any loss which would entitle them to damages. Even if the patient does suffer from the risk materializing, the case is not clear-cut. Can the surgeon not argue 'Even if I had told the patient, he or she would have consented to the operation and suffered the harm'—in other words, that the injury would have occurred even if fuller information had been provided? The validity of such an argument was raised in the following important decision.

> **KEY CASE**   *Chester v Afshar* [2004] 4 All ER 587
>
> Ms Chester, a journalist, was suffering from persistent lower back pain. She consulted Mr Afshar, a consultant neurosurgeon. During the consultation, he advised surgery to remove three spinal disks. Ms Chester agreed to undergo the operation with Mr Afshar at the next available opportunity, which was a few days later. What was said at the consultation was in dispute. The trial judge preferred the evidence of Ms Chester, who explained that she had concerns about the risks of the proposed operation, but that all Mr Afshar had said about the dangers of the operation was that he 'hadn't crippled anybody yet'. It was common ground that it was accepted practice among specialists in the field to warn patients due to undergo this operation about the risk of paralysis that could result. There was a 1–2 per cent chance of the risk developing in an operation of this kind. When Mr Afshar carried out the operation in what was found to be an entirely appropriate way, Ms Chester suffered from severe pain and motor impairment as a result.
>
> The key issue before the House of Lords was that Ms Chester stated that if she had been told about the risks connected with the operation, she would not have consented to undergo the

---

[327] [2015] EWHC 3135 (QB).

procedure immediately, but would have sought a second, or even third, opinion. For Mr Afshar, it was argued that Ms Chester had no claim. Mr Afshar had not operated negligently and although he should have informed her of the risk, even if he had informed her of the risk, she would still have undergone the operation. Although she would not have had the operation at the same time as she did, she would have had (she accepted) the operation at some point. The operation would have carried the same risk of the paralysis developing as it did when she undertook it. In other words, Ms Chester was in no worse position as a result of the failure to inform her of the risks than that in which she would have been had she been told of the risks.

The majority of the House of Lords rejected this argument. It was held that there was a specific loss for Ms Chester: she had lost the chance of having the operation on another day, when she might not have developed the paralysis. The majority focused on the policy that doctors had to be liable if they failed to respect their patients' rights to know about the risks attendant on the operations. Even if there were difficulties in establishing causation, a doctor who had not properly informed a patient about risks should be liable to pay damages to the patient.

The minority applied the traditional causation principle. Lord Bingham did not accept that it was just for a claimant to be awarded a substantial level of damages when it could not be shown that he or she was any worse off as a result of the negligence. Lord Hoffmann said that the operation in this case could be analogized to a game of roulette: the chances of winning (or losing) were the same whichever day someone played. It was the same with the chances of the operation causing paralysis. Ms Chester's paralysis could not therefore be said to have resulted from Mr Afshar's negligence.

This decision is significant. It would not have been particularly controversial if the facts of the case had indicated that, had she been informed of the risks, Ms Chester would not have had the operation. Then, it would have been easier to show that the defendant's negligence had caused her loss. However, here, the evidence was she would have consented to the operation, but at a different time. At the heart of the majority's judgment is a finding that Mr Afshar's negligence should not go unpunished. Lord Hope emphasized that the law of tort in this area had the function of protecting patients' rights (to choose whether or not to have treatment). He explained that:

> If it is to fulfil that function it must ensure that the duty to inform is respected by the doctor. It will fail to do this if an appropriate remedy is not given if the duty is breached and the very risk that the patient should have been informed about occurs and she suffers injury.[328]

But notice that the majority did not throw causation entirely out of the window. If the evidence had indicated that, had she been informed of the risk, she would still have agreed to the operation at the time and place where she had it, then there would have been no claim.[329] Her evidence indicated that, if told of the risk, she would have sought a second opinion and therefore had the operation at a later time. It seems that the majority presumed that had she had the operation at another time, she would not have suffered the injury.

The difficulty facing the majority and minority in *Chester* was this: the real loss to the patient was the loss of the opportunity to make an informed decision for

---

[328] At [54].   [329] *Meiklejohn v St George's NHS Trust* [2014] EWCA Civ 120.

herself—an infringement of her rights of autonomy and right to human dignity. Such 'ephemeral' losses are not recognized as wrong in tort law. To award her nothing would be to show lack of respect for these losses, but to award her the losses that flowed from her injuries seemed to the minority to award her too much. It is interesting to note that, in *Beary v Pall Mall*,[330] the Court of Appeal held that *Chester v Afshar* was not of general application to the law on negligence and was influenced by the special importance of protecting the rights of patients in the medical context. José Miola[331] argues, however, that the law should recognize the loss of autonomy as a legal harm. He explains:

> if we are going to prioritise autonomy and state that Ms Chester has a right to be informed of the material risks, then we should be bold and assert that not to be informed of them is therefore a harm in itself.

Note, however, that that argument would mean she should be entitled to damages even if the operation had been a complete success.

14 Ethics and autonomy

For many medical ethicists, autonomy has become the most fundamental ethical principle in the medical arena. For too long, patients have been treated by medical professionals as 'objects to be mended'. By emphasizing the principle of autonomy, we can move from a 'doctor knows best' perspective to an approach that recognizes the rights of the patient.[332] After all, it is the patient's body, even if the doctor does know best. Anyway, even if we accept that a doctor has expertise in what works well in medicine generally, only the particular patient knows what is important to them and their body.

Despite these arguments, in recent years, there has been a growing body of writing concerned by the pre-eminence of autonomy in medical ethics. There are some who, while recognizing the importance of autonomy, claim that it should not block out consideration of other important values. There are others who argue that, although autonomy is important, the concept of autonomy traditionally used by commentators is an inappropriate one and alternative ways of understanding autonomy have been proposed.[333]

Before looking at the views of those troubled by the pre-eminence of autonomy, it is useful to expound the principle of autonomy and why it is valued.

14.1 The importance of autonomy

In 1914, the highly respected American judge, Cardozo J, recognized the importance of autonomy: 'Every human being of adult years and sound mind has a right to determine what shall be done with his own body; and a surgeon who performs an operation without his patient's consent, commits an assault.'[334] However, much as the medical profession might believe a procedure to be in a patient's best interests or may even be

---

[330] [2005] EWCA Civ 415.   [331] Miola (2017).   [332] P. Foster (1998).
[333] For example, Taylor (2009).   [334] *Schloendorff v New York Hospital* (1914) 105 NE 92.

morally required for a patient, it is still seen as morally wrong to force that treatment on the patient. It must be that patient's choice to receive the treatment.[335]

Professor Kennedy has put the point eloquently:

> [I]f the beliefs and values of the patient, though incomprehensible to others, are of long standing and have formed the basis for all the patient's decisions about his life, there is a strong argument to suggest that the doctor should respect and give effect to a patient's decision based on them ... To argue otherwise would effectively be to rob the patient of his right to his own personality which may be far more serious and destructive than anything that could follow from the patient's decision as regards a particular proposed treatment.[336]

It is also perhaps notable that the rise of autonomy has been matched with a lack of confidence about declaring what is or is not in a person's best interests.[337] With an increasing lack of trust in medical expertise and a breakdown in agreed moral values, it has become highly controversial to declare what is or is not in a patient's interests. What might be good treatment for one person might not for a different person with different values and lifestyle. We need to replace paternalism with an assessment of what the individual patient wants. Hence, we have the 'triumph of autonomy'.[338]

Supporters of autonomy emphasize the value that each of us puts on being in control of our destiny and being able to decide how to live out our version of the 'good life'.[339] One person may want to dedicate his or her life to the watching of football and the drinking of beer. To others, that may be a bad way of life, but we must respect each person's decision as to how he or she wishes to live that life, unless that decision causes harm to others. The idea of someone else coming along and telling you what to do with your life, and how to live it, is repellent to most people. Many people will agree with Isaiah Berlin, who stated:

> I wish my life and decision to depend on myself, not on external forces of whatever kind. I wish to be the instrument of my own, not of other men's act of will. I wish to be a subject, not an object; to be moved by reasons, by conscious purposes, which are my own, not by causes which affect me, as it were from outside.[340]

14.2 Challenges to the pre-eminence of autonomy

We should start by emphasizing that nowadays few people reject the importance of autonomy. The dispute is over whether it should be the sole or primary ethical principle governing medical ethics. Charles Foster, in his book subtitled *The Tyranny of Autonomy in Medical Ethics and Law*, complains that 'modern debates in medical ethics are often very boring', in that autonomy has come to be widely regarded as the sole principle.[341] He writes: '[A]ny society whose sole principle is autonomy is unreflective, shallow and dangerous.'[342] In fairness, there are very few academic medical lawyers who would claim that autonomy is the sole principle at play in medical law and ethics.

---

[335] Wicks (2016).   [336] Kennedy (1991a: 56).   [337] Tännsjö (2013).   [338] Foster (2009 and 2014).
[339] See further Chapter 1.   [340] Berlin (1961: 131).   [341] Foster (2009: 17).
[342] Foster (2009: 181).

A number of challenges have been made to the paramountcy of autonomy. First, some critics have suggested that it should not be held that all autonomous decisions demand respect. John Keown argues:

> The capacity to choose brings with it the responsibility of making not just any old choice, but choices that do in fact promote, rather than undermine, human flourishing. Given the legitimate diversity of lifestyles and life-choices which are consistent with human flourishing, many choices are consistent with human well-being. We should, therefore, think carefully before restricting another's autonomy. But it is difficult to see why patently immoral choices, choices clearly inconsistent with human well-being, merit any respect. In other words, an exercise of autonomy merits respect only when it is exercised in accordance with a framework of sound moral values.[343]

Supporters of autonomy would reply that the difficulty with such an argument is in identifying what decisions are 'consistent with human flourishing'. This has a different meaning for different people. Some people might say that trainspotting is inconsistent with that aim, but it is an activity greatly valued by some. Should we not leave each person to work out his or her own version of human flourishing? On the other hand, does Keown not have a point: just because a decision is made autonomously does not mean that it is a valuable one deserving of great respect. Is the decision to spend a life reading pornography one deserving of respect? As Onora O'Neill has pointed out, letting people act out their autonomous wishes can lead to disastrous results.[344] Sarah Conly writes 'when individuals engage in behavior that undercuts their own chances of happiness, state interference may be justified'.[345] Indeed, it is notable that even those taking a strong autonomy-based line scrutinize very carefully the capacity of a person who wants to make a decision that will cause a serious harm.[346] That shows that the line between promoting autonomy and promoting well-being is not as straightforward as it might at first appear.[347]

A second challenge to the pre-eminence of autonomy is the argument that autonomy is very much a Western, perhaps even North American, way of looking at the world. The 'American dream' promotes the freedom of all individuals to seek the best for themselves. But other societies have placed great weight on cooperation and the pursuit of community goals. In other words, there is a danger that we elevate an American value into a high ethical principle without regard to its cultural roots.[348] Indeed, this point can be developed further. If you choose to live your life according to certain moral values and seek to live in a community that holds fast to certain principles, these will involve restrictions on your choice. There can therefore be a tension between retaining free choice and respecting autonomy (in the sense of building up a system of values to live by as part of your vision of the 'good life').[349]

A third challenge is that the emphasis on autonomy overlooks other important values.[350] There is a danger that autonomy ignores issues of obligations owed to others, the pursuit of community goals, notions of justice in healthcare decisions, and the importance of relationships in the lives of others.[351] Some who make this suggestion have promoted the notion of 'relational autonomy', a concept that will be explored later.[352]

---

[343] Keown (2002: 53). See West (1985) for a similar argument from a feminist perspective.
[344] O'Neill (2002: 20).   [345] Conly (2012).   [346] Flamme and Forster (2000).
[347] Molyneux (2009).   [348] Holm (1995).   [349] Montgomery (2006).
[350] McCall Smith (1997).   [351] Herring (2013b).   [352] Foster and Herring (2012).

But all supporters of autonomy agree there are limits to autonomy, most significantly that we can restrict your behaviour if you want to do something that harms someone else. Sarah Conly argues that principle applies to harm to the self too: 'If it is permissible, even obligatory, to stop me when I do something that seriously interferes with someone else's chances of achieving the life he wants, I think it is equally permissible, and perhaps obligatory, to save me from myself.' That analogy might be questioned: there is a difference in choosing to harm yourself and choosing to harm another. In the former case you have consented to suffer the harm, but not the latter.[353]

A fourth challenge is to question to what extent healthcare decisions can be said to be autonomous. We shall consider the reality of 'consent giving' shortly, but there it will be noted that patients are often willing to agree to whatever their expert doctor suggests. 'Rituals of consent' have replaced true autonomous decision making, it is suggested.[354] A rather different point is that whether a patient consents or not may depend on a host of factors that means that the consent does not reflect a real choice by that patient. In one study, patients were offered two alternative treatments and were told of the percentages of people who survived the treatments; 18 per cent of people selected the first treatment. The same group were then offered the two treatments and were told the percentage of people who died (that is, the same statistic presented differently). This time, 44 per cent of people selected the first treatment.[355] In other words, although it may appear that a patient is exercising autonomy, in fact the choice that he or she makes may be influenced by a host of external factors. Sarah Conly[356] gives the example of a person ordering a large serving of fries. She questions whether such a person really wants a large serving. At least she suggests that such a decision is normally a result of mistaken thinking:

> As has by now been discussed convincingly and exhaustively (notably by Nobel Prize-winning Daniel Kahneman and Amos Tversky), we suffer from common, apparently ineradicable tendencies to 'cognitive bias,' which means that in many common situations, our decision-making goes askew. These biases are many and varied, but they have in common that they interfere with our appreciation of even quite simple facts, and lead us to choose ineffective means to our ends.[357]

Returning to the fries example: few people really want to become unhealthy and so many regret their decision to order the large fries later.[358] Such a flawed decision does not deserve respect. Some fries lovers might want to take issue with her assessment!

14.3 Which autonomy?

If you say 'we should respect people's decisions' that can become problematic if a person has competing decisions. John Coggon has listed three versions of autonomy:

1. Ideal desire autonomy—leads to an action decided upon because it reflects what a person should want, measured by reference to some purportedly universal or objective standard of values.

---

[353] Eyal (2015).   [354] Ploug and Holm (2013); Tauber (2003: 484).
[355] Schwab (2007).   [356] Conly (2012).   [357] Conly (2014).
[358] She is arguing in favour of portion control, rather than banning fries, claiming that people will be just as happy with a small portion as a large one.

2. Best desire autonomy—leads to an action decided upon because it reflects a person's overall desire given his own values, even if this runs contrary to his immediate desire.

3. Current desire autonomy—leads to an action decided upon because it reflects a person's immediate inclinations, ie what he thinks he wants in a given moment without further reflection.[359]

Similarly, Alasdair Maclean discusses three broad conceptions of autonomy: 'The libertarian approach is to see autonomy simply as self-determination. The liberal view requires the inclusion of rationality. The communitarian approach would be to require autonomy to have some substantive moral content.'[360] As these authors demonstrate, it is foolhardy to assume that all autonomous wishes carry the same moral weight. A considered autonomous decision, based on full knowledge of the facts and reflecting a person's underlying and enduring values, might be thought to be deserving of greater moral weight than the decision based on mistakes or the one that is inconsistent with the values by which the person lives his or her life.[361] If that view is accepted, then, at least in ethical terms, not all autonomous decisions deserve the same level of protection.[362] This then opens up an approach that allows us to say that where a patient's decision is going to cause him or her serious harm, then that decision will need to be richly autonomous, and if it is not fully autonomous, we need not comply with it. Indeed, this may be what we are witnessing in the case law on vulnerable adults, at which we looked earlier in the chapter.[363] There, the impaired decisions of people with capacity are not followed because they represent only a severely impaired exercise of autonomy.

The issue can also be presented as an issue of competing decisions. If a person decides they would like to have an operation, but whenever they see the doctor's needle become terrified and say they do not want the procedure, what would it meant to promote their autonomy? Is respecting their decision not to have the injection autonomy enhancing, or respecting their decision to have the treatment? As this discussion shows it is not always a question of whether to respect autonomy or not, but which autonomous decision to respect.

One solution to this issue is to use 'soft paternalism'[364] where we seek to determine the goals of the patient and seek to ensure we reach those, even if that means going against the decision the patient makes about the 'means' to that goal. So imagine a patient has an infection and wants to get better, but believes 'fresh air' will heal her and so refuses medication. We might say her real goal is to get better and giving her medication against her wishes will help her reach that goal. We just have to be paternalistic about the best way of reaching that goal.

14.4 Can one be autonomous?

What does it mean to be autonomous? Jesse Wall[365] has argued to act autonomously it must be shown a person is able:

(i)   to act free from undue interference or influence of others (the freedom condition);

[359] Coggon (2007b: 235). See Trout (2013) for a case against placing weight on current desires.
[360] Maclean (2009: 11).   [361] J. Craigie (2011).
[362] Gilmore and Herring (2011); Coggon (2012).
[363] See under the heading '7.2 Vulnerable adults'.   [364] Kniess (2016).   [365] Wall (2017).

(ii) to exercise the capacity for rational thought and cognition (the competence condition); and

(iii) to act according to the beliefs, values, and commitments that the person identifies or endorses as their own beliefs, values, and commitments (the authenticity condition).

Mackenzie and Rogers to similar effect argue, to be able to exercise autonomy, we need to display the following characteristics.[366]

- *Self-determination* This refers to the ability:

   … to determine one's own beliefs, values, goals and wants, and to make choices regarding matters of practical import to one's life free from undue interference. The obverse of self-determination is determination by other persons, or by external forces or constraints.[367]

- *Self-government* This refers to the ability:

   … to make choices and enact decisions that express, or are consistent with, one's values, beliefs and commitments. Whereas the threats to self-determination are typically external, the threats to self-governance are typically internal, and often involve volitional or cognitive failings. Weakness of will and failures of self-control are common volitional failings that interfere with self-governance.[368]

- *Having authenticity*

   [A] person's decisions, values, beliefs and commitments must be her 'own' in some relevant sense; that is, she must identify herself with them and they must cohere with her 'practical identity', her sense of who she is and what matters to her. Actions or decisions that a person feels were foisted on her, which do not cohere with her sense of herself, or from which she feels alienated, are not autonomous.[369]

Their point is that if these conditions are not fulfilled then a person cannot really be taken to have chosen a course of action for themselves. Others have imposed values upon them or they are not able to use their values to make decisions for themselves.[370] Imagine, a woman who is in a relationship of domestic abuse. She has reached a position where she simply obeys her partner on every issue. In such a case respecting her decisions is not respecting her autonomy. The problem is that if we require all of the conditions that Wall or MacKenzie and Rogers require, one might question how often anyone can meet all of these criteria and so be richly autonomous.[371]

To similar effect Julian Savulescu suggests that only rational decisions deserve respect under the principle of autonomy. He explains they are rational if and only if P makes the decision:

---

[366] Mackenzie and Rogers (2013).   [367] Mackenzie and Rogers (2013: 43). See also Wertheimer (2012).
[368] Mackenzie and Rogers (2013: 44). See Bock (2012) for a discussion of how such considerations work with a religious individual.
[369] Mackenzie and Rogers (2013: 45).   [370] Ahlin (2017).
[371] For further discussion, see Freyenhagen and O'Shea (2013).

while in possession of all relevant, available information, without making relevant, correctable error of logic and vividly imagining what each state of affairs would be like for P.[372]

The problem is that if that is the test then few decisions would be rational.

Arguments of this kind have led me to suggest that 'it is implausible that a large majority of people have capacity to make important medical decisions'[373] and question the presumption in favour of people having capacity. Few, if any, of us really understand enough information; are able to use the information rationally; based on principles we have adopted to be able to claim to be acting autonomously. However, if we find few people have capacity it might be thought that this would open the door to rampant paternalism. But that is not necessarily so. You might think doctors and judges are as bad at making decisions as anyone else. So the questioning of the presumption of capacity is not necessarily an argument in favour of paternalism, but rather a suggestion we need to find other reasons, apart from autonomy, for respecting people's decisions about their lives.

15 The United Nations Convention on the Rights of Persons with Disabilities

The previous section considered whether it might be more accurate to assume no one has capacity. A very different challenge is to suggest we should assume everyone has capacity. Even those who may be thought to lack capacity can be enabled to make decisions. Ginerva Richardson[374] uses the United Nations Convention on the Rights of Persons with Disabilities (CRPD) to make this point:

> Under the CRPD, the approach is very different. The emphasis has moved from substitute to supported decision-making. Decisions are no longer to be made, however benignly, on behalf of the person with disability; instead she is to be supported and encouraged to make her own decisions. In its purest form there is no point beyond which legal capacity is lost. There is no binary divide. Article 12 of the Convention provides:
>
> (1) 'States Parties reaffirm that persons with disabilities have the right to recognition everywhere as persons before the law.'
>
> (2) 'States Parties shall recognize that persons with disabilities enjoy legal capacity on an equal basis with others in all aspects of life.'
>
> These two paragraphs can be read as requiring the law to give the same status and respect to decisions made by people with mental disabilities, however great the impact of those disabilities on their decision-making, as it gives to the decisions made by others. *Legal* capacity should not be dependent on *mental* capacity.[375]

The Committee on the Rights of Persons with Disabilities has adopted a line similar to Richardson's and called on rejection of capacity tests and the use of the best interests approach. Instead we should focus on the 'will and preference' of every person.[376] The committee states that 'at all times, including in crisis situations, the individual autonomy and capacity of persons with disabilities to make decisions must be respected'. They argue that even if a person has mental impairments their will and preferences must

---

[372] Savulescu (2001).   [373] Herring (2016b).   [374] Richardson (2012).
[375] Richardson (2013: 88).
[376] Donnelly (2016); see also Series (2015), Gooding (2016), and Dawson (2015).

be respected. It may be that in some cases they will need support from family, friends, or professionals to articulate their will and preferences, but once those are ascertained they deserve no less protection than those of a person with capacity.

This is a dramatic argument and not without problems.[377] One is that there will be some cases where even with extensive support the person is unable to present a view. A patient in a coma would be one example. So there may be some cases where some kind of substitute decision making is required. A second is the difficulty we have seen several times in this chapter about determining what precisely someone's will is if they have conflicting wishes. If a patient says 'I don't want those red pills because red is the colour of the devil and they are evil', are they rejecting pills that are evil or are they rejecting the red pills (which are not evil)? What does it mean to respect a decision which has no connection with the reality?

Another concern is with the idea of supported decision making. Can we be sure if relatives or friends are involved to ascertain P's will that what we are discovering is in fact P's wishes rather than the views of their relatives? Will professionals feel compelled to ascertain 'will' where there is none really?[378]

Finally, the UN Convention requires states to protect disabled people from abuse.[379] To leave a person to suffer greatly on the basis that that was their choice, when in fact they had no understanding of the impact of their decision, is to uphold their rights, it is to deny them their rights, not to uphold them.

16 Balancing protection and autonomy

So far we have been looking at rather extreme alternatives to the current law: presuming few (if any) have autonomy; and assuming everyone does. More moderate options would be to suggest that we should find a way of taking into account respect for autonomy and protection from harm.

One option is 'risk-relative capacity'.[380] This is a suggestion that the degree of risk may affect how strictly we apply a test of capacity. So if P wants to make a decision that might cause him or her significant harm, then we will require a lot of evidence to be persuaded that P has capacity. However, if the decision carries little risk, then we can be rather lax in applying such a test. The proposal is a controversial one and many commentators feel that it is inappropriate because a person either understands the issues or does not, and the degree of risk should not affect an assessment of his or her comprehension.[381]

An alternative argument is to suggest, as Professor Gunn has pointed out, that capacity and incapacity are not 'concepts with clear a priori boundaries. They appear on a continuum ... There are, therefore degrees of capacity.'[382] I have argued that we need a more nuanced approach for those in the hinterland of capacity, so that we can offer some protection for those only just having capacity who are endangering themselves, but pay

---

[377] See Donnelly (2016) for an excellent discussion.
[378] See Case (2016) on the role of psychiatrists in assessment.
[379] See Clough (2015) for a helpful discussion.
[380] Lawlor (2016) Gilmore and Herring (2011); DeMarco (2002); Cale (1999).
[381] See Herring (2008c) for further discussion.   [382] Gunn (2004: 9).

greater respect to the wishes of those who lack capacity, but only just.[383] As Jesse Wall and I have argued:

> To put it another way, we should not assume that autonomy is an 'all-or-nothing concept'. A richly autonomous decision requires full protection and the patient has the right to have their refusal respected, however serious the consequences. Where, however, the decision is only marginally autonomous, then it may be sufficient to deserve respect in cases where what the patient wants to do something that is not particularly harmful. A weakly autonomous decision may, therefore, not be sufficient to justify doing an act that will lead to serious harm.[384]

It may be that the jurisdiction that is being developed in relation to vulnerable adults is providing a way of protecting those on the borderline of capacity.[385]

17 Relational autonomy

In light of the concerns about autonomy, some have argued that rather than abandon autonomy, we need to find a new way of understanding it. One of the most popular of these is the notion of 'relational autonomy'.[386] At the heart of this approach is a rejection of the idea that we live our lives as unconnected individuals. The traditional notion of autonomy promotes the concept of an isolated patient deciding for himself what is in his best interests (the image of 'the male in the prime of his life'[387]), whereas in fact we live lives based on interdependent relationships.[388] We therefore need to recognize that, for most patients, the question is not simply 'What is best for me?', but rather 'Given the responsibilities that I owe to those in relationships with me and the responsibilities owed to me by others, what is the most appropriate course of action?'[389] We need a vision of autonomy that promotes the values of love, loyalty, friendship, and care.[390] We need to examine patients' choices in light of the relationships within which they live and the feelings of worry, concern for others, and obligation that they may have.[391]

In the medical context, this means that we should not regard decisions as simply decisions for the patient, but consider the impact of the decision on those with whom they are in relationships.[392] One example of this is a study into treatment for breast cancer in which the women with partners regarded the treatment decision as a joint one with their partners, rather than one only for them.[393]

Some supporters of traditional autonomy argue that supporters of relational autonomy have misunderstood traditional liberal autonomy and that it was never intended as an individualistic concept. Indeed, liberals accept that, for many individuals, the meaning of their lives is shaped by their relationships and communities.[394] However, there is a

---

[383] Herring (2009a). See also den Hartogh (2016).   [384] Wall and Herring (2015).
[385] See Herring (2016).
[386] Herring (2013; 2009e); De Clercq, Ruhe, Rost, Elger (2017); Dochin (2001); Agich (2003).
[387] Dochin (2001).   [388] Herring (2000: 278).   [389] West (1997).
[390] Mackenzie and Stoljar (2000). See Gilbar and Miola (2014) for an argument that relational autonomy is particularly effective for those from non-western backgrounds.
[391] Dodds (2000).   [392] Herring (2008b).   [393] R. Gilbar and O. Gilbar (2009).
[394] Singer (1993).

danger within relational autonomy that the wishes of the individual can be too easily overridden by the needs of the 'community'. Christman has argued:

> Just as conceiving of persons as denuded of social relations denies the importance of such relations to the self-understandings of many of us at various times in our lives, to define persons as necessarily related in particular ways similarly denies the reality of change over time, variability in self-conception, and multiplicities of identity characteristic of modern populations.[395]

In particular, there is a concern that relational autonomy could be used to reinforce the traditional caring roles that women have played in our society or to trap individuals into decisions prescribed by a culture to which they do not subscribe.[396] The example of the breast cancer research may highlight such concerns: should women be influenced in what treatment to receive for breast cancer by the views of their partners?

In a helpful discussion on relational autonomy, Natalie Stoljar considers a woman deciding whether to take hormone replacement therapy (HRT) for menopausal symptoms.[397] Such a woman is likely to be given all of the relevant medical facts:

> However, the decision-making process will likely be influenced by factors in addition to a weighing up of the medical evidence that is presented to the woman, including her education, race, and class; her conception of herself and her unique experience of menopause; cultural norms such as that looking young is attractive and valued whereas looking old is unattractive and devalued; the attitude of family members to the symptoms of menopause; the support of family members for the woman's decision; and so on. The complexity of all these factors and the uncertainty experienced by the woman in weighing them up may lead to diminished self-trust. Informed consent, as an opportunity concept, is inadequate to ensure that agents *exercise* their preference formation with the required subject-referring attitudes. The process of preference formation that we call informed consent is therefore not sufficient for autonomy.[398]

With these concerns in mind, Stoljar advocates the following:

> Taking relational autonomy seriously suggests that in addition to securing informed consent, health care providers have an important role to play in promoting patient autonomy. Providers must be alert to the social conditions that affect patients' capacities for autonomous reasoning. For example, internalized norms may undermine an agent's sensitivity to the options that are available to her; and cultural or family expectations may erode a patient's 'self-referring attitudes' and lead to diminished self-confidence and self-esteem. The provider must therefore take positive steps to counteract these effects, for instance, encourage imaginative reflection on different options and create the conditions in which patients truly feel authorized to speak for themselves.[399]

Critics may raise concerns about this kind of approach. Should we assume that a woman who makes a decision in line with social expectations about women lacks capacity? Is that not demeaning to women? Or is Stoljar correctly acknowledging that our claims to autonomy too often ignore that our wishes are as much, if not more, influenced by social expectations and assumptions as they are by our own values and wishes?

---

[395] Christman (2004: 145). See also Tauber (2003).   [396] MacKinnon (1987).
[397] Stoljar (2011).   [398] Stoljar (2011: 21).   [399] Stoljar (2011: 22).

18 **Autonomy in practice**

To some, although the theoretical case for emphasizing autonomy is strong, there are inevitable difficulties when the concept is put into practice. Following a diagnosis and suggestion of treatment, very few patients will disagree with the proposal. Patients may consent, but feel that they have no real choice. Those who are weaker, less articulate, or more malleable than others can have their autonomy 'used against them'. One sociologist has written of 'the modern clinical ritual of trust',[400] whereby a patient is given information about an operation to which a patient accedes with little understanding of what is proposed or even an appreciation that he or she has a choice. In other words, despite grand visions of autonomy, in practice, far from being an expression of someone's image of the good life for themselves, consent is little more than a formality.[401] There is an additional concern that evidence suggests the values of the person making the capacity assessment can impact on whether a patient is found to have capacity or not.[402]

19 **Nudging**

If we assume for the moment, that autonomy should be respected, might it nevertheless be appropriate to seek to persuade the patient to act in the best way[403] or nudge the patient to reach the right decision?[404] Nudges are very much in vogue in current economic and political thought. They involve encouraging, but not forcing, people to make good choices. Examples can range from putting healthy options at the front of a buffet and unhealthy options difficult to reach; or putting pictures of cancer tumours on packets of cigarettes. As these examples show, someone is not forced to eat healthily or give up smoking, they are just 'nudged' in that direction. As Savulescu[405] argues, nudges can enhance autonomy:

> If I promise myself a treat if I complete a boring task, I have autonomously chosen to complete the boring task. The incentive is enhancing my motivation to complete the task I have chosen. The more I value the incentive, the greater the enhancement, but my autonomous choice remains.

However, as Savulescu accepts this example is one where a person chooses to nudge themselves. It might be argued it is where others, unknown to the individual, nudge you that the problem arises. Levy[406] suggests that nudges that provide information are acceptable, but nudges that 'bypass our capacities for deliberation' (e.g. subliminal advertising) are not.

This can be applied in a medical context. Is it appropriate for a doctor to 'steer' a patient towards a wise choice by presenting what they think is the best option in the most attractive way?[407] Or should doctors try and present information neutrally? Given that many people go to doctors for advice and recommendations it would seem odd if doctors could not advocate for what they regard as the best option, even while leaving the ultimate choice to the patient.

---

[400] Wolpe (1998).   [401] Heywood, Macaskill, and Williams (2010).
[402] Hermann, Trachsel, and Biller-Andorno (2015); Griffiths and West (2015).
[403] Griffiths and West (2015).
[404] Heywood, Macaskill, and Williams (2010); Hermann, Trachsel, and Biller-Andorno (2015); Griffiths and West (2015).
[405] Savulescu (2017).   [406] Levy (2017).   [407] Dunn (2016).

FEMINIST PERSPECTIVES

Consent

Feminist writers on consent have tended to fall into one of three camps, although many feminists see strengths in all three positions.[408]

(i)   There are those who greatly welcome the emphasis on autonomy, believing that, in the past, women were too easily seen as subject to the paternalistic power of medicine.[409] Women were regarded as incapable of making decisions for themselves and wise doctors were needed to make decisions for them. Autonomy should therefore be welcomed as giving women a voice in their treatment and providing them with power in the medical context.

(ii) Many of those supporting the notion of 'relational autonomy' mentioned earlier[410] have written from a feminist perspective.[411] Traditional visions of autonomy have been seen as 'masculine' by emphasizing values of independence and self-sufficiency that are alien to the lives of many women.[412] By contrast, the emphasis that relational autonomy places on the values of relationship, care, and interdependence reflects the values that matter to many women.

(iii) There are feminists who feel that both of the above positions fail to recognize the social context within which women make medical decisions.[413] The oppressive circumstances of women's lives and the social expectations placed on women can lead them to make sacrificial decisions. Until there is greater equality between men and women, there is a danger that women's autonomy will be used against them.

20 Ethics and best interests

As we have seen, if a patient lacks capacity to make a medical decision, the key principle is that the medical team must act in the patient's best interests. At first sight, this may seem so obviously sensible an approach that it is difficult to disagree with it, and that even if one were to disagree, there are few effective alternatives. However, as we shall see, the issue is not as straightforward as it may at first appear.

20.1 Criticisms of the 'best interests' principle

There are a number of criticisms of the 'best interests' principle.[414] Many centre on the vagueness that surrounds the concept of best interests.[415] It has been described as 'empty rhetoric'.[416] Specifically, concerns have been expressed that the phrase is so vague that it can mean whatever one wants it to mean. The judge or medical professional can declare treatment to be in a patient's best interests, with that being no more than a

---

[408] See Tong (1996).   [409] Jackson (2001: ch. 1).

[410] See under the heading '11.3 Alternative versions of autonomy: relational autonomy'.

[411] Sherwin (1998); Mackenzie and Stoljar (2000).   [412] Fineman (2004).   [413] Oshana (1998).

[414] See Holm and Edgamot (2008).

[415] Although Huxtable (2014) makes a powerful argument in favour of a flexible concept of best interests.

[416] Kennedy (1991a: 90). See further Hope, Slowther, and Eccles (2009).

reflection of one person's views. Supporters of the 'best interests' standard might accept that there is an element of subjective evaluation in the assessment, but argue that, in fact, there is widespread agreement about what are the good things in life. Although there are cases in which what is in a patient's best interests may be contested, those are rare and are likely to be difficult cases whatever standard is used.

There is also some debate over whether the 'best interests' standard should take into account the values and principles of the individual person. If a healthcare team is dealing with an incompetent Jehovah's Witness, would it be correct to say that, for that person, it is in his or her best interests not to receive a life-saving blood transfusion? Or should our assessment of best interests be objective and take no account of the particular characteristics of the individual?

Some have criticized the 'best interests' principle for being unduly individualistic. When making decisions for a person without capacity, is it not permissible to take any account of the interests of the person's relatives and family? What should happen if a relative of a patient without capacity will die without blood or even a kidney taken from the patient? The law's 'best interests' principle would appear to suggest that such acts of altruism should not be forced on a person lacking capacity.[417] However, Charles Foster and I have argued that the notion of best interests can be understood as living a 'good life' and that can include displaying a reasonable display of virtue and altruism.[418]

20.2 Who should decide what is in the patient's best interests?

The law takes the view that medical professionals, and ultimately the court, should decide what is in a patient's best interests. This is disputed by some. Although a medical professional may have expertise in medical issues, he or she will not know a patient's religious or ethical views, or what that patient finds pleasurable in life.[419]

Some have argued that the relatives of the patient are better placed to decide what is in the best interests of the individual in question than the medical team.[420] Then again, it might be thought that relatives lack the emotional detachment to make an effective assessment of a patient's best interests. Indeed, relatives might even have conflicting interests in reaching decisions over a relative (for example financial concerns over the cost of care). Also, the assumption that family members know a patient better than anyone else is often untrue. A patient's flatmate may know him or her better than his or her brother, for example.

Another alternative decision maker would be an ethics committee. This could intervene where there is a dispute between the family and the physician. Such a committee could comprise lay members and medical professionals, and act as representative of the wider community in the way that a jury does in a criminal trial. There are, however, concerns that such committees act without the procedural safeguards that courts have.

20.3 Substituted judgement

An alternative to the 'best interests' test that has received support in some quarters is the notion of 'substituted judgement', which is a particularly influential concept in

---

[417] See Cantor (2005: ch. 5).   [418] Foster and Herring (2016).
[419] Veatch (2000). See further Coggon (2008b).   [420] Fan and Tao (2004).

American medical law. This requires the decision maker to decide what the individual would have wanted had he or she been able to make a decision. This involves the decision maker considering whether the person had made comments about how he or she would like to be treated if he or she were to lose capacity. The individual's religious or ethical views may be taken as indicators of the kind of decision that the person would have made if competent. Supporters claim that this approach maximizes autonomy in that it means that we are seeking, as best we can, to determine the decision of the individual over his or her health care.

Critics argue that such a test places undue weight on comments made by an individual perhaps years previously. A dinner conversation in which a person said that he or she 'never wanted to live as a vegetable' can suddenly become the key element in a healthcare decision years later. Worse than this, it can encourage deception, with relatives being encouraged to 'recall' the wishes of the individual. Dresser claims that studies show that people are very bad at predicting what decisions their family or friends would make.[421] The huge controversy in the United States concerning whether to stop nutrition for Terri Schiavo centred in part on disputed claims over what she may or may not have said many years previously.[422] Dresser has claimed that the substitute judgement approach 'is indeterminate enough to permit almost any treatment option preferred by a patient's family, guardian, or physician'.[423]

TO PONDER

Information about fatal conditions

As has been clear throughout this chapter, the right of autonomy plays a central role in medical law and ethics. It is proudly declared that patients should be the ones who decide what treatment they should be given and should be informed about their treatment. But is this always what the general public actually wants? One issue that generates controversy is what a medical professional should do if he or she discovers that his or her patient is suffering from a fatal condition.

One survey of elderly people found that 80 per cent said that they would rather not be told if it was discovered that they were suffering from cancer.[424] It seems that people would rather have a few weeks or months of blissful ignorance than spend the time in terror of the potential impact of the disease. Yet, despite such surveys, when asked in general terms, patients do support a right to know of their medical condition.[425] The difficulty is, of course, that for every patient who expresses a wish for blissful ignorance, there is another patient who would value the time to prepare for his or her death and to 'put my affairs in order'.

A survey of physicians found a notable minority of physicians not telling patients of their life-threatening condition, with a quarter saying that they told patients of life-threatening conditions only 50–90 per cent of the time. Over half of those questioned said that they explained a patient's condition in only general terms.[426] Another survey found that where a doctor did tell a patient of a diagnosis of a terminal illness, the doctor was deliberately over-optimistic in his or her discussion of the prognosis and that this was in fact welcomed by patients.[427]

[421] Dresser (2015).   [422] Koch (2005) discusses this case.   [423] Dresser (1994: 645).
[424] Ajaj, Singh, and Abdulla (2001).   [425] Sullivan, Menapace, and White (2001).
[426] Sullivan, Menapace, and White (2001).   [427] The, Hak, Koëter, et al. (2000).

21 Ethical issues surrounding advance directives

Is it appropriate to pay heed to advance directives (known as 'advance decisions' under the MCA 2005)? A competent person, fearing loss of capacity, might, quite properly, seek to determine how he or she will be treated in the future when lacking capacity.[428] Such an action can be seen as an attempt to ensure that what happens to the person at the end of his or her life is a fitting end to the vision of the good life that he or she has set for himself or herself and by which he or she sought to live.[429] As Dworkin has put it: '[T]hey want their deaths, if possible, to express and in that way vividly to confirm the values they believe most important.'[430] Controversially, Dworkin goes on to say that even if the person lacking capacity is stating that he or she does not want treatment, these wishes are experimental (short-term) interests and can be overridden in the name of protecting the critical (long-term) interests of the earlier competent person. Even ignoring this more controversial suggestion, where there is a clear advance directive, it might be thought obvious to prefer the expressed wishes of the patient, rather than someone else's view about what is best for him or her.

It is not that straightforward, however. There are three main points that are made by opponents of advance directives. First, some claim that the person who makes the advance directive is not the same person as the person who subsequently loses capacity. We are, it is said, a collection and continuity of memories and life stories.[431] In the case of an Alzheimer's patient, although his or her body remains the same, the loss of memory or connection with relatives or friends means that, with the onset of Alzheimer's, a new person has come into being. Or at least it means that there has been such a change of personality and personhood that the competent person is no longer empowered to speak on behalf of the person lacking capacity.[432] Therefore the advance directive made when the person was competent should not have force. Robertson writes as follows:

> The values and interests of the competent person no longer are relevant to someone who has lost the rational structure on which those values and interests rested. Unless we are to view competently held values and interests as extending even into situations in which, because of incompetency, they can no longer have meaning, it matters not that as a competent person the individual would not wish to be maintained in a debilitated or disabled state. If the person is no longer competent enough to appreciate the degree of divergence from her previous activity that produced the choice against treatment, the prior directive does not represent her current interests merely because a competent directive was issued.[433]

Dworkin has replied to such arguments that even if there is some validity in the claim that the person has changed since developing Alzheimer's, the person's 'critical interests' remain.[434] Critical interests are those things that are fundamental to our life story

[428] Gremmen, Widdershoven, Beekman, et al. (2008).   [429] Dworkin (1993). See also Burford (2008).
[430] Dworkin (1993: 211). Dresser (1995) is doubtful that people have such a developed view of the story of their lives.
[431] This is developed from the theories of Parfitt (1984), Dresser (1994; 1995), and Rich (1998). See also Gligorov and Vitrano (2011); DeMarco and Lipuma (2016).
[432] Dworkin (1993: 554); Buchanan and Brock (1990: 152–89). See also Quante (1999).
[433] Robertson (1991: 7).   [434] Buchanan (1998).

(important relationships, career goals, and so on). Being able to determine how the final chapter of our life is to be played out, if we lose capacity, is a critical interest. We should therefore, through advance directives, be able to restrict how we are to be treated if lacking capacity. Indeed, the fact that we allow people to make wills indicates our acceptance of the idea that a person can have some say over his or her interests when capacity is lost.[435] Dresser responds by saying that if a person has lost the capacity to understand his or her critical interests, they should not be given weight.[436] Another line of response to the 'personality change' argument is that, to his or her friends and family, the Alzheimer's patient has not changed his or her identity.[437] The notion that we are only our memories is unduly focused on an individual picture of personal identity, and does not locate the individual within the community of their friends and relatives.[438] A more extreme response is to claim that a person without capacity has no interests in receiving life-sustaining treatment and therefore can, in compliance with an advance directive, be permitted to die.[439] The interests of a competent person in knowing that his or her wishes will be fulfilled is greater than the interests that the person lacking capacity has in being kept alive. Recently, there has been support of a middle path allowing advance decisions to carry some weight, so that they should be followed unless they cause the current individual harm[440] or significant harm.[441]

Second, and more straightforwardly, there is a question mark over whether it is possible for us to predict how we would like to be treated when we suffer loss of capacity.[442] We may imagine that suffering from Alzheimer's would be a horrific experience and yet many sufferers appear to be happy. It has been argued that research suggests that most people suffering from dementia are unaware of their demented state and so do not find the condition degrading or distressing.[443] Are we confident that the person who made the advance directive had sufficient information about what experiencing the condition would be like?[444] People's reaction to death and dying when they are healthy can be very different when they are actually faced with death as an imminent reality.[445] Indeed, evidence suggests that people are likely to underestimate the strength of their desire for medical intervention. It is difficult to imagine all of the possible scenarios in which one might find oneself.[446] You might decide that you would rather die quickly if suffering from a prolonged illness, but would that be your view if, by intervention, you could be kept alive long enough to see your first grandchild born? Further, there are difficulties in determining whether we can be confident that a directive made years previously represents the most recent views of the patient.

Third, some argue that even if an advance directive can be seen as having some weight, our primary obligation towards the person lacking capacity is to show compassion and to seek his or her best interests. That principle cannot be challenged by using a directive.[447] Supporters of advance directives could reply that the person, in making the

---

[435] Burford (2008). Although note that, in English law, under the Inheritance (Provision for Family and Dependants) Act 1975, a court can make orders requiring that the will not be followed if there is inadequate provision for someone with a legitimate claim.

[436] Dresser (2003).

[437] This might mean that there is a difference if the 'second person' is regarded as a non-person (e.g. he or she is in a persistent vegetative state) rather than regarded as a different person: Holland (2003).

[438] Kuczewski (1994).   [439] Kuhse (1999).   [440] Herring (2009d).   [441] Maclean (2006).

[442] See Auckland (2017).   [443] Dresser (2015); Hertogh (2009).

[444] Shaw (2011); Dresser (2003).   [445] Ryan (2000).   [446] Ryan (2000).   [447] Dresser (1994).

directive, has considered whether, when capacity is lost, he or she wished to be treated on the basis of compassion or under the terms of the directive—and has chosen the latter. Rebecca Dresser argues that we must focus on the interests of the patient without capacity, not the person whom he or she once was. She argues:

> [T]he law must also ensure that the present patient does not simply disappear in the shadow of the person she once was. The law must ensure that someone looks carefully at the patient whose fate is now in question. It is the best interests standard that shines the brightest light on the patient in the present … Courts should not permit competent persons to exercise tyranny over their lives as incompetent patients.[448]

If the decision is made to respect advance directives, there is a further question as to how far they should be taken. Generally, it is thought that a directive should be treated in the same way as an expression of a competent person. In other words, it cannot compel doctors to provide a certain form of treatment, but it can restrict what may be done to the patient. Some, however, have questioned whether an advance directive can direct altruistic behaviour. For example, if a patient were to sign a directive stating that, in the event of a relative requiring a kidney, he or she would be willing to donate one, even if he or she had capacity when signing could such a directive be relied upon? One view is that there is no reason why not, given that a competent person would be allowed to make such a donation.[449] Others think that an advance directive cannot be used to authorize treatment that is not in a patient's best interests.[450] Alasdair Maclean has drawn an analogy between the competent person making the advance directive and his or her future demented self, and a parent making a decision for a child.[451] Although he emphasizes that the analogy is not exact, he suggests that an advance directive should be followed, but that it should be open to challenge if following it will cause serious harm to the demented person—just as we allow people to challenge the decisions of a parent that will cause serious harm to the child.

In all of the debate over advance directives, it should not be forgotten that, in fact, few people do try to make advance directives. This may well be because they do not like to think about death or serious illness.[452] Alternatively, it may be that many people are simply happy for decisions concerning their medical treatment to be made by their doctors and family should they lose capacity.[453]

22 Autonomy and the medical professional–patient relationship

The law's approach to medical decision making has an impact on the relationship between the medical professional and his or her patient. Myfanwy Morgan has suggested four models of the doctor–patient relationship, as follows.[454]

- *A paternalist relationship* The physician controls the relationship and decides what is best for the patient.

---

[448] Dresser (1994: 646).   [449] Lewis (2002).
[450] Law Commission Report 231 (1995: para. 5.13).   [451] Maclean (2006).   [452] Stern (1994).
[453] Dresser (1995).   [454] Morgan (2009).

- *A relationship of mutuality* The doctor and patient are equal partners engaged in a sharing of information and ideas designed to produce the best treatment for the patient.
- *A consumerist relationship* The patient is the active and dominant party, demanding treatment and assistance from a doctor whose primary role is to meet the requests of the patient.
- *A relationship of default* In this model, neither party takes a leading role. This normally leads to a non-productive encounter.

As can be seen, an autonomy model could fit within either the mutuality or consumerist models.

The decision in *Montgomery* has had a radical impact on the law's understanding of the doctor–patient relationship. Supporters of the decision argue that it opens up new ways of understanding the doctor–patient relationship. Heywood and Miola[455] suggest that it may have 'redefined the entire basis of the doctor–patient relationship in the eyes of the law'. Herring, Fulford, Dunn, and Handa[456] argue that the decision promotes dialogue between the patient and the doctor:

> The patient needs to understand from the doctor the risks and benefits of the different options available in order to weigh them one with another from the perspective of their own values. But the clinician needs to understand from the patient what matters or is important to him or her. For without such understanding the clinician will have no way of calibrating the information they convey appropriately to the values of the patient in question.

This promotes a process where the doctor and patient work together to find the treatment which will be best in line with the values of the patient.

Not everyone is so supportive of the decision. Critics note that their Lordships portrayed Mrs Montgomery as a powerless, uninformed patient, whereas in fact she was a graduate level-educated professional, who had experience in the health care sector.[457] The doctor was portrayed as imposing her views on the patient, rather than seeking to promote the patient's best interests. The broader point is that there is danger in the approach taken by the court of infantilizing patients and demonizing doctors.[458]

Another concern is that we may be expecting too much of doctors in advising patients. If they are to understand the values of patients, as Herring et al. suggest, are they meant to seek out the religious views of patients? That could be embarrassing and/or complex. For example, even if a patient is a Roman Catholic, it does not follow that they agree with everything the Pope says.[459]

23 The ethics of child treatment

When the decision in *Gillick* was handed down, it was interpreted by some as heralding the emergence of children's rights in the medical arena.[460] In recognizing that a competent child was able to give legally recognized consent to receive contraceptive advice

[455] Heywood and Miola (2017).   [456] Herring et al. (2017).   [457] Clark (2016).
[458] Montgomery and Montgomery (2016).   [459] Brazier and Farrell (2016).
[460] Eekelaar (1986); Gilmore (2009).

and treatment, the case was interpreted by some as meaning that mature children had the same rights to make decisions about their medical treatment as did adults. However, *Gillick* must now be considered in the light of subsequent decisions of the Court of Appeal, which have emphasized that even though the *Gillick* competent child can provide a legally effective consent to treatment (and in that way he or she is treated like an adult), but if he or she refuses treatment, then (unlike adults) consent can be provided by another: a person with parental responsibility, or the courts.

To many, the current law is illogical.[461] To say to a child 'You are mature enough to be able to make a decision about your treatment and we will respect your decision if you consent, but if you refuse, we will enable your decision to be readily overridden' is illogical. If a child is competent to decide about medical treatment, then that is so whether the child says 'yes' or 'no'. It is almost as if the law is saying to children: 'We will respect your right to autonomy, but only if you give the right answer!'

To others, the law does have a certain logic.[462] Rather than seeing *Gillick* as a case about giving children the right to make medical decisions for themselves, the decision should be seen as about preventing Mrs Gillick from depriving her daughters of access to needed medical treatment. Her veto of treatment could be overridden by the competent consent of one of her daughters.[463] The principle underlying the law, then, is that if a doctor believes that a child needs medical treatment, then the law should make it as easy as possible for the doctor to give it. This is done by enabling the doctor to provide the treatment, provided that he or she has the consent of either a person with parental responsibility, or a *Gillick* competent child, or a court. Seen this way, the law is simply promoting what is seen as the guiding principle in relation to children in the law: that the child's welfare should be promoted. However, this principle is not unproblematic. As Andrew Bainham points out:

> The courts are much inclined to speak of the welfare principle as an absolute standard and an unproblematic concept which can act as a panacea for all ills affecting children. This is not altogether surprising since it is they who get to define this content in any given situation.[464]

The debate can appear, then, as a clash between 'child liberationists', who would like to see the law recognize that children have the same rights as adults, and 'child paternalists', who see the law's paramount role as the protection of children's best interests. It appears that the majority of commentators reject 'the extremes' of child liberation or paternalism, and instead seek to develop a model that acknowledges both a child's right to be protected from harm and a child's right to make decisions for him or herself. One theory, which has received widespread support, is that proposed by John Eekelaar.[465] He has developed an approach to children's rights that requires the law to protect three different interests that a child has, as follows.

(i) *Basic interests* These are interests that are central to a child's well-being. They would include the feeding, housing, and clothing of a child. Basic interests also include promotion of the child's physical, emotional, and intellectual care.

---

[461] For example, Bainham (1992).   [462] Lowe and Juss (1993).
[463] It should be emphasized that there was no question in the case that one of her daughters would actually be seeking contraceptive treatment.
[464] Bainham (1987: 339).   [465] Eekelaar (1986; 1994).

(ii) *Developmental interests* These are the interests that a child has to enable him or her to develop as a person. Interests in education or socialization may be included here.

(iii) *Autonomy interests* These are the interests that children have in being permitted to make decisions for themselves.

Eekelaar goes on to argue that where there is a clash between the autonomy interests and the other two, the developmental or basic interests would trump the autonomy interest. In other words, children have an interest in being able to make decisions for themselves unless such a decision would infringe their basic or developmental interests. Children would therefore be able to make what adults might think of as 'bad decisions', but only as long as those are not such bad decisions that they interfere with matters that are central to a child's well-being. This is because the law should seek to allow children to develop into adults with maximum autonomy and maximum ability to decide how to live their lives.[466] In other words, an infringement of a child's autonomy in childhood is justified if necessary to maximize autonomy later in life. Applied to this context, it would mean that children can be prevented from refusing life-saving treatment or treatment without which they would suffer debilitating conditions, because that prevention will increase their autonomy when they become adults. However, such a view may be said to place too much weight on the importance of autonomy, and insufficient weight on the responsibilities and obligations that flow from the child's relationships with others.[467] It may also fail to capture the interests of children being heard and involved, even though autonomy may not be possible.[468]

Where there is a dispute between parents and doctors over medical treatment for children, the parties will, of course, attempt to reach a compromise. If necessary, the courts will be required to resolve the dispute using the welfare principle as the guiding rule. When making such decisions, the courts have emphasized that they will place weight on the views of parents, but the guiding principle will be what is best for the welfare of the child.[469] Indeed, occasionally, there have been cases in which the views of the parents have played a critical role in the courts' decisions.[470] This has been criticized by some as not protecting children's rights.[471] To allow a parent's views to change what would otherwise be ordered in the best interests of the child is unjustifiable.[472] To others, it is a recognition that a child is a member of a family and that his or her welfare is to some extent tied up with that of the family.[473] Indeed, to some, the current law fails to acknowledge adequately the proper position of parents as decision makers for children.[474] *In the Matter of Ashya King (A Child)*[475] parents disagreed with the medical plans for their children and took him from hospital to overseas to seek treatment there. Baker J overturned orders requiring the return of the child and held it was a

> fundamental principle of family law in this jurisdiction that responsibility for making decisions about a child rest with his parents. In most cases, the parents are the best

---

[466] See Herring (2009f) for a challenge to that.   [467] Herring (2009f).
[468] Donnelly and Kilkilly (2011).   [469] *Re A (Conjoined Twins: Medical Treatment)* [2001] 1 FLR 1, 49E.
[470] *Re T (A Minor) (Wardship: Medical Treatment)* [1997] 2 FCR 363. See further Bridgeman (2008).
[471] Freeman (2000).   [472] Freeman (2000).
[473] See the useful discussion of these issues in Bridge (2002).   [474] Engelhardt (2010).
[475] [2014] EWHC 2964. See Bridgeman (2015) for a sensitive discussion of the issues raised in this case.

people to make decisions about a child and the State—whether it be the court, or any other public authority—has no business interfering with the exercise of parental responsibility ...

Crucially in this case Baker J found the plans of the parents to be reasonable. The case does not challenge the principle that the welfare of the child will determine disputes over medical treatment, but it does suggest that if the court deems both the views of the medical team and the parents reasonable, it will side with the parents. This was demonstrated in the controversial decision concerning Charlie Gard, where the parents who wished to pursue experimental treatment for Charlie, against the advice of the medical team, lost their legal battle to authorize his removal overseas to where the treatment was available.[476] The decisions were consistently based on the view that the evidence on what was in Charlie's best interest pointed against authorizing the novel treatment.[477]

The decisions of the courts about whether a child is *Gillick* competent have been criticized by many commentators. It is said by some that the law improperly sets far higher standards of competence for children than it does for adults.[478] Indeed it has been argued that the test for capacity in the Mental Capacity Act 2005 should be used for everyone, including children.[479] Others have claimed that if a child is making a decision with which the court disagrees, then the court declares the child to lack capacity, whereas if the court agrees with the child, then the child is declared competent. There is a particular concern that where a child is expressing religious views as the basis for his or her refusal to consent to treatment, the courts are sceptical and are likely to regard the child as lacking capacity. The judges have stated that they respect teenagers' profession of religious belief, but then state that the child may reject that religion when he or she is older,[480] or that the child, having been brought up within a religion, does not have a wide enough experience of the world to enable him or her to be competent.

24 Conclusion

This chapter started with the relatively straightforward proposition that a medical professional should not treat a patient without his or her consent. However, it has become apparent that the law on consent is far from straightforward. The exact meaning of 'capacity to consent' is a delicate issue: if too strict a line is taken, then we rob a large number of people of their rights of autonomy; if too liberal a line is taken, we may end up attaching great weight to the statements of people who have little understanding of what the issues are. It is one thing to let a competent patient die if he or she has rejected life-saving treatment after a careful consideration of the issues; it is another when a person's rejection is little more than a confused and frightened 'no', with no real understanding of what is going on. Further, the chapter has explored the difficulties in deciding how decisions should be made in relation to those who lack capacity. For children who lack capacity, this involves a delicate balance between the rights of the children and those

---

[476] *Great Ormond Street Hospital v Yates* [2017] EWHC 1909 (Fam). See Bridgeman (2017).
[477] For discussion of whether the views of parents should be followed unless the child suffers harm, see Birchley (2016); Foster (2016).
[478] Bridgeman (1998).   [479] Discussed in Cave (2014).   [480] *Re E* (1990) 9 BMLR 1, 8.

of their parents. For adults lacking capacity, the MCA 2005 has emphasized the 'best interests' test, but has largely left open the question of how a person's best interests are to be ascertained. In recent years the courts have placed increasing weight on the values of the particular patient.

John Coggon[481] has usefully summarized the current position:

For treatment to be lawful it is requisite that:

- It is established to reflect, or at least be consistent with, the patient's personal view of her interests: this may be established through gaining consent, or by reference to proven facts about the patient's values.

- It is judged by reference to professional opinion to be in the patient's best interests: this will be established by reference to the doctor(s) agreeing that the intervention is indicated as a worthwhile intervention because of the benefits—whether therapeutic or otherwise—that it will provide.

- It is judged, by reference to principles of sound public decision-making, to be worth funding through the health care system: this will be established by the particular resource allocation model that governs access to treatment.

As this summary shows, the values of a patient are now key, but they are not the only factor that is taken into account. It also shows that increasingly less weight is attached to whether a patient has mental capacity or not.

QUESTIONS

1. Many competent people do not do everything that they should to promote their health (for example they fail to ensure that they have regular dental check-ups). Should we impose on those who lack mental capacity higher standards of care than most people choose for themselves?

2. In *Re E*,[482] a 15-year-old Jehovah's Witness refused to consent to a blood transfusion. The transfusions were nevertheless authorized by a court. After nearly three years of non-consensual transfusions, E reached the age of majority and his views had to be respected. He died. Does this tell us that the law on children's refusal of medical treatment is wrong? Or that the law on adults is?

3. Consider the following.

   It is one thing to respect a refusal of treatment based on a religious conviction of a devout patient who has long held their religious beliefs. It is another to require us, as the courts have declared, to accept a decision made for 'no reason at all'.[483]

   Does the law pay too much respect to decisions that appear to defy logic?

4. Does the law improperly assume that a decision maker is competent or is not? Would it not be more appropriate to recognize that there is a scale of competence, with

---

481 Coggon (2016).   482 [1993] 1 FLR 386.   483 Stauch (1998: 76).

decisions falling at different places along that line? The weight attached to a decision could then depend on where on the scale of competence the decision maker lay.

5. Is it correct to emphasize the 'principle of autonomy' given that, although great respect is paid to a patient's refusal to consent to treatment, little legal weight attaches to the right to receive treatment that one desires?[484]

6. Consider the following.

    Healing, as we define it, is a form of assistance in making the patient whole again by working through her or his body. If the values of patient welfare and patient autonomy remain in conflict, then authentic healing cannot take place. A physician, therefore, must become both a moderate autonomist and a moderate welfarist.[485]

    Is a compromise view of this kind, between a welfarist and autonomist approach, workable?

7. In May 2005, it was disclosed that a man who had refused treatment for tuberculosis had gone on to infect twelve other people with the disease.[486] When should infectious people be detained?

8. Should doctors perform circumcision on boys where that is not clinically required, but the parents want it? If parents were to want the tips of a finger removed, would we allow doctors to operate to remove that? Is it any different whether the parents are acting for religious or aesthetic reasons?[487]

9. In early 2007, much media attention was paid to an American couple who had decided to keep their severely disabled daughter 'child-sized' by giving her drugs.[488] This would avoid her having periods and make caring easier. Should the doctor have been willing to go along with the parents' wishes? Or is this a case in which making the patient's care easier so that she can stay at home is more important than her interests in growing up?

10. I have written:

    Dependency on others is an aspect of our humanity. From our earliest beginnings we are in relationships of dependency and we are for much if not all of our lives. Sometimes receiving, sometimes giving, care; often doing both. We may look to puff ourselves up on our independence and boast of the rational powers we use to exercise our autonomy. The truth is a little less grand. Many decisions we take are based on little evidence and made based on irrational fears and emotions. Relationships of dependency are central to our lives. We may point to rationality and independence as marking the line between competence and incompetence, but in fact they demonstrate how blurry that line is.[489]

    Do we deceive ourselves into thinking that autonomy is important?

[484] See Graber and Tansey (2005) for a discussion of this issue.
[485] Pelligrino and Thomasma (1988: 32).
[486] BBC News online (9 May 2005b).
[487] See Fox and Thomson (2005) for a discussion of this question.
[488] BBC News online (4 January 2007).
[489] Herring (2009a: 510).

FURTHER READING

A comprehensive bibliography, including all references used throughout the book, is available online at www.oup.com/uk/herringmedical7e/.

For a discussion of the capacity of children to consent, see:

Bridgeman, J. (2015) 'Misunderstanding, threats, and fear, of the law in conflicts over children's healthcare', *Medical Law Review* 23: 477.

Cave, E. (2014) 'Goodbye Gillick? Identifying and resolving problems with the concept of child competence', *Legal Studies* 34: 103.

Gilmore, S. and Herring, J. (2011) '"No" is the hardest word: consent and children's autonomy', *Child and Family Law Quarterly* 23: 3.

McDougall, R. and Notini, L. (2014) 'Overriding parents' medical decisions for their children: a systematic review of the normative literature', *Journal of Medical Ethics* 40: 448.

For issues surrounding autonomy, see:

Beyleveld, D. and Brownsword, R. (2007) *Consent in the Law* (Hart).

Coggon, J. and Miola, J. (2011) 'Autonomy, liberty and medical decision-making', *Cambridge Law Journal* 70: 523.

Conly, S. (2012) *Against Autonomy: Justifying Coercive Paternalism* (Cambridge University Press).

Craigie, J. (2011) 'Competence, practical rationality and what a patient values', *Bioethics* 25: 326.

Fovargue, S. and Mullock, A. (2016) *The Legitimacy of Medical Treatment: What Role for the Medical Exception?* (Routledge).

General Medical Council (2008) *Consent: Patients and Doctors Making Decisions Together* (GMC).

Herring, J. (2009d) 'Losing it? Losing what? The law and dementia', *Child and Family Law Quarterly* 21: 3.

Herring, J., Fulford, B., Dunn, M. and Handa, A. (2017) 'Elbow Room For Best Practice? Montgomery, Patients' Values, and Balanced Decision-making in Person-Centred Clinical Care', *Medical Law Review* 25: 582.

Herring, J. and Wall, J. (2017) 'The nature and significance of the right to bodily integrity', *Cambridge Law Journal* 76: 566.

McCall Smith, A. (1997) 'Beyond autonomy', *Journal of Contemporary Health Law and Policy* 14: 23.

McLean, S. (2009) *Autonomy, Consent and the Law* (Routledge).

Mackenzie, C. and Rogers, W. (2013) 'Autonomy, vulnerability and capacity: a philosophical appraisal of the Mental Capacity Act', *International Journal of the Law in Context* 9: 37.

Maclean, A. (2009) *Autonomy, Informed Consent and the Law: A Relational Challenge* (Cambridge University Press).

Manson, N. and O'Neill, O. (2007) *Rethinking Informed Consent in Bioethics* (Cambridge University Press).

Miola, J. and Heywood, R. (2017) 'The Changing Face of Pre-Operative Medical Disclosure: Placing the Patient at the Heart of the Matter', *Law Quarterly Review* 133: 296.

O'Neill, O. (2002) *Autonomy and Trust in Bioethics* (Cambridge University Press).

Wicks, E. (2016) *The State and the Body* (Hart).

For ethical and legal issues surrounding advance directives, see:

Auckland, C. (2017) 'Protecting Me From My Directive: Ensuring Appropriate Safeguards for Advance Directives in Dementia', *Medical Law Review* (advance access online).

Dresser, R. (2003) 'Precommitment: a misguided strategy for securing death with dignity', *Texas Law Review* 81: 1823.

Gligorov, N. and Vitrano, C. (2011) 'The impact of personal identity on advance directives', *Journal of Value Inquiry* 45: 147.

Heywood, R. (2015) 'Revisiting advance decision making under the Mental Capacity Act 2005: a tale of mixed messages', *Medical Law Review* 23: 81.

Huxtable, R. (2014) 'Autonomy, best interests and the public interest: Treatment, non-treatment and the values of medical law', *Medical Law Review* 22: 459.

Johnston, C. (2014) 'Advance decision making—rhetoric or reality?', *Legal Studies* 34: 497.

Maclean, A. (2006) 'Advance directives, future selves and decision-making', *Medical Law Review* 14: 291.

Maclean, A. (2008) 'Advance directives and the rocky waters of anticipatory decision-making', *Medical Law Review* 16: 1.

For the treatment of patients lacking capacity, see:

Bartlett, P. (2012) 'The United Nations Convention on the Rights of Persons with Disabilities and Mental Health Law', *Modern Law Review* 75: 724.

Buchanan, A. and Brock, C. (1990) *Deciding for Others: The Ethics of Surrogate Decision Making* (Cambridge University Press).

Cantor, N. (2005) *Making Medical Decisions for the Profoundly Mentally Disabled* (MIT Press).

Garwood-Gowers, A. (2005) 'The proper limits for medical intervention that harms the therapeutic interests of incompetents', in A. Garwood-Gowers, J. Tingel, and K. Wheat (eds) *Contemporary Issues in Health Care Law and Ethics* (Elsevier).

Herring, J. and Foster, C. (2016) *Altruism, Welfare and the Law* (Springer).

Lewis, P. (2002) 'Procedures that are against the medical interests of the incompetent person', *Oxford Journal of Legal Studies* 12: 575.

For articles on the Mental Capacity Act 2005, see:

Arstein-Kerslake, A. and Flynn, E. (2017) 'The right to legal agency: domination, disability and the protections of Article 12 of the Convention on the Rights of Persons with Disabilities', *International Journal of Law in Context* 81.

Banner, N. (2013) 'Can procedural and substantive elements of decision-making be reconciled in assessments of mental capacity?', *International Journal of the Law in Context* 9: 71.

Boyle, A. (2008) 'The law and incapacity determinations', *Modern Law Review* 71: 433.

Brosnan, L. and Flynn, E. (2017) 'Freedom to negotiate: a proposal extricating "capacity" from "consent" ', *International Journal of Law in Context* 13: 6.

Clough, B. (2014) '"People like that": Realising the social model in mental capacity jurisprudence', *Medical Law Review* 23: 53.

Clough, B. (2016) 'Anorexia, Capacity, and Best Interests: Developments in the Court of Protection Since the Mental Capacity Act 2005', *Medical Law Review* 24: 434.

Coggon, J. (2016) 'Mental Capacity Law, Autonomy, and Best Interests: An Argument for Conceptual and Practical Clarity in the Court of Protection', *Medical Law Review* 24: 396.

Craigie, J. (2015) 'A fine balance: Reconsidering patient autonomy in light of the UN Convention on the Rights of Persons with Disabilities', *Bioethics* 29: 398.

Donnelly, M. (2011) *Healthcare Decision-Making and the Law* (Cambridge University Press).

Donnelly, M. (2016) 'Best Interests in the Mental Capacity Act: Time to say Goodbye?', *Medical Law Review* 24: 318.

Foster, C., Herring, J., and Doran, I., (2015) *The Law and Ethics of Dementia* (Hart).

Herring, J. (2008a) 'The place of carers', in M. Freeman (ed.) *Law and Bioethics* (Oxford University Press).

Herring, J. (2016) *Vulnerable Adults and the Law* (Oxford University Press).

Hope, T., Slowther, A., and Eccles, J. (2009) 'Best interests, dementia and the Mental Capacity Act (2005)', *Journal of Medical Ethics* 35: 733.

For works on relational autonomy, see:

Mackenzie, C. and Stoljar, N. (2000) *Relational Autonomy* (Oxford University Press).

Maclean, A. (2009) *Autonomy, Informed Consent and the Law: A Relational Challenge* (Cambridge University Press).

Stoljar, N. (2011) 'Informed consent and relational conceptions of autonomy', *Journal of Medicine and Philosophy* 36: 275.

Confidentiality

INTRODUCTION

There is probably no avoiding the National Health Service (NHS) keeping information about patients. The NHS has produced a 'Care Record Guarantee', which explains:

> In the National Health Service in England, we aim to provide you with the highest quality of healthcare. We also aim to gain evidence that will improve health and care through research. To do this, we must keep records about you, your health and the care we have provided to you or plan to provide to you. NHS care records may be electronic, on paper or a mixture of both, and organisations use a combination of working practices and technology to keep to this guarantee.[1]

It might, at first, be thought that the issue of medical confidentiality is straightforward. Healthcare professionals should always keep secret their patients' confidential information and it is as simple as that. As Lord Phillips MR stated in *Ashworth Security Hospital v MGN Ltd*:[2]

> It is well settled that there is an abiding obligation of confidentiality as between doctor and patient, and in my view when a patient enters a hospital for treatment, whether he be a model citizen or murderer, he is entitled to be confident that details about his condition and treatment remain between himself and those who treat him.

However, as we shall see, the issue is complex. Modern healthcare systems would be unworkable if a doctor were never to pass on medical information about patients to other medical professionals. Also, only a moment's thought will allow you to conjure up situations in which even information given in confidence to a doctor should be revealed. For example, if a father confesses to his doctor that he is abusing his child, is the doctor to do nothing?[3]

Current medical practice has certainly made the issue of confidentiality more complex. A patient in a hospital is likely to be treated by a large number of healthcare professionals, each of whom will be dealing with different aspects of his or her treatment. Each one may need to have access to the patient's medical records. Also, internal and external audits of NHS trusts may require managers to have access to at least parts of a patient's medical records to be able to ensure that high standards of treatment are being offered. Further, the inevitable increase in use of computer technology in

---

[1] NHS (2011b: 8).   [2] [2000] 1 WLR 515, 527.
[3] A doctor who did nothing after receiving a report of abuse in 1975 was found not to be negligent when assessed by the standards of doctors at that time: *C v Dr AJ Cairns* [2003] Lloyd's Rep Med 90. The judgment assumes that things would be very different today.

relation to patients' records, while easing the passing of information to those who need to know, makes protecting confidentiality more complex.

Despite these modern pressures on confidentiality, the notion that a doctor should not improperly divulge sensitive information about his or her patient is deeply ingrained. The Hippocratic Oath states:

> Whatsoever things I see or hear concerning the life of men, in my attendance on the sick or even apart therefrom, which ought not to be noised abroad, I will keep silence thereon, counting such things to be as sacred secrets.[4]

Confidentiality is seen as an essential aspect of effective medical treatment. Doctors can give an effective diagnosis only if patients are completely honest with their doctor. Indeed, it is difficult to find anyone working in the medical field who believes that confidentiality is unimportant, even though there are certainly disputes over when confidentiality can properly be breached. However, as we will see later in this chapter, although the principle of confidentiality has received much praise, some believe that it is honoured as much in the breach as in the observance. There have even been complaints that medical ethicists themselves, in their writings, have discussed individual patients' cases, thereby failing to pay sufficient attention to issues of confidentiality.[5]

One important point that is now being taken seriously in the NHS is that confidentiality is not only a negative concept—that is, an obligation on staff not to reveal information; it also contains a positive obligation—that the NHS must take steps to ensure that confidential information is not revealed. This has led some to shift the focus of the discussion away from confidentiality towards the notion of data protection. The emphasis reflects the view that the greater threat to medically sensitive information is not doctors selling our health records to the tabloid press, but hackers entering NHS computers and accessing private information.

The General Medical Council (GMC) has also issued strict guidelines in relation to confidentiality, based on the following principles:

> Confidentiality is central to trust between doctors and patients. Without assurances about confidentiality, patients may be reluctant to seek medical attention or to give doctors the information they need in order to provide good care. But appropriate information sharing is essential to the efficient provision of safe, effective care, both for the individual patient and for the wider community of patients.[6]

The guidance explains that if a doctor is required to make a disclosure, this should be kept to a minimum:

> When disclosing information about a patient, you must:
>
> (a) use anonymised or coded information if practicable and if it will serve the purpose
>
> (b) be satisfied that the patient:
>
>   (i) has ready access to information that explains that their personal information might be disclosed for the sake of their own care, or for local clinical audit, and that they can object, and
>
>   (ii) has not objected

---

[4] Kennedy and Grubb (2000: 1047).   [5] Rogers and Draper (2003).   [6] GMC (2009: 12).

(c) get the patient's express consent if identifiable information is to be disclosed for purposes other than their care or local clinical audit, unless the disclosure is required by law or can be justified in the public interest

(d) keep disclosures to the minimum necessary, and

(e) keep up to date with, and observe, all relevant legal requirements, including the common law and data protection legislation.[7]

The NHS Constitution includes the right 'to privacy and confidentiality and to expect the NHS to keep your confidential information safe and secure'.[8] The Department of Health has published guidelines on the issue of confidentiality within the NHS. But notice, in the following opening statement, how the emphasis is more on fairness of dealing with information than it is on keeping it confidential:

> The NHS is committed to the delivery of a first class confidential service. This means ensuring that all patient information is processed fairly, lawfully and as transparently as possible so that the public:
>
> • understand the reasons for processing personal information;
> • give their consent for the disclosure and use of their personal information;
> • gain trust in the way the NHS handles information; and
> • understand their rights to access information held about them.[9]

These principles and the duties of confidentiality apply to all NHS staff, including volunteer helpers,[10] not only to doctors.

1 The legal basis of confidentiality

Perhaps surprisingly, the legal basis of a medical professional's duty of confidentiality is far from clear. There is no single statute or common law body of laws governing confidentiality. A medical professional who improperly discloses private information can be found to have acted illegally on the basis of a wide range of legal obligations, as follows.

1.1 Contract law

It might be said that to reveal a patient's confidential information is a breach of contract with the patient. However, there is no contract between an NHS patient and anyone caring for him or her. A court might find a special implied contract, but the general view is that this is unlikely. A contract claim would, however, have a greater chance of success in a case involving a private patient.

A breach of contract claim could also arise if (as is likely) infringing patient confidentiality were a breach of the healthcare professional's contract of employment.[11] The claim and any remedy would, however, be open only to the employer, not to the patient.[12]

---

[7] GMC (2009: 13).   [8] NHS (2013a: 10).   [9] DoH (2003a: 4).   [10] DoH (2003a: 16).
[11] *X v Y* [1988] 2 All ER 649.
[12] Unless a patient could claim under the Contracts (Rights of Third Parties) Act 1999.

1.2 **Tort law**

Revealing confidential information could amount to negligence. It is well established that keeping a patient's affairs private is part of reasonable care. A claim could be brought against a medical professional in tort if the professional were either to reveal the protected information or fail to take reasonable steps to ensure that others did not get hold of it.[13] The difficulty in such a claim is, however, damages. Generally, in tort, damages are available only for financial or physical loss. Feelings of embarrassment, for example, would not be a recognized form of financial loss in tort law. Therefore, even if a successful claim could be brought in negligence, only very limited damages might be available.

If the released information were untrue and would lead reasonable people to think less of the patient, then a claim could be brought in defamation. However, this will assist a patient only if the information disclosed is false. Reassuringly for doctors, they also have a defence of 'qualified privilege' if they reasonably believed their statement to be true and have communicated with a person who has a legitimate interest in the relevant information.[14] This would be relevant in a case in which a doctor supplied information in a medical questionnaire for an insurance company that was reasonably believed to be correct, but which was, in fact, not.

The courts are now developing a new tort of breach of privacy, using the Human Rights Act (HRA) 1998. In *Campbell v MGN Ltd*,[15] Lord Nicholls referred to the tort of misusing private information. In *Douglas v Hello!*,[16] Lord Nicholls suggested that there were two causes of action: protecting privacy; and protecting confidential information. The exact extent of the tort of privacy is still being developed. In *Murray v Big Pictures*,[17] it was held that children are entitled to protection of privacy in circumstances in which that could be reasonably expected. That included, in that case, walking down a street to a cafe. Taking a photograph of the child in those circumstances infringed his rights under Article 8 of the European Convention on Human Rights (ECHR) and he was entitled to legal redress. Similarly, Max Mosley successfully sued a newspaper for breach of privacy after it carried stories about his sexual habits.[18]

If a medical professional were to reveal private medical information, this may amount to both an interference with privacy and a breach of confidence. In *McKennit v Ash*,[19] it was held that medical information is 'doubly private' because it is both private information and confidential.

1.3 **Equitable obligations of confidence**

Often, the best option for a patient who wishes to commence a legal claim in respect of a revelation of medical information is to rely on the equitable obligation to respect confidential information. In order for information to be protected by equitable obligations of confidence, four criteria need to be satisfied, as follows.

---

[13] *Swinney v Chief Constable of the Northumbria Police* [1996] 3 All ER 449.
[14] Brazier and Cave (2007: 86).   [15] [2004] UKHL 22, [15].   [16] [2007] UKHL 21, [25].
[17] [2008] EWCA Civ 446.   [18] *Mosley v News Group Newspapers* [2008] EWHC 687 (QB).
[19] [2006] EWCA Civ 1714.

(i) The information must be of a personal, private, or intimate nature.[20] The test for this is whether the person whom the information concerns had a reasonable expectation that the information would be kept private.[21] This will generally be true of medical information. This requirement indicates that if a doctor were to reveal a trivial piece of information (for example what colour socks a patient was wearing), this may be regarded as not protected by confidence. However, it should be noted that the British Medical Association (BMA) has suggested that even the fact that a patient visited a doctor should be regarded as confidential information.[22] In *Campbell v MGN Ltd*,[23] Lady Hale surprisingly stated:

> Not every statement about a person's health will carry the badge of confidentiality or risk doing harm to that person's physical or moral integrity. The privacy interest in the fact that a public figure has a cold or a broken leg is unlikely to be strong enough to justify restricting the press's freedom to report it. What harm could it possibly do?

This statement might be read as suggesting that minor medical complaints are not to be regarded as confidential. However, it is better understood as a statement that, with minor medical complaints, it will not be particularly difficult to find public interest reasons (for example freedom of the press) that justify breaching the confidence.

(ii) The information must be imparted in circumstances imposing an obligation of confidence. It used to be thought that there needed to be shown that there was a confidential relationship between the parties, such as doctor and patient or husband and wife, but now it is clear that all that is required is that a person receives information that he or she knows, or ought to know, is fairly and reasonably to be regarded as confidential or private.[24] There is therefore little doubt that information provided to a doctor by a patient would satisfy this criterion. Indeed, even words spoken in group therapy sessions have been said to be bound by confidence.[25] The duty of confidence will also apply to someone who discovers information and it is clear that the person whom it concerns had a reasonable expectation that it would be kept private.[26] So if a doctor were to tell his wife about a patient's medical condition, she would also be bound by the duty of confidence because she would be aware that the information was confidential in nature. Similarly, if a member of the public were to find medical notes that had been accidentally left on a park bench, the member of the public would be required to keep the information confidential.

(iii) It may be necessary to show that someone will suffer as a result of the release of confidential information about them. This was the basis of the reasoning in *R v Department of Health, ex p Source Informatics Ltd*,[27] which held that the release of anonymized medical information was not a breach of confidentiality. However, it is not

---

[20] *Stephens v Avery* [1988] 2 All ER 477; *Campbell v MGN Ltd* [2004] UKHL 22.
[21] *Campbell v MGN Ltd* [2004] UKHL 22, [21], *per* Lord Nicholls, and [137], *per* Lady Hale. Lord Hope preferred the test of whether it would cause the victim 'substantial offence' (at [92]), but this test was rejected by Lord Hoffmann (at [22]) and Lady Hale (at [135]).
[22] BMA (2004: 167).   [23] [2004] UKHL 22, [157].
[24] *Campbell v MGN Ltd* [2004] UKHL 22, [14], *per* Lord Nicholls, and [85], *per* Lord Hope.
[25] *Venables v MGN Ltd* [2001] 1 All ER 908.
[26] *Attorney General v Guardian Newspapers Ltd (No. 2)* [1990] 1 AC 109, 281, *per* Lord Goff.
[27] [2000] 1 All ER 786.

clear whether this represents the law, because Lord Keith, in *A-G v Guardian (No. 2)*,[28] suggested that even if no one individual were to suffer a specific detriment in relation to the revelation, there could even so be a public interest that supported confidentiality.[29] In other words, even if the revelation did not itself harm a particular person, if it could be said to be likely to cause a public harm (such as that it would lead to a lack of trust in doctors), this could be sufficient to justify protecting the information in equity.[30] Hence it is widely accepted that even if a patient had died, a doctor ought not to make public details of that patient's medical conditions.[31] And, of course, even though someone is no longer a doctor's patient that does not mean the doctor is free to reveal their information.[32]

(iv) Confidence will be breached only if an unauthorized person sees it. It is not necessary to show that the information was made public.[33]

The leading case on breach of confidence is now *Campbell v MGN Ltd*.[34] In which their Lordships emphasized that the right to respect for private and family life under Article 8 ECHR should now be regarded as underpinning the protection of confidentiality. Protection of confidential information is about respecting the autonomy and dignity of individuals.[35] This meant that, in deciding whether the information was protected by the law, it would be necessary to consider whether the information is protected under Article 8 and then whether infringement of the confidence is justified under Article 8(2).[36]

KEY CASE   *Campbell v MGN Ltd* [2004] UKHL 22

Naomi Campbell—and, as Baroness Hale pointed out, 'Even the judges know who Naomi Campbell is'—was photographed leaving a meeting of Narcotics Anonymous (NA). The *Daily Mirror* published the photographs, accompanied by an article praising Ms Campbell's battle with drug addiction and giving details about her treatment. Naomi Campbell sued for breach of confidence. She won at first instance, lost in the Court of Appeal, but won again in the House of Lords. She was awarded £2,500 damages plus £1,000 aggravated damages.

The speeches in the House of Lords, unfortunately, are unclear on the basis of the award. Lord Nicholls talked of the tort of misuse of private information. However, Lord Hoffmann, Lord Hope, and Baroness Hale all talked of equitable breach of confidence. Lord Hoffmann also mentioned a new common law right to protect private information. Lord Carswell talked in general terms about a right to confidentiality, but it is not clear what kind of right he was talking about. This lack of certainty is explicable because none of their Lordships suggested that the law differed depending on

---

[28] [1988] 3 All ER 545.
[29] See also *Bluck v Information Commissioner* (2007) 98 BMLR 1, [15], which stated that, in cases of breach of medical confidentiality, it was not necessary to show detriment.
[30] *Stone v South East Strategic Health Authority* [2006] EWHC 1668 (Admin); *Ashworth v MGN Ltd* [2001] 1 All ER 991.
[31] *Bluck v Information Commissioner* (2007) 98 BMLR 1. See also *Lewis v Secretary of State for Health* [2008] EWHC 2196.
[32] *Re C (A Child)* [2015] EWFC 79.   [33] *A-G v Guardian (No. 2)* [1990] 1 AC 109, 260.
[34] [2004] UKHL 22.   [35] At [53], *per* Lord Hoffmann.   [36] See, e.g., Lord Nicholls at [17].

what classification was used. They were united in agreeing that the law would protect an improper revelation of confidential information, be that through tort, equity, or some unclassified right.

The first issue was whether details about Naomi Campbell's attendance at NA meetings were confidential. Lord Hoffmann explained that the protection of confidential information was about 'the right to control the dissemination of information about one's private life and the right to the esteem and respect of other people'.[37] Their Lordships explained that, in considering what information was confidential, consideration would be given to Article 8 ECHR and the right to respect for private life. In deciding whether information was confidential, Lord Hope suggested that 'the broad test is whether disclosure of the information about the individual ("A") would give substantial offence to A, assuming that A was placed in similar circumstances and was a person of ordinary sensibilities'.[38] However, Lord Hoffmann and Baroness Hale did not approve of this test. They preferred to ask whether a person would have a reasonable expectation that the information would be kept confidential.

Applying this test to the facts of the case, their Lordships agreed that, prima facie, the fact that someone was receiving treatment for drug addiction would be confidential information. However, in this case, Naomi Campbell had made various public statements to the effect that she (unlike many other models) did not take drugs. By so doing, she had made her drug-taking a public matter and so no longer confidential. Alternatively, her statements created sufficient public interest to justify the press correcting the misleading impression that she had created. But the majority of their Lordships then held that her statements did not mean that every aspect of her drug-taking and treatment was now public information. The time, place, and form of drug therapy were still confidential. To the minority (Lords Nicholls and Hoffmann), the article was essentially about Campbell's treatment for drug addiction, and that was not private because she had chosen to make that issue a public one. The information about where and when she was attending treatment was 'unremarkable and inconsequential' (in Lord Nicholls' view). To the majority, revealing the fact that she was attending NA meetings was analogous to informing the public of what medical treatment a celebrity was receiving, which was clearly protected information.

Having decided that the taking of photographs and publication of the story were in breach of confidence, the next question was whether there was a public interest (including freedom of the press) that justified the infringement. Quite simply, this involved a balancing exercise between the right to respect for private life under Article 8 ECHR and the right to freedom of expression under Article 10:

> [T]he right to privacy which lies at the heart of an action for breach of confidence has to be balanced against the right of the media to impart information to the public. And the right of the media to impart information to the public has to be balanced in its turn against the respect that must be given to private life.[39]

In undertaking this balancing exercise, Baroness Hale, for one, did not have great sympathy for either side: 'Put crudely, it is a prima donna celebrity against a celebrity-exploiting tabloid newspaper.'[40] And this might explain why, even though the majority sided with Campbell, the level of damages was small. What seemed to have influenced the majority was that a recovering drug addict is in a vulnerable position, needing all of the support that she can get. The publication of information about her treatment was likely to distress her at what might be a particularly vulnerable time. There was little public interest in the story and therefore the right to privacy trumped the right to freedom of expression.

[37] At [51].   [38] At [52].   [39] At [112].   [40] At [143].

The main disadvantage in relying on the equitable remedy is in relation to the remedies that a court can grant. The primary remedy is an injunction. A court may be willing to prevent a disclosure of confidential information through an injunction if that is necessary in the public interest.[41] This is, of course, useful only to someone who is aware that there is about to be a revelation of confidential information and provides little assistance in a case in which the revelation has already been made. It used to be thought that damages were not available. However, the Court of Appeal in *Cornelius v de Taranto*[42] upheld an award of damages for breach of confidence, and, of course, the House of Lords in *Campbell* did likewise. In neither case, were the sums awarded very large. If the person breaching confidence thereby acquires a profit, it may be that he or she can be made liable to account for those profits to the victim.[43]

1.4 Ownership

It could be argued that a patient owns his or her medical information and therefore can bring a property claim if the information is revealed to others. But in *R v Department of Health, ex p Source Informatics Ltd*,[44] the Court of Appeal rejected an argument that patients own the information about themselves. Indeed, the general view seems to be that it is the NHS trust that owns the records that its staff makes. The trust (rather than the staff) therefore can control the access to that information. That said, in *R v Mid Glamorgan Family Health Services Authority, ex p Martin*,[45] it was emphasized that simply because someone owns records does not mean that they have the right to do what they want with them.

1.5 Criminal law

It has long been held that information is not property that is capable of being stolen.[46] However, the paper on which a medical report is contained could be. So a doctor who handed over a piece of paper with a medical record on it, or an X-ray, to a journalist could be guilty of theft not of the information, but of the piece of paper on which it was written. If the doctor were to telephone a journalist and read out a medical record, there could be no theft conviction. The Computer Misuse Act 1990 also criminalizes 'hacking' into a database to access confidential information. Notably, an offence under that Act is committed by staff who have access to some parts of a database, but who access parts that they are not authorized to access.[47] This means that a healthcare professional is guilty of an offence under the Act if he or she accesses the hospital's database to discover information about a celebrity who is not his or her patient.

1.6 Human rights

The HRA 1998, as discussed in Chapter 1, affects the law in two ways:

• it can be used to direct the interpretation of statute or to develop the common law; and

• it provides a cause of action in its own right.

[41] *W v Egdell* [1990] 1 All ER 835.   [42] (2001) 68 BMLR 62.
[43] *Blake v Attorney-General* [2003] 1 WLR 625.   [44] [2000] 1 All ER 786.   [45] [1995] 1 All ER 356.
[46] *Oxford v Moss* (1978) 68 Cr App R 183.
[47] *R v Bow Street Metropolitan Stipendiary Magistrate, ex p Government of the USA* [2000] 2 AC 216.

1.6.1 *The interpretation of statutes and common law*

Article 8 ECHR, which protects the right to respect for private and family life, also protects confidential information.[48] As the European Court of Human Rights (ECtHR) explained in *Z v Finland*:[49]

> The protection of personal data, not least medical data, is of fundamental importance to a person's enjoyment of his or her right to respect for private and family life as guaranteed by article 8 of the Convention ... Without such protection, those in need of medical assistance may be deterred from revealing such information of a personal and intimate nature as may be necessary in order to receive appropriate treatment and, even, from seeking such assistance thereby endangering their own health and, in the case of transmissible diseases, that of the community.

Article 8 may require states to take positive steps to ensure that medical confidentiality is protected.[50]

Following the HRA 1998, when the courts are interpreting statute or the common law, they should as far as possible do so in a way that is compatible with the protection of confidential information, as required under Article 8. Indeed, we have seen in *Campbell v MGN Ltd* that the House of Lords relied on the ECHR in determining the extent of the confidentiality, and in balancing the right to privacy and the right to freedom of expression. It is permissible to infringe the right to respect for private life if one of the interests listed in Article 8(2) is threatened: it is permissible to disclose confidential information only if to do so is 'necessary in a democratic society' in the interests of 'national security, public safety or the economic well-being of the country, for the prevention of disorder or crime, for the protection of health and morals, or for the protection of the rights and freedoms of others'. This offers a stronger protection for individual rights of privacy than might at first be apparent. First, the word 'necessary' means not only reasonable or convenient, but also that there is some pressing social requirement.

Second, the ECtHR has interpreted the provision to emphasize the notion of proportionality. This means that the extent to which the confidence is interfered with must be the minimum required to protect the countervailing interest. In other words, even if the interests of the protection of public health may justify interfering with the confidentiality of part of someone's medical records, it may not justify revealing them all. In *Re C (A Child)*[51] a psychiatrist wanted to reveal confidential information in order to protect himself against allegations of malpractice she had made in public. It was held that to reveal highly confidential information was disproportionate to his wish to protect his reputation.

In *Z v Finland*,[52] a husband was being prosecuted for a crime. The prosecuting authorities needed to establish when he became aware of his HIV-positive status. The police relied upon his wife's medical records for this purpose. The wife unsuccessfully complained to the European Court that her human rights had been infringed. A number of important points come out of the decision. First, the Court indicated that some kinds

---

[48] Phillipson (2003). See further Wicks (2007: ch. 6).
[49] Application no. 22009/93 (1998) 25 EHRR 371, [95]–[96]. Approved in *Szuluk v UK* (2009) 108 BMLR 190.
[50] *I v Finland* (2009) 48 EHRR 31.   [51] [2015] EWFC 79.
[52] Application no. 22009/93 (1998) 25 EHRR 371.

of medical information were more sensitive than others; information about HIV status was particularly sensitive. The implication is that the more intimate the information, the stronger the countervailing interests had to be to justify revealing it. Second, the Court held that accessing the wife's medical records was justified in the name of pursuing criminal proceedings for a serious offence, but that did not justify making her medical records public. It should have been possible for the evidence to have been made available in the trial without her right to respect for her private life being invaded. In other words, the extent of the invasion of her confidence was disproportionate.

In *MS v Sweden*,[53] the claimant applied for compensation for an industrial injury from social insurance benefits. The Social Insurance Office was sent information in her health records, including an abortion that she had had as a result of the injuries. It was held that this did not infringe her Article 8 rights: the infringement of her rights of privacy was justifiable in the name of checking the accuracy of the data. The officer checking the information was required to maintain the confidentiality of the information. One point that seemed to be given attention by the Court was that the claimant had chosen to apply for the benefit and had therefore raised publicly the state of her health.

1.6.2 *Remedies under the Human Rights Act 1998*

The HRA 1998, section 7, allows someone to sue a public authority that has infringed their Convention rights. It does not allow a claim to be made against an individual. Section 8 permits the court to award damages or to grant such remedy as seems just and appropriate.

1.7 **Statutory obligations**

There are a number of statutes that impose particular obligations in relation to confidential information. The Data Protection Act 1998 is the most significant, although there are a host of other statutory instruments and provisions that impose duties of confidentiality in particular circumstances.[54] For example, a medical professional cannot disclose information about a patient's attendance at a fertility clinic[55] or genito-urinary medicine clinic,[56] even to the patient's general practitioner (GP), without the express consent of the patient.

1.8 **Professional disciplinary procedures**

As well as the law, a variety of professional bodies have issued guidelines on confidentiality. These include the BMA,[57] the GMC,[58] and the Nursing and Midwifery Council (NMC).[59] The NHS has also issued its own code on confidentiality.[60] These guidelines are clearer and more accessible to healthcare professionals than the law. No doubt most professionals simply ensure that they are following the relevant professional guidelines,

---

[53] Application no. 20837/92 (1997) 45 BMLR 1.
[54] For example, NHS Trusts and Primary Care Trusts (Sexually Transmitted Diseases) Directions 2000.
[55] Human Fertilisation and Embryology Act 1990, as amended by the Human Fertilisation and Embryology (Disclosure of Information) Act 1992.
[56] National Health Service (Venereal Diseases) Regulations 1974, SI 1974/29.
[57] BMA (2004).   [58] GMC (2009).   [59] NMC (2009).   [60] DoH (2003a).

rather than attempt to understand the legal position. They make the assumption that if they are following the guidelines, they are acting lawfully. This is probably a reasonable assumption to make. Notably, the courts have on occasion relied upon the professional guidelines when deciding what the legal position was.[61]

We will now introduce two of the most important guidelines.

1.8.1 *The General Medical Council*

The guidelines issued by the GMC also emphasize the importance of ensuring that confidences are respected.[62] The GMC regards the consent of the patient as the primary exception to the principle that confidential information must be kept secret. However, it also accepts that, where secrecy would risk death or serious harm to the patient or another person, disclosure is permitted. The GMC guidance emphasizes that patients should be told at the outset how information about them is to be used. If a patient refuses to permit the sharing of his or her records with others caring for him or her, this must be respected.

The GMC suggests that a disclosure of confidential information is exceptionally justifiable only in the public interest. When deciding whether disclosure is justified, it is necessary to weigh up the benefits of disclosure against its harm 'both to the patient and to the overall trust between doctors and patients'. Further, the guidance states:

> Before considering whether a disclosure of personal information would be justified in the public interest, you must be satisfied that identifiable information is necessary for the purpose, or that it is not reasonably practicable to anonymise or code it. In such cases, you should still seek the patient's consent unless it is not practicable to do so, for example, because:
>
> (a) the patient is not competent to give consent, in which case you should consult the patient's welfare attorney, court-appointed deputy, guardian or the patient's relatives, friends or carers
>
> (b) you have reason to believe that seeking consent would put you or others at risk of serious harm
>
> (c) seeking consent would be likely to undermine the purpose of the disclosure, for example, by prejudicing the prevention or detection of serious crime, or
>
> (d) action must be taken quickly, for example, in the detection or control of outbreaks of some communicable diseases, and there is insufficient time to contact the patient.[63]

1.8.2 *NHS guidelines*

The Department of Health has issued a code of practice designed to ensure the protection of confidential information. At the heart of the guidance is the following principle:

> Patients entrust us with, or allow us to gather, sensitive information relating to their health and other matters as part of their seeking treatment. They do so in confidence

---

[61] *Re C* [1996] 1 FCR 605; *W v Egdell* [1990] 1 All ER 835; *Lewis v Secretary of State for Health* [2008] EWHC 2196.
[62] GMC (2009).   [63] GMC (2009: 37).

and they have the legitimate expectation that staff will respect their privacy and act appropriately. In some circumstances patients may lack the competence to extend this trust, or may be unconscious, but this does not diminish the duty of confidence. It is essential, if the legal requirements are to be met and the trust of patients is to be retained, that the NHS provides, and is seen to provide, a confidential service. What this entails is described in more detail in subsequent sections of this document, but a key guiding principle is that a patient's health records are made by the health service to support that patient's healthcare.[64]

The code makes it clear that duties of confidentiality apply not only to doctors, but also that:

- all NHS bodies and those carrying out functions on behalf of the NHS have a common law duty of confidence to patients, and a duty to support professional ethical standards of confidentiality;

- everyone working for or with the NHS who records, handles, stores or otherwise comes across information has a personal common law duty of confidence to patients and clients and to his or her employer. This applies equally to those, such as students or trainees, on temporary placements;

- health professionals have, by virtue of professional regulation, an ethical duty of confidence which, when considering whether information should be passed on, includes paying special regard to the health needs of the patient and to his or her wishes;

- other individuals and agencies to whom information is passed legitimately may use it only as authorized for specific purposes and possibly subject to particular conditions.[65]

1.9 **Comments on the law**

It must be admitted that the law in this area is not very satisfactory. There have been few cases governing the issue and there appear to be a large number of branches of the law that govern the area. A number of points can, however, be made to reassure the reader. The first is that, as already indicated, professional bodies have provided fairly clear guidance on the obligations of confidentiality and the courts are likely, in areas of doubt, to ensure that the law coincides with professional guidance.

Second, the courts have indicated that, when considering the legal position of confidence, whether the obligation is seen as emanating from contract, tort, or equity, the extent of the obligation will be the same.[66]

Third, the paucity of case law may indicate that this is not an area in which clear legal regulation is required: professional responsibilities appear to protect patients' confidentiality adequately. However, it might be that lack of clarity discourages people from bringing legal proceedings.

---

[64] DoH (2003a: 7).   [65] DoH (2003a: 4.1).   [66] Montgomery (2003: 262).

REALITY CHECK

Confidentiality in practice

As we have seen, in theory, the law takes breaches of confidentiality seriously, but how well is confidentiality protected in real life?

According to David Stone, 'many observers would say that, at ground level, the rights and duties arising from patient confidentiality are honoured more in the breach than the observance'.[67] As he points out, such a large number of people will have access to the records that they cannot realistically be described as private. One writer explains that at least twenty-five and possibly a hundred healthcare professionals and administrative personnel at one university hospital deal with a particular patient's records.[68] (But this kind of use of information is probably not objected to by many people.)

The kind of scenario that is more likely to give concern to members of the public is the following mundane case:

> Over a golf match between a dentist and a GP the two men discovered they shared a patient. The GP told the dentist that the patient had had an abortion. The dentist told his wife, who told a friend. The friend mentioned it to the patient.[69]

It is this kind of revelation of personal information to a person's social circle that is the main concern of many patients.[70] Another kind of incident that raises ire in the media is the finding of confidential medical reports in public waste bins or on the street.[71]

Interestingly, people in one survey were not particularly concerned about doctors seeing their medical records, but were unhappy about receptionists receiving it.[72]

An investigation by *The Observer* discovered some troubling breaches of confidentiality, including the following.[73]

- A 68-year-old man was refused a place in a care home when social services found out from his medical records that he was gay.

- A man found out that his niece had a secret abortion when the company for which he worked was asked to do a financial audit of the local health authority. He told her parents, who were very religious.

- A woman was sacked after her GP sent her records to her employer. The notes revealed that she had a history of mental health problems.

- A member of Parliament (MP) was sent the medical records of a constituent without her consent. She found out only when the MP passed the records on to her.

One study[74] found around 2,500 breaches of confidentiality a year, including:

- 50 cases of data being posted on social media;

- 103 cases of data being lost or stolen;

- 251 cases of data being inappropriately shared with a third party;

- 236 cases of data being shared by email, letter, or fax.

---

[67] Stone (2001: 132).   [68] Gillon (1986: 109).   [69] BMA (2004: 167).   [70] Siegler (1982).
[71] See, e.g., BBC News online (9 December 2003).   [72] NHS Information Authority (2002: 6).
[73] Browne (2000).   [74] BBC News Online (2014a).

It may be that attitudes within the NHS towards confidentiality are changing. The NHS has talked about the need to create a 'confidentiality culture'.[75] However, there is at least anecdotal evidence that doctors are often overheard discussing patients' personal medical details on trains,[76] at parties,[77] and in lifts.[78] Interestingly, in the NHS Code on Confidentiality it is seen as necessary to spell out the requirement not to discuss patients' confidential information in public places.[79]

One final point: in hospital, many consultations on the ward take place with only the flimsiest of curtains between patients. These may offer the pretence of privacy, but it is difficult to believe that they ensure that conversations are not overheard.

2 Denying breach of confidentiality

It is arguable that the easiest way in which to look at the law is to consider what defences someone might raise to a claim that he or she wrongfully revealed confidential information, and that is how we shall proceed. There are essentially two kinds of argument that a defendant may make: first, he or she could deny that the disclosure breached confidentiality; second, he or she could accept that there was a breach of confidence, but claim that the breach was justified. We shall look now at the first kind of defence.

2.1 The information is not confidential

It may be argued that the information lacks any element of confidentiality.[80] Really, this is not a defence to a breach of confidence claim, but rather an argument that the information is not protected by the law on breach of confidence. In the House of Lords' decision in *Campbell*, it was held that information is confidential if someone had a reasonable expectation that it would be kept confidential.

It is generally thought that information can acquire its confidentiality from two sources.

(i)   The information is given in the context of a relationship that is of a kind based on an assumption of confidentiality. There is little doubt that the doctor–patient relationship is of this kind.

(ii) The information is itself of a private and intimate kind, and therefore must be kept confidential.

It should be noted that information can be regarded as confidential if it falls in either of these categories.

There are two main issues of dispute. What if information given to a healthcare professional by a patient is trivial? For example, if a law professor tells her doctor that she loves the television programme *Big Brother* and the doctor tells her friend, could this be

---

[75] NHS Information Authority (2002: 6).   [76] Hendricks (2003).   [77] Weiss (1982).
[78] Vigod, Bell, and Bohnen (2003).   [79] DoH (2003a).
[80] See Donnelly and McDonagh (2011) for a discussion of the extent to which medical confidentiality protects patients who have died.

regarded as a breach of confidence, even though love of *Big Brother* is not a particularly intimate piece of information? Is the fact that the doctor acquired the information as a result of the confidential relationship between them enough to render the information confidential?[81] In *R (Stevens) v Plymouth*,[82] it was suggested that 'straightforward descriptions of everyday life' of a patient would not be regarded as confidential. In *R (W) v Secretary of State for Health*[83] a challenge was made to the practice of the NHS passing to the Home Office information about non-resident patients who owed debts to the NHS for treatment. As the information did not contain health data it was not treated as confidential. On the other hand, in *Ashworth Hospital Authority v MGN Ltd*,[84] an argument that information about a patient was too trivial to be protected by confidentiality was rejected, on the basis that confidentiality contained a subjective element. In other words, a person would be entitled to regard a piece of medical information about himself or herself as sensitive, even if most people would not regard it as particularly private. Of course, if the information revealed is not particularly damaging, there is unlikely to be a legal remedy of any significance, even if technically there is a breach of confidence.

Second, what if doctors are given information when they are not acting in their professional capacity? It is generally thought that if a doctor is given private information in his or her role *as a doctor*, it must be kept confidential.[85] For example, if a person at a party takes a doctor aside and asks for some medical advice, then what the person says should be kept confidential. But if the doctor is given information, not as a doctor, but as a piece of gossip between friends (for example if he or she is told that a neighbour is having an affair), then this will not necessarily attract confidentiality, but may do so if it is the kind of information that a reasonable person would expect to be kept confidential.[86] Some commentators argue that if the neighbour, or the person telling the doctor, were a patient of the doctor, that would change the issue and the information would then become confidential.

2.2 The information is no longer confidential

Even if it is accepted that the information was confidential, it might be argued that the information has lost its confidential nature. Confidentiality can be lost if the information has become public. If therefore a patient has revealed his or her medical condition to the press, there can be no complaint if the doctor subsequently reveals that same information.[87] Remember, in *Campbell v MGN Ltd*,[88] by making public statements that she did not take drugs, it was suggested that Naomi Campbell had made some information about her drug-taking non-confidential. As that case shows, however, just because some knowledge about a medical condition has been made public does not mean that others are free to reveal everything relating to the condition and its treatment. Less straightforwardly, in *Stone v South East Strategic Health Authority*,[89] a convicted murderer was found through his crimes to have put himself in the public domain and hence weakened the protection of his right to respect for privacy over his medical information.

[81] BMA (2004: 167) suggests that even if the information is not 'medical', it can still be regarded as confidential.
[82] [2002] 1 WLR 2483.   [83] [2014] EWHC 1532 (Admin).
[84] [2001] 2 All ER 991. See further *Mersey Care NHS Trust v Ackroyd* [2007] EWCA Civ 101.
[85] Kennedy and Grubb (2000: 1062).   [86] BMA (2004: 167) leaves the question open.
[87] See also *Douglas v Hello!* [2001] 1 WLR 992.   [88] [2004] UKHL 22.
[89] [2006] EWHC 1668 (Admin).

2.3 **The disclosure does not breach the confidentiality**

Even though it is admitted that there has been a disclosure of confidential information, it might be argued that the disclosure was not in breach of the obligation not to disclose. There are two main situations in which such a claim could be made, as follows.

(i)   *Consent* Fairly obviously, if the patient is happy for information to be disclosed, then there is no breach of confidence.[90] A husband may, for example, ask a doctor to discuss his medical condition with his wife. The patient should have information about the scope, purpose, and likely consequences of the disclosure.[91]

(ii) *Anonymity* In a highly controversial decision, it was held that the release of confidential information in an anonymized form was not in breach of a duty of confidentiality.[92] It is worth considering the decision in further detail.

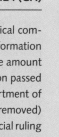

KEY CASE   *R v Department of Health, ex p Source Informatics Ltd* **[2001] QB 424 (CA)**

Source Informatics Ltd was in the business of selling medical information to pharmaceutical companies. It started a scheme under which GPs and pharmacists would pass to the company information about drugs prescribed for patients. This information included the doctor's name, and the amount and name of drug prescribed. The name of the patient was removed from any information passed on. The GPs and pharmacists were given a small sum of money for doing this. The Department of Health issued guidelines that passing on this information (even with the patient's name removed) breached the professional's confidentiality to patients. Source Informatics Ltd sought a judicial ruling on the Department of Health's guidelines. The Court of Appeal held that even though the patients had not consented to the passing of their medical information, because the information was anonymized, there was no breach of confidentiality; nor could the patient claim any property in the prescription forms from which the information was taken or the information itself.

The key passage in the judgment is as follows:

> [T]he confidant is placed under a duty of good faith to the confider and the touchstone by which to judge the scope of his duty and whether or not it has been fulfilled or breached is his own conscience, no more and no less. One asks, therefore, on the facts of this case: would a reasonable pharmacist's conscience be troubled by the proposed use to be made of patients' prescriptions? Would he think that by entering Source's scheme he was breaking his customers' confidence, making unconscientious use of the information they provide?[93]

The answer to the questions in the Court of Appeal's view was clearly 'no'. There was no identifying information and therefore the patient's privacy was not infringed, meaning that the doctors and pharmacists were not acting in breach of their duty of good faith.

---

[90] In *R (Servier) v NICE* [2009] EWHC 281 (Admin), the National Institute for Health and Care Excellence (NICE) wanted to disclose confidential information and was found to be in breach of its legal duties in not seeking the consent of the provider of the information to do so.

[91] GMC (2009: 34).

[92] See also *Department of Health v Information Commissioner* [2011] EWHC 1430 (Admin), in which the Department of Health was required to disclose anonymized data about abortion statistics. Because it was anonymized, it was not 'personal data' and had to be disclosed under the Freedom of Information Act 2000.

[93] At [31], *per* Simon Brown LJ.

The decision in *Source Informatics* is highly controversial. It is important to separate out two questions here. The first is whether the disclosure of anonymized medical information is in breach of confidence; the second is whether the disclosure is justified if necessary to the public interest, for the purposes of medical research.[94] The controversy surrounds the former issue. The Court of Appeal's approach is that because no one can know whose medical details are being looked at, there can be no harm, no invasion of privacy, and therefore no wrong is committed.[95] However, that is debatable. If a nude photograph of a person were published in a newspaper without his or her consent, with the face obscured so the person could not be identified, that person may well feel wronged, even though no one would know it was him or her. The person's privacy would have been invaded, even if no one else but that person were to realize it. Could the same thing not be said about someone's private medical details? The decision has also been criticized on the basis that it appears to suggest that a breach of confidence is a wrong only if there is unfairness or loss to someone, rather than seeing the breach of confidential information being a prima facie wrong for which a justification must be produced.[96]

The Court of Appeal's assumption was that the general public would not object to their medical information being used if it were anonymized. That assumption is contestable. In fact, the research shows a mixed picture, with some surveys suggesting that the general public have no such objection and others that they do.[97] The decision also provides no option for a person who objects to his or her information being used for the basis of particular kinds of research. A patient may have strong moral objections to research in relation to contraception or research that involves animals, and yet have no power to object to his or her medical information being used in such research.[98] A person's information may also be used in a way that (indirectly) harms him or her. The anonymized information might, for example, show that people of a particular ethnic or cultural group were more susceptible to a certain disease, and such a finding could have negative impacts for all members of that group, for example making it difficult for them to obtain mortgages.[99] Further, it may be questioned whether any information can be securely anonymized, given the amount of data held about individuals in government and other databases.[100]

Data that contains the postcode (but not the name) of the patient is regarded by some people as anonymous.[101] The postcode is useful if research is being carried out in an attempt to ascertain whether certain conditions are more prevalent in particular parts of the country. However, some argue that it can be all too easy to discover the identity of a person, given his or her postcode and a few pieces of health information.[102] Critics reply that it is fanciful that someone will seek to discover the identity of individuals from amongst a mass of research data.

---

[94] See Taylor (2011) for further discussion on the use of data for research.
[95] O'Neill (2003); Warnock (1998).
[96] Mason and Laurie (2006: 280). For criticism of its interpretation of the Data Protection Act 1998, see Beyleveld and Histed (2000).
[97] Research by Willison, Kashavjee, Nair, et al. (2003) found that patients drew no distinction between identifiable and anonymous data. But the NHS Information Authority (2002) found patients happy not to be asked for consent if the information was anonymized.
[98] Chester (2003).   [99] Gostin (1995: 521).   [100] Gellman (2010).
[101] GMC (2009) suggests that, to be anonymized information, it must not contain a full postcode.
[102] Chester (2003).

The most fundamental aspect of the decision in *Source Informatics* is its shift in focus from protection of confidential information to fairness of use. As long as the user can show that it was acting in good faith with personal information, it is not acting in breach of confidence. This shift from protecting the privacy of the patient to focusing on the conscience of the user could be highly significant.[103] The decision could even be read as shifting the burden from the user (showing that it had justifiable reasons for using the confidential information) to the patient (being required to show that the use was in bad faith). The potential impact of the decision is therefore enormous. However, the traditional approach—that people have a right to have their private information protected—underpins the professional guidance that has been issued and the Data Protection Act must still be followed.[104] Also, the emphasis that Lord Hoffmann in *Campbell v MGN Ltd*[105] placed on the right to privacy and autonomy as underlying the law on protection of confidential information suggests a very different approach from that promoted by *Source Informatics*.

Those keen to emphasize the importance of confidentiality can try to put a more positive spin on the decision in *Source Informatics*. The Department of Health guidelines state that if information is disclosed, it should be anonymized if possible.[106] A person wishing to reveal personal medical information must now, first, show that there are sufficient reasons for making the disclosure and, second, show why the disclosure cannot be made with the information first anonymized. This is most significant in the area of the use of medical information in research, where it might be thought that only exceptionally would anonymous information not be sufficient for the task at hand. However, there can be difficulties in using anonymous data for research purposes, because it can be harder to ensure that there are no duplicates.[107]

3 Justifying breach of confidence

If it is established that there was a breach of confidence, the defendant may nevertheless claim that the breach was justified. There are several circumstances in which the law would permit a breach.

3.1 Consent

As already indicated, there is no breach of confidence if the patient has consented to the release of the information. In fact, it is rare for patients to be asked explicitly whether they consent to others seeing their information. This is because, often, medical professionals rely on implied consent.[108] When patients agree to be referred to a consultant by a GP, although they do not in so many words consent to the disclosure to the consultant of their medical history, they do so by implication.[109] As we shall see, this 'implied consent' can be taken to authorize the use of information by a wide range of medical personnel.[110] So, more generally, patients who give information to their doctors are presumed to consent to the information being provided to others in the healthcare system in the course of normal medical practice.[111]

---

[103] See the discussion in Laurie (2002: 224).   [104] Laurie (2002: 228).   [105] [2004] UKHL 22, [51].
[106] DoH (2004b: para. 4.5).   [107] Chalmers and Muir (2003).   [108] BMA (2004: 177).
[109] However, a consultant should not pass on a report to a GP against the wishes of a patient: *Birmingham CC v O* [1983] 1 All ER 497.   [110] BMA (2004: 180).
[111] Information Commissioner (2002). For opposition to this view from GPs, see Cole (2009).

The GMC guidance states:

> Most patients understand and accept that information must be shared within the health-care team in order to provide their care. You should make sure information is readily available to patients explaining that, unless they object, personal information about them will be shared within the healthcare team, including administrative and other staff who support the provision of their care.[112]

The difficulty with applying the implied consent model to such a wide range of medical professionals is that it assumes that a patient is aware that the information will be shared.[113] Although this is plausible in relation to the sharing of information between the doctors who are actually dealing with the patient, the justification has been used to justify the Health Service (Control of Patient Information) Regulations 2002, which permit the sharing of anonymized data for research.[114] Is it not a fiction to say that the patient 'consents' to such use of information? This is especially so in circumstances in which the revealing of information is not directly related to the patient's treatment, but includes managers looking at the general running of the hospital. Also, if implied consent is the basis of the law here, does that mean that patients who state that they do not want their records to be viewed by anyone except the medical staff attending them must have those wishes respected?

Such concerns about an implied consent model could lead us in two directions.

(i)   We should continue to accept that consent is the basis of the justification, but we need to make sure that patients are aware how widely their information will be distributed within the NHS and give them an opportunity to object to some of the uses. If they do object, then their wishes must be respected.

The GMC has accepted this approach. Its guidance in relation to clinical audits explains:

> If an audit is to be undertaken by the team that provided care, or those working to support them, such as clinical audit staff, you may disclose identifiable information, provided you are satisfied that the patient:
>
> (a) has ready access to information that explains that their personal information may be disclosed for local clinical audit, and that they have the right to object, and
>
> (b) has not objected.[115]

Similar guidance is issued in relation to research.[116]

(ii)   The alternative approach (which we will consider below) would be to abandon the implied consent model as too artificial and instead suggest that revelation to workers in the healthcare system should be seen as justified in the public interest.

---

[112] GMC (2009: 25).
[113] The Royal College of General Practitioners (2000: 1) is concerned about the reliance on implied consent.
[114] See Taylor (2015) for a more detailed discussion.   [115] GMC (2009: 30).
[116] DoH (2003a: para. 12).

3.2 'The proper working of the hospital'

As we have seen, in a modern hospital, medical information about patients is shared among a bewildering number of people. Accountability, monitoring, and research may require confidential information to be processed by many within a hospital.[117] A proposal to include in the NHS Constitution an assumption that patients consented to medical researchers being permitted to see their medical records was dropped after protests.[118] The breach of confidentiality could be justified on the basis that it is an essential part of the working of a modern national healthcare system.[119] As such, it is justifiable in the public interest that a patient's medical information be available to any worker in the NHS who has a legitimate interest in viewing it. If such a justification were supported, then, arguably, even if a patient were to object, public policy would justify the disclosure. In terms of Article 8 ECHR, it could be said that the breach of the patient's rights under Article 8(1) is justified as necessary in the interests of the state under Article 8(2).

There is little explicit legal support for this approach. In *R v Department of Health, ex p Source Informatics Ltd*,[120] Simon Brown LJ suggested that using confidential information for legitimate NHS purposes was legitimate, even if done against a patient's wishes. However, he left open the question of whether this was because there was no breach of confidence or because there was a public interest justifying the breach. There are also cases in banking law that have accepted an argument that confidential information can be used within a bank if necessary to enable the proper workings of the bank.[121]

3.3 A threat of serious harm to others

Threats of serious harm to others can justify revealing confidential information.[122] There have been few cases dealing with this justification and so it is difficult to state the law with certainty. The most obvious explanation for this exception is that there is a public interest in protecting innocent people from harm and that this outweighs the public interest in protecting confidences.[123] An alternative could be based on the maxim of equity that 'He who comes into equity must come with clean hands'. If a patient poses a risk to others, he or she thereby forfeits the protection of the law on confidence. However, the equitable principle is founded on the notion of conscience and thus cannot explain why a patient who, through no fault of his or her own, poses a risk to others should lose the protection of the law. So the obvious explanation is the most popular one: given the choice between respecting confidentiality or protecting someone from death or serious harm, a medical professional should choose the latter. It is not surprising that this exception is not controversial among most ethicists,[124] practitioners, or members of the public.[125]

What is a matter of some debate, however, is how serious the harm to others must be before a breach of confidentiality is justified. The GMC advice is that there must

---

[117] DoH (1996a: para. 1.2).   [118] Dyer (2009).   [119] BMA (2004: 180).
[120] [2000] 1 All ER 786.   [121] *Tournier v National Provincial and Union Bank of England* [1924] 1 KB 461.
[122] For a rejection of this claim on ethical grounds, see Kipnis (2006).
[123] *Saha v GMC* [2009] EWHC 1907.
[124] Morgan (2001: 166) thinks it will be very rare that the threat will be of sufficiently serious harm.
[125] Jones (2003).

be a serious risk of serious harm.[126] The British Psychological Society's guidelines for psychologists require only a 'risk of harm'.[127] The Department of Health guidelines suggest:

> Murder, manslaughter, rape, treason, kidnapping, child abuse or other cases where individuals have suffered serious harm may all warrant breaching confidentiality. Serious harm to the security of the state or to public order and crimes that involve substantial financial gain or loss will also generally fall within this category. In contrast, theft, fraud, or damage to property where loss or damage is less substantial would generally not warrant breach of confidence.[128]

NHS guidance suggests that there must be a risk of serious harm to others and not only to the patients themselves.[129] The BMA guidance suggests that a risk of assault or a road traffic accident are sufficient to justify disclosure of confidential information, but not solely a financial loss.[130] However, it went on to point out that this division between a threat of harm to person and property is not that straightforward. Serious fraud of the NHS delays treatment for patients and can thereby be said to cause physical harm.

The problem, as the BMA has pointed out, is that it is difficult for a medical professional to know whether the risk to others would be judged sufficiently serious to justify an interference until the courts rule on the issue. This can leave the professional in an 'invidious position'.[131]

The leading case on this exception is the following.

KEY CASE   *W v Egdell* [1990] 1 All ER 835

W had been convicted of manslaughter in connection with the extremely violent killing of five people. He was being detained in a secure hospital under the Mental Health Act 1983. Dr Egdell was asked to prepare a report for a mental health review tribunal, which was considering whether W should be released. The doctor's report indicated that W was extremely dangerous. He went on to say that those caring for him did not appear to appreciate his dangerousness, particularly his interest in high explosives. When W's solicitors saw the report, they decided to drop their application to the tribunal. Dr Egdell wanted to send a copy of his report to the Home Office and the medical director of the hospital caring for W. W applied to stop him disclosing the report. The Court of Appeal held that the disclosure of the report to those parties was justified. The Home Office and the hospital staff were not aware of W's dangerousness, and the public interest justified the disclosure. It was legitimate to breach confidence where there was a real risk of significant harm to others.

Importantly, Bingham LJ emphasized that the Court was not saying that W's confidentiality was not protected at all:

> [Dr Egdell] could not lawfully sell the contents of his report to a newspaper ... Nor could he without a breach of the law as well as professional etiquette, discuss the case in a learned article or in his memoirs or in gossiping with friends, unless he took appropriate steps to conceal the identity of W.[132]

---

[126] GMC (2009). The BMA (2004: 190) suggests that serious harm can include psychological harm.
[127] British Psychological Society (2002: 4).   [128] DoH (2004b: 11).   [129] DoH (2010).
[130] BMA (2004: 190).   [131] BMA (2004: 190).   [132] At 841.

This case reveals some important limitations on the justification based on a threat of death or serious harm to another.

(i)   It must be shown that there is a real and serious risk of danger to the public. The risk must be of significant harm, probably of a physical kind, to a victim. Also, that risk must be a serious possibility and not merely a fanciful one.

(ii) The risk must be an ongoing one.[133] The fact that there was a past risk to the public would not, it seems, be sufficient.[134]

(iii) The disclosure had to be to appropriate people with a legitimate interest in the matter. In *W v Egdell*, the Court of Appeal approved of the disclosure to the hospital and the Home Office. A disclosure to members of the press would probably not be regarded as lawful. However, there might be cases in which revealing information to the public would be appropriate (for example if a dangerous patient were to escape from a secure hospital). Disclosure of confidential information to regulatory bodies such as the GMC is permissible, if disclosure is necessary to enable them to ensure that the public is protected from professional misconduct.[135]

(iv) Any disclosure must be restricted to the minimum necessary to protect the public.[136] To use the example just mentioned, if a dangerous patient were to escape from a secure hospital, although it may be justifiable to inform the public that the patient posed a particular risk, for example towards elderly women, it would not be necessary for all of his medical history or details to be made public. However, in *Stone v South East Strategic Health Authority*,[137] it was held that partial disclosure of the report, which contained details of a convicted murderer's mental health, would be misleading and so the full report should be made available. In *Saha v GMC*,[138] the fact that disclosure was required to the GMC, a body that would ensure that the information was kept confidential, was an important point in finding the disclosure requirement justified.

What is the position where a patient has informed his or her doctor that he or she intends to kill or to cause serious harm to another and the doctor decides to keep quiet about this? If the patient does go on to kill or cause serious harm, can the doctor be sued? An American decision, *Tarasoff v The Regents of the University of California*,[139] discusses the issue. P was receiving therapy at a hospital in the University of California at Berkeley. He told his therapist, a Dr Moore, that he was going to kill his former girlfriend, Tatiana Tarasoff, when she returned from her holidays. The doctor informed the police, who detained P, but released him when he promised not to harm Tatiana. The doctor took no steps to warn Tatiana herself. P killed Tatiana on her return from her holidays. The Supreme Court of California, by a majority, held that Dr Moore owed Tatiana a duty of care. Where a doctor is aware that one of his or her patients poses a serious danger of violence to another, he or she incurs an obligation to use reasonable care to protect the intended victim. Dr Moore had failed to do this.

---

[133] In *R v Harrison* [2000] WL 1026999, it was held that a doctor owed no duty of confidentiality in respect of threats to kill made by a defendant. See also *R v Kennedy* [1999] 1 Cr App R 54.
[134] *Schering Chemicals v Falkman Ltd* [1981] 2 All ER 321.
[135] *Re A (A Minor) (Disclosure of Medical Records to GMC)* [1999] 1 FCR 30; *Woolgar v Chief Constable of Sussex Police and UKCC* [1999] 1 LMLR 335.   [136] *X v Y* [1988] 2 All ER 649.
[137] [2006] EWHC 1668 (Admin).   [138] [2009] EWHC 1907.   [139] (1976) 17 Cal 3d 358.

It is far from clear whether that decision would be followed in England and Wales. The general view seems to be that it would not,[140] because normally, in tort law, someone is not responsible for the acts of a third party.[141] In *Palmer v Tees Health Authority*,[142] it was held that a health authority that was caring for a man did not owe a duty of care to a woman who he killed. One of the reasons given was that there was no way in which the health authority could foresee that its patient would kill this woman. This might suggest that the case would have been decided differently had he posed a risk to an identifiable individual.

3.4 Child protection

In a similar vein to the exception just mentioned, confidence can be breached if there is evidence that a patient may have been abusing a child.[143] The GMC has suggested that not only may doctors make a disclosure in order to protect a child from abuse, but that they *must* do so:

> If you believe that a patient may be a victim of neglect or physical, sexual or emotional abuse, and that they lack capacity to consent to disclosure, you must give information promptly to an appropriate responsible person or authority, if you believe that the disclosure is in the patient's best interests or necessary to protect others from a risk of serious harm. If, for any reason, you believe that disclosure of information is not in the best interests of a neglected or abused patient, you should discuss the issues with an experienced colleague. If you decide not to disclose information, you should document in the patient's record your discussions and the reasons for deciding not to disclose. You should be prepared to justify your decision.[144]

This could also be justified in terms of Article 8 ECHR, in that the patient's rights under that Article are properly infringed because disclosure is necessary in the interests of others (that is, the child). Not only that, but the child's rights under Article 3 ECHR may also impose a positive obligation on the state to protect children and vulnerable adults from abuse.[145]

3.5 Assisting police investigations

Perhaps surprisingly, there is no general obligation on healthcare professionals to disclose confidential information even if requested to do so by the police.[146] There are a few specific circumstances in which they must. They are bound to provide the police, on request, with any information that would identify a driver alleged to have committed a traffic offence.[147] Even if not specifically requested, they are bound to disclose to the police suspicions that a person has been involved in terrorist activities.[148] It should be added that medical professionals should not obstruct a police investigation, but that an offence will not be committed by failing to answer police questions, provided that the medical professional has a lawful excuse (for example that the information requested is confidential).[149]

Although there are only limited circumstances in which there is a *duty to* disclose information, there are circumstances in which the information *may* be disclosed. The

---

[140] Miers (1996); Morris and Ashead (1997).   [141] *Smith v Littlewoods* [1987] AC 241.
[142] [2000] PIQR 1.   [143] *Re M* [1990] 1 All ER 205, 213; DoH (1999a: para. 7.27).
[144] GMC (2009: 63).   [145] Choudhry and Herring (2006).
[146] *Sykes v DPP* [1962] AC 528, 564 (Lord Denning).   [147] Road Traffic Act 1988, s. 172.
[148] Terrorism Act 2000, ss 19 and 20.   [149] *Rice v Connolly* [1966] 2 All ER 649.

Crime and Disorder Act 1998, section 115, permits the disclosure of confidential information to, inter alia, a chief officer of police. However, this power should be used only where the patient has consented or there is a strong public interest in disclosure.

The BMA and Department of Health have suggested that doctors should consider disclosing information in circumstances in which all of the following are true:[150]

- the offence is grave (for example murder, manslaughter, rape, hostage-taking, causing death by dangerous driving);

- the prevention or detection of the crime will be seriously delayed or prejudiced without the disclosure;

- the disclosed information will be used only for the detection and prosecution of the alleged criminal; and

- any material released will be destroyed once it has been used.

In *Initial Services Ltd v Putterill*,[151] Lord Denning appeared to suggest that disclosure of any crime committed or contemplated is permitted. If this is correct, it means that a doctor who discloses information concerning a minor crime is not acting illegally, but is acting contrary to professional guidance. That said, until we have further guidance, it is not safe to declare with confidence what the law is.

3.6 Public debate and press freedom

Can a breach of confidentiality be justified on the basis that the disclosure is in the public interest because it promotes public debate? Two cases that illustrate the issues well are the following.

KEY CASE   *X v Y* [1988] 2 All ER 649

A newspaper discovered that two doctors were being treated for AIDS. A hospital sought an injunction to prevent the publication of the information. The newspaper accepted that it had obtained the information in breach of confidence, but argued that it was important that there was a public debate over the issue. The judge argued that the public interest (which was not to be confused with things in which the public were interested) had to be weighed against:

(i)   the principle that hospital records should remain confidential;

(ii) the public interest that employees should not be encouraged to disclose confidential information to newspapers (in other words, prohibiting the publication might deter employees from passing on confidential information to newspapers in the future); and

(iii) the public interest in ensuring that AIDS sufferers can use hospitals without fear that their condition will be made public.

Taking these factors into account, the judge concluded that the newspaper should not publish the information. The judge noted that there was already wide-ranging debate about AIDS and that the information in question would add little to it.

---

[150] BMA (2004: 23–4).   [151] [1968] 1 QB 396, 405.

> **KEY CASE** *H (A Healthcare Worker) v Associated Newspapers Ltd and N (A Health Authority)* [2002] Lloyd's Rep Med 210 (CA)
>
> H, a healthcare professional, tested positive for HIV. The health authority (N) proposed to notify all of his patients and invite them to undergo an HIV test if they so wished. H sought an injunction to prevent N from notifying his patients. He argued that the risk to patients of HIV was very low and insufficient to justify a breach in his confidentiality. *The Mail on Sunday* got to hear about the dispute and H successfully applied for an injunction to prevent the publication of any details identifying him, his speciality, or N. On the hearing for the full injunction, Gross J upheld the ban on publishing H's identity, but would have allowed the naming of N and H's specialism. H appealed to the Court of Appeal, arguing that it would be easy for people, knowing his specialism and the name of the health authority, to discover his identity. The Court of Appeal held that H's name and N's identity should be kept secret. The Court accepted the argument that H's identity would otherwise be too readily discovered. In particular, it was concerned that his patients would discover the news before being contacted by N and being offered the appropriate counselling. However, H's specialism could be named, because that raised particular issues that were relevant to a legitimate debate about the risks of HIV.

It is a notable aspect of *H (A Healthcare Worker) v Associated Newspapers Ltd* that the Court attached particular significance to the protection of press freedom guaranteed by Article 10 ECHR. This right led the Court to require clear harm to justify an interference with this right:

> We would view with concern any attempt to invoke the power of the court to grant an injunction restraining freedom of expression merely on the ground that release of information would give rise to administrative problems and a drain on resources. Such consequences are the price which has to be paid, from time to time, for freedom of expression in a democratic society.[152]

In weighing up the freedom of expression and protection of privacy in a case in which medical records have been improperly acquired, the court should consider *both* the interests of the individual patient and the interests of the hospital in ensuring the confidentiality of its records.[153]

3.7 For the best interests of a person lacking capacity

If a person is lacking capacity, then it is generally thought that it is permissible to disclose confidential health information to those caring for him or her, or others if that is necessary for his or her proper care.[154] However, this exception should be interpreted strictly. As the BMA has stressed, just because a patient is lacking capacity, this should not lessen the protection that is accorded to his or her right of confidentiality.[155]

---

[152] *H (A Healthcare Worker) v Associated Newspapers Ltd* [2002] Lloyd's Rep Med 210, [141].
[153] *Ashworth Hospital Authority v MGN Ltd* [2002] UKHL 29, [2002] 4 All ER 193.
[154] *F v W Berkshire Health Authority* [1989] 2 All ER 545.
[155] BMA (2004: 178); DCA (2007: para. 4.56).

3.8 **Discovery**

If a person is bringing or plans to bring legal proceedings against another, he or she can apply for all relevant information to be disclosed. However, this is not an absolute right.

In *D v NSPCC*,[156] the plaintiff sought from the National Society for the Prevention of Cruelty to Children (NSPCC) documents indicating the name of the person who had alleged that she had been committing child abuse. The court refused to order disclosure of the information. It was felt that it was necessary to weigh up the plaintiff's interest in discovering her accusers, so that she could, if appropriate, bring legal proceedings against them, with the public interest in encouraging people who have suspicions about child abuse to alert appropriate authorities, without fear that doing so could lead to legal proceedings being taken against them. The balance fell against ordering disclosure. The same approach might be taken if a person were seeking another's medical records for the purposes of using it in litigation: would the interest in protecting confidentiality outweigh the importance of enabling a person to have access to relevant documents in the course of legal proceedings? The reasoning in *D v NSPCC* would not be directly applicable because the issue there was a special immunity known as 'Crown immunity', which applies to bodies acting in the public interest. Nevertheless, a similar approach may well be adopted by the courts when considering infringement of an individual's rights of confidentiality.

3.9 **Good faith disclosure**

The Court of Appeal, in *R v Department of Health, ex p Source Informatics Ltd*,[157] suggested that there is a breach of confidence only if the breach affects the conscience of the discloser.[158] In other words, if the revelation of the secret information is in good faith, then there is no breach of confidence. It is not clear, however, that this represents the law. It does not sit easily with *Swinney v Chief Constable of Northumbria Police*,[159] which suggests that a breach of confidence does not need to be deliberate and can be negligent.[160] More significantly, Lord Hoffmann in *Campbell v MGN Ltd*[161] in the House of Lords, stated that the modern understanding of breach of confidence was that it was not based on a 'good faith' requirement imposed upon the recipient of the information, but rather that it focused on the protection of human dignity and autonomy of the person with which the information was concerned.

3.10 **Other public interest reasons**

The exceptions mentioned so far can be said to be justifiable in the public interest. There may be, in addition to those already discussed, a 'catch-all exception' that a breach of confidence can be justified in the public interest. When relying on the general public interest, the medical professional must be persuaded that it is necessary to reveal

[156] [1978] AC 171. [157] [2000] 1 All ER 786.
[158] The role of conscience in breach of confidence was also emphasized in *Campbell v MGN* [2003] QB 633, in the Court of Appeal, and *Stephens v Avery* [1988] 2 All ER 477.
[159] [1996] 3 All ER 449. [160] See also Grubb (2000), who questions this part of the judgment.
[161] [2004] UKHL 22, [51].

non-anonymized data and that it is not practical to obtain the consent of the patient.[162] The NHS Code states that public interest disclosure could be justified if:

- Disclosure would be in the public interest; AND
- The purpose of the disclosure cannot be achieved with anonymized information; AND
- There is no statutory basis for disclosure; AND
- Patient consent has not been given because:
  - It is not practicable to ask the patient(s) for consent, e.g. because, for example, there are no up-to-date contact details for the patient, or the matter is urgent and the patient cannot be contacted; OR
  - It would be inappropriate to ask the patient(s) because, for example, they lack the capacity to give consent, or they are suspect(s) who should not be informed that they are under criminal investigation; OR
  - The patient(s) have been asked for consent and refused.[163]

Interestingly, the Code includes 'in public interest' cases in which there is a 'clear benefit to the public'.[164] That might include the use of patient information for research.

In *R v Crozier*,[165] a psychiatrist instructed by the defendant in an attempted murder case disclosed his report to the prosecution after a judge sentenced the defendant to prison, not having been told of the report. Once the judge was informed about the report, the defendant was sentenced to a hospital order and orders were made under the Mental Health Act 1983. The court held that this disclosure was justified in the general public interest in ensuring that appropriate sentences were imposed in criminal cases.[166] In *R (Axon) v Secretary of State*,[167] Silber J rejected an argument that there was a public interest in infringing a child's right to confidentiality in order to inform her parents that she was seeking an abortion. Indeed, Silber J suggested quite the reverse: the public interest was in respecting the confidentiality of the information.

3.11 Special statutory provisions

There are special statutory provisions that permit, or even require, confidential informa-tion to be disclosed. To give a couple of examples: a doctor treating a drug addict must give details about the person to the Home Office;[168] and the Public Health (Control of Disease) Act 1984 states that cholera, plague, relapsing fever, smallpox, and typhus shall be notifiable diseases, which means that if a doctor finds a patient with such a disease, he or she must notify the government. Similarly, some kinds of venereal disease[169] and food poisoning are notifiable. Controversially, details of terminations of pregnancies under

---

[162] GMC (2009: para. 1).   [163] NHS (2010: 6).   [164] NHS (2010: 8).
[165] (1990) 12 Cr App R (S) 206.
[166] Disclosure of medical reports might also be justifiable in order to protect the economic well-being of the country: *MS v Sweden* (1997) 45 BMLR 133.
[167] [2006] EWHC 37 (Admin).
[168] Misuses of Drugs (Notification of Supply to Addicts) Regulations 1973, SI 1973/799.
[169] *Lee v South West Thames Regional Health Authority* [1985] 2 All ER 385.

the Abortion Act 1967 must be given to the Chief Medical Officer.[170] Since 2002, only a patient's NHS number, date of birth, and full postcode are required, not her name.[171]

The National Health Service Act 2006, section 251(1), permits the disclosure of medical information for research purposes without a patient's consent. This section provides:

(i) The Secretary of State may by regulations make such provision for and in connection with requiring or regulating the processing of prescribed patient information for medical purposes as he considers necessary or expedient—

(a) in the interests of improving patient care, or

(b) in the public interest.

Further, under section 253(1), powers are given in an emergency to require healthcare professionals to disclose information without consultation with patients.[172] This is a controversial provision because, potentially, it provides a significant inroad into protection of medical confidentiality.

Much depends on what kind of regulations will be issued by the Secretary of State. He or she must consult with the Care Quality Commission (CQC) before issuing any regulations.

The CQC has the job of overseeing arrangements created under section 251. The following principles underpin its approach to requests to use data:

a. People have personal interests and responsibilities as patients, users of services, service providers and also as citizens.

b. Within health and social care services:

- The interests of patients and service users come first;

- Informed consent and personal autonomy should underpin the provision of health and social care; and

- The right information should be available to the right people at the right time to provide individual care whilst preserving confidentiality.

c. It is in people's interests to have:

- Appropriate and accessible care, which promotes health, social welfare and public safety;

- A sound research base on which to build and improve effective services; and

- Well managed and cost effective services.

d. Professionals work within a legal framework and professional guidance.[173]

The CQC has made it clear that section 251 of the National Health Service Act 2006 will not be allowed to be used only to make access to medical data easier. It will have to be shown that there is no other practical way in which to get to the data and that it is not possible to use anonymized data.

Section 251 has been criticized. The BMA has complained that it is 'very general' and that more guidance is required on how to apply it. It is justified by others on the basis

---

[170] Abortion Regulations 1991, SI 1991/499.   [171] DoH (2002a).
[172] See Grace and Taylor (2013) for a detailed discussion.   [173] Care Quality Commission (2011: 4).

that, if large-scale research needs to be carried out, it is not practical to obtain the consent of each and every person. If that were done and only the information of those who consented could be used, this would skew the sample. On the other hand, researchers have complained that the procedures to obtain approval to carry out large-scale studies are 'sluggish' and an improper restriction on research.[174]

There is also increasing concern with the development of the NHS Care Data plan that consent for the sharing of information will be presumed, unless the patient goes to the trouble of objecting. In particular there are concerns that it is the hope of selling the data for profit which is driving the scheme.[175]

3.12 Extent of disclosure

One point that has already been emphasized at several points bears repeating—that is, that even if there is a justifiable ground for disclosure it must be shown that:

(i)   the person to whom the disclosure was made was an appropriate person[176]—so although, in a certain case, disclosure to the police may have been justified, if the disclosure was to a journalist, this may be unlawful;[177] and

(ii) the disclosure was to the minimum amount necessary under the justification—so if anonymized disclosure would have adequately protected the public interest, then only anonymized disclosure is permitted.

4 The Data Protection Act 1998

The Data Protection Act 1998 covers the processing of personal data.[178] The Act is not restricted to computerized records; it covers all personal data stored in systems (be they electronic or on paper) that enable information about someone to be readily accessible. At the heart of the Act are eight cardinal principles, which are set out in Schedule 1, Part 1, of the Act:

(1) Personal data shall be processed fairly and lawfully and, in particular, shall not be processed unless—

   (a) At least one of the conditions in Schedule 2 is met, and

   (b) in the case of sensitive personal data, at least one of the conditions in Schedule 3 is also met.

(2) Personal data shall be obtained only for one or more specified and lawful purposes, and shall not be further processed in any manner incompatible with that purpose or those purposes.

---

[174] Turnberg (2003).   [175] Sterckx and Cockbain (2014).
[176] In *Woolgar v Chief Constable of Sussex Police and UKCC* [1999] Lloyd's Rep Med 335, the police contacted the then UK Central Council for Nursing, Midwifery and Health Visiting (UKCC)—now the NMC—after they had concerns over the claimant's behaviour.
[177] Although on whether a journalist is required to reveal his or her sources, see *Mersey Care NHS Trust v Ackroyd* [2007] EWCA Civ 101, discussed in Sandland (2007).
[178] The Data Protection Act 1998 was passed to give effect to the European Directive on Personal Data 1995 (EC Directive 95/46/EC).

(3) Personal data shall be adequate, relevant and not excessive in relation to the purpose or purposes for which they are processed.

(4) Personal data shall be accurate and, where necessary, kept up to date.

(5) Personal data processed for any purpose or purposes shall not be kept for longer than is necessary for that purpose or those purposes.

(6) Personal data shall be processed in accordance with the rights of data subjects under this Act.

(7) Appropriate technical and organisational measures shall be taken against unauthorised or unlawful processing of personal data and against accidental loss or destruction of, or damage to, personal data.

(8) Personal data shall not be transferred to a country or territory outside the European Economic Area unless that country or territory ensures an adequate level of protection for the rights and freedoms of data subjects in relation to the processing of personal data.

Health records are classified as 'sensitive personal data' and are subject to special protection. A health record is defined under section 68(2) as:

... any record which:

(a) consists of information relating to the physical or mental health or condition of an individual, and

(b) has been made by or on behalf of a health professional in connection with the care of an individual.

All information in health records is regarded as sensitive personal data, whether it relates to minor injuries or much more intimate information.[179] Sensitive personal data can be 'processed' (for example consulted or used) only if a series of special conditions are met. These include the following:[180]

(a) The patient has given explicit consent to the information being used.

(b) It is necessary to process the information to protect the vital interests of the patient.

(c) Where the data is in the public domain.

(d) A health care organization or professional needs to use the information to obtain legal advice or in the course of legal proceedings.

(e) The processing of the information is necessary for the purposes of statutory or government functions.

(f) It is necessary for medical purposes and the information is used by a healthcare professional.

(g) Processing of medical data or data relating to ethnic origin for monitoring purposes.

(h) Processing in the substantial public interest, necessary for the purpose of research whose object is not to support decisions with respect to any particular data subject

---

[179] Information Commissioner (2002).
[180] The full list is to be found in Data Protection Act 1998, Schs 1 and 3.

otherwise than with the explicit consent of the data subject and which is unlikely to cause substantial damage or substantial distress to the data subject or any other person.[181]

It is the responsibility of the 'data controller' to ensure that these obligations are complied with. However, all those who use protected information are required to comply with the terms of the legislation. Anyone who obtains or discloses information without the consent of the data controller commits an offence.[182] If a person has suffered damage or loss as a result of a violation of the 1998 Act, he or she can receive compensation. There is also an obligation on health organizations to protect the security of health records. The Information Commissioner has the power to issue an enforcement notice requiring specific steps be taken to ensure compliance of data.[183] Individuals can ask the Information Commissioner to assess whether the Act is being complied with.[184] It is a criminal offence to fail to comply with a notice.[185] The Information Commissioner also has the function of preparing good practice guidance.[186]

5 Problem issues

We now look at some particular areas in relation to confidentiality that have proven particularly controversial.

5.1 Genetic information: informing relatives

Genetic information has become increasingly important and the extent to which it should be kept confidential is a highly topical issue.[187] Consider the following two scenarios, which indicate why the issue can be complex.

(i)   A couple are considering having a child, but are aware that there may be genetic diseases in the family history. They seek medical advice on what risks there are that any child of theirs will inherit a condition. The doctor, to advise them properly, will need the medical history of their parents. If the couple's parents refuse to co-operate, can the doctor access the parents' notes so as to advise the couple?

(ii) In treating X, a doctor discovers that X suffers from a genetically inherited illness and therefore that it is likely that X's relatives do too. The doctor wishes to advise the relatives of that risk, but X objects to this. If the doctor were to go ahead and inform the relatives, would the doctor be infringing X's rights to confidentiality?

It is notable that, in both of these cases, if the doctor maintains confidentiality, he or she is not thereby putting people at risk of harm; rather, he or she is denying them the option of treatment or advice that might otherwise have been available. We now have some indication of how the court might resolve such a case.

---

[181] The Data Protection (Processing of Sensitive Personal Data) Order 2000, SI 2000/417, added (g) and (h).
[182] DPA 1998, s. 55.   [183] DPA 1998, s. 40.   [184] DPA 1998, s. 42.   [185] DPA 1998, s. 47.
[186] DPA 1998, s. 51(3).
[187] Foster, Herring, and Boyd (2015); Weaver (2015); Gilbar (2005); Pullen (1990); Nuffield Council on Bioethics (1993); Genetic Interest Group (1998).

KEY CASE   *A, B, C v St George's* **[2015] EWHC 1394 (QB)**

Nicol J rejected a claim brought by children of a man who had been diagnosed with Huntington's disease, but who had asked his doctors not to tell his children of the diagnosis. That refusal meant that the children could not have themselves tested, although they later accidentally found out the information. Nicol J held that the doctors were not under a duty under the law of tort to tell the children, although it would not be a breach of confidentiality if they were told.

In his judgment Nicol J highlighted the fact that the case involved a condition for which there is no treatment. That was significant because, as Nicol J noted, it was not clear if people would want to know they might have inherited the condition if there was no treatment available. This made it all the harder to claim there was a positive duty on doctors to inform relatives. This may leave open the option in a future case for the courts to decide there is a duty if the condition was a treatable one and would be confident that relatives would want to know of the risk.

Montgomery suggests that, going back to first legal principles, the law does not normally require people to provide benefits to others, but simply not to harm them.[188] This might suggest that the law would require confidentiality to be preserved. He goes on to suggest, however, that this might be one situation in which the law should depart from its normal approach and adopt a less individualistic one. With similar ideas in mind, Loane Skene has contrasted two approaches that could be taken to this topic, as follows.[189]

(i)   *A legal approach* This emphasizes individual rights of privacy of particular patients.

(ii) *A family approach*[190] This focuses on the care of patients with genetic illness. It places less weight on individual rights, and emphasizes the concerns of the community and families. Patients should be treated as members of a family, not as isolated individuals.

While many who take a 'family approach' are in favour of sharing information on the basis that it does not belong only to the tested family member, but also to all members of the family, not everyone takes that approach. Carol Smart has argued that, sometimes, secrecy in families helps to maintain and build relationships.[191] One question that is immediately raised is whether the issues surrounding genetic information are any different from those surrounding other medical information. Loane Skene suggests a number of differences, including the following.[192]

• For genetic tests to be accurate, it is necessary to test members of the patient's family.

• The issue of consent to the tests is complex, because the results will not be certain and will be predictive of an illness perhaps developing quite some time in the future.

---

[188] Montgomery (2003: 277).   [189] Skene (1998).
[190] Skene (1998) described this as a 'medical approach', but in Skene (2001) stated that she preferred the term 'family approach'.
[191] Smart (2010).   [192] Skene (1998).

- There may be significant social and legal consequences that flow from a test.
- The result of the test may have significance for other members of the family.[193]

Gostin and Hodge are critical of any attempt to provide special protection for genetic information.[194] They argue that a genetic predisposition to a particular illness is no different from a predisposition to an illness that a person might have from other causes. They go on to argue that it would be quite wrong if the legal position in relation to a woman whose breast cancer was linked to genetic factors were to be any different from a woman whose breast cancer was the result of other factors. One response to this is that it is not the position of the woman that is different, but rather the claims, if any, that can be made by her relatives. Another point to emphasize is that it is far more likely that women will receive genetic tests and so that any obligation to share that information with wider family members will fall disproportionately on women.[195]

Some commentators have argued that genetic information is essentially joint information co-owned by all of the members of the family; therefore genetic information disclosed in the course of treatment of one patient should be shared with other members of the family if it affects them.[196] But this has been challenged. Liao argues that the likelihood that because one person has a genetic condition, another will also, depends on the condition in question.[197] He therefore challenges the description of genetic information about a genetic condition as 'familial information'.

Schedule 4, paragraph 9, of the Human Tissue Act 2004 permits the Human Tissue Authority to authorize the use of X's tissue to obtain medical information that will be used for the benefit of X's relative, even if X did not consent.[198] We do not know yet whether the Authority will authorize such use, and if it will, what conditions might be attached. Further, the courts are yet to discuss the issues relating to genetic confidentiality and families. So all that it is possible to do at the moment is outline a number of ways in which the law could address the issue.

5.1.1 *The traditional confidentiality approach*

It could be argued that issues surrounding genetics should be addressed in line with the normal rules on breaching confidentiality.[199] This would suggest that only where there is a high risk of significant harm to another is it proper to breach confidentiality.[200] So the arguments in favour of informing a patient's relatives are stronger the greater the risk of the relative suffering from the illness, the greater its severity, and the more likely it is that having the information will enable the relative to receive effective treatment for the condition.[201] Hence the GMC advises:

> [A] patient might refuse to consent to the disclosure of information that would benefit others, for example, where family relationships have broken down, or if their natural children have been adopted. In these circumstances, disclosure might still be justified

---

[193] But see Mason and Laurie (2006: 207) for an argument that other kinds of medical test results can also carry significance for family members.

[194] Gostin and Hodge (1999).   [195] Melo-Martín (2006).   [196] Parker and Lucassen (2004).

[197] Liao (2009).   [198] Lucassen and Kaye (2006) discuss the issue in depth.

[199] Bell and Bennett (2001).

[200] Grubb (1999) suggests that the courts, at some point, will recognize a legal duty on doctors to tell relatives in such a case.

[201] Ngwena and Chadwick (1993).

in the public interest. If a patient refuses consent to disclosure, you will need to balance your duty to make the care of your patient your first concern against your duty to help protect the other person from serious harm. If practicable, you should not disclose the patient's identity in contacting and advising others of the risks they face.[202]

Laurie has suggested that, in considering disclosure of genetic information to a relative, the following factors should be considered:

- the availability of a therapy or cure;
- the severity of the condition and the likelihood of onset;
- the nature of the genetic disease;
- the nature of any further testing that might be required;
- the nature of the information to be disclosed;
- the nature of the request (for example testing for the individual's health or for diagnostic purposes for a relative);
- the question of whether disclosure can further a legitimate public interest; and
- the question of how the individual might react if offered unsolicited information (for example whether any advance directive has been made).[203]

Critics of the traditional approach claim that it is individualistic and fails to take into account that we are not isolated people, but live in a web of family relationships.[204] Most people would want family members to whom they were close to be told of medical information that was relevant.[205] Informing family members will support and encourage family bonds, whereas the individualist traditional approach threatens them. However, it should be borne in mind that what we are discussing here is whether a doctor should provide information to a patient's family against the patient's wishes. Where the patient is happy for his or her family to be informed, there are no particular legal difficulties.

5.1.2 A Human Rights Act 1998 approach

A similar solution could be reached if the issue were to be examined from the perspective of the HRA 1998. A patient would have the right for his or her genetic information to be kept secret under Article 8 ECHR,[206] but that right could be interfered with if necessary to protect the interests of others, as set out in Article 8(2). It should be emphasized that the infringement can be justified under Article 8(2) only if it is in accordance with the law. So anyone seeking to rely on Article 8(2) to justify an interference in someone's rights of confidentiality would need to point to a statutory or common law permission to do so. It is likely that only if another was going to suffer a serious harm would the breach of private life involved in breaching genetic confidentiality be justified. It might be argued that, because genetic information might be regarded as even more private—more connected with the most intimate part of a person—even stronger reasons are required to justify its disclosure than are normally required to justify disclosure of medical information.

---

[202] GMC (2009: 69).   [203] Laurie (2002).
[204] Gilbar (2004).   [205] Benson and Britten (1996).
[206] *A London Borough Council v (1) Mr and Mrs N* [2005] EWHC 1676.

5.1.3 *The right not to know*

Laurie has emphasized that as well as the patient having a right of confidentiality, the court should also take into account that the relative could claim a right *not* to know the information.[207] The 'right not to know' has been recognized in the European Convention for the Protection of Human Rights and Dignity of the Human Being with regard to the Application of Biology and Medicine, Article 10(2) of which states: 'Everyone is entitled to know any information collected about his or her health. However, the wishes of individuals not to be so informed shall be observed.'

At first, the notion of a 'right not to know' sounds strange.[208] But imagine this: you have a 10 per cent chance that you will develop a genetic disease for which there is no known cure or treatment. If you are told this, your life might be blighted by the knowledge, living in terror of this illness, seeing signs of it in every twinge or strange feeling in your body, and yet you might never develop the disease. With this in mind, you might, quite rationally, decide that it would have been better for you not to have known of this genetic risk. It is therefore rational for someone to say: 'I do not want to be told of risks of illnesses, unless that knowledge will enable me to take preventative action.'[209] Where, in a case like this, it is both in your best interests and in accordance with your autonomy not to be told of a risk it seems clear the right to know should be protected. Harder are cases where a person does not want to know, but the decision is irrational or poses a risk to others.[210] Of course, it would also be rational to say that you would want to know of the risks so that you can plan your life accordingly.[211] The difficulty is, of course, that most people do not think about the issue. We end up, usually, trying to guess whether or not a person would want to be told about a certain risk. To overcome this problem, Laurie proposes that we focus on the right of privacy rather than a right not to know.[212] This idea is one at which we will look later.

5.1.4 *A property approach*

A very different approach would be to say that a person's genetic data belongs not only to himself or herself, but also to his or her relatives.[213] There is some research suggesting that this is how such information is understood by members of the public.[214] After all, someone's genetic information can say as much about their relatives as it does about themselves. In the terms of the Data Protection Act 1998, a daughter, for example, can claim that information held about her mother is information held about her.

5.1.5 *A duty approach*

Another solution would be to insist on the preservation of medical confidentiality, but place a legal duty on the person tested to inform his or her family of any risks that they

---

[207] Laurie (2014). See also Foster and Herring (2011).   [208] Takala (1999).
[209] See Andrews (2001: 31–40) for evidence that, after being informed of a risk of serious illness, patients suffer psychological illness. One study—Almqvist (1999)—found that suicide rates among those informed that they have Huntington's disease is ten times higher than the United States' average.
[210] Young and Simmonds (2016).   [211] Hietala, Hakonen, Aro, et al. (1995).
[212] Laurie (2002). See also Ngwena and Chadwick (1993).
[213] *R v Department of Health, ex p Source Informatics Ltd* [2000] 1 All ER 786 suggests that a patient does not 'own' his or her medical information.
[214] Kent (2003).

face in the light of the test.[215] The NHS could even consider making it a condition of genetic testing that the patient agrees that relatives will be informed of any relevant information.[216] However, the approach suffers from the difficulty that we do not normally require people to bear such a duty to warn relatives of dangers to their health.[217] There is no obligation on a person to warn his or her sister of the dangers of smoking, for example. Gilbar has suggested that, before testing is carried out, all family members who may be affected should agree whether or not they wish to be informed of the results.[218]

5.1.6 *The public health approach*

Gostin and Hodge have argued that the collection, study, and dissemination of genetic information can achieve important public health goals.[219] The more we can learn about the genetic causes of various diseases, the more we can do to put in place programmes of education or treatment to prevent or ameliorate these illnesses. There are therefore dangers that, in treating genetic information as some kind of especially privileged information, we shall lose out on a host of gains. As they ask:

> [I]s the value of collecting genetic information so important to the achievement of communal goods that the law ought not to promise absolute or even significant levels of privacy? Perhaps the law should simply require that genetic data be acquired, used, and disclosed in orderly and just ways, consistent with the values of individuals and communities.[220]

5.2 **Genetic privacy: insurance**

Another controversial issue concerning genetic information is its use for insurance purposes.[221] An insurance company offering someone life insurance would clearly want to know genetic information about that person, so that a precise calculation can be made as to whether he or she is a good or a bad risk for life insurance purposes. However, if genetic information were to be made available to insurers, this would mean that some people would, in effect, be unable to acquire life insurance. This would also probably mean that these people would not be able to take out a mortgage. Being denied life insurance, then, can have a severe impact on someone's life.[222] Concerns of this kind led the Human Genetics Commission in May 2001 to impose a three-year moratorium preventing insurers seeking access to genetic test results,[223] where the figure involved was less than £500,000. The Association of British Insurers (ABI), which represents the majority of insurance companies, has voluntarily agreed a five-year ban on requesting genetic information for other policies.[224] The Human Genetics Commission has asked

---

[215] See Brassington (2011b) for an argument that you might have a duty to remain ignorant in order to protect the confidentiality of other family members.
[216] Genetic Interest Group (1998).   [217] King (1999).   [218] Gilbar (2004; 2005).
[219] Gostin and Hodge (1999). See also Harmon and Chen (2012).   [220] Gostin and Hodge (1999: 8).
[221] McGlennan (2000).   [222] Laurie (2002: 138).
[223] There is one exception and that is for tests relating to Huntington's chorea: DoH (2000f).
[224] Laurie (2002: 137).

the government to pass legislation specifically to protect genetic privacy and to outlaw discrimination on the grounds of genetic make-up.[225]

In many ways, the issue over insurance depends on what values should underlie life insurance. Is our society one that is willing for the majority of people to pay slightly higher life insurance premiums, so that genetic information can be kept confidential? Or do we believe that each person is entitled to be assessed for life insurance on his or her own merits? This will mean that those with a genetic make-up predisposing them to various illnesses will have to pay much higher premiums and that those with 'healthy' genetic make-up will pay slightly lower premiums.[226] One MORI poll suggests that four out of five members of the general public thought that genetic information should not be used for insurance purposes.[227]

5.3 Domestic violence and child abuse

What if a patient reveals that his or her children are the victims of abuse by her partner?[228] There seems to be near-universal agreement that, in the case of child abuse, the doctor must break confidence if that is necessary to protect the children. Where the adult patient is himself or herself the victim of abuse, the position is more debatable. The GMC guidance refers to cases in which the patient lacks the capacity to consent to disclosure.[229] It may be that an adult victim of domestic violence will have the capacity to consent or not, but that the 'serious harm' ground will justify the disclosure in cases of serious domestic violence.

It has been argued that victims of domestic violence and child abuse have rights under the HRA 1998 to protection from abuse.[230] This might make it particularly hard not to justify disclosure.

5.4 Confidentiality and child patients

The issue of confidentiality and children was considered in Chapter 4.[231] Young people aged 16 or 17 are regarded as adults for purposes of consent to treatment, and are therefore entitled to the same duty of confidence as adults.[232] The Data Protection (Subject Access Modification) (Health) Order 2000[233] states that competent children can prevent their records from being disclosed to parents, where they are able to appreciate the nature of the application for access to the records.

Children under the age of 16 who have the capacity and understanding to take decisions about their own treatment are entitled also to decide whether personal information may be passed on, and generally to have their confidence respected (for example they may be receiving treatment or counselling that they do not wish their parents to know about). In other instances, decisions to pass on personal information may be taken by a person with parental responsibility in consultation with the healthcare professionals involved.[234]

[225] Human Genetics Commission (2007). Genetics discrimination was not included in the grounds of discrimination in the Equality Act 2010.
[226] Rothstein (1998).   [227] MORI (2001: para. 7.2).   [228] Jecker (1993).
[229] See earlier in the chapter, under the heading '3.4 Child protection'.
[230] Choudhry and Herring (2006).   [231] See also Loughrey (2008).
[232] *Torbay BC v MGN Ltd* [2003] EWHC 2927 (Fam).   [233] SI 2000/413, art. 5.
[234] DoH (2004b: 4.10).

More problematic are cases in which the child who is not competent to consent to treatment asks the doctor not to tell his or her parents. There is no clear case law authority. There is much to be said for the view that the key question is whether the child is competent to reach a decision about confidentiality.[235] Just because a child is not competent to decide about a medical treatment does not mean that the child is not competent enough to reach a decision about whether or not his or her parents should be informed. If the child is competent to decide that the parents should not be involved, the doctor must follow the child's wishes. However, it has also been suggested that if a child is lacking capacity to reach the medical decision, then there is no duty of confidentiality. Kennedy, supporting this view, argues that the basis of the obligation of confidence is about enabling autonomous decision making.[236] If the child is unable to make the decision, then autonomy is not at issue. However, there is an argument that confidentiality is not about autonomy, but privacy rights, and these rights exist whether or not the person is autonomous.[237]

5.5 Carers

When family members or friends are caring for someone, they may want to find out information about the person for whom they are caring. Hopefully, that person will be willing to share, but he or she may not, or he or she may not be able to give consent. This can put carers in a difficult position. The GMC guidance states:

> You may need to share personal information with a patient's relatives, friends or carers to enable you to assess the patient's best interests. But that does not mean they have a general right of access to the patient's records or to have irrelevant information about, for example, the patient's past healthcare. You should share relevant personal information with anyone who is authorized to make decisions on behalf of, or who is appointed to support and represent, a mentally incapacitated patient.[238]

The NHS Code of Practice states:

> Carers often provide valuable healthcare and ... every effort should be made to support and facilitate their work. Only information essential to a patient's care should be disclosed and patients should be made aware that this is the case. However, the explicit consent of a competent patient is needed before disclosing information to a carer. The best interests of a patient who is not competent to consent may warrant disclosure.[239]

This advice is somewhat vague. It does seem to permit carers to be given information if necessary to assess a patient's best interests—but it is not clear how much wider it goes. Does a wife looking after her husband have a right to know whether he is dying? Does a friend looking after a confused neighbour have a right to know if that neighbour is suffering from dementia? There is plenty of evidence that carers are providing a substantial amount of day-to-day care without really knowing the diagnosis or prognosis of the person for whom they are caring.[240]

Those supportive of carers being more readily given access to information that they need for their caring role might make two arguments. One would be that, if involved

[235] Montgomery (1987).   [236] Kennedy (1991a: 111–17).   [237] Loughrey (2003).
[238] GMC (2009: 23).   [239] NHS (2013a: 12).   [240] Herring (2013: 181).

in a substantial amount of care, they become in effect part of the medical team, and so should be entitled to the information on that basis. Indeed, carers involved in heavy caring responsibilities might feel it odd that they are excluded from the information that they need when a medical professional, with much less contact with the patient, will have ready access. Alternatively, it might be argued that carers' lives have become intertwined with those of the patients, meaning that there is no clear distinction as to which person the medical information relates to.[241]

6 Legal remedies in confidentiality cases

Few cases on confidentiality appear in the law reports. This is primarily because of the limited nature of the remedies available.[242] There are basically two on offer: damages; or an injunction to prevent publication. The problem is that damages are only rarely available if there has been no financial loss to the patient. However, only rarely is there a pecuniary loss to the patient.[243] The revelation of medical information may cause embarrassment and loss of social standing, but rarely financial loss. Notably, in the *Campbell* case, only £2,500 damages plus £1,000 aggravated damages were awarded.

Injunctions to prevent publication, meanwhile, are useful only where it is known that the information is about to be revealed. In most cases, the patient learns of the breach of confidentiality only when it is too late. Even where it is not too late, the claimant will face an uphill task persuading the court that his or her right to respect for private life justifies an infringement of the freedom of the press.

It may be argued that the present inadequacies of legal remedies are incompatible with an individual's rights under Articles 6 and 8 ECHR, and so open to challenge through the HRA 1998.

If someone does breach confidentiality, it is more likely that the remedy against them will be disciplinary procedures brought by their employer and professional body. For such procedures, there is no need to show that the patient suffered a financial loss as a result. It has been suggested that the fact that confidentiality is widely respected is not a result of the availability of legal remedies, but rather the widespread acceptance of its ethical basis among those working in medicine.

7 Access to information

A doctor must maintain medical records as part of care for his or her patients. So far, we have been discussing the obligation on doctors to keep a patient's records secret, but a patient may also want to see the information kept about him or her. The NHS Constitution is clear: 'You have the right of access to your own health records. These will always be used to manage your treatment in your best interests.'[244] However, there is

---

[241] Herring (2013: 182); Gilbar (2012).
[242] Stauch and Tingle (2002: 260).   [243] *Cornelius v de Taranto* (2001) 68 BMLR 62.
[244] NHS (2009a: 8).

no common law right to see your healthcare information;[245] however, there are various statutory rights to see the information.[246]

7.1 The statutory provisions of access to records

The Data Protection Act 1998 is by far the most important piece of legislation governing this area, but others will be briefly mentioned first. It should also be noted that Article 8 ECHR protects the right of access to medical records and therefore that legislation should be interpreted in a way that is compatible with that right.[247]

The relevant statutes include the following.

(i) *The Human Rights Act 1998* In *KH v Slovakia*,[248] the ECtHR recognized that access to medical records was part of the right to respect for private and family life under Article 8 ECHR. As a result of the HRA 1998, legislation and common law should be interpreted, in so far as is possible, in recognition of that right. Remember, however, that Article 8 rights can be interfered with if justified under Article 8(2), for example if doing so is necessary to protect the interests of a third party.

(ii) *The Supreme Court Act 1981* If a person has commenced or is likely to commence litigation that has some prospect of success, then he or she has a right to 'discovery' of relevant evidence, including documents. These can include medical records. If disclosure would harm a patient, then those documents can be shown only to the patient's medical advisers.[249]

(iii) *The Access to Medical Reports Act 1988* This Act applies to reports supplied by a medical practitioner for the purposes of insurance or employment. The subject of such a report (the patient) has the right to see them, veto their release, and to append comments if he or she believes the report to be inaccurate. Doctors are entitled to refuse access if there are concerns that allowing it would be likely to cause serious harm to the physical or mental health of the person seeking it or to others, or to protect a doctor's informant.

(iv) *The Access to Health Records Act 1990* The 1990 Act gives a right of access to patients to all manual health records since 1 November 1991. The 1998 Data Protection Act has, in fact, rendered the 1990 Act obsolete, except in relation to deceased persons, who are not covered by the 1998 Act.

(v) *The Data Protection Act 1998* Patients have rights of access to their health records under the Data Protection Act 1998, sections 7 and 8. A person can be informed whether his or her personal data is being processed, be given a description of the data, and be told the purposes for which it is being processed and the classes of people to whom it will be disclosed. Most significantly, he or she is entitled to a copy of the records in an 'intelligible form'. This includes, where necessary, an explanation of any terms

---

[245] *R v Mid Glamorgan Family Health Services Authority, ex p Martin* [1995] 1 All ER 356, criticized in Dermot Feenan (1996).
[246] See Kaye, Kanellopoulou, Hawkins, Gowans, Curren, and Melham (2013) on rights of access to one's genome.
[247] *McGinley and Egan v UK* (1998) 27 EHRR 1.
[248] Application no. 32881/04, ECtHR, 29 April 2009.   [249] Section 33(2).

used.[250] Once they have seen their records, patients are entitled to require the data controller to stop processing the information if doing so would cause substantial and unwarranted distress to the patient or another.[251] The patient has the right to have the information rectified if it is wrong.[252]

There are two important limitations on the right of access under the Data Protection Act 1998 and they are:

(a)   where the disclosure would cause serious harm to the physical or mental health of the patient or another[253]—but a healthcare professional must confirm that this applies and the BMA guidance suggests that it will be 'extremely rare' for this exception to apply;[254] and

(b)   if the data disclosed would reveal information about another person—so if, on a man's medical records, there were a statement about his wife's concerns about him, that section of the record could not be revealed.

Normally, of course, another person cannot use the 1998 Act to obtain the record of another. However, a parent with parental responsibility can obtain the records of his or her child, or a person managing the affairs of a person lacking capacity can access the relevant files, unless either person has provided information in the expectation that it will not be disclosed. So if a child has seen a doctor on his or her own and talks on the basis that his or her parents will not find out what he or she says, then this need not be disclosed.

In *Roberts v Nottinghamshire Healthcare NHS Trust,*[255] a patient at a high security psychiatric hospital sought access under the 1998 Act to a psychological report on him. The court held that the Trust was not required to produce the report. Good reasons had been provided to the court and these did not need to be disclosed to the applicant.

The leading case on common law rights of access to medical records is the following.

KEY CASE   *R v Mid Glamorgan Family Health Services Authority, ex p Martin* **[1995] 1 All ER 356**

Martin sought from the medical authorities all of his personal health and social work records, which had been made while he had been a patient at a number of different hospitals. The hospitals concerned were willing to disclose the records to Mr Martin's medical advisers, but not to him directly.

It was held by the Court of Appeal that health authorities and doctors owned the medical notes. They could deny a patient access to the notes if that was in his or her best interests. This might be, for example, if disclosure could be detrimental to the patient's health. The offer to disclose the notes to Mr Martin's medical advisers was the most that could be expected. Sir Roger Parker LJ stated:

> I regard as untenable the proposition that, at common law, a doctor or health authority has an absolute property in medical records of a patient, if this means, which it appears to do, that either could make what use of them he or it chose. Information given to a doctor by a

---

[250] Section 8(2).   [251] Section 10.   [252] Section 14.
[253] Data Protection (Subject Access Modification) (Health) Order 2000, SI 2000/413, art. 5.
[254] BMA (2004: 217).   [255] [2008] EWHC 1934 (QB).

patient or a third party is given in confidence and the absolute property rights are therefore necessarily qualified by the obligations arising out of that situation.[256]

But he regarded as equally untenable that a patient had an unfettered right of access to his or her records. He then stated:

In my view the circumstances in which a patient or former patient is entitled to demand access to his medical history as set out in the records will be infinitely various, and it is neither desirable nor possible for this or any court to attempt to set out the scope of the duty to afford access or, its obverse, the scope of the patient's rights to demand access. Each case must depend on its own facts.[257]

The lawyers were permitted to use the documents only for the purposes of advising on and undertaking legal proceedings.

The NHS Care Record Guarantee states:

When we receive a request from you in writing, we must normally give you access to everything we have recorded about you. We may not give you confidential information about other people, or information that a healthcare professional considers likely to cause serious harm to the physical or mental health of you or someone else. This applies to paper and electronic records. However, if you ask us to, we will let other people see health records about you.[258]

7.2 Should there be a right to see one's medical records?

Those who support such a right claim four particular benefits, as follows.[259]

(i) *Improved accuracy and general quality of records* Certainly, there are concerns about the quality of information in medical records.[260] If a patient could check records, then this would be one way of improving the accuracy of records. It might also mean that the records would be kept more efficiently and would not include inappropriate comments about patients.[261] The press is often full of reports of offensive remarks being made in people's medical records. The BMA records a case in which a medical record originally referred to a patient as a 'silly old bat', although this was altered to read 'still holds bottle'.[262]

(ii) *Relief of patient's anxiety* Some patients are convinced that they are suffering from illnesses that they are not or that their doctors are hiding the truth from them. A right to access their health information may allay such fears.

(iii) *Improved communication* If patients are entitled to see their healthcare information, then the records will need to be presented in a clear way that is readily understandable to patients. This might be in the best interests of everyone.

[256] At [21]. [257] At [22]. [258] NHS (2011b: 4). [259] Gilhooley and McGhee (1991).
[260] Information Policy Unit (2004). The National Patient Safety Agency Plan 2003–04 found 1,742 incidents in which patients had suffered as a result of bad medical records.
[261] BMA (2004: 199).
[262] BMA (2004: 218). No doubt there are worse things written on medical records.

(iv) *Increased trust* Openness in dealings between patients and their doctors may persuade patients to be more open with doctors and doctors to be more open with patients.

There are, however, those who are opposed to opening up medical records.[263] It is argued that, inevitably, such records contain complex medical terminology and too easily lead to misconceptions, and may even exacerbate the worries of an over-anxious patient. It is feared that doctors may then have to become involved in lengthy discussions explaining the records to their patients. It may, of course, be regarded as a good thing that doctors explain to patients the details of their medical conditions.

REALITY CHECK

Medical acronyms

It should not be thought that medical records will contain only medical information. A BBC News report found the following acronyms and other phrases used in people's records:[264]

CTD–'Circling the Drain' (a patient expected to die soon)

GLM–'Good Looking Mum'

GPO–'Good for Parts Only'

TEETH–'Tried Everything Else, Try Homeopathy'

UBI–'Unexplained Beer Injury'

NFN–'Normal for Norfolk'

FLK–'Funny Looking Kid'

GROLIES–'*Guardian* Reader of Low Intelligence in Ethnic Skirt'

TTFO–roughly translated as 'Told To Go Away'

LOBNH–'Lights On But Nobody Home'

'Pumpkin Positive'–Implying that a penlight shone into the patient's mouth would encounter a brain so small that his or her whole head would light up

8 The ethical issues

We have so far concentrated on the legal position, which is generally based on the assumption that medical professionals should not breach confidence. But what are the ethical arguments that might support such an assumption?

8.1 Arguments in favour of confidentiality

8.1.1 *Consequentialist arguments*

Consequentialist arguments rely on the benefits and disadvantages that flow from confidentiality. It is argued that, if confidentiality is promised, patients will be willing to

---

[263] Ross (1986).   [264] BBC News online (18 August 2003).

be completely honest with their doctors, and to discuss all of their symptoms and past history.[265] This will mean that the best diagnosis and treatment can be offered. This will benefit both patients and the general public. It will also ensure that there is an efficient and organized healthcare system. Murphy has argued in favour of confidentiality, because it encourages 'talk' between the patient and the medical professional.[266] In other words, it encourages a model whereby the doctor and patient discuss and agree on an appropriate course of treatment, rather than the doctor providing a monologue setting out the problem and proposed solution, which the patient must simply accept or reject.

All of the arguments in the consequentialist model, however, assume that patients are aware of the obligations of confidence under which medical professionals operate and rely on them. Whether this is true is a matter of debate.

8.1.2 Deontological arguments

Confidentiality is a fundamental principle that should be respected. It has been argued: 'The right to control who knows the things about us which we regard as private is integral to our sense of self and sense of identity.'[267] Others ground the right in terms of the right to autonomy: that people should have the ability to live their lives as they choose. This is possible only if private matters are being kept secret by those to whom they are divulged. Capron argues that a breach of confidence involves a lack of respect for reserve and solitude.[268] Others emphasize not privacy, but fidelity. In other words, a breach of confidence is quite simply a breach of a promise.[269] The obligation of confidence can also be seen as a reflection of the fact that patients must submit themselves and their futures to the professional.[270]

8.1.3 Public/private benefits

As can be seen from the points above, some arguments in favour of confidentiality are in terms of the public good: it aids an effective healthcare system. When confidentiality is broken, not only does that harm the individual concerned, but it also has an impact on the general public's willingness to trust medical professionals and this can harm the health of the nation.[271] Other arguments focus more on the 'private' issues: the rights and harms of the particular individual concerned.

It is, of course, quite possible to claim that there are both public and private claims that can be made in favour of confidentiality, and it would be wrong to emphasize one more than the other.[272] In other words, when a doctor breaks a duty of confidentiality not only is there a wrong done to the individual patient, but there also is a public harm, because patients generally lose trust in the medical profession. Until recently, the case law on the equitable protection of confidential information emphasized the public interest in protecting confidential information as of more importance than the private

---

[265] There are psychological studies that support the argument that guaranteeing confidentiality will lead to greater honesty and openness: McMahan and Knowles (1995).
[266] Murphy (1998).   [267] O'Brien and Chantler (2003: 37).   [268] Capron (1991).
[269] Beauchamp and Childress (2009).   [270] Sokolowski (1991).
[271] Hall (2002) emphasizes the importance of trust in good medical practice.
[272] Childress and Beauchamp (2009).

interest in maintaining confidence.[273] However, it may be that the understanding on the basis of confidentiality has shifted after the HRA 1998. Indeed, the House of Lords held in *Campbell v MGN Ltd*[274] that privacy, dignity, and autonomy provided the basis of medical confidentiality.

It is arguable that the recognition of confidentiality as a private right will make it more difficult to justify a disclosure on the basis of the public interest.[275] If confidentiality is seen as being in the public interest, it is easier to justify an infringement by reference to other public interest claims than it would be if the claim were seen as being a private individual's right.[276] Also, if put in terms of the public benefit, there are concerns that some groups of people could assert that they have a stronger claim than others.[277] It might, for example, be argued that it is more in the national interest that the medical records of top politicians be kept confidential than those of benefit claimants.

8.2 Arguments against confidentiality

There are very few people who actually believe that confidentiality does not deserve protection at all. But there is a considerable body of opinion holding that far too much respect is paid to the notion of confidentiality. Paterson argued that the emphasis on confidentiality was an interference with research.[278] Indeed, the impact on research has led some to claim that 'privacy is bad for your health'.[279] Professor Gostin has explained the problem well:

> Because significant levels of privacy cannot realistically be achieved within the health information infrastructure currently envisaged by policymakers, we confront a hard choice: should we sharply limit the systematic collection of identifiable health care data in order to achieve reasonable levels of informational privacy? The result of that choice would be to reduce considerably the social good that would be achieved from the thoughtful use of health data. Alternatively, we may decide that the value of information collection is so important to the achievement of societal aspirations for health that the law ought not promise absolute or even significant levels of privacy at all, but rather should require that the data be used only for authorized and limited purposes.[280]

He argues that, in a modern healthcare system, the notion of confidentiality between patient and doctor is outdated. Instead, we have to focus on protection of records and ensuring that any medical data (however acquired) is used for proper purposes.

Rubinstein makes the point that emphasizing confidentiality too strongly carries risks:

> Inherent in the privacy advocates' rejection of the public duty paradigm is a refusal to recognize, in exchange for the vast improvements in medical care, a correlative responsibility on the part of the individual, as a potential consumer of health care services, toward the community. As individuals rely on their right to be let alone, they shift the burden on others in the community to accept the responsibility for providing the data needed to advance medical and health policy information. Their individualist vision threatens the entire community, because when particular segments of the community opt out of participation as data subjects, the resulting value of the research is

---

[273] *W v Egdell* [1990] 1 All ER 835; *X v Y* [1988] 2 All ER 649.   [274] [2004] UKHL 22.
[275] Lee (1994: 291).   [276] Lee (1994: 292).   [277] Murphy (1998).
[278] Paterson (2001); Al-Shahi and Warlow (2000).   [279] O'Grady and Nolan (2004).
[280] Gostin (1995: 454).

questionable, and many worthwhile protocols could be abandoned on that basis. Thus, a policy that requires consent before each use of health data might have unintended and undesirable consequences for our medical care and health policy.[281]

8.3 Public views

Surveys among the general public in relation to confidentiality might make depressing reading for those who are concerned about the present protection of confidential information. First, the surveys suggest that the public has high confidence in the way in which the NHS protects confidentiality.[282] Second, the surveys suggest that people are not particularly concerned about the fact that a large number of people within the NHS may need access to their data,[283] although there is much unease about information being given to people outside the NHS.[284]

However, the picture is more complicated than this. Although the public are pleased with the way in which their medical records are kept secret, in fact the general public have little idea how the information is in fact used.[285] For example, only 16 per cent of those questioned in one large survey realized that their information could be revealed to hospital managers. Further surveys indicate that when the public are asked if they are happy for their medical details to be used in 'medical research', there is much unease, although they tend to be much happier when asked if they would be willing for their records to be used in a particular project (for example to research the causes of cancer).[286] A team researching asthma and angina, who decided to write to individuals asking consent to use their medical records, found that 9.8 per cent refused. This indicates that an assumption that nearly everyone wants to help in medical research is ill-founded, even when the research might be regarded as uncontroversial.[287]

Surveys do give us some picture of what kind of medical issues people are particularly sensitive about. Not surprisingly, these relate to termination of pregnancy and mental health issues.[288] This might support an argument that medical records should be divided up into general records, readily available for anyone in the NHS with a legitimate reason for seeing them, and a sensitive part, which could be examined only on a 'need to know' basis. One study looked at this option and found much support among the general public, but 60 per cent said that they would want their information to be put in the sensitive part.[289]

9 Informational privacy

Laurie has argued that the law should move away from focusing on the notion of confidentiality and instead focus on the right to informational privacy.[290] He explains the difference between the two concepts in this way:

---

[281] Rubinstein (1999: 227).   [282] National Health Service Information Authority (2002).

[283] Adams, Budden, Hoare, et al. (2004).

[284] NHS Information Authority (2002); van de Creek, Miars, and Herzog (1987).

[285] National Health Service Information Authority (2002).

[286] The Welcome Trust and Medical Research Council (2001).

[287] Baker, Shields, Stevenson, et al. (2000).

[288] National Health Service Information Authority (2002).

[289] National Health Service Information Authority (2002).

[290] Laurie (2002: ch. 7). For further discussion on the nature of privacy, see Neill (2002).

Informational privacy is concerned with the control of personal information and with preventing access to that information by others. An invasion of informational privacy occurs when any unauthorized disclosure of information takes place. Confidentiality is a subset of this privacy interest, and is breached when confidential information which is the subject of the relationship is released to parties outside the relationship without authorization. Informational privacy is wider than this in that it requires no relationship to exist.[291]

Laurie sees privacy as creating and respecting a 'state of separateness' for individuals: '... the protection of a private sphere around oneself.'[292] It is important for people living in society to have their 'own space'. This may involve a physical space, but also a psychological one. This is possible only if people are able to control who has access to information about them and what information they find out about themselves. Laurie is aware that this might sound as if he is advocating a highly individualist vision of society, which pays no attention to relationships between people. However, he says that the protection of privacy is important to enable relationships to flourish.[293]

So what exactly is the difference between 'confidentiality' and 'informational privacy'? The differences appear to include the following.

(i)   The classic definition of confidentiality requires there to be a confidential relationship between the parties. It therefore does not readily apply where a party acquires private information about another outside the context of such a relationship. There are no such difficulties for the notion of informational privacy, which does not depend on any kind of relationship.[294]

(ii)   The idea that a party has a right not to know a piece of information can be readily included within the notion of informational privacy. It cannot easily fit into the notion of breach of confidence.

(iii) Laurie suggests that an understanding of a right to information privacy, when combined with a proprietary right over medical information about a person, will give a person appropriate control over his or her medical details. In particular, it will mean that a person can have ongoing control over how his or her records are used. Laurie is concerned that, with breach of confidence, once consent is given for the public use of the information, then the protection is lost.

 A SHOCK TO THE SYSTEM

The following shows that it is possible to respect confidentiality *too* much.

In January 1999, the US state of Maine enacted a strict law prohibiting the passing of medical information without a patient's written consent.[295] Heavy fines would be placed on those who violated the rules. The law was soon found to be impracticable: relatives of patients who telephoned for updates could not be given any information; florists found it impossible to deliver flowers; priests could not discover the whereabouts of patients to administer religious rites; doctors found it difficult to consult over problems with patients; delays occurred because labs refused to give the results of tests over the telephone.

---

[291] Mason and Laurie (2006: 224).   [292] Laurie (2002: 128).
[293] See Andorno (2004), who develops the right not to know from autonomy rather than privacy.
[294] Micholowski (2004: 16–18).   [295] See C. Scott (2000).

There is also some evidence that in the UK, following the Data Protection Act 1998, some healthcare trusts became so nervous of infringing the Act that they refused to provide information to outside bodies, even where to do so would be uncontroversial.[296]

10 Conclusion

A survey of patients across European countries found that they regarded confidentiality as 'very important' and one of their highest priorities when consulting doctors.[297] And if the professional guidelines are anything to go by, healthcare workers take the duty of confidentiality seriously. Yet there is little doubt that medical confidentiality is under threat. In practice, the flimsy curtain in hospitals, with medical notes at the end of a bed, mean that, in that setting, confidentiality is little protected.[298] The desire to ensure that the NHS is run effectively and efficiently means that managers and administrators need to have access to records to an extent never needed before. Further, computerization of health records will inevitably increase and with it the difficulties of ensuring that the information is kept secure.[299] Insurance companies seek ever more intimate medical information about people looking for life insurance.[300] It is not surprising that some commentators have described confidentiality as a 'decrepit concept'.[301]

This ambiguity over the notion of confidentiality is also found in the shift of language in some court cases[302] and professional guidance[303] from talk of a duty of confidentiality towards a discussion of the fairness of use of information. Maybe this is realistic: the NHS cannot promise that your information will not be disclosed to anyone else, but it can promise that your information will be dealt with fairly. But there are counter influences. The HRA 1998 appears to classify protection of private information as a human right.[304] Especially in the area of genetic information, there is widespread unease about the way in which such information is used. Also, there is increasing concern at the lack of trust between patients and doctors, which is central to an effective healthcare system. A reaffirmation of the importance of confidentiality could be seen as one way of restoring that trust.[305]

QUESTIONS

1. Proposals to take DNA profiles of every baby born in the UK have been rejected by the Human Genetic Commission.[306] What ethical issues would be raised by such a database?[307]

---

[296] Boyd (2003).   [297] Grol, Wensing, Mainz, et al. (1999).
[298] Okino Sawada, Mendes, Correia, et al. (1996).
[299] Gostin, Hodge, and Burghardt (2002). See Anderson, Brown, Dowty, et al. (2009) for claims that it will not be possible for computerized health records to comply with data protection requirements.
[300] The Royal College of General Practitioners (2000) is concerned about this.   [301] Siegler (1982).
[302] *R v Department of Health, ex p Source Informatics Ltd* [2000] 1 All ER 786.   [303] NHS (2007b: 1).
[304] Evans and Harris (2004) are concerned at the shift away from protecting confidentiality as a right.
[305] Clarke (2002).   [306] BBC News online (31 March 2005).   [307] See Gibbons (2007).

2. There are plans for all medical records within the NHS to be computerized. Is this a concern? How should the balance be struck between the importance of keeping information confidential and ensuring that medical professionals have ready access to the medical information necessary to treat a patient?[308]

3. Should the law do more to distinguish between different kinds of medical information? It might, for example, be argued that we could distinguish non-intimate medical information (such as the fact a person has broken a leg) from intimate information (such as the fact a person has had an abortion). Would that be a useful distinction?

4. Can you think of any medical information about yourself that you would rather not know? How can the law respect that wish?

5. Does it matter whether the protection of medical confidential information is regarded as a matter of private rights or public interest or both?

6. One survey suggested that patients were less concerned about the fact that information about them might be stored on a database than that their information might be given to commercial bodies for marketing or other purposes.[309] Should the law focus on the use of information rather than its storage?

FURTHER READING

A comprehensive bibliography, including all references used throughout the book, is available online at www.oup.com/uk/herringmedical7e/.

Generally, on the protection of confidential medical information, see:

Andorno, R. (2004) 'The right not to know: an autonomy based approach', *Journal of Medical Ethics* 30: 435.

Case, P. (2003) 'Confidence matters: the rise and fall of informational autonomy in medical law', *Medical Law Review* 11: 208.

Kipnis, K (2006) 'A defense of unqualified medical confidentiality', *American Journal of Bioethics* 6: 7.

Pattenden, R. (2003) *The Law on Professional Client Confidentiality* (Oxford University Press).

Skene, L. (2001) 'Genetic secrets and the family', *Medical Law Review* 9: 162.

Sterckx, S. and Cockbain, J. (2014) 'The UK National Health Service's "innovation agenda": Lessons on commercialisation and trust', *Medical Law Review* 22: 221.

Taylor, M. (2011) 'Health research, data protection, and the public interest in notification', *Medical Law Review* 19: 267.

---

[308] Shenoy and Appel (2017).
[309] Baird, Jackson, Ford, et al. (2009).

On the protection of genetic information, see:

Gibbons, S. (2009) 'Regulating biobanks: a twelve-point typological tool', *Medical Law Review* 19: 1.

Gilbar, R. (2012) 'Medical confidentiality and communication with the patient's family: legal and practical perspectives', *Child and Family Law Quarterly* 24: 199.

Laurie, G. (2002) *Genetic Privacy: A Challenge to Medico-Legal Norms* (Cambridge University Press).

Lowrance, W. (2012) *Privacy, Confidentiality, and Health Research* (Cambridge University Press).

Widows, H. and Mullen, C. (eds) (2009) *The Governance of Genetic Information: Who Decides?* (Cambridge University Press).

6

Contraception, Abortion, and Pregnancy

INTRODUCTION

Few topics arouse greater passion than those surrounding abortion and the regulation of pregnancy. In the United States, the issue of abortion is of enormous political significance; in the UK, less so. Whether as a political matter or a moral one, it creates heated argument. The reason is that, for those on either side of the debate, the stakes could hardly be higher: on the one hand, there are those who regard abortion as the murder of the most innocent and vulnerable human beings; on the other, there are those who claim that access to abortion is a crucial part of the battle towards women's equality and is a fundamental human right.[1] For them, abortion and fertility decisions should be made by the woman alone, and should not be interfered with by the state.[2] Indeed this can make it difficult to present a 'non-biased' discussion of the law. The questions you start with and the framing of the question can reflect a particular approach.[3]

The law, as we shall see, seeks to strike a somewhat uneasy balance between recognizing that the foetus has some interests, reinforcing medical control over pregnancy and birth control, and protecting the rights of the pregnant woman. In all of the fascinating theoretical debate, it must not be forgotten that these issues affect millions of women in the UK. It has been claimed that, in the UK, nearly 50 per cent of pregnancies were unplanned.[4] By the time they are aged 45, a third of all women in the UK will have had an abortion.[5]

Before looking at the issue of abortion, we will consider contraception.

1 Contraception: its use and function

It is often claimed that the wide availability of effective contraception has done more to emancipate women than any other social development. Women's control over their fertility is now sometimes taken for granted. A 2015 UN report found that worldwide 64 per cent of women of reproductive age were using contraception.[6] For the UK the rate was 81.3 per cent.[7] Access to effective contraception is regarded by some as a fundamental human right.[8]

---

[1] See Sifris (2010), who regards abortion as a basic part of a right to health care.
[2] Kaposy (2011) suggests that the abortion debate reflects two completely different world views.
[3] Priaulx (2017).   [4] Bury and Ngo (2009).   [5] Education for Choice (2013).
[6] United Nations (2015).   [7] National Statistics (2009a).   [8] Eriksson (1993).

The most common forms of contraception are:

- the condom;
- the intra-uterine device (IUD);
- injectable contraceptives;
- the female contraceptive pill;
- sterilization; and
- natural methods.[9]

It is not emphasized often enough that there are serious disadvantages to all of these forms of contraception. In a survey covering seven countries, a substantial majority of women were dissatisfied with all of the available methods of contraception.[10] Two leading clinical experts working in the UK have stated: '[T]here is a real need for new methods of contraception to be developed that are more effective, easier to use, and safer than existing methods.'[11] It is remarkable that the most commonly used method of birth control worldwide is sterilization of women.[12] The United Nations Report found that worldwide 19 per cent of women in relationships relied on sterilization.[13] New techniques of sterilization mean that the operation is less invasive than it once was and is highly reliable, yet its permanence[14] and degree of invasion mean that it is hardly ideal.

The other forms of contraception also have disadvantages. The pill, although popular, can carry unpleasant side effects and there have been persistent concerns with long-term health risks associated with it. The pill has been linked to breast cancer, cervical cancer,[15] and thrombosis.[16] That said, many believe that these risks are overstated.[17] Certainly, the pill has been used for more than forty years, without there being a clearly established link between the pill and illness for most women. The other disadvantage of the pill is that it requires users to ensure that they take the pill daily. Some people find the discipline required to remember to do this challenging.

A major problem with all forms of contraception is reliability. The success rates of the different forms of contraception vary. One study by the respected Alan Guttmacher Institute found the following percentages of those using these methods who became pregnant in the first year of use:

- withdrawal—15–28 per cent;
- rhythm—14–57 per cent;
- spermicide—13–55 per cent;
- condom—6–51 per cent;
- pill—3–27 per cent;
- female sterilization—0.5 per cent; and
- male sterilization—0.1–0.2 per cent.[18]

---

[9] Natural methods do not use devices or medication, but depend on ensuring that sexual intercourse is at a time when the woman is not fertile or requiring the man to withdraw before ejaculation.
[10] Snow, Garcia, and Kureshy (1996: 8).   [11] Baird and Glasier (1999: 969).
[12] Blank (1991: 16).   [13] United Nations 2015.
[14] Although it is possible to try to reverse sterilization, this involves major surgery and is not always successful.
[15] BBC News online (4 April 2003).   [16] Grabrick, Hartmann, Cerhan, et al. (2000).
[17] Baird and Glasier (1999: 969) claim that the pill has an excellent safety record.
[18] Alan Guttmacher Institute (2004: 16).

One practical consequence of these failure rates is that, in about three-quarters of pregnancies ended by abortion, the woman was using some form of contraception at the time of conception.[19] The National Institute for Health and Clinical Excellence (NICE) has recommended that wider use be made of reversible long-acting contraception.[20]

Despite a widespread perception of sexual promiscuity, a major government survey found that, of those aged 16–69, 75 per cent of men had had only one sexual partner in the year prior to the interview and 11 per cent had had no sexual partners.[21] For women, the corresponding statistics were 78 per cent and 13 per cent. It is notable that, of those seeking advice from National Health Service (NHS) contraceptive clinics, 89 per cent were women.[22] Sadly, contraception still seems to be regarded as largely a 'woman's responsibility'.

2 The availability of contraception

In 1925, the House of Lords held, in a libel action, that to describe contraception as 'monstrous and revolting to human nature'[23] was a fair comment. Lord Denning, in *Bravery v Bravery*,[24] suggested that a sterilization that is done 'so as to enable a man to have the pleasure of sexual intercourse, without shouldering the public interest attaching to it' was contrary to public policy and degrading to the man. But the judges gradually moved with the times and, in *Gillick v West Norfolk and Wisbech Area Health Authority*,[25] Lord Scarman held that contraceptive medical treatment is 'recognized as a legitimate and beneficial treatment in cases where it is medically indicated'. There would be widespread agreement with the statement made by Munby J in *R (Smeaton) v The Secretary of State for Health*:[26]

> It is, as it seems to me, for individual men and woman, acting in what they believe to be good conscience, applying those standards which they think appropriate, and in consultation with appropriate professional (and, if they wish, spiritual) advisers, to decide whether or not to use IUDs, the pill, the mini-pill and the morning-after pill. It is no business of government, judges or the law.

In fact, the law does regard contraception as part of the state's business. Contraceptives are medical products that must be licensed by the Medicines and Healthcare products Regulatory Agency (MHRA) of the European Medicines Agency (EMA) before use.[27] Also, the National Health Service Act 2006, Schedule 1, paragraph 8, places a duty upon the Secretary of State, who:

> . . . must arrange, to such extent as he considers necessary to meet all reasonable requirements, for—
> (a) the giving of advice on contraception,
> (b) the medical examination of persons seeking advice on contraception,

[19] *R (John Smeaton on behalf of SPUC) v The Secretary of State for Health* [2002] 2 FCR 193, [215].
[20] NICE (2005b).   [21] Office of National Statistics (2007).
[22] NHS Information Authority (2015c).   [23] *Sutherland v Stopes* [1925] AC 45.
[24] [1954] 1 WLR 1169, 1173. The other members of the Court of Appeal were not in agreement with his comments.
[25] [1985] 3 All ER 402, 418.   [26] [2002] 2 FCR 193, [396].
[27] Medicines Act 1968, s. 19; Medicines for Human Use Regulations, SI 1994/3144; EC Council Directive 65/65/EEC.

(c) the treatment of such persons, and

(d) the supply of contraceptive substances and appliances.

In effect, it means that anyone should be able to access contraception.

It must not, however, be thought that there are no barriers to accessing contraceptive treatment. First, the oral contraceptive pill is available only under prescription or from pharmacists.[28] This is because, for people with certain medical conditions, it can carry serious side effects, and it is thought that the pill should be used only under medical supervision. However, condoms and, significantly, post-coital contraception is available over the counter at a pharmacy. The second barrier is cost: although contraception provided under prescription is free, as is contraception (including condoms) provided at family planning clinics, when purchased at a supermarket, a packet of twelve condoms can cost around £10. Although, to many, these barriers appear small, as we shall see they are significant to some young people.

Sterilizations are available on the NHS, although about one third are carried out privately. In 1999, there were 64,422 vasectomies and 41,300 tubal occlusions. The number of sterilizations carried out by the NHS had dramatically fallen by 2015–16 to 11,113 vasectomies for men and 13,858 sterilizations for women.[29] This might, in part, be explained by an increase in the use of long-acting contraceptives. According to McQueen[30] women under 30 who have not had children find it very difficult to obtain sterilizations, with medical professionals saying they are too young and may regret the decision. He notes that men seem to find it easier to access sterilization, suggesting gendered assumptions about sterilizations are playing a role.

There is also widespread use of 'emergency contraception', for which, in 2015/16, there were 291,000 prescriptions—a 40 per cent drop from 484,000 in 2004/5.[31] Research suggests that those requesting emergency hormonal contraception are not using it as an alternative to other methods.[32] It is available from a pharmacist without a prescription to those over the age of 16.[33]

3 Teenage pregnancy rates

For every 1,000 girls under the age of 15–17 in England and Wales, 21.0 became pregnant in 2015.[34] The rate has been falling dramatically in recent years. In 2013, it was 24.5. The estimated number of conceptions to women aged under 16 was 3,455, compared with 4,648 in 2013.

One study found that 25 per cent of people did not use contraception during their first experience of sexual intercourse.[35] If these figures sound high, it is because they are. England and Wales has the highest teenage pregnancy and teenage parenthood rates in Europe[36]—the highest by some distance. The teenage pregnancy rate is twice that of Germany, three times that of France, and six times that of the Netherlands.

---

[28] Jarvis (2008) argues in favour of this, explaining that requiring GPs to see patients enables them to encourage the use of long-acting contraception. See Grossman (2008), who argues the pill should be available without prescription.

[29] NHS (2016).   [30] McQueen (2017).   [31] NHS (2016).

[32] Glasier and Baird (1998).

[33] The Prescription Only Medicines (Human Use) Amendment (No. 3) Order 2000, SI 2000/3231.

[34] ONS (2017c).   [35] BBC News online (2 July 2007).   [36] ONS (2014).

The British Medical Association (BMA) has acknowledged that there is a 'clear need' to improve access to contraception.[37] Although contraception is widely available, young people find it difficult to access it. Why is this? Again, the reasons are unclear. It may be they are not aware that it is available free of charge or that they are concerned about confidentiality. There may even be practical difficulties getting to see a general practitioner (GP) out of school hours.

A SHOCK TO THE SYSTEM

A multimillion-pound UK government programme to discourage teenage pregnancy was abandoned in 2009 after it was found those who attended the programme were more likely than similar women who did not attend to have sex early, not to use contraception, and to become pregnant.[38]

4 Abortion and contraception

At the heart of the legal regulation of fertility is a distinction between abortion and contraception. If a technique is classified as producing an abortion or miscarriage, its regulation is entirely different from where it is classified as a contraceptive. As we shall see later in this chapter, there is a host of detailed regulations governing abortion.

The following decision is now the leading authority on the distinction.[39]

KEY CASE   *R (John Smeaton on behalf of SPUC) v The Secretary of State for Health* **[2002] 2 FCR 193**

The Society for the Protection of the Unborn Child (SPUC) sought to challenge the legality of the Prescription Only Medicines (Human Use) Amendment (No. 3) Order 2000,[40] which permitted the sale of the morning-after pill without prescription. The Offences Against the Person Act 1861, sections 58 and 59 (creating the offence of procuring a miscarriage), mean that substances that cause miscarriage or abortion may be administered only if two doctors certify that the conditions set out in the 1967 Abortion Act are satisfied. Otherwise, the use of such substances is, in principle, potentially criminal. The question for the court was whether the morning-after pill is such a substance. If it is, then it would be an offence for a pharmacist to provide it and an offence for the woman to take it, unless all of the formalities required by the Abortion Act were complied with.

To answer the question, Munby J explained the 'medical facts':

Put very simply, there are two key stages in the biological process following sexual intercourse:

(i)   The first is fertilisation. This takes place after the man's sperm and the woman's egg have met in the fallopian tube. It is a process which commences hours, or even days, after sexual intercourse. The process itself takes many hours.

---

[37] BMA (2004: 228).   [38] BBC News online (7 July 2009).
[39] See Keown (2005a) for a critique of this decision.   [40] SI 2000/3231.

(ii) The other key stage is implantation. This takes place after the fertilised egg has moved into the womb. It involves a process by which the fertilised egg physically attaches itself to the wall of the womb. The process does not start until, at the earliest, some four days after the commencement of fertilisation. The process of implantation itself takes some days.[41]

The SPUC argued that any procedure that caused the loss of a fertilized egg was procuring a 'miscarriage' and that contraception involved procedures that prevented fertilization. So the Society's argument was that something that prevents a fertilized egg implanting itself in the wall of the womb is an abortifacient and not a contraceptive. The morning-after pill (and indeed the normal contraceptive pill) operates, in some cases, to prevent fertilization and in others to prevent implantation. However, the morning-after pill (and the normal pill) cannot work once the fertilized eggs are implanted.

The SPUC argued that the word 'miscarriage', at least as understood in 1861, included preventing implantation. The aim of Parliament in 1861 was to prohibit all attempts to abort, from the moment of fertilization. This argument was rejected by Munby J for two main reasons:

(i) As a matter of law, the decision must ultimately turn not on what the word 'miscarriage' was understood to mean in 1861 but rather on what it means today.

(ii) Whatever it may or may not have meant in 1861 the word 'miscarriage' today means the termination of an established pregnancy, and there is no established pregnancy prior to implantation. There is no miscarriage if a fertilised egg is lost prior to implantation. Current medical understanding of what is meant by 'miscarriage' excludes results brought about by the pill, the mini-pill or the morning-after pill. That is also, I should add, the current understanding of the word 'miscarriage' when used by lay people in its popular sense.[42]

It followed that the SPUC's arguments failed, and the morning-after pill was a form of contraceptive and not abortion for the purposes of the legislative scheme.

Part of Munby J's reasoning was based on the social benefits of the availability of emergency contraception. He accepted the point that: 'Emergency contraception is safe, simple and effective. Abortion is both medically and psychologically invasive.'[43] All of the evidence was that if emergency contraception were not available, the number of abortions would greatly increase, and this, he thought, would be a bad thing. Also, he pointed out that if the SPUC's arguments were accepted, then use of the contraceptive pill itself, where it operated to prevent implantation (as opposed to conception), would be criminal. The pill is used by millions of women and it could not be Parliament's intention that its use was unlawful.

The effect, then, of Munby J's judgment in this case is that the line between contraception and abortion is not pre- and post-conception, but before and after implantation.[44] As Sally Sheldon[45] has written this may prove problematic as many modern forms of contraceptive drugs can operate post-implantation. She suggests the current distinction based on implantation is looking increasingly Victorian and out of touch with modern forms of birth control.

[41] At [62].   [42] At [67].   [43] At [66].
[44] See Jones and Stammers (2009) for arguments against this conclusion.   [45] Sheldon (2015).

5 Contraception and children

We have already indicated that a doctor is permitted to provide contraceptive advice to those under the age of 16. However, the position is not quite as straightforward as stated. The leading decision on the issue is the following.

> **KEY CASE**   *Gillick v West Norfolk and Wisbech Area Health Authority* [1986] AC 112
>
> Mrs Gillick sought to challenge the legality of a Department of Health circular that permitted doctors to provide contraceptive advice and treatment to those under the age of 16 without parental permission. The House of Lords held that it was lawful for a doctor to do so, provided that the child is sufficiently mature to understand the medical, social, and family issues involved, and the child can provide an effective consent. Therefore, maturity and the ability to understand the issues determined whether a person was competent, rather than age. The majority emphasized that even if a child's parents do not want the child to have contraceptive advice, it was still open to a doctor to provide the advice if the child was competent to make the decision.
>
> Some commentators have seen a distinction between the approach of Lord Fraser and Lord Scarman in the case. Lord Fraser emphasized that the doctor can treat a *Gillick* competent child with contraceptive treatment only if to do so would be in her best interests. However, Lord Scarman makes no reference to 'best interests'. It may be that this is because Lord Scarman thought it self-evident that a doctor would act only in a way that benefited his or her patient. An alternative interpretation is that there is a difference: Lord Scarman thought that a doctor could treat a competent child seeking treatment unless to do so would harm the child; while Lord Fraser thought that the doctor would have to be convinced that the treatment benefited the child.
>
> Their Lordships dealt with two other issues. First, it was emphasized that a doctor owes a child patient a duty of confidentiality. The doctor should not inform the child's parents of the visit. Second, their Lordships responded to an argument that the provision of contraception to an under-age person could be regarded as a criminal offence of assisting in the commission of a child sex offence. The House of Lords held that the doctor could not be guilty of an offence because he or she did not intend the child to engage in sexual intercourse. Although a controversial piece of reasoning, this issue has now been addressed by the Sexual Offences Act 2003, and so it is not necessary to consider this aspect of their Lordships' judgment further.

As *Gillick* makes clear, a doctor can provide contraceptive advice and treatment to someone under the age of 16 if the child has sufficient maturity and intelligence to understand the issues involved, and is therefore competent to give consent to the treatment provided. There may also, it appears from Lord Fraser's speech, be a requirement that any treatment provided is in the child's best interests. Because the House of Lords appeared to approve of the general social policy of making contraception available to competent sexually active minors, it may be thought to complicate a GP's job unnecessarily if he or she is to consider whether or not the contraception is in the child's 'best interests'. There have been reports of children as young as 10 being given the contraceptive pill.[46]

[46] BBC News online (9 May 2005a).

There is still the issue of potential criminal liability as an accessory to a sexual offence. This is addressed in the Sexual Offences Act 2003. The concern is that, by providing contraception, a doctor might be said to be aiding or abetting the commission of a child abuse offence. Section 73 of the Act states:

(1) A person is not guilty of aiding, abetting or counselling the commission against a child of an offence to which this section applies if he acts for the purpose of—

(a) protecting the child from sexually transmitted infection,

(b) protecting the physical safety of the child,

(c) preventing the child from becoming pregnant, or

(d) promoting the child's emotional well-being by the giving of advice,

and not for the purpose of obtaining sexual gratification or for the purpose of causing or encouraging the activity constituting the offence or the child's participation in it.[47]

This makes it clear that if a doctor is acting to protect the child's health, he or she will not be guilty as an accessory to a criminal offence against the child if he or she provides contraceptive advice or treatment.

6 Contraception, sterilization, and those lacking capacity

6.1 Contraception and those lacking capacity

The leading case on whether an adult has the capacity to consent to receive contraception is *A Local Authority v Mrs A and Mr A*[48] (discussed in Chapter 4). In that case, it was held that it was necessary to show only that the person understood the proximate issues relating to contraception: the reason for contraception; how contraception works and the likelihood of pregnancy if contraception is not used; the different types of contraception; their effectiveness; their side effects; the advantages and disadvantages of each; and the ease of changing contraception. Bodey J rejected an argument that it was also necessary to show that the individual understood the broader issues surrounding pregnancy and the realities of bringing up a child. He explained that to require this would 'risk a move away from personal autonomy in the direction of social engineering'.[49] His concern was that it would become too easy to say that someone it was thought would not be a good mother did not really understand what motherhood was about. However, that raises the issue of whether a decision about contraception that is made with no real understanding of the broader consequences is really an autonomous decision.[50]

Bodey J was clearly also influenced by pragmatic considerations. He explained that to test whether a woman had properly understood what caring for a child would be like would be unrealistic in the real world. In family planning clinics or doctors' clinics, there was not enough time to assess whether a patient appreciated what it would be like to raise a child.

---

[47] See also Sexual Offences Act 2003, s. 16(3).   [48] [2010] EWHC 1549 (Fam).
[49] At [63].   [50] See Keywood (2011) for an excellent analysis of this case.

Notably, in that case, although it was decided that Mrs A lacked capacity to make the decision about contraception, it was ruled not to be in her best interests to be compelled to have it.[51] It was held to be preferable to seek to persuade her to agree to have the contraception voluntarily. That may be contrasted with *A Mental Trust v DD*[52] where receiving the contraceptive injection was so important to her best interests that the court authorized the use of force if necessary to ensure she received it.

6.2 The law and sterilization of those lacking capacity

Is it ever appropriate to sterilize a person without his or her consent? At first, this appears a horrific suggestion, but it is a reasonably common practice. In the not-too-distant past, it was part of eugenics, whereby it was thought appropriate to sterilize 'undesirables' to prevent them producing children who would be similarly undesirable. Eugenics was seen as a way of ensuring that only the best kind of human beings survived. This kind of thinking was revealed by the judgment of Justice Oliver Wendell Holmes in *Buck v Bell*: 'It is better for all the world if instead of waiting to execute degenerate offspring for crime, or to let them starve for their imbecility, society can prevent those who are manifestly unfit from continuing their kind.'[53] Few were more enthusiastic about eugenic sterilization than the Nazi regime, which sterilized up to 3.5 million people.[54] Nowadays, few people openly support eugenics, but it is thought appropriate to sterilize people lacking capacity because to do so would be in their best interests. Nowadays, with the possibility of long-acting contraception, it is rarer for full sterilization to be necessary.

The legal position on sterilization is as follows. If a doctor wishes to sterilize a patient, the normal rules on consent apply. So if the patient is an adult and has capacity, he or she cannot be sterilized without consent.[55] If a patient lacks capacity, and a doctor believes that a sterilization would be in the patient's best interests and is the least intrusive way of protecting the patient's interests, then the sterilization can be performed.[56] Approval of the court must be obtained first.[57] This will now be governed by the Mental Capacity Act (MCA) 2005. In determining whether sterilization is in a patient's best interests under section 4, the MCA 2005 Code of Practice states that the courts should follow the approach that they have developed in the earlier case law, which was also based on ascertaining the best interests of the patient.[58] However, the House of Lords in *F v West Berkshire Health Authority*[59] emphasized that if the sterilization is for non-therapeutic reasons (that is, it is not required to treat a medical condition), then a court declaration that the sterilization would be lawful should be sought.[60] In the case of a child, this could be an application made under the Children Act 1989 or under the wardship jurisdiction. In the cases of an adult lacking capacity, the court can declare a sterilization lawful under the MCA 2005, section 15.[61] There is no need to obtain court

---

[51] See Herring (2010b) for criticism of this conclusion.   [52] [2014] EWCOP 44.

[53] 274 US 200 (1927), 207.   [54] Lombardo (1996: 12).

[55] The test of capacity to consent to or refuse treatment is set out in the Mental Capacity Act 2005: see Chapter 4.

[56] This is now emphasized by the MCA 2005, s. 1(6).   [57] DCA (2007: para. 8.18).

[58] DCA (2007: para. 8.22).   [59] [1989] 2 All ER 545.

[60] *Practice Direction 9E* under the Court of Protection Rules 2007.

[61] *A Local Authority v K* [2013] EWHC 242 (COP).

authorization if there are therapeutic reasons for the sterilization (for example to deal with excessive menstruation or to deal with cancer),[62] as long as the sterilization is the least intrusive way of dealing with the medical problem.[63]

It is not quite clear what the legal position is where a doctor fails to obtain a court order authorizing sterilization that is not for therapeutic purposes. Technically, the court order made in this kind of case is a formal declaration that the procedure is lawful. In other words, it does not render a procedure lawful; it simply confirms the legal position. It may therefore be that a doctor who fails to obtain a court order will be breaching professional guidelines, but otherwise will be acting criminally only if it could be shown that the procedure was not in the patient's best interests.

Where an application is made to authorize sterilization, the decision will be made simply on the basis of what is in the best interests of the patient. This approach was established in the following case.

KEY CASE   *Re B (A Minor) (Wardship: Sterilisation)* [1987] 2 All ER 206

The House of Lords was faced in this case with a 17-year-old with the mental age of a child aged 5 or 6. The issue before their Lordships was the legality of her proposed sterilization. Their Lordships held that the key question was simply what was in her best interests. Lord Hailsham, giving the leading judgment, focused on the terror and distress that the 17-year-old would face were she to become pregnant. He stated that she had no maternal instincts and that she would not be able to care for the child. Lord Bridge was careful to emphasize that the case was not based on eugenics. He stated that the only consideration was what was in B's best interests. In taking this line, he rejected the approach of the Canadian Supreme Court in *Re Eve*.[64]

Re Eve concerned the proposed sterilization of a 21-year-old woman. She suffered from learning difficulties and had struck up a friendship with a man. The point was made that the only reason for the operation was to prevent Eve from becoming pregnant. The Court was heavily influenced by concerns that sterilization may be used for eugenic reasons. It was emphasized that Eve was no more likely to suffer from a pregnancy than other women. The personal hygiene problems associated with menstruation were troublesome, but no more so than other matters of personal hygiene. The Court emphasized the point that the operation was irreversible. Maintaining the physical integrity of a human being ranked highly. A non-therapeutic sterilization was a 'grave intrusion' on a person's rights. It could therefore never be lawful.

This approach was rejected by Lord Bridge on the basis that it could require a court to make an order that was not in a patient's best interests. This was unacceptable:

This sweeping generalization [that non-therapeutic sterilizations should not be performed] seems to me, with respect, to be entirely unhelpful. To say that the court can never authorize

---

[62] *A NHS Trust v K* [2012] EWHC 2922 (COP).

[63] *F v F* (1991) 7 BMLR 135; *Re SL (Adult Patient) (Medical Treatment)* [2000] 1 FCR 361. If the case is near the boundary line between therapeutic and non-therapeutic, it should be referred to the court: *Re S (Sterilisation)* [2000] 2 FLR 389, 405.

[64] [1986] 2 SCR 388.

> sterilization of a ward as being in her best interests would be patently wrong. To say that it
> can only do so if the operation is 'therapeutic' as opposed to 'non-therapeutic' is to divert
> attention from the true issue, which is whether the operation is in the ward's best interests,
> and remove it to an area of arid semantic debate as to where the line is to be drawn.[65]

The courts have emphasized that because the best interests are to be the sole consideration, there are two other factors that should not be taken into account:

• The court should not take into account the interests of those people who are caring
  for the patient.[66] So, for example, an argument by those caring for a mentally ill
  woman that sterilization should be performed because of the extra burdens that the
  carers would face were she to become pregnant could not be a reason for providing
  sterilization. That said, the court might consider an argument that the burdens of
  supervising the woman who was not sterilized would be so great that the carers would
  fall ill and be unable to offer care. It should also be noted that the court will often
  be given information by carers from which it will decide what is in a patient's best
  interests. This might be thought to give the carers 'power' to present the image of
  the patient to the court in a way that is likely to lead to the order that they are seeking
  being made.

• The courts will not take into account eugenic considerations.[67] So the fact that the
  person might have a disabled child is not a relevant consideration.[68]

Those are the factors that are *not* taken into account, but what *is* to be considered? In
Re F (A Mental Patient: Sterilisation),[69] it was emphasized by the House of Lords that
the 'best interests' test was not the same as the *Bolam* test. In other words, it would not
be enough to show that there was a respectable body of medical opinion in support of
sterilization, but the court had to be persuaded considering all of the arguments that the
procedure would be in the patient's best interests.[70]

In deciding whether the operation is in the best interests of an individual, the court
will consider not only the medical issues, but also the broader ethical, social, moral, and
welfare considerations.[71] In deciding whether or not to authorize the sterilization, the
following factors have been mentioned by the courts.[72]

• Professional opinion is usually taken into account. Rarely will the court decline to
  authorize the sterilization where it has the approval of all of the professionals involved.
  In the few cases in which the court has refused to grant a declaration, the professional

[65] [1987] 2 All ER 206, 217.
[66] *Re B* [1987] 2 All ER 206. Although, in *Re HG* [1993] 1 FLR 588, the 'legitimate concerns' of the
patients' carers were a relevant consideration.
[67] *Re B* [1987] 2 All ER 206.
[68] *Re X (Adult Sterilisation)* [1998] 2 FLR 1124, 1129; *Practice Note (Official Solicitor: Declaratory
Proceedings: Medical and Welfare Decisions for Adults who Lack Capacity)* [2001] 2 FLR 158, App. 1.
[69] [1990] 2 AC 1.
[70] *Re A (Medical Treatment: Male Sterilisation)* (2000) 53 BMLR 66.
[71] *Re S (Sterilisation: Patient's Best Interests)* [2000] 2 FLR 389, 401.
[72] In *Re S (Sterilisation: Patient's Best Interests)* [2000] 2 FLR 389, 403, it was held that the 'best interests'
test was the same as the welfare test used in wardship.

opinion has been divided.[73] However, the Court of Appeal has emphasized that it is for the court, not the doctors, to decide what is in the best interests of the patient.[74]

- Sterilization will be approved only if it is a 'last resort'.[75] This is because forcing sterilizations on people lacking capacity infringes their rights under Articles 3 or 8 of the European Convention on Human Rights (ECHR).[76] So, if the court is to be persuaded that sterilization is appropriate because a pregnancy would be too distressing for the patient, then it will need to be shown that alternative means of avoiding pregnancy are not appropriate.[77] Therefore successful applications tend to include evidence that the contraceptive pill is not appropriate for some reason.[78] However, the courts do not appear to be at all strict on this ground. In *Re P*,[79] although the patient was successfully using an oral contraceptive at the time of the hearing, sterilization was approved because it was felt that there was a risk she might not take the pill regularly in the future. A court may be persuaded that the controlling of severe menstrual bleeding justifies sterilization rather than other forms of contraception.[80]

- The court will need to be persuaded that any alleged risk of pregnancy is not fanciful. Applications are therefore often supported by evidence that the patient is showing an interest in members of the opposite sex, or is involved in an intimate relationship, or even that she is 'attractive'.[81] In *Re W*,[82] it was held that the risk of pregnancy was slight, but the sterilization was approved because it was supported by the medical experts. In *Re HG*,[83] sterilization was approved even though there was no evidence that the woman was sexually active. More recent decisions seem to take a stricter line.[84] In *Re LC*,[85] Thorpe LJ refused to approve of a proposed sterilization because he believed that the patient's carers were constantly supervising her and therefore that she was adequately protected from the risk of pregnancy.[86]

- The ability of the person to care for any child born following a pregnancy is a factor sometimes mentioned by the court.[87] This is said to be relevant where the child will have to be removed from the patient soon after birth and that this action would cause the patient great distress.

Usually, consideration of these factors leads the court not to approve sterilization. Although in one notable recent case, approval was granted.

---

[73] For example, *Re D* [1976] 1 All ER 326; *Re LC* [1997] 2 FLR 258 (in which the patient's key social worker opposed the operation).

[74] *Re A (Medical Treatment: Male Sterilisation)* [2000] 1 FCR 193.

[75] *Re B* [1987] 2 All ER 206, 218, *per* Lord Oliver.

[76] *Re A (Medical Treatment: Male Sterilisation)* [2000] 1 FCR 193.

[77] *A Local Authority v K* [2013] EWHC 242 (COP).

[78] In *Re P (A Minor) (Wardship: Sterilisation)* [1989] 1 FLR 182.

[79] [1989] 1 FLR 182.

[80] *Re Z (Medical Treatment: Hysterectomy)* [2000] 1 FCR 274, in which it was said that her periods brought her nothing but pain and discomfort. But is there anything unusual in that?

[81] *Re P (A Minor) (Wardship: Sterilisation)* [1989] 1 FLR 182; *SL v SL* [2000] 2 FCR 452.

[82] [1993] 1 FLR 381.   [83] [1993] 1 FLR 588.

[84] *Re S (Medical Treatment: Adult Sterilisation)* [1998] 1 FLR 994; *Re LC (Medical Treatment: Sterilisation)* [1997] 2 FLR 258.

[85] [1997] 2 FLR 258.

[86] See also *Re S* [1998] 1 FLR 944, in which a sterilization was not approved because there was insufficient proof of a risk of pregnancy.

[87] *Re X* [1999] 3 FCR 426; *Re M (A Minor) (Wardship: Sterilisation)* [1988] 2 FLR 497.

> ### KEY CASE   *A NHS Trust v DE* [2013] EWHC 2562 (Fam)
>
> DE had a very low intelligence quotient (IQ), with a mental age of between 6 and 9. He lived with his parents, whose care for him was strongly praised by the judge. They had helped him to have a remarkable degree of autonomy and independence. DE had formed a long-term relationship with a woman, MB, who also had learning difficulties. The judge noted that the social worker 'told the court how very unusual it is to see such an enduring relationship between two significantly learning disabled people, it is she said remarkable and very *precious* and should be valued and protected in their interests'. MB had become pregnant and her child had been taken into care. This had caused enormous disruption and distress to MB and DE, and to their families. DE's parents wanted him to have a vasectomy.
>
> Eleanor King J agreed. She accepted that, given his mental difficulties, it was not effective for DE to use a condom. Without a vasectomy, his meeting with MB would need to be supervised and he would lose autonomy. Further, without the vasectomy, DE's parents would suffer anxiety and strain. That would not be in DE's best interests.

Approval was also recently granted in *Cambridge University NHS Foundation Trust v BF*[88] for surgery that would have rendered a woman who lacked capacity infertile. However, that was because that was necessary as part of treatment for a tumour.[89] Without surgery her prognosis was six months. MacFarlane J stated: 'The loss of the ability to bear children is a matter of great moment in circumstances where that loss is irreversible and where BF has explicitly stated that it is her wish to have children.' Nevertheless, without the surgery she would die and not be able to have children anyway.

6.3 Criticisms of the courts' approach

There have been many who have been critical of the courts' approach to these cases. Their objections include the following.

- The courts are too readily finding a patient to lack capacity.[90] In *Re P*,[91] the judge accepted that P might have the mental capacity to marry, but she did not have the mental capacity to decide about a sterilization. This appears out of line with the normal approach to consent in medical law, under which even people with some mental difficulties are permitted to make decisions for themselves, provided that they have a basic understanding of the issues.

- The courts are simply too ready to declare a sterilization as necessary. Although the courts say that they will authorize a sterilization only as a last resort, in fact the courts are far more willing to grant sterilizations than might appear from their rhetoric.[92]

---

[88] [2016] EWCOP 26.
[89] In fact during the procedure it because clear it was possible to preserve her fertility while removing the tumour.
[90] Jackson (2001: 54); Lee and Morgan (1988).   [91] [1989] 1 FLR 182.
[92] Montgomery (1989).

For example, as Jackson, points out, it is surprising that the courts have authorized sterilizations without requiring evidence that the individual is fertile.[93]

- The law puts much weight on the distinction between a therapeutic and non-therapeutic sterilization. This distinction is not always an easy one to draw.[94] In some cases, the courts have accepted as a reason for sterilization the distress caused by menstruation. Some commentators have firmly rejected the view that menstruation should be regarded in this way as an illness.[95]

- The 'best interests' rhetoric is so vague that it enables a judge to reach a decision based on his or her own values.[96] It therefore fails to protect patients' rights adequately.

- Montgomery has argued that 'eugenics' arguments have been 'introduced through the back door'.[97] He points to *Re M*,[98] in which Bush J held that there was a 50 per cent chance that the patient, were she to become pregnant, would conceive a child suffering a mental handicap, and that if she did so, she would have to have an abortion and this would cause her harm. Justice Bush insisted that this was not a eugenics argument because it was based on concerns about the patient's welfare. However, to Montgomery, this method of reasoning has become a 'routine means of bypassing the restriction on eugenic considerations'.

- Brazier and Cave have expressed the concern that sterilization of the mentally ill provides an easy means of covering up sexual abuse.[99] In institutional settings, it is difficult to ensure that there is no sexual abuse between patients, or between staff and patients, and there are concerns that it is even routine. Sterilization means that staff do not need to be overly concerned about the issue because it is unlikely to come to light through pregnancies. They suggest that proper policing of institutions should mean that sexual abuse is avoided and that therefore there is much less need for sterilization.[100]

- The law fails to pay sufficient attention to the fact that any case of involuntary birth control violates a person's freedom to make reproductive choices for himself or herself.[101] Emily Jackson argues:

  My argument is, however, that honourable intentions will invariably fail to offer adequate justification for the non-consensual and permanent removal of an individual's reproductive capacity. That the sterilization of mentally incapacitated women without their consent is not generally perceived to be an egregious and violatory act reflects, I argue, a web of negative assumptions about the sexuality and possible future maternity of women with mental disabilities.[102]

  Notably, one study found that 68 per cent of mentally disordered women disapproved of their sterilization, and felt stigmatized and degraded.[103]

- The law purports to be gender neutral. However, it is difficult to justify the sterilization of a man as being in his best interests, there being no danger of pregnancy for

---

[93] Jackson (2001: 63).   [94] Hale (1996: 25).   [95] Cica (1993).   [96] Peterson (1996: 64).
[97] Montgomery (2003: 400).   [98] [1988] 2 FLR 497.   [99] Brazier and Cave (2007: 287).
[100] Indeed, sterilization offers no protection from STDs.   [101] Jackson (2001: 42).
[102] Jackson (2001: 55).   [103] Cepko (1993).

him.[104] This makes it far easier for the courts to authorize the sterilization of women than men. This might be said to be an example of double standards.

Underlying many of the criticisms is the view that to sterilize a person without his or her consent is a major invasion of that person's rights and dignity.[105] Freeman refers to 'the rights we have we have simply by virtue of being human. The right to reproduce is one of these rights. Involuntary sterilization, save where it is carried out for exclusively medical reasons, denies an aspect of humanity.'[106] Only in the most unusual of cases will that be justifiable. A representative of MENCAP is reported as saying of the *Re B* decision that, now, mentally disabled girls have been reduced to the status of pets, which can be neutered at will.[107]

However, to supporters of the approach under current law, the loss of ability to reproduce is hardly a grave invasion of a person's rights if he or she is unable to appreciate the nature of the right or to exercise it in a responsible way. It is easy to take the high moral ground and demand respect for the rights of the mentally incompetent, but that may leave them and their carers to suffer the consequences of unwanted and distressing pregnancies. Should the courts pay more attention to the high-minded musings of theoreticians or the wishes of those caring for the mentally disordered day by day?[108] Some commentators have suggested that the reality is that if we take a strict line in protecting the rights of reproductive freedom and do not sterilize, this will lead to an infringement of the freedom of movement and association of mentally disordered people. This is because if they are not sterilized, they will need to be supervised and have their movements restricted to a far greater extent than they would if they were sterilized.[109] This, in turn, leads to a debate over the importance of reproductive freedom. Is reproductive ability a key aspect of a woman's identity? Or is that to reinforce childbearing as an essential part of being a woman? Or is the law here enforcing a construction of idealized motherhood, with only the 'good mothers' being permitted to reproduce?[110]

7 Tort liability and contraception

A number of tort law issues can arise in connection with contraception. They include the following.

7.1 Contraception and side effects

A doctor prescribes the pill without warning of potential side effects. This is, prima facie, negligent.[111] However, if a patient claims that taking the pill has caused her to suffer medical conditions about which she was not informed, she faces an uphill task in establishing that the pill caused the medical condition.[112]

---

[104] *Re A (Medical Treatment: Male Sterilisation)* [2000] 1 FCR 193.
[105] Cleveland (1997).   [106] Freeman (1988: 75).
[107] Brian Rix, quoted in Brazier and Cave (2007: 285).
[108] Scott (1986). See Scroggie (1998) for a sympathetic look at why parents seek sterilization for their mentally disordered children.
[109] Keywood (1998).   [110] Bridgeman and Millns (1998: 342).
[111] *Pearce v United Bristol Healthcare NHS Trust* [1999] PIQR 53.
[112] *Vadera v Shaw* (1999) 45 BMLR 162.

7.2 Defective contraception

In *Richardson v LRC Products*,[113] a condom split and a woman who became pregnant as a result failed in her action against the manufacturer. She claimed that the condom was a defective product. The claim failed for three reasons.

(i) It had not been shown that the product was defective in the sense that it failed to provide the protection that 'persons generally are entitled to expect'.[114] Justice Kennedy pointed out that people were not entitled to expect that any method of contraception would be 100 per cent effective.

(ii) The woman had known that the condom had broken, but not taken the morning-after pill.

(iii) The *McFarlane*[115] decision (at which we will look shortly) had made it clear that damages were not available for raising a child.

In *Wootton v J Docter Ltd*,[116] a claim against a pharmacist who had given a customer a different contraceptive pill from that which she had been prescribed failed on the basis that the difference in pill did not significantly increase the risk of pregnancy.

7.3 Mistaken sterilization

In *Devi v West Midlands Area Health Authority*,[117] a woman went into hospital for a minor gynaecological procedure. By mistake, she was sterilized. Her religion outlawed sterilization or contraception. She received £4,000 for the loss of the ability to conceive and £2,700 for the neurosis caused by the knowledge of what had been done to her. In *Biles v Barking Health Authority*,[118] in which a woman was wrongly advised that she needed a sterilization, the claimant was awarded £45,000. This award in part was to fund in vitro fertilization (IVF) treatment.

7.4 Negligence in sterilization

If a patient is sterilized in a defective way, then has sexual intercourse leading to a pregnancy, can legal proceedings be brought against the doctor? There are quite a number of difficulties that would face such a claim.[119]

First, it would need to be shown that the failed operation caused the pregnancy. This is normally easily shown. It might be argued that the sexual intercourse, rather than the failed sterilization, caused the pregnancy, but the courts have not accepted such arguments, unless at the time of the sexual intercourse the applicant was aware that the sterilization was not effective.[120] The courts have also firmly rejected an argument that if a woman becomes pregnant following a failed sterilization, she has a duty to have an abortion, and if she chooses not to do so, then she cannot sue.[121]

---

[113] [2000] Ll Med Rep 280.   [114] The wording of the Consumer Protection Act 1987, s. 3.
[115] *McFarlane v Tayside Health Board* [1999] 3 WLR 1301.
[116] [2008] EWCA Civ 1361.   [117] [1980] 7 CL 44.
[118] [1998] CLY 1103.   [119] Hoyano (2015) provides an excellent analysis of the issues.
[120] *Sabri-Tabrizi v Lothian Health Board* (1997) 43 BMLR 190, a Scottish case, but one that is likely to be followed south of the border.
[121] *Emeh v Kensington, Chelsea and Fulham Area Health Authority* [1984] 3 All ER 1044, 1053; *McFarlane v Tayside Health Board* [1999] 4 WLR 1301, 1301, *per* Lord Slynn, and 1317, *per* Lord Steyn.

Second, it would need to be shown that the doctor owed the claimant a duty of care. There would be no difficulty if the doctor had treated the woman herself, or her and her partner together. Where it was the woman's partner whose vasectomy was unsuccessful, it needs to be shown that the doctor who carried out the operation owed the woman a duty of care. This will be shown if the doctor is aware that the woman is a partner of the patient. However, in *Goodwill v British Pregnancy Advisory Service (BPAS)*,[122] a doctor was held not to owe a duty of care to a woman who started a relationship with the man three years after the operation.

Third, it would need to be shown that the doctor was negligent. Two claims could be made here. It could be said that the procedure was negligently performed, in which case the normal law governing whether the performance of an operation was negligent would apply (see Chapter 3). Alternatively, it might be claimed that the doctor had made a negligent misstatement. This may be an assurance that the operation has been a success when it was not, or a failure to encourage the parties to use contraception until tests have confirmed that the operation is a success, or a failure to warn the parties of the small risk that the operation has not succeeded. In the case of such claims, the normal test for deciding whether a failure to give medical information was negligent will apply: was the risk such that no responsible body of medical opinion would have failed to give a warning, or is the risk so substantial that the court feels that whatever medical opinion may be, it is one of which a patient should be warned?[123] It is established that it is not negligent for a doctor not to warn a couple of the 1 in 2,000 chance that a sterilization operation of a man will reverse itself years later.[124] Professional bodies have stated that women should be warned of the 1 in 200 risk that sterilization will not work.[125]

Fourth, it would need to be shown that the claimant had suffered a loss. This has proved the most difficult issue. If the woman miscarries or suffers a stillbirth, she will be able to claim for her pain and suffering, although the sums awarded will not be high. If she decides to have an abortion, she could claim for medical expenses connected with the abortion, and for pain and suffering, and any loss of income. Again, the sum awarded is unlikely to be high. The greatest difficulty comes with cases in which the woman gives birth.

A child cannot bring a 'wrongful life' claim. In other words, it is not possible for the child to sue the doctor who negligently performed the sterilization. In essence, the courts have found morally repugnant the claim that a child should not have been born.[126] This is so even where the child has been born seriously disabled.[127] In *Criminal Injuries Compensation v First Tier Tribunal*[128] the Court of Appeal upheld a ruling that a child born as a result of incest, who had a genetic condition, could not claim injuries for being the victim of a crime. Henderson LJ stated:

> The injury of which he complains is, in truth, a complaint about the genetic inheritance which made him the unique person who he is. That is not a complaint of an injury sustained by him, because he, the person allegedly injured, has never existed in an uninjured

---

[122] [1996] 1 WLR 1397.
[123] *Sidaway v Bethlem Royal Hospital Governors* [1985] 1 All ER 643; *Pearce v United Bristol Healthcare NHS Trust* [1999] PIQR 53.
[124] *Newell v Goldenberg* [1995] Med LR 6.   [125] RCOG (1999).
[126] *MacKay v Essex Area Health Authority* [1982] QB 1166.
[127] For further discussion, see Scott (2013).   [128] [2017] EWCA Civ 139.

state. On analysis, his real complaint would have to be that he should never have been conceived at all. A complaint of that nature, however, is not a claim for personal injury, but a claim for wrongful existence, which . . . is not one which the law can recognise . . .

The woman can seek damages for the pregnancy and birth if it was her sterilization that failed. This can include medical expenses and money to compensate for the pain and suffering in connection with pregnancy and childbirth. In *Walkin v South Manchester Health Authority*,[129] it was confirmed that a pregnancy could be regarded as a personal injury (although Roch LJ had 'some difficulty' with that conclusion[130]). A loss of earnings can also be claimed. Similarly, she can recover for expenses associated with the birth.

But what about the costs of raising the child? Generally, the courts have been extremely reluctant to award damages for the raising of the child. There are a number of reasons for this: it might harm the child to find out that his or her birth led to litigation rather than happiness;[131] and there is a public policy against describing the birth of a child as a 'loss' to parents, because it is not possible or desirable to weigh up the joy that the child will bring its parents against the costs of parenthood. The leading case is *McFarlane v Tayside Health Board*,[132] which classified the claim for child-rearing costs as a claim for pure economic loss and stated that the normal rules of tort that applied to such claims should be used. This required proof that the loss be foreseeable, that there be a relationship of sufficient proximity between doctor and claimant, and that it should be fair, just, and reasonable to impose a duty of care in the circumstances. The House of Lords decided that it would not be fair, just, or reasonable to impose a duty of care in such a case. At the heart of their Lordships' reasoning was a moral judgement that the birth of a child should be regarded as a blessing and joy, not a harm. As Lord Millett put it:

[I]f the law regards an event as beneficial, plaintiffs cannot make it a matter for compensation merely by saying that it is an event they did not want to happen. In this branch of the law at least, plaintiffs are not normally allowed, by a process of subjective devaluation, to make a detriment out of a benefit.[133]

This reasoning has been criticized.[134] Emily Jackson argues: 'Where a patient has decided to have an operation in order to irrevocably remove the possibility of conception, it seems perverse to argue that they should regard the failure of this surgery as a blessing.'[135]

A second strand of reasoning is that the level of damages that would be awarded would be out of proportion with the wrongdoing of the doctor.[136] While it is true that the amount of money required to raise a child could be substantial, the argument is not one that is normally used in tort law. A driver who, through a moment of carelessness, renders another a paraplegic will not be heard to say that the level of damages necessary to compensate the victim is out of proportion to the degree of negligence. But it may be that behind this point is a point of public policy. Weir points out that, if such claims

[129] [1995] 1 WLR 1543.   [130] At 1553.   [131] [1997] SL 211, *per* Lord Gill.
[132] [1999] 3 WLR 1301.   [133] At 1346.   [134] Priaulx (2007a: ch. 1).
[135] Jackson (2001: 35–6).
[136] *McFarlane v Tayside Health Board* [1999] 3 WLR 1301, 1340, *per* Lord Clyde.

are allowed, we 'transfer to reluctant parents for the upbringing of healthy brats the re-sources needed by hospitals to cure the sick'.[137] While this is true, this kind of argument could be used to deny nearly any claim against the NHS brought by a patient who has suffered loss at the hands of a negligent medical staff.

Subsequently, in *Greenfield v Irwin*,[138] an attempt to claim that the Human Rights Act (HRA) 1998 required English law to provide compensation for raising the child was rejected. It was also argued that, even if there could be no claim for the costs of raising the child, a claim could be made for the loss of earnings caused by a parent giving up work to raise the child. This argument was unsuccessful too.

In *Rees v Darlington Memorial Hospital NHS Trust*,[139] a sterilization was performed negligently on a woman with a severe visual impairment. A healthy child was born. *McFarlane* was unsuccessfully challenged in the House of Lords. Unanimously, it was decided that it would be wrong to reverse a House of Lords' decision only four years after it had been made. It was agreed by all of their Lordships that sterilization cases were a special exception to the normal rules of tort law. Lord Bingham, for the majority, was willing to award £15,000 for the affront to the woman's autonomy caused by the steriliza-tion. This was not money to compensate for the expense of raising the child, but for her loss of opportunity to live her life in the way that she had wished and planned. The fact that the mother was disabled was not a reason for departing from the approach taken in *McFarlane*.

But what if the child were born disabled? The House of Lords in *McFarlane* expressly left this issue open. In *Parkinson v St James*,[140] a woman gave birth to a disabled child following a negligent sterilization operation. In a notable speech by Hale LJ, the em-phasis was placed on the fact that to cause a woman to become pregnant against her will was an invasion of bodily integrity. This interference with personal autonomy would continue while the mother raised the disabled child. In the light of *McFarlane*, the Court of Appeal was willing to award damages for the costs over and above the costs of raising a non-disabled child. It must be admitted that the arguments used in Hale LJ's judgment would point to an overruling of *McFarlane*. In *Rees*,[141] the House of Lords considered the *Parkinson* decision. Lords Steyn, Hope, and Hutton approved of the decision; Lords Bingham and Nicholls disapproved it. Lord Scott thought that the decision was wrong on its facts in that he thought that damages should be awarded only if the sterilization had been requested specifically to avoid the birth of a disabled child. Lord Millett did not express a view. So the correctness of the approach in *Parkinson* is unclear.[142]

In *Groom v Selby*,[143] a woman was sterilized, although the clinician failed to notice that she was pregnant at the time. By the time, the pregnancy was spotted it was too late (in her view) to have an abortion. The child was born healthy, but three weeks after the birth developed meningitis, owing to an infection picked up during the birth. The Court of Appeal followed the *Parkinson* approach and awarded damages for the raising of the disabled child.

---

[137] Weir (2000b: 131).   [138] [2001] 1 WLR 1279.   [139] [2004] AC 309.
[140] [2002] QB 266.   [141] [2004] AC 309.
[142] See Priaulx (2004) for an interesting discussion of the issues raised.
[143] (2002) 64 BMLR 47.

8 Ethical issues concerning contraception

Many of the ethical issues relating to contraception are tied up with one's response to the question 'When does life begin?'[144] Contraceptives that cause the destruction of a fertilized egg are rejected as immoral by those who see fertilization as the beginning of human life. We shall be discussing the question of when life begins when we look at abortion. Much of the writing specifically on contraception has been written from a feminist or religious perspective. We shall consider these next.

FEMINIST PERSPECTIVES

To many feminists, contraception has been heralded as a major contribution to women's liberation. Bristow, writing 'in praise of the Pill', stated:

> Whatever the Pill's faults, 50 years on from the time it was first synthesised it remains the best form of contraception that we have; and it seems unlikely that, without it, the struggle for women's equality would have come so far, so fast.[145]

Contraception has done much to give women freedom over their lives. The ability to control whether and when to have children is treasured by many women.

However, contraception is not without its feminist critics. We have already noted that there are concerns over the health risks associated with the pill, and developing better forms of contraception appears to be low on the list of priorities for medical research. A different concern is that contraception can be seen as of benefit to men in that it renders women sexually available without men having to bear the financial cost of child support. Pollock argues that current forms of contraception make women available for men's pleasure, through contraception that poses a risk to women's health.[146]

It has been suggested that women who use contraception can be stigmatized in a way that works against women's interests. MacKinnon writes: 'Using contraception means acknowledging and planning the possibility of intercourse, accepting one's sexual availability, and appearing non-spontaneous. It means appearing available to male incursions.'[147]

Gilder has argued that men are yet to grasp the psychological impact of birth control:

> [F]ew males have come to psychological terms with the existing birth control technology; few recognize the extent to which it shifts the balance of sexual power further in favour of women. A man quite simply cannot now father a baby unless his wife is fully and deliberately agreeable . . . Throughout the centuries, men could imagine their sexual organs as profoundly powerful instruments . . . Male potency was not simply a matter of erectile reliability; it was a full weapon of procreation. Women viewed male potency with some awe, and males were affirmed by this response. This masculine attribute is now completely lost. The male penis is no longer a decisive organ in itself . . . A man's penis becomes an empty plaything unless a woman deliberately decides to admit a man's paternity.[148]

It is noticeable that, in a survey of successful programmes reducing teenage pregnancy and the spread of STDs, not one of them had an impact on men's behaviour.[149] This indicates that women still bear the brunt of keeping sex safe.

[144] Marquis (2008).   [145] Bristow (2002).   [146] Pollock (1985: 66).
[147] MacKinnon (1987: 95).   [148] Gilder (1986: 106).   [149] Kirby (2009).

A VIEW FROM ABOVE

Religious views on contraception

Many religions have no objection to contraception. The most vocal opposition to it comes from the Roman Catholic Church, which has consistently opposed the use of artificial means of contraception. Pope Paul VI explained:

> God has wisely disposed natural laws and rhythms of fecundity which, of themselves, cause a separation in the succession of births . . . [This teaching] is founded upon the inseparable connection, willed by God and unable to be broken by man on his own initiative, between the two meanings of the conjugal act: the unitive meaning and the procreative meaning.[150]

The Roman Catholic Church does, however, permit the use of natural birth control methods such as *coitus interruptus* and others. To some, the distinction drawn between 'natural' and 'unnatural' methods of contraception is artificial, suggesting that even using the 'rhythm method' can be said to cause the destruction of embryos.[151]

The argument behind the Church's approach is that the purpose of sexual intercourse should not be pleasure, but the production of children. Gormally explains:

> [I]f I engage in contraceptive intercourse I undermine in myself the disposition to recognise that the good of sex is essentially connected with children. I act on the assumption that it has a separate meaning which makes good and adequate sense of it. This is to act as if there is a true good of sexual activity apart from marriage.[152]

Some Catholic writers have argued that contraception should be regarded as a decision against the coming into being of a new life, which is a decision against a basic human good.[153] But others have responded to this by saying that, to many people, the use of contraception is about deciding when it would be the right time to produce a new life, rather than a decision against life altogether.[154] The Catholic view has also been objected to on the basis that it would appear to say that there is nothing good about sex between an infertile couple.

Although this is the official teaching of the Church, there is evidence that, in fact, most Roman Catholics do practise artificial means of contraception.[155] Further, the teaching has been criticized by leading Catholic theologians.[156] The official position has been strongly criticized by those who say that it works particularly harshly in developing countries where condom use needs to be encouraged to prevent the spread of HIV and to control population growth.[157] Nevertheless, the Papacy has taken a firm line against contraception and its prohibition remains the formal doctrine of the Church.

The Islamic view of birth control is hotly debated.[158] At the strict end, there is a ban on all use of contraceptives;[159] at the more liberal end, there is less opposition. However, most Muslim traditions do emphasize that procreation within marriage is a religious duty, and therefore sterilization is nearly always objected to by Muslims.

Jewish approaches to contraception are also divided. The Orthodox position is that male contraception (for example the condom) is not permitted, but female contraception may be permitted for health reasons (such as danger to the health of the mother or the potential child). Conservative and Reform views tend to have no opposition to the use of contraception between married couples.

---

[150] Pope Paul VI (1968: 300).   [151] Moore (2001: 163); Bovens (2007).
[152] Gormally (1997b: 1).   [153] Grisez, Boyle, Finnis, et al. (1988).   [154] Moore (2001: 167).
[155] Sander (1993).   [156] Barth (1998); Burtchaell (1998).   [157] Curran (1982).
[158] Deuraseh (2003).   [159] Ebrahim (2000).

9 An introduction to abortion

Abortion is one of the most controversial issues of our time. This is, in a way, surprising given that it is, in the words of one leading commentator, 'a simple, routine and frequently performed operation'.[160] Indeed, it is estimated that 35–40 per cent of all women in England will have at least one abortion during their lives.[161] A recent study found that 16.2 per cent of all pregnancies were unplanned, in 29 per cent the woman was ambivalent about becoming pregnant, and only 55 per cent were planned pregnancies.[162] But to some commentators, abortion has become too readily available, with women treating 'babies like bad teeth to be jerked out just because they cause suffering'.[163] According to the most vehement opponents of abortion, we are witnessing via abortion the mass murder of the most vulnerable members of our societies (unborn children). To others, abortion is a fundamental human right that is an essential aspect of the move towards greater equality between men and women. To force a woman to go through with a pregnancy against her wishes would be the most profound violation of her body and autonomy.

We tend, in the UK, to take abortion and good maternity care for granted. It has been estimated that, worldwide, some 44,000 women die each year from unsafe abortions and 6.9 million are hospitalized.[164] Of all pregnancies worldwide, it is thought that 25 per cent are ended by abortion.[165]

The forms of abortion include the following.

- *The abortion pill* This drug (mifepristone) is taken in early pregnancy and procures a miscarriage by blocking the hormone needed to enable a fertilized egg to implant.

- *Vacuum aspiration abortion* A tube is inserted through the cervix up into the womb. The tube is used to suck out the contents of the womb, thereby destroying the foetus.

- *Evacuation and curettage* In this procedure, the woman's cervical canal is enlarged and the womb then emptied by suction or scraped out with a curette.

- *Intact dilation and extraction ('partial birth abortion')* The foetus is extracted into the vagina and the contents of the skull are sucked out. This kills the foetus. The body is then removed.

The 'morning-after pill' and IUD are sometimes listed in medical writings as forms of abortion, but under the law they would be contraception, rather than abortion.[166]

REALITY CHECK

In 2012, for women resident in England and Wales:

- The total number of abortions was 190,406—4.2 per cent lower than in 2006 (193,737).

- The age-standardized abortion rate was 16.0 per 1,000 resident women aged 15–44. This is the same as 2015 and 9.1 per cent lower than in 2006 (17.6).

- The abortion rate was highest for women at the age of 22 (at 27.9 per 1,000).

---

[160] Jackson (2002: 72).
[161] Furedi (1998: 161). See also http://www.1in3campaign.org/; http://mybody-mylife.org/.
[162] Wellcome Trust (2013).   [163] Hansard, HC (Series 5) vol, 732, col, 1100 (22 July 1966).
[164] Alan Guttmacher Institute (2017).   [165] Alan Guttmacher Institute (2017).
[166] *R (John Smeaton on behalf of SPUC) v The Secretary of State for Health* [2002] 2 FCR 193.

- The highest rate in 2015 was for women at the age of 21 (at 28.7 per 1,000).

- The under-16 abortion rate was 1.7 per 1,000 women and the under-18 rate was 8.9 per 1,000 women. Both lower than in 2015 (2.0 and 9.9 per 1,000 women respectively) and in the year 2006 (3.9 and 18.2 per 1,000 women respectively).

- Ninety-eight per cent of abortions were funded by the NHS. Of these, over two-thirds (68 per cent) took place in the independent sector under NHS contract, as was the case in 2015 (68 per cent).

- Ninety-two per cent of abortions were carried out at under 13 weeks gestation and 81 per cent were carried out at under ten weeks, which is slightly higher than in 2015 at 80 per cent, and considerably higher than 2006 at 68 per cent.

- Medical abortions accounted for 62 per cent of the total. This is higher than in 2015 (55 per cent), and more than double the proportion in 2006 (30 per cent).

- There were 3,208 abortions (2 per cent) carried out under ground E (risk that the child would be born 'seriously handicapped'). This is similar to 2015 when there were 3,213 (2 per cent) abortions carried out under ground E.

Thirty-eight per cent of abortions in 2016 were to women who had had one or more previous abortions; the same proportion as in 2015.[167]

10 Abortion: the law

The legal attitude to abortion is that it is a criminal offence, although the Abortion Act 1967 provides an extensive defence to any criminal charge.

10.1 Criminal offences

The starting point for the law on abortion is the criminal law.[168] Most abortions will be a criminal offence unless there is a statutory or common law defence. The criminal offences in relation to abortion are the following.

(i) *Offences Against the Person Act 1861, section 58*

Every woman, being with child, who, with intent to procure her own miscarriage, shall unlawfully administer to herself any poison or other noxious thing, or shall unlawfully use any instrument or other means whatsoever with the like intent and whosoever, with intent to procure the miscarriage of any woman, whether she be or not with child, shall unlawfully administer to her or cause to be taken by her any poison or other noxious thing, or shall unlawfully use any instrument or other means whatsoever with the like intent, shall be guilty of an offence, and being convicted thereof shall be liable to imprisonment.

There are a number of points to notice about this section. The first is that the offence can be committed by the pregnant woman or by someone else. The second is that if

---

[167] All of these statistics come from the Department of Health (2017a).
[168] For a discussion of the law, see Keown (1988) and Grubb (1990).

the woman is being charged, she must actually be 'with child', but if another person is charged, there is no need to show that the woman is 'with child'. This means that if a woman who is not in fact pregnant, but believes herself to be, consults a friend and together they attempt to use an instrument to procure a miscarriage, then the friend,[169] but not the woman, could be guilty of the offence.[170] The third is that the offence is committed only where the defendant intended to procure a miscarriage: so a pregnant woman who takes illegal drugs, foreseeing that by doing so she may cause a miscarriage, but not wanting to, will not commit the offence.

(ii) *Offences Against the Person Act 1861, section 59*

Whosoever shall unlawfully supply or procure any poison or other noxious thing, or any instrument or thing whatsoever, knowing that the same is intended to be unlawfully used or employed with intent to procure the miscarriage of any woman, whether she be or not be with child, shall be guilty of an offence and being convicted thereof shall be liable to imprisonment for a term not exceeding five years.

This offence prohibits the supply of drugs, substances, or instruments for use in unlawful abortions. Notice that, for this offence, there is no need to show that the woman was actually pregnant. In *R v Ahmed*,[171] a husband brought his wife (who spoke little English) to a clinic seeking to arrange an abortion for her (without her consent). The clinic realized that the wife did not understand what was proposed and so refused to perform the procedure. His conviction under section 59 was overturned on appeal because he was not supplying, or procuring the supply of, anything.[172]

(iii) *Infant Life (Preservation) Act 1929, section 1*

(1) Subject as hereinafter in this subsection provided, any person who, with intent to destroy the life of a child capable of being born alive, by any wilful act causes a child to die before it has an existence independent of its mother, shall be guilty of felony, to wit, of child destruction, and shall be liable on conviction thereof on indictment to penal servitude for life:

Provided that no person shall be found guilty of an offence under this section unless it is proved that the act which caused the death of the child was not done in good faith for the purpose only of preserving the life of the mother.

(2) For the purpose of this Act, evidence that a woman had at any material time been pregnant for a period of 28 weeks or more shall be prima facie proof that she was at the time pregnant of a child capable of being born alive.

These offences can be committed by anyone, including the pregnant woman, a doctor, or anyone else, such as the boyfriend of the mother. This offence can be committed only where the foetus is 'capable of being born alive'.[173] It will be noted that, under subsection (2),

[169] *R v Price* [1968] 2 All ER 282.
[170] An argument could be made that, in such a case, the woman has committed an attempted offence.
[171] [2010] EWCA Crim 1949.
[172] The court mooted the possibility that a charge under the Offences Against the Person Act 1861, s. 58, might have been successful, relying on the words 'other means'. A better possibility would be a charge of attempted assault occasioning actual bodily harm.
[173] See Davis (2011) for a detailed discussion of the 'born alive' rule, especially when applied to conjoined twins.

a foetus of twenty-eight weeks' gestation or older is presumed to be capable of being born alive. This is only a presumption and could be rebutted if it could be shown that, for example, an older foetus was not actually capable of being born alive or that a younger one was. According to Jonathan Montgomery, it is generally assumed in medical circles that foetuses of twenty-four weeks' gestation are capable of being born alive.[174] The phrase 'capable of being born alive' was defined in *Rance v Mid-Downs Health Authority*[175] as 'breathing and living by its breathing through its own lungs alone, without deriving any of its living or power of living by or through the connection to its mother'.

10.2 Common law defences

In *R v Bourne*,[176] it was accepted that there was a common law defence of necessity for a doctor facing a criminal charge of procuring a miscarriage. The case involved a well-known surgeon who performed an abortion without charge on a girl who was aged 14 and had been violently raped. The abortion was said to be justified as performed 'in order to save a woman's life'. The decision left the law in a somewhat uncertain state, although disputes over the extent of the common law defence are of little importance now, because it will not be wider than those provided under the Abortion Act 1967. In other words, whenever the common law defence of necessity provides a defence, so does the Abortion Act 1967.

10.3 The Abortion Act 1967

The Abortion Act 1967 sets out the circumstances in which an abortion is legal. There are special rules in cases in which an abortion is urgent,[177] but normally there are four requirements, as follows.

(i)   Abortions may be carried out only under the authority of a registered medical practitioner. In fact, all that the Act requires is that the doctor, having decided that the grounds for the termination are made out and deciding on the method of abortion, be on call and responsible for the woman's treatment throughout the procedure. Other healthcare professionals, such as nurses, can carry out the actual abortion.[178]

(ii)   Abortions can be carried out only in an NHS hospital or another approved place (such as a private clinic).[179]

(iii) Two medical practitioners must agree that one of the statutory grounds permitting abortion is made out.[180] In 2012 it was found out that some doctors were pre-signing blank abortion forms. That is not permissible.[181] It is not necessary for both doctors to see the woman, but they need to have 'sufficient information specific to the woman seeking a termination to be able to assess whether the woman satisfies one of the lawful grounds under the Abortion Act'.[182]

---

[174] Montgomery (2003: 391).   [175] [1991] 1 All ER 1230, 1241.   [176] [1939] 1 KB 687.
[177] Abortion Act 1967, s. 1(4).   [178] *RCN v DHSS* [1981] 1 All ER 545.
[179] Abortion Act 1967, s. 1(3).
[180] House of Commons Science and Technology Committee (2007) and Royal College of Obstetricians and Gynaecologists (2010a) suggest that the law should be changed, so that only one signature should be required.
[181] BMA (2017).   [182] DoH (2014).

(iv) All abortions must be notified to the relevant authorities. Certificates have been produced on which the doctors must set out their opinions as to the grounds that justify the abortion. There are further forms relating to the abortion requiring details about the method of abortion used.[183]

The statutory grounds are the most contentious requirements, but before looking at them, it is worth noting the following general points.

• The Abortion Act does not, on its face, provide a 'right to abortion' in any sense. A woman can have an abortion only if two doctors are satisfied that the grounds for an abortion are made out. The Act does not recognize that because a woman has chosen to have an abortion, her choice must be respected.

• The Act focuses on the opinion of the doctors. It is not, in fact, necessary to show that one of the statutory grounds was actually made out; it is sufficient that the doctors were of the opinion that it was. In other words, if the doctors in good faith mistakenly believed that one of the grounds existed when it did not, the abortion will still be lawful. This emphasizes that abortion is seen as a medical decision.[184] If the doctors are persuaded that an abortion is appropriate, it is not for non-medical people to seek to challenge that decision. Indeed, George Baker P stated:

[N]ot only would it be a bold and brave judge . . . who would seek to interfere with the discretion of doctors acting under the [Abortion Act 1967], but I think it would really be a foolish judge who would try to do any such thing, unless possibly there is clear bad faith and an obvious attempt to perpetrate a criminal offence.[185]

• It is extremely difficult to show that an abortion was illegal, because it is necessary to show that the doctor did not believe that one of the statutory grounds was made out. One of the very few cases in which a conviction has been upheld was *R v Smith*,[186] in which a doctor carried out a private abortion. The evidence suggested that he had made no internal examination of the patient and had not inquired into her personal history or situation. The only entry in the doctor's notes was that she was depressed. The jury convicted on the basis that the doctors had not in good faith formed the opinion that the termination was justified under one of the statutory grounds.

The statutory grounds for an abortion are found in section 1 of the Abortion Act 1967, as amended by the Human Fertilisation and Embryology Act 1990,[187] which states:

(1) Subject to the provisions of this section, a person shall not be guilty of an offence under the law relating to abortion when a pregnancy is terminated by a registered medical practitioner if two registered medical practitioners are of the opinion formed in good faith—

[183] Abortion Regulations 1991, SI 1991/499.
[184] Grubb (1990).   [185] *Paton v BPAS* [1978] 2 All ER 992, 996; *C v S* [1987] 1 All ER 1230.
[186] [1974] 1 All ER 376.
[187] An attempt to introduce a requirement for independent counselling before abortion into the Health and Social Care Bill 2011 failed. It is sometimes alleged that abortion is linked to mental health problems for women, but there is no clear evidence of this: RCOG (2008).

(a) that the pregnancy has not exceeded its twenty-fourth week and that the continuance of the pregnancy would involve risk, greater than if the pregnancy were terminated, of injury to the physical or mental health of the pregnant woman or any existing children of her family; or

(b) that the termination is necessary to prevent grave permanent injury to the physical or mental health of the pregnant woman; or

(c) that the continuance of the pregnancy would involve risk to the life of the pregnant woman, greater than if the pregnancy were terminated; or

(d) that there is a substantial risk that if the child were born it would suffer from physical or mental abnormalities as to be seriously handicapped.

(2) In determining whether the continuance of a pregnancy would involve such risk of injury to health as is mentioned in paragraph (a) or (b) of subsection (1) of this section, account may be taken of the pregnant woman's actual or reasonably foreseeable environment.

We shall now look at the four individual grounds in more detail.

10.3.1 *Risk to physical or mental health*

Section 1(1)(a) of the Abortion Act 1967 requires that:

> . . . the pregnancy has not exceeded its twenty-fourth week and that the continuance of the pregnancy would involve risk, greater than if the pregnancy were terminated, of injury to the physical or mental health of the pregnant woman or any existing children of her family.

Two things are required here: first, that the two registered medical practitioners are of the opinion that there is risk to the physical or mental health of the pregnant woman or her existing children; and second, that the risk of harm is greater than that which would occur if the pregnancy were terminated.

What is 'mental health' in this context? This is unclear. It clearly includes recognized mental conditions, such as depression. But would it include emotional upset? Also unclear is the meaning of 'risk'. Does the possibility of a mental condition have to be likely, or only a possibility? Until we see these questions raised and resolved in court, we do not know the answers.

Section 1(2) states that, in considering the risk to physical or mental health, the woman's 'actual and foreseeable environment' in relation to the risk can be taken into account.[188] If the woman is a teenager with limited family or social support, this would be an important factor to consider. It has even been suggested that it would permit an abortion to be carried out on the basis of the sex of the foetus if serious social or cultural harm would be caused to a woman by the birth of a child of a particular sex and if this could be said to have an adverse impact on her mental health.[189] Such a suggestion is, however, controversial.

The reference to the health of the pregnant woman's existing children is interesting. What is envisaged is a case in which the woman's care for her newborn will mean that her existing children's physical or mental health will be affected. This might most readily be

---

[188] Abortion Act 1967, s. 1(2).   [189] Morgan (1998).

demonstrated where the mother has a severely disabled child who requires continuous care, which might be severely affected by any new child. There is debate over what is meant by 'children of the pregnant woman's family'. The use of this phrase, rather than 'any children of the pregnant woman', suggests that the mother's stepchildren could be included; indeed, perhaps any children living with her.

Section 1(1)(a) can be relied upon only if the pregnancy has not exceeded its twenty-fourth week.[190] In practice, it can be difficult to find doctors willing to perform an operation on this ground where the pregnancy exceeds sixteen weeks.[191] But from when does this time period run? Kennedy and Grubb suggest four different dates on which the 'clock could start running':

(i)   the first day of the woman's last period;

(ii) the date of conception—up to fourteen days later than (i);

(iii) the date of implantation—up to ten days later than (i);

(iv) the date of the woman's first missed period—about four weeks after (i).[192]

None of these is entirely satisfactory. Approaches (ii), (iii), and (iv) all suffer from uncertainty, because we cannot be sure precisely when they occur. If a court were required to face this issue, it could take a number of approaches. One would be to consider what method most medical practitioners use for assessing the length of the pregnancy. This would lead to support for approach (i).[193] An alternative way of finding an answer is to ask why Parliament chose this twenty-four-week time limit. The answer appears to be that Parliament believed that twenty-four weeks from conception was the time at which a child would be capable of surviving if born.[194] This leads Murphy to support (ii), although arguably Murphy's view appears to be better designed to date the age of the foetus, rather than the length of the pregnancy.[195] A further difficulty with this argument is that it is nowadays thought that twenty-two weeks or less is the date at which a foetus can be viable. Kennedy and Grubb argue in favour of (iii).[196] They suggest that (i) leads to the 'absurd conclusion' that a woman is pregnant from the day on which she missed her last period, which cannot be true. Also, because the statute deals with criminal liability, it would be wrong to interpret any ambiguity in a way that works against a potential defendant.

10.3.2 *Grave permanent injury*

Section 1(1)(b) of the Abortion Act 1967 requires that 'the termination is necessary to prevent grave permanent injury to the physical or mental health of the pregnant woman'. It should be noted that this ground is significantly harder to prove than that under section 1(1)(a). Although both involve mental and physical harms, section 1(1)(b) is harder to satisfy in three ways:

(i)   the harm must be grave;

(ii) the harm must be permanent; and

(iii) the harm must be an injury.

---

[190] The House of Commons Science and Technology Committee (2007) decided that there was no medical evidence to justify reducing this time period.
[191] Furedi (2000).   [192] Kennedy and Grubb (2000).
[193] Montgomery (2003: 386) supports this approach.
[194] House of Commons Science and Technology Committee (2007).
[195] Murphy (1991).   [196] Kennedy and Grubb (2000: 1423). See also Grubb (1991).

The fact that this ground is significantly harder to prove reflects the fact that, under it, an abortion can be carried out twenty-four weeks or more after the pregnancy commences. Remember that the Act does not require a doctor to show that the abortion was actually necessary to prevent the injury, but that the doctors believed in good faith that it was. Paragraph (b) is different from (a) in that it does not specifically require the doctor to decide that the risks of continuing the pregnancy are greater than the risks of an abortion. However, the word 'necessary' is important here: if the risks of an abortion are greater than the risks of the pregnancy continuing, it can hardly be said that the abortion is necessary to prevent a grave and permanent injury.

10.3.3 *Risk to life*

Section 1(1)(c) of the Abortion Act 1967 requires that 'the continuance of the pregnancy would involve risk to the life of the pregnant woman, greater than if the pregnancy were terminated'. This ground justifies an abortion where the medical practitioners believe that the pregnancy involves a risk to the life of the woman. It therefore is not necessary to show that continuing the pregnancy will lead to the death of the woman; only that it might and that an abortion will reduce any risks to the woman's life.

10.3.4 *Abnormalities*

Section 1(1)(d) of the Abortion Act 1967 requires that 'there is a substantial risk that if the child were born it would suffer from physical or mental abnormalities as to be seriously handicapped'. Notably, this ground has no time limit and therefore it is permissible for a very late abortion to be performed on this basis.

This ground could be explained on two bases. First, on the basis of the well-being of the child, it could be argued that if the child will suffer appalling handicaps, it would be better for the child not to be born.[197] However, it may be noted that serious handicaps may fall well short of those that we might consider appalling. Second, it might be explained on the basis that raising a severely disabled child will impose such heavy burdens on parents that they should not be compelled to take them on.

It should be emphasized that the risk must be substantial and the handicap must be serious. This limits the width of the ground. The meaning of 'substantial' is disputed. Gillian Douglas has suggested that, in considering whether the risk is substantial, consideration can be given to the severity of the disability being faced.[198] Others claim that it would be strange if the meaning of 'substantial' were to alter depending on the nature of the disability. The guidance issued by the Royal College of Obstetricians and Gynaecologists (RCOG) suggests 'whether a risk is substantial depends upon factors such as the nature and severity of the condition and the timing of diagnosis, as well as the likelihood of the event occurring'.[199] It is also unclear whether the woman's view on whether the disability would be serious is relevant.[200] One study found a wide variation among those practising in the field over the relevance of the mother's view and how severe the disability needed to be to fall within paragraph (d).[201]

---

[197] *Mackay v Essex Area Health Authority* [1982] QB 1166.   [198] Douglas (1991: 94).
[199] RCOG (2010b: 8).   [200] Scott (2005).   [201] Statham, Solomou, and Green (2006).

The RCOG guidance also gives some suggestions on what might be regarded as a serious handicap. It includes the following:

- assisted performance: the need for a helping hand—that is, the individual can perform the activity or sustain the behaviour, whether augmented by aids or not, only with some assistance from another person; and

- dependent performance: complete dependence on the presence of another person— that is, the individual can perform the activity or sustain the behaviour, but only when someone is with him or her most of the time.[202]

The RCOG guidance lists the following factors that should be considered:

- the potential for effective treatment, either *in utero* or after birth;

- on the part of the child, the probable degree of self-awareness and of ability to communicate with others;

- the suffering that would be experienced;

- the probability of being able to live alone and to be self-supportive as an adult; and

- on the part of society, the extent to which actions performed by individuals without disability that are essential for health would have to be provided by others.

It is generally thought that this definition of serious handicap is a broad one. The ground has been relied upon to justify the abortion of a foetus that would have been born with a cleft palate.[203] The RCOG has issued guidance on cleft palates and abortion, which states:

> The issue of fetal abnormality is a sensitive one since there are differing interpretations of what constitutes a serious handicap. The evidence outlined above show that cleft lip and/ or palate are, in some cases, indicators of serious congenital malformations.[204]

It therefore refuses to provide general guidance except that each case needs to be dealt with on an individual basis. However, as the RCOG acknowledges, 'we do not have sufficiently advanced diagnostic techniques to detect malformations accurately all of the time and it is not always possible to predict the "seriousness" of the outcome'.[205] The BMA suggests that, in deciding whether this ground is made out, the doctor should consider:

> . . . the probability of effective treatment, either in utero or after birth; the child's probable potential for self awareness and potential ability to communicate with others, the suffering that would be experienced by the child when born or by the people caring for the child.[206]

Morgan, arguing for a narrow interpretation of this ground, suggests that consideration could properly be given to the case law on severely disabled newborns and the circumstances in which it is legitimate not to offer them treatment.[207] There has also been some debate as to whether a more serious handicap is required if the pregnancy is very well developed, while a less serious handicap would suffice earlier on.[208]

---

[202] RCOG (2010b).
[203] A cleft palate is described by the Cleft Lip and Palate Association (2005: 1).
[204] RCOG (2008: 4).   [205] RCOG (2008: 5).   [206] BMA (2004: 242).
[207] Morgan (2001).   [208] RCOG (2008).

10.4 **Emergency abortions**

Under the Abortion Act 1967, section 1(4):

> Subsection (3) of this section, and so much of subsection (1) as relates to the opinion of two registered medical practitioners, shall not apply to the termination of a pregnancy by a registered medical practitioner in a case where he is of the opinion, formed in good faith, that the termination is immediately necessary to save the life or to prevent grave permanent injury to the physical or mental health of the pregnant woman.

This covers situations in which there is a medical emergency and the abortion must be carried out immediately to prevent injury to the physical or mental health of the woman. In such a case, the termination can be carried out by one doctor and the abortion need not take place in an approved place.

10.5 **Where abortions can take place**

Section 1(3) of the 1967 Act states:

> Except as provided by subsection (4) of this section, any treatment for the termination of pregnancy must be carried out in a hospital vested in the Secretary of State for the purposes of his functions under the National Health Service Act 2006 or the National Health Service (Scotland) Act 1978 or in a hospital vested in a Primary Care Trust or a National Health Service trust or an NHS foundation trust or in a place approved for the purposes of this section by the Secretary of State.

This means that an abortion, even if based on one of the permitted grounds, will be illegal if the abortion does not take place in one of the permitted places. A private clinic requires the approval of the Secretary of State to carry out abortions. Specific approval is required if abortions are required for pregnancy after the twentieth week. Abortions after the twenty-fourth week can be carried out only in an NHS institution.

These provisions are straightforward, although complexities arise concerning the 'morning-after' drug RU-486, known as 'mifepristone'. This drug blocks progesterone (the female hormone), and that causes the surface of the endometrium to be shed and prevents implantation. However, the drug can also be taken to dislodge a fertilized egg that has implanted. Following *Smeaton*,[209] it can therefore operate as a form of abortion. The drug has been licensed, although its conditions require that it can be administered only at a hospital. The problem is that the pill is normally given to the woman at a hospital, who will take it and leave about two hours later. The drug will take effect up to forty-eight hours later. The question is whether her 'treatment' is taking place in a licensed place.

The issue was considered in *British Pregnancy Advisory Service v Department of Health*,[210] in which Supperstone J held that treatment included not only diagnosis and prescription of the drug, but also the taking of it. However, he held that any actual abortion was the result of treatment and was not itself treatment. This means that if abortion is by medication, then the medication must be taken in a licensed place, but the woman

---

[209] *R (John Smeaton on behalf of SPUC) v The Secretary of State for Health* [2002] 2 FCR 193.
[210] [2011] EWHC 235 (Admin).

may return home and the actual termination may occur there. Kate Greasley argues that although the decision is understandable as a matter of statutory interpretation, it showed little sympathy for women seeking an abortion.[211] As she notes, the pill can start to have effect a short time after taking it. That might be on the way home as a result of the decision. The benefit of Supperstone J's interpretation is that the medical team can be confident that the medication has been taken and control who has access to it.

10.6 'Abortions' that fail or in which the patient is, in fact, not pregnant

It might be thought the Abortion Act 1967 must provide protection from criminal liability where the requirements of the Act are complied with, but the attempted abortion fails, or it turns out that the patient is, in fact, not pregnant.[212] However, this is far from straightforward. The difficulty is that the Abortion Act 1967 provides protection in cases 'where the pregnancy is terminated'. Discussing these words, *obiter*, in *Royal College of Nursing of the UK v DHSS*,[213] Lord Wilberforce took the view that it was fanciful to think that Parliament intended the 1967 Abortion Act to cover unsuccessful abortion or attempted abortions where there is no pregnancy. However, Lord Diplock thought that it could not have been the intention of Parliament to render criminal those who are involved in an abortion, where the abortion is unsuccessful. Lord Edmund-Davies thought that such cases would not be criminal, not on the basis that they would be covered by the Abortion Act 1967, but that they would not be guilty of an offence under the Offences Against the Person Act 1861. Whether a court follows Lord Diplock's or Lord Edmund-Davies's reasoning, it is hard to imagine a court convicting someone involved in an attempted abortion that would have been lawful had it resulted in a successful termination.

10.7 Selective reduction

There is much debate over the legality of selective reduction. This procedure takes place in cases in which a woman is pregnant with multiple embryos, and one or more of those embryos are destroyed in order to allow the others to develop healthily or to preserve the health of the woman. It is particularly common where a number of embryos have been implanted in a woman as part of infertility treatment. As we shall see in Chapter 7, the maximum number of embryos that can be implanted in infertility treatment is three. A crucial point to notice is that, when selective reduction is performed, the destroyed foetus is absorbed into the mother's body and is not expelled.

There are two issues here. The first is whether the procedure constitutes a miscarriage and is therefore potentially an offence contrary to the Offences Against the Person Act 1861, section 58. It is arguable that the natural meaning of 'miscarriage' is that the foetus is expelled from the mother and that therefore a selective reduction would not be a miscarriage. John Keown has argued that it is.[214] He argues that the meaning of miscarriage relates not to the destination of the foetal remains, but rather to the failure of gestation.

---

[211] For further discussion of the case, see Greasley (2011).
[212] In such cases, those involved could face a charge of attempting to procure a miscarriage.
[213] [1981] AC 800.   [214] Keown (1987). See also Price (1988).

Even if the procedure falls within the 1861 Act, there is an argument that it is covered by the 1967 Act. Section 5(2) of the 1967 Act, as amended by the 1990 Act, states:

> For the purposes of the law relating to abortion, anything done with intent to procure a woman's miscarriage (or, in the case of a woman carrying more than one foetus, her miscarriage of any foetus) is unlawfully done unless authorized by section 2 of this Act and, in the case of a woman carrying more than one foetus, anything done with intent to procure her miscarriage of any foetus is authorized by that section if—
>
> (a) the ground for termination of the pregnancy specified in subsection (1)(d) of that section applies in relation to any foetus and the thing is done for the purpose of procuring the miscarriage of that foetus, or
>
> (b) any of the other grounds for termination of the pregnancy specified in that section applies.

This means that foetal reduction is permissible if it falls under the foetal abnormality ground or where there is a risk to the mother without the reduction. Kennedy and Grubb take the view that section 5(2) does not permit an abortion on the ground that it being a multiple pregnancy increases the risk to the foetuses that the mother carries, but arguably a risk that the foetuses will be lost is nearly always a risk of causing harm to the mother.[215]

10.8 Abortions in which the child is born alive

If the abortion procedure fails and a child is born alive, then the doctors must act reasonably towards him or her. Remember: to be 'born alive' means that the child must be outside the mother and capable of independent existence. Indeed, to kill a child born alive could be murder.[216] Failing to provide the born child with a reasonable level of medical care might lead to a murder or manslaughter conviction. However, in many cases, the child may be so ill that not providing medical care will be deemed in the child's best interests.[217] The summary of the advice from the RCOG is that:

> A fetus born alive after termination for a fetal abnormality is deemed to be a child and must be treated in his or her best interests and managed within published guidance for neonatal practice. A fetus born alive with abnormalities incompatible with long-term survival should be managed to maintain comfort and dignity during terminal care.[218]

10.9 Reporting abortions

The Abortion Regulations 1991[219] provide the forms that need to be completed by the practitioners involved with an abortion. One interesting point revealed by these forms is that their format permits the two medical practitioners to state different grounds for the abortion. In other words, it indicates the abortion is lawful if the two practitioners agree that one of the statutory grounds is made out, even if they cannot agree

---

[215] Kennedy and Grubb (2000).
[216] The Abortion Act 1967 provides no defence to a charge of murder or manslaughter.
[217] See further the discussion in Chapter 9.   [218] RCOG (2010b: 7).   [219] SI 1991/499.

which one. The Abortion (Amendment) (England) Regulations 2002[220] introduced a change to the form, which means that rather than the patient's name being put on the form, her patient identity number and postcode are used. The forms are used to collate statistics on abortion, although it is not quite clear why this should be so. There are no other operations for which the government centrally collects information of this kind. Even with the 2002 Regulations, it might be felt that patients' confidentiality is inadequately protected. However, in *Department of Health v Information Commissioner*,[221] the Department of Health was required to disclose anonymized data about abortion statistics under the Freedom of Information Act 2000. The fact that it was anonymized meant that it was not 'personal data', which is protected from disclosure.[222]

10.10 The involvement of non-doctors in abortions

In *Royal College of Nursing of the UK v DHSS*,[223] the meaning of 'when a pregnancy is terminated by a registered medical practitioner' was considered. The majority of their Lordships took the view that the Abortion Act 1967 was designed to ensure that the abortion is carried out with all proper skill and in hygienic conditions. It did not require every part of the procedure to be performed by a doctor. Lord Diplock explained:

> [T]he requirements of the subsection are satisfied when the treatment for termination of a pregnancy is one prescribed by a registered medical practitioner carried out in accordance with his direction and of which a registered medical practitioner remains in charge throughout.[224]

There is a problem here with the drug RU-486 mentioned earlier. If the woman takes the drug, is the termination 'by a medical practitioner'? The problem arises particularly in cases in which the miscarriage produced by the drug occurs at home.[225] However, relying on *Royal College of Nursing*, it could be argued that if the woman is taking the medication under the guidance of the doctor, this should be regarded as analogous to other situations, such as nurses carrying out the doctor's instructions.

11 Conscientious objection

Of course, abortion is a highly controversial issue. Inevitably, there will be medical practitioners who have moral objections to the procedure.[226] The Abortion Act 1967, section 4, makes it clear that if someone has a conscientious objection to abortion, they are not under a legal duty to participate in any treatment authorized by the Act. This is subject to some limitations. First, it should be noted that section 4 does not affect the

---

[220] SI 2002/887.   [221] [2011] EWHC 1430 (Admin).

[222] For further discussion, see McHale and Jones (2011).   [223] [1981] AC 800.

[224] At 821.

[225] There is some evidence that women would like to have the option of a 'home abortion': see Hamoda, Critchley, Paterson, et al. (2005). The House of Commons Science and Technology Committee (2007) argued that this should be permitted.

[226] The BMA (2004) says that it is neutral on the ethical debate surrounding abortion. Although see BMA (2007d), which argues that, in the first trimester, the consent of the woman alone should be sufficient in law to justify abortion.

duty of a doctor to perform an abortion if that is necessary to save the life, or to prevent permanent injury to the physical or mental health, of a pregnant woman. So if a patient's life is in danger or she is at risk of serious injury, the doctor's conscience does not provide a defence to any legal action that may result from him or her not acting. Of course, in many cases, a doctor with a conscientious objection in such a case will be able to find a colleague to carry out any necessary surgery.

Second, the Act does not remove the duty on a doctor to advise. Therefore, if a patient visits a GP wanting to discuss an abortion, but the GP has conscientious objections to abortions, he or she should still refer the patient to another practitioner.[227]

Third, section 4 does not affect the duties owed to those who have had an abortion. For example, if, owing to a negligently performed abortion, a woman required a blood transfusion, a doctor could not refuse to participate in the blood transfusion because of his or her objections to abortion.

The leading case on section 4 is the following.

KEY CASE   *Greater Glasgow Health Board v Doogan* [2014] UKSC 68

The key question before the Supreme Court was the meaning of the phrase 'to participate in any treatment authorised by this Act' in section 4 of the Abortion Act 1967. Following a restructuring of a hospital in Glasgow abortion services were to be provided through the Labour Ward. Some mid-wives in that ward had conscientious objection to abortion and they wanted reassurances that they would not be required to play any role in abortion. In particular that they would not be 'delegating, supervising and/or supporting staff to participate in and provide care to patients through the termi-nation process'. The decision of the Health Board was that section 4 only applied to one-to-one care and that the objecting midwives could be expected to delegate and supervise and support other staff performing abortions. The midwives sought judicial review of that decision.

The Supreme Court sided with the Health Board and interpreted the section 4 exception to be limited to cases of person to person involvement in an abortion. The Court held that the treatment authorised by the Act is the whole course of medical treatment, which 'begins with administra-tion of the drugs designed to induce labour and normally ends with the ending of the pregnancy by delivery of the foetus, placenta and membrane'. Lady Hale asserts further that '[o]n any view [the term "to participate in"] would not cover things done before the first drug is administered'. Participation, therefore, did not cover care after an abortion or before the administration of the drugs. The basis of the narrow reading was not so much in policy terms due to a reading of the wording of the statute. Lady Hale summarized her reasoning in this way:

In my view, the narrow meaning is more likely to have been in the contemplation of Parliament when the Act was passed. The focus of section 4 is on the acts made lawful by section 1. It is unlikely that, in enacting the conscience clause, Parliament had in mind the host of ancillary, administrative and managerial tasks that might be associated with those acts.

---

[227] *Barr v Matthews* (1999) 52 BMLR 217, although it is unclear whether this is a legal duty.

It is important to note that the Supreme Court held that a claim based on Article 9 of the European Convention on Human Rights could still be made by a midwife if in the circumstances of a particular case reasonable accommodation for religious belief had not been made. Lady Hale held the Article 9 arguments were context specific and so could not impact on the general reading of section 4. This means it is still open for a midwife to claim that the hospital could easily have found someone else to carry out the role which was contrary to her belief but failed to do so. Supporters of the decision will claim that too wide an interpretation of section 4 could make running a hospital unworkable.[228] A line must be drawn somewhere and putting it between direct involvement in the procedure and subsidiary care is a reasonable place.[229]

The issue of conscientious objection is wider than abortion, but we will discuss it here because that is the context in which it most often arises. The issue of whether the law should permit medical professionals to refuse to be involved in abortions (or other controversial procedures) has generated heated debate.[230]

Part of the debate surrounds the meaning of 'conscientious objection'. There might be many reasons why a medical professional may not want to be involved in a procedure: they may feel tired; they may think the patient undeserving; they may think this treatment ineffective or a waste of resources. We could not allow any kind of objection to being involved suffice as an justification for not doing one's job and most supporters of conscientious objection certainly would not. They argue there is something special about 'conscientious objection' that makes it different from other reasons to object. Brock suggests:

> Deeply held and important moral judgments of conscience constitute the central bases of individuals' moral integrity; they define who, at least morally speaking, the individual is, what she stands for, what is the central moral core of her character. Maintaining her moral integrity then requires that she not violate her moral commitments and gives others reason to respect her doing so, not because those commitments must be true or justified, but because the maintenance of moral integrity is an important value, central to one's status as a moral person.[231]

This seeks to distinguish between beliefs a person has that are central to their 'moral integrity' and beliefs that are not core beliefs. Your feminist principles might be core to who you are, but your belief that hazelnut yoghurt is the best flavour ever might not. Neal and Fovargue argue it is important that health care professionals act as moral agents. They require them to morally assess what they are doing and to ensure they are not forced to act in ways 'that undermine the coherence of an individual's agency'.

To be required to act in a way one believes is gravely wrong is a major interference in one's rights.[232] If someone takes the view that abortion is 'murder' they will strongly object to supervising or supporting its practice, as well as participating in it.[233] Gerrard provides an alternative argument claiming that it is beneficial to society to have healthcare with a range of ethical views, representing a cross section of society, and that will include people with profound objections to certain procedures, such as abortion.[234]

---

[228] Wicclair (2009 and 2017).
[229] For further discussion see Fovargue and Neal (2015), Ekin (2016), Montgomery (2015), and Miola (2015).
[230] Wicclair (2013).   [231] Brock (2008).
[232] Lamb (2016). Lafollette (2017) suggests respecting another conscientious objection is a matter of moral courtesy rather than rights.
[233] Stammers (2017).   [234] Gerrard (2009).

Those who oppose conscientious objection might do so from three main perspectives. First, there are practical concerns.[235] If all those who have conscientious objection were allowed to refuse to participate in controversial procedures would the system break down?[236] At the moment, in relation to abortion, it does not seem to create unsurmountable problems.[237] An objecting GP is required to refer a patient to a GP who is willing to facilitate abortions and there are a sufficient number to provide an effective service. However, this relies on conscientious objectors being willing to refer patients. There is, Cowley suggests, something odd about that. He says that 'the duty [to refer] would be tantamount . . . to the objecting GP saying: "I don't kill people myself, but let me tell you about the guy down the street who does" '.[238]

Second, there are moral arguments. Savulescu and Schuklenk say:[239]

> Doctors must put patients' interests ahead of their own integrity . . . If this leads to feelings of guilty remorse or them dropping out of the profession, so be it. As professionals, doctors have to take responsibility for their feelings . . . The place to debate issues of contraception, abortion and euthanasia is at the societal level, not the bedside . . .

They go on to say that doctors who, for example, refuse to be involved in provision of contraception are acting unprofessionally. Schuklenk and Smalling[240] argue: 'Forcing patients to live by the conscientious objectors' values constitutes an unacceptable infringement on the rights of patients.' Sometimes the argument is that religious beliefs should be a private matter and not impact on people's public roles.[241]

Third, there are concerns going back to the definition of conscientious objection.[242] How do we know if a person who refuses to participate in a procedure is acting out of conscience or just does not fancy the idea of it? One possibility is to require doctors with an objection to appear before some kind of tribunal which would need to be persuaded that they had a genuine objection and good reasons for their objection.[243] This is what happens typically when at wartime and conscription is used, but someone wishes to conscientiously object. However, one may wonder whether this would be an effective or meaningful exercise. And what would the committee be asking: are these objections reasonable?[244] Or are they genuine?[245] It would not be easy to answer either question.[246] But if we don't ask whether an objection is reasonable do we have to respect the conscience of the racist and the misogynist, for example?[247]

12 Actions to prevent abortion

If a person wishes to oppose an abortion, is he or she able to seek an injunction to prevent it from being performed? It appears not. The leading decisions are as follows.

(i)   In *Paton v Trustees of the British Pregnancy Advisory Service*,[248] a husband sought an injunction to prevent his wife from having an abortion without his consent. Sir George

---

[235] Giubilini and Savulescu (2017). See also Minerva (2017).
[236] Wilkinson (2017).   [237] Maclure and Dumont (2017).   [238] Cowley (2017).
[239] Savulescu and Schuklenk (2014).   [240] Schuklenk and Smalling (2017).
[241] For a rejection of that see Sulmasy (2017).   [242] Clarke (2017).   [243] Card (2014).
[244] Liberman, A. (2017).   [245] Cowley (2016).   [246] Vacek (2017); Oderberg (2017a and b).
[247] Ancell and Sinnott-Armstrong (2017).   [248] [1979] QB 276.

Baker held that the father had no right to such an injunction. Indeed, he noted that the 1967 Act did not even require a father to be consulted or notified before an abortion took place. He did not, however, rule out the possibility that a court might order an abortion not to take place where a doctor was clearly acting in bad faith. Mr Paton also sought to argue that even if he did not have standing to prevent the abortion as the father, he could intervene to prevent it on behalf of the foetus. This argument failed because the foetus was said not to have any legal standing in the eyes of the law.

(ii) In *C v S*,[249] a man sought to prevent his partner having an abortion. The approach in *Paton* was followed, with Sir John Donaldson MR stating that even where it was claimed that the abortion would be illegal (that is, that the doctor was acting in bad faith), the matter should be left to the Director of Public Prosecutions or the Attorney-General. The court also rejected the man's attempt to claim to represent the foetus on the ground that the foetus could not be a party to the proceedings. He failed in the English courts and took the case to the European courts. The European Commission of Human Rights held that not only did he have no right to prevent the abortion, but neither did a father have even a right to be notified that an abortion was going to take place.[250] Even if the failure to notify him amounted to an interference with his rights to respect for his family life under Article 8(1) ECHR, such interference could be justified under Article 8(2) as necessary to protect the rights of the mother.

(iii) In *Jepson v The Chief Constable of West Mercia Police Constabulary*,[251] a curate learned of a case in which an abortion had been carried out on the disability ground. The alleged 'serious disability' was that the foetus suffered from a cleft lip. She notified the Crown Prosecution Service (CPS), which, after an investigation, decided not to prosecute. The curate sought a judicial review of the decision. She was given leave to bring the application. The CPS, in the face of her application, decided to reinvestigate the case, but decided, after a thorough review, that there was no evidence that the doctors concerned had not formed in good faith the view that the child would be seriously handicapped.[252]

These cases demonstrate that if someone wishes to object to an abortion being performed, it is highly unlikely that they will be found to have standing to bring the matter before the court, be they claiming in their own right (for example as a 'father' of the foetus) or claiming on behalf of the foetus. Any challenge to the legality of an abortion should be brought by the Attorney-General or the CPS.[253] If an individual wishes to challenge a decision not to prosecute, then judicial review of that decision is a possibility.

13 Abortion and adults lacking capacity

What is the position where the pregnant woman is incompetent and not able to decide whether or not she wants an abortion? The issue is resolved by applying the normal legal principles in relation to incompetent people. In *Re SB (A patient; capacity to consent to termination)*,[254]

[249] [1988] QB 135.
[250] See also *Re SB (A patient: capacity to consent to a termination)* [2013] EWHC 1417 (COP).
[251] [2003] EWHC 3318.   [252] Scott (2005) discusses in detail the issues raised by this case.
[253] See BBC News online (7 October 2013) for complaints that doctors who were alleged to have performed abortions based on the gender of the child were not prosecuted.

discussed in Chapter 4, a woman with bipolar disorder was found to have capacity to decide about her abortion. It seems that the Court strived to find her as having capacity so that she could make the decision. Holman J stated:

> It seems to me that this lady has made, and has maintained for an appreciable period of time, a decision. It may be that aspects of her reasons may be skewed by paranoia . . . My own opinion is that it would be a total affront to the autonomy of this patient to conclude that she lacks capacity to the level required to make this decision.[255]

The doctor can perform the abortion if that is in the best interests of the patient. It is not required to obtain a court order before carrying out the operation,[256] although if there is a division among medical opinion,[257] or perhaps if the incompetent person or her family is strongly opposed to an abortion, it might be appropriate to seek a court order.[258] In *Re SS (Adult: Medical Treatment)*,[259] a schizophrenic woman (S) who was twenty-four weeks' pregnant was being detained under the Mental Health Act 1983. She had had four children previously. There was conflicting evidence over whether it was in S's best interests to have an abortion or to continue the pregnancy. S was strongly in favour of a termination. S would not be able to look after any child born and so it would be likely that the child would be removed. Wall J, in deciding against an abortion, placed weight on the fact that S was nearly twenty-four weeks' pregnant,[260] which meant that the abortion procedure would be painful and traumatic, especially if done without the patient's understanding. He took the view that this would be more traumatic than giving birth and having the baby removed. As the following case shows the court will attach particular weight to the past views of a person who has lost capacity.

KEY CASE   *Re CS (Termination of Pregnancy)* [2016] EWCOP 10

CS had been in a relationship with a man who was alleged to have abused her. She became pregnant and told friends and relatives she wanted an abortion. She arranged to attend an abortion clinic but before she went she was assaulted by her partner and suffered a serious brain injury, as a result of which she could not retain information. At times she said she wanted the baby, but each time she then said she wanted a termination.

Baker J found that CS lacked capacity to make the decision about the termination. A 'best interests' assessment was therefore required under the Mental Capacity Act 2005. Baker J placed particular weight on the fact that prior to the brain injury she had wanted a termination and made an appointment to do so. Her sister and mother believed that if CS had capacity she would want a termination. CS's present wishes were fluctuating and hard to determine and so could not carry significant weight. It was also noted there were risks of injuries and particular falls, if the pregnancy were to continue. Overall it was in her best interests for the termination to take place.

---

[254] [2013] EWHC 1417 (COP).   [255] At [32].   [256] *Re SG* [1993] 4 Med LR 75.
[257] *Re SS (Adult: Medical Treatment)* [2002] 1 FCR 73.
[258] Stauch and Wheat (2004: 232).   [259] [2002] 1 FCR 73.
[260] At [62]. Wall J was critical of the fact that the pregnancy had been allowed to develop so far before seeking court involvement.

One controversial issue is whether a pregnant woman in a coma can be kept on a life support machine solely for the purposes of allowing her foetus to be kept alive and, in due course, born.[261] To some, once the mother had died, she has no interests,[262] or she has some interests and these are outweighed by the interests of the unborn child. To others, to permit the mother to be kept alive in this way is an affront to her dignity: it is to use her as little more than a 'fetal container'.[263] Yet another view is that the key issue should be what the woman's wishes were whilst she was alive. If this approach is taken, some argue that, especially if the pregnancy is well advanced, it can be presumed that the mother wanted to take the pregnancy to term if she had not made her views known in advance.[264]

14 Abortion and minors

In 2016, there were 1,564 abortions involving children under the age of 16 in England and Wales, a notable drop from 2014 when there were 2,339.[265] Where the pregnant woman is under the age of 16, the normal rules in relation to medical treatment of children apply. This means that if the child is assessed to be *Gillick* competent and consents, it is permissible for a doctor to perform the operation on her if the doctor assesses that to be in the interests of the child. There is no need for the doctor to obtain parental consent. This was confirmed in *R (Axon) v Secretary of State*,[266] in which a mother claimed that she had a right under the HRA 1998 to be informed or consulted if her daughter were to seek an abortion. Indeed, Silber J held that a young person seeking advice from a doctor on reproductive issues has a strong right of confidentiality. Further, there was an important public interest in ensuring that young people had access to confidential abortion and contraceptive advice.[267]

This approach was also taken in *An NHS Trust v A, B and C*.[268] A had just turned 13 years old. Applying the *Gillick* test for capacity (see Chapter 4) Mostyn J found that A understood the options open to her, the risks attached to them, and their implications. As a result A had capacity to make the decision and so it was for 'A to decide what she wishes to do'. It is interesting to note that unlike other cases where children consent to medical treatment the court did not make a determination that the abortion was in the best interests of the child. Indeed Mostyn J seemed to take the view that as A had capacity she could make the decision. It is not surprising that judges would rather avoid having to make a determination about whether an abortion promoted a child's welfare or not.

The Department of Health has issued guidelines that recommend that doctors encourage children to discuss the issue with their parents, relatives, or another responsible adult.[269] However, the guidance makes it clear that this is not a requirement.

---

[261] See a case in Ireland where this occurred: *PP v Health Service Executive* [2014] IEHC 622. A thorough discussion of the issue can be found in Heywood (2017); Sperling (2006) and Peart, Campbell, and Manara (2000).

[262] De Gama (1998) strongly rejects such a claim.   [263] Purdy (1990).

[264] Sperling (2006) argues that we should require very strong evidence that this was what the woman wanted before relying on this argument.

[265] DoH (2015a).

[266] [2006] EWHC 37 (Admin), discussed in Herring (2017c); Bridgeman (2006) and Taylor (2007).

[267] For evidence that illegal underground abortions are still performed in the UK, see BBC News online (23 November 2007).

[268] [2014] EWHC 1445 (Fam).

[269] DoH (2004b). Herring (1997b) provides arguments in favour of such an approach.

Technically, if the child is judged *Gillick* competent and does not want an abortion, it is permissible for a doctor still to carry out the abortion if that is consented to by someone who has parental responsibility for her and the doctor assesses the abortion to be in the girl's best interests. It is hoped that no doctor would want to perform an abortion in such a case.[270] What if the girl is incompetent? The issue then is simply whether the doctor believes the abortion is in the best interests of the patient. If he or she does, and someone with parental responsibility for the child consents, then there is no need for the doctor to obtain the approval of the court before doing so.

15 A right to abortion

As will be clear from the above discussion, English law does not formally acknowledge a woman's right to an abortion. It is for the doctor to decide whether an abortion is appropriate and whether one of the statutory grounds is made out. In practice, it might be argued that if a woman wants an abortion, then, provided that she is in the early stages of pregnancy, she is likely to find a doctor who will authorize an abortion. So, whatever the appearance of the law, it might be said that practice operates as if there were a right to an abortion, even if formally there is not. The issue has recently been considered by the European Court of Human Rights (ECtHR).[271]

KEY CASE   *A, B and C v Ireland* [2010] ECHR 2032

Three women, A, B, and C, argued that their rights under Articles 2, 3, 8, and 14 ECHR had been breached because they had to travel to England in order to have an abortion. Irish law does not permit abortions, save in a very limited number of cases, but does allow women to travel abroad to have an abortion. The three cases raised slightly different issues. By and large, the claims failed.

- A was a recovering alcoholic and her children were in care. She became pregnant and felt unable to care for the child, so wanted an abortion. She travelled to England, but had to do so alone and in secret to avoid social services finding out, because she feared that this would affect the contact she had with the children in care.

- B became pregnant, despite taking the morning-after pill. Her doctors were concerned that her pregnancy might be ectopic (it was not, as it transpired). She travelled to England for an abortion.

- C became pregnant while recovering from cancer. She could not find a doctor who could advise her on whether the pregnancy posed a risk to her health or life. In relation to C, the court upheld the complaint that the Irish law failed to provide a sufficiently clear regulatory regime to inform the applicant whether she could have an abortion. She had an abortion in England.

---

[270] See Harrington (2014) for a strong criticism of this state of the law.
[271] For an excellent discussion of the approach to abortion in the ECtHR see Fenwick (2014) and Goold (2015).

In all three cases, the ECtHR held that Article 8 was engaged. However, it upheld the right of Irish law to prohibit abortion, stating 'that the impugned prohibition in Ireland struck a fair balance between the right of the first and second applicants to respect for their private lives and the rights invoked on behalf of the unborn'.[272]

However, the Court upheld C's complaint. Where a state does permit abortion, the circumstances in which a person could have an abortion had to be clear. In C's case, C had not been able to ascertain whether it would have been lawful for her to have an abortion in Ireland. This infringed her Article 8 rights.

This judgment will be a disappointment for those who hoped that the ECHR could be used to recognize a right to abortion. However, it does not, as some commentators have suggested, shut the door on recognition of a right.[273] First, it should be noticed that the Court recognized that abortion engaged Article 8 rights. It did therefore, in one sense, recognize a right to an abortion. It is just that the Court found that there could be good reasons for interfering in the right.[274] The Court in *A, B and C* held that 'legislation regulating the interruption of pregnancy touches upon the sphere of private life', which included 'the right to personal autonomy, personal development and to establish and develop relationships with other human beings and the outside world', as well as a 'person's physical and psychological integrity'.[275] In *R (A) v Secretary of State for Health (Alliance for Choice)*[276] the Supreme Court held that the requirement for women from Northern Ireland to pay for abortions in England did interfere with their rights under Article 8, but that interference could be justified in order to preserve the balance of powers between the countries of the UK. The Department of Health subsequently announced they would no longer require payment.

Second, the decision does recognize that, where abortion is permitted, the right must be clearly defined and exercisable.

Third, the Court placed much weight on the doctrine of the margin of appreciation. It noted that Ireland's approach to abortion was more conservative than other signatories to the ECHR. Nevertheless, it felt that, on such a controversial issue, Ireland should be permitted to adopt its own approach. It was notable that the ECtHR placed weight on the fact that the views of the Irish people supported a restrictive approach to abortion. The implication of the judgment is that if the views of Irish people change, it will be harder to justify the current law on abortion.

The European Court recently returned again to the question of abortion. In *P and S v Poland*,[277] a 14-year-old girl was raped and became pregnant. Although Polish law allowed abortion following pregnancy, she encountered great difficulty in accessing it. In particular, a range of doctors refused to perform the abortion on religious grounds. It was held by the European Court that states had to ensure that patients were not denied, on the basis of

---

[272] At [241].   [273] McGuinness (2011); Ronchi (2011).
[274] Confirmed in *R (A) v Secretary of State for Health (Alliance for Choice)* [2017] UKSC 41.
[275] *A, B and C v Ireland* [2010] ECHR 2032, [106]–[107].
[276] [2017] UKSC 41.   [277] Application no. 57375/08 [2012] ECHR 1853.

conscientious objection by healthcare professionals, access to treatment to which they were legally entitled. The girl had not been given clear advice on how to obtain the abortion to which she was entitled. Article 8's protection for the right to respect to private and family life covered decisions to become or not become a parent. The Court then went further and found that the way in which the girl had been treated breached Article 3, having regard to all of the circumstances, including the procrastination in dealing with her case, the lack of objective counselling, and the fact that she had been separated from her mother.

16 Discussion of abortion law in the UK

There are a number of themes that run through the legal treatment of abortion. One is the medicalized model of abortion, in which the judgement of doctors is key to the legality of abortion procedures. As Sheldon puts it: '[I]if the law aims to protect and entrench any rights it is not those of the woman (nor indeed those of the foetus) but rather those of the doctor.'[278] Indeed, the wording of the Act does not even require the woman to consent to the abortion. By contrast, in other countries, abortion is seen as a private matter for the woman alone.[279]

The historical explanation of the English abortion law can be found in the debates surrounding the Abortion Act 1967. As Sheldon's analysis of these demonstrates, much weight was placed by campaigners in favour of the Act on the image of a woman at the end of her tether, desperate for an abortion without which she and her family may be plunged into despair.[280] This image meant that the woman was regarded as barely competent, and therefore that the doctor had to be the one to decide that the abortion was appropriate and help to make the decision for the confused woman. In fact, Sheldon goes so far as to claim that, far from being a liberalizing measure, the 1967 Act was about putting in place a more rigorous and subtle system of medical control over women's fertility.[281] She argues that the Act means that the abortion decision is made by the doctor. She argues that the decision should be made by the woman: '[A]ny system of abortion must decide on one person who should be empowered to make such a decision. It seems to me that this can only be the pregnant woman.'[282] Marie Fox has made the interesting point that regarding abortion as a medical issue has had one benefit for pregnant women, in that it has produced an obstacle for men seeking to challenge the legality of an abortion.[283] The matter is one for medical experts, rather than lay people, and so any outsider seeking to challenge abortion is unlikely to succeed.

Despite these points, there is general agreement that, in practice, a woman who is seeking an abortion, at least in the first three months of pregnancy, will face few obstacles to obtaining one.[284] Many doctors appear to operate on the principle that if a woman wants an abortion, she should have one. To some, then, the criticisms of Sheldon and others fail to appreciate that the Act is, in a sense, a benign fiction. Whatever the Act says, in truth, a woman who wants an abortion, at least in the first three months, will get one. But such points may overlook the symbolic power of the wording of the

---

[278] Sheldon (1997: 42).   [279] Lee (2003).   [280] Sheldon (1997: 38–41).
[281] Sheldon (1997: 30).   [282] Sheldon (1997: 4).   [283] Fox (1998).
[284] Lee (2002) argues that, after sixteen weeks, few doctors are willing to agree to an abortion, and in many areas only a few will terminate pregnancies after the twelfth week.

Act. Abortion is not widely seen as an entitlement and, if anything, carries stigma. Interestingly, in a major research project looking at why pregnant teenagers reach a decision over abortion, the researchers found that most made the decision on the basis of what was best for the unborn child. In other words, the abortion decision was seen by these young women not as a matter of their rights, but rather in terms of the rights of the child.[285] The message still sent is that pregnant women are not able to make decisions about their own bodies and this reinforces medical power.[286] As Sheldon points out, the meeting between the pregnant woman and her doctor is one that is pervaded with the doctor's power:

> . . . first at the level of a technical control of the means of avoiding reproduction, secondly at the level of decisional control—policing who should (and who should not) be allowed the possibility of an abortion, thirdly at the level of paternalistic control (where the benevolent doctor will enforce her views through 'persuasion'), and lastly at the level of a normalising control exercised in the medical interview over women seeking abortion.[287]

A different interpretation of the Abortion Act is that its regulation is surprisingly loose. The decisions are made in private, there are no prior notification requirements, and there are very limited grounds upon which a legal challenge can be made to the decision of the patient. It can be argued that the Act was specifically designed to enable the routine use of abortion in an attempt to reduce the number of 'unwanted children'.

There is a lively debate on whether abortion should be decriminalized. The BMA, the Royal College of Obstetricians and Gynaecologists, and the Royal College of Midwives have all called for decriminalization.[288] Sheldon[289] argues the legal framework is 'rooted in the punitive, conservative values of the mid-Victorian era' and requires reform. The argument is not primarily about particular prosecutions, but primarily about the stigmatizing message that abortion is criminal. In fact, there have not been many cases of people charged with abortion-related offences. They can broadly be broken down into three categories.

First, there are cases of people providing abortion services outside the terms of the Abortion Act 1967. For example in *R v Kaur*[290] a 51-year-old woman, Gurpreet Kaur, was sentenced to twenty-seven months in prison for supplying abortifacients. The case came to the attention of the authorities as some of the women who took the abortifacients fell ill.

Second, there are cases where people have sought to procure abortions or miscarriages of a woman without her consent. In *R v Ahmed*[291] the defendant sought to arrange at a health clinic an abortion for his non-English speaking wife, without her realizing what was being done. In *R v Erin*[292] a doctor ground up medication in his lover's drink without her knowledge in an attempt to produce a miscarriage. There are also cases where a defendant has assaulted a pregnant woman and caused a miscarriage and he can be charged in relation to the assault on the woman and procuring the miscarriage.[293]

---

[285] Lee, Clements, Ingham, et al. (2004: 16).   [286] Lee (2002).
[287] Sheldon (1997: 73). Contrast Wyatt (2000), who sees, in abortion cases, doctors working with pregnant women on an expert–expert level to reach an appropriate decision for the woman.
[288] Campbell (2017).   [289] Sheldon (2016 a and b).   [290] [2015] EWCA Crim 2202.
[291] [2010] EWCA Crim 1949.   [292] BMA (2017).
[293] *Attorney-General's Reference (No. 3 of 1994)* [1998] AC 245, although in that case the child was born alive and so a manslaughter charge was established.

Third, there have been cases where women have terminated their own pregnancies. In *R v Catt*[294] a 35-year-old woman purchased medication over the Internet and took it to procure a miscarriage. She then buried the body. She was convicted of procuring her own miscarriage and sentenced to eight years' imprisonment, subsequently reduced to three-and-a-half years. The BMA refers to the case of Natalie Towers, a 24-year-old woman who was sentenced to two-and-a-half years for procuring her own miscarriage when 32–34 weeks' pregnant, again purchasing the medication online. In both cases the court was told that the women had mental health issues.

The argument in favour of decriminalization has both a practical and theoretical aspect. The practical point is that 'the current threat and stigma of criminal sanctions may deny some women access to services, where healthcare professionals are reticent, or are not permitted, to be involved in all aspects of the provision of a safe abortion service'.[295] It is not clear whether professionals are deterred from being involved in an abortion for fear of criminal prosecution, although in the *Catt* case the woman had sought an abortion and been told one could not legally be provided. Perhaps a more common issue, is that:

> Criminalisation of abortion reflects a deep mistrust of women (and doctors) being able to make moral choices. It denies women fundamental rights to make decisions about their own bodies. Abortion should be treated in the same way as other medical decisions.[296]

That is a slightly odd argument because normally surgery will be seen as a criminal offence, which can be justified by the consent of the woman. Perhaps the argument is that the fact there is specific legislation criminalizing it creates a particular stigma against it.

The arguments in favour of retaining at least some criminalization relate to the first two categories of cases. It seems we need some kind of offence to deal with cases where pregnant women have their pregnancies terminated without their consent or where unsafe abortions are being offered unnecessarily. While some of the prosecutions of women who have ended their own pregnancies seems unduly harsh it may be better to amend the law so that pregnant woman who end their own pregnancies cannot be guilty of an offence, or make greater use of prosecutorial discretion, rather than making all abortion lawful.

17 Abortion: the reality

As already mentioned, 98 per cent of abortions were funded by the NHS in 2014, but 68 per cent of those were carried out in private establishments, under an NHS contract.[297] However, the rate of use of NHS facilities varies around the country.

By far the most common ground for an abortion is section 1(1)(c): the risk to physical or mental health. In 2017, 97 per cent of abortions were performed on that ground.[298] This has led some to claim that, in effect, there is abortion 'on demand'.[299] Some doctors have even argued that because carrying a pregnancy to term always carries health risks, it is arguable that there is always less risk to a woman's health in a termination than with continuation of the pregnancy. Whether such an argument would be accepted by

---

[294] [2013] EWCA Crim 1187.   [295] BMA (2017).   [296] BMA (2017).   [297] DoH (2017a).
[298] DoH (2017a).   [299] *RCN v DHSS* [1981] 1 All ER 545, 554, *per* Lord Denning MR.

a court is a matter of debate.[300] But if it were, it would suggest that the grounds for a lawful abortion exist in the first twenty-four weeks of every pregnancy.

As we have seen, English and Welsh law does not formally recognize a right to abortion on demand. However, it would be accurate to state that while the law enables there to be abortion on demand, it does not ensure that there is. A woman can have an abortion only if she can find a doctor who is willing to comply with her wishes.[301] There is little difficulty for a woman who is able to afford private medical treatment. If a woman is relying on the NHS, then the limited number of doctors in her vicinity could mean that if a couple of them are unwilling to agree to her request for an abortion (for example because they have a conscientious objection to such a procedure), then her choices become limited. Of course, with some perseverance and determination, every woman in the UK can find a doctor relatively close by who will be willing to arrange the abortion, but for some that may require quite some effort at a vulnerable stage of their lives. Sheldon argues that doctors' views still play a significant role in restricting or enabling access to abortion.[302]

Despite the generally widespread availability of abortion, those who are supporters of abortion provision still have concerns over the quality of it, including the following.

- *Availability* There appears to be few problems with women wanting an abortion, but finding it unavailable. However, there can be difficulties where an abortion is sought after the first trimester (that is, the first three months). Then, the number of NHS facilities willing to provide an abortion is smaller and some women have to travel long distances to access them.

- *Delay* There is some evidence of lengthy delays in some abortion cases.[303] It was reported that, in some cases, women have had to wait up to seven weeks for an abortion.[304] The government's recommendation is that there should be no longer than a three-week wait.[305]

- *Counselling and attitudes of healthcare professionals* One report looking at young women's experiences with abortion services found that, generally, the professionals whom they encountered were non-judgemental and respectful of their choice. However, a minority complained about being 'over-counselled' about the pros and cons of the abortion decision; others complained that there was not enough time in which to talk about their decision.[306] In one case, a young woman complained that her GP had tried to change her mind about having an abortion.[307] In fact, a slightly commoner complaint was of GPs encouraging those who did not want to have an abortion to consider one.[308] The BMA guidance on abortion says that 'doctors should ensure that the decision is supported by appropriate information and counselling about the options and implications'.[309]

- *Scanning* Being required to go through a scan prior to the abortion was disturbing for some mothers.[310] Understandably, for some, this *was* seen as a way of criticizing the decision that they had made.

---

[300] Sheldon (1997: 53–74).   [301] Clarke (1989).   [302] Sheldon (1997).
[303] Lee, Clements, Ingham, et al. (2004: 3).   [304] BBC News online (22 January 2007).
[305] DoH (2003c).
[306] Lee, Clements, Ingham, et al. (2004: 27). See Woodcock (2011) for a further discussion.
[307] Lee, Clements, Ingham, et al. (2004: 27).   [308] Lee, Clements, Ingham, et al. (2004: 27).
[309] BMA (2007d: 11).   [310] Lee, Clements, Ingham, et al. (2004: 35).

18 **The legal status of the foetus**

English law is clear that a foetus is not a person until it is born.[311] Baker P went further and stated: 'The foetus cannot, in English law, in my view, have any right of its own at least until it's born and has a separate existence from the mother.'[312] But that does not mean that a foetus is 'a nothing'. In *Attorney-General's Reference (No. 3 of 1994)*,[313] the House of Lords rejected an argument proposed by the Court of Appeal that a foetus should be regarded as part of the mother, equivalent to a leg or an arm. Instead, Lord Mustill declared that a foetus is a unique organism.[314] This, of course, leaves much open to question.

The courts, perhaps understandably, have sought to avoid the controversial issue of the status of the foetus and tend to talk more about what a foetus is *not*, rather than what a foetus *is*, but it seems that we can say the following.

(i)   The foetus is not a person. Only at the point of birth does the foetus become a person.[315] But once the child is born, he or she can sue for injuries suffered while he or she was a foetus.[316]

(ii)   The foetus is protected by sections 58 and 59 of the Offences Against the Person Act 1861, and by the Abortion Act 1967.[317]

(iii)   The foetus does not have rights that can be enforced by other people.[318]

(iv)   The foetus is not simply part of the mother.[319]

(v)   In *St George's Healthcare NHS Trust v S*,[320] Judge LJ stated that a 36-week-old foetus is 'not nothing: it is not lifeless and is certainly human'.[321]

(vi)   It is not possible to bring proceedings 'in the name of the foetus'.[322]

(vii)   A foetus cannot be made a ward of court.[323]

(viii) The foetus has interests that are protected by the law.[324]

(ix)   A foetus could not be abducted. So a man could not prevent a pregnant woman from travelling out of the country.[325]

The following cases give a flavour of how the courts deal with the foetus.

(i) **Evans v Amicus Healthcare Ltd**[326]   The Court of Appeal heard a dispute over what should happen to a frozen embryo created using the gametes of a couple who were

---

[311] See Alghrani and Brazier (2011) for a helpful discussion.
[312] *Paton v BPAS* [1978] 2 All ER 987, 989.   [313] [1998] AC 245.
[314] An approach approved by the Court of Appeal in *CP (a child) v First-tier Tribunal (Criminal Injuries Compensation)* [2014] EWCA Civ 1554.
[315] *CP (a child) v First-tier Tribunal (Criminal Injuries Compensation)* [2014] EWCA Civ 1554.
[316] Under the Congenital Disabilities (Civil Liability) Act 1976. In *Burton v Islington Health Authority* [1993] QB 204, it was explained that the foetus's potential claim crystallizes at birth.
[317] *Re SB (A patient: capacity to consent to a termination)* [2013] EWHC 1417 (COP).
[318] BMA (2004: 227).   [319] *Attorney-General's Reference (No. 3 of 1994)* [1998] AC 245.
[320] (1998) 44 BMLR 160, 163.
[321] For discussion and criticism of this comment, see Fovargue and Miola (1998).
[322] *Paton v BPAS* [1978] 2 All ER 987.   [323] *Re F (In Utero)* [1988] Fam 122 (CA).
[324] Judge LJ in *St George's NHS Trust v S* (1998) 44 BMLR 160. See also *R v Gibson* [1990] 2 QB 619, in which an artist who displayed two earrings created from freeze-dried human foetuses of between three and four months' duration was convicted of the offence of a conspiracy to outrage public decency.
[325] *Re J* [2006] EWHC 2199 (Fam).   [326] [2004] 3 All ER 1025.

undergoing assisted reproductive treatment. The case is discussed in detail in Chapter 7. Essentially, the man wanted the embryo destroyed, while the woman wanted to keep the embryo. The woman sought to argue that the rights of the embryo should be taken into account in their dispute. Lord Justice Thorpe felt that the position in English law was so clear that he did not even need to hear the barristers' arguments on the issue:

> In our domestic law it has been repeatedly held that a foetus prior to the moment of birth does not have independent rights or interests: see *Re F (In Utero)* [1988] (Fam) 122 and *Re MB (Medical Treatment)* (1997) 2 FLR 426. Thus even more clearly can there be no independent rights or interests in stored embryos. In this respect our law is not inconsistent with the decisions of the ECHR. Article 2 protects the right to life. No Convention jurisprudence extends the right to an embryo, much less to one which at the material point of time is non-viable.[327]

It is possible that Thorpe LJ dealt with this issue a little too quickly. Although it is clearly established that the foetus has no interests that can trump the rights of autonomy or bodily integrity of the mother (as the cases he cites shows), this does not mean that the foetus has no rights at all.

(ii) ***Attorney-General's Reference (No. 3 of 1994)***[328] The case involved a man who stabbed a pregnant woman, injuring both her and her foetus. The child was subsequently born, lived for a short while, and then died. The man was charged with murder. The House of Lords emphasized that murder involved the killing of a human being; therefore the killing of a foetus was not murder. However, once the foetus was born alive, it was a person. The man had therefore, in this case, killed a person. He was not guilty of murder, because he lacked the necessary intention to kill or to cause grievous bodily harm to the victim, but could be guilty of manslaughter.

Lord Mustill had the following to say about a foetus. He first rejected the view expressed in the Court of Appeal that the foetus should be regarded as part of the mother:

> The emotional bond between the mother and her unborn child was also of a very special kind. But the relationship was one of bond, not of identity. The mother and the foetus were two distinct organisms living symbiotically, not a single organism with two aspects. The mother's leg was part of the mother; the foetus was not.[329]

He went on to say:

> [T]he foetus does not (for the purposes of the law of homicide and violent crime) have any relevant type of personality but is an organism sui generis lacking at this stage the entire range of characteristics both of the mother to which it is physically linked and of the complete human being which it will later become . . . I would, therefore, reject the reasoning which assumes that since (in the eyes of English law) the foetus does not have the attributes which make it a 'person' it must be an adjunct of the mother. Eschewing all religious and political debate I would say that the foetus is neither. It is a unique organism.[330]

(iii) In ***CP (a child) v First-tier Tribunal (Criminal Injuries Compensation)***[331] CP was born with foetal alcohol spectrum disorder, caused by her mother's excessive

---

[327] At 1027.   [328] [1998] AC 245.   [329] At 275.   [330] At 256–7.
[331] [2014] EWCA Civ 1554.

drinking of alcohol while pregnant. It was claimed the mother was aware of the dangers, but drank excessively anyway. On CP's behalf an application was made for compensation from the Criminal Injuries Compensation Authority (CICA). They award compensation to certain victims of crime. The CICA refused to grant compensation on the basis that CP's condition was not the result of a crime of violence. CP sought a judicial review, claiming that she had been the victim of the offence under section 23 of the Offences Against the Person Act 1861: unlawfully administering to any other person any poison or noxious thing so as to inflict grievous bodily harm.

The Court of Appeal confirmed that the foetus was not another person in the eyes of the law so at the time of the drinking it could not be said the mother was administering a poison to another person. The crime alleged had occurred to the child in utero and although it became manifest post-birth the actual injury had been sustained prior to birth.[332] It could not, therefore, be said that CP was a person who had been the victim of a crime.

There has been much debate over whether the foetus can claim protection under the ECHR.[333] The issue has been considered in the following case.

KEY CASE   *Vo v France* [2004] 2 FCR 577 (ECtHR)

Ms Vo attended a routine antenatal appointment. Owing to a mix-up over names, a doctor thought that she was present for the removal of a contraceptive coil. In attempting this procedure, he ruptured her amniotic sac and, as a result, the pregnancy had to be terminated. The doctor was charged with negligently injuring or killing the foetus. Under French law, the courts found that he could not be guilty of criminal offences against the foetus. The case was brought before the ECtHR. The claim was that the absence of a criminal remedy to punish the unintentional destruction of the foetus meant that the foetus's right to life under Article 2 ECHR was inadequately protected.

The majority (fourteen to three) found that French law did not violate the foetus's rights under Article 2. The majority, however, refused to make a clear ruling on the status of the foetus under the Convention. It was confirmed, as had been held in previous cases, that the foetus was not a person and so was not directly protected by Article 2. However, it was left as an open question whether the foetus could claim a version of right to life under Article 2. The Court explained that even if the foetus did have such a right, it would be limited by the mother's rights and interests. The majority took the view that, when the right to life begins and becomes protected by the Convention, it comes within 'the margin of appreciation' and that each European country can decide the legal status of the foetus for itself. This meant that although it was not contrary to the Convention for French law not to protect the foetus in criminal law, it would also not be contrary to the Convention for another country to protect the foetus. However, the Court held that there was common ground between European states that the potentiality of the foetus and its capacity to become a person required protection in the name of human dignity. The majority went on to suggest that even if Article 2 were to be held to protect the foetus, still its rights would not be improperly interfered with by not providing a criminal offence, because the foetus could be protected under the civil law.

---

[332] The application may have had more success if the alleged crime had been that of inflicting grievous bodily harm under s. 20 of the Offences Against the Person Act 1861 if it could be said the grievous bodily harm had been caused post-birth.

[333] Stauch (2001); Ford (2008). See *Paton v UK* (1980) EHRR 408 (EComHR); *Open Door Counselling and Dublin Well Woman v Ireland* (1992) 18 BMLR 1 (ECtHR).

In dissenting speeches, judges criticized the majority for not being willing to make a clear finding on whether or not the foetus was protected within Article 2. They were adamant that it would be perfectly possible to hold that a foetus was protected under Article 2, but still uphold a right to abortion. It could, for example, be argued that a case in which a pregnant woman harms her foetus is entirely different from that in which a third party does so (Judge Rees). Judge Rees argued that the civil law protection was inadequate. Judge Mularoni pointed out that if the foetus did not have any rights, then there would be no need for there to be special legislative provisions relating to abortion. The fact that all European countries had such legislation indicated that there was a consensus that the foetus had some kind of rights.

The issue came before the Grand Chamber in *A, B, C v Ireland*,[334] which confirmed *Vo*:

A broad margin was specifically accorded to determining what persons were protected by Article 2 of the Convention: the Court had conclusively answered in its judgments in *Vo v. France* and in *Evans v. the United Kingdom* that there was no European scientific or legal definition of the beginning of life so that the question of the legal protection of the right to life fell within the States' margin of appreciation.

The failure of the Court to make a determinative ruling on the status of the foetus has led Ken Mason to state that 'the reader is likely to feel, by analogy, that it had been a long journey to the pub with no beer'.[335] As he points out, English law at present has produced the odd result that if a foetus is so badly injured that the foetus dies in the womb, there is no murder or manslaughter, but if the foetus is less seriously injured and is able to be born alive, but then dies from his or her injuries, then there could be an offence of murder or manslaughter. Katherine O'Donovan criticizes the decision for being overly concerned with the interface with abortion law.[336] She sees the case as involving an interference with the woman's right to bodily integrity, given that this was a wanted pregnancy. Such a wrong to the mother should be recognized in the law, she argues.

19 Abortion ethics

19.1 Introduction

Few areas of medical law and ethics are more controversial than abortion. Many people fall into one of two camps:

• those who emphasize a 'woman's right to choose' whether or not to terminate her pregnancy, to whom abortion is a fundamental aspect of personal freedom to decide what happens to person's body; or

• those who emphasize a right to life of the unborn child, to whom abortion is tantamount to murder.

Hence we have the well-known division between the 'pro-choicers' and the 'pro-lifers'.

[334] Application no. 25579/05 [2010] ECHR 2032, [185].
[335] Mason (2005: 106).   [336] O'Donovan (2006).

As may appear from this summary, it is often difficult for the two camps to reach any consensus. They appear to be emphasizing two utterly different principles. Public debates on abortion can sometimes appear to involve each side simply repeating to the other its key principles. The entrenchment is enhanced by the fear that both sides have in 'giving an inch'. Once a pro-lifer agrees that there may be some cases in which abortion is legitimate, it becomes difficult for him or her still to maintain that the life of the foetus is as valuable as the life of an adult. Similarly, once a pro-choicer accepts that sometimes a woman should not be permitted to abort, he or she is taken to admit that it is not simply a matter of choice for a woman.[337]

Before going any further, it is worth emphasizing that this is an area of the law in which some commentators distinguish between what is moral and what should be illegal. It is, for example, a perfectly respectable view to believe that abortion is (or nearly always is) immoral, but that the law should leave the choice up to the individual.[338] There are plenty of examples of where the law permits individuals to act in a way that might be regarded as being immoral. A far rarer view would be that abortion is morally justified, but should be illegal. That view might be supported by someone who believes that the state needs to increase its population, or that the claims of infertile couples wishing to adopt outweigh the rights of pregnant women. That said, for many people, the moral and legal positions are interlinked. If you believe that a foetus is a person, it is difficult then to explain why you think that person can be lawfully killed.

As already indicated, one's starting point in looking at the debate depends on one's view of the issue. Pro-lifers would want to start with the right to life of the foetus; pro-choicers, with the right to choice of the woman. We will start by looking at the position of the foetus, because if you conclude that the foetus has no right to life or no interests to be protected, that is practically the end of the debate.

19.2 The status of the foetus

What status should the foetus have? This question takes us to the issue of personhood (see Chapter 1, 19.1). It raises many of the issues here and it is worth reading that section again. Before looking at some of the answers to that question, we must point out that many people object to it. They argue that you cannot look at the foetus without looking at the woman as well. We should be asking what status the pregnant woman and foetus have together.[339] Even if it is the wrong question, it is one about which there has been much discussion, and so we will address it: what status should the foetus have?

Before looking at the answers to this question, it is appropriate to have a woefully brief biology lesson. Conception takes place while the sperm enters the ovum (egg). Fertilization actually takes place quite some time later (up to twenty-four hours later). The conceptus then moves from the fallopian tube into the womb and attaches to the womb lining. This is sometimes known as 'implantation'. The next point of significance occurs about fourteen days after the conception and is known as a 'primitive streak'. Another time of significance is viability. This is when the foetus is capable of living outside of the mother. This, with present technology, can be at twenty-two weeks. At

---

[337] Hursthouse (1987).   [338] Boonin (2002: 5).   [339] Herring and Chau (2007).

about twenty-six weeks, a foetus is capable of experiencing pain and has basic responses to external stimuli.[340] Birth normally occurs about thirty-eight weeks after conception.

Before looking at these views, it might be worth drawing a distinction between saying that a foetus is 'human' and saying that it is a 'person'.[341] There seems to be general agreement that the foetus is living (it is growing and developing) and that it is human (it can hardly be said to belong to another species). The debate is over whether the foetus is regarded as a person.

We will now consider some of the views as to the status of the foetus.

19.2.1 *The foetus is a person from the moment of conception*

The view that the foetus is a person from the moment of conception is one taken by many people opposing abortion, especially those writing from a religious perspective. However, it also has its supporters among those who have no explicit religious affiliation. We will now consider only the secular reasoning that supports the view.

It is important to look at three kinds of argument that can be made about conception being the start of personhood.

(i)   It can be claimed that the foetus is a person at the point of conception.

(ii) It can be claimed that, because we do not know when life begins, the safest assumption is that life begins at conception.

(iii) It can be claimed that, at the point of conception, the foetus is not yet a person, but has the potential to be a person, and therefore should be treated in the same way as a person.

We will focus on the first two arguments in this section, before moving then onto the third in the next.

One common argument in favour of regarding a foetus as a person from the moment of conception is that, at that point, the entire genetic make-up of the person is complete.[342] Apart from growing and developing, there is nothing that will be added or taken away in genetic terms from the person.[343] The embryo is the same physical organism that develops into a person. It is therefore 'one of us'.[344] Against such an argument it could be said that a corpse is the same human organism that the live person was. However, we do not attach the same moral status to a corpse and a live person.[345] Opponents may also reply that, in fact, it is not until the forming of the primitive streak that this is so. Alternatively, they may argue that it is not 'genetic' identity that creates personal identity, but psychological wholeness. Because adults have no psychological links with the foetuses that they were, they cannot be regarded as the same people, whatever genetic links may exist.[346] That reply will be rejected by supporters of the conception view because it exaggerates the importance of our psychological wholeness to our identity. A mentally ill person may lack psychological wholeness, but he or she is still a person.

Christopher Kaczor, in one of the best recent presentations of the 'pro-life' perspective, argues that 'each human being has inherent moral worth simply by virtue of the kind of being it is'.[347] He goes on to argue:

---

[340] Wyatt (2000: 1).   [341] Fortin (1988).   [342] Beckwith (2007).   [343] Finnis (1995b).
[344] Wolf-Devine and Devine (2009: 86).   [345] Reiman (2007).   [346] Heathwood (2011).
[347] Kaczor (2011: 105).

> A human embryo is properly classified as an individual human being rather than a collection of human cells, a member of the kind Homo sapiens rather than simply a 'heap' of cells of human origin. A shaving of your skin may contain living human cells, but the skin shavings as a group are just an uncoordinated heap, whereas you are a self-developing and self-integrated whole whose various parts (skin, eyes, arms, blood) serve the whole. Skin cells are merely parts of a human being without a dynamic, intrinsic orientation to develop towards maturity in the human species. By contrast, the human embryo is a whole, complete organism, a living individual human being whose cells work together in a coordinated effort of self-development towards maturity. If all human beings are persons, then the human embryo is a person.[348]

Opponents, as we shall see, will prefer the view that personhood is generated from the capacity to do or to experience certain things, rather than from a genetic constitution. Kaczor disagrees and argues that we have good reason to value foetuses as human persons, even though they may have fewer capacities than non-human animals. He claims that there is 'an important difference between eating a hamburger and a Harold burger, even if Harold, due to his mental handicap, was no more intelligent than a cow'.[349]

There is a more technical difficulty with Kaczor's argument. Stretton notes:

> The vast majority of the cells in the very early embryo go towards the creation of the placenta and amniotic sac rather than the later embryo. Thus we cannot identify the very early embryo with the later embryo, because the very early embryo has a better claim to being identical with the placenta or amniotic sac.[350]

This means that it is not necessarily conception that creates the moment at which the embryo becomes a complete organism.

A slightly different argument is that, apart from conception, there is no other clear point in time at which it is possible to say that a foetus's personhood begins. Koop writes as follows:

> My question to my pro-abortion friend who will not kill a new born baby is this: 'Would you kill this infant a minute before he was born, or a minute before that, or a minute before that, or a minute before that?'[351]

Such an argument assumes that there must be a clear point in time at which a foetus becomes a person and that it is conception that provides the clearest point at which to draw the line. There is no other point in foetal development that is as dramatic as conception and as clear an indicator of the beginning of life.

One reply to such an argument is that we should not assume that there needs to be a clear moment in time at which life begins. We know that there is a difference between day and night, even though there are times of the day when it is unclear whether night has started or finished. But in response it might be said that while it might be easily accepted that daytime and night-time are relative concepts, we believe that something either is or is not a person—that an entity either does or does not have a right to life.[352] Another criticism that could be used against an argument like that made by Koop is that, in fact, conception is not the 'bright line' event that it is sometimes portrayed to

---

[348] Kaczor (2011: 105). See also Lee (2004).   [349] Kaczor (2011: 106).
[350] Stretton (2008: 797).   [351] Koop (1978: 9).   [352] Boonin (2002: 35).

be; rather, conception and fertilization take place over a period of time (normally about twenty-two hours) and it might be as difficult to pinpoint the moment during the conception process at which personhood begins as it is for other theories to pinpoint when life begins.[353] Another argument against this 'line drawing' argument is to ask whether it is sensible to draw a distinction between the sperm and egg a few seconds before fertilization and the conceptus produced shortly afterwards.

Those who disagree with the argument that personhood begins at conception, as well as making the responses mentioned already, could also make the following argument: '[It] is striking that the usual fate of the fertilized human egg is to die.'[354] It has been estimated that fewer than 15 per cent of fertilized eggs will result in a birth.[355] This might be taken as an argument that setting personhood at conception means that the vast majority of people die within a few days. Some see this as a strong argument against conception being the start of personhood. However, in reply to such points, it has been asked: would we say that, in an impoverished country where there was an infant mortality rate of 90 per cent, the children born were of lower moral status than those born in a country where there was a much lower infant mortality rate?[356] There still seems something rather odd with a definition of personhood in which so many people die within a few days.

A final point to note is that if personhood starts at conception, then many forms of contraception would become immoral—namely, all those that operate after conception, including the contraceptive pill.[357] It would also mean that all forms of embryo research and IVF practices that involved discarding embryos would probably be immoral. Such consequences lead some to argue that we cannot accept this conception view. But if the view is correct, should we shy away from it only because of its 'undesirable consequences'?

19.2.2 *The foetus has moral claims based on its potential*

A different kind of argument in favour of treating the foetus as a person from the moment of conception is that even accepting that, at conception, a foetus is not a person, it has the potential to become a person. We must therefore respect the foetus not for what it is, but for what it has the potential to become. By killing foetuses, we are depriving them of the future lives that they would have. The deprivation of future life is the essential wrong in killing.[358] We must therefore treat the foetus as if it were a person.[359] This focus on potential, rather than current abilities, might note the following analogy: a sleeping person does not cease to be a person because he or she is not currently using his or her capacities; it is the potential to use them that gives the person his or her life value.[360] So too with the foetus.

---

[353] Williams (1994). Ford (2002: 55) simply responds that it is at the end of fertilization that personhood begins. Gonzalez (2016) uses the point of implantation. See further Oderberg (2008) and Eberl (2000; 2007); in response, see Deckers (2007a).

[354] The words of Professor Brown, reported in *Smeaton* [2002] 2 FCR 193, [129].

[355] Harris (2003a). This figure is disputed: Kaczor (2011: 131) suggests that it is 50 per cent.

[356] Beckwith (2005). Keown and Jones (2008) respond that the fact that nature allows this to happen does not give us moral warrant to destroy foetuses.

[357] This operates either to prevent fertilization or implantation.

[358] For a challenge to that view, see Strong (2008 and 2009), although cf. Di Nucci (2009).

[359] Marquis (2006; 2002; 1989); Wilkins (1993); P. Lee (1996 and 2007). For a rejection of the argument, see Savulescu (2002b).

[360] For further discussion, see Cox (2011) and Finnis (2013).

Christopher Nobbs has developed a version of this argument suggesting that the greater the likelihood the foetus will become a person, the greater the value that it has.[361] Hence less value attaches to a conceptus and much more value to a foetus just prior to birth.[362]

Inevitably, such an argument has its critics. We do not normally treat someone who has the potential to be something as if he or she has acquired it. You might have the potential to qualify as a doctor, but that does not mean that we should treat you as though you are a qualified doctor. A seriously ill person has a high likelihood of dying, but that does not mean that we should treat him or her as dead.[363] Taking the potentiality argument to its logical limits might entail one saying that refraining from sexual intercourse is depriving someone of a potential future.[364] Further, whether it is wrong to deprive someone of a future about which he or she has no awareness is debatable.[365] It is arguable that it is worse to kill a human with a self-conscious future than to kill one who has no such awareness.[366] This would suggest that, although killing a foetus may be a wrong, it is not as wrong as killing a child or adult.[367] And if a person who has no awareness of the value of his or her future cannot be harmed by being killed, does that mean that a person in a temporary coma (or in a depressed suicidal state) has no right not to be killed?

A different reply to the potentiality argument is that it could apply to a couple who have undergone IVF treatment and decide not to use their stored gametes to produce an embryo, or even a couple who decide not to have sex at a time when a woman was fertile. These couples too could be said to have deprived someone of a future,[368] although it might be said in reply that, in such a case, an identified individual is not deprived of a future.[369]

Of course, the potentiality view is criticized by those who are adamant that a foetus is a person from conception. Finnis argues that 'he or she is a human being and human person with potential, not merely potential human person or potential human being'.[370]

19.2.3 Playing it safe

The 'playing it safe' argument is probably best considered when all of the arguments over the status of the foetus have been considered. But it will be discussed here because it is a powerful argument in favour of emphasizing conception. Let us imagine that you have read all of the writings on the status of the foetus and your conclusion is simply that you do not know whether the foetus is a person or not. You might then have sympathy with Brazier's comments:

> Perception of the status of the embryo derives in many cases from the presence or absence of religious belief . . . The dispute reaches stalemate . . . The humanity of the embryo is unproven and unprovable. But that acts both ways. Just as I cannot prove that humanity

[361] Nobbs (2007).   [362] See also Card (2006).   [363] Clune (2011).
[364] Savulescu (2002b); Clayton Coleman (2013).
[365] M. Brown (2000). Stretton (2000) argues that something cannot have intrinsic value if it is not valued by other people.
[366] McMahan (2002).
[367] Dworkin (1993: 19) argues: 'Whether abortion is against the interests of a foetus must depend on whether the foetus itself has interests at the time the abortion is performed, not whether interests will develop if no abortion takes place.'
[368] Savulescu (2002b).   [369] Marquis (2006).   [370] Finnis (1994: 14).

was divinely created and that each and every one of us possesses an immortal soul, so it cannot be proved that it is not so.[371]

If we do not know when a foetus becomes a person, it is possible that a foetus is a person at conception—so is it not better to resolve the doubt in favour of life?[372] In other words, is it far better to treat a non-person as a person than to treat a person as a non-person? In reply, it might be asked whether this is a strong enough justification to compel a woman to go through an unwanted pregnancy, with all of the bodily invasion and loss of autonomy that results. Thomson has argued that, given the lack of consensus on the status of the foetus, the law should prefer liberty.[373] She offers three principles:

> First, restrictive regulation [of abortion] severely constrains women's liberty. Second, severe constraints on liberty may not be imposed in the name of considerations that the constrained are not unreasonable in rejecting. And third, the many women who reject the claim that the fetus has a right to life from the moment of conception are not unreasonable in doing so.[374]

Beckwith argues that we would not allow a shooting range to operate if it was close to a school and there were a small chance that a child would be killed; therefore we should not allow abortion if there is a small chance that a foetus is a person.[375]

That analogy is not exact, however, because those who are prevented from being shot are not suffering a severe lack of liberty as a result. Stretton suggests that a closer analogy would be forbidding the driving of cars because of the small risk of death.[376] But Friberg-Fernros[377] responds by saying we would think it appropriate to lock up a person who may have an deadly infectious disease that threatened the lives of others.

19.2.4 *The foetus becomes a person at fourteen days*

Those who support the view that the foetus becomes a person at fourteen days (when the primitive streak appears) tend to support it with the kind of arguments that have been made above in relation to relying on conception.[378] However, they argue that it is at fourteen days, rather than conception, that the embryo becomes a distinct entity.[379] It is, for example, not until fourteen days that it is clear whether the embryo will divide and form two people (twins).[380] It is only then that we can be confident that we have, at least in genetic terms, an identified person.[381] One difficulty with this view is that it does not provide a precise moment in time at which human life starts. The exact moment of the primitive streak is unclear.

19.2.5 *Quickening/human appearance*

Historically, the moment at which the foetus 'quickened' was regarded as of moral and social significance. This was the time at which the mother could feel the foetus

---

[371] Brazier (1990a: 134). See further Brazier (2013).
[372] See Smith (2008) for a development of such an argument.
[373] Thomson (1995).   [374] Thomson (1995: 20).   [375] Beckwith (2007: 60).
[376] Stretton (2008: 793).   [377] Friberg-Fernros (2014).
[378] Nathanson (1979: 216).
[379] McMahan (2002: 82). Warnock (1998: 64) sees the development of the primitive streak at fourteen days' gestation as signalling that the foetus acquires a special moral status, although not personhood.
[380] Burgess (2010).
[381] See Oderberg (2008) and Curtis (2011) for a rejection of the argument that the possibility of twins means that personhood does not begin at conception.

moving inside her. This was seen by some as the moment at which life begins. With modern technology and scans, it is possible to see images of the foetus at an early stage. Expectant mothers looking at books with pictures of how their foetus might look are understandably excited at the stage (normally about eight weeks) when the foetus starts to look recognizably human. Much was made of pictures appearing to show a foetus waving and smiling.[382] Nowadays, although these points in time are no doubt of emotional importance, few people suggest that they should carry moral significance.[383] John Burgess suggests that the crucial point should be six weeks, when a rudimentary cardiovascular system starts to function.[384] His argument is that because death is marked by the stopping of the heart beating, the start of life should be marked at the first heartbeat. Penner and Hull see the moment as being that at which receptors in the brain appear, which is at around twenty-three weeks' gestation.[385]

19.2.6 *The foetus becomes a person at viability*

To some commentators, it is the moment of viability that is crucial.[386] That is the moment at which the foetus becomes capable of existing independently of the mother (with appropriate medical support)—in other words, the time at which, if prematurely born, the child would be capable of living, which is currently about twenty-two weeks' gestation.[387]

The significance that may be attached to viability can result from two different kinds of arguments:

(i)　at viability, the foetus becomes a person; or

(ii)　at viability, the mother is entitled to withdraw her support of the foetus (she can have the foetus removed), but not in such a way as to kill the foetus.

We will focus on the first argument here. The second kind of argument is an argument about the responsibility of the mother to the foetus, rather than the moral status of the foetus as such.

The notion of viability is seen as important by some because it marks the transition from being a human entity dependent on another for survival to being someone capable of independent life. The foetus has, at that point, sufficient independence to be regarded as clearly separate from the mother. Elizabeth Wicks argues that it is the point at which there is 'integrative function of a human organism'.[388] David Jensen[389] argues that the timing of birth depends on a range of intrinsic factors, not necessarily related to the physical nature of the foetus, while viability clearly focuses on the capacities of the foetus itself.

The notion of viability as a criterion for life is not without its critics. Some are simply critical of the uncertainty: it can be very difficult to know whether a foetus could survive outside the mother.[390] Others argue that it might mean that the moment at which a foetus becomes a person depends when in history, and even where in the world, you live. A 26-week-old foetus may be viable in the UK, but would not be in a developing

---

[382] Kirklin (2004) claims that these images are, in a way, deceptive.
[383] Gillon (2001a).　　　[384] Burgess (2010).　　　[385] Penner and Hull (2008).
[386] For example, Jensen (2015); Lee, Ralston, Drey, et al. (2005).
[387] As Gillon (1989) points out, technology with artificial incubators could develop so that, from conception, a foetus could be deemed viable. See Alghrani (2008) for further discussion.
[388] Wicks (2010: 78).　　　[389] Jensen (2015).　　　[390] Cave (2004: 15).

country with limited medical facilities.[391] Should the moral status of the foetus depend on where on the planet the mother is located?[392] A further argument concerns the meaning of 'viability'. A premature foetus may be viable if placed in an incubator and receiving full-time nursing care, but such a baby is utterly dependent on others to provide the essentials for life. Being completely independent from others is, in fact, not possible (if ever) until the child is several years old.

19.2.7 *The foetus becomes a person at sentience*

A popular approach is to argue that a foetus becomes a person when it develops sentience, or is capable of sensation[393] or desires.[394] This may be between twenty to twenty-four weeks' gestation, although that is debated.[395] One way of justifying this approach is to argue that we should base our approach to the question 'When does life begin?' on the answer to the question 'When does life end?' There is much support for the view that brain death (the cessation of brain activity) should be the mark of death. If so, it is arguable that life should therefore be said to begin at the point at which brain activity starts.[396] John Harris has put the argument this way: 'I argue that the moral status of the embryo and indeed of any individual is determined by its possession of those features which make normal adult human individuals morally more important than sheep or goats or embryos.'[397]

As we shall see, such an approach could, in fact, also lead to the view that life does not begin until some time after birth. What makes someone a person is not merely sensation or sentience (an animal can experience these), but rather being a 'rational self-conscious being', and that does not start until some time after birth. We will discuss this view next. From Kaczor's perspective (mentioned earlier), a person's life should be valued not for what he or she does or thinks, but for what he or she is: a living person.[398] Indeed, it has been suggested that seeing brain activity as being the start of life creates an artificial divide between the brain and the body. There is also a concern voiced by some that if sentience is seen as the criterion for life, then, as foetal science develops, it may be that foetal sentience will be found to start at an earlier and earlier point in time.

19.2.8 *The foetus becomes a person at birth*

There is no doubt that birth is a dramatic event in human life. To some, it is the most natural moment at which to see the foetus as having its own existence. It is the point at which the child becomes an entirely separate entity from the mother. Further it is the point at which the child is able to engage with the world. As Achas Burin[399] puts it, during pregnancy: 'there is a fundamental disjunct—the world is prevented from showing itself to the foetus, and the foetus cannot access the world'. That all changes on birth.

There are others, however, who see birth as essentially an arbitrary occasion. It is clearly of great significance to the mother and her relationship to the foetus, but does it alter the status of the foetus? Why does a 30-week-old foetus who has been born and

---

[391] Kaczor (2012: 70) refers to Amilia Taylor, born at twenty-one weeks' gestation.
[392] Watt (2002b) develops this argument.   [393] Martin (2006).
[394] Steinbock (1992: 5). Martin (2006) contains a detailed discussion of when foetuses can feel pain.
[395] Boonin (2002); BMA (2007d).   [396] Savulescu (2002b).   [397] Harris (1998: 79).
[398] Kaczor (2011).   [399] Burin (2014).

kept alive in an incubator have a different moral status from a 30-week-old foetus that is yet to be born? Where they are living is different, but should that alter their moral status? As Charles Foster has argued, should a journey of a few centimetres down the birth canal make a huge difference to the moral status of the foetus?[400] In response, it might be said that the law often has to use apparently arbitrary points in time to ascribe statuses (for example an 18th birthday).[401] Another response, explored later, is that birth gives rise to a fundamental change in the relationship between the baby and mother, and society generally, and this alters its legal and moral status.[402]

19.2.9 *Personhood does not begin until some time after birth*

One view that appears to have growing support is the view that someone is not a person until they are 'a rational and self-conscious being'. This means that a foetus is not a person.[403] Nor indeed is a newborn infant.[404] Peter Singer has written:

> If the fetus does not have the same claim to life as a person, it appears that the newborn baby does not either, and the life of a newborn baby is less value to it than the life of a pig, a dog, or a chimpanzee is to the nonhuman animal.[405]

The shocking conclusion, if this argument were accepted, would be that infanticide (the killing of babies) is permissible.

In a highly controversial article, Giubilini and Minerva suggest precisely that.[406] Because a newborn baby has not acquired sufficient attributes to become a person, 'post-birth abortion' should be permitted. As mentioned in Chapter 1, this article attracted considerable public attention and controversy.[407] However, as the authors maintained, there is a logic to its approach if one accepts that what generates human personhood is the acquiring of capacities. Of course, some will use the issue of infanticide precisely to argue against such an approach. As Jacqueline Laing somewhat acerbically comments:

> Whether or not we are exercising our capacities or abilities, are in pain or desirable to third parties are insufficient grounds on which to judge human moral value. So too are qualities like evincing rationality, capacity for self-reflection or moral sensibility, characteristics that exclude many professors of moral philosophy for a lifetime. Even human dignity does not fluctuate and should not be regarded as fluctuating.[408]

Another response might be to claim that babies do have some of the moral characteristics that mark personhood, such as the capacity to form desires (they do cry when hungry).[409]

Andrew McGee also points to the powerful instinct to love one's offspring, which helps to form the basis of our moral codes:

> Our lives are defined in large part in terms of our relationships with our loved ones and, especially, our offspring. The value we afford to human life therefore stems from the central role our loved ones play in our lives, and the meaning they give to them.[410]

Indeed, the powerful reaction against Giubilini and Minerva's article may support McGee's claim. McGee's claim, then, is that these deeply held instincts can properly

[400] Foster (2009). For a rejection of that view, see Herring (2011b).
[401] Norrie (2000: 226).   [402] Herring (2011b).   [403] Kuhse and Singer (1985: 133).
[404] Tooley (1983).   [405] Singer (2000: 160).   [406] Giubilini and Minerva (2013).
[407] Schüklenk (2013).   [408] Laing (2013: 337).   [409] McGee (2013).
[410] McGee (2013: 337).

form the foundation of moral claims. And it is interesting to note that Giubilini and Minerva defend their article as an exercise in logic.[411] McGee's comments perhaps help to make sense of the claims of the prominent ethicist Robert George that the arguments in favour of infanticide are simply 'moral madness'.[412] Indeed, he does not see the issue as worthy of discussion, because 'anyone should immediately be able to see that killing infants because they are unwanted is unacceptable'.[413] But critics will reply that gut instinct reactions will not do and that we need to provide a coherent argument as to why babies are morally different from foetuses.[414]

To many, the shock is such that the argument must immediately be rejected.[415] However, there is undoubtedly a logic to the argument. If we are looking at what makes an entity distinctly human, the traditional religious answer would be 'a soul'. But if that view is rejected, it is difficult not to conclude that capacities such as rationality and self-consciousness are the most obvious hallmarks of people.[416] Newborn babies appear to lack these. Is our rejection of infanticide therefore based on a failure to think clearly and on sentimental attachments to babies? Or is it that the supporters of such a view have taken their logic to extremes? Anne Maclean argues that:

> We treat babies in certain ways and not in others; not for example, as if their lives were at our disposal. Bioethicists demand for what reason we do so, but there is no reason—or, to put the same point differently, their being babies is the reason, all the reason in the world.[417]

Jeff McMahan, taking a view similar to that of Kuhse and Singer, argues that those suffering severe mental illness do not have the status of people, because they lack an awareness of self or an ability to think rationally.[418] Eva Feder Kittay argues:

> . . . creating a category of moral status extended to certain human beings (along with unspecified, hypothetical others) based on intrinsic valued properties but denied to other human beings is dangerously close to the harmful exclusions of racism and pernicious nationalism.[419]

19.2.10 *Gradualist view*

Perhaps the most popular answer to the status of the foetus is an attempt to move away from having to locate a point in time at which the foetus becomes a person towards recognizing that the status of the foetus changes during pregnancy.[420] As Greasley[421] explains:

> there is no reason to assume a sharp threshold exists between the absence and presence of personhood status, since there is no good reason to think that personhood is the kind of property that emerges wholly and instantaneously.

---

[411] Giubilini and Minerva (2013b).   [412] George (2013a).
[413] George (2013b: 229). See also Finnis (2013).
[414] McMahan (2013b).   [415] Maclean (1993: 22).
[416] Lockwood (1985: 10). Harris (1999) suggests that, to be a person, you must be capable of valuing your own existence.
[417] Maclean (1993: 36).   [418] McMahan (2002).   [419] Feder Kittay (2005: 131).
[420] For example, Feinberg (1992: 49).   [421] Greasley (2017: 147)

If this is accepted then we need not identify a particular point at time in which person-hood is acquired. Rather the status of the foetus gradually emerges over time. The older the foetus, the greater the respect due to it.[422] The Polkinghorne Committee argued for 'a special status for the living human foetus at every stage of its development which we wish to characterize as a profound respect based on its potential to develop into a fully formed human being'.[423] Others talk of the foetus moving from being a human organism, to a human being, to being a person.[424] Indeed, it has been argued that we should not base our discussion around what is or is not a person, but rather around the moral relevance of particular characteristics.[425]

Such arguments seek to drive a middle way between saying not that a foetus is a person or a nothing, but rather that a foetus is somewhere in between. Some add that such a view enables us to say that, as the foetus grows older, the foetus acquires an increasing measure of respect, until it reaches the status of a person.[426] Mackenzie argues that this accords with the experiences of pregnant women, which change as their pregnancy progresses:

> Firstly, from the perspective of the woman, the foetus becomes more and more physically differentiated from her as her own body boundaries alter. Secondly, this gradual physical differentiation . . . is paralleled by and gives rise to a gradual psychic differentiation, in the experience of the woman, between herself and the foetus . . . Thirdly, physical and psychic differentiation are usually accompanied by an increasing emotional attachment of the woman to the foetus, an attachment which is based both in her physical connection with the foetus and in anticipation of her future relationship with a separate being who is also intimately related to her.[427]

Gradualists will typically claim that although the foetus gradually acquires moral status, the law needs to have a clear marking point at which it becomes a person for legal purposes. Birth provides that clear marker, at a time by which the foetus has typically acquired a sufficient number of markers of personhood.

This middle view of the foetus might be said to accord with the real views of many of the protagonists in the debate.[428] Many staunch pro-lifers are willing to concede that abortion is not as bad as murder,[429] and many staunch pro-choicers would be unhappy with the idea of a woman carrying out an abortion at thirty-eight weeks' gestation without a good reason. Does this not suggest that, in fact, many pro-lifers do accept that foetal life is not exactly equal to adult life and that many pro-choicers do accept that foetal life has at least some value? As Wolf points out, many people's attitudes to foetuses depends on whether the foetus is wanted: 'So what will it be: Wanted fetuses are charming, complex, REM-dreaming little beings whose profile on the sonogram looks just like Daddy, but unwanted ones are mere "uterine material"?'[430]

One major difficulty for the gradualist view is that, once a person is born, we do not normally accept the idea that he or she is 'more' or 'less' human. The idea that a person with a mental disorder is less human than someone else is repugnant. We treat all born

---

[422] BMA (2004: 228).   [423] Polkinghorne (1989: 9).
[424] This approach is discussed in Fortin (1988).   [425] Beauchamp (1999).
[426] See the discussion in Sanger (2004).
[427] Mackenzie (1992: 148–9). See further Stychin (1998).   [428] Quinn (1984).
[429] Although not Wolf-Devine and Devine (2009: 99).   [430] Wolf (1995: 4).

people as people, full stop. So why are we willing to accept that foetuses can have degrees of personhood?

19.2.11 *The relational view*

To another group of commentators, much of the discussion on the status of the foetus is misguided. We cannot consider the status of the foetus in isolation from that of the woman.[431] She is not simply a foetal container.[432] Rather, our discussion should focus on the relationship between the mother and foetus: they are both two and one.[433] Any dealings with the foetus must be mediated by the woman.[434] Dworkin puts it this way:

> [H]er foetus in not merely 'in her' as an inanimate object might be, or something live but alien that has been transplanted into her body. It is 'of her and is hers more than anyone's' because it is, more than anyone else's, her creation and her responsibility; it is alive because she has made it come alive.[435]

Seymour argues that, instead, we need to emphasize the relationship between the foetus and woman. He explains that the key feature of the relationship approach is 'its emphases on the shared needs and interdependence of the woman and her foetus, whose relationship is seen as characterized by "[c]onnectedness, mutuality, and reciprocity"'.[436] The alternative, he suggests, involves setting up the interests of the foetus in conflict with the interests of the mother.[437] Camilla Pickles argues instead for a 'not-one/not-two approach'. This relational approach means:

> Focus should be squarely on the pregnancy relationship as expressing in inseparable unit between a woman and the unborn and this structure requires that when the law is applied to this relationship it should advance a healthy relationship which fosters female autonomy and foetal interests.[438]

Catherine Mackinnon argues that 'the only point of recognizing fetal personhood, or a separate fetal entity, is to assert the interests of the fetus *against* the pregnant woman'.[439] Mackinnon, however, also argues that it is wrong to see the foetus as simply like a body part of a woman: 'Physically, no body part takes as much and contributes as little. The fetus does not exist to serve the woman as her body parts do . . . No other body part gets up and walks away on its own eventually.'[440] We need an approach that recognizes the intimacy of the relationship between the two.

As Dawn Johnsen points out, there are dangers with presenting the interests of the foetus and the woman as separate: 'By creating an adversarial relationship between a woman and her fetus, the state provides itself with a powerful means of controlling women's behaviour during pregnancy, thereby threatening women's fundamental rights.'[441]

---

[431] Herring (2011b).   [432] Annas (1986).   [433] Seymour (2000); Herring (2000).
[434] Gallagher (1987); Gibson (2007).   [435] Dworkin (1993: 55).
[436] Seymour (2000: 190), quoting L. De Gama (1993: 114–15).
[437] Jackson has objected to the phrase 'maternal–foetal' conflict on the basis that the pregnant woman is not yet a mother and because there is rarely a conflict between the two, but rather between the mother and a third party.
[438] Pickles (2017: 320).   [439] Mackinnon (1991: 1315).
[440] Mackinnon (1991: 1316).   [441] Johnsen (1986: 599).

I have argued that the relational approach provides a way of looking at pregnancy issues in the way in which women do:

> The abstracted weighing of the interests of the fetus/baby and woman pays no account of the complex interactions between them; and between them and those who are in relationship with them; not to mention the broader social context which has such an impact on the actual and perceived moral and legal obligations that are imposed. We need to move from an idealised analysis and listen to voices of women faced with pregnancy decisions and decisions concerning birth and children. There we usually find not the language of status, rights, viability or choice: but the language of despair; ecstasy; interconnection and guilt. The language is that of relationships: seeking to do the right thing 'for everyone'. It is there we need to start the legal and moral analysis of pregnancy and find the significance of birth.[442]

Opponents of the relationship approach argue that to focus on the relationship between the two rather than to separate out the interests, despite its worthy aims, is misguided. How can we discuss the maternal–foetal relationship in any meaningful way without deciding whether a foetus should be regarded as equivalent to a strand of her hair,[443] or has the same status as an adult person? Others are concerned that emphasis on the relationship rather than the interests of those involved might too easily lead to an overriding of the woman's rights, especially given the strong image that motherhood holds in our society.[444] Or the argument may go the other way: that a focus on regarding the foetus and woman 'as one' gives the woman a say in how the relationship should progress, thereby downplaying the protection of the foetus.

Certainly, it is true that the relationship approach does not necessarily point in a particular direction in the abortion debate and could even be used to support abortion. Petcheksy argues:

> A feminist challenge to fetocentrism has to assert that, while some fetuses may become at some point transplantable, no fetus is actually viable. Fetuses are biologically dependent on a pregnant woman and will be physically and socially dependant on her after birth. This dependence provides the basis for both her moral obligation to regard the fetus with care and her moral right to decide whether to keep it.[445]

The relationship approach has received some support from pro-life feminists. They emphasize what are seen as the feminist values of nurturing, caring, and the value of life.[446] Wolf-Devine argues that there is:

> . . . a prima facie inconsistency between the ethics of care and abortion. Quite simply, abortion is a failure to care for one living being who exists in a particularly intimate relationship to oneself. If empathy, nurturance, and taking responsibility for caring for others are characteristic of the feminine voice, then abortion does not appear to be a feminine response to an unwanted pregnancy.[447]

---

[442] Herring (2011b: 109–10).
[443] Warren (1992) suggests that abortion is morally equivalent to cutting one's hair.
[444] Fovargue (2002).   [445] Petcheksy (1984: xii).
[446] Wolf-Devine and Devine (2009); Castonguay (1999); Maloney (1995).
[447] Wolf-Devine (1989: 121).

19.2.12 *Property model*

The property model sees the foetus as the property of the mother. Mary Ford explains the benefits of this approach:

> By treating the foetus as the property of the pregnant woman, it allows us to under-stand why the law should only protect the foetus against the actions of third parties, and not against the actions of the woman herself. Within a property framework, she is entitled to dispose of her property without legal interference, and she is also entitled to seek compensation from—and criminal sanctions for—those who interfere with her property.[448]

Ford denies that this approach leads to the conclusion that the foetus has no interests. By regarding it as a piece of property, it is recognized as having value and interests that should be protected by the law. However, harms to the foetus are seen as harms to the mother. A problem with this approach is that it may not accord with any woman's own understanding of pregnancy. At least in the case of a wanted pregnancy, few women will regard their foetuses as analogous to their microwaves—although one response to that would be that no legal approach can hope to capture the experience of pregnancy properly.

19.2.13 *Conclusions on the moral status of the foetus*

It is tempting to conclude that all of the theories outlined above have 'problems'.[449] Some lead to what would be widely regarded as undesirable consequences, such as the legality of infanticide or the illegality of the contraceptive pill; others appear to rest on uncertain or arbitrary distinctions, such as whether the foetus is born or the current state of technology. In the end, the question of when life begins depends on what mean-ing and value you give to life, and because there are so many answers to these questions, it is not surprising that there is such dispute over when life begins.

19.3 **The right to choose**

Many pro-choicers reject the argument that the foetus has any rights or interests until birth and argue that what is important is the right of autonomy and bodily integrity of the woman. Such a view is relatively straightforward: if a foetus has no interests of its own until birth, then it is difficult to think of any convincing arguments that would justify denying that women have a right to abortion.[450]

More difficult is the position of a person who wishes to argue that a foetus is a person or has interests that deserve protection, but that these are trumped by the woman's right to autonomy or bodily integrity. The debates over the legitimacy of such a view have been dominated by a hugely influential article by Judith Jarvis Thomson.[451]

---

[448] Ford (2005b: 263).   [449] Gillon (2001a).
[450] Some have argued that pregnant women are not aware of the psychological harm that abortion can cause and therefore do not give informed consent. Whether abortion causes psychological harm is much debated: see Dadlez and Andrews (2010).
[451] Thomson (1971).

19.3.1 *Jarvis Thomson's violinist*

At the heart of Thomson's article is the following hypothetical example:

> You wake up in the morning and find yourself back to back in bed with an unconscious
> violinist. A famous unconscious violinist. He has been found to have a fatal kidney ail-
> ment, and the Society of Music Lovers has canvassed all the available medical records and
> found that you alone have the right blood type to help. They have therefore kidnapped
> you, and last night the violinist's circulatory system was plugged into yours, so that your
> kidneys can be used to extract poisons from his blood as well as your own. The director
> of the hospital now tells you, 'look, we're sorry the Society of Music Lovers did this to
> you—we would never have permitted it if we had known. But still, they did it, and the
> violinist is now plugged into you. To unplug you would be to kill him. But never mind,
> it's only for nine months. By then he will have recovered from his ailment, and can safely
> be unplugged from you'.[452]

Thomson assumes that you will say that you are entitled to unplug yourself. She expects
that you would agree that if you were an extremely virtuous person, you may be willing
to make the sacrifice and remain plugged in, but that it is not something that you should
be legally compelled to do. Many people have accepted this analysis. Thomson then
argues that if you agree with her on that scenario, then you must agree that abortion
likewise is permissible. In the same way as you think that your right to bodily integrity
means that you do not have to remain plugged into the violinist, you should also think
that you do not have to remain pregnant. If, however, you feel that the person plugged
into the violinist should not be permitted to unplug himself or herself, then the article
offers you no arguments in favour of abortion.

Many have found Thomson's argument to be highly persuasive. But also there are
many who seek to distinguish her scenario from the abortion debate.[453] Some of the
points that they make are as follows.

(i) *Responsibility*

Thomson's analogy involves a person who is kidnapped and forced into being linked up
to the violinist. This is analogous only to pregnancy following rape.[454] So some commentators have taken the view that whilst Thomson's analogy creates a powerful case to
justify abortion in the case of rape, it is unconvincing in other cases.[455]

Thomson foresees this objection and produces another analogy:

> Suppose it were like this: people-seeds drift about in the air like pollen, and if you open
> your windows, one may drift in and take root in your carpets or upholstery. You don't
> want children, so you fix up your windows with fine mesh screens, the very best you can
> buy. As can happen, however, and on very, very rare occasions does happen, one of the
> screens is defective; and a seed drifts in and takes root. Does the person-plant who now
> develops have a right to the use of your house? Surely not—despite the fact that you vol-
> untarily opened your windows, you knowingly kept carpets and upholstered furniture,
> and you knew that screens were sometimes defective.[456]

---

[452] Thomson (1971: 132).
[453] Wiland (2000) provides a useful summary. See also the excellent discussion in Taylor (2009).
[454] Tooley (1983: 45).   [455] Meilaender (1998).   [456] Thomson (1971: 137).

Here, Thomson is arguing that a woman should not be regarded as responsible for the foetus's vulnerable position where she has taken precautions against the child being born.[457] She argues that a foetus has no rights to use a woman's body without her consent.[458] In cases of contraceptive failure, clearly the woman has not consented. Using a different analogy, Thomson argues that the fact that a householder has left their windows open does not give a burglar the right to enter and remain in the house.[459] Her point here is to argue that a woman who has sex cannot thereby be taken to have accepted being pregnant.

Some commentators do not find these seed or burglar analogies very convincing. Meilaender argues that the womb is the natural place for a foetus to be; it cannot be seen as similar to an invader or intruder.[460] Marquis argues that a burglar is responsible for entering a house and can be removed by force, while a foetus is not responsible for being in a womb.[461] Others reply that the fact that a woman has known that using contraception is not 100 per cent reliable means that she has undertaken the risk of pregnancy and so is responsible for the foetus.[462] Warren modifies Thomson's violinist analogy to one in which you have joined the Society of Music Lovers and accepted that, in the event of a violinist's illness, there will be a lottery and you will have a 1 in 100 chance of having to be plugged into the violinist for nine months.[463] In such a case, if you are selected, you are morally bound to remain plugged in, because you took on the responsibility by joining the society. Similarly, if you decide to engage in sexual intercourse, you voluntarily undertake the risk of pregnancy. But others are not convinced by this. It can be argued that you cannot give away in advance your right to bodily integrity.[464] Just because a person agreed to provide ten sessions of bone marrow transplant treatment does not mean that we would force him or her to continue if the person were to change his or her mind midway through.[465] Boonin suggests that, in the end, this comes down to a question of society's conventions: do we, as a society, agree that a woman who engages in sexual intercourse thereby takes on the responsibility for any foetus thereby created?[466] He suggests that we do not. But not everyone will agree. Marquis argues that a mother is responsible for her foetus:

> All mammals have mothers. A fetus is a mammal. Therefore, a fetus has a mother. Only the pregnant woman qualifies to be the mother of the fetus within her. All mothers are parents. All parents (unless exceptional circumstances obtain) have serious, special duties of care to their children . . . Therefore, all pregnant women have serious, special duties of care to their children. Fetuses are children. Therefore, all pregnant women have serious, special duties of care to their fetuses.[467]

In assessing this argument, it should be recalled that, normally, a parent is entitled to hand over his or her children to be cared for by local authorities if the parent does not wish to care for them any longer. That option is not available for a pregnant woman. But where does that leave us?

---

[457] Thomson does not make it clear how she would deal with a case in which a woman had sexual intercourse without using contraception.
[458] Thomson (1971: 138).   [459] Thomson (1971: 58). See also Manninen (2010).
[460] Meilaender (1998).
[461] Marquis (2010). Although it is worth noting you would be permitted to remove even a sleepwalking or insane burglar.
[462] See the discussion at Steinbock (1992: 78).   [463] Warren (1973).   [464] Long (1993: 189).
[465] Kamm (1992).   [466] Boonin (2002: 164).   [467] Marquis (2010: 65).

It is helpful to separate out two ways this could be expressed.[468] First, it might be said that the woman has through having sex caused the foetus to come into existence in a precarious state and owes a duty because she has put the foetus in that harm. This might be analogous to an obligation one might put on a driver to stop and help a cyclist they have accidentally knocked over. Second, it might be said the duties arise from being in a position to offer help. We might more generally say if someone is in great need and you are in a position to offer them care, you have a duty to do so. This might apply if someone is out for a walk in the mountains and comes across someone injured. The first claim is based primarily on the idea of having a causal link to the harm. The second is on the ability of the person to provide care. In English law generally there is a not a duty to rescue based simply on the fact you are in a position to assist.

As to the first, it might be claimed that the pregnant woman is not like the motorist who has knocked over the cyclist. First, her causal link to the precarious position the foetus is in is less clear. She has not done anything to the foetus. Nor is it clear that as a result of her action the foetus is in a worse position than the foetus would be otherwise. Indeed but for the sex there would be no foetus. In any event even if there is a causal link so too is the man responsible. Further while the act of driving in to the cyclist inevitably harms the cyclist, the action of sex has only a risk of harming the foetus.

The care-based responsibility is however limited by the requirement of reasonableness. The walker might be expected to phone for help or undertake basic steps to help. They would certainly not be required in any legal system to endanger themselves or undertake highly burdensome activities, although it might be considered heroic if they did.

(ii) Killing v letting die

Another distinction between Thomson's violinist analogy and abortion is that, in the case of the violinist, by unplugging yourself, you are letting the violinist die.[469] While in some methods of abortion, you are killing the foetus (for example, by cutting it up).[470] However, that is rare, as most methods of abortion effectively release the foetus from the womb, which looks like an omission (a withdrawal of assistance) rather than an active act of killing. You might think that the analogy works with most forms of early abortion, but not the forms used in later abortion which can be seen as directly killing the foetus. However, the issue is even more complicated than that.

First, the validity of this argument depends in part on whether you think there is a difference between an act and an omission. The arguments concerning this distinction are found in Chapter 9. As we note there, there are many philosophers who find the distinction one of little or no moral significance, although it plays an important role in the law.

Second, you are responsible in the criminal law in England for an omission if there is a duty to act. Could it not be said that a pregnant woman has special duties to the foetus? So, to some, the crucial distinction between pregnancy and the violinist analogy is that the violinist is a stranger to you, while the woman is no stranger to her foetus.

---

[468] See McDanile (2015) for a helpful discussion.
[469] But Tooley (1983: 43) argues that unplugging is an act.
[470] Brody (1975: 27–30); Alward (2002). It may be argued that, in other forms of abortion (which involve prising the foetus away from the womb, thereby creating a miscarriage), the analogy would be convincing.

The argument here is that a stranger owes no duty to another. To use yet another of Thomson's analogies:

> If I am sick unto death, and the only thing that will save my life is the touch of Henry Fonda's cold hand on my fevered brow, then all the same, I have no right to be given the touch of Henry Fonda's cool hand on my fevered brow.[471]

However, parents, unlike strangers, do owe a duty to act reasonably in order to protect their children from danger.[472] Pro-choicers might respond to such an argument by saying that even parents are not required to give a kidney or even blood if necessary to save the child's life.[473] So even though we do put duties on parents to protect their children, this will never be such as to require an interference with bodily integrity.

Even if we see the later abortion as an act, it might still be argued that an act which kills another can be permitted if it is performed in self-defence. We will explore the issue further shortly.

(iii) Intention

Another distinction that some seek to make surrounds the concept of intention. In the case of the violinist, when you unplug yourself, you do not intend to kill the violinist.[474] You would be delighted if somehow he were to manage to survive, although you realize that this is unlikely. However, in the case of abortion, most procedures are done with the purpose of killing the foetus. If the foetus survives *in utero*, the abortion will be regarded as a failure. Even if the woman does not want the baby to die, she is consenting to a process that will inevitably result in the foetus's death.[475] Such an argument relies on the doctrine of 'double effect', which we shall discuss in Chapter 9, and the controversial distinction between foresight and intention. Also, it appears arguable that at least some women having an abortion would be happy if the foetus were to be born alive, as long as they were no longer pregnant. Presumably, some would then consent to adoption.

Interestingly, Thomson's article has also been criticized by those who are pro-choice. These critics have made the following arguments.

(i)   The article does not emphasize the fact that only women get pregnant. In other words, the violinist analogy overlooks the point that abortion can be justified as part of the equality between the sexes.[476] To look at abortion without looking generally at the position of women and mothers in society is to miss much of the context within which the abortion debate must take place.[477]

(ii) Thomson appears to accept that it is selfish to abort. Her argument is that the law does not expect people to be 'good Samaritans' and to go the extra mile for other people; rather, the law requires that we are 'minimally decent Samaritans'. This implied criticism of those who choose to have abortions is objected to by some.[478]

(iii) Thomson is wrong to assume that it is wrong to detach oneself from the violinist. Kamm has argued that unplugging the violinist simply returns him to the position in which he would have been before he came into contact with you.[479] This was

---

[471] Thomson (1973: 31).   [472] Beckwith (1992).
[473] See the discussion in Shrage (2003: 63).
[474] Finnis (1973). See, by way of reply, Thomson (1973).   [475] Lee (1996).
[476] Jaggar (2009).   [477] Markowitz (1990).   [478] Markowitz (1990).   [479] Kamm (1992).

support to which he had no right. So, by unplugging him, you are not harming him, but returning him to the position in which he was initially. Similarly, in relation to abortion, no wrong is done to the foetus through abortion; the foetus is simply returned to the position in which it would have been without the woman's sustenance.

(iv)   Thomson's article is based on the assumption that a foetus is a person—an assumption that Thomson makes absolutely clear she is making only for the purpose of the article. But some pro-choice critics think that she moves too quickly from accepting that the foetus is a person to saying that a foetus has a right to life. It is arguable that if a person's existence is dependent on the body of another, that person cannot assert his or her right to life against the other. The foetus's life is dependent on the mother's support and this is something to which it has no right[480]—although it may be replied, as has already been argued, that a woman who engages in intercourse thereby accepts a risk that a foetus will be created and therefore has responsibilities towards it.[481]

19.3.2 *Self-defence/duty to rescue*

One theme underlying the debate surrounding the Thomson article that is worth bringing out more clearly is whether abortion should be regarded as a 'failure to rescue' the foetus or a killing of it in self-defence. If one regards abortion as a positive action that kills the foetus, then the analogy will be with self-defence; if abortion is seen as a withdrawal of support, this will be regarded as failure to aid, and the analogy will be with rescue. It may be necessary to draw a distinction between the forms of abortion. If abortion is seen as a failure to rescue, it is harder to justify its criminalization than if it is seen as an act of killing done in self-defence.

At first, the idea that abortion can be regarded as an act of self-defence might seem strange. The argument is that the woman is defending herself against the pain, injuries, indignities, and bodily intrusion that can accompany a pregnancy. McDonagh writes:

A woman's bodily integrity and liberty is just as violated by preborn life that implants itself, using and transforming her body for nine long months without consent, as she is when a born person massively imposes on her body and liberty without consent, as in rape, kidnapping, slavery, and battery.[482]

Hale LJ (as she then was) has written eloquently of the impact of pregnancy in *Parkinson v St James and Seacroft University Hospital NHS Trust*:[483]

From the moment a woman conceives, profound physical changes take place in her body and continue to take place not only for the duration of the pregnancy but for some time thereafter. Those physical changes bring with them a risk to life and health greater than in her non-pregnant state . . . along with those physical changes go psychological changes . . . some may amount to a recognised psychiatric disorder, while others may be regarded as beneficial, and many are somewhere in between . . . Along with these physical and psychological consequences goes a severe curtailment of personal autonomy.

[480] Kamm (1992).   [481] McMahan (2002).   [482] McDonagh (1996: 169).
[483] [2001] 3 WLR 376, 381. See also her speech in *R (A) v Secretary of State for Health (Alliance for Choice)* [2017] UKSC 41.

Literally, one's life is no longer just one's own but also someone else's . . . continuing the pregnancy brings a host of lesser infringements of autonomy related to the physical changes in the body or responsibility towards the growing child.

Such an argument has difficulties. Normally, killing in self-defence is justified only to avoid a threat of death or very serious injury, and it may be questioned whether the effects of pregnancy are sufficiently grave to justify a killing. Further, at the time of the abortion, the threat is not of imminent harm as is normally required for the operation of the defence. Finally, self-defence normally involves a defence against a blameworthy aggressor and the foetus, it might be thought, is hardly that. Can the foetus be regarded as posing an unjust threat to the woman? That is alien to most women's understanding and experience of pregnancy.[484] Or should we ask whether it would be unjust not to permit the mother to expel the risk posed by the foetus?

If abortion becomes more a question of whether the woman is under a duty to rescue, it appears easier to justify abortion. Even though, generally, English law does require parents to rescue their children, the degree of physical invasion involved in pregnancy is unlike any normal obligation to rescue. Indeed, we do not require parents to donate a kidney that their child needs.[485] Should we therefore require a woman to go through her pregnancy? There is no other area in law in which someone can be compelled to go through anything like the bodily invasion that pregnancy involves, even if that is necessary to save a life.

19.3.3 Dworkin

Ronald Dworkin has suggested that, despite appearances, there is less disagreement between the 'pro-choice' and 'pro-life' camps than might at first appear.[486] He starts by claiming that those in both camps 'overstate' their positions. Pro-choicers do not believe that a foetus is a 'nothing' that has no moral value, nor do most pro-lifers really believe that the death of a foetus is as serious as the death of a person. Although they do not realize it, both camps are emphasizing the sacredness of life, albeit different aspects of life's sacredness. He suggests that there are two things that make life sacred: the natural investment in life; and the human investment in life. He explains that, by the 'natural investment' in life, he is thinking of the wonder and awe created by new life represented by the evolutionary process (or, if you prefer, the creative power of God). By contrast, the 'human investment' is the effort and love put into a life by the person himself or herself and by other people. This is why he suggests we see the death of an elderly person as less of a tragedy than the death of a teenager. Elderly people have seen a return for the investment that they and others have put into their lives through the richness of experience that they have enjoyed during that life. On the other hand, in relation to the teenager, the return on the investment has only just begun.

Dworkin thinks that this distinction between the different kinds of investment in life is key to the divisions over the abortion debate. He argues:

> If you believe that the natural investment in a human life is transcendently important, that the gift of life itself is infinitely more significant than anything the person whose life

---

[484] Shrage (2003: 68).   [485] Scott (2002: 90).
[486] Dworkin (1993). See Greasley (2016) for an excellent discussion.

it is may do for himself, important though that may be, you will also believe that a deliberate premature death is the greatest frustration of life possible, no matter how limited
or crippled or unsuccessful the continued life would be. On the other hand, if you assign
much greater relative importance to the human contribution to life's creative value, then
you will consider the frustration of that contribution to be a more serious evil, and will
accordingly see more point in deciding that life should end before further significant
human investment is doomed to frustration.[487]

Dworkin sees the key question as being: 'Is the frustration of a biological life, which
wastes human life, nevertheless sometimes justified in order to avoid frustrating a
human contribution to that life or to other people's lives, which would be a different
kind of waste?'[488]

Although many have found Dworkin's contribution to the debate extremely useful,
it has, of course, not produced universal agreement. It would be surprising if Dworkin
had managed to articulate the issue in such a way that those who had been warring over
the issue for so long were to 'lay down their arms' in realization that their only real
disagreement was over the nature of the concept of sanctity. Those who take a 'pro-life'
view find that Dworkin too easily dismisses their argument.[489] Certainly, his view that
most pro-lifers would accept that abortion in a case of rape is permissible overlooks
the firm line consistently taken against abortion in such circumstances by the Roman
Catholic Church (arguably the most influential body in the pro-life movement) that
abortion is impermissible even in the case of rape.[490] Keown argues that Dworkin's view
appears to suggest that lives with greater investment in them are of more value than
those without.[491] That would suggest that the life of a newborn baby who required
intensive care by a substantial number of people would be of greater value than that of
a healthy newborn because of the greater investment in his or her life. Could that be
correct, he asks? Dworkin's idea of 'investment', however, includes not only matters of
input, but also 'added value', and therefore he distinguishes the life of the baby in intensive care and the 'normal' baby.

Those who take more of a pro-choice line have expressed concern that his emphasis
on the value of the foetus is misplaced. No doubt the human foetus creates feelings of
awe and wonder, but so too does the human egg or sperm and yet these are not seen as
having some special sacred position.[492]

19.3.4 Privacy, equality, or bodily integrity

So far, we have been a little vague on the question of precisely what right(s) of the
woman it is said justify overriding the interests, if any, of the foetus. Three candidates
are most often promoted.

- *The right to privacy* This is the argument that the issue of abortion should be a private issue for the woman herself. It involves grave moral, social, and personal issues
that are for her, and no one else, to decide.[493]

[487] Dworkin (1993: 138).   [488] Dworkin (1993: 140).   [489] Bradley (1993).
[490] Kingston (1996).   [491] Keown (1994b: 675).   [492] Boonin (2002: 31).
[493] In *Tysiac v Poland* (2007) 22 BHRC 155, the ECtHR accepted that not permitting abortion could
interfere with a woman's right to private life.

- *The right to bodily integrity* This focuses on the extent to which pregnancy can be said to constitute a bodily invasion of the woman. A pregnant woman, like anyone else, has the right to control what happens to her body; abortion is a central part of this right. Indeed, it could be claimed that being forced to continue a pregnancy against her wishes amounts to subjecting a woman to torture or inhuman or degrading treatment.[494]

- *The right to equality* Abortion plays a central role in tackling the disadvantages that women face when compared to men. The significance of abortion can be appreciated only when seen in the context of the oppression and restriction of women. Catherine MacKinnon puts it this way: '[A]bortion promises to women sex with men on the same reproductive terms as men have sex with women.'[495] We should not forget that, as Jaggar notes: 'Often women do not control sexual intercourse, often they have no access to contraception, often their access to pregnancy and birthing care is limited, and usually they are responsible for raising any children they may bear.'[496] Another point that is often overlooked is that there are strong links between domestic violence and abortion.[497] In one study, 20 per cent of women seeking an abortion had been assaulted by their partner in the previous year.[498]

Pro-choice advocates have disagreed over which right it is best to emphasize. Some of the issues in that debate will be discussed now.

The benefit of the privacy approach is that it emphasizes that the abortion decision is for the woman alone.[499] The views of the father of the foetus, her doctor, or indeed the 'moral majority' are irrelevant. Indeed, it is a common argument of the pro-choice camp that the pro-life supporters are seeking to impose their religious beliefs on others. However, some have seen weaknesses with the privacy approach. First, it does not appear to require the state to ensure that there are proper abortion facilities.[500] If abortion is a private matter, then its obligations can be limited to not prohibiting women from attending abortion clinics; it would mean that the state would not be required to ensure that abortions are available.[501] By contrast, if abortion is seen as an aspect of equality or bodily integrity, it is easier to establish an obligation on the state to provide abortion facilities.

Second, simply regarding the issue as one of choice appears to underplay the issues involved. Abortion is not just a 'lifestyle choice'; rather, it concerns matters intimately involved with the body of the woman. This is a factor that the right to bodily integrity emphasizes.

Third, to see the issue simply as one of privacy ignores the fact that the issue of abortion is one that is of special significance *to women*. Indeed, to many commentators, it is not possible to understand the issues surrounding abortion without appreciating the wider forms of oppression under which women live.[502] As Bridgeman puts it:

> Neither the unpleasant side effects nor risks to health of contraception, the lack of social provision to assist in the cost of bringing up a child which forces a woman to choose to abort, nor the physical and emotional pain of high-tech, low-success fertility treatments are acknowledged. The focus upon choice makes the circumstances in which women make decisions about pregnancy and child birth irrelevant.[503]

---

[494] Although, in *Tysiac v Poland*, a woman who was denied an abortion, despite pregnancy posing a serious risk to her eyesight (a risk that materialized in the form of severely impaired eyesight), was held not to have had her Article 3 ECHR rights interfered with.

[495] Mackinnon (1987: 99).   [496] Jaggar (2009: 133).   [497] Aston and Bewley (2009).

[498] Aston and Bewley (2009).   [499] Fox (1998b).   [500] Mackinnon (1987: 96–7).

[501] Clarke (1989); Kingdom (1991).   [502] Thomson (1998).   [503] Bridgeman (1998: 86).

Some pro-choice advocates dislike the emphasis on rights. We have already mentioned the relationship-based perspective on abortion, which seeks to emphasize the relationship between the foetus and the mother. Such a view is concerned that a strong emphasis on rights is liable to underplay the importance of the foetus. Himmelweit stated:

> Their [rights] ultimate flaw resides in the inability of a liberal rights position to cope with caring, interdependent relationships. This means that a position which is based on the individual rights of the woman alone, inevitably appears self-centred and inhumane. Basing the claim for access to abortion on women's individual rights has forced feminists to maintain a hopelessly insensitive position on the status of the foetus.[504]

19.3.5 Regret

One argument that is commonly used against abortion is that women later regret it. Indeed, pro-life websites often include accounts from women who wish that they had not had an abortion.[505] The argument is used to indicate that abortion harms women and that, on reflection, women realize that abortion is wrong. Kate Greasley argues that this is not a convincing argument.[506] She claims that regret is not necessarily associated with acceptance of wrongdoing. For example, a parent may regret his or her children leaving home to go to university; that regret does not mean that the parent has done anything wrong.[507] A divorce may be regretted, even while acknowledging that it was right to end the relationship. Regret and acceptance that the wrong decision was made are not the same thing. Notably, a study in the US found that 95 per cent of women reported believing the abortion was the 'right decision' for them, even though there were feelings of regret.

19.4 Is criminalizing abortion practically desirable?

Even a hardened opponent of abortion could take the view that making it illegal would, in fact, do little to stop the practice. Rendering abortion illegal would simply send the practice underground.[508] For example, although abortion is officially illegal in Chile, it has been estimated that up to 300,000 illegal abortions are performed each year.[509] Jaggar states that Latin America has 'the world's strictest abortion laws and also the highest abortion rates'.[510] The concern is that these backstreet abortions are likely to endanger women's lives and open them up to exploitation. In Nepal, it is estimated that six women die each day as a result of illegal abortions;[511] worldwide, 47,000 maternal deaths a year are said to result from illegal abortions.[512] So, to some, whatever the moral arguments, the practical consequences of rendering abortion illegal would be so disastrous that we should not go down that route. However, those who take a strict pro-life view might argue that if rendering abortion illegal were to mean that only a few hundred

---

[504] Himmelweit (1998: 49).

[505] One study of women who had first-trimester abortions found 72 per cent stating that more harm than good came from the abortion: Greasley (2012).

[506] Greasley (2012).   [507] This is not an example that she uses.

[508] Although there still seem to be illegal underground abortions in the UK: BBC News online (23 November 2007).

[509] Cases-Becerra (1997).   [510] Jaggar (2009: 165).   [511] IPPF (1999).

[512] Alan Guttmacher Institute (2011).

fewer abortions were carried out, that would be worthwhile, even if it also meant some women dying as a result of illegal abortions.[513]

19.5 The role of 'fathers' in abortion

As we have seen, the law has granted 'fathers' few rights in the abortion debate.[514] They do not even have a right to be consulted, let alone to veto, an abortion decision. Their legal position is no stronger if they seek to institute legal proceedings in the name of the foetus, rather than their own. Most commentators accept that this is correct. Feminists in particular have emphasized that the decision should be one for the woman alone. However, it might be argued that if we wish to encourage fathers to play a larger role in contraception and the raising of children, then fairness requires an acknowledgement of their interests in the abortion decision. This has led one leading feminist commentator to suggest that men should at least play a role in the counselling process.[515] It might also be argued that if a couple decide to have a child together the father has some kind of autonomy interest in the child being produced.[516] However, it is hard to see how that could ever be strong enough to defeat the woman's bodily integrity rights. When considering the strength of these arguments, it should be borne in mind that pregnant women are at greater risk of violence from their partners than non-pregnant women.

 A VIEW FROM ABOVE

Religious perspectives on abortion

The Roman Catholic Church and many other Christian denominations have taken a strong line against abortion, with Pope Paul VI calling abortion an 'abominable crime'.[517] For them, personhood begins at 'ensoulment'—the moment at which an entity develops a soul.[518] This is usually taken to be at conception. However, it should be noted that, at different points in history, Christian theologians have pointed to different stages of pregnancy as being the moment of ensoulment.[519] The one concession that the Catholic Church is willing to make in the context of abortion is that if there is a very serious threat to the mother's life if the pregnancy continues, then abortion is permissible.[520] The Anglican Church is generally opposed to abortion, but states that there may be a few strictly limited cases in which abortion is morally preferable.[521]

Islam also takes a strong view against abortion. An embryo, from conception, is seen as having a right to life, and hence abortion is murder.[522] An interesting side consequence of this view is that if a pregnant woman is given a death sentence, it must be postponed until after she has given birth.[523] Some Muslims take a more moderate view, accepting that although abortion is wrong, it may be permissible, or at least not punishable, early in the pregnancy.

Judaism has generally taken a less strict line against abortion.[524] This is in part because, in Jewish thought, it is not until birth (or at least until the greater part of the child is outside the

---

[513] Watt (2000b).
[514] See Collier (2011) for a helpful discussion of the role of fathers in pregnancy generally.
[515] Fox (1998b).   [516] Di Nucci (2014).   [517] Pope Paul VI (1977).
[518] Moreland and Rae (2000).   [519] Maguire and Burtchaell (1998).   [520] See Lee (2004).
[521] Church of England (2005).   [522] Ebrahim (2000).   [523] Ebrahim (2000).
[524] Sinclair (2003: ch. 1).

mother) that the foetus becomes a person. Although not regarded as a person, there is still an offence of foeticide, which is normally regarded as an offence that a third party commits if, for example, he or she causes a mother to miscarry. Of course, there are many writing from a Jewish perspective who oppose abortion.

There is some debate over the appropriate Buddhist approach to abortion. It appears that the majority view is that life begins at the moment of rebirth: when a previous life enters the embryo. This is widely taken to be at conception.[525] Others think that life does not begin until much later and that Buddhists should not object to abortion.[526]

Hindus generally oppose abortion, because it is seen as contravening the principle of *ahimsa* (non-violence). The general approach is that the course of action that will do least harm to the mother, the father, the foetus, and society should be chosen. There may therefore be circumstances in which abortion is permitted. It should also be noted that, among Hindus in India, abortion appears widespread.

PUBLIC OPINION

In a later poll, MORI (2011) 70 per cent of people questioned agreed that women had the right to choose about abortion free from government interference.[527] Of those questioned, 46 per cent disagreed and 23 per cent agreed with the suggestion that it should be harder for women to obtain an abortion; 53 per cent agreed that 'a woman should not have to continue with her pregnancy if she wants an abortion'. A poll in 2013 found that 44 per cent believed that life began at conception and 17 per cent believed it began at birth.[528] Perhaps surprisingly only 8 per cent said they did not know when life began. Although only 7 per cent were in favour of banning abortion.

20 Particularly controversial abortions

Let us assume, for now, that the pro-choice arguments have been found the most persuasive. Does this mean that every abortion must be lawful, or are there special arguments in relation to particular kinds of abortion? The following are regarded as particularly problematic kinds of abortion.

20.1 Late abortions

A study into second-trimester abortions (between thirteen to twenty-four weeks' gestation) found a range of reasons why the abortion occurred later in the pregnancy. In some cases, it was a delay in a woman recognizing that she was pregnant; in others, a late discovery of foetal abnormality; in others, a change in the woman's relationship status; some were caused by worry about what the abortion involved; in other cases, the delay

---

[525] Keown (2002: ch. 1).   [526] LaFleur (1992).   [527] MORI (2011).   [528] YouGov (2013).

was the result of delays in service provision.[529] Late abortions can be seen as particularly controversial for a number of reasons.[530]

(i)   For those who regard personhood as beginning at viability or sentience, then, by the time of a late abortion, the foetus may have become a person.

(ii)   It would be possible to take the view that although a nine-month pregnancy is demanding too great a sacrifice of a woman who is unwilling to make it, if the pregnancy is well advanced and there are only a few weeks left, it may not be an inappropriate burden to place on a woman to save the life of the foetus.

(iii) It could be claimed that there comes a point at which the woman, by delaying an abortion, has waived her right to an abortion.[531]

(iv)   Finally, if the foetus is viable, it can be claimed that although the woman has the right to withdraw her support and nurturance, she has no right to kill the foetus.

However, for some pro-choice advocates, however far along the pregnancy, it is still the woman who should choose what happens during the pregnancy and whether a termination is appropriate.[532] Alternatively, she is entitled to remove an invasion of her bodily autonomy whether that is to last many months, or a few hours.

20.2 Abortion and disability

If a woman learns that the child she is carrying is severely disabled, she may decide to have an abortion.[533] Many people will find such a decision understandable. However, the issue is a controversial one, especially if the disability is not severe. Imagine a woman who finds that the foetus she is carrying suffers from Down's syndrome and she then opts for an abortion. Is she not thereby saying that Down's syndrome children are better off dead?[534] If so, is such a view not deeply offensive to those suffering from the syndrome and a law that respects such a decision (by permitting abortion) equally offensive? If we would not permit someone to abort on sexist grounds (for example because they did not want to have a girl), should we permit abortion decisions that are based on discriminatory attitudes towards disability? Interestingly, amongst younger people in particular, disability is not regarded as an acceptable reason for termination. In one survey, only 11.4 per cent of young people thought Down's syndrome to be acceptable reason for termination.[535] Only 47 per cent of those aged 15–24 thought physical handicap an acceptable reason for abortion.[536] Richard Dawkins caused an outcry when on social media he had this advice for a pregnant woman whose foetus had been tested as having Down's syndrome: 'Abort it and try again. It would be immoral to bring it into the world if you have the choice.'[537]

---

[529] Ingham, Lee, Clements, et al. (2008).
[530] See Greasley (2014a) for an insightful discussion of the conviction of Kermit Gosnee in the United States for a series of late-term abortions.
[531] See discussion in Regan (1979).
[532] See Lee (2007) for a powerful consideration of current debates over later abortions.
[533] There were 3,208 abortions on this ground in 2016 (DoH 2017a).
[534] S. McGuinness (2013b); Field (1993). See also Lindemann Nelson (2007); Mahowald (2007); Asch and Wasserman (2007).
[535] Lee and Davey (1998: 21).   [536] Furedi (1998: 166).   [537] Dawkins (2013).

A parliamentary inquiry on the issue found that many parents reported feeling that, following a discovery of foetal disability, there was a strong steer towards abortion from the medical professionals.[538] It noted that 90 per cent of babies with a definite diagnosis of Down's syndrome had been aborted in 2011.

We have already mentioned that, in the past, abortion of disabled foetuses was justified on eugenics grounds. Our society now firmly rejects such eugenics arguments. However, there is a concern that, in the past, we practised public eugenics; now, we practise private eugenics.[539] In other words, although the establishment does not seek to prevent the birth of disabled people directly, by encouraging expectant mothers to undergo tests for foetal abnormality and making abortion readily available if a disability is discovered, in effect eugenics is being practised.[540] There are also concerns that, once a test reveals an abnormality, people feel pressurized to have a termination.[541] Victoria Seavilleklein lists the pressures that women face if presented with the results of a prenatal test:

> [T]he normalization of technology combined with a cultural desire for information, cultural assumptions about women and mothers being responsible for health combined with the misperception of medical technology as promoting the birth of a healthy child, the categorization of pregnant women into risk categories with technology offering risk reduction and reassurance, and medical and societal values that determine which choices will be supported and made available to pregnant women.[542]

All of these pressures, she suggests, mean that it does not necessarily follow that offering the test increases the choices that women have.

There is some research that medical professionals advising women in these cases overemphasize the difficulties connected with raising a disabled child.[543] Some disability groups point to what they regard as the disparity between the effort and funding put into prenatal testing for disability and that put into improving the lot of disabled people.[544] Nor is it only serious disabilities that are involved here. We have already mentioned a case in which abortion was performed because the foetus had a cleft lip, and some foresee a time when fixation with personal appearance will mean that even the most 'trivial blemish' will be regarded as a reason for abortion.[545]

Some argue that disability is a social construct and should never be perceived as a ground for abortion. It is not the person's body that is the problem; it is society's failure to provide properly for disabled people. This argument was raised and discussed in Chapter 1. The point here would be that allowing abortion on the disability ground would be relying on a distinction (between disability and health) without meaning. Notably, there is research suggesting that parents of disabled children are more worried about the social stigma attached to disability than about the impact of the physical limitations.

In supporting the permissibility of abortion on the grounds of foetal disability, Jackson argues that:

> Disability should not be a legitimate reason for choosing between people, but a fetus does not have legal personality and so rules that prohibit discrimination cannot be said to apply in utero. It is perfectly plausible to think that a disability makes a life less satisfying without believing that a person with that disability is less valuable.[546]

---

[538] Bruce (2013).   [539] Parens and Asch (2000).   [540] Field (1993).   [541] Tomlinson (1999).
[542] Seavilleklein (2009: 69).   [543] Alderson (2002).   [544] Shakespeare (1999).
[545] Gosden (1999: xiv). This is just implausible according to Jackson (2001: 97).
[546] Jackson (2001: 98).

Furedi and Lee argue that:

> A woman who opts for this kind of abortion is not making a social or political statement about the abnormality, or about people with that disability. She is making a statement about herself; what she feels she can cope with and what she wants.[547]

In other words, the abortion decision should simply be regarded as the mother's choice.[548] Priaulx argues that there should be no discrimination between a woman carrying a late-term healthy foetus and a late-term foetus suffering disability.[549] Both women should have equal control over their pregnancies.

Those who oppose the foetal disability ground could argue that it should be removed from the list of circumstances in the Abortion Act 1967 in which abortion is legal. Alternatively, it might be argued that these arguments show the difficulties that can arise once the reasons behind a woman's abortion decision are opened up to scrutiny from other parties. This leads to the argument that therefore it would be better to allow a woman to abort, without any consideration of the reasons behind her decision.[550]

20.3 Abortion and sex selection

What about the decision to abort a foetus on the basis of its sex?[551] The Department of Health is clear: 'Abortion on the grounds of gender alone is illegal.'[552] However, it goes on to explain that some disabilities are sex-linked and so if the abortion is performed to avoid disability, rather than on gender grounds it would be permitted. The BMA[553] has suggested another situation in which sex of the foetus might be a legitimate part of the justification for the abortion:

> Doctors may come to the conclusion, in a particular case, that the effects on the physical or mental health of the pregnant woman of having a child of a particular sex would be so severe as to provide legal and ethical justification for a termination.[554]

Dubuk and Coleman estimate that, in the UK, up to 100 abortions each year are carried out on the basis of foetal sex alone.[555] Worldwide, it appears that there is a preference for boys.[556] It has been suggested that India is 40 million women short of the number that a normal sex ratio would produce.[557] Should the law take the view that although generally abortion may be regarded as a private decision of the woman, where she reaches her decision for reasons that amount to discrimination on the grounds of sex, she should not be permitted to abort?[558] Notably, there is an increasing reluctance in some hospitals to tell a woman the sex of the baby that she is carrying for fear that the information could

---

[547] Furedi and Lee (2001: 124). See also Furedi (2001).
[548] Scott (2003). See Smith (2007) for a discussion of abortion and neonaticide for severe disability.
[549] Priaulx (2007b).   [550] Savulescu (2001a).
[551] Greasley (2016). Sex is now identifiable at twelve weeks' gestation: Gosden (1999). See BBC News online (7 October 2013) for a refusal of the Director of Public Prosecutions to prosecute in a case of alleged gender-based abortion.
[552] DoH (2014).
[553] It is notable that the DoH (2014) does not include this argument in their discussion.
[554] BMA (2017a).   [555] Dubuk and Coleman (2007).
[556] Jackson (2001: 107–9).   [557] Gosden (1999: 47).
[558] Moazam (2004) provides an interesting discussion of the difficulties that feminists encounter in dealing with this issue.

be used as the basis for an abortion decision. Emily Jackson insists that the abortion decision is for the woman to take, and even if it is one of which we do not approve, that does not mean that she should be compelled to carry on an unwanted pregnancy.[559] The correct response to the issue of sex selection, she argues, is to educate people against it. To Derek Morgan, however, to allow sex to form the basis of an abortion decision is to violate a fundamental principle of equality between men and women.[560] Others question whether women who choose to abort on the basis of sex selection are making a genuinely autonomous choice.[561] It is also worth emphasizing that tests might establish the sex of the child, but not the gender the child will choose to live. It might be argued that it is potentially misleading to tell parents whether their child is a boy or a girl.[562]

21 Pregnancy and childbirth

There have been great medical advances in the treatment of pregnancy and foetal medicine. In the past, pregnancy and childbirth carried a significant risk of death, and indeed still do in many parts of the world. But in the UK, pregnancy for most women carries few risks and the number of children lost during pregnancy or childbirth has decreased. The advances in foetal medicine have been remarkable. Further, there has been an emphasis on social support for pregnant women. Pregnant women are exempt from prescription charges during pregnancy and for twelve months after they have given birth. Classes, obstetric services, and a wide range of support services are available during pregnancy, birth, and the months after childbirth.[563] Pregnant woman are offered some protection under employment law, which, for example, makes it illegal for an employer to dismiss a female worker on the grounds that she is pregnant.

However, with modern-day medical approaches to pregnancy come some concerns. First, the ability of medicine to provide treatment and even surgery for the foetus has encouraged the notion that the foetus, like the mother, is a patient. Some are concerned that, in this way, the mother's interests are easily lost.[564] A focus on the interests of the foetus alone easily leads to a model that promotes the maternal–foetal conflict. On the other hand, foetal medicine has meant the birth of healthy (or healthier) babies for women wanting to give birth. It has also led to a wider social awareness of factors that can harm a foetus, such as pollution and cigarette smoke.[565]

Second, there is a concern over the 'medicalization' of pregnancy. In 2005–06, only 47 per cent of deliveries were 'normal' (defined as those without surgical intervention, the use of instruments, induction, epidural, or general anaesthetic).[566] Some argue that pregnancy, which should be a natural, straightforward process, has been 'pathologized' into a kind of illness. Ann Oakley writes:

---

[559] Jackson (2001: 110). As she points out, it would be easy to invent a different reason for an abortion if she were told that the foetus's sex was an unacceptable reason. See also Zilberberg (2007).
[560] Morgan (2001).   [561] Rogers, Ballantyne, and Draper (2007).   [562] Browne (2017).
[563] Although Jackson (2001: 116) states that there are regional variations in the standards of obstetric services available.
[564] McLean (1999: 48).
[565] There is evidence that a child is able to suffer pain at least by the twenty-sixth week of gestation: Wyatt (2000: 1).
[566] Richardson and Mmata (2007: vii).

[W]hen antenatal care began [its purpose] was to screen a population of basically normal pregnant women in order to pick up the few who were at risk of disease or death. Today the situation is reversed, and the object of antenatal care is to screen a population suffering from the pathology of pregnancy for the few women who are normal enough to give birth with the minimum of midwifery attention.[567]

Pregnant women must regularly meet with medical professionals, who will be monitoring them and encouraging or discouraging certain forms of behaviour. Despite the movement in support of natural childbirth and home births, fewer than 4 per cent of births take place at home.[568] Although women are usually encouraged to 'take control' of the birthing process, this is often presented as being the doctor letting her do so.[569] All of this disempowers the woman. The perception created is that she lacks the expertise and technology to deal with her pregnancy, and needs healthcare professionals to assist her. Again, these concerns need to be weighed up against the benefits of the medical supervision in terms of improved health of the mother and baby.[570] The delicate balance between advising, supporting, and empowering is a difficult one to make. The Department of Health's document *Changing Childbirth* puts it this way:

> The woman must be the focus of maternity care. She should be able to feel that she is in control of what is happening to her and be able to make decisions about her care, based on her needs, having discussed matters fully with the professionals involved.[571]

Many feel that this is a statement of ideal rather than of practice.[572]

Third, there is a particular concern at the rate of pregnancies that end in a Caesarean section operation (26.2 per cent for 2014).[573] The rate recommended by the World Health Organization (WHO) is 10–15 per cent.[574] The general view appears to be that what has changed is not the medical condition of pregnant women, but a number of factors.[575] One is fear of litigation. Where there are complications during birth, it is often seen as 'safer' to perform a Caesarean section immediately than to allow the birth to continue. It is also quicker, cheaper, and easier to perform a Caesarean section than to assist a woman through what might be a painful and lengthy natural birth. The popular press has even suggested that some women request a Caesarean section to avoid the pain of labour: they are 'too posh to push'.[576] This appears to be a myth with no empirical support, but it is noticeable that the two most expensive private maternity hospitals do have some of the highest rates of Caesarean sections (at 34 per cent and 38 per cent).[577] The Maternity Care Working Party points out that: 'The NHS pays a high price for this trend towards surgical birth. But women and their families pay an even higher price in the form of delayed postnatal recovery, increased risks, and

---

[567] Oakley (1984: 213).
[568] Richardson and Mmata (2007: vii), but there is wide variation around the country.
[569] Jackson (2001: 118).
[570] Fitzpatrick (2003) is a little sceptical about the benefits that such treatments offer.
[571] DoH (1989: 21).
[572] For a survey of women's unhappy experiences during childbirth, see BBC News online (13 June 2005a).
[573] Health and Social Care Information Centre (2015).   [574] RCOG (2001a).
[575] Nordic countries have been able to reduce their Caesarean rate significantly, without harmful consequences: RCOG (2001a).
[576] NHS (2010b).   [577] Jackson (2001: 117).

post-surgical discomfort and fatigue.'[578] NICE has now issued guidance on the use of Caesarean sections and has emphasized that maternal preference is an important factor to take into account. It is considering whether all women should be given the option of a Caesarean section.[579]

A fourth issue is the widespread use of prenatal tests. Less than 1 per cent of British pregnant women receive no prenatal tests[580] and research indicates that many women do not realize that routine screening is optional.[581] The explicit aim of the tests is to ascertain whether there are abnormalities or concerns with the foetus. On the one hand, there are those who argue that the primary purpose of the tests is to enable a couple to abort a child who it is predicted will be disabled. This raises the issue of abortion and disabled foetuses, which we discussed earlier. On the other hand, there are those whose concern is that the tests, and particularly scans, are really designed to emphasize to the mother that she is carrying 'a child' and thereby reinforce the huge number of concerns about what an expectant mother should or should not eat or do.[582] This all increases medical control over pregnant women. But all of these concerns must be weighed up against the improvements in the health of newborn babies, which for many women is crucial. Many pregnant women will want to know what they can do or avoid doing to improve the health of their foetus.

22 Regulating pregnant women

We now know that a foetus can be harmed by the conduct of the mother during pregnancy. For example, inappropriate use of alcohol, illegal drugs, and food can damage a foetus.[583] Less well known is that the father's behaviour can also affect the foetus. If, for example, he had been misusing drugs before intercourse, this can damage his sperm and thereby cause harm to any child born. Further, environmental factors, such as pollution or the cleanliness of hospitals, can harm a child before birth. Should we seek to limit other people's behaviour in order to protect the foetus? It is the mother on whom most attention has been focused (a point noteworthy in itself).[584] Should we, for example, imprison a drug-using mother to ensure that her unborn child does not suffer from the consequences of her drug use, as has happened in the United States?[585]

Perhaps the first point to make is that the idea that inappropriate drug or alcohol use leads to harm to the foetus is a little simplistic. Research has shown that 70.9 per cent of 'poor' women drinking more than three units of alcohol a day gave birth to a child suffering from foetal alcohol syndrome, while for wealthier people the rate was 4.5 per cent.[586] This suggests that there is more to foetal alcohol syndrome than simply misuse

---

[578] Maternity Care Working Party (2001: 6).   [579] NICE (2011).
[580] Graham, Smith, Kamal, et al. (2000: 157).   [581] Kolker and Burke (1994: 5).
[582] Jackson (2001: 121).
[583] See Seymour (2000: 223) for a useful summary of the ways in which maternal behaviour can cause harm to the foetus. It is well established that smoking during pregnancy can harm the foetus: Hultman, Sparen, Takei, et al. (1999). More controversial are suggestions that a vegetarian diet—North and Golding (2000)—or depression—Hultman, Sparen, Takei, et al. (1999)—are harmful.
[584] Meredith (2005).
[585] Cave (2004: ch. 3) provides a useful discussion of the use of the criminal law in the United States in these kinds of cases.
[586] Bingol, Schuster, Fuchs, et al. (1987).

of alcohol. But that should not distract from the fact that drug and alcohol misuse by pregnant women can harm their foetuses.

It might be thought that if you take the view that the foetus does not become a person until birth (or afterwards), the issue is straightforward: the foetus cannot make any claims on the woman. However, this would be too easy an answer. First, even if the foetus is not a person, you might still believe that it has interests that deserve protection.[587] Second, it might be argued that even if intervention is not justified in the name of the foetus, protection is justified in the name of preventing harm to the child who will be born and suffer from the effects of the woman's actions during pregnancy. Third, it might be argued that there are broad social objectives, such as saving expenses for the NHS, that justify intervention.

Let us assume that we have a clearly established harm, be that to the foetus or the child who will later be born. Does that justify imposing legal restrictions on the woman's lifestyle? Those who argue not tend to use three types of argument. The first is that, because of the closeness of the relationship between the woman and the foetus, and all of the sacrifices that the woman has and will make for the foetus, the law cannot demand anything more from her.[588] As Eekelaar notes, there is an important difference between pregnant women and parents of children here.[589] With parents, if their lifestyle choices are harming children, the criminal law may be appropriate. This is because we can say to a parent of a child, 'You are free to live your life in this way if you choose, but if you do, then you must ensure that your child is cared for by someone else' (for example by the local authority or a relative). But for a pregnant woman, there is not this option (unless you are attracted by the argument that the woman has the option to abort if she wishes to continue her alcohol intake, for example). But this still leaves Scott arguing that a woman cannot refuse to have treatment for the foetus's benefit if she is refusing for a trivial reason.[590]

A second argument is that such legal intervention would be counter-productive. If a pregnant woman who was taking drugs or excessive alcohol knew that she was thereby committing an offence, she may decide not to seek medical help at all. Further, it is unlikely that many addicted to alcohol or drugs would change their behaviour in the light of potential criminal sanctions. 'What kind of society do we want?', Robertson asks: 'In the worst-case scenario, special pregnancy police will be commissioned to monitor women for pregnancies, and then survey their behaviour; if they err, they are stigmatised, shamed, fined or incarcerated.'[591]

A third argument is to emphasize that the legal response to such arguments appears to have been especially directed towards women. Men whose lifestyles have meant that their sperm is 'damaged' and who thereby harm the child escape liability.[592] The wider ways in which society may be said to cause harm to foetuses often go unchallenged, although it has even been reported that makers of French wine are facing legal action in connection with children born with birth defects, based on the fact that their products do not contain clear warnings about the dangers of drinking alcohol while pregnant.[593]

---

[587] Norrie (2000: 227) points out that things can be protected even though they are not people and even if they do not have interests (for example listed buildings).

[588] Herring (2000: 281).

[589] Eekelaar (1988). See also the reasoning of the Canadian Supreme Court in *Winnipeg Child and Family Services v G* (1997) 152 DLR 193.

[590] Scott (2003: 114).   [591] Robertson (1994b: 180).

[592] Daniels and Golden (2000) discuss in detail the ways in which fathers can harm their offspring through their lifestyle choices prior to conception.

[593] Burgermeister (2004).

In conclusion, many writers have accepted there is an argument that a pregnant woman is under a moral obligation not to engage in behaviour that will cause avoidable harm to the child once born.[594] But few British academic commentators have argued that that duty should be turned into a legal one.[595] The strongest legal response would be the removal of the child at birth, the justification being that the behaviour of the woman during pregnancy indicates that she poses a risk to the well-being of the child after birth.[596] It is through education, encouragement, and support that we are more likely to prevent these kinds of harmful behaviour than through the criminal law.[597] Finally, it should not be forgotten that, in the words of one obstetrician, most pregnant women 'would cut off their heads to save their babies'.[598]

23 Caesarean section cases

One topic that has attracted much attention from commentators and courts is the issue of enforced Caesarean sections.[599] The kind of case under discussion is one in which the pregnant woman in labour is told that, without a Caesarean section, her life and that of the foetus are in severe danger. The woman is, however, adamant that she does not want the operation. Some first-instance decisions have indicated that an operation could be performed.[600] The legal position is now clear after the judgments of the Court of Appeal in *Re MB (An Adult: Caesarean Section)*[601] and *St George's Healthcare NHS Trust v S*.[602]

> **KEY CASE** *St George's Healthcare NHS Trust v S* [1998] 3 All ER 673
>
> S was thirty-five weeks pregnant and suffering from various complications, including pre-eclampsia. She was told that she needed to have a Caesarean section operation. She was adamant that she wanted the child to be born naturally, even if that meant that she and/or the child would die. Her doctors were clear that she was competent to make decisions. Nevertheless, the hospital detained her under the Mental Health Act 1983, section 2. An application by the NHS Trust to a court, seeking authorization for the operation against her consent, was made and Hogg J granted the declaration sought. A baby girl was born as a result. S did not seek to resist the performance of the operation, because to do so would be undignified. S sought judicial review of the hospital's actions and appealed against Hogg J's decision.
>
> The Court of Appeal allowed the appeal, and declared that the detention and administration of treatment had been unlawful. Judge LJ warned of the dangers in concluding that a patient was incompetent or mentally ill simply because her decision appeared irrational or bizarre. Her depression

---

[594] But note the view of Jackson (2001: 115): 'Every pregnant woman should . . . be allowed to decide for herself the nature and the scope of the obligations she chooses to assume towards her developing fetus.'

[595] Cave (2004); Seymour (2000: 239); Norrie (2000); Brazier (1999b).

[596] *D v Berkshire CC* [1987] 1 All ER 29.   [597] Cave (2004: ch. 6).   [598] Quoted in Rhoden (1987: 1959).

[599] Much has been written on these cases, including: Scott (2002); Wells (1998); Herring (2000); Brazier (1997); Plummer (1988); Draper (1996); Widdett and Thomson (1997); Weaver (2002).

[600] Wells (1998: 250).

[601] [1997] 2 FLR 426, discussed in Michalowski (1999).

[602] [1998] 3 WLR 936. Fox and Moreton (2015) is an excellent discussion of the case law.

was not a mental condition of the kind required by the Mental Health Act 1983. Having found that S was competent, the Court of Appeal found the case straightforward, in legal terms. Judge LJ explained:

> [I]n our judgment while pregnancy increases the personal responsibility of a woman it does not diminish her entitlement to decide whether or not to undergo medical treatment. Although human, and protected by the law in a number of different ways . . . an unborn child is not a separate person from its mother. Its need for medical assistance does not prevail over her rights. She is entitled, not to be forced to submit to an invasion of her body against her will, whether her own life or that of her unborn child depends on it. Her right is not reduced or diminished merely because her decision to exercise it may appear morally repugnant.[603]

Therefore if a competent pregnant woman refuses to consent to medical intervention, it cannot be imposed upon her even if, without it, she and the foetus will die.

So the first question in the legal analysis is whether the woman is competent. If she is and refuses to consent to the Caesarean section, then it is illegal to perform it and a court will not authorize its performance.[604] The courts have explicitly rejected an argument that it is lawful to carry out the operation in such a case in order to save the life of the foetus. If the woman is not competent, then doctors can carry out the operation having regard to the best interests of the woman. The interests of the foetus are not to be taken into account. There will be little difficulty, therefore, in ordering the Caesarean section if that is necessary to save the incompetent woman's life. But if the benefit of the Caesarean section is solely for the benefit of the foetus, then it may not be performed.

The courts continue to hear cases about Caesarean section cases. In five recent cases: *Re AA*;[605] *Royal Free NHS Foundation Trust v AB*;[606] *Re P*;[607] *Great Western Hospitals NHS Foundation Trust v AA*;[608] and *University Hospital NHS Trust v CA*,[609] the women were found to lack capacity to consent and the declarations sought by the medical team permitting Caesarean section were granted. It is possible to detect a difference between the cases. In *Re AA*[610] the best interests' assessment focused on the medical evidence of a 1 per cent chance of a ruptured womb which the medical team thought justified performing the Caesarean. By contrast in *Great Western Hospitals NHS Foundation Trust v AA*[611] the primary focus at the best interests' stage was not the medical evidence but rather what the woman would have wanted had she not been affected by her mental disorder. The evidence of her family was she wanted to produce and care for the child. In *Royal Free NHS Foundation Trust v AB*[612] Hayden J held that forcing a Caesarean section was 'draconian' but could be justified if the court determined it was what the woman would have wanted had she had capacity. In *Re P*[613] particular weight was put on the

---

[603] At 692.
[604] See Kukla, Kuppermann, Little, et al. (2009) for an argument that the law needs to do more to ensure that women are able to make a genuine choice.
[605] [2012] EWHC 4378 (COP), discussed in Warmsley (2014).
[606] [2014] EWCOP 50.   [607] [2013] EWHC 4581 (COP).
[608] [2014] EWHC 132 (Fam).   [609] [2016] EWCOP 51.
[610] [2012] EWHC 4378 (COP), discussed Warmsley (2014).
[611] [2014] EWHC 132 (Fam).   [612] [2014] EWCOP 50.   [613] [2013] EWHC 4581 (COP).

fact that a vaginal delivery carried a serious risk the child would be born disabled and it would not be in P's interests to have to raise a disabled child. In *University Hospital NHS Trust v CA*[614] although P strongly opposed a Caesarean section, if a vaginal delivery was attempted it was extremely likely that an emergency Caesarean section would be required, which would be far more traumatic than a planned one.

The law, as set out above, therefore emphasizes the importance that is attached to the autonomy of the pregnant woman. Indeed, that was central to the seminal *Montgomery v Lanarkshire*[615] decision where the doctor was found to be negligent for not offering the claimant the option of a Caesarean section. Whether or not autonomy should be granted such pre-eminence is a matter for debate, which we discussed in Chapter 4. The current state of the law raises concerns from a variety of perspectives.

(i) Some commentators have complained that the courts too easily find a woman undergoing labour to be incompetent. The courts have been willing to find a woman incompetent because of the emotional stress and pain of labour.[616] Because almost any labour involves stress and pain, it might be thought that this, in effect, will mean that every woman in labour can be found incompetent. Indeed, some have argued that the construction of motherhood is such that any pregnant woman who does not want to consent to an operation to save her foetus's life will be regarded as incompetent.[617] This means that a pregnant woman has a harder task in establishing competency than a man.[618] Further, some women may not realize that they can say 'no'.[619] If so, the loud trumpeting by the courts of autonomy will mean little. On the other hand, it has also been argued that if the principle of autonomy is to be elevated to the extent that respecting it can mean the death of the woman and her foetus, then the law should ensure that the refusal of life-saving treatment is a fully free and informed decision.[620]

(ii) In many of the cases in which the court has ordered that the Caesarean section go ahead despite the opposition of the woman, she has afterwards expressed great gratitude that the courts reached the decision that they did.[621] Does this demonstrate that there are dangers that the present law places too much weight on the 'momentary' wishes of the woman?[622] Or is this argument too easy a way of justifying paternalism?

(iii) There have been grave concerns that judges are often faced with these cases at a stage when they have become an emergency, giving the courts little time in which to assess the issues properly.[623]

(iv) To some, the emphasis on the right of the pregnant woman overlooks her responsibilities. Kluge writes:

---

[614] [2016] EWCOP 51.   [615] [2015] UKSC 11, discussed in depth in Chapter 4.
[616] *Rochdale v C* [1997] 1 FCR 274; Widdett and Thomson (1997).
[617] Diduck (1993) expresses concerns that any woman who is not acting as the idealized 'mother' is therefore incompetent.
[618] Widdett and Thomson (1997).   [619] Donohoe (1996).
[620] Herring (2000).   [621] For example, *Re L (Patient: Non-consensual Treatment)* [1997] 2 FLR 837.
[622] See the discussion in Wells (1998: 250).
[623] Wells (1998: 62).

By voluntarily allowing the fetus to become a person, possessed of a right to life, the mother had de facto accepted the conditions accompanying that action—which is to say, since she was aware of the dependent nature of the fetuses and children (or ought to have been thus aware) she had, through her action, voluntarily accepted the responsibilities attendant on the fact of such dependence and thereby has de facto subordinated her right to otherwise unhindered autonomy, to the right to life of the fetus.[624]

But Scott replies that:

[A] woman who elects not to abort and thereby chooses to carry a fetus to term is not at the same time undertaking to do *whatever* is required to prevent harm to the fetus and ensure that it is live-born and in good health, notwithstanding her moral duties to do all she can.[625]

(v) As already mentioned, the courts, when considering the best interests of the incompetent patient, will not consider the interests of the foetus. Some think that the court, however, needs to take on board the point that if the mother has taken the pregnancy through to the stage of labour, she can be taken to have wanted the foetus to be born alive, and that therefore, in that sense, the interests of the foetus should be considered, because the foetus's welfare is important to the mother's well-being.[626] But even in the light of these concerns, given the current law on consent, the present law should not be surprising. If a 6-year-old child needs a donor kidney, a parent cannot be compelled against his or her wishes to provide one. Indeed, even if the child needs only some blood, a parent could not be compelled to donate that. So why should a pregnant woman be required to undergo a Caesarean section operation for the foetus?

24 Conclusions

Your views on the topics discussed will determine what you regard as the main theme of this chapter. To some, we will have seen the shocking failure of our legal system to protect the most vulnerable members of our society (unborn children) from being killed. To others, we will have seen the struggle for control over women's bodies, especially during pregnancy. Although women now have some control over their reproductive bodies, this control is said by some only to be to the extent that it is permitted by the male-dominated legal or medical establishment.[627] For those seeking a middle path of respecting the interests of the foetus and the rights of the mother, the exact balance appears elusive and uneasy.

---

[624] Kluge (1998: 205). See also Robertson (1983: 456).
[625] Scott (2002: 273).
[626] Jackson (2001: 136) is critical of the willingness of the courts to order Caesarean sections where the patient is incompetent, especially where the decisions appear to have taken into account the well-being of the foetus. In reply, it could be argued that a pregnant woman who has carried her pregnancy to labour can be taken to wish, if possible, for the birth of a healthy child: Herring (2000: 277).
[627] Thomson (1998).

QUESTIONS

1. Consider this statement:

   > Choosing to carry a pregnancy to term and give birth to a child is undoubtedly one of the most significant decisions a woman will ever take, and it is not, in my opinion, one that anyone else should be able to either veto, or force upon her.[628]

   Do you think that this is a guiding principle that should be applied to all of the topics discussed in this chapter?

2. Apparently, some clinics will now offer 'lunchtime abortions', for which procedure women will spend only an hour or two in a clinic. Is this shocking or an important step towards recognizing the right to abortion?

3. Think about the following:

   > And suppose we've let him be born in the first place, not plucked him out, or sucked him out, untimely ripped from the womb. Many of us have a death like this on our conscience: the children that might have been, the embryos. A murdered foetus: not to be equated with a murdered child. And yet, and yet. There are no weighing-scales for the guilty heart.[629]

   Do you think that there needs to be a greater awareness among all those involved in the abortion debate of the trauma experienced by those affected by abortion? Or should the message be that abortion is a simple standard medical procedure?

4. Ronald Dworkin, a leading supporter of abortion rights, argues that:

   > [I]n a better society, which supported child rearing as enthusiastically as it discourages abortion, the status of a fetus probably would change, because women's sense of pregnancy and motherhood as creative would be more genuine and less compromised, and the inherent value of their own lives less threatened.[630]

   Do you agree?

5. In the popular literature, a common pro-life argument is to point out that, in line with current medical practice, it is likely that Beethoven would have been aborted: what geniuses are being lost to the human race through the practice of abortion? Hare makes the point in a more personal way: we are glad that we were not aborted and so we should not abort others.[631] Harris replies:

---

[628] Jackson (2001: 71).   [629] Morrison (1997: 55–6).   [630] Dworkin (1993: 57).
[631] Hare (1975).

To choose not to have a child with inherited syphilis is not to decide that the world would be better off without Beethoven. It is as senseless to bemoan the fact that we have elected not to create 'a Beethoven' as it would be to celebrate the fact that, by practising contraception, we have just prevented the birth of a Hitler.[632]

Dawkins rejects the argument, saying that it could even be used to oppose a woman resisting rape on the basis that the rape might produce a Beethoven.[633] McLachlan replies to such arguments that there is a difference between killing someone and not bringing someone into existence.[634] Are these profitable lines of argument?

6. If a woman is offered a scan, but through medical negligence she is not told of an apparent disability, should she be able to claim damages based on the argument that, had she known of the child's disability, she would have had an abortion?[635]

7. For those who believe that an embryo has some kind of moral status, there are some difficult questions that will arise in the future. What status should be attached to an entity that is a mixture of human and non-human gametes, or a creation that is a bit of embryo (for example a 'headless clone')?[636]

8. If there were a fire in a fertility clinic and it was possible to save only either a two-month-old baby or a hundred frozen embryos, would not even the most ardent pro-lifer save the baby? Does this not show that, in fact, pro-lifers do not really think that embryos have an equal right to life as babies?[637]

9. If technology were to develop so that a foetus could be removed from a mother and grown in an artificial environment until it was viable, would that alter the ethical issues surrounding abortion?[638]

FURTHER READING

A comprehensive bibliography, including all references used throughout the book, is available online at www.oup.com/uk/herringmedical7e/.

For book-length discussions of abortion, see:

Beckwith, F. (2007) *Defending Life: A Moral and Legal Case against Abortion Choice* (Cambridge University Press).

Boonin, D. (2002) *A Defense of Abortion* (Cambridge University Press).

Dworkin, R. (1993) *Life's Dominion* (HarperCollins).

George, R. and Tollefsen, C. (2008) *Embryo: A Defense of Human Life* (Doubleday).

Greasley, K. (2017) *Arguments about Abortion* (Oxford University Press).

Kaczor, C. (2011) *The Ethics of Abortion* (Routledge).

Lee, E. (2002) *Abortion: Whose Right?* (Hodder and Stoughton).

---

[632] Harris (2001: 61).   [633] Dawkins (2007: 399).   [634] McLachlan (2009b).
[635] This issue is discussed in detail in Scott (2003).   [636] See Watt (2007) for a discussion.
[637] See Deckers (2007c) and Mathison and Davis (2017) for a discussion of such a scenario.
[638] See Jackson (2008) for a provocative discussion.

Sanger, A. (2004) *Beyond Choice* (Public Affairs).

Sheldon, S. (1997) *Beyond Control: Medical Power and Abortion Law* (Pluto).

Tooley, M., et al. (2009) *Abortion: Three Perspectives* (Oxford University Press).

Leading articles on abortion include:

Fenwick, D. (2014) ' "Abortion jurisprudence" at Strasbourg: deferential, avoidant and normatively neutral?', *Legal Studies* 34: 214.

Finnis, J. (1973) 'The rights and wrongs of abortion', *Philosophy and Public Affairs* 2: 117.

Greasley, K. (2012) 'Abortion and regret', *Journal of Medical Ethics* 38: 705.

Greasley, K. (2016) 'Is sex-selective abortion against the law?', *Oxford Journal of Legal Studies* 36: 535.

Mackenzie, C. (1992) 'Abortion and embodiment', *Australasian Journal of Philosophy* 70: 136.

Manninen, B. (2013) 'The value of choice and the choice to value: expanding the discussion about fetal life within prochoice advocacy', *Hypatia* 28: 663.

Marquis, D. (2006) 'Abortion and the beginning and end of human life', *Journal of Law, Medicine and Ethics* 34: 16.

McGuinness, S. (2013b) 'Law, reproduction, and disability: fatally "handicapped"?', *Medical Law Review* 21: 213.

Priaulx, N. (2017) 'The Social Life of Abortion Law: on Personal and Political Pedagogy', *Medical Law Review* 25: 73.

Scott, R. (2005) 'Interpreting the disability ground of the Abortion Act', *Cambridge Law Journal* 64: 388.

Sheldon, S. (2016) 'The Decriminalisation of Abortion: An Argument for Modernisation', *Oxford Journal of Legal Studies* 36: 334.

Sifris, R. (2010) 'Restrictive regulation of abortion and the right to health', *Medical Law Review* 18: 185.

Thomson, J. (1971) 'A defense of abortion', *Philosophy and Public Affairs* 1: 47.

West, R., Murray, J., and Esser, M. (2014) *In Search of Common Ground on Abortion* (Ashgate).

For discussion of the regulation of pregnancy, see:

Cave, E. (2004) *The Mother of All Crimes* (Ashgate).

Fovargue, S. and Miola, J. (2016) 'Are We Still Policing Pregnancy?' in C. Stanton, S. Devaney, A-M. Farrell, and A. Mullock (eds), *Pioneering Healthcare Law: Essays in Honour of Margaret Brazier* (Routledge).

Halliday, S. (2016) *Autonomy and Pregnancy* (Routledge).

Meredith, S. (2005) *Policing Pregnancy: The Law and Ethics of Obstetric Conflict* (Ashgate).

Seymour, J. (2000) *Childbirth and the Law* (Oxford University Press).

Sperling, D. (2006) *Management of Post-Mortem Pregnancy: Legal and Philosophical Aspects* (Aldershot).

The status of the foetus is examined in:

Burin, A. (2014) 'Beyond pragmatism: Defending the "bright line" of birth', *Medical Law Review* 22: 494.

Ford, M. (2005b) 'A property model of pregnancy', *International Journal of Law in Context* 1: 261.

Ford, M. (2009) 'Nothing and not-nothing: law's ambivalent response to transformation and transgression at the beginning of life' in S. Smith and R. Deazley (eds), *The Legal, Medical and Cultural Regulation of the Body* (Ashgate).

Ford, N. (2002) *The Prenatal Person* (Blackwell).

Fox, M. and McGuinness, S. (2016) 'The science of muddling through: Categorising embryos' in A. Mullock et al. (eds), *Pioneering Healthcare Law: Essays in Honour of Margaret Brazier* (Routledge).

Herring, J. (2011b) 'The loneliness of status: the legal and moral significance of birth' in F. Ebtehaj, J. Herring, M. Johnson, and M. Richards (eds), *Birth Rites and Rights* (Hart).

Morgan, L. and Michaels, M. (1999) *Fetal Subjects, Feminist Positions* (University of Pennsylvania Press).

Warren, M. (1997) *Moral Status: Obligations to Persons and Other Living Things* (Oxford University Press).

Watt, H. (2016) *The Ethics of Pregnancy, Abortion and Childbirth: Exploring Moral Choices in Childbearing* (Routledge).

Compulsory sterilization is considered in:

Freeman, M. (1988) 'Sterilising the mentally handicapped' in M. Freeman (ed), *Medicine, Ethics and the Law* (Stevens).

Keywood, K. (2002) 'Disabling sex: some legal thinking about sterilisation, learning disability and embodiment' in A. Morris and S. Nott (eds), *The Gendered Nature of Health Care Provision* (Dartmouth).

Keywood, K. (2015) 'People Like Us Don't Have Babies: Learning Disability, Prospective Parenthood and Legal Transformations' in J. Herring and J. Wall (eds), *Landmark Cases in Medical Law* (Hart).

Negligent sterilization and wrongful birth is discussed in:

Hoyano, L. (2015) 'McFarlane v Tayside Health Board' in J. Herring and J. Wall (eds), *Landmark Cases in Medical Law* (Hart).

Priaulx, N. (2007a) *The Harm Paradox: Tort Law and the Unwanted Child in an Era of Choice* (Routledge).

7 Reproduction

INTRODUCTION

We live in interesting times. Consider some of these headlines:

- 'US "pregnant man" has baby girl';[1]
- '21-year-old fathers seventh child';[2]
- 'Mixed-sex human embryo created';[3]
- 'Twins born to own gran fly home';[4]
- 'Mother, 53, has baby for daughter';[5]
- 'UK considers bulk sperm imports';[6]
- 'Yes to cloning with two mothers';[7]
- 'Woman, 67, to be "oldest mum yet" ';[8]
- 'Couple having four babies by two surrogates';[9]
- 'Men should bank sperm early as quality diminishes alarmingly with age';[10]
- 'First three parent baby born to infertile couple';[11]
- 'The genius sperm bank';[12]
- 'Baby girl born to dead mother';[13] and
- 'Sperm bank turns down red-heads'.[14]

Such headlines generate a range of responses. Some people are terrified, some are amused, and others, impressed with the wonders of modern science. What is clear is that the days when there was one 'simple' way of producing children are long past. Technological advances have given us a wide range of options for creating children. The first 'test tube baby' was born in 1978, but now, in the UK, one in fifty children born is a result of medically assisted conception.[15] With the scientific developments have come a host of complex legal and ethical difficulties. Henry Greely has written a book entitled, *The End of Sex*, foreseeing a time when the 'natural' way of producing children will no longer be used.[16] These will be considered in this chapter. The starting point, however, is the issue of infertility, for it is that which has spurred the technological advances—although, increasingly, assisted reproduction is being used by those who do not suffer infertility.

---

[1] BBC News online (3 July 2008).   [2] BBC News online (2 July 2006).
[3] BBC News online (3 July 2003).   [4] BBC News online (26 July 2004).
[5] BBC News online (30 September 2005).   [6] BBC News online (21 October 2003).
[7] BBC News online (8 September 2005).   [8] BBC News online (3 May 2005).
[9] BBC News online (28 October 2013).   [10] *Daily Telegraph* (2015).
[11] BBC News online (18 January 2017)
[12] BBC News online (15 June 2006). Some readers of this book may be suitable candidates: http://www.geniusspermbank.com/.
[13] BBC News online (12 January 2009).   [14] HFEA (2015).   [15] Jackson (2001: 161).
[16] He imagines sex may still be used for other purposes!

1 Infertility

1.1 What is infertility?

A common definition of 'infertility' is that a couple has failed to conceive after twelve months of unprotected sexual intercourse, or has suffered three or more miscarriages or stillbirths.[17] However, the World Health Organization (WHO) suggests that there should be two years of unprotected sexual intercourse without conception before an infertility diagnosis is made. Indeed, it is notable that half of those couples who have had unprotected sexual intercourse for twelve months in an unsuccessful attempt to have a child are, in fact, able to go on to have children without medical intervention.[18] This has led some to claim that the 'assisted reproduction industry' uses an unduly broad definition of infertility in order to increase the number of potential clients.[19] That said, it should be noted that the age of the couple can have a significant impact on the chances of success of assisted reproductive treatment, and a couple who delay seeking assistance might be reducing their chance of the treatment working.

1.2 What are the rates of infertility?

Infertility affects around 16 per cent of couples.[20] In the UK, around 3.5 million people are affected. Around 52,288 women received fertility treatments in 2014 in the UK.[21] Overall 36.3 per cent of treatments resulted in a pregnancy, although the success rate depends on a broad range of factors.[22]

1.3 What are the causes of infertility?

The exact cause of infertility is unknown. There is, no doubt, a plethora of different reasons, ranging from obesity,[23] smoking, heavy alcohol use,[24] tight underwear, using laptops,[25] and hot baths,[26] to delaying the age at which women seek to start a family.[27] There is some evidence that the rate of infertility is increasing.[28] What is unknown is what causes these problems to arise.

1.4 Responses to infertility

Some people find unwanted childlessness profoundly distressing. The lengths to which people are willing to go financially, emotionally, and physically in order to have a child using assisted reproduction demonstrate that vividly. This is particularly so given the low rates of success of many forms of reproductive assistance. Donor insemination, for example, has a failure rate of around 66 per cent.[29] For women treated with embryos created from their own fresh eggs using IVF the success rate is 33.6 per cent per cycle.[30] However, that depends on age: for women aged 45 or over, it is 2.2 per cent. With a success rate like that, it is extraordinary that people are still willing to try.

---

[17] Jackson (2001: 162).   [18] Jackson (2001: 162).   [19] Faludi (1992: 47).   [20] NHS (2017c).
[21] HFEA (2016).   [22] HFEA (2016).   [23] BBC News online (23 June 2005).
[24] National Collaborating Centre for Women's and Children's Health (2004).
[25] BBC News online (5 March 2007).   [26] BBC News online (5 March 2007).
[27] Templeton (2000).   [28] BBC News online (23 June 2005).
[29] HFEA (2016).   [30] HFEA (2016).

The Canadian Royal Commission wrote of the experiences of some of those who were infertile:

> There is often a loss of self-esteem mixed with feelings of grief, anger, and sometimes guilt about the source of the infertility. Many also experience a sense of isolation from family members and friends. People told us that infertility is not something that is easy to deal with and move on from, because having children is so firmly embedded in the everyday social and family interactions in which most of us take part. As friends and siblings go through life, milestones in their children's lives—school events, graduations, weddings, the birth of grandchildren—continuously remind those without children of their childlessness.[31]

Others have written that, for infertile couples, 'the painful gap occupied by the fantasy baby haunts their daily relationship'.[32] Some women regard it as one of their primary roles to produce and raise children, and so experience infertility as, in a sense, a failure to be a 'real woman'. Men similarly regard infertility as a lack of manliness.[33] The sadness is that many infertile couples would make wonderful parents. As Wall J noted:

> The Family Division, unfortunately, is all too used to the fact that nature often makes most fecund those least able properly to exercise parental responsibility, whilst at the same time denying parenthood to those who would undertake it conscientiously.[34]

It must be emphasized that many people do not regard infertility as a tragedy. They may have no wish to have children; infertility may even be a boon, because it avoids the difficulties of contraception and the burdens of parenthood. Others accept infertility as their 'lot', without experiencing childlessness as a huge loss. Certainly, there are many who would fiercely reject the idea that women should regard reproduction as a primary role or that fertility should be needed by men as a confirmation of their sexual identity.[35] As this indicates, it is perhaps dangerous to categorize 'infertility' as a straightforward concept. Its meaning, impact, and treatment, if any, will vary from person to person.[36] Fertility has social consequences too. Even today, some commentators bemoan the low numbers of children being born in the UK and argue that something must be done to increase the birth rate.[37] Yet others argue it is immoral and irrational to want to have children, given our overpopulated world.[38] There has even been debate over whether assisted reproduction is economically beneficial to the state by producing more children who will go on to be taxpayers![39]

2 The concept of reproductive autonomy

Key to the theoretical disputes surrounding the issue of reproductive technology is the concept of 'reproductive autonomy'.[40] Unfortunately, although it is a phrase that is much bandied about, its meaning is far from clear.[41] First, it is necessary to distinguish between 'reproductive liberty' and the 'reproductive autonomy'.

---

[31] Canadian Royal Commission on New Reproductive Technologies (1993: 171).
[32] Raphael-Leff (2002: 223).   [33] Hardy and Yolanda Makuch (2001).
[34] *Evans v Amicus Healthcare Ltd* [2003] 3 FCR 577, [318].
[35] Morgan (1998).   [36] Phillips (2002).   [37] Häyry (2004).   [38] Heitman (2002).
[39] Connolly, Hoorens, and Ledger (2008).
[40] Quigley (2010); Priaulx (2008); Purdy (2006); Robertson (1986).
[41] See Murphy (2009) for a powerful critique of the concept.

- *Reproductive liberty* refers to the idea that one's reproductive choices (when, where, how, and with whom to have children) should be a private matter in which the state should not interfere.[42] It would therefore be wrong if the state were to seek to prevent a woman from reproducing on the grounds that it thought she would be a bad mother. Likewise, it would be wrong of the state to prevent a couple from seeking access to IVF treatment on the basis that the state believed they would make inadequate parents. It is also used to support a woman's right to abortion. However, reproductive liberty is essentially a negative concept: it prevents the state from interfering in people's reproductive choices—but it does not give people rights to treatment, for example.

- *Reproductive autonomy* refers to all of the ideas contained within the notion of reproductive liberty, but goes further. Decisions about whether or not to have children are profoundly important and intimate for individuals, and for many are central to how they wish to live their lives. The state should therefore, so far as practicable, assist couples who need treatment or help to have children. Infertility, in this way, may be seen as analogous to a serious disease, which the National Health Service (NHS) has an obligation to treat. This concept then places positive obligations on the state to provide treatment for those suffering from infertility. Notice that, even in its strongest manifestation, the right to reproductive autonomy is not a right to a child, but a right of access to facilities so that one can try to have a child.

As will be appreciated, these concepts of reproductive liberty or reproductive autonomy cover a wide range of reproductive issues: from contraception to abortion; from cloning to sex selection of the embryo for implantation.[43] Further, there is dispute over what 'reproduction' means in this context. In particular, are we discussing the right to produce a child or the right to rear a child? Steinbock has questioned whether a person's interest in the production of a genetically related child is of a sufficient weight to ground a right.[44] She suggests that the interest will be strong enough only if the person wishes not only to produce the child, but also to raise him or her.[45]

It is also notable that much of the discussion about reproductive autonomy has centred on the rights of women. Erin Nelson writes: 'Reproduction takes places in a context within which women's bodies, needs and interests have a central role. Reproductive activity is literally located within women's bodies.'[46] This does not mean that men do not have reproductive rights, but given, at least in our current state of technology, that reproduction inevitably involves a woman's body it is understandable why the interests of women dominate.[47]

We need to look a little more closely at some of the arguments that might be used to justify reproductive liberty or autonomy.

2.1 Arguments in favour of reproductive autonomy or liberty

2.1.1 *The harm principle*

This principle, developed from the writings of John Stuart Mill, has received widespread support. At its simplest, it declares that the state should accept as lawful any activity unless

[42] Harris (1998). [43] Nelson (2013). [44] Steinbock (1995). [45] Quigley (2010).
[46] Nelson (2013).
[47] Although see *R (Rose) v Thanet Clinical Commissioning Group* [2014] EWHC (Admin) 1182 which rejected an argument that policies which treated storage of eggs and sperm differently amounted to sex discrimination.

it causes harm to others, even if it is regarded as immoral. This principle would support non-intervention by the state unless it could be shown that the reproductive choice would harm someone else. For example, making reproductive cloning illegal could be supported under this principle if it were to harm people, but not on the basis that it was 'unnatural' or 'immoral'.[48] Similarly, if a couple wanted to pay for assisted reproductive treatment we should let them, even though we might think it is not a good decision for them.[49] Trickier is an argument the couple should not be allowed treatment because the child who will be born will be harmed. The difficulty is first it might be hard to know if the couple will be good parents or not. The second is that if we are looking at the harm to the child, is it plausible that it would be better for the child not to be born, than to be born to undesirable parents? This is the so-called 'non-identity problem' and we shall return to it later.

2.1.2 Discrimination: the principle of equal treatment

This holds that there should be no disadvantage suffered by those who are infertile as compared to fertile couples. This principle leads John Harris to argue:

> It seems invidious to require that people who need assistance with procreation meet tests to which those who need no such assistance are not subjected. If we are serious that people demonstrate their adequacy as parents *in advance* of being permitted to procreate, then we should license all parents. Since we are evidently not serious about this, we should not discriminate against those who need assistance with procreation.[50]

Part of the debate concerning this issue is the argument made by some that infertility should be regarded as a kind of disability.[51] The argument is that infertility is a disease that impairs normal functioning.[52] The state should do all that it can to limit the negative impact of this disability. But to some, being unable to have a child is not a disability.[53] We might like to be good-looking, to have fast cars or a big house, but that does not mean that we are disabled if we do not have them, even if we want them very much; similarly, we are not 'disabled' if we are not able to have a child.[54] To suggest so is to reinforce the view that childbearing is an essential role of womanhood, some argue. Baroness Mary Warnock has sought to develop a moderate position: that there is no right to fertility treatment, but that, for some, infertility creates a great need, and therefore an expectation, but not a right, that that medical need will be met by the NHS.[55]

2.1.3 The intimate nature of the procreation question

Those supporting the right to procreative autonomy often emphasize how important reproductive decisions are to individuals.[56] They are, it has been said, similar to rights to freedom of religion because they involve issues of a profound kind that go to an individual's sense of identity.[57] Onora O'Neill has argued that the analogy with freedom of speech or religion is misleading, because reproduction involves the creation of another person, and therefore the interests of that person must inevitably come into play in the formation and boundaries of any alleged right.[58] That point, which is a good one, might

---

[48] See Blackford (2006) for an attempt to give some philosophical meat to the notion that a practice is unnatural.
[49] Harris (2015a).   [50] Harris (2005a: 292).   [51] RCOG (2010b).   [52] Brazier (1998: 75).
[53] Lauritzen (2014).   [54] Warnock (2002: 50).   [55] Warnock (2002: 52).
[56] Robertson (1994); Walker (2003).   [57] See Alghrani and Harris (2006).   [58] O'Neill (2002).

be thought to mean that an interference in the right is more easily justified, rather than being an argument that the right does not exist before.

The significance of procreation may also be reflected in Article 12 of the European Convention on Human Rights (ECHR), where it is said that: 'Men and women of marriageable age have the right to marry and to found a family, according to the national laws governing the exercise of this right.'[59] The Court of Appeal, in *R v Secretary of State for the Home Dept, ex p Mellor*,[60] held that this Article did not give an absolute right to assisted reproductive services or impose obligations on the state to provide them. However, that view was rejected by the Grand Chamber of the European Court of Human Rights (ECtHR) in *Dickson v UK*.[61] In that case, it was held that, for an infertile couple, access to assisted reproductive services was engaged by Article 8 ECHR. In *SH v Austria*,[62] the ECtHR acknowledged that 'the right of a couple to conceive a child and to make use of medically assisted procreation for that purpose is also protected by Article 8, as such a choice is an expression of private and family life'. However, the Court went on to state that, under Article 8(2), a state may be able to provide good reasons to interfere in that right, and where it did, the Court would, given the controversial nature of the issue, respect the margin of appreciation.[63] While a state may well have good reasons to deny access to IVF in certain cases, the restrictions had to be justified.

2.1.4 *Reproductive autonomy or liberty*

As already indicated, there is a dispute between those that view reproductive rights as negative (preventing the state from interfering in reproductive decisions) and those that view them as positive (the state must, as far as is reasonable, enable people to carry out their reproductive choices by supplying services and support). It must be admitted that even the most ardent supporters of reproductive autonomy rights do not claim that these are absolute rights.[64] A person's reproductive choice may need to be limited in the name of countervailing interests. If, for example, there are other more pressing calls on NHS resources, it may not be possible to provide NHS fertility treatment to all who need it. Further, it might be argued that the state has a desperate need for foster and adoptive carers. We should, therefore, encourage infertile couples to look after children who have no parents.[65] An argument the other way is that offering assisted reproductive services to same-sex couples can ensure they are not disadvantaged as compared to same-sex couples.[66] This, however, leaves open the question of how strong this right is. In other words: what degree of public interest will justify interference in it?

2.1.5 *The importance of the biological link*

Underlying many of these issues is whether one regards it as legitimate or important to have a child to whom one has a genetic link. That is at the heart of the argument over

---

[59] For a useful discussion, see Eijkholt (2010). The rights could also be said to be an aspect of someone's private life and so protected by the right to respect for private and family life in Article 8: Blyth (2003).

[60] [2001] 2 FCR 153.   [61] Application no. 44362/04 (2008) 46 EHRR 41.

[62] Application no. 57813/00 [2011] ECHR 1878, [82], discussed in McGuinness (2013a).

[63] See Sanderson (2013) for criticism of the decision, particularly as the state laws there had a harsher impact on women than men.

[64] Robertson (1994).   [65] McTernan (2015).

[66] McTernan (2015) believes on this basis there is a case for offering same-sex but not opposite sex couples assisted reproduction.

whether infertile couples should be encouraged to adopt or foster a child. That is only a valid alternative if one believes that no or little significance should be attached to the biological link. On the one hand there are those who claim it is natural to want a child with a biological connection and even an evolutionary urge to take particular care of one's biological children. Moschella argues that the genetic link 'in and of itself constitutes an intimate personal relationship that gives rise to a special, personal obligation to love and (in most circumstances) raise one's genetic children . . . '.[67]

Against such a view is the argument that parenthood should not be seen as a matter of biological connection. I have argued:

> Parental status should be earned by the care and dedication to the child, something not shown simply by a biological link. It is the changing, of the nappy; the wiping of the tear; and the working out of maths together that makes a parent, not the provision of an egg or sperm.[68]

Those who take such a view might suggest that the state should not be seen to suggest the biological link is important in parenthood. To do so undermines the position of adoptive and foster parents. Indeed, if someone was living with children biologically related to them and had adopted children, we would think it was very wrong to treat the children differently. Roache argues it can be harmful for a parent to try and have a child who is 'like them'.[69]

A compromise position on this debate is suggested by Di Nucci[70] who suggests that it should be seen as not objectionable to prefer children biologically related to you, but it should be promoted. This might lead to a conclusion that the state should not prevent people using IVF, but it should not be positively encouraged, at least while there are children needing adoption or fostering.

2.2 Arguments against reproductive autonomy or liberty

There are those who reject the arguments put forward by those supporting reproductive autonomy rights. These objections can be divided between those who object to assisted reproductive technology (ART) generally, and those who object on other grounds— and we will consider the latter first.[71]

Conservatives might accept that reproductive choices are valuable and important, but only within the context of marriage. To reproduce outside that context (for example if a single woman were to want to raise a child) is irresponsible. It is a choice that does not deserve the respect that is due to a right. Supporters of such an approach would accept the idea of 'reproductive liberty', but restrict it to those seeking to raise children within the traditional context of marriage. O'Neill would not go that far, but argues against a right to procreate willy-nilly. She writes: 'Reproduction aims to create a dependent being, and reproductive decisions are irresponsible unless those who make them can reasonably offer adequate and lasting care and support to the hoped-for child.'[72] If an individual wishes to procreate, but has no intention of taking responsibility for the

[67] Moschella (2016: 105).   [68] Herring (2013b: 121).   [69] Roache (2016).
[70] Di Nucci (2016).
[71] See also Laing and Oderberg (2005), who argue that the harms to society caused by assisted reproduction mean that the state is not required to provide reproductive services.
[72] O'Neill (2002: 62).

resulting child, then there is no right to do that.[73] However, supporters of the right to assisted reproductive autonomy would note that a fertile couple are able to produce a child, even though they may have no intention of raising him or her. Should infertile couples be denied that freedom?

One difficulty over the right to procreative freedom is where the corresponding duty lies. If we have a right to reproduce, on whom does the burden to meet that right fall? Surely the government is not under a duty to run a national stud and/or surrogacy service?! However, one reply is that it is perfectly proper that one can have a right to something, even if there is no corresponding duty. Elaine Sutherland suggests that such a right should be understood as a right not to be deprived of the opportunity to procreate.[74] But putting it that way, it looks more like procreative liberty rather than a procreative right.

3 Criticisms of assisted reproduction

To many, the 'miracle' of assisted reproduction has brought enormous joy into their lives through a child they thought they would never have. It might be thought difficult to object to procedures that create new life and produce such happiness, yet the main objections to assisted reproduction are as follows.

3.1 Unnaturalness

One complaint is that assisted reproduction is unnatural. It is 'playing God' and interfering in nature's most precious activity: the creation of life.[75] Life and its beginnings should be kept as a mysterious and sacred process, rather than babies designed or produced.[76] Babies should be gifts, not products to be created or destroyed at will. As one group of Catholic bishops put it: 'Increasingly, children are seen as the object of "consumer choices", rather than as new human beings to be accepted unconditionally.'[77] Jacqueline Laing and David Oderberg argue that assisted reproduction commodifies life.[78]

To supporters of ART, these points are vague and/or meaningless. As Jackson[79] points out, it is common for couples to have sexual intercourse deliberately at the time of ovulation in order to increase the chances of conception. No one objects to this 'designing' of the production of children. Indeed, a lot of medicine can be seen as an interference in what would otherwise be a 'natural' process.

3.2 Harm to the embryo

Many forms of ART involve the creation of a number of embryos, from among which two are normally selected and implanted. Where the treatment is successful, or the couple decide to stop the treatment, this leaves spare embryos, which, if not used, are destroyed.[80] This is strongly objected to by those who regard embryos as having a right

---

[73] O'Neill (1979).   [74] Sutherland (2003).   [75] Watt (2002a).
[76] Gormally (2004).   [77] Catholic Bishops' Conference (2004: 2).
[78] Laing and Oderberg (2005).   [79] Jackson (2001).
[80] Karnein (2012) suggests spare embryos should be made available for adoption. Murphy (2015) presents arguments against that.

to life or having a profound symbolic importance.[81] Of course, it would be possible to meet this concern. Regulations could permit only the creation of single embryos, which would then have to be placed immediately in a woman. This would mean that there would be no need to store and then destroy embryos. However, that would greatly reduce the chances of the procedure working. Alternatively, all spare embryos could be made available for donation to other couples.[82]

3.3 Donated sperm

Some concerns focus on the use of donated sperm in some forms of ART.[83] The objections centre on the separation between the social and genetic fatherhood.[84] To set about deliberately generating a situation in which the child will be raised by a man who is not his or her biological father is seen as departing too greatly from the traditional setting in which children should be raised. However, many children nowadays are raised by a man who is not their genetic father (a stepfather). There is no evidence that such children suffer greatly from this (as opposed to from the separation of their parents).

3.4 'Child welfare'

Assisted reproduction leads to a higher rate of multiple births than normal sexual intercourse. In England and Wales, of births following IVF treatment, one in six were multiple births in 2014.[85] Multiple births create a greatly increased danger to mother and children, summarized by the HFEA as the following:

- mothers have a higher risk of miscarriage and other complications in pregnancy;
- the babies are more likely to be premature and to have low birth weights;
- the risk of death within the first week of life is more than four times greater for twins than for a single baby; and
- the risk of cerebral palsy is five times higher for twins and eighteen times higher for triplets than for a single baby.[86]

In addition, the cost for the NHS of multiple births is huge. A complaint among some practitioners is that private IVF is used to produce multiple births, which create vast costs for the NHS owing to the extra care necessary.[87] It is for this reason that the HFEA is encouraging single embryo transfer.

3.5 The cost of failure

The public image of IVF is the joyful production of a new 'miracle baby'. This public face masks much private grief. There are official figures on the number of children born

---

[81] Catholic Bishops' Conference (2004: para. 8).   [82] Savulescu (2003a).
[83] It should be noted that only 1,916 women received donor insemination and 487 babies were born as a result in 2008: HFEA (2011b).
[84] Giesen (1997: 260).   [85] HFEA (2016).   [86] HFEA (2011b).
[87] Braude and El-Toukhy (2011).

using assisted reproduction, but none on the number of couples for whom the experience has produced only false hopes, huge expense, deeply invasive procedures, and unbearable sadness.[88] It must not be forgotten that the rates of success of assisted reproduction are not high. It is remarkable that ART has become so widespread without a firmer research basis. In 2014, around 75 per cent of IVF treatments did not result in a baby,[89] although the success rate varies by age.

FEMINIST PERSPECTIVES

Assisted reproduction

Perhaps not surprisingly, there is no single 'feminist' response to assisted reproduction. The response from radical feminists has tended to oppose assisted reproductive techniques and we will examine that first, although, as we shall see, other feminists have been more supportive.

Feminists are concerned that ART reinforces the message that a woman's primary purpose is to be a mother. It perpetuates the message that reproduction is essential for women and that invasive procedures are justifiable if a woman is unable to meet that role. As Callahan and Roberts put it, 'reproduction-assisting technologies . . . contribute to the subordination of women by continuing to tie the value of women to reproduction'.[90] If a woman is infertile, the message from society should not be 'You must get that fixed', but rather 'That is unimportant'. Women's desperation to use assisted reproduction simply reflects wider society's assumptions about the role of women. We need to challenge those assumptions, not reinforce them. If we were to live in a society in which childlessness was a 'respectable' choice, we could be confident about women's choice to use assisted reproduction.[91] As Emily Jackson points out, however, although it is often said that women who use assisted reproduction are not 'genuinely' consenting, we do not tend to say the same thing about women who conceive 'naturally'.[92] Is this not a further example of double standards? Is not the choice to have a child through assisted reproduction as open to societal pressure as any decision to have children?

There is concern about the power that assisted reproductive technology gives to the medical professionals (often male). Rosi Braidotti suggests that 'the test-tube babies of today mark the long-term triumph of the alchemists' dream of dominating nature thorough their self-inseminating, masturbatory practices'.[93] Even if that is a bit much, there is a widespread feeling among women using ART that they end up with their bodies being treated as laboratories.[94] All indignities and pain involved in using the woman's body are justifiable for the ultimate goal of producing a child. And it *is* normally women's bodies that suffer all of the invasion, even where the cause of the infertility rests with the man, and such invasion is normally at the hands of male doctors. As Corea states: 'Reproductive technology is a product of the male reality. The values expressed in the technology—objectification, domination—are typical of male culture. The technology is male-generated and buttresses male power over women.'[95]

Of course, not all feminists agree with such arguments. Some argue that they lead to the conclusion that no woman should decide to have children. Does a fertile woman having sexual intercourse reinforce the mother role any more or less than a woman having assisted reproduction?

[88] Franklin (1997).   [89] HFEA (2016).   [90] Callahan and Roberts (1996: 1211).
[91] Maclean (1993: 30).   [92] Jackson (2001).   [93] Braidotti (1994: 88).
[94] Corea (1985).   [95] Corea (1985: 4).

Jennifer Parks argues that there is nothing in ART itself that is inevitably anti-women, but that its use reflects tensions within society.[96] She argues that:

[I]t simultaneously produces two contradictory images of what families are and can be: on one hand, it promotes a radical conception of family as unbounded by traditional, 'age-appropriate', heterosexual limits; on the other hand, it reinforces the primacy of reproductive functioning that one typically associates with traditional heterosexual families.[97]

ART therefore has the potential to be liberating, but also oppressive.

Another feminist response is that opposition to ART is voiced by feminist intellectuals who are not listening to what women actually want. Listening to our infertile sisters, some feminists argue, will lead us to appreciate their needs and position much better. Assisted reproductive technology has done much to improve the reproductive options for women. Increasing reproductive autonomy for women, it is said, cannot amount to being anti-feminist.

Some feminists also see great hope in assisted reproduction as a means of challenging the traditional image of a family. Assisted reproductive technology offers single women and lesbian couples the hope of having a child, which would otherwise not be possible.[98] Indeed, a feminist opposing assisted reproduction may end up in the uncomfortable position of having to accept that the only legitimate way to conceive children is through male–female sexual relations.

Another feminist argument used against assisted reproduction is that it reflects a preoccupation with the genetic link.[99] What drives some couples (and especially fathers) to use assisted reproduction is the desire to have a child who is 'their own'—in other words, one who has a genetic link to them. Some feminists suggest that we need to challenge this argument that it is genetics that makes someone a parent. They argue that it is day-to-day caring that makes someone a parent, whereas others feel that this is to ignore the powerful feelings that some people have concerning the genetic link.

Perhaps, then, for feminists, the advances of ART are a 'double-edged sword'.[100] Do we respect women's wishes to have children and to promote their reproductive autonomy, or do we reject such desires as a result of patriarchal thinking? It has been suggested that reproductive technologies are the wrong responses to the wrong problems.[101] The problem for a feminist response to infertility is that feminism would not want to support the situation that our society is currently in: one in which childlessness is regarded as an unattractive option, especially for women, and in which great store is placed on genetic links. Certainly, if we are to take the notion of reproductive autonomy seriously, the option of childlessness needs to be as facilitated as much as the option of child rearing.

4 The different techniques

We will discuss here only the lawful techniques that are available. Reproductive cloning is presently illegal, but will be discussed later in this chapter.

---

[96] Parks (2009).   [97] Parks (2009: 22).   [98] Lublin (1998).
[99] Wilkinson and Williams (2016).   [100] Stanworth (1988: 16).   [101] Smart (1993: 223–4).

4.1 **Cryopreservation**

Sperm, eggs, and embryos can be frozen. This means that donors' sperm can be tested, or embryos frozen, so that they can be implanted at the optimum time in a woman's cycle. It is also used for individuals who are about to undergo surgery or treatment that will render them infertile, so that they can retain the option of reproduction in the future. The freezing of eggs carries serious risks of failure, although technological advances are improving the success rate of doing so.

4.2 **Intrauterine (or assisted) insemination by husband/partner**

In an intrauterine (or assisted) insemination by husband/partner (AIH/AIP) procedure, a husband or partner's sperm is placed inside the woman, where it fertilizes an egg. The technology available through intra-cytoplasmic sperm injection (ICSI), at which we will look shortly, means that AIH/AIP is now rarely used, unless the man's sperm has been frozen in advance.

Assisted insemination with sperm of a living husband or partner is specifically excluded from the kinds of treatment that require a licence under the Human Fertilisation and Embryology Act 1990.

4.3 **Donor insemination**

Donor insemination (DI) is used where the woman has no partner, or her partner is infertile. It involves the insemination of sperm from a donor into a woman, via her vagina, into the cervical canal or into the uterus itself. It is normally used as a last resort. The use of ICSI means that even low-quality sperm can now be used where, in the past, donor insemination would have been the only option.

4.4 **Egg (oocyte) donation**

Egg donation is necessary where the woman has no healthy eggs. A woman willing to donate eggs will have hormonal treatment and then eggs will be surgically retrieved from her. This is an uncomfortable and invasive procedure, certainly more so than the donation of sperm. The donated eggs can be fertilized with the sperm of the woman's partner, or donated sperm, and are then put into her uterus.

4.5 **In vitro fertilization**

In an IVF procedure, hormonal treatment is used to stimulate the overproduction of eggs. These are removed from the ovarian follicles and placed in a culture, which matures them further. Then, in a Petri dish, they are fertilized with sperm (that of her partner or donated sperm) and the resulting zygotes are either frozen or placed back into the woman's uterus.

4.6 **Gamete intra-fallopian transfer**

In a gamete intra-fallopian transfer (GIFT) procedure, eggs are retrieved as in IVF, but the eggs are mixed with sperm and returned to the fallopian tubes, with the intent that fertilization will take place there. Technically, this procedure does not require a licence, but it will very rarely be attempted in unlicensed clinics.

4.7 Intra-cytoplasmic sperm injection and sub-zonal insemination

Intra-cytoplasmic sperm injection (ICSI) and sub-zonal insemination (SUZI) involve the injection of a single sperm into an egg with a very fine needle. If fertilization is successful, the fertilized egg is then transferred to the woman's uterus in the same way as in an IVF procedure. The ICSI technique is particularly useful where the sperm cannot naturally penetrate the egg or where it is of poor mobility. Procedures involving ICSI now account for 52.6 per cent of all IVF treatment.[102]

The SUZI procedure is similar, but involves micro injections of a small number of sperm.

4.8 In vitro maturation

In vitro maturation (IVM) is a new form of treatment that has been used only occasionally in England. It involves removing an immature egg from a woman's ovaries and then maturing it in a laboratory, before it is fertilized and then returned to the woman's womb.[103]

5 Regulation

Assisted reproductive technologies are regulated by the Human Fertilisation and Embryology (HFE) Act 1990, which created the Human Fertilisation and Embryology Authority (HFEA). The HFEA issues guidance on ARTs and licenses their use.

In the UK, we have become quite used to the idea that scientists wishing to carry out reproductive treatment or research require a licence from a government agency, but from a worldwide perspective, it is a controversial stance to take. The ability of the government to restrict what scientists can or cannot research, or what treatments a doctor can offer a patient, is seen in some countries as improper government intrusion. Nevertheless, the UK's regulation of this area is well established and is regarded by many in the world as a model system.[104] But what is the justification for regulation?

The advantage of regulation is that it provides a flexible approach to this controversial area. The HFEA can respond reasonably quickly to advances in medical technology or novel moral issues, whereas it can be slow for Parliament to pass legislation in response to changing circumstances. The HFEA is also able to provide regulation that is free from political pressure: it is less likely to be influenced by a campaign from the tabloid press than politicians might. Veronica English has listed

---

[102] HFEA (2014).
[103] For future developments, including uterus transplantation, see Alghrani (2016).
[104] Deech (2003).

what she regards as the four main advantages of having regulation under a body such as the HFEA:

(i)   it protects patients;

(ii)   it allays public concerns;

(iii) it provides an environment within which scientific progress can flourish; and

(iv)   it protects IVF practitioners against claims of unethical behaviour.[105]

Martin Johnson has listed the parties whose interests regulation needs to protect:

(i)   the embryo *in vitro*;

(ii)   children deriving from these embryos;

(iii) patients (especially women, but also partners, donors, surrogates);

(iv)   society (the public interest); and

(v)   the health team (doctors, counsellors, nurses, biomedical scientists).[106]

Johnson is concerned that the interests of the embryo have come to dominate the issue of regulation, without proper thought being given to what regulation is seeking to achieve and how the different interests can be balanced.

The disadvantages of regulation include the dangers of 'slippery slopes': by considering each new case 'on its merits', there is a danger that the wider picture will be lost. An apparently reasonable decision will be made on each occasion, with the change made from previous cases being minimal, but we will end up at a place at which we did not want to be. There are also claims that the HFEA is not adequately responsive to public opinion and that there is no way of readily holding it to account for its decisions. Finally, there are the costs of regulation, which are ultimately passed on to the consumer, and this may increase the number of people for whom ART is not available for financial reasons.

The HFEA has two primary purposes: to ensure that assisted reproductive treatment and research is ethical and to ensure that it is safe. The Authority produces guidelines that govern licensed clinics. It does not normally consider individual cases, unless they raise particularly complex problems. There are twenty-two members of the Authority appointed by the UK Health Minister, made up of both lay and medically or legally qualified individuals. The HFEA operates as a licensing body for clinics that wish to offer ARTs and for researchers wishing to conduct research on embryos. A clinic that receives a licence will face a full inspection at least every three years and interim inspections on other occasions. Licensed clinics must abide by codes of practice issued by the HFEA.[107]

It is possible to divide up activities in the areas of ART and research into three categories:

(i)   those that are unlawful;

(ii)   those that are lawful only if the clinic has a licence in respect of those activities; and

(iii) those that are lawful and do not require a licence.

We shall now look at these separate categories.

---

[105] English (2006: 304–8).   [106] Johnson (2007).   [107] HFEA (2017).

5.1 Activities prohibited by the HFE Act 1990

The HFE Act 1990 renders certain activities unlawful and does not permit the HFEA to license them. They include the following.

- An embryo cannot be stored for more than fourteen days after the mixing of the gametes (at which time the primitive streak will have appeared).[108] This means that although research can take place on embryos up until the fourteenth day, the HFEA has no power to authorize the storage of an embryo beyond that time.
- It is unlawful to place an embryo that is not a 'permitted' embryo in a woman.[109] The definition of a 'permitted embryo' allows the HFEA to issue regulations that would allow embryos to be created using animal gametes.[110]
- It is unlawful to place a human embryo in a non-human animal.[111]
- The use of eggs taken from embryos in fertility treatment is forbidden.[112]

Keeping or using an embryo under any circumstances in which regulations prohibit its keeping or use is unlawful.[113] It is unlawful to alter the genetic structure of any cell while it forms part of an embryo.[114]

5.2 Activities permitted only if performed under a licence

The HFE Act 1990 also outlaws certain activities, although it enables the HFEA to provide a licence for them that renders them lawful.

- The storage of an embryo is lawful only if carried out under a licence issued by the HFEA.[115]
- The storage and use of gametes can lawfully be carried out only under a licence issued by the HFEA.[116] This includes, since the HFE Act 2008, those offering courier services delivering sperm to women's homes. In 2009, two men were prosecuted after setting up an Internet site that offered £450 for a 'door to door' service for sperm delivery.[117]

5.3 Activities that do not require a licence

There are, of course, other activities involving assisted reproduction that do not require a licence. This is any process that does not involve the creation of an embryo outside the human body or the storage of any gametes. 'Do it yourself insemination', using fresh

---

[108] HFE Act 1990, s. 4(3).
[109] HFE Act 1990, s. 3(2). A permitted embryo is defined in s. 3ZA.
[110] See later in the chapter, under the heading '14.4 Hybrids and cybrids'.
[111] HFE Act 1990, s. 3(3).   [112] HFE Act 1990, s. 3A.   [113] HFE Act 1990, s. 4(2).
[114] HFE Act 1990, Sch. 2, para. 1(4).
[115] HFE Act 1990, ss 3 and 4. It is otherwise a criminal offence: HFE Act 1990, s. 41.
[116] Section 4 prohibits the storage and use of human gametes. There are special exemptions where the storage of gametes is for the researching or developing of pharmaceutical and contraceptive products, or for teaching, under the Human Fertilisation and Embryology (Special Exemptions) Regulations 1991, SI 1991/1588.
[117] Jones (2009).

sperm and a turkey baster (or similar instrument), is not subject to regulation. It would, of course, be difficult to police a law that made it illegal for someone to give someone else their fresh sperm.

5.4 Mitochondrial Replacement Therapy

The Human Fertilisation and Embryology (Mitochondrial Donation) Regulations 2015 for the first time permitted Mitochondrial Replacement Therapy. This is used for women whose eggs carry mitochondrial diseases. A donor egg is used and the 'heart' of it is removed and replaced with the nucleus from the would-be mother's egg. The resulting egg is primarily material from the mother but the mitochondrial DNA is from the donor. The egg is fertilized with sperm from the would-be mother's partner (or donor sperm). The significance of this procedure is that because the mitochondrial DNA is coming from the donor, any mitochondrial disease is not passed on.[118] The child will be technically genetically related to three people, even if the predominant genetic contribution will be from the would-be mother and sperm donor. The regulations make it clear that the donor of the egg will not be the mother of the child.[119] The mother will be the woman who gives birth to the child and fatherhood is determined by the normal rules.

It might be thought that the benefits of the regulations are clear: they offer women who carry mitochondrial diseases the chance of a healthy baby. However, concerns have been expressed at the fact it will require more donated eggs[120] and may cause confusion for children born with a genetic link to three people.[121] What this new technology does show is that we have moved beyond the position that any child born will result from the equal genetic contributions of one man and one woman.[122]

5.5 The paramountcy of consent

A key principle in the HFE Act 1990 is that gametes or embryos may not be used without the consent of the provider(s). So if a couple have had embryos frozen, these can be stored only with the couple's consent. If they ask for the embryo to be destroyed, then it would be unlawful for the clinic not to do so. However, there is a maximum limit of ten years on the storage of embryos and gametes.[123] An embryo can be stored for up to fifty-five years if the couple in question are infertile or likely to become infertile.

The most controversial issue surrounding consent is where a couple have created frozen embryos, but disagree over whether or not the embryo should be destroyed.[124] That issue was addressed in the following controversial case.

---

[118] See Chau and Herring (2015) and de Melo-Martin (2017); Harris (2016) for a more detailed discussion.
[119] Controversially, the child will not have a right to know the identity of the donor. See the discussion in Brandt (2016) and Appleby (2015).
[120] For an argument that egg donors are not being protected in the regulation see Dickinson (2013 and 2017); Rulli (207) and Bayliss (2017).
[121] Saunders (2015); Bayliss (2017); Scully (2016 and 2017).   [122] Liao (2016).
[123] The Human Fertilisation and Embryology (Statutory Storage Period for Embryos and Gametes) Regulations 2009, SI 2009/1582. See Jackson (2016) for criticism of this.
[124] Harris-Short (2009); Shenfield (2000); Daar (1999).

KEY CASE   *Evans v Amicus Healthcare Ltd* [2004] 3 All ER 1025

In October 2001, Natalie Evans and Howard Johnston, who were engaged, underwent IVF treatment. It was discovered that Natalie Evans had tumours on her ovaries. Her ovaries had to be removed as soon as possible, and she was required to make a decision quickly on whether she wanted
any ova removed and frozen. There were three main options: that she freeze her ova; that her eggs
be fertilized with donated sperm and frozen; or that her ova be fertilized with Mr Johnston's sperm
and then frozen. She chose the last option, a decision that she would subsequently deeply regret.
There were two main reasons why: the first was that ova do not freeze well and many do not survive; the second was that Mr Johnston assured her that he wanted to be the father of her children,
that they were not going to split up, and that she should not be negative. Six eggs were harvested,
fertilized, and frozen. Later that month, her ovaries were removed. In May 2002, the couple separated and Mr Johnston wrote to the clinic asking it to destroy the embryos. Ms Evans sought an
order preventing their destruction.

The Court of Appeal found the case straightforward in legal terms, deciding against Ms Evans
and authorizing the destruction of the embryos. The decision was reached primarily on the basis
of the interpretation of the HFE Act 1990. That Act makes it clear that a licensed clinic is permitted to store an embryo that has been brought about in vitro only if there is effective consent
by each person whose gametes were used to bring about the creation of the embryo.[125] Although
Mr Johnston had consented to the original storage of the sperm and its use in fertilizing the egg, he
had now withdrawn his consent and so the clinic was no longer permitted to store it. Lord Justice
Thorpe explained: '[T]he clear policy of the Act is to ensure continuing consent from the commencement of treatment to the point of implant.'[126] The Court of Appeal also emphasized the fact
that the consent form signed by Mr Johnston and Ms Evans stated that the embryo could be used
for the treatment of 'myself [Ms Evans] together with a named partner [Mr Johnston]', clearly indicating that they were agreeing to treatment as a couple.

It was not only the wording of the statutory provisions that convinced the Court of Appeal that
this was the correct interpretation of the Act. The Court emphasized that there were two principles
underlying the Act:

(i) the welfare of any child born by treatment was to be of fundamental importance; and

(ii) licensed clinics were able to store gametes only with their providers' informed consent, which
     was capable of being withdrawn at any point prior to the transfer of the embryos to the
     woman receiving treatment.

Both of these principles supported the conclusion that the embryos should be destroyed. As to the
first, it was not in the child's interests to be born to a father who did not want the child to be born.
As to the second, it clearly required the destruction of the embryo.

The Court of Appeal also considered whether the Human Rights Act (HRA) 1998 required the
Court to reinterpret the 1990 Act in a way that was consistent with the parties' rights under the ECHR.
The Court quickly concluded that the embryo had no rights under the Convention. As to the Article 8
rights to respect for private and family life, it was noted that Ms Evans's right to reproduce had to
be balanced against Mr Johnston's right not to reproduce. This was problematic because it involved
'a balance to be struck between two entirely incommensurable things'.[127] In essence, the Court of

---

[125] HFE Act 1990, Sch. 3, paras 6(3) and 8(2).   [126] At [37].   [127] At [66].

Appeal felt that the HFE Act had taken a reasonable approach between balancing these rights and so it could not be said to be incompatible with the Convention, although had the Act permitted Ms Evans to implant the embryo, this too might have been compatible with the Convention.

The Court divided on whether the law discriminated against Ms Evans on the grounds of disability (her infertility). In essence, the argument was that, for a fertile woman, once the man has given his sperm, he has no right to stop the birth of the child that may result. The HFE Act 1990 meant that an infertile woman faced the risk that the man who provided the sperm could prevent the birth of the child. Arden LJ accepted this argument. Thorpe and Sedley LJ thought that this did not constitute discrimination, arguing:

> [I]t is not the Act which discriminates against Ms Evans on this ground [infertility]. It is the Act which, conditionally, seeks to reverse nature's discrimination. What are under attack in these proceedings are the conditions on which it does so.[128]

However, all three agreed that even if there was discrimination, it was justifiable in order to protect Mr Johnston's rights.

Ms Evans took her case to the ECtHR and the Grand Chamber.[129] Both courts accepted that Ms Evans's right to private life under Article 8 was applicable to the case. The ECtHR explained that this case involved 'sensitive moral and ethical issues', and that there was 'no clear common ground amongst the member states'.[130] This meant that states had a wide margin of appreciation of this issue. The law of the UK, in not allowing Ms Evans to implant the embryo, did not infringe the Convention, although neither would a law that would have allowed her to use the embryo. The European courts accepted that, in this case, there was a clash between the Article 8 rights of Mr Johnston and those of Ms Evans. In essence, Ms Evans was asserting the right to be a parent and Mr Johnston, the right not to be a parent. The law of the UK had struck a balance between these two rights that could not be said to exceed its margin of appreciation. It was important in cases of this kind that there was legal certainty and that there was public confidence in the provision of assisted reproductive services. Both of these policies justified the UK's approach.

The case, as an interpretation of the HFE Act 1990, was relatively uncontroversial. However, the human rights issues were less straightforward. The Court of Appeal's conclusion that the Article 8 rights of Ms Evans and Mr Johnston were approximately equal is also controversial. Although both the alleged right to implant the embryo, and thereby to become a mother, and the alleged right to destroy the embryo, and thereby to avoid becoming a father, could be said to be an aspect of the right to respect for private and family life under Article 8, this did not mean that the alleged rights were equal. Many people will agree with Thorpe LJ that these were incommensurate. Only the most hard-hearted can fail to find sympathy with Ms Evans being denied the only chance that she had to have a child of her own. But many will also sympathize with Mr Johnston's principled objection to becoming a father against his wishes. One could go back to what is at the heart of the rights claimed here. In essence, this is the right of autonomy: the right to live your life as you wish. It is common to talk in terms of encouraging people to find and live out their version of the 'good life', free from interference from the state. This provides us some benchmark against which to measure these competing rights. Would it be a greater setback to their version of living their 'good life' for Ms Evans to

---

[128] At [72].   [129] Application no. 6339/05 [2006] ECHR 200.   [130] At [62].

be denied having the child she so desperately wanted, or for Mr Johnston to have to live his life knowing that there was a child of his whom he did not know and in whose life he was not able to play an effective role?[131]

What the case most certainly demonstrates is the importance of ensuring that couples are properly counselled before embarking on treatment, to ensure that they have considered the consequences of the forms they are signing.[132] While, since that case, the forms have been clearer, it is still not possible for the parties to give their consent irrevocably.[133] That is justified on the basis that parties should have the freedom to change their mind.

The *Evans* case can be contrasted with *Warren v Care Fertility (Northampton) Limited*[134] where a woman's husband died when he was 32. Earlier he had provided some sperm samples for possible future reproductive use with his wife. However, the form he signed only allowed the sperm to be used for three years. By the time he had died the period had run out. The clinic wanted to destroy the sperm because there was no on-going consent to its storage. Hogg J disagreed. Although the wording of the HFE Act said that the man's written consent was required that had to be read in the light of the Human Rights Act 1998. Hogg J held:

> [Mrs Warren] has the right to decide to become a parent by her deceased husband, which would accord with his wishes, and the written consent he gave.

She was reinforced by her conclusion that even if formal written consent was absent it was clear the husband would have wanted his wife to be able to use it. Indeed the clinics were at fault in not offering him the option of signing for a longer period of consent. This suggests that the courts will strive to ensure that where the consent of the parties is clear the legislation will not prevent them fulfilling their reproductive plans.[135] This overall emphasis on the reality of consent can also be seen in *R (IM) v HFEA*[136] where the Court of Appeal allowed an appeal against the refusal of the HFEA to permit parents to export the eggs of their deceased daughter. Although Ouseley J had found there was no concrete evidence that the daughter had consented to this prior to her death, the Court of Appeal disagreed. There was evidence the daughter had said she wanted her mother to 'carry my babies'. The Court of Appeal thought Ouseley J had also been too strict about what information the daughter needed to know before giving consent. This decision indicates that the court will take a broad-brush approach in seeking to determine whether or not there was consent.

6 Criticisms of the HFEA

We will now consider the criticisms that have been made of the HFEA. Although they amount to a long list, it should be emphasized at the start that, in fact, the HFEA has many supporters. It has overseen the regulation of a highly controversial and rapidly expanding area of science, without obviously losing the support of the general public or

---

[131] Harris-Short (2010), Dochin (2009), C. Morris (2007), Lind (2006), Alghrani (2005), and Sheldon (2004) discuss the reasoning in the cases.
[132] See HFEA (2013c).   [133] Sozou, Sheldon, and Hartshorne (2010) argue that should be an option.
[134] [2014] EWHC 602 (Fam), discussed in Herring (2014b).
[135] See also *Re A* [2015] EWHC 2602 (Fam) where incorrect completion of paperwork did not render the storage unlawful where it was clear the parties intended their material to be stored.
[136] [2016] EWCA 611.

Parliament.[137] Indeed, it is cited around the world as a model of regulation. So although more space will be dedicated to its criticism than to its praise, this reveals only the fact that critics tend to be more vocal than supporters.

6.1 **Quality control concerns**

There is a wide variation in the success rates of different clinics around the country. This has led to complaints that the HFEA is failing to ensure that there is sufficiently high quality across the board and is failing to advise patients of the differences in services offered. In *Re A*[138] Munby P referred to 'widespread incompetence' in the fertility sector, when examining seven cases of malpractice. He questioned whether the HFEA was effectively regulating the field. The HFEA acknowledges that it can appear that there is wide variation in the success rates of clinics. Of course, such statistics must be treated with some caution. Some clinics may be willing to take on couples who are 'difficult cases' with a low chance of success and others may be stricter in their selection criteria. There may also be other socio-economic factors that influence a clinic's success rate. A low rate does not necessarily indicate bad practice. That said, the levels of difference are so great that it is difficult to avoid the conclusion that there must be a difference in the quality of service being offered.

6.2 **'Adverse events'**

There have been a number of 'adverse events' at licensed clinics.[139] These include accidental destruction of gametes or embryos.[140] Between April 2011 and March 2012, there were 571 errors at licensed clinics.[141]

6.3 **'Pro-life concerns'**

Predictably, the HFEA has been criticized by pro-life groups for not adequately promoting respect for the embryo.[142] It has been too ready to permit research and ART that involves the destruction of embryos, which are regarded by many as having a right to life. The complaint is sometimes made that the HFEA is under the thumb of scientists wishing to make ever greater advances, without protecting the interests of the unborn child.

6.4 **Restrictions on research**

From another perspective, the HFEA has been criticized for being too restrictive. A leading critic with this point of view has been Lord Robert Winston, who has described the HFEA as 'incompetent'.[143] He has complained about the organization being too bureaucratic and hindering research.[144] For example, he states that his clinic, which

---

[137] See Callus (2007) on attitudes among the general public towards the HFEA.
[138] [2015] EWHC 2602 (Fam).   [139] HFEA (2014).
[140] *Yearworth v North Bristol NHS Trust* [2009] EWCA Civ 37.   [141] HFEA (2014).
[142] SPUC (2000).   [143] BBC News online (10 December 2004).   [144] Winston (2005).

handles just over 1,000 patients a year, has to employ two people full time just to deal with the paperwork required by the HFEA. The HFEA's investigations are haphazard, he complains, with the same procedures being praised by one inspection team and then criticized by another.[145] It is perhaps fair to add that these kinds of complaints echo those made by any professional subject to outside inspection.

6.5 A conflict in roles

There are concerns that the HFEA is in the difficult position of both regulating and advising clinics. The HFEA is required both to enforce the provisions of the HFE Act 1990 and to issue regulations, while at the same time advising the government whether there are problems with the legislation.[146] This is seen as particularly problematic because one of the requirements to be a member of the HFEA is that one is broadly sympathetic to the aims of the 1990 Act.

7 Access to treatment

If we were to take the right to reproductive autonomy seriously, then anyone who came forward for treatment would have a right to it unless there were very strong reasons why they should not.[147] In fact, in England and Wales, there are a number of barriers to accessing treatment and we shall consider these now.[148] The National Institute for Health and Clinical Excellence (NICE) has admitted that there are problems: 'NHS funding for investigation of infertility is generally available but there is wide variation and often limited access to NHS-funded treatment, particularly assisted reproduction techniques.'[149]

We shall now explore some of the barriers to access to assisted reproduction.

7.1 Financial restrictions

Perhaps the major bar to ART at present is financial. The NHS provision of assisted reproduction is patchy and currently there is no consistent approach taken. In 2014, only 41.3 per cent of IVF treatment was funded by the NHS, although that was an increase on the 2006 figure of 25 per cent.[150] In many areas, the NHS offers no assisted reproductive treatment and therefore couples seeking it must use the private sector. Of course, that is an option only for those with the funds to pay for it. At around £5,000 for a cycle of IVF, it is not cheap.[151] Even where the treatment is offered on the NHS, there can be significant waiting times. The government has admitted that whether or not one receives assisted reproductive treatment under the NHS can be a 'postcode lottery' and is seeking to take steps to prevent that result.[152]

---

[145] Winston (2005).
[146] House of Commons Science and Technology Committee (2005: para. 209).
[147] Peterson (2005b).
[148] See Riley (2007).   [149] NICE (2010: 4).   [150] HFEA (2016).   [151] NHS (2017).
[152] DoH (2009g); NICE (2011). Lee, Macvarish, and Sheldon (2014) found there was still wide variation in provision around the country.

NICE has looked at the issue of provision of assisted reproductive services in the NHS, and has recommended that a woman who satisfies either of the following two criteria should be offered up to three cycles of IVF:[153]

- she has been trying to get pregnant through regular unprotected intercourse for two years; or
- she has not been able to get pregnant after twelve cycles of artificial insemination.

There is no need to wait if tests show that IVF is the only way in which a woman is likely to become pregnant.

For women aged 40–42, all four of the following criteria should be met:

- she has been trying to get pregnant through regular unprotected intercourse for two years, or she has not been able to get pregnant after twelve cycles of artificial insemination;
- she has never had IVF treatment before;
- she shows no evidence of low ovarian reserve (that is, the eggs in the ovary are low in number or low in quality); and
- she has been informed of the additional implications of IVF and pregnancy at this age.

To satisfy this requirement will impose a significant financial burden on primary care trusts.

The NHS has admitted that it is yet to meet the NICE guidelines and that there is no consistent approach:

> NHS trusts across England and Wales are working to provide the same levels of service. However, the provision of IVF treatment varies across the country and often depends on local CCG policies. Priority is often given to couples who don't already have children.[154]

Even the most ardent supporter of reproductive autonomy would accept that it is not realistic for the NHS to offer unlimited reproductive treatment to everyone who wants it. Margaret Brazier reminds us that calls for reproductive autonomy must be matched by other calls on NHS resources:

> [O]ne woman's right to reproduce would have to be weighed against her mother's right to preventive care to ensure breast cancer is detected early enough, against her grandmother's need for a hip-replacement, against perhaps her great grandmother's life itself.[155]

As this quote indicates, there is a real danger that, for all the bold talk of reproductive autonomy, it may not be affordable under the NHS. The right of reproductive autonomy in this context will therefore join that shameful list of rights that are rights for the rich alone. And if they are rights for the rich alone, should they be called 'rights' at all?

---

[153] NICE (2013). Although Krajewska (2015) finds only 30 per cent of PCTs do abide completely by the NICE guidance.
[154] NHS (2013e: 2).   [155] Brazier (1998: 74).

7.2 **The welfare of the child**

Before a clinic can provide infertility treatment to a couple or individual, it must consider the HFE Act 1990, section 13(5), which states:

> A woman shall not be provided with treatment services unless account has been taken of the welfare of any child who may be born as a result of the treatment (including the need of that child for supportive parenting, and of any other child who may be affected by the birth).

The Human Fertilisation and Embryology Act 2008 amended this provision. Previously, clinics had been required to consider the 'need of that child for a father'. This was seen to create a bar for single women and lesbian couples.[156] The requirement to consider the need for 'supportive parenting' might still mean that a clinic may refuse to offer services to a single woman with a limited social support network,[157] but it should not work against a lesbian couple.

Despite the reforms in the 2008 Act, the clinic must still assess whether providing the service will result in the welfare of the child.[158] The Code states the centre should refuse treatment if it:

(a) concludes that any child who may be born or any existing child of the family is likely to be at risk of significant harm or neglect, or

(b) cannot obtain enough information to conclude that there is no significant risk.[159]

That suggests that the focus of the clinic's enquiry is whether there is a risk of harm or neglect, rather than asking whether the applicants will be good parents. The factors they should consider include:

(a) past or current circumstances that may lead to any child mentioned above experiencing serious physical or psychological harm or neglect, for example:

   (i) previous convictions relating to harming children,

   (ii) child protection measures taken regarding existing children, or

   (iii) violence or serious discord in the family environment

(b) past or current circumstances that are likely to lead to an inability to care throughout childhood for any child who may be born, or that are already seriously impairing the care of any existing child of the family, for example:

   (i) mental or physical conditions,

   (ii) drug or alcohol abuse,

   (iii) medical history, where the medical history indicates that any child who may be born is likely to suffer from a serious medical condition, or

   (iv) circumstances that the centre considers likely to cause serious harm to any child mentioned above.

When considering a child's need for supportive parenting, centres should consider the following definition:

> Supportive parenting is a commitment to the health, wellbeing and development of the child. It is presumed that all prospective parents will be supportive parents, in the

---

[156] Riley (2007: 87).   [157] Krajewska (2015).
[158] HFE Act 1990, s. 13(6), also requires counselling for the couple.   [159] HFEA (2017: para. 8.15).

absence of any reasonable cause for concern that any child who may be born, or any other child, may be at risk of significant harm or neglect. Where centres have concern as to whether this commitment exists, they may wish to take account of wider family and social networks within which the child will be raised.[160]

For supporters of reproductive autonomy rights, these provisions are objectionable, on the following grounds.

(i)   They require the clinic to assess the parental fitness of infertile individuals wanting to have children, when we do not do this for couples who wish to have children by means of sexual intercourse. There is, in this way, an improper discrimination against infertile people.

(ii) It requires the clinic to ask an unanswerable question: how can anyone know whether someone else will make a good parent or not? This is guesswork and the test is simply an invitation to prejudice. In any event, clinicians are not social workers and have no training in assessing parenting skills. Even if they did have the skills, how are they to get evidence to make an effective decision?

(iii) The test is meaningless. This is commonly known as the 'non-identity' problem.[161] How can you assess the interests of a person who will never come into being? Or put another way, how can it not be in the interests of the child to be born?[162] Perhaps this might be the case if the child's life were destined to be a short life full of pain, but in that event no clinic would offer treatment. The section does not explain precisely what the clinic is meant to be asking itself. The section states that the child's welfare need only be taken into account; it is not a 'paramount consideration', as is often the case in the law relating to children.[163] This seems to suggest that it might be appropriate to give treatment even if, in some sense, this was not in any potential child's interests. But can that have been Parliament's intention?

(iv) The provisions appear to be rarely used to deny treatment. It has been reported that clinics have used this provision to deny treatment in up to only 0.3 per cent of cases.[164]

(v)   The provision fails to pay adequate attention to the human rights of the parties. In *Dickson v UK*,[165] the Grand Chamber of the ECtHR found that denying a prisoner access to IVF infringed his and his partner's Article 8 ECHR rights. However, it should be recalled that Article 8 rights are not absolute rights and can be interfered with if necessary in the interests of others. Denying IVF treatment is therefore likely to constitute a breach of Article 8 rights unless it can be justified. However, it is very likely that a court would decide that foreseeable harm to a child born would be justification.

The logic of the arguments in favour of reproductive autonomy would be that there should be no restrictions on who can receive reproductive assistance. So even if there were a couple seeking treatment with a history of child abuse, they should receive

[160] HFEA (2017: para. 8.11).   [161] Boonin (2014); Lawlor (2015).
[162] Smajdor (2014). Although, at least one philosopher argues that it is true of everyone that it would have been better for them not to have existed: Benatar (2006b).
[163] Children Act 1989, s. 1.   [164] House of Commons Science and Technology Committee (2005: 96).
[165] Application no. 44362/04 (2008) 46 EHRR 41.

treatment. After all, if they were fertile, there would be nothing that the state could do to stop them having children. Of course, in such a case, the baby may be removed from the couple at birth. Hence Emily Jackson has written:

> [I]f we respect the procreative choices of alcoholics, and people with a record of violence and abuse, even when we know that their children are likely to be disadvantaged, is it disingenuous to require infertile people to satisfy a conceptually incoherent version of the welfare principle prior to reproducing?[166]

Opponents of reproductive autonomy question whether it can be right to provide treatment to a couple deliberately, knowing they cannot care for their child and that their child will be removed from them soon after birth.[167] We do not prevent utterly unsuitable people from conceiving children naturally because we cannot—but where we can, we should.

To others, the present law is too weak to be of use. Some support a far stricter approach on who can receive assisted reproductive help. As in adoption, we should be confident that the couple are in a stable relationship and are fit to raise the child well.[168] Others reject the analogy with adoption. In adoption, the state has taken into its care a child whose parents cannot care for him or her and is looking for alternative carers. In such a scenario, the state has a responsibility to find the best possible carers. In the case of assisted reproductive treatment, there is no equivalent responsibility on the state. The analogy should be with children conceived by sexual intercourse, where there is no attempt to regulate who can become a parent.

7.3 Lesbian couples

When the HFE Act 1990 was passed, the possibility of a lesbian couple receiving assisted reproductive treatment was a highly controversial issue. It is less so now.[169] The Adoption and Children Act 2002 permits same-sex couples to adopt a child and the Marriage (Same Sex Couples) Act 2013 provides full official recognition for same-sex relationships. Evidence suggests that children raised in lesbian households do not suffer as compared with children raised by opposite-sex couples.[170] That said, most of the studies have involved relatively small numbers of children and it would be wrong to suggest that the case has been made beyond reasonable doubt. Interestingly, one study found that, on average, children benefited from a greater degree of involvement from the mother's same-sex partner than that which a child raised by an opposite-sex couple received from his or her father.[171] Although it is clear that clinics do offer lesbian couples assisted reproductive treatment, there is evidence that some lesbian couples are deterred from approaching clinics for fear of how they will be treated, and that they prefer to use unregulated methods.[172] The HFEA Code of Practice makes it clear that people should not be discriminated against based on their sexual orientation.[173] It seems that the 2008 Act reforms and new Code of Practice have enabled a larger number of lesbian couples seeking to use assisted reproductive services.[174]

---

[166] Jackson (2001: 195). See also Alghrani and Harris (2007).
[167] McMillan (2014).   [168] Overall (2014), discussing surrogacy.
[169] See Smith (2013) for a detailed discussion of legal responses to lesbian parents.
[170] Brewaeys (2003).   [171] Brewaeys, Ponjaert, van Hall, et al. (1997).   [172] Wallbank (2004).
[173] HFEA (2017: para. 8.7).   [174] Secretary of State for Health (2014).

7.4 **Age**

There is some debate over whether or not age should be a factor in deciding whether or not to offer treatment.[175] The HFEA Code of Practice states simply that 'patients should not be discriminated against on grounds of gender, race, disability, sexual orientation, religious belief or age'.[176] The NICE guidance recommendations apply only to women aged below 42. However, those guidelines will not affect women seeking treatment. However, one survey found that only 35 per cent of clinics used that age as their upper age limit for offering treatment.[177] It is clear that most clinics will not offer treatment to older women, and particularly to post-menopausal women.[178] As already mentioned, the success rate of IVF dramatically drops as a woman reaches the age of 40. In *R v Sheffield Area Health Authority, ex p Seale*,[179] it was held that a ban on women over the age of 35 receiving ART was justified on the basis that the chances of treatment being successful decreased once a woman was over that age. There are, however, reports of a woman aged 67 becoming a mother using ART in Romania.[180]

It is important to distinguish two reasons why age may be relevant: the first is that the chances of success of assisted reproductive services greatly reduce as age increases;[181] the second is that any child born may suffer from having a parent older than normal. Lord Robert Winston has suggested that: 'Children should reasonably expect that their parents should be young enough to indulge in the pursuits which are all part of growing up with their family.'[182] Critics respond that there are no such considerations when a couple is seeking to have a child 'naturally'. No one questions whether they are too old to have children.[183] In particular, men have been known to father children at a great age: mine worker Les Colley is said to have fathered a child at the age of 93. This is rarely seen as irresponsible, but rather a sign of the father's continuing virility. Indeed, it has been pointed out that, not many decades ago, a woman's average life expectancy was 47 and so there was by no means a guarantee that a mother would live to see her child's teenage years.[184] Would we say that it was immoral for mothers in that era to have given birth?

A factor that has received less attention is young women seeking assisted reproductive treatment. Apparently, teenagers have been seeking assisted reproductive treatment, having not been able to conceive after more than two years of sexual activity.[185] Notably, the NICE guidelines put the lower age at which their guidelines should apply at 23.

7.5 **Genetic conditions**

If the parents suffer from a genetic condition and if granted assisted reproductive treatment, there is, say, a 25 per cent or 50 per cent chance that the child born will inherit the condition, does that justify not providing the couple with treatment? The requirement in the Code that the couple be not discriminated against on the grounds of their disability may mean that the clinic could not take this factor into account.[186] Again, the point could be made that if they were fertile, there would be no restriction on

---

[175] See Goold and Savulescu (2009), Cutas (2007), and Biggs (2007b) for a discussion of the issues raised by enabling older women to become mothers.
[176] HFEA (2013c: para. 8.7).   [177] Brown (2005).   [178] Lee, Macvarish, and Sheldon (2014).
[179] (1994) 25 BMLR 1.   [180] Cutas (2007).   [181] De Wert (1998).
[182] Quoted in Harris (1999: 20). Harris comments that he expects that the remark would be offensive to disabled parents.
[183] Goold (2017).   [184] Jackson (1999).   [185] Anon (2004a).   [186] HFEA (2017: para. 8.7).

them producing a child through sexual intercourse. Should there be one imposed because they need medical assistance? Certainly, some commentators have suggested that it would be immoral to have a child, knowing that child was likely to suffer from a disadvantageous genetic condition.[187]

8 Parentage

8.1 The legal position

In family law, the rules as to who is the parent of a child used to be relatively straightforward.[188] The woman who gives birth to the child is the mother and the man presumed to be the genetic father was the father.[189] The presumptions used in relation to paternity (that the husband of the mother was the father of the child) are less important now that DNA tests can be performed if there is any question over paternity. However, these rules do not operate satisfactorily in the context of assisted reproduction and so the HFE Act 1990 developed some special rules in relation to paternity.[190] These can be summarized as follows.

(i)   The mother is the woman who gives birth to the child even if she became pregnant using donated eggs.[191] So even though the woman does not have a genetic link to the child, the fact that she has carried the child through pregnancy and given birth entitles her to be the mother. In a case involving donated eggs, the donor will have no legal rights in respect of the child.

(ii)   Who is the child's father in cases involving donated sperm? We need to consider four categories of man in the event that a woman gives birth using donated sperm.

   (a)   *The sperm donor* Where a donor's gametes are used in accordance with his consent, as required by Schedule 3, he is not to be treated as the father of the child.[192] A sperm donor therefore need not fear potential claims under the Child Support Act 1991 or other parental liabilities.

   (b)   *The husband of the woman* Under the HFE Act 2008, section 35, if a married woman gives birth using donated sperm, then her husband will be treated in law as the father of the child unless he can prove that: (1) he is not the genetic father of the child; and (2) he did not consent to the placing of the embryo into his wife. As the standard practice for clinics is to require the written consent of a married patient's husband, it will be very rare for a husband not to be treated as a father under this provision.

   (c)   *The civil partner or wife of the woman* [193] Section 42 of the HFE Act 2008 states:

---

[187] Purdy (1999).

[188] In family law, an important distinction is drawn between being a parent and having parental responsibility. Here, we are simply considering who will be regarded as a parent.

[189] HFE Act 2008, s. 33.

[190] Jones (2007) provides a useful discussion of the rules of paternity. See McGuinness and Alghrani (2008) for a discussion of the way in which the current law deals inadequately with transsexual people who use assisted reproduction.

[191] HFE Act 2008, s. 33.   [192] HFE Act 2008, s. 41.

[193] These provisions will be amended when the Marriage (Same-Sex Couples) Act 2013 comes into force to include married same-sex couples.

If at the time of the placing in her of the embryo or the sperm and eggs or of her artificial insemination, W was a party to a civil partnership or marriage, then subject to section 45(2) to (4), the other party to the civil partnership or marriage is to be treated as a parent of the child unless it is shown that she did not consent to the placing in W of the embryo or the sperm and eggs or to her artificial insemination (as the case may be).

Notice that the civil partner or spouse will not be the father or mother of the child, but the 'parent'. This seems odd, but reflects the law's traditional approach that a child can have only one mother and one father.[194]

(d) ***The partner of the woman*** If the woman is not married or has not entered a civil partnership, but lives with a partner, then that partner (male or female) can be a parent if the so-called 'agreed parenthood conditions' apply.[195] These require that the partner and the woman agreed that the partner would be a parent of the child born using these procedures. The HFEA Code of Practice states:

Where a woman is seeking treatment using donor sperm, or embryos created with donor sperm, her male partner will be the legal father of any resulting child if, at the time the eggs and sperm, or embryos, are placed in the woman or she is inseminated, all the following conditions apply:

a)   both the woman and the male partner have given a written, signed notice (subject to the exemption for illness, injury or physical disability) to the centre consenting to the male partner being treated as the legal father,

b)   neither consent was withdrawn (or superseded with a subsequent written notice) before insemination/transfer, and

c)   the patient and male partner are not close relatives (within prohibited degrees of relationship to each other, as defined in section 58(2), HFE Act 2008).[196]

There is a similar provision for female partners.

(iii) A child can be legally fatherless. If a child is born with the use of donated sperm, and the mother is unmarried and without a partner, then the child will have no father. However, in *Re R (A Child)*,[197] Hale LJ said that it is in a child's interests, if possible, to have a father. Not least, perhaps, so that the child will have a greater chance of receiving adequate child support.

(iv) The 2008 Act, in sections 39 and 40, provides that, in certain circumstances, a deceased person can be a parent of a child. These sections require that, before his death, the man consented to his gametes being used by the woman to produce a child. In *L v HFEA*,[198] Charles J suggested that removal of sperm from a dead person without his consent infringed his human rights and could amount to a criminal offence.

(v) A child cannot have more than one mother or one father (save in the case of adoption). As we have seen, the law does allow a woman's female partner to be a parent, but not a mother.

The following case illustrates the complexities that can arise in applying these rules. Although decided before the 2008 Act, a similar result would now be reached.

---

[194] See McCandless and Sheldon (2010) for a helpful discussion.   [195] HFE Act 2008, s. 44.
[196] HFEA (2013c: para. 6.11).   [197] [2003] 1 FCR 481, [27].   [198] [2008] EWHC 2149 (Fam).

KEY CASE   *Leeds Teaching Hospital v A* [2003] 1 FLR 1091

Mr and Mrs A and Mr and Mrs B both attended an assisted conception clinic in Leeds to receive infertility treatment. For both couples, the intention was to use the eggs of the wife and inject into them the sperm of the husband. Owing to a mistake, Mrs A's eggs were mixed with Mr B's sperm. The resulting embryo was placed in Mrs A and healthy twins born. The mix-up with the sperm came to light because Mr A and Mrs A were white, while Mr and Mrs B were black. DNA tests confirmed that Mr B was the genetic father of the twins. Mr B had no contact with the twins and did not wish to play an active role in their lives. Mr A, however, was happy to perform the role as father and wished to be legally recognized as such.

The key question for the court was who should be regarded as the child's father. At the heart of Dame Butler-Sloss's reasoning is the holding that, as a basic principle, the genetic father of a child is the legal father of the child, unless there is a statutory provision that displaces that principle. This meant that Mr B was to be regarded as the father of the child unless there was a provision in the HFE Act 1990 that led the court to conclude otherwise.

The court first considered Mr B's position and considered whether he could claim not to be a father because he was a sperm donor under section 28(6)(a). The difficulty that the court found in accepting this argument was that the section applies only where the sperm is used in accordance with the donor's consent. In this case, it had not been: he had consented to the use of his sperm to fertilize one of his wife's eggs. He therefore could not rely on section 28(6)(a).

The court then considered whether Mr A could claim to be the father relying on section 28(2). He was, after all, the husband of the mother and he had consented to her receiving the treatment. However, the court rejected this argument. Although he had consented to her receiving treatment, he had not consented to her receiving *this treatment* (that is, an embryo using another man's sperm). He therefore could not claim to be the father under section 28(2).

What about Mr A claiming to be the father under section 28(3), based on the fact that he was receiving treatment services together with his wife? Dame Butler-Sloss concluded that section 28(3) applied only to unmarried couples and so could not be relied upon by Mr A.

This led to the conclusion that Mr B was the legal father of the child. Mr and Mrs A were, however, free to adopt the child, terminating Mr B's parental status.

8.2 What should make someone a parent?

The rules on assisted reproduction and parenthood are controversial, and highlight the complex issue of what makes someone a parent.[199] There are four main theories, as follows.

(i) *Genetic link* There are those who argue that we should take a strict approach and declare that a parent is the person with the genetic link to the child.[200] That would mean that the sperm donor was the child of the father. Some may find that unpalatable, but quite simply that is the truth. As Daniel Callahan has put it: 'Fatherhood,

---

[199] See McGuinness and Alghrani (2008) and Horsey (2007) for a useful discussion.
[200] Moschella (2014).

because it is a biological condition, cannot be abrogated by personal desires or legal decisions.'[201] Supporters of this view would object to the allocation of parenthood in the HFE Act 1990. They would suggest that husbands and partners of women who become pregnant using donated sperm should be given parental responsibility, but not receive the status of being a parent.[202]

A slightly different argument is that we have responsibilities towards our genetic offspring. A sperm donor who therefore gives his sperm with no concern about any resulting child is not showing sufficient respect for this moral responsibility.[203] The HFE Act encourages such irresponsibility. However, it might be thought that, in giving sperm to a responsible licensed clinic, a donor can be confident that it will be used to assist a couple who desire a child and will care for him or her.

(ii) *Social parenthood* There are those who argue that what makes someone a parent is not a mere biological link, but rather the day-to-day caring for the child: washing, feeding, clothing, and educating him or her. It is the doing of the work of parenthood that earns the title of 'parent', not the genetic link, which may indicate no more than a 'one-night stand'. This approach would generally be supportive of the provisions in the HFE Act. For example, we can presume that the husband or partner of a woman undergoing IVF will undertake some of the jobs of parenthood, while the sperm donor will not. To declare the husband the father is therefore justifiable.

(iii) *The intended parent* There are those who argue that the person who is intended by those involved to be the parent should be the parent.[204] Again, this theory can be used to explain some of the provisions in the HFE Act. The sperm donor is not intended by anyone involved to be the father, while the husband or partner is. The HFE Act can be said to ensure that the intended father is the father. Critics of this approach criticize its vagueness, however: you cannot decide to become a parent of a child only by intending to do so.

(iv) *Causation* Rebecca Probert has argued that those who are the primary cause of the child, or who are best held as being responsible for the production of the child, should be regarded as the parents.[205] She accepts there may be many causers of a child: a sperm donor; the medical team; and the couple seeking treatment. However, she regards the couple as being the primary causers and therefore to be regarded as parents of a child born using donated sperm.

The complex notions of 'what is a parent' may be threatened by yet further technological advances. Reproductive cloning and the use of artificial gametes[206] provide the possibility of children being born genetically related to two people of the same sex, or indeed of being genetically related to only one person or more than two people.[207] Our 'cereal box' family assumption that each child has one mother and one father may not last very long.

---

[201] Callahan (1992a: 739).
[202] See also Weinberg (2009) for an interesting discussion on the moral obligations of sperm donors.
[203] Benatar (1999). See the reply in Bayne (2003).   [204] Horsey (2010).   [205] Probert (2004).
[206] Newson and Smajdor (2005).   [207] See, for further discussion, Jackson (2008).

9 Gamete donation: anonymity

An issue of great controversy is whether children born using donated sperm should be able to discover the identity of the sperm donor.[208] Until recently, such children had access to only the most limited of information: a child could discover whether he or she was born as a result of donated gametes and whether he or she was related to a person whom he or she intended to marry.[209] However, section 31ZA of the HFE Act 1990 provides children with access to a far greater range of information, although the regulations apply only prospectively: to all donations from 1 April 2005. Children born as a result of donations after that date can apply, once they have reached the age of 18, to discover identifying information including:

- the donor's name (and name at birth, if different) and address;
- the donor's date of birth and the town or district of birth;
- the appearance of the donor;
- a short statement about the donor; and
- information about other children born using his donated sperm.[210]

The regulations will *not* render a sperm or egg donor a parent in the eyes of the law, *nor* will they mean that he or she becomes liable for child support or takes on other financial responsibilities. All that they mean is that the donor's identity can be discovered by a child.

This change in the law may not have as great an impact as may be thought. This is because children have no right to be told that they were born as a result of IVF.[211] Of course, if a child does not know that he or she has been born using donated sperm, he or she will not realize that he or she could request the identity of the sperm donor. In fact, very few children are told about their genetic origins. In one study, 41 per cent of children conceived by egg donation and 28 per cent of those conceived by sperm donation had been told.[212] These percentages are higher than a survey around twelve years earlier which found less than 10 per cent of children born using donated sperm were told.[213] The difference in figures for egg and sperm donation are interesting. One explanation is it reflects the greater weight men place on genetic connection. Another explanation is that where egg donation is involved, there may be a greater degree of sharing of information, because almost one third of egg donors are known to the couple before the donation.[214]

The arguments in favour of allowing children access to the identity of their sperm donor 'fathers' or egg donor 'mothers' include the following.

(i)   The identity of one's genetic parents forms a key part of many people's sense of themselves.[215] This is reflected in, for example, the extent to which adopted people will try to find their genetic parents. Children born using donated sperm have

---

[208] Blyth, Crawshaw, and Speirs (1998).
[209] For donations since 1 July 2004, a wider range of non-identifying information, such as hair colour, can be provided.
[210] Their number, their sex(es), and their year(s) of birth.
[211] The HFE Act 2008 did not change this. HM Government (2007a) preferred educating parents about the benefits of telling their children, rather than compelling them to do so.
[212] Murphy and Turkmenda (2014).   [213] Golombok (2002).
[214] Abdallah, Shenfield, and Latarche (1998).   [215] Siegel, Dittrich, and Vollmann (2008).

spoken of being 'incomplete' without the full knowledge of their genetic origins. However, it is not clear from research whether giving identifying information creates the feelings of completeness for which these individuals hope.[216] The stories of donation are not likely to be as dramatic as those surrounding adoption, but are more likely to reveal a student donating sperm to generate beer money.[217]

(ii) A person's genetic background can nowadays contain important medical information. Denying access to information identifying a sperm donor would deprive an individual of important information about their medical background. However, it may be that the medical information could be provided in a way that would not reveal the identity of the donor, in the sense of giving their name.

(iii) Children have a right not be deceived as to their genetic origins (as recognized in *R (Rose) v Secretary of State for Health*[218]). John Eekelaar has asked whether anyone would like to be brought up deceived as to their genetic origins.[219] He thinks not. On the other hand, one might argue that there are occasions on which we would rather not know the truth. Would one want to know the genetic truth if it would destroy the image of the happy childhood with which one has grown up?

(iv) There does appear to be, amongst the general public, a genuine concern that a child born using donated sperm might meet and fall in love with someone born from sperm from the same donor (a blood half-brother or sister).[220] Although this fear may be generated more by the stories in soap operas than by statistics, openness about genetic background would alleviate this concern.

The arguments against allowing children access to the information include the following.

(i) Donors have a right of privacy. It is noticeable that the new regulations apply only prospectively and so donors who, in the past, donated on the understanding that their identity would be kept secret will have their rights respected, unless the HRA 1998 provides a challenge. In future, donors will be made aware that children born using their sperm will be able to discover their identity and so donors can hardly claim an infringement of rights if the information is disclosed.

(ii) Couples who used donated sperm may be very wary about their children being able to discover their genetic origins. Such information may undermine family relationships if the child does not regard his or her legal father as his or her 'real father'.[221] There is evidence that, when Sweden changed its law removing the anonymity of sperm donors, a large number of Swedish couples seeking donation went abroad to countries that retained the anonymity.[222] Of course, whether the wishes of infertile couples should trump the 'rights of the child to know her genetic origins' is a matter of debate.

(iii) The removal of anonymity would create a significant disincentive for people to donate. Supporters of the new regulations claim that although the kinds of people who wish to donate may change, there will not be a significant drop in the numbers donating. This can be a problem, in particular because, at present, there are attempts to 'match' the donor and the infertile person, so that the donor and person will be from the same ethnic group and even (apparently) have the same

---

[216] Turner and Coyle (2001); McWhinnie (2001).
[217] Deech (1998).   [218] [2002] EWHC 1593 (Admin).   [219] Eekelaar (1994).
[220] Edwards (1999).   [221] Roberts (2000).   [222] Jackson (2001: 213).

hair colour.[223] It appears that there has been a significant drop in the number of donors coming forward since the Department of Health announced its proposals in relation to anonymity.[224] The number of new registered sperm donors fell from 422 in 1993, to 254 in 1998. However, since 2005, the number of new donors has increased year on year, and in 2011, there were 501 registered donors and in 2014, 587.[225] Still, the HFEA accepts that there are severe shortages of sperm and eggs, and long delays.[226] In 2014 the UK Sperm Bank was set up to encourage donors. It closed in 2016 having recruited only seven donors.[227]

The HFEA has said that a single donor should not provide gametes for more than ten children.[228] One option to deal with shortages has been to use 'bulk imports' of sperm from Denmark.[229] In 2011, 7 per cent of all registered donors lived in Denmark and had been recruited to donate sperm![230] If the beer adverts are correct and the Danes get nasty when learning of the export of their beer, who knows what their reaction will be if they get to hear of this?!

The shortage of sperm and the identification of donors has also led an increasing number of couples to seek treatment overseas.[231] Again, it is Denmark that is a popular venue.[232] The sperm there is tall, blond, and anonymous.

The sperm shortage has led some to criticize the removal of anonymity. Ilke Turkmendag, Robert Dingwall, and Therese Murphy argue:

> The removal of anonymity has had identifiable detrimental effects: donors are reluctant to donate, UK clinics cannot meet the demand for gametes, there are long waiting lists for patients who wish to get treatment, and increasing use of international travel to avoid the law. None of these consequences were unforeseen or unpredictable.[233]

(iv) There are those who argue that we should reject the idea that genetic parenthood is of importance. What makes a parent is not a genetic link, which may be at most the result of the most casual of relationships, but rather the day-to-day, hands-on aspects of parenting. A man with no genetic link to a child can be just as good a father as one who has none.[234] To encourage people to think that genetic links are important is to encourage an outdated idea of parenthood. Feelings of being incomplete without knowledge of one's genetic identity are social constructions and need to be challenged, not pampered.[235] As Harris points out, any two people share 99.9 per cent of their genes; indeed, we share 50 per cent of our genes with bananas.[236] The notion that one's genetic link with one's parents is of significance must therefore be challenged. However, whether socially conditioned or not and however illogical or not, the strong desire for knowledge of children born using donated sperm cannot be denied.[237]

[223] Anon (2004a).   [224] House of Commons Science and Technology Committee (2005: para. 152).
[225] HFEA (2014).   [226] HFEA (2011d).   [227] BBC News (26 October 2016).
[228] HFEA (2011f). This restriction has been questioned: Millibank (2014).
[229] BBC News online (21 October 2003).   [230] HFEA (2013b).
[231] See Beers (2015) and Jackson et al. (2017) on the broader issues around reproductive tourism.
[232] BBC News online (20 May 2011).   [233] Turkmendag, Dingwall, and Murphy (2008: 211).
[234] Golombok, Jadva, Lycett, et al. (2005).   [235] Harris (2003a).   [236] Harris (2003a).
[237] See Fortin (2009) for an excellent discussion of the arguments.

10 Payment for gamete donation

The HFEA does not prohibit the payment or giving of benefit in return for gametes, but it is permitted only if authorized by directions issued by the HFEA. The HFEA has recommended that donors can receive payment in kind, in the form of discounts for assisted reproductive services. Sperm donors are normally paid reasonable expenses and for lost earnings. Small sums used to be paid to sperm donors. However, the European Tissues and Cells Directive requires that gametes should be supplied only on a not-for-profit basis.[238] Article 12 of the Directive says that 'donors may receive compensation which is strictly limited to making good the expenses and inconveniences related to the donation'.

There has been some debate over whether donors of gametes should be paid.[239] The stopping of payments and the removal of anonymity has led to a change in the kind of people donating. The HFEA explains: 'Today's sperm donors are much more likely to be family men in their 30s than the old stereotype of hard-up medical students.'[240]

Fox argues that the payment of donors would degrade the practice of reproduction, particularly if different amounts were paid depending on the characteristics of the donor:

> A market in the stuff of reproduction reduces offspring characteristics to a scalar metric, whereby the market worth of a designer child can be expressed in the same terms as designer clothes . . . To appraise the worth of reproductive goods on a common scale of fungible value is thus to make the stuff of babies exchangeable, tradable, and rankable.[241]

By contrast, the argument may be made that a failure to pay reflects a lack of recognition of the work that is involved in egg donation.[242]

If a woman seeking IVF is unable to afford the treatment, she may be asked whether she is interested in donating her eggs in return for a reduction of the costs of the IVF treatment. Critics claim that calling this 'egg sharing' disguises the reality that this is payment for eggs.[243] There are also, it is claimed, a host of potential psychological difficulties with the idea. What if the woman engages in egg sharing and, while her treatment is unsuccessful, the treatment using her eggs succeeds for someone else? Despite these concerns, one study found that 65 per cent of women who had engaged in egg sharing would be willing to do it again.[244] However, one might be concerned by the 35 per cent who would not.[245]

11 Surrogacy

11.1 The definition of 'surrogacy'

'Surrogacy' was defined in the Warnock Report as 'the practice whereby one woman carries a child for another with the intention that the child should be handed over after birth'.[246] In practice, the child is handed over within a day of the birth.[247] A distinction is often made between a partial and a full surrogacy: in a partial surrogacy, the eggs

---

[238] Directive 2004/23/EC.   [239] Daniels (2000); Draper (2007).
[240] HFEA (2005c: 11).   [241] Fox (2008: 164).
[242] Case (2009). See Pattinson (2012), who calls for a national donation system for gametes.
[243] Lieberman (2005).   [244] Ahuja, Mostyn, and Simons (1997).
[245] Wilkinson (2013), who provides a powerful exploration of the issue around egg donation.
[246] Warnock (1984: para. 8.1).
[247] Jadva, Murray, Lycett, et al. (2003); MacCallum, Lycett, Murray, et al. (2003).

of the commissioning mother are fertilized and placed into the surrogate; whereas in full surrogacy, the surrogate mother's eggs are used, and so she is both the genetic and gestational mother. Official figures suggest there were 167 surrogate births in 2014, although there may be many more that are not officially recorded.[248]

11.2 Is surrogacy legal?

It is not illegal to enter into a surrogacy arrangement, but there are a series of criminal offences connected with surrogacy.

- It is unlawful to negotiate or arrange a surrogacy arrangement on a commercial basis.[249] This does not prevent non-commercial groups from facilitating surrogacy arrangements and there are some organizations that do this. These offences cannot be committed by the surrogate mother or commissioning parents.[250] The offences could be committed by a commercial organization seeking to facilitate surrogacy arrangements.
- It is unlawful for anyone to advertise surrogacy services.[251]
- It is unlawful to make an offer that constitutes a reward or profit for the gestational mother, although she can be offered payment of expenses.[252]

Essentially, then, if a surrogacy arrangement is organized by an individual or a non-commercial body and there is no payment, surrogacy is legally permitted. However, even then, the surrogacy arrangement is not enforceable. The Surrogacy Arrangements Act 1985, section 1A, makes this absolutely clear: 'No surrogacy arrangement is enforceable by or against any of the persons making it.'

It may be that those involved in a surrogacy arrangement wish to use a licensed clinic to assist in the conception. This is permissible, but the HFEA Code of Practice requires clinics to:

> . . . take into account the possibility of a breakdown in the surrogacy arrangement and whether this is likely to cause a risk of significant harm or neglect to any child who may be born or any existing children in the surrogate's family.[253]

The clinic should also ensure that the parties are aware of the legal issues, consider whether there is likely to be a dispute concerning the child, and take into account the likely effect of the arrangement upon the child or a child of the family.[254]

11.3 What is the legal position if a child is born under a surrogacy arrangement?

When a child is born using surrogacy, the parental issues are dealt with as follows.

- The mother is the woman who carried the child.[255]
- The commissioning mother is not the mother, even if her eggs were used.
- The father will be the genetic father, unless he is a sperm donor using a licensed clinic.

---

[248] Hoyle (2015).   [249] Surrogacy Arrangements Act 1985, s. 2(1).

[250] Surrogacy Arrangements Act 1985, s. 2(2).   [251] Surrogacy Arrangements Act 1985, s. 3.

[252] *Re C (Application by Mr and Mrs X)* [2002] EWHC 157 (Fam).   [253] HFEA (2013c: para. 8.12).

[254] Brinsden, Appleton, Murray, et al. (2000).

[255] Contrast the position in California: see *Johnson v Calvert* 851 P 2d 776 (Cal, 1993), in which the commissioning couple were said to be the parents.

If the child is handed over and the commissioning parents wish to become recognized as the parents, they have two main options: adoption; or a parental order.

A parental order can be applied for under the HFE Act 2008, section 54. According to section 54 in order to obtain the order, the following must be shown.

(i)   Either the sperm, or eggs, or both, must have come from the commissioning couple.

(ii)   The commissioning couple must be married, civil partners, or living as partners in an enduring family relationship.[256]

(iii)   The child must be living with the commissioning couple.

(iv)   The surrogate must consent to the order.

(v)   Any parent of the child must consent to the order.[257]

(vi)   The court must be satisfied that no prohibited payment has been made, unless authorized by the court.[258]

(vii)   The applicants must have applied within six months of the birth.

(viii) The applicants must be at least 18 years old.

(ix)   The order will be in the welfare of the child.[259] This is to be the court's paramount consideration.[260]

However, in a series of cases the courts have been willing to overlook the fact that one or more of these requirements are not met. In *Re X (A Child) (Surrogacy: Time Limit)*[261] the couple applied some two years and two months after the birth of the child; well over the six-month limit in section 54. The court was willing to overlook this and make an order. The difficulty the court faced was that the couple had arrived in England having used a surrogate mother in India. If the court did not make a parental order the child would be living with the couple without any proper legal authorization. It was clearly in the child's welfare to make an order. Taking a similar approach the courts have been willing to make a parental order even though the couple have separated;[262] the application was brought three years after the birth, rather than the required six months;[263] or the surrogate's could not be found and so her consent could not be provided. The current position is well summarised by Russell J:

> when a child's welfare demands that a parental order is made it can only be refused in the 'clearest case of the abuse of public policy'.[264]

---

[256] The couple cannot be within the prohibited degree of relationships (e.g. siblings). See *A v P* [2011] EWHC 1738 (Fam) for a case in which a parental order was made even though the commissioning father had died shortly before the birth.

[257] That would normally include any husband or civil partner of the surrogate.

[258] HFE Act 2008, s. 54(8). The courts have been notably willing to grant parental orders even where substantial sums have passed hands, especially where this has been done overseas: *Re L* [2010] EWHC 3146 (Fam).

[259] Human Fertilisation and Embryology (Parental Orders) (Consequential, Transitional and Saving Provisions) Order 2010, SI 2010/986.

[260] *Re L* [2010] EWHC 3146 (Fam).   [261] [2014] EWHC 3135 (Fam).

[262] *A and B (No 2) (Parental Order)* [2015] EWHC 2080 (Fam).

[263] *AB and CD v CT (Parental Order: Consent of Surrogate Mother)* [2015] EWFC 12 (Fam).

[264] *Re A and B (Children) (Surrogacy: Parental Orders: Time Limits)* [2015] EWHC 911 (Fam).

So far there has only been one case where the courts have insisted that the section 54 requirements be fulfilled strictly. That was *Re Z (A Child: HFEA: Parental Order)*[265] where a single man had arranged for an overseas surrogate to carry a child for him and he wanted a parental order to be made in favour of him alone. The requirement in section 54 for there to be two applicants was seen as indispensable as it was a 'fundamental feature' of the legislation. No real explanation was offered by Munby P for why this requirement was fundamental and the others were not. Subsequently in *Re Z (A Child) (No. 2)*[266] the government conceded that sections 54(1) and (2) of the HFEA 2008 are incompatible with the rights of the father and child under Article 14 in conjunction with Article 8, in so far as they prevent the father from obtaining a parental order on the sole ground of his status as a single person, as opposed to being part of a couple.[267]

In these cases we see judges heavily influenced by the wish to promote the welfare of the child and being willing to read over legislative requirements in order to protect the child. However, a rather surprising aspect of this string of cases is the limited consideration of adoption. Even if a parental order is made, adoption is available. It is striking that the court preferred to stretch the statutory language of parental orders, rather than encourage the parties to apply for an adoption order.[268]

In the event of a dispute between the commissioning couple and the surrogate over who should care for the child, the matter is likely to be brought before the court by means of an application for a residence order (that is, an order determining where the child should live).[269] The court will make the order based on what will best promote the child's welfare.[270] Where the child has lived to date is likely to be an important factor.[271] If the surrogate has given birth to the child and cared for the child since birth, it is unlikely that the court would order the child to be handed over to the commissioning couple, unless there is evidence that the surrogate mother poses a serious risk to the child.[272] On the other hand, if the surrogate has handed over the child to the commissioning couple and then, some time later, changes her mind and seeks a court order that the child be returned to her, it is unlikely that she will succeed.[273]

11.4 The arguments in favour of surrogacy

The following are some of the most popular arguments used in favour of surrogacy.

(i)   The main argument in favour of surrogacy is autonomy. If a woman wishes to be a surrogate mother, why should she not be allowed to be?[274] She is not harming anyone else. Quite the opposite: her actions will bring great joy to the commissioning couple.

(ii) Surrogacy is inevitable and has occurred since biblical times. If it were outlawed, this would simply lead to a black market in surrogacy. It is better to permit it and regulate it, rather than to send it underground.[275]

---

[265] [2015] EWFC 73.   [266] [2016] EWHC 1191 (Fam).
[267] See Horsey (2016) for a helpful review of the literature.
[268] Perhaps the reason is that would have involved the local authority adoption agencies becoming involved.
[269] Children Act 1989, s. 8. Remember that, if no application is brought, the woman who gives birth will be the child's mother: HFE Act 2008, s. 33.
[270] *Re TT* [2011] EWHC 33 (Fam); *Re N (A Child)* [2007] EWCA Civ 1053.
[271] *Re TT* [2011] EWHC 33 (Fam).   [272] *A v C* [1985] FLR 445.
[273] *Re ME (Adoption; Surrogacy)* [1995] 2 FLR 789.   [274] Freeman (1999).   [275] Freeman (1999: 10).

(iii) Surrogacy widens the variety of family forms. Gay couples can now arrange for the production of a child; a single man can arrange for a child to be born for him to care for; grandparents can use the sperm of their deceased son to produce the grandchildren that they would otherwise never have.[276] Of course, whether these kinds of developments are a welcome break from the traditional nuclear family or a misuse of technology is a matter for debate. As Cook, Day Sclater, and Kaganas put it:

> Surrogacy, then, perhaps more than any other reproductive practice, throws into sharp relief our anxieties about the future(s) of the family. It threatens accepted views of what a family is, of gender-appropriate parental behaviour, and of our ideas of what is natural in the realm of reproductive behaviour.[277]

11.5 The arguments against surrogacy

The following are some of the most common arguments raised against surrogacy.

(i)   The situation is potentially harmful to children, in that it is liable to produce litigation over them.[278] A surrogate mother may form a strong attachment to the child and be unwilling to hand the child over.[279] Whether that is likely to happen may be questioned.[280] Two studies of surrogate mothers found a significant majority saying that they felt no special bond between them and the child.[281] Further, from the limited data on surrogacy in the UK, it appears that disputes over a child are rare[282] and, so far, there have been no reported cases in the UK of a commissioning couple refusing to accept a baby.[283]

(ii) Surrogacy exploits surrogates.[284] There is evidence, especially in the United States where large sums are paid to commercial surrogate companies, that surrogate mothers are required to undertake risky work for inadequate care.[285] It has even been said to be analogous to slavery.[286] There are particular concerns in this regard now that surrogacy has become international.[287] In the Warnock Report, it was argued 'it is inconsistent with human dignity that a woman should use her uterus for financial profit'.[288] However, supporters of surrogacy might point out that we do generally allow people to do things that we think foolish or even exploitative.[289] Many of these concerns are based on the view that for a woman to give up a baby to whom she has just given birth is unnatural and that she would do so only if desperate for money.

(iii) An argument specifically against the paying of surrogates is that the practice becomes too close to 'baby selling'. This may be seen as objectionable in itself; it is

---

[276] Laurance (2000). See also Carroll (2013) and Rao (2013).
[277] Cook, Day Sclater, and Kaganas (2003: 5). See also Mackenzie (2007).
[278] For example, *W v H (Child Abduction: Surrogacy) (No. 2)* [2002] 2 FLR 252.
[279] Tieu (2009).   [280] Hanna (2010).
[281] Jadva, Murray, Lycett, et al. (2003); MacCallum, Lycett, Murray, et al. (2003).
[282] Dodd (2003) found only 2 per cent of surrogacy cases in which there were disputes; Brazier (2003b: 3.38) found between 4 per cent and 5 per cent.
[283] Van der Akker (1999).
[284] The arguments receive careful analysis in Wilkinson (2016), Tieu (2009), Callahan and Roberts (1996), and Purdy (1989).
[285] Ince (1984).   [286] Roberts (1986).   [287] Parks (2010).   [288] Warnock (1984: 45).
[289] Steinbock (1988: 44).

MEDICAL LAW AND ETHICS

argued that, once the child discovers the circumstances of his or her birth, he or she will be greatly distressed. It might also be said to transform surrogacy from essentially an altruistic exercise into a commercial one.[290] Michael Freeman has said that payment to a surrogate is not buying children, but recompense for 'a potentially risky, time consuming and uncomfortable process'.[291] We pay the medical staff who enable the surrogacy; why should we not pay the woman who carries the child?

11.6 Should surrogacy contracts be enforced?

If surrogacy is permitted, there is still the question of whether or not we should enforce surrogacy contracts. In other words, if the surrogate mother refuses to hand over the child at birth, should she be forced to? One of the most common arguments in favour of this is that a surrogacy contract should be treated like any other contract and should be enforced in the same way.[292] This, however, is not as convincing an argument as it first sounds. The normal remedy for a breach of contract is the payment of damages. The argument might therefore be that if the surrogate mother does not hand over the baby she should pay damages (e.g., any expenses incurred by the commissioning couple), but it does not mean she should be required to return the baby. An alternative argument is that the commissioning couple started the process by which the baby came into being and may have contributed genetic material to the child. A recognition of their commitment to the child should justify making the order. However, one might think the physical and emotional commitment of the surrogate through the experience of pregnancy will trump such a claim.[293]

11.7 Reform of surrogacy

Margaret Brazier chaired a review into surrogacy in 1997.[294] It considered in particular whether mothers should be allowed to receive payment, whether an agency should be created to regulate surrogacy arrangements, and whether there was a need for legislative change. Its main findings were as follows.

(i)   Surrogacy contracts should continue to be unenforceable.

(ii) Only legitimate and proven expenses should be paid to a surrogate mother. If illegitimate expenses were paid, then a parental order should not be made.

(iii) All surrogacy agencies should be registered with the Department of Health, but no commercial agency should be allowed.

(iv) There should be a code of practice issued, which governs the practice of surrogacy agencies.

The report proved controversial and the government has not taken any steps to implement it. In 2005, the government initiated a consultation exercise, which included questions on whether the law on surrogacy needs to be reformed, but no significant reforms resulted.[295] It seems that there is widespread agreement that there should be

---

Brazier (1999c: 345).   [291] Freeman (1999: 9).   [292] Straehle (2016).
Gerber and O'Byrne (2015); Baier (2015)
Brazier, Campbell, and Golombok (1998).   [295] DoH (2005e).

some kind of regulation.[296] Surrogacy carries at least as many risks as IVF and yet is unregulated, at least when performed outside of a clinic. What has proved elusive is a form of regulation that is acceptable to all. Should surrogacy be promoted, tolerated, or discouraged? Should we regard the commissioning couple as the parents of the child from the moment of birth? Why should a commissioning couple have a greater claim to a child than a couple wanting to adopt a child who might be assessed as more suitable than the commissioning couple?[297] Unfortunately, it may take a scandal to spur the government into regulation and the resolving of these questions.[298]

12 Preimplantation genetic screening

The usual procedure for couples using IVF is to create a number of embryos and implant them one or two at a time into the woman. The question that we will consider here is whether it is permissible to select which, from among the embryos created, will be implanted.[299] There is generally no objection to a selection being made on the basis of which embryos are most likely to survive to birth, but more controversially a couple who are at risk of having a child with a genetic disability may wish to select an embryo that does not carry that disability. This requires an assessment of the different embryos to see if they carry the desirable or undesirable characteristic. This is known technically as preimplantation genetic screening (PGS) and requires a licence from the HFEA. A total of 578 of the IVF treatment cycles started in 2013 involved the use of PGS.[300]

The 1990 Act sets out the circumstances in which PGS is permitted. This includes 'to establish if an embryo has an abnormality that might affect its capacity to result in a live birth' and 'to avoid a serious medical condition'.[301] The practice is controversial and the HFEA will allow it only for a strict set of reasons.[302] The HFEA Code of Practice explains:

> Preimplantation genetic diagnosis (PGD) can be carried out for a heritable condition only in two circumstances:
>
> - where there is a particular risk that the embryo to be tested may have a genetic, mitochondrial or chromosomal abnormality, and the Authority is satisfied that a person with the abnormality will have or develop a serious disability, illness or medical condition, or
> - where there is a particular risk that any resulting child will have or develop a gender related serious disability, illness or medical condition. A condition is gender related if the Authority is satisfied that it affects only one sex, or affects one sex significantly more than the other. In the first situation, PGD may be carried out to establish whether the embryo has the suspected abnormality; in the second, PGD may be carried out to establish the sex of the embryo.[303]

---

[296] Warnock (1984: para. 8.18) expressed the concern that regulation might be seen as official endorsement.
[297] Overall (2015).   [298] Horsey (2015) for an excellent discussion of reform possibilities.
[299] See Krahn (2011) for a discussion of the use of PGD for Down's syndrome.
[300] HFEA (2016).   [301] HFE Act 1990, Sch. 2, para. 1ZA.
[302] See the discussion in Gilbar (2009), Gavaghan (2007), and Scott (2006).
[303] HFEA (2017: 10.2)

The HFEA is clear that it is not possible to select an embryo which will be likely to develop a serious physical or mental disability or other medical condition.[304]

The Human Genetics Commission argues in favour of a liberalizing of the law on preconception genetic testing, noting that testing of babies and children for possible genetic conditions is seen as generally uncontroversial.[305] The Commission argues that 'there are good reasons why earlier testing is favoured over later testing, as it facilitates wider patient choice and improved access to information supporting reproductive decision-making'.[306]

Supporters of PGD make some of the following arguments. First, some argue that the question of which embryos a woman chooses to implant should be up to her—that it is an aspect of her reproductive autonomy.[307] No one should prevent a woman from selecting her embryos as she chooses, just as no one could interfere with the decisions of a woman to have sexual relations with a dark-haired man in the hope that the baby born would have dark hair.

Second, there are those who argue that zygotes have no moral status, and therefore that decisions about them and their disposal carry no weight.[308]

Third, there are those who argue that there is a basic moral obligation to avoid harm to others. If therefore it is possible to choose an embryo that will not suffer the harm of having an undesirable characteristic of his or her parents, we should do so. Indeed, there is even an argument that genetic screening should be compulsory in order to ensure that a disadvantaged child is not born.[309] We would regard a parent who, through negligence, failed to give her child the necessary medical treatment and whose child suffered a disability as a result as a neglectful parent. Her behaviour might even be a criminal offence. Is it any different if a parent fails to provide prenatal genetic testing or treatment for a child so that he or she avoids a disability?[310]

The reasons why PGD may be used vary and, because they raise slightly different arguments, it is worth considering them separately.

12.1 Disability

If a couple choose from among their embryos those that do not carry a gene for, say, cystic fibrosis, we can presume that those embryos carrying this gene will be discarded. But what does that say about the attitude revealed towards people suffering from cystic fibrosis? Is it not revealing a discriminatory attitude? In the most obvious way, the statement is that a life with cystic fibrosis is not worth as much as a fully healthy person's life. Should we allow couples to exhibit such an attitude and allow medical staff to act on it?[311] Or, rather, is it the message that is being sent by a society that encourages the use of tests for disability that is most concerning?[312] Does it not perpetuate the promotion of the myth of idealism as to human nature: that any child who is not perfect can be rejected by a parent? Further it reduces people to their disabilities and encourages the treatment of others simply by looking at their disability.[313] However, it might be replied

---

[304] HFEA (2017).   [305] Human Genetics Commission (2011).
[306] Human Genetics Commission (2011: 3).   [307] Harris (1998: 133).   [308] Holm (1998).
[309] BBC News online (19 May 2005b).   [310] Hammond (2010).
[311] Kaplan (1999); Peterson (2005a).
[312] Asch and Wasserman (2007).
[313] Soniewicka (2015).

that it is proper to seek to ensure that those with disabilities are not disadvantaged, while at the same time seeking to prevent disabilities where possible.[314] A parent may therefore legitimately prefer a child without that disadvantage than a child with. There is, after all, a difference between saying that a life with a characteristic is one that is not worth living and saying that it would be better not to have that characteristic. People routinely take steps to avoid becoming disabled (for example by taking safety measures), and in doing so are choosing to try to avoid disability. Is that sending a negative message about disability?[315] Adrienne Asch has argued that parents should be given full information about the characteristics of the embryos and allowed to choose.[316] She objects to the fact that particular characteristics (that is, those connected with 'disability') are selected and highlighted as disadvantages, and suggests that all of the facts about each embryo should be given to parents to let them make a choice, without indicating that medicine regards some characteristics as harmful and others as not. However, one response is that as those not selected never come into existence they cannot be regarded as being harmed.[317]

Even more controversial is the question of whether a couple should be allowed to choose to have the embryos that carry a disability. The HFEA currently does not allow that.[318] Say, for example, a deaf couple wished to select an embryo that was likely to be born deaf, rather than a child who could hear. Should that be permitted?[319] Supporters of a strong right to procreative autonomy might be compelled to say 'yes'. After all, a person could, by selecting a sexual partner, seek to increase the chances of a child having a disability, and that could not be prevented. To others, deliberately choosing a child who will be at a disadvantage when compared to other children is simply wrong. If a couple were to have a deaf child whose deafness could be 'cured' and the couple refused to allow the child to be treated, would that not be wrong?[320] However, it might be replied that, in selecting a deaf child, no one is being harmed. This makes it different from a case in which a particular child is rendered deaf.[321]

These arguments, however, assume that deafness is a 'disability' that we need to 'cure'. The debate centres on what can be regarded as an acceptable range of conditions for the proposed child to have.[322] There is little consensus on that.[323] After all, in other contexts, we give parents a broad discretion as to how to raise children, including allowing them to raise children in ways that are harmful.[324]

12.2 Sex selection

The HFEA does not allow embryo selection on the basis of sex unless there is a genetic illness related to sex and therefore the sex selection is performed in order

---

[314] Asch (2003); Mahowald (2007).   [315] Malek (2010).   [316] Asch (2003).
[317] Walker (2014).   [318] HFEA (2017: 10.4)   [319] Anstey (2002).   [320] Kahane (2009).
[321] Hope and McMillan (2012).
[322] For an interesting survey of the views of hearing children of deaf parents on the issue see Mand, Duncan, Gillam, et al. (2009). Most are opposed to using genetic selection in order to avoid or ensure deafness.
[323] See the useful discussion in Hull (2006).   [324] Murphy (2011).

to avoid a risk of a particular condition.[325] As a result, the HFEA will not accept sex selection for social reasons.[326] These would include 'family balancing' (to have a family that has children of both sexes)[327] or to replace a dead child with a child of the same sex.

Supporters of reproductive autonomy argue that sex selection should be permitted as an aspect of a person's right to control his or her reproduction.[328] After all, there is plenty of folk law about what to do if one wants a boy or a girl when engaging in sexual intercourse. No one suggests that it is improper to try to use these methods.

The objections to sex selection include the following.

(i) *Demographic impact* The concern is that the ratio between male and female will skewed. In some countries (India and China are often given as examples), the ratio of boys to girls is 107:100 or even higher, and this is said to be caused by the abortion of girls.[329] However, there is no reason to believe that sex selection would lead to such a skew in the UK. Indeed, it is perfectly possible that couples would prefer girls to boys. In any event, there would be a noticeable demographical impact only if a large number of parents were to engage in sex selection, and this is unlikely.

(ii) *International implications* There is a concern that if sex selection were to be permitted in the UK, it would make it difficult for the UK to object to the procedure in other countries where it is being used in an unacceptable way.

(iii) *Psycho-social impacts* There is a concern that a child born as a result of sex selection will suffer psychological problems. The child may fear that he or she was selected only on account of his or her sex.[330] We simply do not know if children would have these feelings or, if they did, whether that would be harmful.

(iv) *Sex discrimination*[331] There is an argument that allowing people to choose the sex of their child will pander to their sexist beliefs and attitudes. People should be encouraged to accept children regardless of their sex. Further, it may be said that the selection of children on the basis of sex reveals an overemphasis on the importance of sex differences.[332]

(v) *Public opinion* The HFEA report found widespread feeling among the members of public consulted against sex selection: of those questioned, 80 per cent thought that people should not be allowed to select on the basis of sex for social reasons.[333] A common feeling was that parents should love their children whatever their characteristics.[334]

The following case demonstrates how instances of sex selection can give rise to complex issues.

---

[325] HFE Act 1990, Sch. 2, para. 1ZA, specifically allows embryo testing for the purpose of avoiding a 'sex related serious medical condition'.
[326] See Seavilleklein and Sherwin (2007) for a disturbing account of the range of sex selection services available online and internationally.
[327] See Wilkinson (2008) for an interesting discussion of the ethical issues surrounding 'family balancing'.
[328] McCarthy (2001).   [329] House of Commons Science and Technology Committee (2005: 135).
[330] Baldwin (2005). See the reply by Harris (2005b).   [331] Dickens (2002); Robertson (2003).
[332] See the discussion in Wilkinson (2008).   [333] HEFA (2004b: 25).
[334] See Herrisone-Kelly (2007) for a discussion of such arguments.

> ### REALITY CHECK
>
> **The Masterton case**
>
> In 1999, Alan and Louise Masterton from Monifieth near Dundee lost their youngest child, a 3-year-old daughter, Nicole, in a bonfire accident. The loss was particularly tragic because they had been trying for fifteen years to have a girl and Nicole's arrival had therefore been a huge joy. The Mastertons, who have four sons, campaigned for the right to rebuild their family with a daughter. They were adamant that they did not want to replace Nicole, but did want a daughter. Louise Masterton had been sterilized after Nicole's birth. The Mastertons wanted the HFEA to permit them to undergo IVF and use PGD to ensure that they had a daughter. The HFEA would consider the issue only if a clinic applied for a licence. However, the Mastertons could find no clinic that would take them on. The Mastertons eventually travelled to Italy and spent £30,000 on IVF treatment, but unfortunately they were able to produce only a male embryo, which they donated to another couple. Female embryos that were implanted were lost.
>
> In 2001, the HFEA did apologize to the Mastertons for mishandling their case. It should, in the unusual circumstances of the case, have considered the couple's direct appeal to it.[335]

12.3 'Trivial reasons'

What about selection for reasons that appear 'trivial': hair or eye colour, for example?[336] In one sense, it may be argued that this is more acceptable. Say that a parent selected an embryo on the basis that he or she wanted a curly-haired child rather than a straight-haired one. It could not be suggested that this indicates a view that children with straight hair have lives not worth living, or be an expression of a prejudicial attitude, in the way that a decision based on disability can be perceived. To Harris, such choices can be left to parents:

> It seems to me to come to this: either such traits as hair colour, eye colour, gender, and the like are important or they are not. If they are not important why not let people choose? And if they are important, can it be right to leave such important matters to chance?[337]

It should be added that, at present, it is not technically possible to use PGD to select for traits such as intelligence, height, hair colour, or sexuality, although it might be possible in the future.[338]

In response, Scott has argued that while parents have legitimate interests in avoiding a child who will be born seriously impaired, their interests are not seriously implicated where the decision is over insignificant matters.[339] Indeed, allowing parents to make decisions over trivial matters could lead to a shallow view of what parenthood is about or create unrealistic expectations in parents about what their children will be like. Either of these would harm children.

---

[335] BMA (2004: 297).
[336] BBC News online (2 March 2009) reports that a US clinic is offering to allow parents to select eye and hair colour for their babies.
[337] Harris (1999: 29).
[338] House of Commons Science and Technology Committee (2005: 143).   [339] Scott (2006).

12.4 Saviour siblings

The emotive term, 'saviour siblings', has come to be used for cases in which the parents of a sick child wish to have another child whose tissue can be used to provide a treatment for the condition of the sick sibling.[340] It is officially known as preimplantation tissue typing.

The following case highlights some of the issues involved.

KEY CASE *Quintavalle (on behalf of Comment on Reproductive Ethics) v HFEA [2005] UKHL 28*

The House of Lords was asked to consider the legality of the HFEA's licence to permit a clinic to use human leukocyte antigen (HLA) typing to test embryos for stem cells that could provide a cure for a couple's son. Under the HFE Act 1990, section 3(1), it is a criminal offence to bring about the creation of an embryo, except under licence from the HFEA. The proposed treatment involved the creation and use of an embryo, and required a licence, which the authority granted. The granting of the licence was challenged in the court by the group Comment on Reproductive Ethics (CORE). Its application succeeded before Maurice J, but failed before the Court of Appeal and the House of Lords.

The key provision was section 11 of the 1990 Act, which permitted the HFEA to license certain activities. In Schedule 2, paragraph 1(3), these included '(d) practices designed to secure that embryos are in a suitable condition to be placed in a woman or to determine whether embryos are suitable for that purpose'. The HFEA argued successfully before their Lordships that the word 'suitable' meant 'suitable for the woman to whom the services are provided'. The mother was entitled to regard an embryo as suitable only if it was compatible for treatment of her sick son. CORE argued that this is too wide an interpretation of the provision and would allow the HFEA to license treatment to test for a whole range of idiosyncratic wishes, such as hair colour. The interpretation of paragraph 1(3) advanced by CORE was that 'suitable' meant that the child would be healthy and free from abnormalities. This would allow PGD to test for abnormalities, but not to test for whether the child's tissue matched a sibling's.

This argument was rejected. First, it was pointed out that although the HFEA's interpretation meant that a licence could be given for frivolous reasons, there was no reason to believe the HFEA would grant such a licence. Second, and more importantly, the HFE Act was designed to leave these complex moral issues with the HFEA. The Act was structured to outlaw some things (such as the cloning of an embryo), but to leave other things open to the HFEA to license if it thought it appropriate to do so. The issue in this case was not outlawed specifically in the Act and therefore was licensable by the HFEA. If Parliament felt that the HFEA was using its powers improperly, it was for Parliament to reform the HFEA.

It is worth emphasizing that the House of Lords approached this case by addressing the narrow legal issue of whether the HFEA had statutory authority to license the treatment. The ethics of it, or whether it would be lawful to use the tissue of any resulting child, were not considered in any detail.

---

[340] For an excellent analysis see Taylor-Sands (2014 and 2016). See also Jackson (2016).

The HFE Act 2008 amended the 1990 Act to make it clear that embryo testing to ensure that an implanted embryo may be a 'saviour sibling' is permitted. Paragraph 1ZA(d) of Schedule 2 of the 1990 Act allows a testing where:

> . . . a person ('the sibling') who is the child of the persons whose gametes are used to bring about the creation of the embryo (or of either of these persons) suffers from a serious medical condition which could be treated by umbilical cord blood stem cells, bone marrow or other tissue of any resulting child, establishing whether the tissue of any resulting child would be compatible with that of the sibling.

There, are however, limitations on the use of PGD for the use of selecting 'saviour siblings'. First, the statute makes it clear that it can be used only in the case of siblings. An 'embryo' who would be the cousin of a child with a serious medical condition could not be selected. Second, paragraph 1ZA(1)(d) makes it clear that selection cannot be performed if it is planned that a whole organ (for example a kidney) is to be donated. The plan must be to use the umbilical cord blood stem cells, bone marrow, or other tissue, from a child.[341] That is not to say that a child cannot donate an organ to a sibling; it is simply saying that the child cannot be selected at the embryo state for such a purpose.

When deciding the appropriateness of preimplantation tissue typing in any particular situation, consideration should be given, by the clinic, to the condition of the affected child, including:

(a) the degree of suffering associated with their condition

(b) the speed of degeneration in progressive disorders

(c) the extent of any intellectual impairment

(d) their prognosis, considering all treatment options available

(e) the availability of alternative sources of tissue for treating them, now and in the future, and

(f) the availability of effective therapy for them, now and in the future.[342]

In cases of saviour siblings, consideration should also be given to the possible consequences for any child who may be born as a result, including:

(a) any possible risks associated with embryo biopsy

(b) the likely long-term emotional and psychological implications

(c) whether they are likely to require intrusive surgery as a result of the treatment of the affected child (and whether this is likely to be repeated), and

(d) any complications or predispositions associated with the tissue type to be selected.[343]

Consideration should also be given to the family circumstances of the people seeking treatment, including:

(a) their previous reproductive experience

(b) their views and the affected child's views of the condition

---

[341] For an excellent general discussion on issues surrounding collection of cord blood see Devine (2010).
[342] HFEA (2017: 10.25).   [343] HFEA (2013c: para. 10.25).

    (c) the likelihood of a successful outcome, taking into account:

        (i)   their reproductive circumstances (i.e., the number of embryos likely to be available for testing in each treatment cycle, the number likely to be suitable for transfer, whether carrier embryos may be transferred, and the likely number of cycles)

        (ii) the likely outcome of treatment for the affected child

    (d) the consequences of an unsuccessful outcome

    (e) the demands of IVF/preimplantation testing treatment on them while caring for an affected child, and

    (f) the extent of social support available.[344]

Critics of 'saviour siblings' claim that it involves bringing a person into being for the sole purpose of assisting his or her sibling. This infringes the principle that people should not be used solely as a means to an end. Supporters could reply to this in two ways. One would be to argue that, in fact, to save the life of one's sibling is beneficial to the donor, or at least not harmful to him or her.[345] Alternatively, they could argue that it is extremely unlikely that parents would treat the saviour sibling simply as a source of tissue. It would be hard to believe that parents would 'discard' a saviour sibling once treatment of the existing child had been effective. The child is being created to be loved in his or her own right, as well as to assist the sibling. A slightly different argument is that the child, when older, might perceive himself or herself to have been created as merely a means to save his or her sibling. This could cause psychological problems, particularly if the matching had not worked out.[346] Again, these are only possible dangers and we do not know how likely they are to be realized. The 'saviour sibling' might be as likely to feel delighted that he or she was able to save, or to attempt to save, another life and regard it as having enriched his or her own.[347] John Harris has argued that guesses about possible emotional harms for the 'saviour sibling' do not justify denying treatment that would save a life.[348] Another issue that the courts may need to address at some point is the legal liability that could arise if a 'saviour sibling' is created, but does not provide a cure.[349]

13 Cloning

13.1 Introduction to cloning

Cloning raises high emotions. To some, extending the possibilities of human reproduction beyond normal sexual intercourse is terrifying, raising profound questions about our identity. To others, cloning provides exciting possibilities of enabling couples, who would be unable to have them otherwise, to have children and offers the hope of a treatment for diseases for which, at present, there is no hope of a cure. Now that the cloning of people is feasible and there have been some claims that humans have been

---

[344] HFEA (2017: par 10.26).   [345] Spriggs (2005).   [346] Delatycki (2005).
[347] Foster and Herring (2016); Strong, Kerridge, and Little (2014).   [348] Harris (2002).
[349] See Chico (2006) for a discussion of the issues that could arise.

cloned,[350] predictions about the effect of cloning have moved well beyond the realm of science fiction. But the question of whether or not to clone is one that has attracted much attention and this has led, in many cases, to a polarization of views.

13.2 The definition of 'cloning'

The US President's Council on Bioethics defined cloning in this way:

> The asexual production of a new human organism that is, at all stages of development, genetically virtually identical to a currently existing or previously existing human being. It would be accomplished by introducing the nuclear material of a human somatic cell (donor) into an oocyte (egg) whose own nucleus has been removed or inactivated, yielding a product that has a human genetic constitution virtually identical to the donor of the somatic cell.[351]

A clone, then, is a group of cells that have identical DNA sequences to the 'parent' group of cells. Almost all of the clones that have been produced so far are not true clones, because their non-chromosomal (mitochondrial) DNA is different from that of the 'parent', even though their chromosomal DNA is identical. Clones are currently created by cell nucleus replacement (CNR). This involves a nucleus from a cell being placed into an egg, thereby activating it. Cloning therefore opens up a number of reproductive possibilities. Because sperm is not required, it offers hope for a man who wants to have genetic offspring, but is unable to produce sperm. It would also enable a lesbian couple to produce a child genetically related to them both.

It is common to draw a distinction between reproductive and therapeutic cloning. Although the same process is used to create an embryo in each case, the difference lies in the motivation behind the process.

- In reproductive cloning, the aim is produce a child. Having produced the cloned embryo, the plan would be to transplant it into the womb to develop.

- In therapeutic cloning, there is no intent to produce a child. The cloned embryo is created in order to produce cells that will be transplanted into someone who suffers from some kind of disability or condition. The cloned embryo may also be created for research purposes.

13.3 Legal responses to human cloning

The HFE Act 2008 permits the licensing of some forms of human cloning, but only for the purposes of research. It is not permitted for a cloned embryo to be implanted in a woman.

13.4 Arguments in favour of reproductive cloning

The key argument in favour of permitting cloning is reproductive autonomy, a concept with which we are now familiar. If we accept that people have free choice over when

---

[350] BBC News online (20 May 2005). Certainly, a monkey embryo has been cloned, and this means that human reproductive cloning is not far off: BBC News online (14 November 2007).
[351] President's Council on Bioethics (2002: 33).

and how to reproduce, cloning should be open to them, unless there are some powerful state interests against allowing it.[352] The arguments over cloning therefore tend to have centred on the strengths or weaknesses of the arguments against it.

Supporters of reproductive cloning argue that cloning enables people, who otherwise would be unable to do so, to have children.[353] Couples who otherwise would have to use donated gametes can have a child who is genetically related to both of them. For this reason in particular, lesbian couples might welcome the technology. It would even be possible for a woman to use a cell from her own body to implant into one of her own eggs.[354] Although the media might portray cloning as being used by people trying to produce the 'perfect baby', in reality it is more likely to be used for couples for whom reproductive cloning offers the only hope of a child.

13.5 Arguments against cloning

Here, we will examine the arguments that have been made against cloning. It will be emphasized that the arguments are stronger against some forms of cloning than others.

(i)   It is widely accepted that to attempt human cloning with the present state of scientific knowledge would pose unacceptable risks.[355] The rate of miscarriage in attempted cloning of animals has been high,[356] and there is a real risk that any child successfully produced would suffer from illnesses or diseases. However, it may be only a matter of time before the success rate of gestation improves and concerns over the future of cloned children are overcome. Harris rejects the argument that, at present, the dangers of reproductive cloning are too great to authorize it.[357] He points out that, with normal sexual intercourse, 80 per cent of fertilized eggs 'die', and between 3 and 5 per cent of embryos have an abnormality. In the light of such statistics, he suggests that the chances of reproductive cloning producing a healthy child do not look too bad. Lane argues that as long as the products of human cloning would have a minimally decent life, cloning should be permitted, even if the cloned child would be likely to suffer some form of disability.[358] Perhaps a commoner view is that until the rates of disability likely to result from cloning are similar to those associated with traditional sexual reproduction, human cloning to produce a child should not be attempted.

(ii) From an evolutionary perspective, it is possible to argue that cloning will limit the genetic diversity of the gene pool, rendering the human race more susceptible to extinction resulting from a particular disease or virus.[359] This argument, however, would carry weight only if cloning were to become the primary means of reproduction. Even if cloning is permitted, the number of cloned people is likely to remain small, and so the impact of cloning on the human gene pool will be minimal.

(iii) Some commentators have claimed that one has a right to be genetically unique.[360] Jim McLean has stated: 'An artificially cloned human being would have been

---

[352] Foley (2002).

[353] Although see Jensen (2008) for an argument that a desire to have a genetically related child is not a good enough moral reason to justify cloning.

[354] Harris (2002: 81).   [355] DoH (2005e).   [356] Golton and Doyal (1998).

[357] Harris (2001: 111).   [358] Lane (2007).   [359] Gardner (2003).

[360] For example, Williamson (1999).

denied the right to be the product of a genetic blueprint having two different sources.'[361] The argument is that each person has a right to have his or her own genetic make-up, which is independent of others. This is because our genetic make-up is regarded as the core to our humanity.[362] To guarantee an individual's unique status and separateness from their parents, it is crucial that a child is a combination of genetic material from both parents.[363] Joyce Havstad argues that '[t]hese individuals ought to be free to pursue this right by not having their opportunities drastically limited, as would happen if parents forced them to assume another's identity instead of allowing them to create their own'.[364]

To some commentators, however, such a claimed right to genetic uniqueness is difficult to justify. Nature itself permits individuals to share DNA: identical twins, for example.[365] Further, the idea that one cannot have a unique personality, identity, and character because another person shares one's genes is unconvincing, again as twins show.[366]

In response to these points, the genetic identity argument could be rephrased in terms of disturbing the structure of the family. The House of Lords Committee put it this way:

> If the cell nucleus from the father were used, for example, the child would be the genetic son of its grandparents, the genetic sibling of its uncles and aunts and the genetic uncle of its cousins. The range of ambiguities introduced into family relationships by cloning from a close relative would be large and the possibility for emotional confusion and uncertainty—not only on the part of the cloned child—considerable.[367]

(iv) Some have argued that children have the right to choose an open future. Even if there is no biological reason for this,[368] a cloned person may believe that he or she is genetically pre-ordained to be like his or her clone.[369] The pressure that a cloned person will feel to be like—or indeed unlike—his or her clone will deprive the cloned person of the right to be an individual and to live out his or her own version of life. In reply, it might be said that even a child born using normal reproduction may feel destined to have some of his or her parents' characteristics and pressure to follow, or not to follow, in his or her parents' footsteps. Sean Pattinson argues that although reproductive cloning itself does not harm an individual, behaviour after the birth, for example, in pressurizing the clone to behave in a particular way, would.[370] He asserts therefore that this argument is not against reproductive cloning per se, but against treating the clones, once born, in a particular way. Again, the example of twins could be considered: pressures that one twin may feel to be like (or unlike) the other are not regarded as some kind of infringement of the twins' human rights.[371]

(v) Some suggest that cloning is likely to work against the interests of women.[372] The argument is that cloning is likely to be particularly attractive to infertile men. The risks, pains, and discomfort of ova stimulation, ova retrieval, and embryo transfer necessary for cloning will all fall on women, in addition, of course, to the burdens of gestation and childbirth. It has been claimed that, for each human cloning

---

[361] McLean (1998: 26).   [362] Kass (1998).   [363] Meilaender (1998).
[364] Havstad (2010: 76).   [365] Harris (2004b).   [366] Prainsack and Spector (2006).
[367] House of Lords Select Committee on Medical Ethics (1994: 34).
[368] Savulsecu (2005).   [369] Holm (1998).   [370] Pattinson (2002b).
[371] As Harris (2005a: 35) points out, 1 in 270 births is a twin.   [372] Mahowald (2006).

attempt, there will be a need for several hundred ova,[373] and there is a high risk of late foetal deaths in cloned embryos.[374] All of these will impose extra burdens on women. There are also wider concerns that reproductive technologies such as cloning increase and perpetuate the exercise of medical and patriarchal power over women's bodies.[375] Such concerns, however, must be weighed against the strong desire of those women for whom cloning may be the only option, such as lesbian couples, to have children. To address these concerns, supporters of cloning may call for regulation to ensure that women do not become only 'vessels' in the hands of medical professionals, but argue that there is nothing in the nature of human cloning that necessarily demeans women.

(vi) A study of public attitudes to cloning found a widespread feeling that the practice of cloning was unnatural.[376] It would disrupt a child's lineage, which is an important part of identity. Helen Watt has said that children would be treated more like products whose genetic make-up is selected in advance, rather than as a gift.[377] Leon Kass has argued that society's natural repugnance of cloning reflects a sound intuition concerning the profound principles of things that people hold dear.[378] Supporters of cloning have questioned whether merely feelings of disgust, per se, are sufficient to justify outlawing an activity. Feelings of repugnance that are not supported by moral arguments should not form the basis of law.[379]

(vii) One way of dealing with questions of this kind is to ask whether a child would choose to be born cloned. Sonia Harris-Short argues that people would not.[380] The question could, however be phrased: would you rather be born cloned than not exist at all? The answer to that question is likely to be 'yes'. Burley and Harris suggest that only if the harms could be said to blight the life of the child could they be said to justify prohibiting cloning.[381]

 A VIEW FROM ABOVE

Religious views on cloning

Some of the most vocal opponents of human reproductive cloning have been those writing from a religious perspective. Indeed, the religious concerns on this issue reflect the objections that many religious people have to the whole area of assisted reproductive treatment.

There are a set of concerns based on the 'sanctity of life' doctrine and the belief that life starts from conception. This leads to a rejection of any method of reproduction that involves the destruction of, or lack of respect for, the embryo.[382] These issues are discussed in detail in Chapter 8, so they will not be repeated here.

Those writing from a religious perspective are often concerned with the way in which reproductive technologies, and in particular cloning, involve 'playing God'. Some emphasize

[373] National Academy of Sciences (2002).   [374] Smolin (2002).   [375] Petchesky (1979).
[376] The Wellcome Trust (1998: 13–14). See Foster (2011), who puts the argument in terms of human dignity.
[377] Watt (2002b). See also Finnis (1998a).   [378] Kass (1998).   [379] Tribe (1998); Rao (2002).
[380] Harris-Short (2004).   [381] Burley and Harris (1999).
[382] See Ibrahim (2000), who emphasizes this point from an Islamic perspective.

that God intended reproduction to take place through sexual intercourse between married people. Attempting to create children in other ways is an unnatural effort to thwart the divine plan. Richardson, for example, argues that God intended reproduction to involve the cooperation of two parties in an act of mutual love and that cloning undermines that.[383] There are also concerns that cloning will challenge the notion that each person has been created by God as part of 'His plan'.[384] Assisted reproductive technology and cloning are seen as ways in which children become regarded as commodities to be bought or produced, rather than as gifts from God.

However, others do not see it in this way and argue that God gave talent to individuals so that it can be used to better the lot of humankind. There should be no more objection to medicine being used to cure infertility than there is to its use in dealing with other forms of illness. Assisted reproductive technology should be regarded as a gift from God rather than as a challenge to God's purposes. Indeed, it may be said to fulfil the biblical command to 'be fruitful and multiply'. Such reasoning is found particularly among Jewish scholars.[385]

14 Therapeutic cloning and embryo research

We will discuss therapeutic cloning and embryo research together, because they raise similar issues. Both involve the creation of an embryo in order to assist in research, or to assist the treatment of others.

14.1 The status of the embryo

This issue has already been extensively discussed in Chapter 6. It will be recalled that there are a wide variety of views on the moral status of the embryo,[386] ranging from the point of view that an embryo is a person with as much of a right to life as any other human being, through to the view that the embryo is no more than a collection of cells of no particular moral significance.

The HFE Act 1990 allows research to be licensed on embryos until the formation of the primitive streak. That is taken to occur no less than fourteen days after fertilization. Baroness Warnock, whose report led to the 1990 Act, has explained her view in this way:

> [B]efore fourteen days, the embryo, or pre-embryo as it was scientifically known, was a loose cluster of first two, then four, then sixteen cells, undifferentiated. An undifferentiated cell could develop into any of the types of cell that go to make up the human body, and some of them would not become part of the embryo at all, but would form the placenta or the umbilical cord. After fourteen days, there begin to appear the first traces of what will become the central nervous system of the embryo, the primitive streak.[387]

---

[383] Richardson (1998).   [384] See Fadel (2002).   [385] Dorff (1998).

[386] See, e.g., Polkinghorne (2004) and Brooke (2004). For a discussion on whether cloning has altered the debate over the moral status of the embryo, see Cameron and Williamson (2005) and Harris and Santon (2005).

[387] Warnock (2002: 35).

The fourteen-day period has also been supported on the basis that it is close to the time at which the embryo may be able to experience pain.[388] It is also the time at which the embryo is a coherent entity and it is clear that there are not going to be twins.

The HFE Act imposes a number of important restrictions on the use of embryos in research, including the following.

(i)   An embryo cannot be stored or used for research after the primitive streak, which is taken to be fourteen days from the mixing of gametes.[389]

(ii) The use or storage of an embryo requires a licence and licences can be issued by the HFEA only for certain purposes, including promoting advances in treatment of infertility, miscarriages, contraception, or causes of congenital diseases.[390] The HFE Act 2008 has added three new purposes to the original five set out in the Act: increasing knowledge about the development of embryos; increasing knowledge about serious disease; or enabling any such knowledge to be applied in developing treatments for serious disease.

(iii) It is not permitted to mix human and animal gametes, or to place a human embryo in a non-human animal, except as permitted by the HFE Act 2008.[391] (We will look at this later in the chapter.[392])

(iv) The HFEA will consider licences for research only if a research ethics committee has approved the research.

Controversially, the HFE Act permits research not only using embryos that are 'spare' following infertility treatment, but also embryos that are specifically created for research.[393] The significance of this is that it permits research into therapeutic cloning.

Most people who support research involving embryos, including the Warnock Committee, whose report underpins the HFE Act, require that embryos be treated with respect. Many will share John Polkinghorne's view that:

> The very early embryo is entitled to a deep moral respect because of its potential humanity, so that it is not just a speck of protoplasm that you can do what you like with and then flush it down the sink; but it is not yet fully a human being.[394]

However, deep moral respect is a troublesome concept in this context.[395] In what way is it respectful of an embryo to carry out experiments on it and then discard it? The House of Lords Select Committee on Stem Cell Research concluded that the HFE Act does demonstrate respect for the embryo used in research, for example by allowing embryo research to be performed only where no alternative means is available and only for one of the permitted purposes.[396]

---

[388] Warnock (1984: paras 11.19–11.21).   [389] HFE Act 1990, s. 3(3)(a) and (4).
[390] These are listed in HFE Act 1990, Sch. 2, paras 3 and 3A(2).
[391] HFE Act 1990, s. 3(3)(b) and (d).
[392] See under the heading '14.4 Hybrids and cybrids'.
[393] Notably, the European Convention for the Protection of Human Rights and Dignity of the Human Being with regard to the Application of Biology and Medicine (the Convention on Human Rights and Biomedicine, or the Bioethics Convention), Art. 18, does not permit states to create embryos specifically for research, and that is a major reason why the UK has not signed this Convention.
[394] Polkinghorne (2004: 594).   [395] See, e.g., Brazier (1999a); Brownsword (2003c).
[396] Brownsword (2002).

John Harris makes the point that 'nature' itself is no great respecter of embryos.[397] He points out that, for every successful pregnancy involving natural sexual intercourse, five embryos are lost or miscarried:

> One obvious and inescapable conclusion is that God and/or nature has ordained that 'spare' embryos be produced for almost every pregnancy, and that most of these will have to die in order that a sibling embryo can come to birth. Thus the sacrifice of embryos seems to be an inescapable and inevitable part of the process of procreation.[398]

Indeed, Harris argues that if one really believes that embryos are people from conception, you should not engage in sexual intercourse because of the very high risk that an embryo will be created, not implanted, and therefore destroyed.[399] The absurdity of such a conclusion leads him to determine that we cannot believe that an embryo has the status of a person.

14.2 Should the law permit the use of embryos in research, and if so, when?

Generally, the issues here are similar to those discussed in Chapter 6.[400] Those that take a strong 'pro-life' view will often oppose embryo research, while those who are more 'pro-choice' will support it.[401] But for some, the link between the issues is not straightforward. Consider the following viewpoints.

(i) *The agnostic* If someone is wholly undecided about the status of the embryo, then a perfectly respectable position for them to take would be this:

> I cannot oppose abortion because it would be wrong for me to require a woman to undergo a pregnancy against her wishes and the interference in her rights that would constitute, based on my doubts over the correct status of the foetus. On the other hand, in relation to embryo research, because no one else's rights are being infringed, my doubts predominate and lead me to argue that research should not be carried out on embryos.

Note, however, that the assumption that no one else's rights are interfered with if embryo research is prohibited might be challenged. Are the interests of those whose diseases would be cured if embryo research were carried out not interfered with if research is banned?

(ii) *The aborted foetus* A strong opponent of abortion may still be able to justify research on an aborted foetus. Although he or she may regard the abortion as abhorrent, it might be arguable that, because it has happened, at least some good should come out of the tragedy, and if medicine can be advanced by research on the aborted embryo, so be it.[402] Of course, this would restrict the kind of research that could be performed.

---

[397] Harris (2002).   [398] Harris (2002: 129).
[399] Chan and Harris (2010).
[400] See Harman (2007) and Pugh (2014) for a useful discussion of the differences in the issues raised by embryo research and abortion.
[401] Although see Deckers (2007b) for further discussion.   [402] Harris (1998a).

(iii) *The potentiality argument* One of the arguments put forward for why a foetus deserves moral respect is that, 'left to its own devices', the embryo would become a human being. Abortion is wrong because it interferes with the potential person. Arguably, an embryo created in a laboratory is in a different position: it will not develop into a person if left alone. This could lead someone to conclude that the moral status of the embryo in the womb is not the same as that of the embryo in 'the test tube'.[403]

(iv) *The significance of the mother* Isabel Karpin is critical of those who assume that the status of the embryo in the mother and in the research lab is the same:

> The embryo is only connected with its potential for personhood by female embodiment. Those who wish to make the argument that all embryos have equivalent value do so only be rendering the female body irrelevant. In order to do this, a complex process of disappearing has to take place. It we return the female body to visibility then the basis of the discussion is fundamental changed.[404]

Amel Alghrani and Margaret Brazier argue that if the foetus is outside the mother (for example in a lab or artificial womb), the foetus should be recognized as having independent interests that should be given weight.[405]

(v) *The 'some value' argument* Someone might believe that an embryo, while not having the moral status of a person, has some moral standing.[406] While that moral status might be insufficient to justify outlawing abortion, it might mean that embryos should not be used in research.[407]

14.3 Therapeutic cloning

Therapeutic cloning is the cloning of an embryo to make the cells, tissue, or organs of that embryo compatible with a proposed recipient. The intention normally is that the embryo will never develop beyond the fourteen days mentioned in the HFE Act 1990. The technology offers potential treatments for diseases such as diabetes, Alzheimer's disease, and Parkinson's disease.[408] The controversial nature of the procedure is immediately apparent because it involves embryos being created and used merely to provide genetic material for a person, and then being disposed of.[409]

One greatly disputed issue is whether it is necessary to use embryonic tissue for therapeutic cloning. This has focused particularly on the use of embryonic stem cells.[410] For some of those who think that embryos have some moral value, the potential benefits of research are too speculative to justify using embryos in research.[411] Some people argue that developing stem cell lines from the umbilical cords of children at birth, or from the

---

[403] This was the approach taken by the Irish Supreme Court in *Roche v Roche* [2009] IESC 82, in which it was held that an embryo in utero was protected by the right to life, but not an embryo that was in a laboratory. See Agar (2007) and Kuflik (2008). See also the discussion in Brazier (2006b).
[404] Karpin (2006: 603).
[405] Alghrani and Brazier (2011). Smajdor (2012) makes the argument that we should develop artificial wombs as soon as possible.
[406] Farsides and Scott (2012) found that researchers using embryos believed embryos to be of some value.
[407] See Savalescu and Perrson (2010), an argument rejected in Chan and Harris (2010).
[408] DoH (2003c).   [409] Halliday (2004).   [410] See Morgan (2007) for an excellent discussion.
[411] Woods (2008).

tissue of adults, is just as effective.[412] Indeed, recently, it became possible to produce pluripotent cells, which may well mean that developing cell lines from embryos is now unnecessary.[413]

14.4 **Hybrids and cybrids**

The HFE Act 2008 will now bring hybrid and cybrid embryos within the scope of the HFEA.[414] Licences may permit their creation subject to the requirement that the project is necessary or desirable for the purposes described in legislation.[415]

The 2008 Act inserts a new section 4A into the 1990 Act:

(1) No person shall place in a woman—

   (a) a human admixed embryo,

   (b) any other embryo that is not a human embryo, or

   (c) any gametes other than human gametes.

(2) No person shall—

   (a) mix human gametes with animal gametes,

   (b) bring about the creation of a human admixed embryo, or

   (c) keep or use a human admixed embryo, except in pursuance of a licence.

(3) A licence cannot authorise keeping or using a human admixed embryo after the earliest of the following—

   (a) the appearance of the primitive streak, or

   (b) the end of the period of 14 days beginning with the day on which the process of creating the human admixed embryo began, but not counting any time during which the human admixed embryo is stored.

(4) A licence cannot authorise placing a human admixed embryo in an animal.

So the Act allows the creation of admixed embryos only up until fourteen days and does not allow such an embryo to be placed in a woman. The creation of an admixed embryo is permitted only if done under a licence.

It seems that surveys of public opinion are against the creation of hybrid embryos for the purposes of research.[416] However, when the public are asked whether they support the use of hybrid embryos for research into treatment of a specific condition (such as Parkinson's disease), then the percentages change significantly and a majority support their use.[417] The Act avoids the difficult questions about whether a cybrid embryo is human. Perhaps that is only an issue that will need to be addressed if ever a cybrid is brought fully to life.[418]

---

[412] Catholic Bishops' Conference (2004). Although see Solbakk and Holm (2008) for a discussion of the difficulties in separating out the ethical debates from debates over how likely such research is to be effective.
[413] Holm (2008).
[414] For general discussions, see Academy of Medical Science (2011); Camporesi and Boniolo (2008); Munzer (2007).
[415] *R (Quintavalle) v HFEA* [2008] EWHC 3395 (Admin) found that the creation of hybrids was permissible even before the 2008 Act came into effect.
[416] Jones (2009).   [417] HFEA (2007a).   [418] Bernat (2008).

15 Genetic enhancement and eugenics

So far, we have been discussing circumstances in which a couple select an embryo from the embryos that their gametes have produced. But now, we will discuss whether it is permissible for a couple to manipulate the genetic make-up of an embryo before it is implanted.[419] It is common to draw a distinction between manipulation that is designed to remove a genetic abnormality, so that the embryo has an average health, and manipulation that is designed to enhance the embryo's characteristics (for example, to make the embryo especially intelligent or strong). Amongst the general public, there appears to be much more sympathy for couples who wish to give birth to children who do not have disabilities or disorders than for couples who wish their child to have some enhanced characteristic.[420] Some people look forward to a 'wonderful new world of genetically and pharmaceutically augmented, ultra-intelligent, long-lived super-persons'.[421] Interestingly, when two artists put up an advert in an American shopping mall for a 'biotech boutique' offering genetic modifications for people (for example, increased machismo or creativity), they were inundated with enquiries.[422]

A rather different issue is whether a parent could select a characteristic that he or she may think desirable, but which others do not.[423] A much discussed situation is deaf parents selecting an embryo to produce a deaf child.[424] Supporters of such a choice emphasize that it would be wrong to say that such a selection has harmed the child: the child in question is not injured or made worse off by the selection or resulting birth, given that the only alternative for the child would be not to exist at all.

The law is clear: the HFEA is not permitted to grant a licence authorizing the alteration of the genetic structure of a cell that forms part of an embryo.[425] To do so would be illegal. The HFE Act 1990, Schedule 2, paragraph 3(4), does permit regulations to be passed by Parliament that allow the alteration of the genetic structure of embryonic cells, but only for the purposes of research.

Not only is genetic modification of embryos therefore against the law, but the technology to do so is also at a very early stage. However, as it advances, the issue is likely to become controversial. If the law were to be relaxed, one option would be to draw the distinction mentioned above: allowing the removal of disadvantages, but prohibiting the enhancement.[426] This, however, assumes that we can agree on what an 'advantage' or 'disadvantage' is.[427] Whether being gay, religious, or temperamental are beneficial or negative characteristics is a matter on which there is no consensus.[428]

Some of those who oppose enhancement sometimes argue that what are improper are alterations to the body that go beyond what is 'natural'. So replacing a lost arm is not enhancement, but rather returning a body to its natural state.[429] By contrast, adding a 'bionic' third arm to a healthy body would be improper. This still relies on a notion of what is natural and leaves the question of whether assisting a person with a congenital

---

[419] See Savulescu and Bostrom (2008) and Gordjin and Chadwick (2009) for excellent discussion of the issues. Note that it may be quite some time before technology enables us to 'enhance' humans in some of the ways discussed: Harris (2011a).

[420] Richards (1999).   [421] Lewens (2009: 11).   [422] Fox (2008).

[423] An excellent discussion is found in Wilkinson (2010).

[424] Fahmy (2011); Shaw (2008).   [425] HFE Act 1990, Sch. 2, para. 1(4).

[426] Farrelly (2004); Pattinson (2002b: 103).   [427] Buchanan, Brock, Daniels, et al. (2000).

[428] Lewens (2009).

[429] See Holtug (2011) for a rejection of the distinction between enhancement and treatment.

illness is departing from what is natural *for them*. Sorensen suggests that there is nothing wrong in 'bringing out the best in people', but that what are objectionable are genetic interventions that 'change the identity of the individual'.[430] But that distinction is not clear: would producing a child who could run unusually fast be changing his or her identity?

For Stephen Wilkinson, there is a key difference between altering the characteristics of a child (for example turning a hearing child into a deaf one) and selecting, from among a number of embryos, a hearing embryo over a deaf one. The latter is acceptable, while the former is not.[431] Not everyone will be convinced by this distinction, especially if they regard embryos as having a special status. Is not the deaf embryo that is not selected, and is therefore likely to be destroyed, harmed? This argument, however, is more an argument against the use of multiple embryos in assisted reproduction generally than an argument against selection.

Much of the ethical debate has focused on whether parents should be permitted to enhance the abilities of their children prenatally. Sandel, opposing this, argues:

> To appreciate children as gifts is to accept them as they come, not as objects of our design, or products of our will, or instruments of our ambition. Parental love is not contingent on the talents and attributes the child happens to have . . . [W]e do not choose our children. Their qualities are unpredictable, and even the most conscientious parents cannot be held wholly responsible for the kind of child they have. That is why parenthood, more than other human relationships, teaches what the theologian William F May calls an 'openness to the unbidden'.[432]

While the approach to parenting that he advocates may be admirable, it leaves open the question of whether those parents who are seeking to enhance their children are doing something so wrong that the law ought to intervene.

Another alternative would be to give parents the choice: they can determine whatever changes to their children's genetic structure that they wish.[433] This would permit a couple to amend their child's genetic structure to be deaf, for example. Many would find that repugnant, but the strict logic of a reproductive autonomy rights perspective would support it. Some have reached an almost opposite conclusion: that there is a duty to engage in genetic intervention to prevent or to ameliorate serious disability or illness.[434] It has been argued that just as it would be seen as horrific to release a substance into the world which created a new disability, it is wrong to deliberately choose to create a deaf child.[435]

Julian Savulescu goes even further and promotes what he calls 'procreative beneficence', which urges parents to select the best children that they can produce.[436] His strongest argument is that parents should select to ensure that their children do not have 'a deep obstacle to human flourishing'.[437] Critics of such a view might argue that this assumes that we can determine what is good or not for a person, that having lives and personalities that are a mixture of good and bad makes our existence more rewarding, that it will lead to children suffering from the over-hyped expectations of their parents,

[430] Sorensen (2009).   [431] Wilkinson (2010).   [432] Sandel (2007: 12).
[433] Savulescu (2001c).   [434] Buchanan, Brock, Daniels, et al. (2000).
[435] Sparrow (2015). Although see Wasserman (2015).
[436] Savulescu (2001c; 2006). See Bennett (2014) for a critique.   [437] Kahne and Savulescu (2010).

and that it overlooks the importance of wider societal influences on what makes a good life.[438] For example, Savulescu assumes that increased intelligence will lead to increased well-being, but that might be disputed.[439] Some argue that even if Savulescu's arguments demonstrate the permissibility of enhancement, they do not demonstrate that it is an obligation.[440] Rebecca Bennett argues that it is wrong to assume that, because parents have a responsibility to produce the best life for their children, there is an obligation to produce the best children.[441] Indeed, she argues that the principle of procreative beneficence is, in effect, eugenics. Disabled people make important contributions to the cultural, educational, and social life of our communities.[442] It would be just as wrong to seek to eradicate a particular disability as it would be to eradicate a religious or ethnic group. A different response for critics would be to ask whether it is possible to know what the 'best' child one could produce would be.[443] To impose on people an obligation to produce the best child is impossible, given the widely divergent views on what makes a life good. Further, why must parents produce the best for that child? Should they not be obliged to produce the child that is best for society?[444] Or indeed is the whole idea of parenthood that one loves one's child as they are?[445] And should not parents be learning from their children as much as moulding their children into a particular identity?[446]

Hanging over this whole debate are concerns about eugenics,[447] and particularly memories of the Nazi regime's desire to produce a 'pure Aryan race'. This is seen as so revolting to many that any procedure that begins to raise the spectre of such a desire must be prohibited. Another concern about allowing enhancement is that it might produce injustices if there is not equal access to the possibilities offered.[448] As Walter Glannon puts it:

> [I]t would involve unfair access to enhancement technology based on ability to pay; it would involve an unacceptable social cost in the form of mental impairment as a side-effect in some people; it would threaten to undermine equality as one of the bases of self-respect, social stability and solidarity; and it would threaten to undermine individual autonomy and responsibility.[449]

So the concern is that richer parents could ensure that their offspring were superior in many ways to the offspring of those who could not afford enhancement.[450] Further, encouraging enhancement might mean that those who were disabled or non-enhanced would suffer a particular disadvantage.[451] It also might be seen as signalling a move from parents accepting and loving their children unconditionally towards children being seen as projects in which parents can 'succeed'.[452] A similar concern is that if we were to produce an enhanced race of people ('post-humans' as some commentators have called them), they would end up oppressing us.[453] There are also arguments that society works better if people have a range of different skills and abilities.[454]

---

[438] Parker (2007).   [439] Saunders (2015). How happy do you think your lecturers are?!
[440] Saunders (2015); Brassington (2009).   [441] R. Bennett (2009).   [442] Wasserman (2015).
[443] Karpin and Mykitiuk (2008).   [444] Elster (2011).   [445] Draper (2014); Gheaus (2016).
[446] Herring (2017).   [447] Glover (1998).
[448] Douglas and Devolder (2013); Lev (2011).   [449] Glannon (2001: 107).   [450] Sorensen (2009).
[451] Holm (2009).   [452] See Wilkinson (2011) for a discussion of this argument.
[453] See discussion in Agar (2010). Or at least might we find it hard to relate to each other: Agar and McDonald (2017).
[454] Gyngell and Douglas (2015).

If we were to enhance them so that they were not only 'super-human', but also 'super-kind', of course, that might not happen.[455] But that creates further problems.[456] If we enhance people so that they are especially moral, does that deprive them of the choice to be immoral, which in turn casts doubt on whether they are truly good people, if they have no choice about it?[457] Further, do we not need people with different moral qualities?[458] We might not want a brain surgeon to be particularly empathetic as that may interfere in their job, even if generally empathy is a good thing.[459] Agar[460] raises the concern that with moral enhancement a minor error can create a huge wrong. A person who is slightly over-empathetic might become deeply depressed, for example. These concerns have led some to suggest that rather than talk about moral enhancement, we should consider whether enhancement to make people more socially useful should be considered.[461]

A final issue is this. Imagine a world in which every person was genetically engineered to be perfect physical and intellectual specimens. Sparrow argues that if we selected only the best embryos, we would select only women (for various reasons, including that they live longer).[462] Would the human race be any happier or better off? Would a world without people with Asperger's syndrome or Down's syndrome really be a better place?[463] Some have suggested that part of the joy and value in life is the struggle to reach physical or intellectual heights. If we are born with these, what will people do with their lives?[464] Completing a marathon would not be rewarding if one were genetically enhanced so that it was no longer a challenge.[465] This might suggest that more limited enhancement is permissible; for example, within the current normal variation that people achieve, but not enhancement to create super-humans.[466]

16 Conclusion

Technological advances have dramatically increased the range of options available for reproduction. This has thrown up a large number of difficult legal and ethical issues which have been discussed in this chapter. First, there are questions about who is the father and mother of a child produced by technological means, if indeed we should stick with such gendered names for parenthood. Do we need to move beyond the heteronormative model of one mother and one father to recognize the biological and social complexities that surround parenthood? Second, there are questions about what the role of the state should be in reproductive technologies. Should the state be providing any reproductive services at all? If it should, should it provide them to everyone or try and restrict these to people who will be good, or adequate, parents? Third, how are we to respond to the possibility of altering the genetic make-up of embryos? A popular approach is to draw a line between the removal of disabilities which is permitted and the enhancement of people which should

---

[455] Persson (2012); Persson and Savulescu (2013 and 2015).   [456] See Chan and Harris (2011).

[457] Chan (2017); DeGrazia (2014); Rakic (2013). Harris (2013 and 2016) argues that moral enhancement is not possible.

[458] Gyngell and Douglas (2017).   [459] Wasserman (2014).   [460] Agar (2015).

[461] Fabiano and Sandberg (2017). See discussion in Hauskeller (2016).

[462] Sparrow (2010). Kahane and Savulescu (2010) and Harris (2011) disagree.

[463] Walsh (2010) and Wilkinson (2015).   [464] Holland (2003: 152).   [465] Tännsjö (2009).

[466] Kahane and Savulescu (2015).

not. However, that line may not be sustainable. Further, it is under serious challenge from disability activists who argue it portrays disability in a negative way. As has been seen from the discussion in this chapter, these are complex and controversial issues.

QUESTIONS

1. Should people be allowed to buy children? Many people find the notion repugnant, but for many, expensive IVF or surrogacy is the only way in which they can have children. Are these people, in effect, buying children? Or what about reports of churches offering pregnant women considering abortion money to persuade them to carry the child to term and then to arrange adoption?[467]

2. It has been suggested that, in our society, choosing to be childless is an act of unimaginable selfishness.[468] Do you agree? Is it selfish not to have children? There is even an argument that it is morally indefensible to have children; the argument is that not having children means leaving the situation morally neutral. Having children is more likely to produce unhappiness than happiness. It is therefore immoral to have children and immoral to provide services to help people to have children.[469] Are you persuaded?

3. Consider this example. A woman, aged 62, went to Los Angeles and used IVF to become pregnant with her brother's sperm. Apparently, this was an attempt to win a dispute over an inheritance with other members of her family.[470] Does this indicate that any claim to reproductive autonomy must have some limits?

4. Agar tells of a repository of the sperm and eggs of the most able and active individuals from around the world.[471] These are then available for sale or research. Should there be more of these? Why should we not use only the gametes that contain the very best genetic material?

5. Consider the following argument.

   Even if our genes could be manipulated to make our behaviour conform to a morally perfect course of action in every situation, it is unlikely that we would want it. Most of us would rather make autonomous choices that turned out not to lead to the best course of action. This is because of the importance of moral growth and maturity that come with making choices under uncertainty. The dispositions that we cultivate on our own, imperfect as they are, make our lives valuable to us.[472]

   Do you agree? Is this a convincing argument against attempts to 'improve' embryos?

6. According to one study, one in twenty-five men are raising children to whom they are not genetically related, but believe that they are.[473] Does that matter? Why should it matter to someone whether the man who has acted throughout their life as a father was genetically related to them?

---

[467] Compare Brazier (1999c) and Landes and Posner (1978) on this issue.
[468] Callahan and Roberts (1996: 1225).
[469] See Häyry (2004) and Bennett (2004).   [470] Warnock (2002: 48).
[471] Agar (2004: 1).   [472] Glannon (2005: 113).   [473] Ives and Draper (2005).

7. Is there any weight in the argument that because there is so much money available surrounding ART, with private clinics charging large sums, there is a danger that the 'reproductive industry' is exaggerating its success rates?[474] Why else is there so little information about success rates? Why is there so little effort put into finding ways in which couples can avoid becoming infertile?

8. One of the difficulties facing the HFEA is that, as Brazier has pointed out, 'British law . . . displays contradictions, no single, coherent, philosophy underpins the law's response to reproductive medicine'.[475] She notes that the embryo is seen as deserving of respect and yet, at least until the fourteenth day, she wonders whether it is 'in reality treated differently from laboratory artefacts'?[476] Is it possible to respect a foetus *and* to permit its destruction?

9. Devolder and Savulescu argue that reproductive cloning should not be permitted, but that there is a moral duty to research therapeutic cloning.[477] Would you agree? Does the fact that the 'abnormality' rate for children born following traditional reproduction is 6 per cent[478] support the case for requiring all couples to reproduce with assisted reproduction?

10. There are news reports on men who offer fresh sperm donation privately.[479] This is unregulated by the HFEA (because there is no storage).[480] Should it, or could it, be regulated?

11. Quigley talks about (legal) drugs known colloquially as 'professor's little helpers', which, it is claimed, help to improve a person's cognitive skills and academic performance.[481] Would you be more or less impressed by an academic who produced a work having taken the pills?! Would it make any difference if the enhancement had occurred pre-birth? Is there a difference between enhancement of mental facilities and physical ones?

12. In *A and B v A Health and Social Services Trust*,[482] a white couple gave birth to non-white children after a mistaken use of donated sperm. They sued for damages and failed. Do you think that they should have succeeded?

13. Harris[483] writes:

    It is doubtful that natural sexual reproduction, with its risk of sexually transmitted disease, its high abnormality rate in the resulting children, and its gross inefficiency in terms of the death and destruction of embryos (estimated to be one in three to one in five deaths per live birth), would ever have been approved by regulatory bodies if it had been invented as a reproductive technology rather than simply 'found' as part of our evolved biology.

Should we forbid sexual reproduction?

[474] Callahan and Roberts (1996).   [475] Brazier (1999c: 197).   [476] Brazier (1999c: 198).
[477] Devolder and Savulescu (2006).   [478] Harris (2014).
[479] BBC News online (18 September 2009).   [480] See also online at www.feelingbroody.com/.
[481] Quigley (2008).   [482] [2011] NICA 28.   [483] Harris (2016).

FURTHER READING

A comprehensive bibliography, including all references used throughout the book, is available online at www.oup.com/uk/herringmedical7e/.

On the general issues raised in this chapter, see:

Alghrani, A. and Brazier, M. (2011) 'What is it? Whose is it? Repositioning the fetus in the context of research', *Cambridge Law Journal* 70: 51.

Alghrani, A. and Harris, J. (2006) 'Reproductive liberty: should the foundation of families be regulated?', *Child and Family Law Quarterly* 18: 191.

Boonin, D. (2014) *The Non-Identity Problem and the Ethics of Future People* (Oxford University Press).

Brownsword, R. (2008) *Rights, Regulation and the Technological Revolution* (Oxford University Press).

Deech, R. and Smajdor, A. (2007) *From IVF to Immortality* (Oxford University Press).

Donchin, A. (2011) 'In whose interest? Policy and politics in assisted reproduction', *Bioethics* 25: 92.

Gerber, P. and O'Byrne, K. (2015) *Surrogacy, Law and Human Rights* (Routledge).

Goold, I. (2017) 'Postponing Motherhood: Ethico-Legal Perspectives on Access to Artificial Reproductive Technologies' in L. Francis (ed), *Oxford Handbook of Reproductive Ethics* (Oxford University Press).

Harris, J. and Holm, S. (2004) *The Future of Reproduction* (Oxford University Press).

Horsey, K (2011) 'Challenging presumptions: legal parenthood and surrogacy arrangements', *Child and Family Law Quarterly* 22: 449.

Horsey, K. and Biggs, H. (eds) (2007) *Human Fertilisation and Embryology: Reproducing Regulation* (Routledge).

Horsey, K. (2015) *Revisiting the Regulation of Human Fertilisation and Embryology* (Routledge).

Jackson, E. (2008) 'Degendering reproduction', *Medical Law Review* 16: 346.

Krajewska, A. (2015) 'Access of single women to fertility treatment: a case of incidental discrimination?', *Medical Law Review* 23: 620.

Laing, J and Oderberg, D. (2005) 'Artificial reproduction, the welfare principle, and the common good', *Medical Law Review* 13: 328.

Lublin, N. (1998) *Pandora's Box: Feminism Confronts Reproductive Technology* (Rowman and Littlefield).

McTernan, E. (2015) 'Should Fertility Treatment be State Funded?', *Journal of Applied Philosophy* 32: 227.

Murphy, T. (2009) 'The texture of reproductive choice', in T. Murphy (ed), *New Technologies and Human Rights* (Oxford University Press).

Nelson, E. (2013) *Law, Policy and Reproductive Autonomy* (Hart).

Priaulx, N. (2008) 'Rethinking progenitive conflict: why reproductive autonomy matters', *Medical Law Review* 16: 169.

On cloning, see:

Harris, J. (2004b) *On Cloning* (Routledge).

Klotzo, J. (2004) *A Clone of Your Own* (Oxford University Press).

Macintosh, K. (2005) *Illegal Human Beings* (Cambridge University Press).

President's Council on Bioethics (2002) *Human Cloning and Human Dignity* (PCBE).

Soniewicka, M. (2015) 'Failures of imagination: disability and the ethics of selective reproduction', *Bioethics* 29: 557.

On genetic enhancement/selection issues, see:

Agar, N. (2004) *Liberal Eugenics* (Cambridge University Press).

Agar, N. (2012) *Humanity's End* (MIT Press).

Bennett, R. (2014) 'When intuition is not enough: Why the principle of procreative beneficence must work much harder to justify its eugenic vision', *Bioethics* 28: 447.

Buchanan, A. (2011) *Better than Human: The Promise and Perils of Enhancing Ourselves* (Oxford University Press).

Douglas, T. and Devolder, K. (2013) 'Procreative altruism: beyond individualism in reproductive selection', *Journal of Philosophy and Medicine* 38: 400.

Gavaghan, C. (2007) *Defending the Genetic Supermarket* (Cambridge University Press).

Haker, H. and Beyeveld, D. (2000) *The Ethics of Genetics in Human Reproduction* (Ashgate).

Hammond, J. (2010) 'Genetic engineering to avoid genetic neglect: from chance to responsibility', *Bioethics* 24: 10.

Harris, J. (2016) *How to be Good: The Possibility of Moral Enhancement* (Oxford University Press).

Herring, J. (2017c) 'Parental Responsibility, Hyper-parenting and the Role of Technology' in R. Brownsword, E. Scotford, and K. Yeung (eds), *The Oxford Handbook of Law, Regulation and Technology* (Oxford University Press).

Hofmann, B. (2017) '"You are inferior!" Revisiting the expressivist argument', *Bioethics* 31: 1.

Kahane, G. and Savulescu, J. (2015) 'Normal human variation: refocussing the enhancement debate', *Bioethics* 29: 133.

Pattinson, S. (2002b) *Influencing Traits before Birth* (Dartmouth).

Persson, I. and Savulescu, J. (2012) *Unfit for the Future: The Need for Moral Enhancement* (Oxford University Press).

Savulescu, J. (2006) 'In defence of procreative beneficence', *Journal of Medical Ethics* 33: 284.

Walsh, P. (2010) 'Asperger syndrome and the supposed obligation not to bring disabled lives into the world', *Journal of Medical Ethics* 36: 521.

Wilkinson, S. (2010) *Choosing Tomorrow's Children: The Ethics of Selective Reproduction* (Oxford University Press).

8 Organ Donation and the Ownership of Body Parts

INTRODUCTION

For several weeks in 2001, two news stories were prominent in the media. Both showed crying parents torn with love for their children. One involved parents who had discovered that parts of their children had been removed after death without consent and stored for research purposes. To them, the bodies of their children had been defiled and abused without their permission. The other story concerned parents of seriously ill children in urgent need of a transplant, without which the children would die; they were appealing for people to donate organs.[1] These two news stories capture some of the issues in this chapter. On the one hand, there is an acceptance of the importance of retaining bodily integrity, even of a deceased person, but on the other, there is the urgent need for organs to be transplanted and bodily material to be used for research, so that cures for diseases can be found.

Until recently, it was the topic of organ donation that dominated the debates over the legal regulation of bodily parts and products. Although organ donation is still a very important topic, a host of other issues have risen to prominence in recent years. Does a patient have any control over bodily material removed during an operation? If a scientist uses bodily samples to develop a wealth-creating discovery, do the people from whom the samples originate have any claim to the proceeds? Can, and should, it be possible to patent DNA sequences?

The starting point for the issues raised concerning the legal regulation of bodily material is now the Human Tissue Act 2004.

1 The Human Tissue Act 2004

The Human Tissue Act (HTAct) 2004 was passed following the scandals at Bristol Royal Infirmary and the Royal Liverpool Children's Hospital (Alder Hey) in 1999–2000, the details of which were revealed in the Kennedy and Redfern Inquiries. What was discovered was that the retention of body parts and organs from dead children was common and widespread. This was often done without the consent or knowledge of the parents. On some occasions, parents were misled as to what they were consenting to, or, where they agreed to a post-mortem subject to certain conditions, these conditions were sometimes ignored. Some parents had agreed to the retention of 'tissue', understanding that to refer to tiny pieces of a child's body, not appreciating that, in medical circles, the term was taken to include whole organs.

---

[1] Herring (2002: 43).

The public outrage at what had happened was enormous. Margaret Brazier and Emma Cave describe it in this way:

> In some cases infants were literally stripped of all their organs and what was returned to their families was an 'empty shell'. In a horrifying number of cases organs and tissue retained were simply stored. They were put to no good use. In some of the most tragic instances the whole of a foetus or still born infant was kept and stored in pots.[2]

The doctors concerned believed that there was nothing improper in what they were doing. The removal of organs and bodily material can be justified on a number of medical grounds: it may be necessary to establish the cause of death, to diagnose the diseases from which the patient was suffering, to discover whether there were environmental causes of death, or to ensure that any lessons in relation to treatment of the relevant condition are learned.[3] It is useful for doctors to have a collection of organs and body parts to which to refer in the course of research, education, or preparing for other operations. It would, of course, be helpful for a surgeon about to operate on a heart with a particular abnormality to have a look at a heart with a similar abnormality in a collection of stored samples. Further, banks of samples of bodily material can assist in research that seeks to discover what, if any, genetic form may predispose someone toward a particular disease.[4] As the Chief Medical Officer has pointed out:

> There have been many occasions in the past where the study of tissue after death had led to discoveries in medical science which have resulted in the saving of lives and the relief of suffering. This has particularly been so in the field of cancer research.[5]

In addition to the belief that the retention of organs was important for the progression of science, it was thought that to ask parents' permission in this regard would only have added to the parents' distress. The views of the hospitals involved were described in the Kennedy Report as 'institutional paternalism'.[6] It seems that there was an element of 'what they don't know won't hurt them' in the surgeons' attitudes. But also there was a genuine belief that whether they buried the whole of their child's body or most of it would not really bother parents. Why waste a good example of a deformed heart by burying or cremating when it could be used to save lives and progress science?

Outrage greeted the disclosures of what had been done in the two hospitals, which was regarded by many, and particularly by the parents involved, as utterly unacceptable.[7] Interestingly, many of the parents involved stated that they would have consented had they been asked. Their objection was that the doctors had treated the bodies of the children with contempt by plundering them for organs without seeking anyone's consent.[8] As one father, Paul Bradley, put it: '[W]e feel it was criminal, what was done. It is how we felt, that it was very contemptuous what was done, to the dignity of our child that her body has been, as we see it, invaded and body parts stolen.'[9]

Mavis Maclean has emphasized that, for a parent who has seen their child die in hospital, the feelings of hopelessness and guilt can be enormous.[10] That final duty of the parent, to ensure a proper burial of their child, becomes the most painful and important of tasks. To be prevented from doing that properly, because the body of the child has

---

[2] Brazier and Cave (2007: 470).   [3] Chief Medical Officer (2001: 5).
[4] Chief Medical Officer (2001: 5).   [5] Chief Medical Officer (2001: 6).   [6] Morrison (2005).
[7] Retained Organs Commission (2004: para. 2).   [8] Brazier and Cave (2007: 471).
[9] Maclean (2001: 80).   [10] Maclean (2001: 80).

been decimated, can create feelings of failure, anger, and violation. To discover that parts of their children's bodies were put in yellow sacks and put on a tip revealed an attitude that the bodies of loved ones were considered rubbish.[11]

Worse was to follow. A census carried out by the Chief Medical Officer for England (in 2000)[12] and the Isaacs Report (in 2003)[13] found that the kinds of practices at Alder Hey and Bristol were widespread across the country. It was discovered that some 54,000 organs and body parts of children or foetuses had been retained, mostly without proper consent having being obtained.[14]

As well as disclosing the practice of organ retention, the reports also found the law to be unclear and inconsistent. It became apparent that new legislation was required and the HTAct 2004 followed.

At the heart of the Act is the notion of consent: bodily material can be retained or used only with the consent of the individual, or, in the case of children, their parents. The point is this: it may be that many people will share the attitude that the doctors had in these cases. Does it matter very much if a little bit of a body is retained for the benefit of science? But some people do object. There are, for example, those with religious beliefs that demand that a body be buried whole. To them, it can matter enormously whether the body is buried complete. To respect the different views about bodies that people hold, we should require consent.

1.1 The coverage of the Act

The government has explained the purpose of the HTAct 2004 in the following way:

> The purpose of the Act is to provide a consistent legislative framework for issues relating to whole body donation and the taking, storage and use of human organs and tissue. It will make consent the fundamental principle underpinning the lawful storage and use of human bodies, body parts, organs and tissue and the removal of material from the bodies of deceased persons. It will set up an over-arching authority which is intended to rationalise existing regulation of activities like transplantation and anatomical examination, and will introduce regulation of other activities like *post mortem* examinations, and the storage of human material for education, training and research. It is intended to achieve a balance between the rights and expectations of individuals and families, and broader considerations, such as the importance of research, education, training, pathology and public health surveillance to the population as a whole.[15]

The Act is restricted in its general coverage in four important ways.

- Part I of the Act does not apply to the removal of human material from humans, but rather the storage and use of the material.[16] The Act is not designed to deal with complaints that a doctor improperly performed an operation or did so without proper consent (which are covered by the tort of negligence), but rather the way in which material is stored or used, after removal.

- The Act deals only with certain kinds of human material. It does not deal with other animals, nor with some kinds of human material (for example sperm, eggs, embryos). It does not cover photographs or other images of human material.[17]

---

[11] Chief Medical Officer (2001: 18).   [12] Chief Medical Officer (2001).
[13] HM Inspector of Anatomy (2003).   [14] DoH (2001h).   [15] DoH (2004f: para. 5).
[16] HTAct 2004, s. 9.   [17] Human Tissue Authority (2014).

- The Act deals only with the storage and use of human material for particular purposes.

- Part 1 of the Act is not intended to affect the way in which a coroner carries out his or her duties.[18]

1.2 Section 1: lawfully storing or using bodily material

The HTAct 2004 opens with a definition of what can lawfully be done with relevant materials (that is, certain bodily materials).

The Act makes it lawful to do any of the following:

- to store or use a whole body;
- to remove, store, or use human material from a deceased person; and
- to store and use human material from living people.

These activities are lawful provided that:

- there is the necessary consent; and
- the act was done for a 'Schedule 1 purpose'.

We need to clarify some of the terms used in this summary.

1.2.1 'Human material'

The Act governs 'relevant material'. Under the HTAct 2004, section 53, relevant material is tissue, cells, and organs of human beings, excluding gametes, embryos outside the body, and hair and nails from a living person. Cell lines are also excluded by virtue of section 54(7), as is any other human material created outside the human body. Doubt has also been expressed whether the term covers the different organisms and bacteria that live in the human body but may not technically be human.[19] However, the definition of 'human materials' is broad and a single cell can be classified as bodily material.

1.2.2 'Appropriate consent'

Consent must be given to the storage or use for the particular purpose in question.[20] So, for example, the fact that there is appropriate consent for the storage of an organ for the purposes of transplantation does not authorize the storage of the organ for research. However, if a patient is willing for his or her material to be used in 'research', it is not necessary to obtain his or her consent for every individual research project. Consent can be specific (e.g., only for a particular research project) or for a generic project (e.g., for an as yet undefined project).[21] A person can place conditions upon their consent.[22] Consent can be withdrawn at any time.[23] Consent can be given orally, except in cases involving anatomical examination and public display, where it needs to be signed and witnessed.[24]

---

[18] HTAct 2004, s. 11.   [19] Herring and Chau (2013a).
[20] See McHale (2006a) for a useful discussion of the notion of appropriate consent.
[21] Human Tissue Authority (2017a: para. 29).   [22] Human Tissue Authority (2017: para. 48).
[23] Human Tissue Authority (2017: para. 51).
[24] Human Tissue Authority (2017: para. 57); Human Tissue Authority (2017b).

What does 'consent' mean in this context? Positive consent is required; a failure to object is insufficient.[25] Whether a person has capacity to consent is governed by the general law on consent, as discussed in Chapter 4. The Human Tissue Authority (HTA) Code of Practice on Consent states:

> For consent to be valid it must be given voluntarily, by an appropriately informed person who has the capacity to agree to the activity in question. The person should understand what the activity involves, any reasonable or variant treatment and, where appropriate, what the material risks are. The test of materiality is 'whether, in the circumstances of the particular case, a reasonable person in the patient's position would be likely to attach significance to the risk, or the doctor is or should reasonably be aware that the particular patient would be likely to attach a significance to it'.[26]

But who can give consent?

(i) *Adults* Under the HTAct 2004, section 3, in the case of competent adults, appropriate consent can be provided only by the individual himself or herself. The normal law on consent, as set out in Chapter 4, applies.

(ii) *Deceased adults* In the case of a deceased adult, the consent or non-consent of the deceased can come from three sources.

- *The deceased* If the deceased has made his or her views clear, then those determine the question. Where the use of human tissue involves storage for the purposes of public display or anatomical examination, there must be consent in writing.[27] However, for all other activities under the Act, there is no need for the decision to be in writing. The decision must have been in force immediately before the person died. So, for example, if the deceased had indicated that he or she was happy for his or her body to be used for medical research, but shortly before his or her death indicated that this was no longer his or her wish, then there will be no effective consent.

- *An appointed representative* If the person has died without expressing a decision about how his or her bodily material is to be used and he or she has appointed a 'representative', the representative can make decisions on the deceased's behalf. The appointment must comply with the requirements in section 4. The representative can be appointed orally or in writing (for example under a will).

- *The person in the closest 'qualifying relationship'* If the person has died without expressing a decision and has not appointed a personal representative, then the person who is in the closest 'qualifying relationship' can make the decision. Section 27(4) ranks the qualifying relations in this order: (a) spouse or partner; (b) parent or child; (c) brother or sister; (d) grandparent or grandchild; (e) child of a person falling within paragraph (c); (f) stepfather or stepmother; (g) half-brother or half-sister; (h) friend of long standing. If there are two people of the same rank, then only the consent of one is required.[28]

---

[25] Human Tissue Authority (2017a: para. 30).   [26] Human Tissue Authority (2017a: para. 40).

[27] HTAct 2004, s. 2(5). See Human Tissue Authority (2017b) for guidance on public display.

[28] In HM Government (2007a), it was acknowledged that the absence of aunts and uncles from this list was causing problems in practice.

(iii) ***Children*** The law on consent in relation to children is set out in the HTAct 2004, section 2.[29] If the child is competent, then he or she may consent.[30] Indeed, a competent child can make an advance decision concerning his or her consent and such a decision must be respected.[31] If the child is not competent, then a person with parental responsibility will be able to consent for the child.[32] Thus a person with parental responsibility could consent that his or her child's organs be used for transplant, but only where the competent child had not expressed his or her views.[33] If the child has died without anyone having parental responsibility, then someone in a 'qualifying relationship' can consent to the removal of the material, and its storage and use.[34]

(iv) ***Adults lacking capacity*** Where an adult lacks capacity, consent can be deemed in certain circumstances under the Human Tissue Act 2004 (Persons who Lack Capacity to Consent and Transplants) Regulations 2006.[35] These permit the storage and use of relevant material for a 'Schedule 1 purpose' if that is in the best interests of the person who lacks capacity.

1.2.3 A Schedule 1 purpose

A person's act is made lawful by the HTAct 2004, section 1, if he or she is acting for a Schedule 1 purpose. The Schedule divides these purposes into two parts. We shall see why shortly.

PART 1

Purposes requiring consent: general

1 Anatomical examination.

2 Determining the cause of death.

3 Establishing after a person's death the efficacy of any drug or other treatment administered to him.

4 Obtaining scientific or medical information about a living or deceased person which may be relevant to any other person (including a future person).

5 Public display.

6 Research in connection with disorders, or the functioning, of the human body.

7 Transplantation.

PART 2

Purposes requiring consent: deceased persons

8 Clinical audit.

9 Education or training relating to human health.

10 Performance assessment.

11 Public health monitoring.

12 Quality assurance.

---

[29] Children are people under the age of 18.   [30] Human Tissue Authority (2017a: para. 87).
[31] Where the consent concerns anatomical examination or public display, the child's consent must be in writing and witnessed.
[32] Chapter 4 explains who has parental responsibility for a child.
[33] Human Tissue Authority (2017a: para. 90).
[34] HTAct 2004, s. 2(7). For discussion, see Lyons (2011b).   [35] SI 2006/1659.

Under section 1(1), the following can be done with appropriate consent for any of the twelve purposes:

(a) the storage of the body of a deceased person for use ... other than anatomical examination;

[...]

(c) the removal from the body of a deceased person for use ... of any 'relevant material' of which the body consists or which it contains.

The following can be done with appropriate consent for a purpose in Part 1 of Schedule 1:

(d) the storage for use ... of any relevant material which has come from a human body.

The following can be done for a purpose in Part 2 of Schedule 2, even without consent:

(e) the storage for use ... of any relevant material which has come from the body of a deceased person;

[...]

It should be noted that there are special provisions dealing with the storage of bodies for anatomical examinations.[36]

Where a person is using bodily material for a purpose other than one approved in Schedule 1, then, according to its Explanatory Notes, the 2004 Act does not apply. So an artist removing part of a corpse to use in a sculpture will not have done an act covered by the 2004 Act. The Act will not render such an act legal or illegal. However, the artist could still be guilty of, for example, the offence of theft.

1.3 Storage and use of human material without consent

A key principle in the Act is that someone's relevant material can be used only with their consent. But there are eight situations in which it is lawful to store and use human material even though there is no consent. These are as follows.

(i) *A Schedule 1, Part II, purpose (such as education, training, and audit)* As already mentioned, there is no need for 'appropriate consent' where human material from a live person is stored for a purpose in Part II of Schedule 1 of the Act—that is, if it is stored or used in connection with clinical audit, education, and training in relation to human health, performance assessment, public health monitoring, or quality control. Research is not included in this list, although the line between research and education and training may be blurred. The reason for these exceptions is that the use of material for these purposes is seen as intrinsic to the proper conduct of the patient's treatment or the health of the nation.[37] Note that the exception does not apply to human material taken from a deceased person.

(ii) *The HTA deems that there is consent* The HTA has the power to deem that there is consent where it is not possible to trace the individual from whom the material originated.[38] The Authority is likely to use this power only where tissue relating to a

---

[36] HTAct 2004, s. 1(2) and (3).
[37] DoH (2004f: para. 13). McHale (2006a) discusses whether a person whose material is used for research without his or her consent can claim interference with his or her human rights.
[38] HTAct 2004, s. 7.

relative of a patient could be used for genetic testing purposes to assist in the diagnosis or treatment of a patient. It has the power to deem consent where it is satisfied that material has come from the body of a living person, that it is in the interests of another person to obtain scientific or medical information about the individual, and that there is no reason to believe that the individual has died or has made a decision not to consent to the use of material. There is also power for the Authority to deem consent where reasonable attempts have been made to get a person to decide what he or she wants to happen to his or her human material and yet the person has not made a decision.

(iii) *A High Court order* A High Court can order that appropriate consent is to be deemed for 'research purposes in connection with disorders, or the functioning of the human body'.[39] These orders can cover the storage of 'relevant material' from the body of a living or a deceased person, and the removal and use of 'relevant material' from a body. The order will be made if it is in the public interest. However, the government has stated that this power is to be used only in the most exceptional of cases.[40]

(iv) *Storage for research purposes* If 'relevant material' from living bodies is stored for the purpose of research in connection with disorders or the functioning of the human body, then consent is not required, provided that:

(a) the research has been ethically approved in line with regulations issued by the Secretary of State; and

(b) the material has been anonymized so that it is not possible to identify the person from whom the material originates.[41]

This is an extremely important provision. Notably, it permits the use of material for research even where the patient positively objects. Hopefully, where a patient has voiced an objection, the researchers will choose not to use his or her material. Note that this does not justify the removal of material without the consent of the patient. It therefore covers material that has been removed with consent, for example material removed during an operation.

(v) *Surplus material* If material has been removed in the course of treatment, diagnostic tests, or research, then that material can be dealt with as waste and there is no need to obtain consent before disposing of it.[42] So a tumour removed in the course of an operation can be disposed of without the explicit consent of the patient. It will be taken that consent to the operation will include consent to the disposal of the tumour.

(vi) *Imported material* Consent is not required where the body or material has been imported from overseas.[43] If therefore a hospital receives a consignment of organs for research purposes from, say, Denmark, it is not for the English hospital to ensure that it has consent from those from whom the organs originated. It is presumed that the law regulating the country of origin will provide adequate protection for their citizen's rights.

(vii) *Existing holdings* If a hospital or surgeon has bodies or material that were held for a Schedule 1 purpose immediately before the Act came into force, consent is not

---

[39] HTAct 2004, s. 7(4).   [40] Price (2005a: 801).   [41] HTAct 2004, s. 1(7)–(9).
[42] HTAct 2004, s. 44. HTA (2017a: para. 25) says it is good practice to get consent for disposal.
[43] Special provisions mean that a body or material that is exported and then imported cannot rely on this exception; otherwise, this could provide too ready a way around the terms of the Act.

required.[44] The HTA has issued a Code to deal with the storage, use, and disposal of existing holdings.[45]

(viii) *Coroners' activities* The functions of the coroner are not covered by the Act. A coroner may therefore authorize the retention of organs without complying with the provisions of the 2004 Act.

As can be seen from this list, there are a large number of exceptions to the principle that a person's bodily material cannot be used without his or her consent.

The following case illustrates that not every eventuality can be covered and demonstrates how the court dealt with the issue by relying on its inherent jurisdiction.

KEY CASE   *CM v Executor of the Estate of EJ* [2013] EWHC 1680 (Fam)

A doctor, CM, was driving home when she came across the body of EJ, who was bleeding profusely. She attempted emergency first aid, but EJ died. CM's hands become covered in EJ's blood. CM was worried that she may have become infected and started anti-retroviral medication, which made her ill. She wanted to obtain a sample of EJ's blood for tests. A family member was willing to give consent and the coroner was happy to approve, but it was unclear what legal authorization could be given to allow the use of the samples. The court held that this would have to be under the inherent jurisdiction, which was available because a closest relative had given consent and the coroner was agreed. Here, the court would use the inherent jurisdiction because CM had acted out of humanity and would otherwise suffer the uncertainty of not knowing whether she was diseased. There was also a public interest in enabling CM to return to work. The tests were ordered. The report notes that the tests were completed and returned negative.

1.4 **The Human Tissue Authority**

The HTAct 2004, Part 2, set up the HTA, the remit of which covers the removal, use, storage, and disposal of human material.[46] The Authority has set up a scheme under which a licence is required for a range of activities connected with human tissue. It is an offence to conduct the activities without a licence.[47] Where a body breaches the terms of a licence, the licence may be revoked. The Authority has also produced codes of practice in connection with dealings with human tissue.[48] The HTA has no power over actions performed for criminal justice purposes, such as coroners' post mortems.[49]

The HTA's remit includes:

- the storage and use of human bodies and tissue, and the removal of tissue from human bodies, for scheduled purposes;

- the import and export of bodies and human tissue for scheduled purposes; and

- the disposal of human tissue, including imported tissue, following its use in medical treatment or for scheduled purposes.

---

[44] HTAct 2004, s. 9(4).   [45] Human Tissue Authority (2017c).
[46] Human Tissue Authority (2017g) describes the recent work of the Authority.
[47] Human Tissue Authority (2017g) reports that more than 573 main sites and 288 satellite sites have been licensed.
[48] Human Tissue Authority (2017e).   [49] HT Act 2004, s. 39; Human Tissue Authority (2017d).

In respect of the matters within its remit, the HTA has the following responsibilities.

- It must provide information for the general public and the Secretary of State.
- It must issue codes of practice.[50] These cover, amongst other things, consent, communicating with relatives post-mortem, import and export, and the disposal of tissue.
- It is in charge of the licensing system. A number of activities in relation to human tissue can be performed only with a licence and anyone seeking a licence has to apply to the HTA. The activities requiring a licence include the following:

  - storage and use of human bodies for anatomical examination and related research;
  - the carrying out of post-mortem examinations, including removal and retention of human tissue;
  - removal of human tissue from the body of a deceased person for other scheduled purposes, except transplantation;
  - storage and use of human bodies or parts for public display; and
  - storage of human tissue for other scheduled purposes, for example human tissue banking for transplant purposes or research.

- The HTA also has the job of carrying out inspections to ensure that the terms of the HTAct and the conditions of any licences are being complied with. The HTA is required to ensure that licensing and inspection are 'proportionate', and not unduly 'burdensome'. The HTA is given flexibility to decide how to carry out its duties of inspection and licensing.

The Authority has set out four guiding principles which it applies to its work:

'(i) Consent

Consent and the wishes of the donor, or where appropriate their nominated representatives or relatives, have primacy when removing, storing and using human tissue. This means:

a) human tissue, or bodies of the deceased, should be used in accordance with the expressed wishes of donors or their relatives;

b) donors and their relatives should be given the information they need to be able to make a decision that is right for them;

c) those seeking consent should do so with sensitivity and an appreciation of the particular circumstances in each case.

(ii) Dignity

Dignity should be paramount in the treatment of human tissue and bodies. This means:

a) the dignity of the donor should be respected at all times;

b) there should be mechanisms in place to protect bodies and human organs and tissue from harm;

c) the privacy of the individual should be maintained;

---

[50] Human Tissue Authority (2017a–e).

d) the disposal of human tissue should be managed sensitively and the method of disposal should be appropriate to the nature of the material;

e) disposal of human tissue from the deceased should, where possible, be in line with their wishes, if known, or the wishes of the deceased person's relatives;

f) where human tissue is imported, importers should endeavour to ensure that it is sourced from a country that has an appropriate ethical and legal framework.

(iii) Quality

Quality should underpin the management of human tissue and bodies. This means:

a) practitioners should be competent, have undertaken appropriate training and work with care in accordance with good practice and other relevant professional guidance;

b) practitioners' work should be subject to a system of governance that ensures the appropriate and safe storage and use of human tissue and which safeguards the dignity of the living or deceased;

c) premises, facilities and equipment should be clean, secure and subject to regular maintenance;

d) proper and accurate records and information should be maintained to ensure full traceability of human tissue and bodies of the deceased and donor tissue;

e) patient data should be held securely and confidentially.

(iv) Honesty and openness

Honesty and openness should be the foundation of communications in matters pertaining to the use of human tissue and bodies. This means:

a) communication with a donor, or person from whom consent is being sought, should be open, honest, clear and objective;

b) serious incidents involving human bodies and tissue should be subject to rigorous investigation to ensure that lessons are learned and the risk of reoccurrence is minimised;

c) establishments should adopt a policy of candour and transparency when dealing with serious incidents, as well as meeting their other, statutory and professional, duties of candour where appropriate;

d) discussions about medical investigation or treatment are kept entirely separate from discussions relating to consent for scheduled purposes;

e) establishments should be open and transparent in relation to arrangements for charging and reimbursement.'

1.5 Criminal offences

There are several criminal offences created by the HTAct 2004.

1.5.1 *Failure to obtain 'appropriate consent'*

Section 5 states that:

> (1) A person commits an offence if, without appropriate consent, he does an activity to which subsection (1), (2) or (3) of section 1 applies, unless he reasonably believes—
>
> (a) that he does the activity with appropriate consent, or
>
> (b) that what he does is not an activity to which the subsection applies.

Section 1 has already been described and covers storage or use of a whole body or bodily material, or removal, storage, or use of human material from a deceased person. This means that it would now be a criminal offence for a doctor to retain a child's organs without consent—the kind of behaviour at Alder Hey that caused such uproar. The maximum sentence for this offence is three years, regarded as very high by some, but thought by the government to be appropriate in the most flagrant of breaches.[51]

The defence of 'reasonable belief' is important. It would mean that if, for example, a doctor were to be convinced by a written document that a patient had consented to the use of his or her body, but in fact that document was forged, the doctor could not be prosecuted. Of course, what will amount to a 'reasonable belief' will depend on the circumstances.

1.5.2 *A false representation of consent*

It is an offence for anyone to represent falsely that there is 'appropriate consent' or that an activity does not require consent for the purposes of the Act, if the person knows the representation to be false, or does not believe it to be true.[52]

1.5.3 *Failure to obtain a death certificate*

It is a criminal offence for someone to store or use a body for anatomical examination without a death certificate.[53] There is a defence for someone who believes that there is a death certificate, or that he or she is doing something not covered by the Act.

1.5.4 *Using or storing donated material for an improper purpose*

A person who uses or stores donated material commits an offence unless it was done for one of the following purposes:

(a) a purpose detailed in Schedule 1,

(b) the purpose of medical diagnosis or treatment,

(c) the purpose of decent disposal, or

(d) a purpose specified in regulations made by the Secretary of State.[54]

There is a defence if a person reasonably believes that he or she was not dealing with donated material.[55]

---

[51] Price (2005a: 809). [52] HTAct 2004, s. 5(2). [53] HTAct 2004, s. 5(4).
[54] HTAct 2004, s. 8(4). [55] HTAct 2004, s. 8(2).

1.5.5 *Analysis of DNA without consent*

An offence is committed if a person has any bodily material intending that the DNA is to be analysed without 'qualifying consent' unless the results are for an 'excepted purpose'.[56] There are four 'excepted purposes', as follows.

- The general excepted purposes are listed as:

  (a) the medical diagnosis or treatment of the person whose body manufactured the DNA;

  (b) purposes of functions of a coroner;

  (c) purposes of functions of a procurator fiscal in connection with the investigation of deaths;

  (d) the prevention or detection of a crime;

  (e) the conduct of a prosecution;

  (f) purposes of national security;

  (g) implementing an order or direction of a court or tribunal, including one outside the United Kingdom.[57]

- Another exception is under order of the High Court for the purposes of medical research.

- There are complex provisions allowing analysis for certain purposes in respect of existing holdings.

- Where the bodily material is taken from a living person, the DNA can be used without consent for, inter alia:

  (i) research,

  (ii) clinical audit,

  (iii) education,

  (iv) performance assessment,

  (v) under direction from the Human Tissue Authority,

  (vi) for the benefit of another person.[58]

The fact that 'qualifying consent' is sufficient where one of the exceptions does not apply is significant because it means that consent to the use of bodily material for a scheduled purpose under the HTAct will be taken as consent to DNA analysis.

1.5.6 *Trafficking human tissue for transplantation*

There are offences connected with the selling or trafficking of human tissue for transplantation.[59] We will be considering these in greater detail later in the chapter.[60]

---

[56] HTAct 2004, s. 45.   [57] HTAct 2004, Sch. 4, Part 2, para. 5(1).

[58] The Human Tissue Act 2004 (Persons who Lack Capacity to Consent and Transplants) Regulations 2006, SI 2006/1659, provide exceptions where the individual lacks capacity.

[59] HTAct 2004, s. 32; Human Tissue Authority (2009h).

[60] See under the heading '8 Selling organs'.

1.5.7 *Unlicensed activities*

Carrying out licensable activities without holding a licence from the HTA is an offence.[61] There are also lesser related offences, such as failing to produce records, or obstructing the Authority in carrying out its powers or responsibilities.[62]

1.6 **Miscellaneous provisions**

- Section 43 of the 2004 Act makes it clear that it is lawful for hospital authorities to take steps to preserve the organs of deceased persons whilst appropriate consent to transplantation is sought.[63]
- Section 44 provides for the disposal of human material that is no longer to be retained.
- Section 47 creates a power for certain national museums to transfer human remains out of their collections if they think it appropriate to do so.

2 **Comments on the Human Tissue Act 2004**

The HTAct 2004 is attempting to strike a delicate balance. On the one hand, it recognizes the importance of ensuring that there is effective consent to the removal and use of human tissue. On the other hand, there is a recognition that the use of human tissue is enormously important for research into medical illnesses and for training.[64] The need to restore public trust in genetic research and the collection of human biological samples[65] must not be bought at the cost of severely hampering research into fatal diseases.

While in its draft form, the Act went through a number of amendments in its passage through Parliament. Many of these amendments were inserted in response to concerns by scientists and medical professionals that the burdens placed on them were too great.[66] Nevertheless, there have been criticisms made about the legislation and ambiguities that include the following.

2.1 **What is a criminal offence?**

There is an ambiguity that unfortunately strikes at the heart of the HTAct 2004. As we have seen, section 5(1) states: 'A person commits an offence if, without appropriate consent, he does an activity to which subsection (1), (2) or (3) of section 1 applies.' Section 1(1) opens:

(1) The following activities shall be lawful if done with appropriate consent—

    (a) the storage of the body of a deceased person for use for a purpose specified in Schedule 1, other than anatomical examination,

[...]

The ambiguity arises in a scenario in which a person is storing the body of a deceased person for a purpose not listed in Schedule 1 (for example to turn a body into a private

---

[61] HTAct 2004, s. 16.   [62] HTAct 2004, s. 16.   [63] For objections that this section inadequately protects autonomy and is a back door to presumed consent donation, see Bell (2006).
[64] Genetic Interest Group (2004).   [65] Human Genetics Commission (2006).
[66] For research on how the legislation might affect the day-to-day work of professionals, see McLean, Campbell, Gutridge, et al. (2006) and Wilton (2007).

art exhibit). Whether or not this is an offence turns on the meaning of 'an activity to which subsection (1) applies'. In section 1(1)(a), for example, is the activity simply the storage of a body of a deceased person, in which case the defendant would be guilty, or is the activity 'storage of a deceased person for a Schedule 1 purpose', in which case the defendant would not be guilty of the offence under section 5?

The Department of Health's guide to the Act describes the offences in terms of 'removing, storing or using human tissue for scheduled purposes, without appropriate consent'.[67] This would appear to suggest that if the actions are done for a purpose not included within Schedule 1, then there is no offence committed under the Act, although there may be some other criminal offence (such as theft), but, as we shall see, the circumstances in which some other offence may be committed are unclear. It may be questionable, however, whether there is much sense in making doctors who remove tissues from cadavers for research without consent guilty of an offence, but those who remove bits of bodies for prurient interest possibly not guilty of any offence.

Further, the use of the word 'lawful' in section 1 is unclear. Presumably, the section means that the act will not be unlawful as contrary to the other provisions of the Act, and does not mean that an act under section 1 cannot be unlawful under other legislation or other parts of the law (for example the law of negligence or the Data Protection Act 1998).[68]

2.2 Exceptions to the consent principle

It might be thought from the furore that followed the various scandals preceding the Act, and some of the rhetoric from the government in connection with the Act, that we would have a clear principle that body organs and materials can be retained only with consent. Although this appears as a cardinal principle, the number of exceptions to it means that its paramountcy is greatly weakened. We cannot say to patients 'No human material can be taken from your body without your consent'; we can say only 'No human material can be taken from your body without your consent, unless it is permitted under the HTAct'. Notably, a person's material can be used without his or her consent for training, audit, or teaching. The justification of the exception (that it is 'considered intrinsic to the proper conduct of a patient's treatment or ... necessary for the public health of the nation') will not convince everyone.[69] And why is research not regarded as 'necessary for the public health of the nation'?[70] Is there a clear distinction between education and research? The distinction is made more complex by the fact that, under section 1(7)–(9), use of material for research without consent is permitted if the factors mentioned there—most significantly, anonymization of any sample and approval by a research ethics committee (REC)[71]—are met.

There is perhaps also a question mark over the distinction here between the bodies of the dead and those of the living. Why is it lawful to use material from living bodies for teaching purposes (without explicit consent), but unlawful to do the same thing with material from a cadaver? Of course, with the scandals in mind, the government had at

[67] DoH (2005m).   [68] Zimmern, Hall, and Liddell (2004).   [69] DoH (2004f: para. 13).
[70] Parry, Zimmern, Hall, et al. (2004).
[71] Zimmern, Hall, and Liddell (2004) question whether RECs have sufficient resources to deal with the increased workload that will result from this.

the forefront of their thinking the position of parents and the bodies of their children—but is there a logical distinction between the living and the dead?

2.3 **Rights or utility**

One way of examining what happened at Alder Hey and Bristol is that doctors were relying on utilitarian reasoning—that it would be for the greatest good to remove the tissue and not tell parents what had happened—rather than on a rights-based approach—recognizing the rights of individuals to have control over their bodily material.[72] The HTAct 2004 can be seen as a form of compromise between a rights-based approach and a utilitarian approach. Although, at first, the statute appears to grant clear rights that material cannot be stored or used without an individual's consent, the number of exceptions to this, many of them justified in the name of the public good, indicate the impact of utilitarian reasoning. It may be claimed that this balancing between the rights of individuals and the public good of research (for example) is necessary.[73] Of course, another argument is that any rights analysis requires the rights of the community to be balanced against the interests of the general community.[74]

2.4 **What principles underpin the Act?**

Some commentators have argued that although the HTAct is not explicit about this, it rests on an assumption that people do own their body parts.[75] Pattinson argues:

> We have seen that the 2004 Act grants a negative right to donors and their representatives, which amounts to negative exclusive control over the donor's organs, *and* that that control turns on nothing more than the donor's identity as the source of the organ in question. In other words, a tenet of the 2004 Act is that the relationship between the source and the organ is such that the source is to have exclusive negative control even when the particular use is one that the source has no subjective interest in.[76]

This argument is that the rights given in the legislation make sense and can be justified only if we start from an understanding that we have property rights over our removed body parts. This does not necessarily follow. The legislative rights could be designed to protect autonomy or dignity interests. Perhaps the best that can be said is that the Act is consistent with the view that people have property rights over their body parts.

Notably, section 32(9)(c) of the Act excludes from the prohibition of commercial dealings any material 'which is the subject of property because of an application of human skill'. Dr Chau and I have suggested that this implied that Parliament did not recognize that generally there were property rights in the body.[77] Pattinson disagrees.[78] He believes that the human material belongs to the source by virtue of the fact that people own their body parts. On that view, section 32 could not apply to all bodily property because, otherwise, the exception to the prohibition on commercial dealings would be pointless. The difficulty with that interpretation is the terminology of section 32, which states that the body becomes 'the subject of property' because of

---

[72] Morrison (2005).   [73] Parker (2011).   [74] Harmon and McMahon (2014).
[75] Price (2009b); Pattinson (2011).   [76] Pattinson (2011: 122).
[77] Herring and Chau (2007).   [78] Pattinson (2011).

the skill. That implies that, before the application of skill, the body was not 'the subject of property'. That wording suggests that bodies are not property until skill is exercised upon them.

2.5 **Is the Act practical?**

There will be some who feel that the HTAct 2004 fails to appreciate the difficulties involved in discussing these issues with grief-filled family members. Any approach to relatives soon after the death of a child to discuss in detail post-mortem examinations and research on removed organs cannot be done in a way that does not appear callous and insensitive. The obtaining of consent may be an ideal for which we should strive, but at the 'coal face' it is far from straightforward. One point worth making here is that although organ transplant decisions will need to be taken very soon after death, decisions about post-mortem examinations are much less time-sensitive. This may make more realistic the possibility of sensitively obtained consent.[79]

With such concerns in mind, one suggestion that was made was that the Act should have focused on authorization, rather than consent.[80] The argument is that a parent may feel uncomfortable consenting to the invasion and retention of organs and body parts from his or her child. However, the parent will feel less perturbed by simply permitting the procedure to go ahead. The word 'authorization' is also thought by some to be more appropriate in the case of children: parents should be permitted to authorize treatment, but they cannot be said to consent because it is not their bodily material. Some might think that the subtle distinction between 'authorization' and 'consent' might trouble the academic lawyer, but it is unlikely to be appreciated by a grieving parent.

A different point is that if the requirement as to what constitutes consent becomes too bureaucratic and onerous, this will stifle important medical research.[81] At the very least, the existence of the criminal offences in this area may produce an atmosphere of excessive caution.[82] If consent is too difficult to acquire, there will be fewer bodily materials available for research, and the advance of science will be slowed.

2.6 **The role of parents**

One of the themes that emerged from the various scandals was the importance attached to parents being involved in decisions concerning the bodies of their deceased children. It has generally been assumed that they should be. But is this any more than sentiment? Should the views of parents on what should happen to their children's bodies hamper the advance of science?[83] Brazier has provided some powerful arguments for paying respect to the views of parents:

(1) [T]he child is 'theirs'. She belongs to them. Her body belongs to them. They are still parents, albeit bereaved parents; (2) they are the guardians of the family's values, be they religious or cultural imperatives, or simply personal convictions; (3) robbed of their child, parents need the means to come to terms with the loss of all the joys of

[79] Morrison (2005: 187).   [80] The arguments are discussed in Brazier (2003a).
[81] Nuffield Council (2004).   [82] Parry, Zimmern, Hall, et al. (2004).
[83] See Lyons (2011b) for further discussion.

parenthood. They need some means of regaining control; (4) the parents' own mental health and emotional wellbeing are at stake, and (5) the physical body of a beloved child remains fixed in the mind. Rationally parents know the child does not suffer or bleed. In the imagination, nightmares haunt their sleep.[84]

To others, although it is understandable that we feel enormous sympathy with grieving parents, the law has to rise above 'mere emotion'. Is it right that the particular wishes of parents trump the public interest in carrying out research into childhood illnesses, which in the long term might save the lives of other children? After all, the feelings of grieving parents are not of such legal weight as to prevent a post-mortem. Is it obvious that post-mortems are more in the public interest than research into childhood illness?[85] John Harris has written of the 'quite absurd, if understandable, preoccupation with reverence and respect for bodily tissue that has come to dominate discussions of retained tissues and organs in the wake of the Alder Hey revelations'.[86]

2.7 The definition of 'human material'

Some concern has been expressed at the broad definition of 'human material' in the HTAct 2004. Although there may be widespread acceptance that the removal of organs from cadavers without appropriate consent should be unlawful, should we say the same thing about a minute amount of tissue to be placed on a slide? Would parents of the children involved in the scandals have felt any shock at discovering that a tiny portion of cells were removed?[87] It can be argued that the Act should have drawn a distinction between a sample (a tiny piece of human material) and organs or large pieces of material. Further, it might be asked whether the definition overlooks the fact that the body is made up of material that is not human (but animal or bacterial) and not cellular.[88]

2.8 Ownership of bodily material

The HTAct 2004 does not directly address the question of whether a person owns bodily material once it has been removed. The focus is on consent, rather than property rights, as the guiding principle behind the Act. The implication of the need for consent—and especially the fact that, in some circumstances, material can be removed without consent—might be that a person does not own bodily material taken from him or her during a medical procedure, but if that is correct, it might have been desirable for the Act to say so explicitly.

Section 32(9) refers to human material that has become property by the application of human skill. Unfortunately, it fails to give guidance as to when human material can become property, and if so, who owns it. This is particularly disappointing given that the Act is intended to provide a comprehensive framework for issues relating to the use and storage of bodily material. Whether one can be said to own one's body or parts of it is a vexed legal and ethical issue, and one to which we shall be returning later in this chapter.

---

[84] Brazier (2003a: 31).
[85] See the arguments of Harris (2002).   [86] Harris (2002: 546).
[87] Skene (2002); Mason and Laurie (2001).   [88] Herring and Chau (2013a).

2.9 **Should the deceased's wishes carry any weight?**

It is generally thought that, in relation to cadavers, the wishes of the deceased, if ex-pressed, should be followed.[89] If someone has made it clear that, on death, they do not want their body used for medical research, their wishes should be respected. This principle is reflected in the HTAct. However, that view is not held universally. John Harris has argued that although a person may have an interest in what happens to his or her body after death, that interest should carry only a little weight.[90] In short, this is because, after death, a person cannot be harmed: he or she no longer exists, and al-though his or her interests persist, because the infringement to those interests cannot harm the person (because the person no longer exists), those interests are weak. Given the enormous benefits of medical research, the public interest in enabling researchers to use material from cadavers should outweigh the value of following an individual's wishes. Harris goes on to argue that we regularly dispose of parts of our bodily tissue through bowel movements, combing hair, menstruation, and so on. We should be no more concerned about bits of our bodily material being taken by doctors than we are with these losses of human material. Harris accepts that there are interests in ensuring that the bodies are disposed of in a way that poses no health risk, which respects public decency and attaches appropriate weight to the legitimate interests of the deceased. But there are no further interests than these. He summarizes his arguments provocatively in this way:

> I suggest that considerations for the welfare and interests of the dead and the philosoph-ical attention given to them are self-indulgent nonsense at best, and at worst a crime against humanity. The real issues are the extent of the harm that might be caused by not using tissue, organs, cells, DNA, and other biomaterials from the dead, and the extent of the good that using such biomaterials might achieve.[91]

In reply to Harris's arguments, Brazier has suggested that his views are driven by a 'cold rationality'.[92] She starts by making the point that it is easy to over-egg the claims for research. Many of the organs removed in the Alder Hey and Bristol scandals were simply being stored and not, in fact, being used for ground-breaking research. But at the heart of her argument is that people's views (or the views of their relatives) about how they wish their bodies to be treated after death deserve the highest respect. Their views may represent powerful religious beliefs. As she points out, Judaism, Islam, and some Christian traditions have particular requirements in relation to the disposal of bodies. To prevent the burial of bodies in line with these religious beliefs (by author-izing removal of body parts without consent) would infringe religious rights.[93] As she says, to some, an improper burial will mean awful consequences in the afterlife: 'It is easy to mock such beliefs from an atheist, agnostic or liberal viewpoint. The pain such a belief must produce is acute and life-destroying.'[94]

But it is not only religious sensibilities that concern Brazier. Many people, however 'irrationally', have strong views about how bodies are treated on death:

---

[89] For an excellent discussion on the interests of the deceased over their bodies, see McGuinness and Brazier (2008).
[90] Harris (2002: 537).   [91] Harris (2014).   [92] Brazier (2002: 551).
[93] Brazier (2002: 560).   [94] Brazier (2002: 560).

The image of the newly dead person remains fixed in the minds of most bereaved families. Mutilation of the body becomes a mutilation of that image. Reason may tell the family that a dead child could not suffer when organs were removed. Grief coupled with imagination may overpower reason. Families grieve differently just as they live their lives differently. Respect for family life requires respect for such differences.[95]

To Harris, feelings of this kind are simply irrational and, although deserving of respect, should not lead us to adopt laws that hinder important medical progress. To Brazier, Harris is seeking to impose his view of the world on everyone.

Brazier points out that we allow people to decide where their property should go on their death, through a will, even if they wish to leave their money to a cause that many people would think irrational. Should we not let people make the same decision about their bodies? She is willing to agree that it is good for people to donate their bodies altruistically to medical science, but she points out that we do not force people to be altruistic while they are alive and so we should not do so when they die. She argues that to ignore a person's wishes about his or her body does cause that person harm:

> We live in a world where our welfare depends on the mutual love and solace our families and friends provide for us. We live in the knowledge of death's inevitability. How we will be treated after our death affects our welfare in life.[96]

3 Transplanting of organs

3.1 Introduction

It is useful to start with a brief outline of some of the technical issues relating to organ donation. First, it is necessary to distinguish between the following.

(i) *Live organ donation* An organ is taken from a live person and given to another. Clearly, the kinds of organs for which this is possible are limited. A popular one is a kidney.

(ii) *Cadaver organ donation* In this procedure, an organ is taken from one person shortly after death and transplanted into another.

(iii) *Xenotransplantation* In this procedure, an organ is taken from another animal and used in a human.

REALITY CHECK

Some statistics on organ donation

The number of transplants

In 2016–17, 4,753 patients received an organ that saved their life or greatly improved it. The organs came from 1,414 deceased donors and 1,043 live donors.

Would-be donors

There has been a push to increase the number of names on the NHS Organ Donor Register. In 2016–17, there were 23,600,000 people on the NHS Organ Donation Register, some 36 per cent of the population.

---

[95] Brazier (2002: 566). See *Re JS (A Child) (Disposal of body)* [2016] EWHC 2859 (Fam) where a dying teenager very much wanted to have her body 'frozen' after her death. Her views had to be respected held the judge.
[96] Brazier (2002: 566). See also Brazier (2015).

Those needing organs

Official figures suggest that, by March 2017, there were 6,388 patients on the 'waiting list' for organ transplants. Unfortunately, in 2016–17, 457 died and 875 people were removed from the list, usually because they had become too ill to receive a transplant.

The success rate of organ transplants

For transplants in adult recipients, the five-year kidney transplant survival rates are 87 per cent. The five-year heart transplant survival rate is 71 per cent.[97]

(iv) *Genetically created organs* Scientists are presently working on this technology. The hope is that, at some point in time, an organ will be able to be created in a laboratory from a person's own genetic material that can be used to be placed into his or her body.

(v) *Artificial organs* Some work is being done to create robotic/mechanical organs for transplantation.

3.2 Living donors: the law

If a living donor wishes to donate regenerative tissue (for example blood or bone marrow), there are few legal or ethical objections to this. The main legal issue is whether or not there is genuine consent to the donation. Where, however, non-regenerative donation (for example a kidney) is involved, the issue is more problematic. Our discussion will therefore focus on those cases.

There are three important legal principles here.

- It is not permissible to consent to a procedure that causes death or serious injury.[98] Therefore a parent cannot donate a heart to a child, assuming that the parent will die as a result of the donation. Donation of a single kidney, a segment of a liver, or a lobe of a lung will be permissible if the donor is in good health.

- There must be consent to the procedure. The donor must understand fully the processes involved.[99] In the case of a patient lacking capacity, the donation will be permitted only if it can be shown to be in that person's best interests.[100] Rarely could it ever be shown that the donation of an organ would be in the best interests of a person who lacks capacity.

- The procedure must be permissible under the HTAct 2004.

This final element requires elaboration. The HTAct 2004, section 33, states:

(1) Subject to subsections (3) and (5), a person commits an offence if—

    (a) he removes any transplantable material from the body of a living person intending that the material be used for the purpose of transplantation, and

    (b) when he removes the material, he knows, or might reasonably be expected to know, that the person from whose body he removes the material is alive.

---

[97] All the figures in this box here are from NHSBT (2017).
[98] Law Commission Consultation Paper No. 139 (1995: para. 8.32).
[99] See Glannon (2008) for an argument that the risks associated with donating livers are insufficiently appreciated; cf. Cronin (2008), who disagrees.
[100] MCA 2005, s. 4.

(2) Subject to subsections (3) and (5), a person commits an offence if—

    (a) he uses for the purpose of transplantation any transplantable material which has come from the body of a living person, and

    (b) when he does so, he knows, or might reasonably be expected to know, that the transplantable material has come from the body of a living person.

(3) The Secretary of State may by regulations provide that subsection (1) or (2) shall not apply in a case where—

    (a) the Authority is satisfied—

        (i) that no reward has been or is to be given in contravention of section 32, and

        (ii) that such other conditions as are specified in the regulations are satisfied, and

    (b) such other requirements as are specified in the regulations are complied with.

As this section makes clear, the starting point is that it is illegal both to remove an organ from a living person to transplant into another and to use the organ that has been removed illegally from a living person.[101] To do so could lead to a criminal conviction. However, the removal and use of the organ can be lawful if:

- there are no payments; and
- the regulations required by the HTA have been satisfied.

These two requirements need further clarification.

(i) The organ must not have been subject to 'commercial dealing' of the kind prohibited by section 32. We will be looking at this provision later in this chapter.[102]

(ii) The HTA has issued regulations concerning live donations.[103] The Code of Practice on Donation provides a lengthy list of issues that must be discussed with the proposed donor. These include the risks involved in the donation and the fact that there is no guarantee that the recipient will benefit from being given the organ. Where the donor is genetically or emotionally related to the recipient, provided that he or she has been given the necessary information, and has met with a clinician and an independent assessor, then the donation can go ahead without the specific approval of the HTA. Where, however, the donor is not genetically or emotionally related to the recipient, there is a need for approval from an HTA panel. It must be made clear to the recipient that the identity of the person who will receive their organ will remain confidential.[104] The Code suggests that a psychiatrist must meet with the donor and ensure that there is genuine consent to the donation.[105]

3.3 Children donating organs

There is no case law that deals specifically with the question of children donating organs. The HTAct 2004 itself provides no specific guidance. The HTA has issued a Code of

---

[101] *Re SW* [2017] EWCOP 7.   [102] See under the heading '8 Selling organs'.
[103] Human Tissue Authority (2017f).
[104] There is no need to show the donor will benefit from the donation. See for discussion Williams (2017).
[105] See *Re SW* [2017] EWCOP 7 for a bizarre attempt to get court approval to remove bone marrow from a woman lacking capacity without following the HTA regulations.

Practice in which it is said that living donations from children will be extremely rare.[106] Any donation from a child must be approved by a panel of the HTA. Where organs (whole or part) are to be donated, a court order is required.[107]

The Code does not make special reference to children who are *Gillick* competent[108] or aged 16 or 17 and so it seems that even for them the consent of the court is required. However, in determining whether the donation will be in the donor's best interests, the fact that the child is *Gillick* competent to make the decision and wants to make the donation must weigh heavily in favour of making the order.

It might be wondered whether any donation could be in a child's best interests. However, it is submitted that it can be.[109] First, if the donation were to a sister with whom the child had a close bond and if, without the donation, the sister would die, the courts would have little difficulty in finding that the welfare of the child would be promoted by the donation. This argument may be more difficult to run where the relationship between the child and recipient was more distant. Or, when the child is a newborn sibling, can it be said that the benefit that the child will gain in the future from the relation with the sibling justifies a donation now?

Second, as the Code mentions, the emotional and social benefits must be considered. So against the pain of the donation must be weighed the emotional and psychological benefits that the child may gain from donation.

The House of Lords in *Hashmi*[110] approved of a decision of the Human Fertilisation and Embryology Authority (HFEA) that it was permissible to screen embryos to see if they would have matching tissue for a bone marrow or umbilical cord transplant. Although not addressing directly the legality of taking the marrow or cord for transplant, the authorization of the screening would appear to imply that any subsequent donation could be regarded as lawful.

It is notable that the World Health Organization (WHO) has suggested that there should be a blanket ban on the use of minors as organ donors.[111] In practice, it seems in the UK that child donors are virtually unheard of. In the Eurotransplant catchment area, only five minor living donors have been used.[112] Many would agree with Garwood-Gowers:

> Perhaps the only circumstances in which the incompetent minor should be used . . . is where the donation is a necessity, such as because it is the only feasible option for preserving the life or well-being of a prospective recipient who is a key component in the incompetent minor's own well-being.[113]

3.4 Donors lacking mental capacity

What about the position of an adult lacking capacity, including a patient in a persistent vegetative state (PVS)?

The HTAct 2004, section 6, explains that if an adult lacks capacity to consent to the use or storage of material for the purposes of transplantation, then his or her consent can be deemed in certain circumstances. The donation would also require the approval

---

[106] Human Tissue Authority (2017f: para. 44).   [107] Human Tissue Authority (2009b: para. 47).
[108] See Chapter 4 for a discussion of this concept.   [109] See generally Herring and Foster (2012).
[110] *Quintavalle (on behalf of Comment on Reproductive Ethics) v HFEA* [2005] UKHL 28.
[111] WHO (1994).   [112] Garwood-Gowers (1999: 122).   [113] Garwood-Gowers (1999: 145).

of the court[114] and would require the approval of a panel of at least three members of the HTA where there is no effective consent in place.

The general position on the treatment of people lacking capacity is covered by the Mental Capacity Act (MCA) 2005, which is discussed in detail in Chapter 4. We shall briefly explain here how that Act deals with organ donation.

There are three grounds on which the removal and transplantation of an organ or bodily material can be authorized from an incompetent person.

(i) **An advance directive** If the incompetent person made an advance decision authorizing the transplantation of the organ, it will be possible to rely on that as consent to the donation. However, the MCA 2005 states that an advance decision can relate only to refusal of treatment.

(ii) **A lasting power of attorney (LPA)** The incompetent person may have signed an LPA that has authorized someone to make decisions concerning his or her welfare and that authorized person (the 'donee') has approved of the proposed removal of material for donation. However, as with advance decisions, the legislation permits the donee of the power of attorney only to authorize treatment and donation of bodily material may not be 'treatment'. Further, the donee can authorize only things that are in the best interests of the patient, and it will be rare for a donation to be regarded as in the patient's best interests.

(iii) **The best interests of the patient** The key principle is found in the MCA 2005, section 1(5): 'An act done, or decision made, under this Act for or on behalf of a person who lacks capacity must be done, or made, in his best interests.' So the basic proposition of law is that material can be taken from a person for donation to another if it is in that individual's best interests. A court approval would be required to confirm this was in the person's best interests.[115]

But can it ever be in someone's best interests to donate material? The leading case on the donation of bodily material prior to the passing of the HTAct 2004 was *Re Y*,[116] which is discussed in detail in Chapter 4. In that case, Connell J accepted that it was in a patient's best interests to donate bone marrow to his sibling on the basis that, otherwise, the sibling might fall seriously ill or die, and this would impact on the level of care and support that Y's mother would be able to offer Y—although it should be emphasized that the case involved bone marrow and Connell J was doubtful that his judgment would act as a useful precedent where more invasive surgery was required, as would be the case in a kidney donation, for example.

To some people, in the absence of an advance directive or the decision of an appointed attorney, it is not permissible to use the organs or bodily material of a person lacking capacity—that is, to use the incompetent person as a means of helping another. Ethically, it cannot be right to use such people for the benefit of others: it is simply 'exploitation'.[117] As we have seen in Chapter 4, however, arguments can be made that there are benefits to an incapacitated person from donation: he or she may be receiving care

[114] Human Tissue Act 2004 (Persons who Lack Capacity to Consent and Transplants) Regulations 2006, SI 2006/1659; see also Human Tissue Authority (2009b).
[115] Human Tissue Authority (2017f: para 55)
[116] *Re Y (Adult Patient) Transplant: Bone Marrow* [1997] Fam 110. The case is discussed in Feenan (1997) and Mumford (1998).
[117] Foster and Herring (2016).

from, or may benefit from a relationship with, the donee of the material; the donor may receive better care as a result of the donation; and it might even be claimed that allowing the incompetent person to participate in the 'good' of donation is beneficial for his or her life. In response, others have claimed that forced altruism is not altruism,[118] and that such arguments too easily lead to the use of those lacking capacity as a means to an end for the benefit of other people.

3.5 Living donors: ethical issues

To some, the low levels of live organ donations (the UK has the lowest in Europe) are shocking.[119] Quite simply, people are dying because of our reluctance to welcome and encourage live organ donations. In clinical terms, the likelihood of a successful transplant appears higher where the donor is a live donor,[120] and there is even evidence that recipients prefer to receive organs from live donors rather than cadavers.[121] Indeed, one leading commentator has suggested that live donor transplants should no longer be regarded as a last resort, but should become a major source of organs.[122] However, we have in fact seen an increase in the number of living kidney donors: from 589 in 2005–06 to 1,009 in 2016–17.[123] The vast majority of these are from people who know the recipient. In 2016–17, 1,218 living organ donations were approved by the HTA, but only eighty-eight 'altruistic donations' were approved by the HTA,[124] these being those that involve donors who do not know the people to whom they are donating.

Despite these arguments in favour of encouraging live organ donations, the subject raises some complex ethical issues including the following.

TO PONDER

Donating everything?

The BMA has reported the following case:

Surgeon's refusal to meet a patient's request. Mr P had two sons, aged 33 and 29. Both sons had Alport's syndrome, an inherited condition that causes kidney failure. Mr P successfully donated a kidney to his younger son. His older son, R, received a cadaveric kidney, but the transplant failed. As it had been a poor match, R developed antibodies that made him incompatible with 96 per cent of the population. Finding a suitable kidney was therefore extremely unlikely, unless his parents were suitable donors. Mrs P was told that she was not suitable. Mr P wanted to donate his second kidney to R.

Mr P argued it would be better for him to be on dialysis than his son. He was retired and prepared for the lifestyle change that dialysis would bring. Despite finding support from some doctors, Mr P's request was turned down by three transplant teams. Some of the deliberations of the third team were filmed and shown on television.

---

[118] Keown (1997b).
[119] Choudhry, Daar, Radcliffe-Richards, et al. (2003).   [120] Garwood-Gowers (1999: 37).
[121] Kranenburg, Zuidema, Weimar, et al. (2005).   [122] Garwood-Gowers (1999: 206).
[123] NHSBT (2017).
[124] Human Tissue Authority (2017g). There were eight cases where people had met online and agreed to donate to the other. This suggests a very small number of cases where people seek online potential donors.

Members of the transplant team had mixed views about Mr P's request. Some understood and felt they would want to do the same for their own children. Although some believed that the benefits were one sided, others agreed that there could be emotional benefits for Mr and Mrs P if the transplant was a success for R. There were also concerns about the impact on the family (the younger brother was opposed to the operation) and about how R in particular would feel about the effects on his father's length and quality of life. The resource implications of ending up with two people on dialysis rather than one if the transplant was not successful were also discussed.

The decision rested with the transplant surgeon. Although he knew that Mr P understood the nature and implications of his request, and that he could see ethical and rational justifications for the operation taking place, he knew that ultimately he would feel unable to perform the operation. Mr P was therefore turned down.

As a last resort, Mrs P was tested again to see if she might be a match. Although she had been rejected several times in the past, she was found to be a match.[125]

3.5.1 *Are there any limits to the donation of organs?*

Should the law allow someone to donate an organ if, in so doing, they are liable to suffer a serious injury or even death? Normally, in the criminal law, a person is not permitted to consent to a serious injury unless there is a good reason to do so. Does this pose a problem for live kidney donations? Not necessarily. First, the risk of injury with live donations is small: reported death rates range from 0.03 per cent to 0.06 per cent. The rate of complications for nephrectomy is 2 per cent and wound pain is 3.2 per cent. Great psychological benefits have been found to result from successful donation, although where the recipient dies after the donation, then there can be psychological harm for the donor.[126] In one survey of live donors, only three of the eighty-four donors questioned said that they would not go through with the donation if they had their time again.[127]

Second, the serious injuries are being caused for a good reason: to save the life of another. We permit people to suffer serious injuries in the name of boxing and bungee jumping; should we not allow them to do so in the name of saving a life?

But how far can we take this? Consider the following.

It would even be possible to imagine a more extreme case: a parent wanting to donate a heart to his or her child. That would, of course, entail the death of the parent. But what justification is there for preventing a person who has freely chosen to do so from acting in what many would regard to be a virtuous way that causes no harm to anyone else?[128]

The answer, which will not convince everyone, is that it will infringe the principle of beneficence: that doctors should do no harm. As Austen Garwood-Gowers puts it: 'The justification for law stepping in is not to prevent people voluntarily assuming risk but to prevent others from using the fact that a person has consented as a basis for mutilating them.'[129] In other words, it is not wrong for a parent to wish to save his or her child's life by donating a heart, but it is wrong for the medical team to rely on that consent to justify the procedure.

---

[125] Garwood-Gowers (1999: 49).   [126] Garwood-Gowers (1999: 37).   [127] BMA (2004: 91).
[128] Glannon and Ross (2002).   [129] Garwood-Gowers (1999: 62).

3.5.2 *The importance of a genetic relationship?*

A clear distinction exists between live donors who are genetically linked to the recipient and those who are not. All cases of 'altruistic non-directed donation' must be referred to the HTA for approval. This is not necessary in most cases, in which the donation is to a relative. The assumption is that those who are not genetically related to the recipient are likely to be improperly motivated, probably by money, and so great caution is required. By contrast, with a genetically related donor, we can assume that the donation is motivated by altruism and so is subject to less scrutiny.[130]

    Not everyone is attracted to the distinction. It has been pointed out that even if the donor is genetically related to the recipient, genuine consent may not be present. Indeed, an argument can be made that emotional pressure can be much greater than the pressure created by the offer of money.[131] Further, it is perfectly possible for a stranger to be willing to donate out of a genuine spirit of altruism, rather than it being inevitably a matter of money. For example, a group calling themselves the 'Jesus Christians' see donation of organs to strangers as an important part of showing their love for their fellow human beings and have complained at the difficulties that their members have faced in seeking to donate organs in the UK.[132] Such arguments have led some to claim that we should welcome donations from live donors whether there is a genetic link or not.[133]

3.5.3 *The distinction between regenerative and non-regenerative organs*

To the law and to many commentators, there is an important distinction to be drawn between the donation of regenerative and non-regenerative parts. The donation of bodily material that will automatically be replaced (such as blood or bone marrow) is much less controversial than the donation of an organ that is not replenished (for example a kidney).[134] This means that there is much less regulation of blood and marrow donation, and that the law is happier about authorizing blood or bone marrow donation from people lacking capacity.[135] A few commentators have found the distinction unconvincing. They point out that even non-regenerative organs are constantly changing and remaking themselves.[136] That said, the loss of a kidney can have a potential long-term health impact that cannot be said to be analogous to the loss of a pint of blood.

3.5.4 *Payment*

If we are going to permit live donation, should we accept payment? This is an issue to which we will return shortly, when we discuss the commercialization of the body generally. As we shall see, it is illegal and contrary to professional guidance to be involved in the sale of organs.[137]

---

[130] Although see Moorlock, Ives, and Draper (2014) for a challenge to the assumption that altruism should be seen as a requirement for a live donation, even if it is seen as desirable.

[131] Biller-Andorno and Schauenberg (2001). Although Burnell, Hulton, and Draper (2015), looking at the experience of parents donating kidneys to children, deny any emotional feelings undermine autonomy.

[132] Ronson (2002).

[133] See Roff (2007), who discusses the motives of unrelated organ donors and argues for a greater acceptance that there can be genuinely altruistic motives.

[134] See Catsanos, Rogers, and Lotz (2011) for a discussion of uterus transplants.

[135] See Farrell (2006) for a discussion of the regulation of blood donation.

[136] Herring (2002: 55).   [137] GMC (1992: 2).

For now, we shall simply note that it certainly seems possible to buy organs if one is willing to do so. The ban on the commercial selling of organs in 1989 followed the discovery that kidneys purchased from donors in Turkey were being transplanted to recipients in the UK. Apparently, it is possible to find kidneys for sale on the Internet.[138] They have even appeared on eBay (the Internet auction site).[139] UK doctors have been struck off for trying to arrange organ sales.[140] A journalist who placed an advert on the Internet, purporting to be desperately seeking a kidney, claimed to have been inundated with replies from people in both the UK and the United States.[141] Many of the respondents were in need of medical treatment themselves and were willing to sell a kidney to pay for it. In many developing countries, it is claimed that there is a flourishing trade in organs. In 2007, a man was given a suspended sentence after trying to sell his kidney for £24,000.[142] One survey of public opinion in the United States found that 27 per cent of people would consider selling a kidney—but, of those, 66 per cent would do so only if they were in a serious financial situation.[143]

3.5.5 *Compulsory organ donation*

Should we compel people to be organ donors against their will? At first sight, the idea seems preposterous: would it not be a monstrous suggestion that people could be killed without their consent so that their organs could be used to save the lives of others? Let us imagine that Alfred is in urgent need of a heart transplant and Bertha, in need of a lung transplant. We could kill Charles, and use his heart and lungs to save Alfred and Bertha's lives. Is this not justifiable on the basis that it is better to kill one person in order to save two lives? John Harris, in his article 'The survival lottery', suggests that the proposal would be acceptable if Charles were selected at random (for example by a computer).[144] In response to the argument that it cannot be right to kill an innocent person, he replies that it is wrong to let two innocent people die. In our scenario, Alfred and Bertha are as innocent as Charles. This point causes Harris to accept that a person may not be able to receive an organ under this scheme if he or she is responsible for the failure of the organs (for example as a result of excessive drinking of alcohol).

Harris's proposal has not exactly received universal acclaim, and one can hardly envisage it being part of a political party's manifesto. Nevertheless, an explanation of what is wrong with it has proved harder to articulate. One response is to draw the distinction between killing someone and letting someone die. It is wrong to let Alfred and Bertha die for want of an organ, but a greater wrong is done to Charles by killing him. It could be put in terms of human rights: we have a right not to be killed, but not necessarily a right to receive life-saving treatments. These distinctions turn on the difference between doing an act that kills and an omission that fails to save a patient. As we will see in Chapter 9, this distinction is a controversial one and one that is rejected by many.

Harris's argument is utilitarian and a different response would be to challenge it on its own terms. Although saving the two lives at the cost of one would initially appear to produce a utilitarian benefit, it might be argued that the impact on society of this scheme, with citizens constantly in fear that their 'number may be up', will be such as to outweigh the benefits. Harris suggests that this concern is fanciful: more people are

---

[138] Hayward and O'Hanlon (2003).   [139] BBC News online (26 April 2004).
[140] Dyer (2002).   [141] Hayward and O'Hanlon (2003).
[142] BBC News online (11 May 2007).   [143] Rid, Bachmann, Wettstein, et al. (2009).
[144] Harris (1975). See Øverland (2007) for a discussion of the different forms that such a lottery could take.

killed in cars than would be under his proposal and people do not appear to be too concerned about that. In any event, the scheme could be promoted in a way that encourages people to make sacrifices for others.

3.6 Organ transplants from the dead

Section 1 of the HTAct 2004 permits the removal, storage, and use of organs for transplantation from a deceased person as long as there is 'appropriate consent'.[145] In order to decide this point, it is necessary to consider the following questions.

(i) Has the deceased made a decision whether or not to consent to the transplant, which was in force immediately before his or her death? This decision can be oral or in writing.[146] If the deceased has made a decision, then that must be respected. So, for example, if the deceased has made it clear that he or she wants to donate his or her organs, his or her relative cannot prevent them being removed for that purpose. Similarly, if the deceased has made it clear that he or she does not want his or her organs used, his or her family cannot override those wishes.[147]

(ii) If the deceased has left no views, then the next question is: has the deceased nominated a representative to make decisions? Section 4 of the Human Tissue Act sets out the circumstances in which the nomination can be made. This can be made orally or in writing. If made orally, it must be in the presence of two or more witnesses; if in writing, it must be signed and witnessed.[148] The representative can make the decision in relation to a transplant. The representative must be an adult;[149] the representative can, if he or she wishes, renounce his or her appointment.[150] If two or more people are appointed as nominated representatives, then it is necessary to have the consent of only one of them, unless the terms of the appointment made it clear that they had to act jointly.[151]

(iii) If the deceased has not made a decision and has not nominated a representative, or if the representative is not able to give consent, then the person who stood in the closest 'qualifying relationship' to the deceased immediately before his or her death can make the decision.[152] Section 27(4) ranks the qualifying relations in this order: (a) spouse or partner; (b) parent or child; (c) brother or sister; (d) grandparent or grandchild; (e) child of a person falling within paragraph (c); (f) stepfather or stepmother; (g) half-brother or half-sister; (h) friend of long standing. The person who is highest up the list immediately before the death of the deceased can make the decision. This means that if there is a dispute between the spouse and parent of the deceased, the spouse will be able to make the decision. If the relationship of each of two or more persons to the person concerned is accorded equal highest ranking, it is sufficient to obtain the consent of either or any of them.[153] So if the brother and sister of the deceased were the two people highest in the list, and the brother were to want to approve a donation and the sister did not, the donation could go ahead.

---

[145] HTAct 2004, s. 3, defines 'appropriate consent'.
[146] It seems that there are no formal requirements in this regard: there is no need for the consent to be in writing (for example), as there is where the tissue or material is for anatomical examination: Human Tissue Authority (2017c).
[147] Human Tissue Authority (2009a: para. 32).
[148] HTAct 2004, s. 4.   [149] HTAct 2004, s. 4(10).   [150] HTAct 2004, s. 4(9).
[151] HTAct 2004, s. 4(6).   [152] HTAct 2004, s. 3(6).   [153] HTAct 2004, s. 9(4).

Note the following points about this list. First, notice that the question is the relationship immediately before the death. This means that a former spouse will not fall within the 'spouse' category. Second, there is no position for a stepchild. Third, the category of 'friend of long standing' means that there will be few deceased who will have no one who can provide 'appropriate consent'.

It will be a criminal offence attracting a maximum prison sentence of three years if a surgeon performs an organ transplant from a deceased person without the necessary consent.[154] However, it will be a defence if the person concerned reasonably believed that the appropriate consent had been given.[155] So, if a surgeon were to rely on the consent of a deceased person's spouse to remove an organ for transplant, unaware that in fact the deceased had made a written statement not wanting his or her organs removed for transplant, the surgeon could rely on this defence. But he or she would succeed only if it was reasonable to believe that there was no written statement. This is problematic: to what lengths should a surgeon go to find out whether or not there was a binding decision of the deceased or appointment of a representative? How is a surgeon to know who is the closest relative of the deceased? This is especially problematic given that transplant decisions often have to be made very shortly after death. Hopefully, the word 'reasonable' will be interpreted in light of the difficult position in which a surgeon may find himself or herself. One approach that might appeal is to say that a surgeon is guilty of an offence only if he or she acts unreasonably.[156]

3.7 Special issues and organ donation

3.7.1 Conditional donation

If a person wishes to donate an organ, should he or she be permitted to attach conditions as to who should receive it? For example, if a donor were to state that he or she was willing to donate only if he or she could be assured that the recipient would be of a certain sex, race, or creed, should the proposed donation be rejected?

The official response has been that conditional donation is not permitted. In 2000, it was reported that an organ was accepted by a hospital subject to the condition that it would be used only for a white person. In fact, the person who was 'top of the queue' was a white person and the organ was used for him. In other words, this racist condition had not affected how the organ was used. When news of the case emerged, however, the government declared itself to be shocked and an investigation was undertaken.[157]

The Human Tissue Authority guidance states:

No organ should be transplanted under a form of consent which seeks to impose restrictions on the class of recipient of the organ, including any restriction based on a recipient's gender, race, colour, language, religion, political or other opinion, national or social origin, association with a national minority, property, birth or other status (including characteristics protected under the Equality Act 2010).[158]

[154] HTAct 2004, s. 5(1) and (7).   [155] HTAct 2004, s. 5(1)(b).
[156] Mason and Laurie (2006: 437).   [157] DoH (2000e).
[158] This last reference would include conditions based on age and sexuality.

This is interesting because it seems to permit conditions which are not restricted by a 'status'. Would it be possible to, for example, leave an organ only for those who attended a private school? The Code explains:

> NHS Blood and Transplant (NHSBT) is the body that has legal responsibility for organ allocation across the UK and, as a matter of policy, does not accept organs from deceased donors where any condition is attached. However, requested allocation of a deceased donor organ can be considered if this is carried out in line with NHSBT policy.

It seems, therefore, the Authority thinks that a condition based on one of the listed grounds is impermissible. The NHSBT has taken the policy as a matter of policy not to permit any conditions, although it does not have to take that view. The NHSBT will consider a request for an allocation (if it is in line with the general policy), but not a condition.

The Department of Health has issued guidance on when weight should be attached to the wishes of a person about to whom their organ is given.[159] The guidance suggests that such views should be respected only in rare cases: where the donation is unconditional; where there is evidence of an intention by the deceased to be a living donor; and where there is no other potential recipient whose case merits priority to the requested recipient. It will be rare for these requirements to be met. Where they are not met, the normal rules of allocation of organs should be followed. Douglas and Cronin have questioned the legality of the guidance.[160] As they note, the HTAct 2004 requires the consent of the deceased. If the deceased has consented to the donation of the organ only to a particular person or group of people, it is not clear that the organ can then be used for other people.

What is permitted is a 'paired organ exchange'. Imagine that Mr A and Mr B both need a kidney. Mrs A is compatible with Mr B and Mrs B is compatible with Mr A. In such a case, the couples could agree that, in exchange for Mrs A giving her kidney to Mr B, Mrs B will give hers to Mr A. This has been said to be acceptable by the British Transplant Society,[161] and there is at least one recorded case of this happening in the UK.[162]

3.7.2 'Beating heart donation'

One issue that can cause problems in practice is where organs are removed from a person who is technically dead (that is, brain dead), but has the appearance of being alive because his or her heart is still beating.[163] A distinction can be drawn between:

- *heart-beating donors*, who have died on a life support system and whose death is established by brain stem criteria; and
- *non-heart-beating donors*, who are not on life support and whose death is established by the more traditional criteria (that is, breathing and heartbeat have ceased).

Of the 1,413 deceased donors whose organs were used in 2016–17, 829 were heart-beating (brain dead) donors and 584 were non-heart beating (circulatory death) donors.[164]

---

[159] DoH (2010a).   [160] Douglas and Cronin (2010); Cronin and Douglas (2010).
[161] British Transplant Society (2005). See also Murphy and Veatch (2006), who discuss an American society whose members agree to donate only to other members.
[162] BBC News online (4 October 2007).   [163] Ducharme (2000); Gardiner and Sparrow (2010).
[164] NHSBT (2017).

In Chapter 9 we will be exploring the definition of death, but it is key in the issue of organ transplantation.[165] The point in time at which death is declared, and therefore transplant organs can be removed, can be crucial for the quality of the organs. Critics sometimes claim that 'brain stem death' is 'suspiciously convenient'[166] for medical professionals, because it readily enables the removal of organs.[167] However, other commentators have complained that the legal definition of 'death' has hindered the policy of encouraging organ transplants.[168] It has been argued that, under the 'best interests' test in the MCA 2005, it is proper to treat a patient who has requested that his or her organs be donated in a way that will ensure, where possible, that the organs can be used.[169] It seems from the Code of Practice that the wish to donate can be a factor in deciding precisely when to withdraw treatment:

> For a patient with a life-threatening or life-limiting condition, the clinical team may, in dis-cussion with the relatives, decide to withdraw life-sustaining treatment. This would usually be expected to result in circulatory death with the attendant possibility of donation after cir-culatory death (DCD). Where the patient lacks capacity, any decisions about the timing of withdrawal of life-sustaining treatment or the institution of new therapies or treatments to enable organ donation to proceed must be taken in the patient's best interests. The patient's known wishes with regard to organ and tissue donation, whether recorded or as expressed to relatives, are one factor to include in the assessment of the patient's best interests.

Particular controversy surrounds elective ventilation.[170] This is a technique whereby a person who is on the point of death is put on a life support machine, for the purpose of preserving his or her organs for transplantation. But for the possibility of transplant-ation, life support would not be used. At present, this practice is considered unlawful by the Department of Health, because the patient is being treated in a particular way that gives him or her no benefit.[171] However, the HTA, in its Code of Practice on Donation, states that:

> The HT Act makes it lawful to take minimum steps to preserve part of a body for poten-tial transplantation, including in those situations where it is still being established if a decision on consent has been, or will be, made.[172]

Supporters of the practice have suggested that consent to organ donation can be treated as consent to elective ventilation.[173] Julian Savulescu argues that failing to use elective ventilation so that organs can be used is against patients' 'global interests, fails to respect autonomy, violates principles of distributive justice and is not even in their interests, however narrowly and medically construed'.[174]

3.7.3 *Distribution of organs*

The decision as to who is given an organ is highly sensitive, especially where there may be a number of patients in urgent need of one. There are advisory groups for particular

---

[165] Miller (2009); Campbell (2004).
[166] Holland (2003: 72). See, for a wide-ranging discussion, Lock (2002). See Machado, Korein, Ferrer, et al. (2007) for a look at the history of the notion of brain death and a convincing argument that the concept was not created to assist transplantation.
[167] Linacre Centre (2002).   [168] Coggon, Brazier, Murphy, et al. (2008).
[169] Coggon, Brazier, Murphy, et al. (2008). That would never justify killing a patient, but might justify keeping a patient alive longer than would otherwise be the case.
[170] Gillett (2013); Coggon (2013); Price (1997a).   [171] DoH (2002e: para. 13.13).
[172] Human Tissue Authority (2017f: para. 140).
[173] Coggan, Brazier, Murphy, et al. (2008). See further the discussion in Price (2011).
[174] Savulescu (2013: 129). See Also McGee and Gardiner (2017).

organs, which provide guidance to deal with the allocation of donations. By way of example, the key features of the guidance in relation to kidneys states:

> [A]ll kidneys from deceased heart-beating donors are allocated according to a national system. This is based on five tiers:
>
> - tier A: complete matches for hard-to-match child patients (under 18 years old)
> - tier B: complete matches for other children
> - tier C: complete matches for hard-to-match adult patients
> - tier D: complete matches for other adults and well-matched children
> - tier E: all other eligible patients (adults and children).

Within tiers A and B, children are prioritized according to their waiting time. In the remaining tiers, patients are prioritized according to a points system. Organs are allocated to the patients with the highest number of points.

The score for an individual patient is based on a number of factors:

- time on the waiting list (favouring patients who have waited the longest)
- tissue match and age combined (favouring well-matched transplants for younger patients)
- age difference between donor and patient (favouring closer age matches)
- location of patient relative to the donor (favouring patients who are closer to minimize the transportation time of the kidney)
- three other factors relating to blood group match and rareness of the patient's tissue type.[175]

The system involves a complex granting of points determined by these factors listed.

4 Liability for mishaps from organ transplant

If a person receives an organ that is diseased or otherwise leads to infection of the recipient, is there any legal remedy to the recipient? There is no case law on this issue to date.[176] An action in negligence could certainly been brought if it could be demonstrated that the NHS trust could have discovered the organ's problems through screening procedures. Another possible claim would be under the Consumer Protection Act 1987, because its definition of a 'product' includes human tissue.

5 The lack of organs

For many years now, there has been a shortage of organs available for transplant.[177] There has been a 20 per cent increase in the waiting time for a new donated kidney in the last three years, despite increasing rates of donation.[178] This has been described as

---

[175] NHSBT (2013a).   [176] See Cronin and Douglas (2013).
[177] See Gil-Diaz (2009) for a discussion of the approach in Spain, which has generated a much higher number of organs available for donation.
[178] *The Guardian* (31 July 2011).

a 'terrible and unnecessary tragedy'.[179] To be blunt, many people die because of the shortage of organs. Officially, 457 people died while on the transplant waiting list in 2016–17;[180] 875 people were removed from the waiting list, many because they became too ill to receive organs. Others will have died without even reaching the waiting list.

Talk of a 'shortage' of organs has been criticized by Schicktanz and Schweda, who argue that using the language of shortage assumes that there is a legitimate expectation that there will be extensive donation.[181] They argue that instead each organ should be received with gratitude and regarded as good fortune, rather than there being a right or expectation that organs should be provided.

The following are some of the suggested ways in which it might be possible to attempt to increase the number of available organs.

(i)   *No change* We should retain the current legal system, but do more to increase the numbers of those registering. This could be by means of public education or even by offering incentives for people to donate. We could also do more to persuade doctors to encourage relatives to consider agreeing to the donation of a deceased's organs.

(ii) *Mandated choice* This is an approach that requires citizens to indicate what they want to happen to their organs on their death.

(iii) *No choice* We should move to a system under which, on death, people's organs can be donated regardless of their wishes. This might even involve a system in which live organ donation can be used against a person's wishes.

(iv) *Opt-out* We should move to a system under which it is presumed that a person wishes to donate his or her organs and that, if he or she has not registered an objection, the person's organs will be made available for use. In other words, we should move from an 'opt-in system' (under which you opt in to offering your organs for donation) to an 'opt-out system' (under which you opt out of making your organs available for transplant).

5.1 Keeping the current system

We could seek to persuade more people to register as willing to donate their organs. This could be done by simply making it easier to register. Some increase in numbers has been achieved by allowing people seeking car licences or a Boots 'Advantage Card' to indicate that they wish to join the register.[182] There could also be campaigns of persuasion or education to encourage more people to register. The HTAct 2004, section 34A, requires health authorities to promote awareness of the register. A recent innovation has been that anyone applying for a driver's licence is required to answer a question about organ donation.[183] Controversially, it allows only three answers to the question of whether a person wishes to donate organs on his or her death: 'yes'; 'already on the register to donate'; 'would like to think about it on another occasion'. One cannot register 'no'.[184]

One alternative would be to offer incentives for people to join the register. Those who put their names down as donors would receive priority if they were themselves to need

---

[179] Harris (2003b).   [180] NHSBT (2015).   [181] Schicktanz and Schweda (2009).
[182] Shaw (2017) notes not much information is given to those registering.
[183] *The Guardian* (31 July 2011).   [184] This makes it feasible for relatives to donate.

an organ.[185] Payment (or tax advantages) for organs might also encourage individuals to register as donors or relatives to consent to an organ transplant.[186] There is some debate whether or not payment would be effective.[187] Also, there is an argument that this would rob people of the opportunity to donate altruistically.[188] Supporters of the state paying tax credits or payments claim that the cost would be largely recouped through saved lives and the savings on expenses that arise when dealing with people with organ failures.[189] That economic calculation has been challenged, however.[190]

It has been claimed that part of the blame for the lack of organs lies with health-care professionals, who are reluctant to discuss the issue of organ donation with the relatives of a person who has just died. This reticence is, of course, understandable, and asking grieving relatives for consent to donate organs could very easily be seen as callous. Indeed, it is difficult to raise the issue without feeling that one is placing 'moral blackmail' on the relatives.

5.2 Mandated choice

The idea here is that individuals should be required to indicate a choice as to whether or not they wish their organs to be used for transplant purposes after death.[191] Arguably, the recent use of driving licence applications, requiring the answering of a question about transplantation, has got close to this. Supporters of such a proposal point out that far higher numbers of those who respond to surveys say that they wish to donate than get around to registering their wish to do so. One difficulty with this proposal, however, would be devising the 'punishment' for those who refuse to express a wish.

5.3 Mandatory donation

We referred earlier to John Harris's radical suggestion for a 'lottery' to provide live organ donors to supply organs. It will therefore be of little surprise to learn that he advocates the removal of organs from a deceased regardless of the views of the deceased and/or his or her relatives.[192] He makes the point that we already override the wishes of a deceased in relation to what happens with the body. Post-mortems can be carried out on a deceased whatever objections he or she may have voiced in his or her lifetime. This is justified as being necessary in the interests of the community. If the public interest in post-mortems is sufficient to override the deceased's wishes, why is the saving of lives through transplants not sufficient?[193]

In reply, it is said that to permit the removal of organs against someone's wishes can be a profound violation of their autonomy, especially where their objection is made on the basis of a religious belief. Cronin and Harris, however, reject claims based on autonomy:

> When I am dead I have lost the capacity that it is the point of autonomy and the law to protect. I am no longer able to think critically about preferences, desires or wishes. I am no longer able to make choices. 'I' no longer exist.[194]

While that may be their opinion, not everyone agrees. People who believe in an afterlife might believe that what happens to their bodies does matter. Alternatively, it might be

[185] Hartogh (2010); Nadel and Nadel (2005).   [186] Petersen and Lippert-Rasmussen (2012).
[187] Evans (2003).   [188] Stacey Taylor (2012).   [189] Petersen and Lippert-Rasmussen (2012).
[190] Quigley (2012a).   [191] Chouhan and Draper (2003).   [192] Harris (2003b).
[193] Harris (2003b).   [194] Cronin and Harris (2010: 628).

said that respecting people's autonomy means respecting the choices that they made while living, even if they are now dead.

5.4 'Opt-out'

The proposal for an 'opt-out' scheme has been dealt with last because it has received much support, including from the BMA.[195] Since Alder Hey, some commentators now view an opt-out scheme as not politically acceptable.[196] In 2008, then Prime Minister Gordon Brown made it clear that he supported a change in the law to have an 'opt-out' scheme.[197] However, a report by an expert group that he set up was against the proposal, and it is unlikely the law in England will be changed in the near future.[198]

The Human Transplantation (Wales) Act 2013 has created an 'opt out' system for Wales.[199] Anyone who dies in Wales is deemed to consent to organ donation unless there is evidence that they objected. Under section 4(4) a relative or friend of long standing of the deceased may object to the donation on the basis that they knew the deceased objected. They cannot rely on their own feelings on the matter. They must produce evidence that would satisfy a reasonable person that they know the views of the deceased.

Any consideration of an opt-out scheme raises a number of issues.

5.4.1 A moral obligation to donate

One argument is that we should 'presume consent', because it is morally correct that people consent.[200] The Department of Health has argued: 'If you are prepared to consider accepting a transplant for yourself or your family it seems only fair to play your part in being willing to be a donor.'[201] The problem is that the law does not normally compel people to act in a way that is moral. The moral case for giving money to help to alleviate the condition of the starving does not lead us to conclude that the government should force people to donate. Savulescu disagrees with that response. He argues:

> [Organ donation] is not just an easy rescue, it is a zero cost rescue. Organs are of no use to us when we are dead, but they are literally lifesaving to others. Nonetheless, most people choose to bury or burn these lifesaving resources, and are allowed to. Yet the state extracts death duties and inheritance taxes, but not the most important of their previous assets—their organs.[202]

There may be an argument that a distinction can be drawn between the moral duties of a family member and of a stranger. A parent can be criminally liable for not providing the necessary basics of life to his or her children. Can we extend that to organs?[203] Not automatically. Although parents are required to feed and care for their children, this does not extend to invasions of their bodily integrity of the kind required in organ donation.

5.4.2 'Presumed consent'

To some, an opt-out position is reasonable because we can presume consent.[204] The argument is most commonly made by reference to a number of surveys of public opinion, which

[195] BMA (2005).   [196] Chouhan and Draper (2003).
[197] BBC News online (13 January 2008).
[198] Organ Donation Taskforce (2008a). Although the BMA (2009b) still pushes for presumed consent.
[199] Douglas and Cronin (2015).   [200] Saunders (2010).   [201] DoH (1999b).
[202] Savulescu (2015a).   [203] The issues are well discussed in Glannon and Ross (2002) and Spial (2003).
[204] Organ Donation Taskforce (2008a: 1.12); Hartogh (2011).

indicate that while a majority of people would want to donate organs on their death, only a minority get around to holding a donor card.[205] It is therefore a reasonable presumption that any given person would want his or her organs used at death. We could therefore have a register for those who *object* to their organs being used post-mortem for donation. If a person fails to register an objection, we can presume consent. Another way of putting the argument is that we can create a rule that silence constitutes consent, in the same way as, in a meeting, if the chair asks if anyone opposes a motion and there is no response, it is taken to mean support.[206] This kind of presumed consent could only be justified if it had been clearly communicated to the public and some believe we could never be confident that a sufficiently large percentage of the population were aware of the scheme.[207]

Critics respond that 'presumed consent' is a misnomer.[208] In a case of presumed consent, there is *no* consent. To remove a person's organ without his or her explicit consent is unethical.[209] In particular, it must be recalled that, in a multicultural society, although some people may have no strong views on what happens to their body on death, there are many who have strong religious or cultural influences on what happens after death. To remove organs without explicit consent runs the risk of causing religious or cultural offence.

One way of resolving this debate is to ask 'Which is worse: not to have your organs removed when you would have wanted them to be (which happens under an opt-in system), or to have your organs removed post-mortem when you would not have wanted them to be (which could happen under an opt-out system)?' To supporters of the opt-out system, both are wrong, and given that people are dying because of the lack of organs, we can presume consent. It is more efficient and cost-effective to maintain a register of the small number who wish to opt out of donation than one comprising the majority who are willing to be donors.[210]

5.4.3 Can the interests of the dead outweigh the interests of the living?

If you take the view that an opt-out system would be improper because it would infringe the rights of the deceased, there is still the question of whether the deceased's interests should outweigh those of the potential recipients of the organ. After all, can ignoring or placing little weight on the wishes of the deceased cause them any harm or loss? Some people believe that the dead have no interests. As Harris has put it: 'The dead person cannot be wronged or harmed by the transplant of their organs "against their will" for they have no will—they are not there to be harmed.'[211] Others disagree and argue that we do have an interest in how we are treated in our death. To many people, our death and burial is the final chapter of our stories.[212] How our death is recalled and commemorated is of great importance.[213]

Ruth Chadwick has argued that respecting the interests of the dead can be seen in terms of respecting the interests of the living:

> Duties regarding the dead could be seen as indirectly duties towards living persons, who certainly do have preferences about how the dead should be treated. The preferences of living persons include both those of the loved ones of a dead person who cannot bear to

[205] BMA (2005).   [206] Saunders (2012).   [207] Mackay (2015).
[208] Manson (2013); Price (2003).   [209] Glannon (2008b).   [210] BMA (2005).
[211] Harris (1984: 119). See also Sneddon (2009) and Callahan (1987).
[212] Herring (2002: 56).   [213] McGuinness and Brazier (2008).

think of their friend or relative being disfigured in an organ transplant operation, and the preferences of persons currently alive who do not like the thought of such procedures being carried out on their own bodies after death.[214]

Harris emphasizes that even if we can claim that the dead have interests in how their body will be treated on death, we need to weigh those interests against other interests.[215] He argues:

> We must remember that while the organ donor may have a posthumous preference frustrated, (more of which anon) and her friends and relatives may be distressed and upset, the potential organ recipient stands to lose her very life and her friends and relatives will have grief to add to their distress.[216]

One factor not mentioned by Harris is the feelings of distress that we all might experience if we were to know that we would have no control over how our bodies would be used after our death.[217]

5.4.4 *Would an opt-out scheme actually work?*

Belgium, Italy, and Greece have all moved to an opt-out scheme, and this has increased the number of organs available for transplant.[218] However, the link between an opt-out scheme and increasing organ donation rates is not as straightforward as might at first appear.[219] It is true that, in some countries, the increase has been dramatic.[220] But when Austria moved to an opt-out scheme, this had little impact on the number of donations.[221] A move to an opt-out scheme may therefore have a noticeable impact on donation rates only if it has the support of medical professionals and the general public.[222] In some countries with opt-out schemes, the consent of family members is still sought, and medical teams are reluctant to proceed with transplants against the wishes of a grieving family.[223]

It might be argued that it is possible to increase the number of donors without moving to an opt-out scheme. Noticeably, Spain has dramatically increased its rate of organ donors without moving to an opt-out scheme.[224] It must also be remembered that, as well as the legal structure, a host of other factors can impact on the transplant rate: causes of death;[225] the kinds of organs required; the number of transplant surgeons; and the availability of intensive care beds and staff.[226] The Organ Donation Taskforce also noted the concern that an opt-out scheme might create mistrust between patients and clinical staff.[227] Indeed, the Taskforce expressed the concern that if patients were to cease to trust the system, this would lead to large numbers opting out and even a reduction in the number of organs available.[228] Its preference is to find ways in which to encourage more people to opt in.[229]

---

[214] Chadwick (1994: 58).   [215] Harris (2002).   [216] Harris (2003b: 205).
[217] Hamer and Rivlin (2002).   [218] De Cruz (2001: 552).
[219] Rithalia, McDaid, Suekarran, et al. (2009).   [220] Chouhan and Draper (2003).
[221] New, Solomon, Dingwall, et al. (1994).   [222] English and Sommerville (2003).
[223] De Cruz (2001: 595).   [224] English and Sommerville (2003).
[225] Some causes of death mean that organs are unsuitable for transplant.
[226] English and Sommerville (2003).   [227] Organ Donation Taskforce (2008a).
[228] See Rieu (2010) for criticism of the Taskforce's assessment of the evidence and reasoning.
[229] Organ Donation Taskforce (2008b).

6 The wishes of relatives

Should family members have any say in what happens to a deceased?[230] It is important to realize that family members could be involved in two ways: first, in providing evidence about what the deceased would have wanted; and second, in terms of the interests that they have in their own right. Here, we are talking about the second issue. There are two main issues in this regard: should the views of relatives be able to outweigh the views of the deceased? And should the views of relatives be taken into account in a case in which the deceased has failed to express any views?[231]

It could be argued that ignoring the wishes of relatives runs the risk of turning public opinion against the transplant system. Further, as UK Transplant has pointed out, the cooperation of the relatives of the deceased is often important in uncovering the medical history of the deceased, which is essential if transplants are to be successful.[232] Also, it has been argued that respecting the wishes of relatives is interconnected with respecting the wishes of the deceased, because we can presume that the deceased would not want distress caused to his or her relatives.[233] Even if it is accepted that the wishes of the family do carry weight, there is still the question of whether they are sufficient to outweigh the interests of the person needing an organ and that person's family.[234] There is even an argument that the organs of the deceased can be treated as property, which is inherited by the next of kin.[235] An alternative argument might be that relatives have a right to determine what should happen to the body as part of their right to respect for their family life.[236]

We should bear in mind the fact that some relatives who choose not to donate have feelings of regret later, when they are able to think about the issue more calmly.[237]

PUBLIC OPINION

There is much evidence that most people would be keen for their organs to be used for transplant on their death.

- A 2005 poll for the BBC's *Watchdog Healthcheck* programme found 78 per cent in favour of a shift to presumed consent in respect of organ donation.[238]

- An 2007 NHS Networks poll found 72 per cent favouring an opt-out system.[239]

- A survey for the Organ Donation Taskforce conducted in 2008 found 60 per cent of the public in favour of an opt-out.[240]

- Another survey also found that 90 per cent of those questioned said that they were willing to donate their organs if they died, but in fact only 50 per cent had registered to donate organs.[241] The most common reason given for not registering was not wanting to 'tempt fate'.

---

[230] Wilkinson (2007b); Boddington (1998).
[231] Haddow (2005) looks at what influences family's attitudes to bodies after death.
[232] UK Transplant (2004).   [233] Murphy and Younger (2003).
[234] Cronin (2007).   [235] Voo and Holm (2014).
[236] *Elberte v Latvia*, Application no 61243/08, 13 January 2015.
[237] Sque, Long, and Payne (2005).   [238] POST (2005).   [239] NHS Networks (2007).
[240] Organ Donation Taskforce (2008).   [241] BBC News online (22 August 2004).

A VIEW FROM ABOVE

Religious views on organ donation

UK Transplant (2004c), in a leaflet written with the support of religious leaders representing Buddhism, Christianity, Hinduism, Islam, Judaism, and Sikhism, claims: 'All our major religions support the principles of organ donation and transplantation.'[242]

Pope John Paul II, in an address to the participants of the Society for Organ Sharing, said: 'With the advent of organ transplantation, which began with blood transfusion, man has found a way to give of himself, of his blood and of his body, so that others may continue to live.'[243]

Buddhism takes a neutral attitude towards donation. The choice of whether or not to donate is seen as being up to the individual and there is no 'correct' choice. Some Buddhists (especially followers of Tibetan Buddhism) believe that consciousness may stay in the body for a short time after the heart has stopped beating. For them, there may be difficulties if organ donation procedures are being commenced too soon after death.

Within Judaism, there are strong objections to unnecessary interference with a corpse and there is a need for immediate burial of a complete body. However, the majority view is that organ donation in order to save lives (*pikuach nefesh*) is justifiable. Donation of organs for medical research would be unacceptable.

Islam also takes a strict line against violating a human body. However, the 1996 Shariah Council issued a fatwa permitting organ donation on the basis of necessity. It is justifiable as a means of alleviating pain or saving life.[244]

One faith that has serious concerns about organ donation is the Shinto faith. In that faith, the notions of purity and wholeness of the physical body are important. From the moment of death, the body is seen as impure, and therefore organ donation is normally regarded as inappropriate, because it may injure the relationship between the dead person and the bereaved (the *itai*).

7 Xenotransplantation

Xenotransplantation involves the use of the organs of one species to transplant into an-other.[245] It has been defined by the Department of Health as:

> ... any procedure that involves the transplantation, implantation, or infusion into a human recipient of either live tissues or organs retrieved from animals, or, human body fluids, cells, tissue or organs that have undergone ex vivo contact with live non-human animal cells, tissues or organs.[246]

It is, at present, a complex procedure because of the difficulties of rejection from the recipient. In fact, the procedure is still at an experimental stage.[247] Improvements in drugs that suppress the rejection of the host have meant that only in recent years has

---

[242] UK Transplant (2004c: 23).   [243] Quoted in UK Transplant (2004: 12).
[244] See also Aasi (2003).
[245] Fovargue and Ost (2010), Fovargue (2013b), McLean and Williamson (2005), Fovargue (2005), and Anderson (2007) discuss this topic in detail.
[246] DoH (2006a: 1).   [247] Mason and Laurie (2006: 422).

xenotransplantation become a realistic possibility.[248] The Department of Health has encouraged research into this practice, saying: '[I]t is right to explore the potential of xenotransplantation in a cautious, stepwise fashion … in a controlled research context.'[249]

Anyone who wishes to use xenotransplantation will need the approval of a research ethics committee. The committee will give permission only where strict guidelines are followed.[250] The fact that one of the most successful cases of xenotransplantation involved a man who received a baboon's liver, but lived for only seventy days,[251] demonstrates that to permit the practice would be to make participants 'human guinea pigs' (so to speak). Following technological advances, some scientists claim that it is now safe for pig organs to be used in humans; however, so far there have been no such xenotransplantations in the UK.[252]

As well as the difficulties in actually succeeding in transplanting an organ, there are concerns about the possibility of transferring viruses to humans, and developing new strains of viruses that may severely impact on the wider community.[253] This is an especially significant issue in relation to the question of consent when people are being involved in medical trials based on xenotransplantation.[254] The concern of creating new potentially catastrophic illness leads some commentators to argue against the use of xenotransplantation.[255]

A further issue is whether there are some animals that should not be used for transplantation. There is a widespread feeling that organs should not be taken from primates, because of their special status, even though they, being closest to humans in biological terms, would be the best donors.[256] The pig has therefore become a popular option. Although there is much debate whether or not non-human animals have rights, it should be remembered that even if they do not, that does not mean that they do not have interests that deserve protection.

8 Selling organs

Should we permit people to sell their organs or body parts? The official response has always been a resounding 'no'. It has been a criminal offence to be involved in the sale of organs for several decades now. Doctors who have been found to be involved in organ selling have been struck off the medical register.[257]

8.1 The criminal offences

The HTAct 2004 provides an impressive array of offences connected with the commercial dealing of human material for transplantation. Section 32 contains a series of offences connected with dealing with organs for reward:

(1) A person commits an offence if he—

(a) gives or receives a reward for the supply of, or for an offer to supply, any controlled material;

---

[248] Nuffield Council on Bioethics (1996: 7).   [249] DoH (2006a: 2).
[250] DoH (2006a). For criticism of the guidance, see McLean and Williamson (2007).
[251] Starlz, Fung, and Tzakis (1993).   [252] BBC News online (1 September 2004).
[253] Muir and Griffin (2001).   [254] McLean and Williamson (2005: ch. 7).
[255] Fovargue and Ost (2011).   [256] Fox and McHale (1998).   [257] Dyer (1990).

(b) seeks to find a person willing to supply any controlled material for reward;

(c) offers to supply any controlled material for reward;

(d) initiates or negotiates any arrangement involving the giving of a reward for the supply of, or for an offer to supply, any controlled material;

(e) takes part in the management or control of a body of persons corporate or un-incorporate whose activities consist of or include the initiation or negotiation of such arrangements.

'Reward' here includes giving a financial or other material advantage. It is not therefore possible to bypass these provisions by not paying cash, but providing property or other economic benefit.

There then follows an offence dealing with advertising and soliciting commercial dealings with human material:

(1) Without prejudice to subsection (1)(b) and (c), a person commits an offence if he causes to be published or distributed, or knowingly publishes or distributes, an advertisement—

(a) inviting persons to supply, or offering to supply, any controlled material for reward, or

(b) indicating that the advertiser is willing to initiate or negotiate any such arrange-ment as is mentioned in subsection (1)(d).

The prohibitions on payment for organs are not as strict as might at first appear. Most importantly, in section 32(7), the prohibitions on reward do not apply to expenses in-curred in removing, storing, or transporting the organ. Nor does it include payments to cover the loss of earnings of a person donating an organ. It will remain to be seen how generously the terms 'expenses' and 'loss of earnings' might be interpreted.[258] Certainly, in the context of similar provisions in relation to surrogacy payments, there have been claims that the courts have been very generous in determining the legitimacy of expenses.[259] The NHS suggests that trusts may decide not to pay for lost earnings if those earnings exceed the average national wage.[260]

The offences are committed only where the controlled material 'consists of or includes human cells', but it must be intended for use in transplantation. It does not include gametes, embryos, or 'material which is the subject of property because of an application of human skill'.[261] This last phrase is problematic because (as we shall see shortly) it is far from clear when material becomes 'the subject of property'. Indeed, it is arguable that an organ removed from a person and preserved for later transplant is indeed the subject of property. If this is correct, the section will fail to achieve its aim in rendering illegal the sale of organs.

The HTA, under section 32(3), can designate a person who can lawfully engage in trade in human material. For example, presumably the National Blood Service will be permitted to purchase blood from abroad, if necessary.

---

[258] Payments can be made only by a 'proper authority' (e.g. an NHS trust) and cannot be made by the rela-tives of the recipients: Human Tissue Authority (2009a: para. 43).

[259] See Dickenson (2008) for evidence of how similar provisions have been bypassed in other countries.

[260] NHS (2009b).   [261] HTAct 2004, s. 32(9)(c).

8.2 **The ethical issues**

Although the legal approach is strict, there has been much discussion among ethicists on the issue of organ selling. One starting point is to consider with whom the burden of argument should lay. Is it for those who want to permit organ selling to produce arguments as to why it should be allowed? Or is it for those who oppose it to produce arguments as to why it should not be permitted? For those who think that the sale of organs should be permitted, the starting point is autonomy.[262] If someone wishes to sell their organs, they should be permitted to do so unless there is clear evidence of a harm.[263] As has been argued:

> If the rich are free to engage in dangerous sports for pleasure, or dangerous jobs for high pay, it is difficult to see why the poor who take the lesser risk of kidney selling for greater rewards—perhaps saving relatives' lives or extricating themselves from poverty and debt—should be thought so misguided as to need saving from themselves.[264]

But to others, there is such widespread instinctive unease at the sale of organs that we should rely on our 'gut instincts' that organ selling should not be permitted unless justified by a very good reason.

So what are the arguments for and against organ selling?

8.2.1 *Arguments against permitting organ selling*

(i) *Gains for the rich* There is a concern that, once a market for organs is created, it will be the wealthy who will be able to purchase organs and the poor who will go without. Organ distribution will be on the basis of wealth, not need. This is a grave concern, although it should be noted that it would be possible, for example, to allow only the NHS to purchase organs and then to distribute the organs on the basis of need.[265] In other words, it would not be impossible to devise a scheme that offered an incentive to donate, without benefiting the better off. However, requiring all organs to be purchased by the NHS may do nothing to discourage the 'black market' in organs.[266] Another response is that the availability of private medicine already, in effect, offers the rich access to quicker and higher quality treatment, although we do not like to admit this truth. If money buys you quicker, and therefore potentially, life-saving cancer treatment, why not organs?

(ii) *Vendors are coerced or do not validly consent to the sale of their organs* Opponents of a market in organs are concerned that those who sell their organs are often driven to do so by poverty or threats from debt collectors.[267] Any person wanting to sell his or her kidney must be driven by such desperation that his or her consent should be regarded as invalid. Supporters of a market in organs tend to make two responses. One is to argue that if the market is made lawful, it can be properly regulated, and we can make sure that only those who are genuinely consenting donate. The other is to question whether being driven by poverty into selling an organ is properly described as coercion. People often agree to do things for money that they would not otherwise do. Many people work because of fear of the poverty that they would face if they did not: are they not acting

---

[262] Stacey Taylor (2005).   [263] Fabre (2006).

[264] Radcliffe-Richards, Daar, Guttmann, et al. (1998: 1951).

[265] Harris and Erin (2002).   [266] On the black market in organs, see Jacob (2012).

[267] Malmqvist (2014).

freely? Wilkinson refers to a survey in which 65 per cent of those questioned said that they would sleep with a complete stranger for £1 million.[268] Would we say that these people were not acting voluntarily or were being coerced into acting against their will? In contract law, when considering whether or not a person has entered a contract freely or under duress, the question on which the courts now focus is the legitimacy of the pressure.[269] This question has no uncontroversial answer, but rather than focusing on how pressurized the individual felt, it focuses the mind on the correct issue.

Sometimes, the argument is put in terms of autonomy: does allowing organ sales infringe an individual's rights of autonomy? At first, this may appear a strange claim: allowing organ sales increases the range of options available to someone. Some philosophers have, however, argued that, sometimes, giving people an extra choice can inhibit autonomy.[270] That would be the case if the choice offered were 'self-defeating', in that the result of the choice would end up restricting a person's lifestyle choices.[271] After all, we often decide to avoid giving ourselves a choice, if we think it is a bad choice. A dieter might only buy healthy foods for their fridge, so that when they feel hungry they do not eat unhealthy foods. They might have deprived themselves of a choice, but not in a way they believe to be harmful. Indeed, the dieter might support the government in banning very unhealthy foods on the same basis. This might apply to organ sales. As Rippon puts it 'people in poverty might well have decisive reasons for preferring not to have the legal options that others seek to foist upon them'.[272]

He also argues that the fact that only the desperate sell their organs, indicates that it is rarely a free choice.[273] This raises the issue of whether a sale of one's organ should be regarded as an act that shows disrespect to one's body, or a way of improving one's financial position while saving lives.[274] Imagine a debt collector turning up at your door and having seized all your possessions and with money still outstanding, points to your stomach and says you still have something to sell. This example might be one where as Rippon suggests it might be better for the person not to have the option and go bankrupt, rather than have the option to sell. This argument, however, might overlook the fact that unless the organ can be matched to a particular individual it is of little use. So, it may be unlikely that random people will be forced to sell.[275]

(iii) *Exploitation* Some are worried about the position of those who are willing to donate for money.[276] It has been estimated that, worldwide, at least 7,000 organs are illegally traded each year.[277] Is there not something very wrong with the world that we are content to allow the most impoverished people in the world to sell their organs in an attempt to combat their financial situation?[278] Is that the kind of society in which we want to live?[279] The better argument is not that the donor has no free choice, but rather that the injustice of his or her socio-economic circumstances causes the donor to sell his or her organs. The unfairness of the donor's position pollutes the agreement.[280]

---

[268] Wilkinson (2003: 118).   [269] Herring (2002: 53).   [270] Rippon (2014a).
[271] Hughes (1998).   [272] Rippon (2014a).
[273] Rippon (2014b). See also Radcliffe-Richards (2014) and Dworkin (2014) for responses.
[274] Boyle (1999).   [275] Semrau (2017).   [276] See Greasley (2014) for a useful discussion.
[277] MacKellar (2014).
[278] Kiplon (2014) provides evidence that people from developing countries suffer through the organ market.
[279] Epstein (2011).   [280] Epstein (2011).

When expressed in its strongest terms, opposition to organ selling sees an analogy between organ selling and slavery.[281] Thomas George writes in these terms:

> The evolution of human civilisation has witnessed several periods of gross exploitation of human beings. Slavery, the extermination of six million Jews, and today the transfer of body parts from one living human being to another, for a financial consideration, are part of a continuum of values which sees some human beings as less valuable than others. It is this value system that those of us who oppose the sale of kidneys, seek to change.[282]

The analogy between slavery, Nazi extermination, and organ selling seems far-fetched, to say the least, but it indicates the strength of this view. Lawlor suggests that it is helpful to distinguish taking unfair advantage of a situation, which is improper, from taking advantage of an unfair situation, which may be permissible.[283] Selling organs falls in the latter, rather than the former, he suggests.

Of course, people who are in desperate need might do all sorts of demeaning things to get money. We allow them to undertake dangerous or unpleasant work. Is organ donation any different? Kate Greasley suggests that it is, because organ donation brings an inevitable harm, rather than simply the risk of harm that dangerous jobs bring.[284]

(iv) *Public opinion* It has been suggested that public opinion is so revolted by the idea of selling organs that the law should match this strong opposition. However, in fact, surveys suggest that the opposition may not be as entrenched as assumed. One survey found that between 40 and 50 per cent of those questioned thought it should be permissible to pay for organs.[285] Whatever the figures are, there is a debate over whether feelings of disgust are sufficient to deny treatment to the dying.

(v) *Commercialization of the body* For some, the concern is over the commercialization of the body. Allowing body parts to be bought or sold reduces our bodies to the status that we accord our cars or televisions.[286] This leads to a devaluation of the body and of human life. The body is seen as simply a collection of parts, to be disposed of at will.[287] Is there not something wrong with a society in which an advert for a kidney appeared on eBay and was removed by the managers of the website when the bidding reached US$5.7 million?[288] Donna Dickenson writes:

> The body both is, and is not, the person. But it should never be only a consumer good, an obscure object of material desire, a capital investment, a transferable resource: merely a thing. Our consciousness, dignity, energy and human essence are all embodied, caught up in our frail bodies. The body is indeed like nothing on earth: not no one's thing, but no thing at all.[289]

To many, this is a convincing argument. To others, the notion of 'commercialization of the body' is a hopelessly vague notion.[290] It is difficult to identify a precise harm that it causes.

---

[281] See Lawlor (2011) for a discussion about the meaning of 'exploitation'.

[282] George (2005: 1).   [283] Lawlor (2014).   [284] Greasley (2013a).

[285] Guttmann and Guttman (1993).

[286] See Bjorkmann (2007) for an argument against selling organs that is based on virtue ethics.

[287] Cherry (1999: 9).   [288] Wilkinson (2003: 107).   [289] Dickenson (2008: 34).

[290] Castro (2003b).

(vi) **Harm to altruism** The current system of organ donation encourages and celebrates altruism. This is a virtue that we should seek to uphold, and there is a danger that, if there is a market in organs, fewer people will donate and will instead sell their organs.[291] Stephen Wilkinson responds that it would be wrong to assume that, because there is payment, there is no altruism.[292] People often buy raffle tickets to support their favourite charity—but they may be motivated both by the desire to give to a worthy cause and by the chance of winning. The latter motivation does not negate the former. Similarly, the fact that the government provides tax benefits for those who donate to charity is not thought to undermine the altruism of such donors.[293]

8.2.2 Arguments in favour of permitting organ selling

(i) **Freedom** A commonly cited argument in favour of organ selling is that it causes no harm and people should be permitted to sell their organs if they so wish. It is part of the right of autonomy.[294] We allow people to sell their hair and to engage in high-risk sports, so why not to donate their organs? We even permit people to receive payment for things that society may regard as immoral or improper, such as pornography.

(ii) **An increase in the number of organs available for transplant** It is claimed that if we permit organ selling, it is likely that there will be a larger number of organs available and so lives will be saved.[295] Some have doubted this, however. It is suggested that those who donated in the past out of altruism will be put off donation now that commerciality has sullied the transplantation scene. Of course, this is a matter of guesswork, but the fact that some people are paid to make music does not mean that amateurs are not happy to do so for free. Indeed, because most organ donations are given to relatives, it is unlikely that a person will be deterred from giving an organ to a relative owing to the payment available. Therefore supporters claim that it is safe to assume that allowing a market will increase the number of organs available.[296]

(iii) **Avoidance of exploitation** It has been suggested that permitting organ selling will avoid exploitation. The present system means that donors who have given a valuable resource receive no payment. The professionals involved in the transplant will all receive payment, while the provider of the organ will not.[297] But Hughes has argued that selling organs presupposes and reinforces dependency relations.[298]

(iv) **Avoidance of the 'black market'** Because organ selling is officially illegal, any market in organs takes place underground in a market that has been described as 'rampant'.[299] There is ample evidence that this occurs.[300] This can easily work against the interests of vulnerable donors, who do not complain about bad treatment or non-payment for fear that they will be prosecuted for an offence. Creating a market in organs should mean that donors are paid a fair price and regulations can ensure that their health needs are protected.[301]

[291] Keown (1997b).   [292] Wilkinson (2003).   [293] Herring (2002: 55).
[294] Stacey Taylor (2005).   [295] Erin and Harris (2003).
[296] Radcliffe-Richards, Daar, Guttmann, et al. (1998).
[297] Larijani, Zahedi, and Ghafouri-Fard (2004: 2540).
[298] Hughes (1998).   [299] Larijani, Zahedi, and Ghafouri-Fard (2004: 2539).
[300] Allain (2011).   [301] Castro (2003b).

478 MEDICAL LAW AND ETHICS

8.2.3 A middle view?

It may be that, although organ sales should not be allowed, we should be generous in ensuring that expenses of donors are covered. Garwood-Gowers suggests that such expenses could include:

- the right to fair compensation for the loss of what the material was reasonably worth to the donor, and for the pain and intrinsic and non-intrinsic determinants that stem from the donation;
- the right to free medical care and regular check-ups in relation to the donating;
- the right to fair compensation for the time involved in donation-related activities;
- the right to defrayment/reimbursement of reasonable costs arising from activities pursuant or incidental to the donation; and
- the right to compensation for discrimination stemming from having donated.[302]

9 Face transplants

Recently, several groups of scientists have been able to engage in face transplants.[303] These are used when someone has suffered a severe facial disfigurement; the face of a deceased person is grafted on in place of their own. To some commentators, such transplants do not raise any special legal or ethical issues over and above those that apply to, say, kidney transplants. Michael Freeman and Pauline Jaoude disagree, however, arguing that:

> As an expressive part of our body, it [the face] represents identity in a way no other part of the body does. It is the most intimate, the most individual characteristic of our body. It is what we recognise as ourselves and what others recognise as us.[304]

They fear that it is not possible to give properly informed consent to a face transplant, given that the impact upon one's identity is so significant and the risks of rejection are largely unknown. Further, there are concerns about the family of the donor, because there will be a person with a close resemblance to their departed loved one. Finally, there are concerns about the effect that face transplants, if they become common, will have on the disfigured community.[305] Dickinson asks: '[I]s our beauty-obsessed society medicalising the "problem" of "abnormal" faces—just as cosmetic surgery has turned small breasts and penises into dreadful deformities?'[306]

While all of these are legitimate concerns, whether or not they are sufficient to outlaw the practice is very debatable.[307] It should be recalled that those seeking a face transplant will already have had their faces disfigured and so the impact on identity will already have taken place.[308] The donees are not necessarily, therefore, like those who use cosmetic surgery to 'improve' their 'natural' appearance. Further, to some, those objecting

---

[302] Garwood-Gowers (1999: 192–3).
[303] The technical terminology is 'facial allograft transplantation'.
[304] Freeman and Jaoude (2007: 76). See also Dickinson (2009: 143).
[305] See also Huxtable and Woodley (2005; 2006).
[306] Dickinson (2009: 142).   [307] Agich and Siemionov (2005).
[308] White and Brassington (2008).

to face transplants on ethical grounds are failing to appreciate the pain of facial dis-figurement.[309] Although it might be argued that the ethical issues play out differently when considering cases where a donation will save someone's life as opposed to a case where it will make their life better.[310]

10 The living body as property

10.1 The law

There has been much academic discussion over whether it can be said that our bodies are our property.[311] In truth, the legal position is ambiguous. Gage J accepted that English law was uncertain and unclear.[312] The safest thing that can be said is that there are some respects in which the body can be treated as property and other respects in which it cannot. There is no coherent picture that can be drawn.

The traditional rule has been that there is no property in the human body. This has been understood to represent the common law,[313] although explicit authority for the proposition is, in fact, limited.[314] There were exceptions to the traditional approach. The law appears rather less reluctant to find that separated body parts or products are property. Hair,[315] blood,[316] and urine[317] have all been found to be property for the pur-poses of the Theft Act 1968. Further, in *R v Kelly*[318] and *Dobson v North Tyneside Health Authority*,[319] the Court of Appeal established that if 'work and skill' had been used on a part of a body (for example to preserve it), then it could become property and be owned.

However, the Court of Appeal, in *Yearworth v North Bristol NHS Trust*,[320] has de-clared that the 'no property' rule is outdated and needs to be re-examined. As yet, what is to replace it is unclear.

KEY CASE   *Yearworth v North Bristol NHS Trust* [2009] EWCA Civ 37

The case involved six men who had been diagnosed with cancer. Before receiving chemotherapy treatment, it was recommended that they provide samples of sperm for storage because the treat-ment was likely to affect their fertility. The sperm was stored at the hospital, but owing to an error was not kept at the correct temperature and was rendered useless. The men suffered psychological harm when informed what had happened. They sued the hospital.

The Court held that, because the sperm was not regarded as part of the men's body, their claim could not be brought as a personal injury claim. The question was therefore whether or not the claim could be brought on the basis that the sperm was their property, meaning that bailment could

---

[309] Agich and Siemionov (2005).   [310] Caplan and Purves (2017).
[311] Hardcastle (2007); Herring and Chau (2007); Dworkin and Kennedy (1993); Matthews (1995).
[312] *AB v Leeds Teaching Hospital NHS Trust* [2004] 3 FCR 324, [135].
[313] *Doodeward v Spence* (1908) 6 CLR 906.
[314] The 'no property' rule was largely *obiter dicta*: Magnusson (1998).
[315] *Director of Public Prosecutions v Smith* [2006] EWHC 94 (Admin); *R v Herbert* (1961) 25 JCL 163.
[316] *R v Rothery* [1976] RTR 478.   [317] *R v Welsh* [1974] RTR 478.
[318] [1998] 3 All ER 714.   [319] [1996] 4 All ER 474.
[320] [2009] EWCA Civ 37. See the useful discussion in Skene (2015); Lee (2014); Rostill (2012), Cordell, Bellivier, Widdows, and Noiville (2011), and Laurie and Harmon (2010).

be used. The Court went over the traditional approach of the law towards ownership in body and body parts. It concluded:

> In this jurisdiction developments in medical science now require a re-analysis of the common law's treatment of and approach to the issue of ownership of parts or products of a living human body, whether for present purposes (viz. an action in negligence) or otherwise.[321]

Although the Court thought that the case could be brought within the 'exercise of work or skill' exception in *Doodeward v Spence*,[322] the approach in that case should be abandoned:

> [W]e are not content to see the common law in this area founded upon the principle in *Doodeward*, which was devised as an exception to a principle, itself of exceptional character, relating to the ownership of a human corpse. Such ancestry does not commend it as a solid foundation. Moreover a distinction between the capacity to own body parts or products which have, and which have not, been subject to the exercise of work or skill is not entirely logical. Why, for example, should the surgeon presented with a part of the body, for example, a finger which has been amputated in a factory accident, with a view to re-attaching it to the injured hand, but who carelessly damages it before starting the necessary medical procedures, be able to escape liability on the footing that the body part had not been subject to the exercise of work or skill which had changed its attributes?[323]

The Court concluded that the sperm was the property of the men for the following reasons:

(i)   By their bodies, they alone generated and ejaculated the sperm.

(ii) The sole object of their ejaculation of the sperm was that, in certain events, it might later be used for their benefit. Their rights to its use have been eroded to a limited extent by the Act but, even in the absence of the Act, the men would be likely to have needed medical assistance in using the sperm: so the interposition of medical judgment between any purported direction on their part that the sperm be used in a certain way and such use would be likely to have arisen in any event. It is true that, by confining all storage of sperm and all use of stored sperm to licence-holders, the Act has effected a compulsory interposition of professional judgment between the wishes of the men and the use of the sperm. So Mr Stallworthy can validly argue that the men cannot 'direct' the use of their sperm. For two reasons, however, the absence of their ability to 'direct' its use does not in our view derogate from their ownership. First, there are numerous statutes which limit a person's ability to use his property—for example a land-owner's ability to build on his land or to evict his tenant at the end of the tenancy or a pharmacist's ability to sell his medicines—without eliminating his ownership of it. Second, by its provisions for consent, the Act assiduously preserves the ability of the men to direct that the sperm be not used in a certain way: their negative control over its use remains absolute.

(iii) Ancillary to the object of later possible use of the sperm is the need for its storage in the interim. In that the Act confines storage to licence-holders, Mr Stallworthy stresses its erosion of the ability of the men to arrange for it to be stored by unlicensed persons or even to store it themselves; he also stresses their inability to direct its storage by licence-holders for longer than the maximum period provided by the Act. But the significance of these inroads into the normal consequences of ownership, driven by public policy, is, again, much diminished by

---

[321] At [33].   [322] (1908) 6 CLR 906.   [323] At [41].

the negative control of the men, reflected in the provisions that the sperm cannot be stored or continue to be stored without their subsisting consent. Thus the Act recognises in the men a fundamental feature of ownership, namely that at any time they can require the destruction of the sperm.

(iv) The analysis of rights relating to use and storage in (ii) and (iii) above must be considered in context, namely that, while the licence-holder has duties which may conflict with the wishes of the men, for example in relation to destruction of the sperm upon expiry of the maximum storage period, no person, whether human or corporate, other than each man has any rights in relation to the sperm which he has produced.

(v) In reaching our conclusion that the men had ownership of the sperm for the purposes of their present claims, we are fortified by the precise correlation between the primary, if circumscribed, rights of the men in relation to the sperm, namely in relation to its future use, and the consequence of the Trust's breach of duty, namely preclusion of its future use.[324]

Although it is clear that the Court of Appeal has rejected the traditional approach that a person cannot claim ownership in parts of his or her body unless the 'work and skill' exception applies, it is far from clear when the Court does think a property claim might arise. It listed a number of factors in the judgment, but we do not know yet which of these must be satisfied if a body or body part is to become property that can be owned.[325]

A broad reading would focus on the factor mentioned by the Court that 'by their bodies, they alone generated and ejaculated the sperm'. That factor might apply to a broad range of bodily products. However, the fact that the Court went on to list further factors may indicate that the mere fact that a person generated the bodily product is not sufficient to give rights of ownership.

A very narrow reading would focus on the weight placed by the courts on the obligations under the Human Fertilisation and Embryology (HFE) Act 1990 to store the sperm, and the rights that the Act gave to the men to control what the hospital did with the sperm. That might suggest that ownership would arise only when there are specific legal obligations on others to care for the products in a particular way.

It is suggested that the best reading may be midway between these two and require proof not only that a person produced the bodily product, but that it was kept for a particular purpose in circumstances in which it is reasonable for the law to impose legal rights and duties.[326]

Simon Douglas and Imogen Goold[327] complain that the court moved too quickly:

Whilst the court answered the question 'can sperm form the subject matter of a property right?' in the affirmative, it did not ask the question which logically follows: 'to whom should such a right be allocated?'

As they note the court simply assumed that if there was to be a property right in the sperm it would be held by the men. They helpfully set out the four questions that a

---

[324] At [61].   [325] See Skene (2012) for further discussion.
[326] See Pawlowski (2009) for further discussion.   [327] Douglas and Goold (2016).

court should consider in determining whether a property claim can be made in relation to human material:

(1) Can the biomaterial form the subject matter of a property right?

(2) Should the biomaterial form the subject matter of a property right?

(3) To whom would the property right be allocated?

(4) Would there be any defences to the property right?

10.2 The body as property: ethical issues

To some, to treat the body as other property—as something that can be traded—is to show disrespect to our bodies. Can it be right to suggest that the relationship we have with our televisions should be the same in the eyes of the law as that which we have with our bodies? To allow the commercialization of bodies is to demean them. One response to this is that it may be demeaning to pay people for body parts, but it may be equally demeaning not to pay them.

One response to these powerful arguments is that, however high-minded, they are out of touch with reality. In the Western world, biotech scientists and their employers make large sums of money through research on bits of bodies. Why should they make all of the gains from the body parts, and not the people from whom the samples originated?[328]

The following case raises some of the issues well.

KEY CASE   *Moore v Regents of the University of California* 793 P 2d 479 (Cal, 1990)

John Moore, suffering from hairy cell leukaemia, had his spleen removed. Dr Golde discovered that cells from his spleen contained potentially beneficial properties. He developed a cell line from the spleen, which he eventually sold for US$15 million. The products produced as a result were said to be worth several billion dollars. His research on the spleen was carried out without Moore's consent or knowledge.

Moore brought an action on a claim based on conversion, breach of fiduciary duty, and informed consent. The Californian Supreme Court rejected the conversion claim, declaring that there was no precedent on which to base a claim that a person had property rights in his or her body and that it would be inappropriate for the law now to recognize one. Indeed, to recognize one now would cause difficulties: it would hinder medical research by restricting access to raw materials and lead to a 'litigation lottery'. The prospect of patients 'shopping around' to find who would offer them the best price for their bodily parts or products was not an attractive one. The Court accepted, however, that Moore might have a claim for breach of fiduciary duty.

Dissenting from the majority opinion, California Supreme Court Justice Mosk argued that the law should at least recognize Moore's:

> ... right to do with his own tissue whatever the defendants [including his doctor and the University] did with it: ie he could have contracted with researchers and pharmaceutical companies to develop and exploit the vast commercial potential of his tissue and its products.[329]

---

[328] Gold (1996: 37).   [329] At 488.

The issue of whether the body should be regarded as property or whether some other legal regulation should be used has generated much debate from a variety of perspectives. Before exploring them, it might be useful to summarize some views that have been expressed on the issue, as follows.

(i) We need to assert that we own our bodies. This provides us with a number of important advantages. It means that individuals have control over parts of their bodies when they are removed. It is, for example, possible for a person to sell, bail, or loan body parts. If a body part is wrongfully taken, then the person (or his or her representative) can seek its return. This also means that if profit is made from a body part without a person's permission, he or she can claim compensation for it.

(ii) To regard the body as property is demeaning to the body.[330] There are some things that are too precious to be owned. The principles that should govern bodies are consent, dignity, and respect.[331] These values are not captured by the property model. We therefore need to focus on rights of autonomy or the right to dignified treatment of bodies, rather than on property rights.[332]

(iii) Although there are no moral difficulties to regarding the body as property, there are technical legal ones. To constitute 'property', an item has to possess certain characteristics and be subject to certain kinds of treatment. Because bodies are not transferable or divisible, we cannot treat them as property. Further, rights of property in law come about in a variety of accepted ways (for example as the fruits of labour). So even though we may feel as if our bodies are owned, they cannot be regarded as property in the way in which the term has been understood by property law.[333]

We need now to look at some of the issues about which debate has arisen.

10.2.1 *The nature of property*

To some, there are technical legal difficulties in declaring that the body is property.[334] This issue is complex and it is not possible here to do justice to the notion of property,[335] but a few basic points can be made. The word 'property' is used to describe not only a thing, but also a relationship between a person and a thing. So a book is a piece of property, but to say that the book is 'my property' is to describe a structure of legal rights and obligations between me and my book. When a person owns a piece of property, this usually denotes a number of rights or entitlements, for example the right to use or enjoy the property, the right to exclude others from using the property, and the right to sell or transfer the property to someone else.[336] 'Full-blooded ownership' involves possession of all of these rights. But a lesser form of ownership may involve only some of these rights. Roger Brownsword has argued that the bundles of rights that are most 'proprietal' are the exclusionary ones: those that prevent others taking our property, however strong a moral claim they may have (for example permitting someone to deny a starving person some of their food).[337] These, he suggests, are very much connected with how we see bodies, in that we firmly reject the notion that other people can make claims over our bodies.

It is important to appreciate the flexibility offered by a property approach. As just mentioned, it is possible to describe something as property, but then restrict the property

[330] Munzer (1994).   [331] Brazier (2003a: 479).   [332] See the discussion in Brownsword (2003c).
[333] Harris (1996: 59).   [334] Harris (1996).   [335] See further Davies and Naffine (2001).
[336] Douglas (2014); Quigley (2007).
[337] Brownsword (2002). See, for further discussion, Douglas (2013) and Wall (2013).

rights that can be exercised. A national park is property, but there are severe limitations on how people can use it. The possibility of using trusts provides further ways of controlling the use of property.[338] So one can agree that the body is property, but then have a very strict regime about when and how those rights can be exercised. One could even say that the body was property, but it could not be sold.

Harris has warned of the dangers of faulty lines of reasoning.[339] Just because the law treats our relationship with our bodies in some ways similarly to ownership does not mean that our bodies are property. So, although our bodies are ours, because we can do what we want with them and stop others from doing things with them, this does not mean we 'own' them. It may reflect only rights to be 'left alone' or rights of bodily integrity, rather than rights of ownership. Further, it would be wrong to think that because no one else owns our bodies, we must; it may be that *no one* 'owns' our bodies.

To some, there is a logical problem in saying that we 'own' ourselves, and that there needs to be a clear separation between 'the owner' and 'the owned'.[340] We can say we own our bodies only if we see a clear distinction between 'us' and 'our bodies'.[341] This kind of reasoning leads some to prefer seeing rights in respect of the body flowing from the right of privacy, under which an interference with the body is an interference with the self and a breach of privacy. Radhika Rao argues:

> Property produces a fragmented relationship between the body and its owner, the person 'inside' the body, in contrast with privacy, which creates an indivisible corporeal identity. By uncoupling the body from the person and undermining the unity of the physical being, the property paradigm facilitates fragmentation of the body itself, both literally and figuratively.
>
> ... Privacy theory, on the other hand, forecloses such bodily fragmentation by identifying the person with his or her physical presence. Hence, privacy shields the individual against corporeal invasion and alteration and preserves the unity and integrity of the embodied being.[342]

I have suggested that the property model will give us too many rights. We do not want control rights or responsibility over the vast majority of our waste products or bodily material that is dropped off.[343] It would be absurd if we could be guilty of littering for dropping a hair and burdensome if we were responsible for our waste products. It is true the doctrine of abandonment, which allows a person to divest themselves of their ownership claim, can deal with some of these problems.[344] However, the extent of that doctrine is unclear and as Douglas and Goold[345] argue the law appears to require strong evidence of an intent to abandon. So, it would be odd to give us property rights over all parts of our body when there are few cases where we would want to exercise them.[346]

10.2.2 *The Moore decision and control of removed bodily products*

The decision in *Moore*[347] has generated much comment in this debate.[348] To some, the case illustrates the problem with not adopting the property approach. Vast sums of money

---

[338] Winickoff and Winickoff (2003).   [339] Harris (1996).

[340] For a rejection of this, see Quigley (2012b).   [341] Naffine (1997); Morgan (2001: ch. 6).

[342] Rao (2000: 364).   [343] Herring (2014d).   [344] See Goold (2014).

[345] Douglas and Goold (2017).   [346] Skene (2014).

[347] *Moore v Regents of the University of California* 793 P 2d 479 (Cal, 1990).

[348] See earlier in the chapter, under the heading '10.2 The body as property: ethical issues'.

were made by the scientists involved, but the person who made 'everything possible' was left with nothing. A property approach would ensure that he was adequately rewarded. The difficulty is that the property approach might result in his being over-rewarded. On the facts of that case, if we were to regard the DNA sequence as his and therefore consider that he had a claim to the money produced from his property, then in theory he should be entitled to *all* of the proceeds. Indeed, there is concern that valuable research into stem cell lines and DNA will be hindered if there is a danger of patients claiming an interest in the products.[349] Indeed, lawyers would have a field day if weeks were to be spent in courtrooms attempting to ascertain whose bodily material was used in the creation of a particular product.

Skene has summarized the issues that need to be balanced here in this way:

> We need legal principles that promote healthcare, teaching medical research and the development of new drugs, but at the same time [we need] to take account of people's sensitivity concerning the removal, retention and use of human bodies, excised body parts and tissue.[350]

She believes that the best balance is achieved in relying on autonomy rights rather than property rights in respect of bodily material.

Jesse Wall has made the important point that we should not assume that control interests must be protected by a property regime.[351] It is perfectly possible to agree that a person can control what happens to his or her body, but then to argue that the law should do so through a legislative scheme or a human rights analysis. However, one reply would be that property has a long history of protecting interests and we could be confident it would protect the claims of the owner. A statutory scheme might easily miss out a layer of protection and/or be over-complicated.[352]

10.2.3 *Privacy and dignity interests*

Some argue that the property approach would fail to protect interests that we have in dignity or privacy.[353] Rao, preferring an autonomy-based approach as the way of protecting the body, argues that property rights are useful for protecting market values, but that privacy rights are appropriate for spiritual ones.[354] Our bodies are not merely property; they are the medium through which we interact with the world. Our relationship with our bodies is not one of 'having', but rather of 'existing'.[355] Our bodies are not like machines, which we can manipulate or discard. It could be added that, looking at the *Yearworth* case,[356] the real wrong done to the men was the impact that the destruction of the sperm could have had on their autonomy: one of their life goals of having a child could have been lost. That seems a better description of the wrong done to them than a property-based one.[357]

Some are not convinced by such arguments. Many items of property carry values beyond the material wealth that they represent. Consider wedding rings, for example. As long as we do not regard property as the only way in which a body is valued, we have

---

[349] DoH (2002e: para. 17.20). See Cohen (2007) for a general discussion of research using stem cells.
[350] Skene (2002: 102–3).   [351] Wall (2011 and 2015).   [352] Nwabueze (2016).
[353] Skene (2002); Mason and Laurie (2006).   [354] Rao (2000).   [355] Toombs (1999).
[356] *Yearworth v North Bristol NHS Trust* [2009] EWCA Civ 37. See earlier in the chapter, under the heading '10.1 The law'.
[357] Cordell, Bellivier, Widdows, and Noiville (2011).

few objections.[358] Indeed, it is possible to regard something as property even if there are restrictions on access to it or restrictions on sale.[359]

Further, relying on privacy rights will arguably be too narrow. Privacy is essentially a negative right and is useful in preventing people from acting in a certain way; property rights give positive rights to act in certain ways. Privacy is effective in protecting the body from physical invasion, whereas property rights provide a freedom to use one's body in whatever way one wishes.

Charles Foster argues that the property approach does not capture the dignity interests that we have in our bodies.[360] The following are two examples that he gives.

1. The human ear ashtray: Medical students steal an ear from the cadaver they are dissecting. They varnish it and use it as an ashtray. The cadaver was donated for the purposes of medical education. Liberal though he was, the donor did not regard use of an ear as an ashtray as one of those purposes.

2. The head of an unknown person: Children play football in the street. They are using, not a football, but the head of an unknown and untraceable person which a dog has retrieved from a mediaeval cemetery.[361]

He argues that seeing these examples in terms of property wrongs does not capture the real wrongs taking place. Foster writes:

> In each of the above examples, the only really satisfactory way of describing the real harm is by using language that looks (for many, embarrassingly) like that of dignity. Ears should not be used as ashtrays, or heads as footballs, because it is contrary to the dignity of humans.[362]

Another aspect of this is that the property approach fails to capture the 'me-ness' in an item.[363] If a part of me is given to a doctor, even with my consent, I might still regard it as having a representational value. It is not like a car that I have sold to someone else; it still has especial significance to me. If you believe in such a claim, you might think that the property approach fails to capture this.

10.2.4 *The balance between social and private interests*

There are certainly situations in which society has important social interests in parts of the body. We have already seen in relation to the Human Tissue Act that parts of bodies may need to be retained for education, research, audit, or post-mortems. Property rights tend to privilege the rights of the individual, rather than society. As Larissa Katz puts it, property doctrines

> carve out a position of authority for owners that is neither derived from nor subordinate to any other's. These and other rules create the institutional structure that permits the owner to function as the supreme agenda setter for the resource.

This has led me to argue that property law is not well designed to protect the communal, relational, and society interests that we have in each other's bodies.[364] Douglas and Goold question this using the example of the ownership of the National Gallery in

---

[358] Gold (1996).   [359] Brownsword (2003c).
[360] Foster (2014).   [361] Foster (2013: 7).   [362] Foster (2013: 7).
[363] The phrase was recommended to me by Jesse Wall.   [364] See also Goodwin (2017).

London of artworks. Its property rights allow it to show artworks for public benefit, without fear they could be stolen without legal recourse. But, that is an exceptional situation; normally, artwork owners are perfectly entitled to withhold access to their artwork from others.

10.2.5 *The interconnection of bodies*

The autonomy and privacy approaches are based on an assumption that our bodies are ours. This has been challenged as overlooking the extent to which our bodies are interconnected and interdependent.[365] There are certainly ways in which our bodies are interconnected. During pregnancy, the bodies of foetus and mother are interdependent. Even during childhood, the bodies of the child and parents can be connected: the child is dependent on the parent to do things, but also the parent's body can be connected with that of the child. In many relationships of dependency, the bodies of carer and dependant will be in a relationship of interconnection. If the body of the carer is impaired, this will impact on the body of the person receiving care. Further, our bodies are connected with the world around us: our bodies take in food, liquid, and air, and these are in due course expelled, usually in a modified form. Indeed, our bodies are constantly changing: by the time we die, there is little of us left that is the same as it was when we were born.[366] This has led some commentators to argue that the buying, selling, and giving of organs should be understood as natural and normal, and a process in which people should be involved and in which we can assume that they wish to be involved.[367] It has also been used to make an argument that a property model is not suitable to represent the interconnected nature of bodily material.[368]

Critics of such a view may respond that the examples of bodily interconnection are rare. We do regard our skin as representing an important barrier between ourselves and others. Organ donation is hardly a natural process, because only with the help of powerful drugs are such donations effective.

10.2.6 *A rejection of a single approach*

Much of the writing on this area is at a general level, asking questions such as whether body parts are property. However, perhaps it is wrong to assume that all body parts should be treated in the same way. Most people's attitude towards their excreta is very different from that towards their heart. Tiny bits of our bodies are falling off all of the time, but we do not really worry about them, whereas we might have deep interests in other bits of our bodies. Similarly, the state interests vary in different body parts. The state or society has little interest in what happens to dandruff, but what happens to hearts that could be used for transplant, or bodies that could decay and cause illness, is another matter.[369] All of this might suggest that we should not be tempted to produce a single approach to deal with all body parts, but rather have legislation that can provide particular rules for different body parts in different contexts. That would be an argument in favour of using legislation to regulate the different areas concerned.

---

[365] Herring and Chau (2013); Herring and Chau (2007); Herring (2002); Lindemann Nelson (2011); Harmon and McMahon (2014).

[366] Leder (1999); Shildrick (1997).   [367] Herring (2002).

[368] Herring (2014d) but see Dickinson (2014) for a communal conception of property.

[369] See *Lakey v Medway NHS Foundation Trust* [2009] EWHC 3574 (QB), in which a husband refused to allow the body of his wife to be properly disposed of.

A SHOCK TO THE SYSTEM

BBC News reported the following story.[370]

John Wood's barbecue smoker was auctioned off in 2007 after he fell behind with payments for a storage facility in North Carolina. It was bought by Shannon Whisnant. Mr Whisnant found Mr Wood's amputated leg in the smoker, where Mr Wood had put it following an amputation several years earlier. Mr Whisnant started up a business, charging adults US$3 and children US$1 to have a look at the leg. The police took the leg to see if it was connected to a crime and they handed it to a funeral home, for Mr Wood to pick up. Mr Whisnant demanded that the leg be returned to him, although Mr Wood said that he wanted his leg back. Mr Whisnant suggested a joint custody arrangement, which Wood rejected.

11 Intellectual property

Should it be possible for an individual to claim intellectual property in bodily material: a patent for a string of DNA perhaps?[371] This is a large topic and it is difficult to appreciate it without a grounding in the law of intellectual property. It will therefore not be covered in this book.[372]

12 Conclusion

This chapter has involved some profound questions. What is our relationship with our bodies? Are they ours to do with as we please, or do we need to protect the 'dignity' of our bodies? As technology develops, and it becomes easier to add, extract, and alter not only organs, but also the genetic basis of our bodies, the questions will only increase in complexity. Many people will feel wonder at the advances that are being made, tinged with fear that we might not know all of the consequences of the issues surrounding the transplantation of organs and ownership of bodies.

QUESTIONS

1. Bob Brecher states:

   However much the Turkish peasant who sold a kidney may have needed the money he was paid; however genuinely he may have wished to exercise his autonomy in this enterprising endeavour … however sincere his wish to benefit his family with the proceeds, and however great their need; nevertheless what he did was wrong.[373]

   Do you think it is as simple as that?

---

[370] BBC News online (2 October 2007).   [371] See Gibson (2009) for a detailed discussion.
[372] See Millum (2008).   [373] Brecher (1994: 1001–2).

2. Why do you think that the HTAct 2004 did not adopt as an inviolable principle that material from humans could never be removed or stored without valid consent?

3. Price thinks:

> It would appear that the legislature ultimately moored the statutory framework in the 2004 [Human Tissue] Act to a rationale principally based upon the infringement of personal integrity ie to the validity of the consent governing removal of the tissue (further uses are implicitly consented to ie they are 'part of the deal' in receiving medical treatment). Arguably however, it is philosophically grounded in property rights and interests, even despite the modifications to the Bill obviating the need for consent, but which in any event only apply to non-identifiable tissue as regards research.[374]

Do you agree?

4. Should someone be allowed to donate their heart to their sick child? We glorify those who give up their lives for the sake of others, so why not allow that in the case of organ donation?

5. Consider this statement:

> Each person is the morally rightful owner of himself. He possesses over himself, as a matter of moral right, all those rights that a slaveholder has over a complete chattel slave as a matter of legal right, and he is entitled, morally speaking, to dispose over himself in the way such a slaveholder is entitled, legally speaking, to dispose over his slave.[375]

Do you agree?

6. It is interesting to note that, even among those who are willing to donate other organs, the rate of cornea donation is low.[376] Why do you think this is? What does this tell us about how people understand different parts of the body? Donna Dickenson writes, of hand transplants, 'for the donor's family it's deeply unsettling to think that the hand which once touched you may now stroke another body'.[377] Would you be unsettled?

7. Spital discusses evidence that, in some hospitals, patients who are reluctant to donate organs are given 'medically acceptable' reasons for not donating (for example that their organs will be unusable) to avoid pressure from family or friends.[378] Is that acceptable?

8. In 2009, a man aged 22 died after being denied a liver transplant.[379] He had started drinking at the age of 13 and had become an alcoholic. Should the fact that he became an alcoholic at such a young age mean that his alcoholism should not have been relevant?[380]

9. Surveys suggest that only 1 per cent of young women are happy with their body shape.[381] Also, 20 per cent of men are distressed by their own body shape.[382] Why do we have such bad relationships with our bodies?

[374] Price (2005a: 817).   [375] Cohen (1986: 109). See Edozien (2013).
[376] Kounougeri-Manoledaki (2000).   [377] Dickenson (2009: 143).
[378] Spital (2008).   [379] BBC News online (20 July 2009).
[380] For the professional guidance in such cases, see UK Liver Transplant Group (2009).
[381] BBC News online (21 February 2001).

FURTHER READING

A comprehensive bibliography, including all references used throughout the book, is available online at www.oup.com/uk/herringmedical7e/.

On xenotransplantation, see:

Fovargue, S. (2007) ' "Oh pick me, pick me": selecting participants for xenotransplant clinical trials', *Medical Law Review* 15: 176.

Fovargue, S. and Ost, S. (2010) 'When should precaution prevail? Interests in (public) health, the risk of harm and xenotransplantation', *Medical Law Review* 18: 302.

Fox, M. and McHale, J. (1998) 'Xenotransplantation: the ethical and legal ramifications', *Medical Law Review* 6: 42.

McLean, S. and Williamson, L. (2005) *Xenotransplantation: Law and Ethics* (Ashgate).

On the legal status of the body, see:

Beyleveld, D. and Brownsword, R. (2001) *Human Dignity in Bioethics and Biolaw* (Oxford University Press).

Brazier, M. (2015) 'The body in time', *Law, Innovation and Technology* 7: 161.

Campbell, A. (2009) *The Body in Bioethics* (Routledge).

Dickenson, D. (2009) *Body Shopping: The Economy Fuelled by Flesh and Blood* (Oneworld).

Douglas, S. and Goold, I (0000) 'Property in human biomaterials: a new methodology', *Cambridge Law Journal* 75: 504.

Fabre, C. (2006) *Whose Body is it Anyway? Justice and the Integrity of the Person* (Oxford University Press).

Farrell, A.-M. (2012) *The Politics of Blood: Ethics, Innovation and the Regulation of Risk* (Cambridge University Press).

Fletcher, R., Fox, M., and McCandless, J. (2008) 'Legal embodiment: analysing the body of healthcare law', *Medical Law Review* 16: 321.

Freeman, M. (1997) 'Taking the body seriously?' in K. Stern and P. Walsh (eds), *Property Rights in the Human Body* (Kings College London).

Gibson, J. (2009) *Intellectual Property, Medicine and Health* (Ashgate).

Goodwin, M. (2017) 'Human Rights, Human Tissue: the Case of Sperm as Property' in R. Brownsword, E. Scotford, and K. Yeung (eds), *The Oxford Handbook of Law, Regulation and Technology* (OUP).

Goold, I., Greasley, K., Herring, J., and Skene, L. (2014) *Persons, Parts and Property* (Hart).

Hardcastle, R. (2007) *Law and the Human Body* (Hart).

---

382 BBC News online (12 September 2008).

Herring, J. and Chau, P.-L. (2007) 'My body, your body, our bodies', *Medical Law Review* 15: 34.

Herring, J. (2016c) 'The law and the symbolic value of the body' in C. van Klink, B. van Beers, and L. Poort (eds), *Symbolic Legislation Theory and Developments in Law* (Springer).

Hoppe, N. (2009) *Bioequity: Property and the Human Body* (Ashgate).

Machado, N. (1998) *Using the Bodies of the Dead* (Ashgate).

McGuinness, S. and Brazier, M. (2008) 'Respecting the living means respecting the dead too', *Oxford Journal of Legal Studies* 28: 297.

Nuffield Council on Bioethics (1995) *Human Tissue: Ethical and Legal Issues* (Nuffield Council).

Nwabueze, R. (2016) 'Proprietary interests in organs in limbo', *Legal Studies* 36: 279.

Price, D. (2007) 'Property, harm and the corpse' in B. Brooks-Gordon, F. Ebtehaj, J. Herring, et al. (eds), *Death Rites and Rights* (Hart).

Wall, J. (2015) *Being and Owning* (Oxford University Press).

On issues surrounding organ donation and sale, see:

Cherry, M. (2005) *Kidney for Sale by Owner* (Georgetown University Press).

Cronin, A. and Douglas, J. (2010) 'Directed and conditional deceased donor organ donations: laws and misconceptions', *Medical Law Review* 18: 275.

Cronin, A. and Harris, J. (2010) 'Authorisation, altruism and compulsion in the organ donation debate', *Journal of Medical Ethics* 36: 627.

Farrell, A.-M., Price, D. and Quigley, M. (eds) (2011) *Organ Shortage: Ethics, Law and Pragmatism* (Cambridge University Press).

Gillett, G. (2013) 'Honouring the donor: in death and in life', *Journal of Medical Ethics* 39: 149.

Glannon, W. (2008b) 'The case against conscription of cadaveric organs for transplantation', *Cambridge Quarterly of Healthcare Ethics* 17: 330.

Goodwin, M. (2007) *Black Markets: The Supply and Demand of Body Parts* (Cambridge University Press).

Lindemann Nelson, J. (2011) 'Internal organs, integral selves, and good communities: opt-out organ procurement policies and the "separateness of persons"', *Theoretical Medicine and Bioethics* 35: 289.

Malmqvist, E. (2014) 'Are Bans on Kidney Sales Unjustifiably Paternalistic?', *Bioethics* 28: 110.

Miller, F. and Troug, R. (2012) *Death, Dying, and Organ Transplantation: Reconstructing Medical Ethics at the End of Life* (Oxford University Press).

Pattinson, S. (2011) 'Directed donation and ownership of human organs', *Legal Studies* 31: 322.

Price, D. (2009) *Human Tissue in Transplantation and Research: A Model Legal and Ethical Donation Framework* (Cambridge University Press).

Stacey Taylor, J. (2005) *Stakes and Kidneys: Why Markets in Human Body Parts are Morally Imperative* (Ashgate).

Saunders, B. (2010) 'Normative consent and opt-out organ donation', *Journal of Medical Ethics* 36: 34.

Wilkinson, T. (2011) *Ethics and the Acquisition of Organs* (Oxford University Press).

On organ retention issues and the Human Tissue Act 2004, see:

Brazier, M. (2002) 'Retained organs: ethics and humanity', *Legal Studies* 22: 550.

Devine, K. (2017) *The Umbilical Cord Blood Controversies in Medical Law* (Routledge).

Harris, J. (2002) 'Law and regulation of retained organs: the ethical issues', *Legal Studies* 22: 527.

Price, D. (2005) 'The Human Tissue Act 2004', *Modern Law Review* 68: 798.

You can register to donate your organs online at www.organdonation.nhs.uk

9 Dying and Death

INTRODUCTION

Our attitudes towards death have changed in recent years. In the past, death was simply something that happened to us and had to be accepted. However, with technological developments, it has become possible to exercise greater control over our dying. Many people now wish for a quiet, peaceful, controlled death. Cryo-freezing and remarkable medical advances have even meant that it is possible to consider immortality as a possibility.[1] It may soon be possible to say that death is not something that happens to you, but something that you do.[2] In October 2015 a company director changed his status on a social media website to announce the date he was due to die with assistance in Switzerland.[3] But the extent to which people should have control of their own or another's death is highly controversial. This chapter focuses on questions such as: is it permissible for a doctor to kill patients at their request? What about supplying drugs, so that patients can kill themselves? Does a person have a right to commit suicide?[4]

Very strong views are held on such questions. The academic debate over the legal and ethical issues is marked by heated exchanges in which both sides feel that the other has misrepresented or failed to understand its arguments. Euthanasia and the related issues are topics with which courts have struggled to deal, and more than once the House of Lords has called upon Parliament to legislate on the area.[5]

At the heart of the debate is the nature of death, although that in turn is, to some extent, a debate about the nature of life. To some, death is the ultimate disaster to be avoided at all costs.[6] We must 'Rage, rage against the dying of the night', as Dylan Thomas put it. By contrast, another commentator has suggested that a good death is one marked by serenity and powerfulness, fortified 'by qualities of composure, calmness, restraint, reserve and emotions or passions subdued and securely controlled without being negated or dissolved'.[7] People's attitudes towards death are often marked by their ethical or religious beliefs.[8] Some therefore regard death as no more than a passage to the start of a joyous afterlife. To others, death is the final chapter of their story, which should reflect the values and principles that they have treasured during their lives.[9]

---

[1] Harris (2004a).

[2] For a discussion of this change in attitude towards death, see Battin (1998) and Brooks-Gordon, Ebtehaj, Herring, et al. (2007).

[3] Khomami (2015).

[4] See Herring (2011a) for a more detailed discussion of the issues raised in this chapter.

[5] *R (Nicklinson) v Ministry of Justice* [2014] UKSC 38; *Airedale NHS Trust v Bland* [1993] 1 All ER 821, 880, 885, and 899; *R (Pretty) v DPP* [2002] 1 All ER 1, [96].

[6] Freud (1911).   [7] Kolnai (1995: 151).

[8] See, e.g., Bedir and Aksoy (2011) writing from an Islamic perspective.

[9] For interesting discussions on what might be regarded as a 'good death', see Dekkers, Sandman, and Webb (2002) and Bradbury (2000).

However, the debate can be unfairly caricatured as 'the liberals' versus 'a small group of conservative Christian zealots'.[10] In fact, both religious and secular writings can be found on either side of the debate.

It has become common in recent times to seek a dignified death, and this wish is behind some of the writing advocating the legalization of euthanasia.[11] The kind of death feared by many people was summarized in the *Debate of the Age*:

> Most people fear death, or perhaps more accurately—most people fear dying. The prospect is often one of dying in hospital, perhaps in great pain, wired up to equipment and enduring uncomfortable interventions, suffering indignities and having little or no privacy, being sedated in such a way that there is little or no awareness of circumstances or surroundings, and, no opportunity to say goodbye.[12]

On the other hand, there are some who complain of the false expectation that we should have a 'dignified death experience'.[13] Death is normally ugly and painful, and we should accept this as a fact of life, so to speak. It has been suggested that the wish to promote euthanasia and physician-assisted suicide (PAS) is a sign of the times, reflecting modern obsessions with living a fast-paced life, avoiding relationships of dependency, disliking mystery and ambiguity, and emphasizing costs and efficiency.[14]

When thinking about death, it is easy to see the issue entirely from the perspective of the person dying. Of course, death usually brings with it unspeakable grief for those 'left behind'. Seale has written of the responsibility that relatives feel for ensuring that the deceased dies well.[15] This can be particularly difficult in a case in which the loss is not publicly recognized as a death. Miscarriage or stillbirths can have a huge impact on the parents, but this loss is often not formally acknowledged.[16]

Before looking further at the issues surrounding the legal regulation relating to the end of life, it is worth noting two observations on the debates that have emerged. First, John Coggon has suggested that the arguments over euthanasia are 'a debate that's being done to death'.[17] As he indicates, it is hard to see the debate progressing: the same arguments are repeated by each side, with little sense of a growing consensus.

Second, it is important to recognize that there are other crucial issues around the issue of dying other than assisted dying. As I have written:

> While we debate the rights and wrongs of assisted dying older people are dying in poverty, freezing temperatures, and desperate hunger. So many are neglected by their communities, abandoned by their families, living isolated, socially excluded lives. For many their last months or, if they unlucky, years, are spent in care homes marked by abuse, neglect and over-medication. Recently it seems barely a month goes by without stories of horrific abuse in our institutional settings for the old. But far more common than physical abuse is a setting of utter boredom, with minimal personal interaction. No love. No tenderness. No hope.

With this background do we dare to discuss the right to die? Are those supporting a right to die not concerned at the misery facing so many of our older people which will

---

[10] Yuill (2012: 3), who goes on to offer a secular opposition to assisted dying.
[11] Biggs (2001).
[12] Age Concern (1999: 18). See further Hardwig (2009), who states that, among those who attend his lectures, most fear that death will come too late for them (!).
[13] Nuland (1993: xvi).   [14] Mann (1998).   [15] Seale (1998).
[16] Biggs (1998).   [17] Coggon (2013b: 402).

lead them to request death? Are those opposing a right to die aware of what we are otherwise leaving older people to face? . . . I am saddened at the amount of time, intellectual energy, and political pressure taken up over it, when the far more important issues of trying to improve the lot of older people; improving the quality of palliative care; combating the prevalent ageist attitudes in society are left aside. These are the issues the books need to be written on; the marches organised for and the Internet petitions. Given the way we treated older people, those with mental health issues and the disabled, those who trumpet either sanctity of life or a right to die should be blushing.[18]

REALITY CHECK

Death

There were 525,048 registered deaths in England and Wales in 2016.[19] Of every 1 million males, 11,284 died in 2016, and of every 1 million females, 8,382 died.

Life expectancy continues to rise. A newborn baby boy today in England can expect to live 79.5 years and a newborn baby girl, 83.1 years.[20] The equivalent figures in 1991 were 73.7 and 79.1. However, life expectancy does depend on where you live. Boys born in Kensington and Chelsea can expect to live until 83.3, while for those born in Blackpool the figure is 74.7.

In one survey of general practitioners (GPs), it was found that 63 per cent of deaths in England involved an 'end-of-life decision' by a medical practitioner.[21] Of these, 32.8 per cent involved a medical professional intervening to alleviate pain or undesirable symptoms, with potentially life-shortening effect, and 30.3 per cent were cases in which potentially life-saving treatment was not given. It has been suggested that about 18,000 patients in Britain are medically assisted to die.[22]

While care must be taken when using such statistics,[23] what they reveal is the extent of 'end of life' decision making engaged in by healthcare professionals.

1 What is death?

1.1 Defining 'death'

Defining 'death' is controversial and problematic.[24] The issue raises fundamental questions about our humanity. What is it to be a person? What are the essential elements of life? There are usually no difficulties in deciding whether a person is dead, even if there is disagreement over when death occurred. However, where a patient is in a state involving an absence of consciousness, but is being artificially sustained, a debate may ensue

---

[18] Herring (2013d: 493).
[19] Office for National Statistics (2017d).   [20] Office for National Statistics (2017e).
[21] Seale (2006).
[22] Price (2009).
[23] It may be, for example, that the percentages of euthanasia were under-reported for fear of criminal investigation.
[24] Chau and Herring (2007), Lizza (2006), and Veatch (2005) discuss the issues.

over whether the person is alive. The issue can become of great practical relevance in the area of organ donation, as we noted in Chapter 8. If the view taken is that organs cannot be removed until the person is dead, it is important to know exactly when death occurs. Postponing the removal of organs until a late stage can mean that they cannot be used for transplantation. The issue is also of practical importance in end-of-life care. If a patient has died then there are no legal or ethical difficulties in stopping treatment. If they are still alive that might be another matter.

1.2 The legal definition of death

It is surprising that the legal definition of death has received very little attention from the courts. In *Bland*,[25] Lords Browne-Wilkinson, Goff, and Keith accepted that brain stem death was the definition of death for the purposes of medicine and law. Tony Bland, although suffering from persistent vegetative state (PVS), was not brain stem dead and so was still alive.[26] This was confirmed in *Re A (A Child)*,[27] although interestingly Hayden J went on to say it did not follow that if the family took a different view from the legal definition, that it would be appropriate to conduct a post mortem on the body. He stated:

> The facts of this case are a reminder once again that in a multi-cultural society there has to be recognition that people, particularly those with strong religious beliefs, may differ with medical professionals as to when death occurs. In the Christian, Muslim and Jewish faiths the concept of the 'breath of life' has ancient and important resonance. It is hardly difficult to understand why the still breathing body is regarded as alive, even though 'breath' may be entirely delivered by machine. An insistence on a legally precise definition of death to trigger the involvement of the Coroner, in such challenging circumstances is, in my judgment, so obviously wrong as to be redundant of any contrary argument.

Perhaps the safest statement to make is that, at present, the legal definition of death is taken to coincide with the medical one. So if the issue is raised, a court is very likely to follow the expert medical opinion. The problem is that there is some disagreement over what the medical definition of 'death' is.

1.3 Alternative definitions of death

Although English and Welsh doctors and lawyers appear to have adopted brain stem death as the definition of death, it is important to appreciate that this is only one definition that could be taken and that it is a controversial one.[28] We shall now look at some of the alternative definitions proposed.

(i) *Brain stem death* As already indicated, brain stem death is widely accepted in the UK as the medical definition of death.[29] It is claimed that a person whose brain stem is

---

[25] *Airedale NHS Trust v Bland* [1993] 1 All ER 821. See Foster (2015b) for a helpful analysis of this case.
[26] Confirmed in *Re A* [1992] 3 *Medical Law Review* 303 and *R (Smeaton on behalf of SPUC) v The Secretary of State for Health* [2002] 2 FCR 193, [57].
[27] [2015] EWHC 443 (Fam).
[28] For an extensive criticism of the concept of brain stem death, see Kirkpatrick, Beasley, and Caplan (2010) and Shewmon (1998).
[29] Pallis and Harley (1996).

dead has ceased to live in anything but a mechanical way.[30] At present, the Department of Health's *A Code of Practice for the Diagnosis of Brain Stem Death* sets out in detail the definition of 'brain stem death'.[31] This outlines three requirements that must be met before a doctor makes a diagnosis of brain death, as follows.

(a) It must be concluded that the coma is not the result of reversible causes, such as drug overdose.

(b) It must be demonstrated that the several components of the brain stem have all been permanently destroyed. Significantly, this includes the respiratory centre.

(c) It must be proved that the patient is unable to breathe spontaneously.

The Code suggests that two medical practitioners registered for more than five years and specialists in the field should agree that there is brain death, before pronouncement.[32]

Supporters of brain stem death tend to rely on two main kinds of argument. The first is that, once the brain ceases to operate, then the body loses its integrated whole. A headless chicken may wander around briefly, but most people would regard it as dead, even if having some appearance of being alive.[33] The second is that, once the brain stem has gone, all that gives life value has been lost.[34] Although there may be some technical biological sense in which a body with no brain stem activity is alive, all of the facilities that give life its meaning and preciousness have gone.[35] Some commentators have argued in favour of total brain death so we can be sure there is a complete loss of capacity for sensation or action.[36]

A fundamental attack on the concept of brain death is that it elevates the brain to being the essential organ of the person.[37] The body is made up of much more than the brain, opponents point out. Glannon argues:

> We are not just our brains but subjects whose ordered and disordered states of mind are the products of continuous interaction between and among the brain, body, and the social and natural world. The brain is not the sole cause of the mind but a relational organ that shapes and is shaped by the mind in mediating interaction between the embodied subject and the world.[38]

To declare the body dead when only part of it (the brain) is not working reveals too narrow an understanding of the body. Joffe argues that even if there is brain stem death, many of the other functions of the body (for example growth, excretion, gestation) can continue.[39] Veatch imagines a time in the future in which it would be possible to give a person a brain transplant.[40] He suggests that if a brain stem test were to be used, this would lead to such a person being classified as dead, even though he or she would patently be alive. It has also been argued that a person can be classified as brain dead

[30] Although Karakatsanis and Tsanakas (2002) argue that it is far from proven that the tests for brain stem death show that there is no consciousness.
[31] DoH (1998).
[32] Fost (1999) complains that there is no definite test for brain death.
[33] Although see Miller and Truog (2010).
[34] Sarvey (2016).   [35] Lee and Grisez (2012).
[36] Lee (2016); Condic (2016); Moschella (2016).   [37] Glannon (2009); Joffe (2010).
[38] Glannon (2009: 329).   [39] Joffe (2010).   [40] Veatch (1999: 41).

even though his or her body is warm and breathing, and that this creates too wide a gap between the legal meaning of 'death' and its understanding by lay people.[41]

(ii) *The end of breathing* At one time, death was defined as the moment at which a patient's heart stopped pumping and breathing ceased. However, medical advances have made this definition of death problematic. It is now clear that the stopping of the heart does not lead to an end of brain activity. The point can also be made that even if respiration has stopped, medical intervention, such as the use of a ventilator or electrical stimulation in the case of a heart attack, can save the patient at the door of death.

One prominent supporter of the loss of cardiac function is the Danish Council of Ethics, which preferred it to brain death.[42] The Council took the view that the definition of death is not a technical question, but must be decided in terms of how the community as a whole understands death. It argued that the person in the street would view the stopping of the beating heart as the criterion for death, because the heart is widely seen as a symbol of life.[43] So, even if the notion of the beating heart as the key to life is not logically or philosophically justifiable, it is intuitively felt to be the essential mark of life.

(iii) *The end of the organism* If the body is seen as a 'working organism' with various functions, then it might be possible to define death as when that organism ceases to achieve those functions.[44] The functions of the body might include ventilation, circulation, nutrition, and elimination of waste products. Only once all of these are no longer being performed should the body be said to have died. To opponents of this view, it treats the body like a piece of machinery; most people regard their bodies as more than an organism that takes in and expels air. Such an approach overlooks what most people regard as most important about their bodies: feelings, thoughts, emotions, and the like.

(iv) *Death of every cell* An extreme view would be to declare that a person has not died until every cell in the body has ceased functioning.[45] This would place the point of death at the state when the body has begun to putrefy. It is unlikely that this would be regarded as an acceptable notion by most people.

(v) *Death as a process* Although most people see death as a moment in time, in medical terms death is better seen as a process. Occasionally, there will be a clear instant of death, for example if a person is blown up in an explosion. But where death is 'natural', there is no easy cut-off point at which we can mark the line between a person who is alive and a person who is dead. As one dying patient put it, 'death keeps taking a little bit of me'.[46]

The difficulty with seeing death as a process is that the law, relatives, and professionals require a clear point at time at which someone has died.[47] Proponents of seeing death as a process could, however, suggest that a person could be treated as dead for different purposes at different times. There could be one point in time in the process at which a person is declared dead for the purpose of removal of organs for transplant, but another at which he or she is dead for the purposes of burial or cremation.[48]

---

[41] Byrne and Rinkowski (1999: 42).
[42] Discussed in Rix (1990), Gillon (1990), and Lamb (1990).
[43] Truog (1997: 29).   [44] Lamb (1985).
[45] It would, for example, be possible to use hypostasis (the moment at which blood stops circulating) as the moment at which death occurs.
[46] Quoted in Kafetz (2002: 536).   [47] Stanley (1987).
[48] DuBois (2002) argues that death should be seen as a state, not a process or event.

(vi) *Desoulment* For those of a religious persuasion, death is often defined as the moment at which the soul leaves the body and moves on to the afterlife.[49] Of course, such a definition will be rejected by those who deny the existence of a soul. Even if the existence of a soul is accepted, there is a problem, in that the moment of desoulment is not apparent to humans. It cannot therefore readily provide a basis of a legal or medical test.[50]

(vii) *Consciousness or social interaction* To some commentators, the definition of death should depend on what we understand it is to be human. Some define this as a consciousness of one's self or others, and an ability to interact with other people. Supporters of such an approach would argue that a person who has permanently lost the ability to communicate or to relate to other people, and/or a person who has permanently lost a conscious awareness of himself or herself or his or her surroundings, has lost what is essential to being a human. Such an approach would lead to a far wider classification of death than used at present. For example, those suffering a PVS would be regarded as dead. Even more dramatically, it would classify as dead (or at least non-people) huge numbers of people with severe mental conditions.

(viii) *Choose your own* Bagheri has suggested that, because there are so many definitions of death and they all depend on one's theological, spiritual, or political beliefs, it is best to let each person decide what he or she would like the definition of death to be.[51] This has some attractions as a proposal, although one would need to have some 'fallback' position on which to rely in cases in which someone had failed to indicate what they wanted their definition of death to be. There would also, presumably, be some definitions of death that would be unacceptable, and so not permitted. Would our society find it acceptable if a person were to decide that he or she would be dead if he or she developed dementia?[52] Probably not. Zeiler suggests that there should be a range of alternative acceptable definitions from among which people can select their preferred option.[53]

(ix) *Avoiding the issue of death* One response to the difficulties over defining death is to suggest that we need to look at the question differently, avoiding the question of when death occurs.[54] We could, for example, ask: at what point is it appropriate to authorize burials of bodies? When can organs be removed from a body for transplant to another?[55] When can a person whose body is being artificially ventilated have the machine switched off? It would be possible to have different answers to these questions.

1.4 Choosing between the definitions

In choosing between these different definitions, it is worth considering the following claim by Lamb: 'It is as wrong to treat the living as dead as it is to treat the dead as alive.'[56] The argument is that it is important not only not to mark the point of death

[49] The 'soul', roughly speaking, is the spiritual essence of a person, which continues after death.
[50] For further discussion, see Tonti-Filipinni (2011).
[51] Bagheri (2007).　　[52] Molina, Rodríguez-Ariasand, and Youngner (2008).
[53] Zeiler (2009).
[54] Chau and Herring (2007). See Moschella (2016) for arguments why death should be seen as a single event.
[55] See McGee and Gardiner (2017).　　[56] Lamb (1994: 1028).

too early, but also not to mark it too late. But not everyone will agree with Lamb's suggestion. Treating a dead person as alive may be a waste of resources, or may delay improperly the grieving process for the family—but is it really as serious as burying a person who is alive?[57]

The different definitions of death tend to group into two categories: those that emphasize life as being about conscious awareness; and those that understand the body as a living organism.[58] The problem is that many people regard both understandings of our bodies and lives as valid.[59] One solution could be to accept that we die twice: once when we lose consciousness; once when our biological organism stops functioning.[60] This would be supported by those who argue that we are not only minds, nor are we only bodies; we are 'embodied minds'.[61]

Another difference between the definitions may be the viewpoint from which death is appreciated: that of the dying person, or that of his or her carers. Arguably, brain stem death will be the point at which the dying person will lose all appreciation of life, but cessation of breathing will be the point at which the person will appear to have died to onlookers. However, it should be noted that the stopping of breathing is the most common cause for the brain stem to cease functioning.[62]

A further key issue is *who* should define death? As already mentioned, so far the English courts have tended to follow the medical definition of death. Although this is approved of by some lawyers,[63] others have argued that the philosophical and moral arguments must also be taken into account, and that therefore the courts should not slavishly follow medical opinion.[64] Shah, Truog, and Miller argue that the law should accept that it needs to use a 'fictional' definition of death (brain stem death) for policy reasons, rather than seek to pretend that it is using a 'real' definition.[65]

Finally, in producing a legal definition of death, it is necessary not only to consider philosophical considerations, but also to recognize that the test must be usable and one that accords with the general public's understanding of death.[66] In other words, it may be that the philosophically most desirable definition of death is not usable because it cannot be transformed into a clear and practical test.[67]

2 The law and the end of life

This section will seek to set out the law on a range of 'end-of-life issues', including euthanasia, assisted suicide, and refusal of medical treatment. To understand the legal position, it is necessary to look at the criminal law on murder, manslaughter, and suicide, and the legal position of patients who are refusing life-saving treatment.[68] A helpful

---

[57] Brugger (2016).
[58] Gervais (1986: 15) distinguishes between those who see death as a biological question and those who see it as a moral one.
[59] Holland (2003: 75).   [60] McMahan (1995).
[61] McMahan (2002: 426). See also Shewmon (1998).
[62] Pallis (1990).   [63] Kennedy (1969).   [64] Skegg (1974).
[65] Shah, Truog, and Miller (2011). They explain that being brain dead means that a person is 'as good as dead' even though not technically dead.
[66] Devettere (1990).   [67] Wicks (2010: ch. 7).
[68] There is also health and safety legislation that may be relevant: *R v Southampton University Hospital NHS Trust* [2006] EWCA Crim 2971.

summary of the law governing the end of life was provided by Lord Sumption in *R (on the application of Nicklinson) v Ministry of Justice*:[69]

(1) In law, the state is not entitled to intervene to prevent a person of full capacity who has arrived at a settled decision to take his own life from doing so. However, such a person does not have a right to call on a third party to help him to end his life.

(2) A person who is legally and mentally competent is entitled to refuse food and water, and to reject any invasive manipulation of his body or other form of treatment, including artificial feeding, even though without it he will die. If he refuses, medical practitioners must comply with his wishes . . . A patient (or prospective patient) may express his wishes on these points by an advance decision (or 'living will').

(3) A doctor may not advise a patient how to kill himself. But a doctor may give objective advice about the clinical options (such as sedation and other palliative care) which would be available if a patient were to reach a settled decision to kill himself. The doctor is in no danger of incurring criminal liability merely because he agrees in advance to palliate the pain and discomfort involved should the need for it arise. This kind of advice is no more or less than his duty. The law does not countenance assisted suicide, but it does not require medical practitioners to keep a patient in ignorance of the truth lest the truth should encourage him to kill himself. The right to give and receive information is guaranteed by article 10 of the Convention. If the law were not as I have summarised it, I have difficulty in seeing how it could comply.

(4) Medical treatment intended to palliate pain and discomfort is not unlawful only because it has the incidental consequence, however foreseeable, of shortening the patient's life . . .

(5) Whatever may be said about the clarity or lack of it in the Director [of Public Prosecution]'s published policy, the fact is that prosecutions for encouraging or assisting suicide are rare . . .

The complexity of the law governing this area is revealed by the fact that even this outline will not be accepted by everyone. In particular the first point seems to overlook the point, explored later in this chapter that the state can be under a duty to stop a person committing suicide in certain circumstances.

The details of the law will now be explored.

2.1 Murder

To be guilty of murder, the jury must be persuaded beyond reasonable doubt that:

(i)   the defendant caused the death of the patient;
(ii) the defendant intended to cause death or grievous bodily harm; and
(iii) the defendant cannot successfully raise a defence.

More needs to be said in medical 'end of life' cases about each of these requirements.

[69] [2014] UKSC 38 at [225].

2.1.1 *The defendant caused the death of the victim*

In considering whether the defendant caused the death of the victim, it is necessary to distinguish cases in which it is alleged that it was the act of the defendant that caused the death (for example where the doctor has given a patient a lethal injection) and those in which it is claimed that it was an omission that caused the death (such as if the carer of a terminally ill patient fails to resuscitate him or her when he or she slips into unconsciousness).

(i) *Acts of the defendant causing death* In a murder case, it is necessary to show that the defendant's act was a substantial and operating cause of the death.[70] This means that the doctor's act does not need to be the sole cause of death, but that it must be a substantial cause of death.[71] In other words, if an autopsy were to establish that a patient died from a combination of a disease and the injection of drugs by a doctor, it could still be said that the doctor's act caused the death. This is subject to two caveats. The first is that if the administration of the drug shortened the victim's life by a only few seconds, this may not constitute a substantial cause of death. However, as Devlin J put it in the trial of Dr Adams: 'If the acts done are intended to kill and do, in fact kill, it does not matter if a life is cut short by weeks or months, it is just as much murder as if it were cut short by years.'[72] The second caveat is that the courts are reluctant to find 'normal' medical treatment to have broken the chain of causation.[73] Certainly, where a defendant has stabbed a victim, who has received medical treatment and died, the courts are likely to be convinced that the stabbing did not cause the victim's death only where the medical treatment was 'palpably wrong'.[74]

(ii) *Omissions of the doctor causing death* If the claim is that it was a doctor's failure to treat a patient that caused the patient's death, the situation is a little more complicated. Generally, in the criminal law, a defendant is not criminally responsible for an omission. Many criminal lawyers point out that a defendant who walks past a stranger drowning in a pond without offering help will not be criminally responsible for the stranger's death. However, there are occasions on which those who fail to act may face a criminal prosecution. These are situations in which the defendant owes a duty to the victim, the defendant fails to act in accordance with that duty, and had the defendant acted in accordance with the duty, the victim would not have died when he or she did.[75] However, in *R (Jenkins) v HM Coroner for Portsmouth*,[76] it was emphasized that there was no crime committed if help was not offered to someone who was dying, when he had made it clear that he did not want medical help.[77] It would have been different had he lacked capacity when refusing assistance.

There is normally no difficulty in establishing that a healthcare professional owes his or her patient a duty of care.[78] However, less straightforward is the question of whether

---

[70] *R v Norris* [2009] EWCA Crim 2697.

[71] *R v Cheshire* [1991] 3 All ER 670; *R v Mellor* [1996] 2 Cr App R 245.

[72] Discussed in Palmer (1957).

[73] Tur (2002) argues that normal medical treatment does not break the chain in causation and so a doctor following sound medical opinion cannot be said to cause a patient's death.

[74] *R v Cheshire* [1991] 3 All ER 670.   [75] *R v Stone and Dobinson* [1977] QB 354.

[76] [2009] EWHC 3229 (Admin).

[77] See Herring (2010a) for further discussion of the issues raised.

[78] See Chapter 3.

the doctor is acting in accordance with his or her duty in not providing treatment to a dying patient. Normally, a doctor will be breaching his or her duty in not providing appropriate medical treatment to a dying patient. However, this is not always so. In the following three situations, a doctor will not breach his or her duty by failing to provide treatment to a patient.

(a) If a competent patient does not consent to the treatment, a medical professional need not provide it. Indeed, it is unlawful for him or her to do so.

(b) A doctor is not required to provide treatment if the treatment is not in the patient's best interests.[79] Of course, only exceptionally will it not be in a patient's interests to receive life-saving treatment.[80] In *Airedale NHS Trust v Bland*,[81] Lord Browne-Wilkinson stated:

> [I]f there comes a stage where the responsible doctor comes to the reasonable con-clusion (which accords with the views of a responsible body of medical opinion) that further continuance of an intrusive life support system is not in the best interests of the patient, he can no longer lawfully continue that life support system: to do so would constitute the crime of battery and the tort of trespass to the person.

(c) Where a doctor has to allocate scarce resources between patients and reasonably decides not to offer some patients the resource, there will be no breach. The most obvious example of this would be where several patients urgently need a kidney transplant, but only one kidney is available. In cases involving omissions, it can be very difficult to tell, in the case of a very sick patient, whether he or she died as the result of an inappropriate lack of care or from the medical condition.

2.1.2 *The doctor intended death or grievous bodily harm*

Generally, in criminal law, there are two ways in which a person can be said to 'intend' a result, as follows.

(i) *Direct intent* A person intends a result if it is his or her purpose to produce the result.

(ii) *Indirect or oblique intent* The test developed in the House of Lords' decision in *R v Woollin*[82] is used. The jury is entitled to find that a defendant intended a result if:

(a) the result was virtually certain to result from the defendant's act; and

(b) the defendant realized this.

A doctor who gives a patient a drug in order to kill him or her will intend to kill the patient (direct intent). This is so even if the doctor was motivated by what some people would regard as the 'good' reason of wishing to end the patient's pain. The criminal law, in deciding intention, is interested in the purpose of the defendant, not his or her reasons for that purpose.[83]

If a doctor were to give pain-relieving drugs to a patient with the purpose of reliev-ing pain, but was aware that the drugs would shorten the victim's life, then, applying

---

[79] *A NHS Trust v X* [2014] EWCOP 35.   [80] *R (Burke) v GMC* [2005] 3 FCR 169.
[81] [1993] 1 All ER 821, 882.   [82] [1999] 1 AC 82.
[83] Confirmed in *R (Nicklinson) v Ministry of Justice* [2013] EWCA Civ 961, [26].

the general criminal law, the jury would be entitled to find—but would not have to find[84]—that there was intent. One might predict that few juries would choose to find intent in such a case. It seems, from the reported cases of doctors charged with murder or attempted murder following the administration of pain-relieving drugs, that judges avoid giving the direction on oblique intention that is normally given in criminal law. Instead, juries are told that if the doctor did not intend death, then he or she cannot be guilty of murder.[85]

2.1.3 Defences

To a charge of murder, a defendant may seek to raise a variety of defences, including self-defence and necessity. The defences that are most likely to arise in the context of assisted dying are diminished responsibility[86] or loss of control. These are most likely to be relied upon in a case in which someone who has been caring for a terminally ill relative is suffering from the exhaustion and stress to which caring for someone twenty-four hours a day can lead.[87] It should be noticed that these are only partial defences, and so, if successful, the defendant is still guilty of manslaughter. Significantly, this means that the defendant does not have to receive the mandatory life imprisonment that accompanies a murder conviction.[88]

If the defendant killed the victim intending to go on and kill him or herself as part of a suicide pact, then he or she will have a defence to a charge of murder, but still be guilty of manslaughter.[89] The onus of proof on establishing that the killing was in the course of a suicide pact is on the defendant.

At one time there was speculation that a person who killed someone who wanted to die might be able to rely on the defence of necessity. This defence is only available in very exceptional cases. An exceptional case was *Re A (Conjoined Twins)*,[90] in which it was held that necessity provided a defence to a doctor who killed one conjoined twin in order to save the other. However, in *R (Nicklinson) v Ministry of Justice*,[91] the Court of Appeal refused to apply the necessity defence in the assisted dying context.

Some have argued that a relative who kills a terminally ill person for whom that relative has been caring should be able to rely on a defence of mercy killing, but the law does not recognize such a defence.[92] In *Inglis*,[93] even though a murder conviction was upheld, the Court of Appeal set the minimum sentence at the unusually low level of five years, indicating its sympathy for the plight of the defendant, who had killed her disabled son,

---

[84] *R v Matthews and Alleyne* [2003] 2 Cr App R 30.

[85] Lord Neuberger in *R (on the application of Nicklinson) v Ministry of Justice* [2014] UKSC 38 at [18].

[86] Homicide Act 1957, s. 2.

[87] Dell (1984). See Innes (2002), discussing the case of a 74-year-old husband who killed his wife, who was suffering from motor neurone disease. The judge gave a three-year community rehabilitation order after a conviction of manslaughter on the grounds of diminished responsibility.

[88] See BBC News online (10 October 2008) for a report of an 86-year-old husband who killed his ill wife being given a suspended sentence.

[89] Homicide Act 1957, s. 4.   [90] [2001] Fam 147.

[91] [2013] EWCA Civ 961. A decision by implication approved by the Supreme Court.

[92] *R v Inglis* [2010] EWCA Crim 2637. Huxtable (2007: 172) argues that mercy killing should be a partial defence to murder.

[93] *R v Inglis* [2010] EWCA Crim 2637.

while recognizing that she had committed a serious crime.[94] Lord Neuberger in *R (on the application of Nicklinson) v Ministry of Justice*[95] explained:

> Mercy killing is a term which means killing another person for motives which appear, at least to the perpetrator, to be well-intentioned, namely for the benefit of that person, very often at that person's request. Nonetheless, mercy killing involves the perpetrator intentionally killing another person, and therefore, even where that person wished to die, or the killing was purely out of compassion and love, the current state of the law is that the killing will amount to murder or (if one or more of the mitigating circumstances are present) manslaughter.

2.2 Manslaughter

To be guilty of gross negligence manslaughter, it must be shown that:

(i)   the defendant owed the victim a duty of care;

(ii) the defendant breached the duty of care;

(iii) the breach caused the death of the victim; and

(iv) the breach was so gross as to justify a criminal conviction.[96]

A conviction for gross negligence manslaughter would arise if a healthcare professional or carer were to act, or fail to act, in an extremely negligent way, to the extent that the jury were convinced that a criminal conviction was appropriate.[97] A conviction would only be appropriate if there was an obvious risk of death as a result of what the defendant was doing or not doing.[98] A person who was providing treatment or not providing treatment for a person in a way regarded as appropriate by a respectable body of opinion would not be acting negligently, and so would not be guilty of this offence.[99] It will be noted that there is no need to show an intention to cause injury to the victim.

2.3 Suicide

REALITY CHECK

The official statistics

In Great Britain, there were 5,668 registered suicides in the year 2016; at least one person dies from suicide every two hours.[100] In 2016, for every 100,000 people, 10.1 would have committed suicide. However, much depends on age and gender. For men aged 40–44 there were 23.7 suicides per 100,000 people. Around three-quarters of all suicides are by men. The death toll from suicide is double the death toll from road traffic accidents. Suicide is the leading cause of death in adults under the age of 50.

---

[94] For powerful calls to create a defence of compassionate killing, see Keating and Bridgeman (2012) and Huxtable (2013c). See Biggs (2007c) for a discussion of the criminalization of carers in this context.
[95] [2014] UKSC 38 at [17].   [96] *R v Adomako* [1995] 1 AC 171.
[97] *R v Sellu* [2016] EWCA Crim 1716 suggesting the behaviour would need to be 'truly exceptionally bad' to justify a conviction for gross negligence manslaughter.
[98] *R v Rudling* [2016] EWCA Crim 741.
[99] Using the test set out in *Bolam v Friern HMC* [1957] 1 WLR 582.
[100] Office for National Statistics (2017f).

> **The unofficial statistics**
>
> The figures just quoted are the official statistics. It has been estimated that the true suicide rate is 50–60 per cent higher than the official figure, although naturally it is difficult to get an accurate figure. Coroners are reluctant to record a verdict of suicide unless it is clear that that is what happened. Brock and Griffiths found that, in 2001, open verdicts accounted for 28 per cent and 38 per cent of suicides for men and women, respectively.[101] The official statistics do not include people under the age of 15. It has been estimated that there are around 140,000 suicide attempts each year in the UK. One in five people who attempt suicide will try again, of whom 10 per cent will succeed. More than 5.7 million people called the Samaritans in 2016.[102] Of adults, 20.6 per cent report that they had thought of taking their own life at some point in their lives.[103] It has been estimated that one in fifteen people will attempt suicide at one point in their life.[104]

The law's response to suicide is complex. At one time, suicide was a crime and, bizarrely, attempted suicide potentially carried a sentence of capital punishment![105] The present law, as set out in the Suicide Act 1961, is that suicide and attempted suicide are not crimes.[106] The reasoning behind the decriminalization of suicide was explained by Lord Sumption in *R (on the application of Nicklinson) v Ministry of Justice*:[107]

> The reason for decriminalising suicide was not that suicide had become morally acceptable. It was that imposing criminal sanctions was inhumane and ineffective. It was inhumane because the old law could be enforced only against those who had tried to kill themselves but failed. The idea of taking these desperate and unhappy individuals from their hospital beds and punishing them for the attempt was as morally repugnant as the act of suicide itself. It was ineffective because assuming that they truly intended to die, criminal sanctions were incapable by definition of deterring them.

So it is wrong to suggest the decriminalization of suicide recognized a right to kill oneself.[108] It was about ensuring suicidal people got the support they needed.

However, the 1961 Act does make it an offence if someone intentionally 'does an act capable of encouraging or assisting the suicide or attempted suicide of another person'.[109] So although a patient who took an overdose of tablets in a bid to kill himself or herself would not have committed an offence, the physician who gave the patient the tablets might have done so. To understand further the offence of encouraging or assisting suicide, a number of issues need to be considered.

---

[101] Brock and Griffiths (2003).
[102] Samaritans (2017), although not all of those were suicidal.
[103] Mental Health Foundation (2017).   [104] Mental Health Foundation (2017).
[105] Williams (1957: 274). This was because suicide was seen as murder of the self: *R (Purdy) v DPP* [2009] UKHL 45, [5].
[106] Suicide Act 1961, s. 1; although there have been reports of a woman who repeatedly attempted suicide being given an antisocial behaviour order (ASBO): MacDonald (2006).
[107] [2014] UKSC 38 at [212].
[108] For a discussion of the ethical issues see Vong (2008).
[109] The wording of the 1961 Act was amended by the Coroners and Justice Act 2009.

2.3.1 *What is suicide?*

The general view seems to be that suicide involves someone intentionally killing them-selves.[110] There are two main areas of controversy surrounding the legal definition of 'suicide'. The first is whether it includes omissions: if a person refuses life-saving treat-ment because he or she wants to die, is this suicide?[111]

The second is whether a person who acts knowing that death will result, but who is not acting for the purpose of dying, is committing suicide. The courts are yet to express a clear view on this. Lord Justice Thorpe, in *Secretary of State for the Home Department v Robb*,[112] argued that a prisoner who went on hunger strike and died as a result did not commit suicide. Thorpe LJ did not explain why. It may be because the hunger striker did not intend to die; rather, he wanted his complaints to be dealt with. Or it may be because Thorpe LJ thought that suicide required a positive act. Cholbi has suggested that we create a category of 'self-manslaughter' to cover those who take a risk of killing themselves, but do not intend to do so.[113] Den Hartogh[114] argues it is helpful to distinguish rational suicides (where a person has a rational reason; for exam-ple, they are suffering great pain) and non-rational suicides where there is no rational reason. That distinction is controversial because the definition of pain and rationality are both complex.

2.3.2 *What is 'encouraging' or 'assisting' suicide?*

For a detailed discussion of these terms, you should consult a book on criminal law.

An example of assisting suicide would be providing equipment or advice that would help someone to commit suicide. Encouraging suicide involves urging or supporting another to commit suicide. The offence is committed if a person encourages someone to commit suicide, whether or not they actually do so. To be guilty of the offence, the de-fendant must intend to encourage another to commit, or to attempt to commit, suicide. So the writer of a novel who describes a suicide in a way that helps someone to commit suicide will not be guilty of the offence because (presumably) the writer did not intend to assist or encourage a suicide.

2.3.3 *When will 'aiding and encouraging' suicide be prosecuted?*

In recent years, it has become clear that not every case of assisted suicide is prosecuted by the Crown Prosecution Service (CPS). Following the decision of the House of Lords in *R (Purdy) v DPP*,[115] and *R (Nicklinson) v Ministry of Justice*[116] to be discussed shortly, the CPS was required to produce and then amend a list of factors that will be taken into account when deciding when to prosecute in a case of assisted suicide. It produced the

---

[110] Donnelly (1998) argues that, in fact, the definition of suicide is a highly complex matter.
[111] Lanham (1990) discusses this in detail. Otlowski (1997: 64) thinks that it is possible to commit suicide by omission.
[112] [1995] Fam 127.   [113] Cholbi (2007). See also Williams (2007: ch. 5).
[114] den Hartog (2015).
[115] [2009] UKHL 45. See Greasley (2015) for a helpful analysis.
[116] [2014] UKSC 3438.

following, which provides arguments that would weigh in favour of prosecution and arguments that would weight against:

Public interest factors in favour of prosecution

A prosecution is more likely to be required if:

(1) the victim was under 18 years of age;

(2) the victim did not have the capacity (as defined by the Mental Capacity Act 2005) to reach an informed decision to commit suicide;

(3) the victim had not reached a voluntary, clear, settled and informed decision to commit suicide;

(4) the victim had not clearly and unequivocally communicated his or her decision to commit suicide to the suspect;

(5) the victim did not seek the encouragement or assistance of the suspect personally or on his or her own initiative;

(6) the suspect was not wholly motivated by compassion; for example, the suspect was motivated by the prospect that he or she or a person closely connected to him or her stood to gain in some way from the death of the victim;[117]

(7) the suspect pressured the victim to commit suicide;

(8) the suspect did not take reasonable steps to ensure that any other person had not pressured the victim to commit suicide;

(9) the suspect had a history of violence or abuse against the victim;

(10) the victim was physically able to undertake the act that constituted the assistance him or herself;

(11) the suspect was unknown to the victim and encouraged or assisted the victim to commit or attempt to commit suicide by providing specific information via, for example, a website or publication;

(12) the suspect gave encouragement or assistance to more than one victim who were not known to each other;

(13) the suspect was paid by the victim or those close to the victim for his or her encouragement or assistance;

(14) the suspect was acting in his or her capacity as a medical doctor, nurse, other healthcare professional, a professional carer [whether for payment or not], or as a person in authority, such as a prison officer, and the victim was in his or her care;

(15) the suspect was aware that the victim intended to commit suicide in a public place where it was reasonable to think that members of the public may be present;

---

[117] The Guidance states: 'On the question of whether a person stood to gain (paragraph 43(6) see above), the police and the reviewing prosecutor should adopt a common sense approach. It is possible that the suspect may gain some benefit—financial or otherwise—from the resultant suicide of the victim after his or her act of encouragement or assistance. The critical element is the motive behind the suspect's act. If it is shown that compassion was the only driving force behind his or her actions, the fact that the suspect may have gained some benefit will not usually be treated as a factor tending in favour of prosecution. However, each case must be considered on its own merits and on its own facts.'

(16) the suspect was acting in his or her capacity as a person involved in the management or as an employee (whether for payment or not) of an organisation or group, a purpose of which is to provide a physical environment (whether for payment or not) in which to allow another to commit suicide.

Public interest factors against prosecution

A prosecution is less likely to be required if:

(1) the victim had reached a voluntary, clear, settled and informed decision to commit suicide;

(2) the suspect was wholly motivated by compassion;

(3) the actions of the suspect, although sufficient to come within the definition of the offence, were of only minor encouragement or assistance;

(4) the suspect had sought to dissuade the victim from taking the course of action which resulted in his or her suicide;

(5) the actions of the suspect may be characterised as reluctant encouragement or assistance in the face of a determined wish on the part of the victim to commit suicide;

(6) the suspect reported the victim's suicide to the police and fully assisted them in their enquiries into the circumstances of the suicide or the attempt and his or her part in providing encouragement or assistance.[118]

The CPS made it clear that, in issuing these guidelines, it was not changing the law:

This policy does not in any way 'decriminalise' the offence of encouraging or assisting suicide. Nothing in this policy can be taken to amount to an assurance that a person will be immune from prosecution if he or she does an act that encourages or assists the suicide or the attempted suicide of another person.[119]

The Suicide Act 1961, section 2(4), in stating that the consent of the DPP was required before bringing a prosecution for assisted suicide, had made it clear that it was not necessarily correct to prosecute in every case. This guidance was to assist prosecutors in determining whether a prosecution was appropriate. The CPS emphasized that the list of factors provided had to be used with care:

Assessing the public interest is not simply a matter of adding up the number of factors on each side and seeing which side has the greater number. Each case must be considered on its own facts and on its own merits. Prosecutors must decide the importance of each public interest factor in the circumstances of each case and go on to make an overall assessment. It is quite possible that one factor alone may outweigh a number of other factors which tend in the opposite direction. Although there may be public interest factors tending against prosecution in a particular case, prosecutors should consider whether nonetheless a prosecution should go ahead and for those factors to be put to the court for consideration when sentence is passed.[120]

---

[118] CPS (2015). In *R(AM) v GMC* [2015] EWHC 2096 (Admin) the latest guidance was upheld as compatible with human rights.
[119] CPS (2015: para. 6).   [120] CPS (2015: para. 39).

The decision in *Purdy* and the subsequent guidance has produced some criticism.[121] John Spencer, while supporting a liberalizing of the law, is concerned about the constitutional principles:

> Is it really compatible with the rule of law that, when an Act of Parliament makes a certain form of behaviour a criminal offence, the DPP should in effect decriminalise it, in whole or in part, by saying when it will and will not be prosecuted? The orthodox answer . . . is 'no': once Parliament has created an offence, only Parliament has the authority to redraw its boundaries so that it catches fewer people in its net. For any other organ of the State to attempt to do so is to infringe the first rule of the constitution, which is the supremacy of Parliament.[122]

Responses to the guidelines have been mixed. For the 'anti-euthanasia' lobby, the guidelines are 'dangerous' and open the door, in effect, to legalizing assisted suicide.[123] Penney Lewis is concerned that the guidance, in focusing on what the defendant did, rather than the position of the victim, has fallen between two stools.[124] It fails to protect the vulnerable, while not guaranteeing non-prosecution in appropriate cases:

> The dangers sought to be addressed by the policy focus on the unscrupulous or even abusive family member or friend, and the healthcare professional or activist. The shift of focus away from the victim, and the desire to avoid the appearance of the creation of a regulatory regime, have opened the door to assisted suicide in cases which would not be permitted by most of the existing regulatory regimes, while exposing to the risk of prosecution those with much-needed expertise and those who agree with the victim's decision.[125]

Kate Greasley is concerned that the guidance offers a formal sanctioning of assisted suicide.[126] She prefers the position in law prior to *Purdy*, under which often assisters were not prosecuted, even though officially they were guilty of an offence. Greasley gives two reasons for disliking the formal approach of the guidance:

> Firstly, it carries with it the unwelcome and inescapable symbolism of identifying kinds of life which may not be worth living. Second, it is a significant step towards the cultivation of a social environment in which controlled death is an accessible and normalized option, and in which both internal and external pressure to end one's life may consequently mount. Moreover, there is a clear reciprocal relationship between the first and second concerns. The symbolic statements made through permitting assisted death in certain circumstances may lead to a change in how severely disabled people and those around them view their condition and their options, in turn generating even greater potential for the social pressurization and manipulation of the vulnerable. It is my contention that what we have here is a strong argument for a legal policy of wilful blindness towards assisted suicide-tourism.[127]

In relation to the last point, the policy, in effect, means that relatives can take a seriously ill person to Switzerland, where they can be helped to die. On that Charles Foster has

[121] For example, Finnis (2009).   [122] Spencer (2009: 495). See also O'Sullivan (2015).
[123] Christian Concern (2011).   [124] Lewis (2011).   [125] Lewis (2011: 120).
[126] Greasley (2010).   [127] Greasley (2010: 311).

referred to the acknowledgement 'that there is something intellectually, if not morally, uncomfortable, about getting another country to do your dirty work'.[128]

Supporters of the guidelines argue that they provide a reasonable balance between the competing views. Given the wide range of circumstances in which assisted suicide can take place, it is not possible to provide absolute clarity.

When considering the guidelines, it is important to remember their context. They are setting out when a defendant should be subject to criminal sanctions. That is a slightly different question from considering when assisted suicide is morally appropriate or should be supported by the state. This may explain why, as Lewis notes, the focus of the guidance is on the defendant, rather than the wishes of the victim.[129] It also may explain why, in the guidance, emphasis is put on whether the defendant was motivated by compassion.[130]

2.3.4 *Is there a right to commit suicide?*

There has been some debate over whether there is a right to commit suicide. It is true that the Suicide Act 1961 means that suicide is no longer a crime, but that does not mean that there is a right to do it, as Lord Neuberger in *R (on the application of Nicklinson) v Ministry of Justice*[131] emphasized.

In *R (Purdy) v DPP*,[132] it was held that a decision to commit suicide can fall within the ambit of Article 8 ECHR, which protects the right to respect for private and family life. However, there are two important limitations to add. First, Article 8(2) permits an interference with Article 8 rights. Indeed, their Lordships in *Purdy* were in no doubt that there could be circumstances in which it was necessary to interfere in a person's decision to commit suicide.

Second, it is not clear from their Lordships' judgments whether they were saying that all decisions to commit suicide are protected under Article 8, or only some. Because Article 8 protects 'autonomous choices', it seems unlikely that a decision by a person who lacks capacity is protected by Article 8. That will be so in quite a number of suicide attempts.

In *Rabone v Penine Care Foundation Trust*,[133] Baroness Hale in her speech referred to the 'right to be prevented from taking [one's] own life', which was protected by Article 2, protecting the right to life. Flowing from that right in some cases there is a duty on the state to protect people from committing suicide under the right to life under Article 2. It was held that when someone is in the care of a public authority (for example as a patient in a hospital), the public authority has a duty to take reasonable steps to prevent them from committing suicide. In that case, a young woman was negligently allowed to leave a psychiatric hospital and then committed suicide.[134]

It is difficult to know quite how these different rights balance out. It seems that under Article 8, a person who is terminally ill, and who has made a free and informed choice to commit suicide, has a right to do so. However, that right may be interfered with if the interference is justified under Article 8(2). There is also a right to be protected from

[128] Foster (2015). [129] Lewis (2011). [130] Mullock (2011).
[131] [2014] UKSC 38 at [17]. [132] [2009] UKHL 45. [133] [2012] UKSC 2.
[134] A straightforward negligence claim could be sought if a suicidal person seeks medical help and is given negligent treatment and as a result attempts suicide, although a claim by a spouse who came across the aftermath of the suicide attempt failed in *Morgan v Somerset Partnership NHSFT* A61YP222.

suicide under Article 2, although its scope is unclear. It may be that if someone has made an undoubtedly autonomous decision to kill themselves it would be unlawful for anyone to intervene.[135] However, if a person is in state care or their capacity is lacking or unclear then there is a duty to protect them from suicide.[136]

SHOCK TO THE SYSTEM

In a series of decisions culminating in *Re X (A Child)*[137] Munby J issued a series of judgments relating to a troubled young woman, X, in a secure unit who was due to be released. The staff at the unit were deeply concerned that X would commit suicide on her release. They wrote:

> The care plan to send her back to any community setting, especially [her home town] 'is a suicide mission to a catastrophic level'. Staff do not think it will take more than 24 to 48 hours before they receive a phone call stating that X has made a successful attempt on her life . . . X will not manage in the community . . .she requires long-term adolescent mental health unit input.

Despite these concerns it had not been possible to find appropriate support for her or a place on a mental health unit. Munby J in his judgments pleaded for intention, using surprisingly strong language:

> If, when in eleven days' time she is released from ZX, we, the system, society, the State, are unable to provide X with the supportive and safe placement she so desperately needs, and if, in consequence, she is enabled to make another attempt on her life, then I can only say, with bleak emphasis: we will have blood on our hands.

The only thing offered by the state seemed to be that if the police found her following an unsuccessful suicide attempt she could be taken into custody. He asked: 'Is that really the best the care system and the family justice system can achieve?'

Surprisingly his remarks did not initially lead to any response and at one point Munby J said: 'I might as well have been talking to myself in the middle of the Sahara.' Eventually, a place was found at a suitable unit by NHS England.

2.4 Refusal of medical treatment

The basic legal principle is that it is not lawful to administer treatment against the wishes of a competent person. This is so even where, without the treatment, the patient will die.[138] So if an adult Jehovah's Witness requires a blood transfusion to save his or her life, but refuses to consent to it, then it is impermissible to force it on him or her. That would amount to the criminal offence of battery. In 2013, in *Aintree University Hospital v James*,[139] Baroness Hale confirmed the core principle:

> Generally it is the patient's consent which makes invasive medical treatment lawful. It is not lawful to treat a patient who has capacity and refuses that treatment. Nor is it lawful

---

[135] Richardson (2013).   [136] *Re Z (An Adult: Capacity)* [2004] EWHC 2817.
[137] [2017] EWHC 2084 (Fam).   [138] *St George's Healthcare NHS Trust v S* [1998] 3 All ER 673.
[139] [2013] UKSC 67, [19].

to treat a patient who lacks capacity if he has made a valid and applicable advance decision to refuse it: see [Mental Capacity Act 2005], sections 24 to 26. Nor is it lawful to treat such a patient if he has granted a lasting power of attorney (under section 10) or the court has appointed a deputy (under section 16) with the power to give or withhold consent to that treatment and that consent is withheld; but an attorney only has power to give or withhold consent to the carrying out or continuation of life-sustaining treatment if the instrument expressly so provides (section 11(8)) and a deputy cannot refuse consent to such treatment (section 20(5)).

It is important to appreciate that this is true only where the patient has capacity. So if the physician is convinced that the individual is suffering from such a severe mental condition that he or she lacks capacity to make the decision, then the doctor can provide the life-saving treatment if that is in the best interests of the patient.[140]

The courts have confirmed the right to refuse medical treatment in a striking case.

KEY CASE   *Re B (Adult: Refusal of Medical Treatment)* [2002] 2 FCR 1

Ms B, aged 41, suffered a haemorrhage of the spinal column in her neck. Despite several years of treatment, her condition worsened and she suffered compete paralysis from the neck down. She became entirely dependent on a ventilator. Subsequently, Ms B made it clear that she wanted to have the ventilator turned off, even if that meant that she would die. Her clinicians accepted that Ms B was competent to make the decision, but had grown close to her during the treatment and could not bring themselves to abide by her wishes. Butler-Sloss P confirmed that Ms B was competent to make the decision to withdraw treatment. She reiterated the fundamental principle that 'if . . . the patient, having been given the relevant information and offered the available options chooses to refuse, that decision has to be respected by the doctors. Considerations of the best interests of the patient are irrelevant'.[141] The fact that the doctors felt that her decision was wrong did not give them a reason to ignore it. Remarkably, Butler-Sloss P herself added:

> [Ms B] is clearly a splendid person and it is tragic that someone of her ability has been struck down so cruelly. I hope she will forgive me for saying, diffidently, that if she did reconsider her decision, she would have a lot to offer the community at large.[142]

Because the doctors had not complied with her wishes, they had acted unlawfully, and a small amount of damages had to be paid by the National Health Service (NHS). Ms B was transferred to another hospital, which was to arrange the termination of the ventilation. She died shortly afterwards.

However, it is important to note, that that approach will not necessarily apply to those under 18.

---

[140] *Re MB (Caesarean Section)* [1997] 2 FCR 541.
[141] At [100].   [142] At [95].

KEY CASE   *NHS Foundation Hospital v P* [2014] EWHC 1650 (Fam)

P, aged 17, had taken an overdose of paracetamol and was admitted to hospital. She had a history of self-harming behaviour and had previously been briefly detained under the Mental Health Act 1983. She refused all treatment saying she wanted to die because her 'life was shit'. She was assessed as having capacity as defined by the Mental Capacity Act 2005. P's mother was willing to consent to treatment.

Baker J explained that as P was under the age of 18 the case was to be resolved under the inherent jurisdiction, meaning that P's best interests were the primary concern. He concluded:

> In this case, balancing the competing factors, I have no hesitation in concluding that the balance comes down firmly in favour of overriding P's wishes. I recognise that this is not to be taken lightly. The wishes of a young person aged seventeen and a half are important. They are, of course, entitled to be taken into account as part of her Article 8 rights under ECHR. On the other hand, those rights are not absolute. Here, they are outweighed by her rights under Article 2—everyone's right to life shall be protected by law. The court is under a positive or operational duty arising from Article 2 to take preventative measures to protect an individual whose life is at risk.

Critics of the decision in *NHS Foundation Hospital v P* [143] might ask why the right to life trumps the right to autonomy for children, but not adults. Baker J offered no explanation for why that should be so.

2.5 The impact of the Human Rights Act 1998 and the right to die

Much of the discussion and development of the law on euthanasia or assisted suicide has been based on the Human Rights Act (HRA) 1998.[144] It is helpful to consider the different rights that might be raised.

(i) *Article 2: the right to life* This prohibits the state from killing someone. In *Rabone v Penine Care Foundation Trust*,[145] it was held that the state can be under a duty to prevent a person in its care from committing suicide. Lady Hale went a little further than that in suggesting there was a right to be prevented from committing suicide, even where they had reached the decision to kill themselves with mental capacity. However, the state only has a duty to prevent suicide when the person is in the care of the state (e.g., they are in a prison or state hospital).

In *R (Pretty) v DPP*,[146] it was argued on Ms Pretty's behalf that the right to life in Article 2 ECHR included a right to control the manner of one's death and therefore a right to commit suicide. The House of Lords and European Court of Human Rights (ECtHR)[147] held that Article 2 imposed a duty on the state to protect life and that this could not be taken to include a right to die. The interpretation sought by

---

[143] [2014] EWHC 1650 (Fam).   [144] See Wicks (2007: chs 11 and 12).
[145] [2012] UKSC 2.   [146] [2002] 1 AC 800.   [147] *Pretty v UK* [2002] 2 FCR 97.

Ms Pretty involved too great a stretch of the natural meaning of the words. In fact, Article 2 requires the state to take reasonable steps to protect the life of citizens.[148] So a law that, for example, allowed involuntary euthanasia would risk infringing Article 2.

(ii) *Article 3: the right not to suffer torture or inhuman and degrading treatment* Ms Pretty also argued that, by prohibiting her husband from killing her, the state was inflicting torture or inhuman or degrading treatment upon her. It was held by the ECtHR that even if Ms Pretty's medical condition could be said to amount to torture, inhuman, or degrading treatment, it could not be said that this was inflicted by the state or was as a result of treatment by the state.[149] The Court also stated that the right under Article 3 had to be read alongside the right to life in Article 2. It could not therefore be argued that a person had the right to be killed or helped to die under Article 3, because that would contravene the right to life under Article 2. However, in *R (Burke) v GMC*,[150] the Court of Appeal stated that Article 3 gave a right to be protected from treatment, or a lack of treatment, which would result in dying in avoidably distressing circumstances.

(iii) *Article 8: the right to respect for private and family life* The ECtHR in *Pretty v UK*[151] appeared open to the argument that the right to determine issues surrounding one's death was an aspect of private life. It stated:

> The very essence of the Convention is respect for human dignity and human freedom. Without in any way negating the principle of sanctity of life protected under the Convention, the Court considers that it is under article 8 that notions of the quality of life take on significance. In an era of growing medical sophistication combined with longer life expectancies, many people are concerned that they should not be forced to linger on in old age or in states of advanced physical or mental decrepitude which conflict with strongly held ideas of self and personal identity.[152]

(iv) *Article 9: the right to freedom of thought, conscience, and religion* Ms Pretty argued that she was being prevented from exercising her moral conviction that it would be best if her life were brought to an end. This argument was rejected on the basis that she was not being prevented from thinking or believing what she wished. It was permissible to prohibit actions motivated by a person's beliefs; Article 9 dealt only with acts prohibiting the manifestation of a person's beliefs.

(v) *Article 14: the right to freedom from discrimination* It was argued that to allow people who were physically capable of committing suicide to do so, but to prohibit those physically incapable of committing suicide to arrange for another person to do so, amounted to discrimination on the grounds of disability contrary to Article 14. The European Court accepted that Ms Pretty was discriminated against in this way, but held that there were objective and reasonable justifications for the discrimination—namely, that any law that permitted assisted suicide could lead to vulnerable people being manipulated into killing themselves.

---

[148] *Oyal v Turkey* (2010) 115 BMLR 1.   [149] *Pretty v UK* [2002] 2 FCR 97, [53].
[150] [2005] 3 FCR 169, discussed in de Cruz (2007).
[151] [2002] 2 FCR 97, disagreeing with the House of Lords.
[152] At [65].

Putting these claims together it seems there is a right under Article 8 to self-determination in relation to suicide, but with four caveats. First, it applies only to those with capacity to decide to do so. Second, it appears to be limited to those who have the capacity to carry out the wish to commit suicide. Third, Article 8(2) allows interference in that right if necessary in the interests of others, although the law on that interference must be clear.[153] The right also needs to be read alongside the need to protect the right to life in Article 2. Fourth, the right does not entail a positive duty on the state to help a person to commit suicide.

The Human Rights issues were drawn upon in the following important case in which it was argued that the current English law was incompatible with the European Convention.[154]

KEY CASE *R (Nicklinson) v Ministry of Justice* [2014] UKSC 38

The case was brought by two appellants. The best known was Tony Nicklinson, who died following the hearing of the case at the High Court, but in whose name the litigation continued. He suffered from 'locked in syndrome' and was paralysed below the neck and could not speak. He communicated by blinking to indicate a letter on a board held up by his wife or an eye blink computer. He told the court:

> My life can be summed up as dull, miserable, demeaning, undignified and intolerable . . . it is misery created by the accumulation of lots of things which are minor in themselves but, taken together, ruin what's left of my life. Things like . . . constant dribbling; having to be hoisted everywhere; loss of independence, . . . particularly toileting and washing, in fact all bodily functions (by far the hardest thing to get used to); having to forgo favourite foods; . . . having to wait until 10.30 to go to the toilet . . . in extreme circumstances I have gone in the chair, and have sat there until the carers arrived at the normal time.[155]

The other appellant, known as Martin, also suffered from locked in syndrome. They both appealed against the findings of the lower courts that the current law on assisted suicide did not infringe their human rights. The Director of Public Prosecutions appealed against an order in the Court of Appeal that the prosecution guidance on assisted suicide needed further clarification as it applied to professionals.

The majority of their Lordships (seven of the nine; Lady Hale and Lord Kerr dissenting) rejected an argument that the ban on assisted suicide imposed a 'blanket ban' and so was impermissible under the European Convention on Human Rights. The majority took the view that the European Court of Human Rights had made it clear that the precise regulation of assisted suicide was within the margin of appreciation, meaning that each country could determine for itself the balance of rights on the regulation of assisted suicide under Article 8. The majority held that ideally Parliament would address the issue and determine what balance was appropriate for England. Only if it refused to would it fall to the courts to make the determination.

---

[153] *Gross v Switzerland* [2013] ECHR 429.   [154] See Wicks (2015) for a helpful analysis.
[155] *R (on the application of Nicklinson and another) (Appellants) v Ministry of Justice* [2012] EWHC 2381 (Admin) at [13]. Tony Nicklinson died following the decision of the High Court. He refused all food and nutrition.

The majority held that the court could, in theory, determine that the ban on assisted suicide infringed convention rights, but that Parliament should be given the opportunity to consider amending the law first. Lord Neuberger summarized the conclusion for why as follows:

> First, the question whether the provisions of section 2 should be modified raises a difficult, controversial and sensitive issue, with moral and religious dimensions, which undoubtedly justifies a relatively cautious approach from the courts. Secondly, this is not a case like *Re G* where the incompatibility is simple to identify and simple to cure: whether, and if so how, to amend section 2 would require much anxious consideration from the legislature; this also suggests that the courts should, as it were, take matters relatively slowly. Thirdly, section 2 has, as mentioned above, been considered on a number of occasions in Parliament, and it is currently due to be debated in the House of Lords in the near future; so this is a case where the legislature is and has been actively considering the issue. Fourthly, less than thirteen years ago, the House of Lords in *Pretty v DPP* gave Parliament to understand that a declaration of incompatibility in relation to section 2 would be inappropriate, a view reinforced by the conclusions reached by the Divisional Court and the Court of Appeal in this case: a declaration of incompatibility on this appeal would represent an unheralded *volte-face*.[156]

The majority thought it was not appropriate at this point in time to issue a declaration of incompatibility. However, a majority of five Justices (Lord Neuberger, Lady Hale, Lord Mance, Lord Kerr, and Lord Wilson) indicated that in the future it could hold that the bar on assisted suicide was contrary to the European Convention on Human Rights, as interpreted by the English courts. Of these five, Lady Hale and Lord Mance appeared willing to issue a declaration of incompatibility immediately. However, the other three (Lords Neuberger, Kerr, and Wilson) were not willing to do so at this point in time. However, they gave strong hints that unless compelling new arguments were made they would be minded to make a declaration of incompatibility if Parliament does not act. Lords Sumption, Hughes, Reed, and Clarke appear currently less inclined to issue a declaration of incompatibility, believing the issue to be one for the legislature.[157]

Subsequently, in *R (Conway) v Secretary of State*[158] Beatson LJ offered a neat summary of the three views that appeared in their Lordships' speeches:

> [1] Lord Sumption and Lord Hughes considered that the question of relaxation of section 2(1) was for Parliament, and that Parliament could properly conclude that a blanket ban on assisted suicide was necessary for the purposes of Article 8, and it had already done so.

> [2] Lady Hale and Lord Kerr, who dissented and would have made a declaration of incompatibility, considered that, unless Parliament devised a scheme which admitted of exceptions to section 2(1), the incompatibility would persist although they recognised that Parliament might take a different view and decline to change the law, as the Human Rights Act 1998 allows.

> [3] The position of the remaining five justices fell in between these settled views. Lord Neuberger, Lord Mance and Lord Wilson concluded that the appeal should be disposed

156 At [116].   157 *R(AM) v GMC* [2015] EWHC 2096 (Admin).
158 [2017] EWCA Civ 275

of in the same way but contemplated that circumstances may arise in the future in which an application for a declaration of incompatibility might succeed . . . Lord Neuberger gave four reasons which, he stated, when taken together 'persuaded him that it would be institutionally inappropriate at this juncture, for a court to declare that section 2 is incompatible with article 8, as opposed to giving Parliament the opportunity to consider the position without a declaration. In summary, these were: **(1)** the issue is deeply controversial and sensitive; **(2)** it would not be simple to identify a remedy for an incompatibly; **(3)** Parliament had recently and repeatedly considered section 2 and a Bill was under consideration at the time: **(4)** in the decision in *R (Pretty)* v *Director of Public Prosecutions* [2002] 1 AC 800 the House of Lords had given Parliament to understand that a declaration of incompatibility would be inappropriate.

Although the application for a declaration of incompatibility in *Nicklinson* failed, the Supreme Court did, however, recommend that the DPP review her guidance in so far as it applied to professionals assisting suicide. Following the decision in *Nicklinson* the DPP updated its guidance that it had produced following the *Purdy* decision. The guidance lists factors which will be taken into account when deciding when to prosecute in a case of assisted suicide.[159] The case was taken to the ECtHR which upheld the approach taken by the Supreme Court.[160]

The issue returned to the courts in *R (Kenward)* v *DPP*[161] where there was a challenge to the DPP prosecution guidance as it related to healthcare professionals. The guidance was upheld, with a rejection of an argument that clearer guidance was needed. A more substantial challenge came in the following case.

KEY CASE   *R (Conway) v Secretary of State for Justice* [2017] EWCA Civ 275

Noel Conway sought judicial review to declare section 2(1) of the Suicide Act 1961 incompatible with the European Convention on Human Rights. He was aged 67 and had motor neurone disease. The Divisional Court refused to give him leave and he appealed against that to the Court of Appeal. His life expectancy was between six and eighteen months. He had lost all mobility and needed assistance for everyday activities. He wanted the assistance of a medical professional to end his life in a 'peaceful and dignified way'. His family supported his decision but did not feel able to travel with him to Dignitas in Switzerland.

The Court of Appeal allowed the appeal and returned the case to the Divisional Court so that the application for leave to bring the case could be brought. It was acknowledged that the issues were essentially the same as in *Nicklinson*. However, a key difference was that since that decision, three different bills which would have liberalized the law had been debated in Parliament, but had failed. Beatson LJ held 'since *Nicklinson* Parliament has made a decision not to change the law and the matter is no longer under active consideration means that Mr Conway should be entitled to argue that it is no longer institutionally inappropriate for the court to consider whether to make a declaration of incompatibility, whilst giving due weight to Parliament's recent decision'. In saying

---

[159] CPS (2015).
[160] *Nicklinson v UK* 2478/15 and 1787/15. See the discussion in Wicks (2016).
[161] [2015] EWHC 3508 (Admin).

this the Court of Appeal was not indicating that it thought Mr Conway's case would succeed, rather just that he had enough of an argument that it should be heard. Indeed, perhaps ominously, Beatson LJ concluded by referring to the 'fragility of the prospects of a successful application for a declaration of incompatibility'.

One thing is for sure, we have not heard the end of this issue.

In the English courts the arguments have primarily been about whether persons should be free to obtain assistance in dying. It has been argued before the ECtHR that there is a positive right to be given assistance to die in the ECHR. This was firmly rejected in this case.

KEY CASE *Haas v Switzerland* **Application no. 31322/07 (2011) ECHR 10**

Mr Haas was aged 57 and had suffered from bipolar disorder for nearly twenty years. He wished to commit suicide. After extensive research on the methods, he decided to use sodium pentobarbital, a drug available only on prescription. Despite contacting 170 doctors, none were willing to write him a prescription.

He filed an application with the ECtHR, complaining that his Article 8 rights had been infringed. The state, in exceptional cases such as his, had to provide him with the substances that he needed to determine the manner of his death. His claim failed. The Court confirmed 'that the right of an individual to decide how and when to end his life, provided that said individual was in a position to make up his own mind in that respect and to take the appropriate action, was one aspect of the right to respect for private life' protected by Article 8.[162] However, that right had to be read alongside Article 2, which protects the right to life. States have a margin of appreciation as to how to balance these two rights. Article 2 compels national authorities to take reasonable steps to prevent someone from killing themselves if that decision is not taken freely and with full knowledge.[163] There was therefore no positive obligation on the state to provide measures allowing people a rapid and painless suicide.

Looking at Mr Haas's case, even though he was acting freely and with understanding, the Swiss law requiring a prescription before obtaining lethal drugs pursued the legitimate aim of protecting individuals from taking hasty decisions and preventing abuse.[164] The Court noted that Switzerland did permit assisted suicide, making Mr Haas's case weaker. The Court added that the risk of abuse in legal systems that facilitated assisted suicide 'cannot be underestimated'.[165]

One interesting recent development in the law has been *Koch v Germany*,[166] in which a man who cared for his terminally ill wife claimed that the inability for him to acquire medication to end her life infringed *his* rights to family and private life under Article 8. The argument was accepted, but with the caveats above that the right could be interfered with justifiably.

---

[162] At [52].   [163] At [54].   [164] At [56].
[165] At [58].   [166] (2013) 56 EHRR 6.

2.6 **Human rights arguments to be kept alive**

Usually, human rights arguments are used by those seeking to die, but they can be relevant for those seeking to be kept alive. The leading case on this is the following.

KEY CASE   *R (Burke) v GMC* [2005] 3 FCR 169

Leslie Burke suffered from cerebellar ataxia. This meant that, at some point in the future, he would require artificial nutrition and hydration (ANH). He sought a declaration from the Court to clarify the circumstances in which it would be lawful for doctors to withdraw the feeding and hydration. He was concerned that the guidance issued by the General Medical Council (GMC) on withdrawal of ANH was inconsistent with the law. He did not want ANH withdrawn if he were to become incompetent. He sought a number of declarations from the Court, including, most notably, the following:

(i)   that the withholding or withdrawal of ANH, leading to death by starvation or thirst, would be a breach of Mr Burke's rights under Articles 2, 3, and 8 ECHR, and would be unlawful under domestic law;

(ii) that where a competent patient requests, or where an incompetent patient has, prior to becoming incompetent, made it clear that he or she would wish to receive, ANH, the withholding or withdrawal of ANH, leading to death by starvation or thirst, would be a breach of that patient's rights under Articles 2, 3, or 8, and would be unlawful under domestic law; and

(iii) that the refusal of ANH to an incompetent patient would be a breach of Article 2 unless providing such ANH would amount to degrading treatment contrary to Article 3.

The Court of Appeal declined to give the declaration sought. In part, this was because Mr Burke was not presently incompetent and the issue of his medical treatment in the future was a hypothetical question. Instead, the Court was adamant that a patient did not have a right to demand whatever treatment he or she wanted. It approved of the following propositions promoted by the GMC.

(i)   The doctor, exercising his professional clinical judgement, decides what treatment options are clinically indicated (that is, will provide overall clinical benefit) for his or her patient.

(ii) The doctor then offers those treatment options to the patient, in the course of which the doctor explains to the patient the risks, benefits, side effects, and so on, involved in each of the treatment options.

(iii) The patient then decides whether he or she wishes to accept any of those treatment options and, if so, which one. In the vast majority of cases, he or she will, of course, accept whichever treatment option he or she considers to be in his or her best interests and, in doing so, he or she will or may take into account other, non-clinical factors. However, the patient can, if he or she wishes, decide to accept (or refuse) the treatment option on the basis of reasons that are irrational, or for no reasons at all.

(iv) If the patient chooses one of the treatment options offered to him or her, the doctor will then proceed to provide it.

(v)   If, however, the patient refuses all of the treatment options offered to him or her and instead informs the doctor that he or she wants a form of treatment that the doctor has not offered, the doctor will, no doubt, discuss that form of treatment with the patient (assuming that it is a form of treatment known to the doctor), but if the doctor concludes that this treatment is not clinically indicated, he or she is not required (that is, is under no legal obligation) to provide it to the patient, although the doctor should offer to arrange a second opinion.

The Court was adamant that a patient had no right to demand treatment on the basis of the right of autonomy. The Court of Appeal explained:

Autonomy and the right of self-determination do not entitle the patient to insist on receiving a particular medical treatment regardless of the nature of the treatment. Insofar as a doctor has a legal obligation to provide treatment this cannot be founded simply upon the fact that the patient demands it. The source of the duty lies elsewhere.167

This, however, did not mean there was not a duty to provide ANH. As the Court explained:

Once a patient is accepted into a hospital, the medical staff come under a positive duty at common law to care for the patient . . . A fundamental aspect of this positive duty of care is a duty to take such steps as are reasonable to keep the patient alive. Where ANH is necessary to keep the patient alive, the duty of care will normally require the doctors to supply ANH.168

However, the Court explained that the duty to provide ANH was not an absolute duty. It did not apply where the competent patient refuses ANH or, where the patient is not competent, it is not in the patient's interests to receive ANH. The Court explained:

The courts have accepted that where life involves an extreme degree of pain, discomfort or indignity to a patient, who is sentient but not competent and who has manifested no wish to be kept alive, these circumstances may absolve the doctors of the positive duty to keep the patient alive. Equally the courts have recognised that there may be no duty to keep alive a patient who is in a persistent vegetative state ('PVS').169

However, this did not apply where the patient was competent and wanting to receive ANH. Withdrawing ANH from a competent patient against his or her wishes would infringe his or her right to life under Article 2 ECHR and would amount to murder, except in the unlikely event that ANH would hasten death. If there is doubt over the legality of withdrawing ANH, advice can be sought from the court.

Mr Burke took his case to the ECtHR,[170] where he lost. The Court held that, if he were to lose capacity:

[A] doctor would be obliged to take account of the applicant's previously expressed wishes and those of the persons close to him, as well as the opinions of other medical personnel and, if there was any conflict or doubt as to the applicant's best interests, then to approach a court. This does not, in the Court's view, disclose any lack of due respect for the crucial rights invoked by the applicant.[171]

Commentators have divided on this case. Some commentators have seen the case as correctly upholding the principle that, where a patient is incompetent, doctors must treat him or her in the way that promotes their best interests, and that a patient cannot require

---

[167] At [31].   [168] At [32].   [169] At [33].
[170] *Burke v UK* Application no. 19807/06, 11 July 2006, ECtHR.
[171] At [21].

a doctor to treat him or her in a way that is harmful.[172] Hazel Biggs, on the other hand, sees it as 'a dangerous endorsement of medical paternalism', and as failing to appreciate that there can be a variety of different views on what is in a person's best interests.[173] To prefer the views of the doctor over those of the patient himself or herself is inappropriate.

2.7 'Do not resuscitate' orders

If there are concerns that a patient will need life-sustaining treatment, but that it might not be appropriate to give it, a 'do not resuscitate' (DNR) notice may be attached to the patient's notes.[174] This will avoid doctors needing to make a split-second decision at a moment of medical crisis. It might be thought obvious that if a patient is still competent, he or she should be consulted before such a notice is attached to his or her notes, although only 80 per cent of junior doctors thought this was necessary in one survey.[175] In *R (Tracey) v Cambridge University Hospitals*[176] the Court of Appeal issued some authoritative guidance. It held that patients must be consulted before a Do Not Attempt Cardio-Pulmonary Resuscitation (DNACPR) notice is put on their file. That was said to be required by Article 8 of the European Convention. The requirement applies even if the doctor believes the resuscitation would be futile. The only exception is where the doctor believes that discussing the issue with the patient would cause physical or psychological harm. In *Winspear v City Hospitals Sunderland NHS Foundation Trust*[177] it was held the same approach applies if a patient lacks capacity. If possible the issue should be discussed with the patient and if not a relative. It should be noted that the requirement is a discussion; these decisions are not saying that patients or their families have the right to demand resuscitation attempts if the medical team believe them inappropriate.[178]

3 Applying the law in difficult cases

We have now summarized some of the key legal principles governing the law in relation to end-of-life decisions. It is now necessary to consider some particularly complex cases in which the law is not always easy to apply. We will look at the administration of pain-relieving drugs, the treatment of severely disabled newborn children, and the position of patients suffering from PVS.

3.1 The administration of pain-relieving drugs

It is clear that if a doctor gives drugs to a patient in order to kill him or her and death results, then that can be murder. In *Bland*,[179] Lord Goff reiterated that 'it is not lawful for a doctor to administer a drug to his patient to bring about his death, even

---

[172] Gillon (2004). Indeed, doctors cannot be required to treat patients in any way: *An NHS Trust v L* [2013] EWHC 4313 (Fam).

[173] Biggs (2007a).   [174] *An NHS Trust v L* [2013] EWHC 4313 (Fam).

[175] Schildmann, Doyal, Cushing, et al. (2006).

[176] [2014] EWCA Civ 822, discussed in Samanta (2015) and Auckland (2016).

[177] [2015] EWHC 3250 (QB).

[178] Although see Anthony Pillai (2017) for a concern this will happen as a result of these decisions.

[179] *Airedale NHS Trust v Bland* [1993] AC 789, 865.

if that course is prompted by the humanitarian desire to end his suffering, however great that suffering may be'. But may a doctor lawfully supply pain-relieving drugs to a terminally ill patient, even if a side effect of the drugs will be to shorten the patient's life?[180]

Looking at cases in which doctors have given high quantities of pain-relieving drugs that have resulted in the patient's death, two things stand out: first, how few prosecutions there have been; and second, how rarely those prosecutions result in a conviction. Doctors Carr,[181] Adams,[182] and Moor were all acquitted.[183] It may be that juries are influenced by the kind of attitude expressed by the direction of the judge to the jury in the trial of Dr Moor:

> You have heard that this defendant is a man of excellent character, not just in the sense that he has no previous convictions but how witnesses have spoken of his many admirable qualities. You may consider it a great irony that a doctor who goes out of his way to care for [the deceased] ends up facing the charge that he does.[184]

Lord Neuberger in *R (on the application of Nicklinson) v Ministry of Justice*[185] held that 'a doctor commits no offence when treating a patient in a way which hastens death, if the purpose of the treatment is to relieve pain and suffering (the so-called "double effect")'. That suggests there is a legal rule preventing the conviction of doctors in these cases.

It should not be thought that doctors are never convicted in relation to euthanasia. In *Cox*,[186] a doctor injected a lethal amount of potassium chloride in order to kill a patient who was suffering intense pain from rheumatoid arthritis. The expert opinion was that the drug shortened life and otherwise had no analgesic value. The jury convicted Dr Cox of attempted murder. Cox's prosecution involved a number of elements that made it unusual: the patient was not terminally ill; the drugs injected were non-therapeutic (for example they did not lessen pain or treat symptoms), but their sole effect was to kill; and Cox could not argue that his purpose was to relieve pain. Despite his conviction, it is noticeable that the consequences for him were limited. He was lucky to face the charge of attempted murder and not murder, because a murder conviction carries the sentence of mandatory life imprisonment. With attempted murder, the judge has a discretion, and a suspended sentence was used in this case.[187] Further, the GMC admonished him, but only on the grounds that, although he had acted in good faith, he had not lived up to the high standards expected of the medical profession. Cox's regional health authority continued to employ him, subject to certain restrictions. What seems to have led to the 'weak' response to his conviction is the fact that he was widely regarded as acting out of compassion. Even if his intent was blameworthy, his motivations were not.[188]

---

[180] Confirmed in *R (Nicklinson) v Ministry of Justice* [2013] EWCA Civ 961, [26].
[181] *Sunday Times*, 30 November 1986.   [182] His trial is discussed in Palmer (1957).
[183] See further Kennedy and Grubb (2000: 2115).
[184] Quoted in Dyer (1999: 1306).   [185] [2014] UKSC 38, para. 18.
[186] (1992) 12 BMLR 38.
[187] See also Dr Michael Irwin, who gave his friend sleeping pills so that his friend could kill himself. Dr Irwin was only cautioned by the police, although he was struck off the register of doctors by the GMC: BBC News online (27 February 2005).
[188] Boyd (1998).

> ## REALITY CHECK
>
> The legal position on euthanasia appears straightforward: it is illegal to give a person a lethal dosage of drugs with the intention of killing him or her. But, in practice, how often do doctors engage in euthanasia or assisted suicide?
>
> The following surveys give us some idea.
>
> - One British Medical Association (BMA) survey found that 22 out of 750 doctors said that they had actively ended the life of a patient.[189]
>
> - A survey carried out in 2003 by medix-uk.com reported that, of 1,002 UK doctors, 40 per cent said that they had been asked by patients to assist in suicide or euthanasia, while 55 per cent of doctors thought that a person who had a terminal illness and un-controllable physical suffering should be allowed to engage in physician-assisted suicide (PAS).[190]
>
> - The BMA strongly opposes all forms of euthanasia or assisted suicide.[191] A poll of members of the Royal College of Physicians found 73 per cent opposed to changing the current law on euthanasia and assisted suicide.[192]
>
> - In one study of nurses, only 5 per cent of those interviewed agreed with the statement that 'health professionals already quietly help patients on their way'.[193]
>
> - According to Seale, only 4.6 per cent of doctors felt that the current law inhibits their preferred way of treating patients, and 82 per cent supported the current ban on assisted suicide and euthanasia.[194] Not one GP or hospital doctor said that he or she had taken part in euthanasia or assisted suicide.
>
> - A study into medical end-of-life decisions in the UK in 2007–08 found that 0.21 per cent of deaths in the UK involved voluntary euthanasia, 0.0 per cent involved PAS, and 0.3 per cent, the ending of life without an explicit request.[195] However, it is clear that doctors are very much involved in end-of-life practices. Of deaths, 21.8 per cent followed end-of-life decisions and 17.1 per cent were 'double effect' cases (for example cases in which pain-relieving medication was given, despite its life-shortening properties). Of deaths, 16.5 per cent followed deep sedation.
>
> Although these statistics do not give an entirely consistent picture, it is clear that most doctors face requests for assistance in dying. Clearly, a minority of doctors are willing, to some extent, to assist in someone's death and a higher number would like to be able to do so. However, most healthcare professionals oppose a change in the law.

3.2 Disorders of consciousness

What is the legal position of the doctor who switches off the life support machine of a patient who is in a disorder of consciousness? In the past there was much talk of patient in a 'persistent vegetative state', but that terminology is no longer used. In part because

---

[189] BMA (1996).   [190] Voluntary Euthanasia Society (2003).
[191] BMA (2009c, 2016).   [192] BBC News online (10 May 2006).
[193] *Nursing Times* (2003).   [194] Seale (2006).   [195] Seale (2009).

it is recognized that disorders of consciousness (DoC) cover a spectrum of conditions and one cannot readily separate those in a vegetative state (where is no consciousness) and those in a minimally conscious state (MCS) where there is some discernible evidence of limited awareness.[196] Patients with DoC are not immobile, and retain some cranial nerve and spinal reflexes; these can include visual and auditory stimuli. The degree of responsiveness reflects the degree of consciousness.

The current legal position can be briefly summarized as follows.[197] Patients suffering from DoC are still alive; they have not yet suffered brain death. The switching off of the life support machine will be regarded as an omission. Although the omission may result in the patient's death, it will not be in breach of the doctor's duty to the patient, and so no crime will be committed. The MCA 2005 requires doctors to comply with any effective applicable advance directive issued by a patient that states that he or she does not wish to receive life-sustaining treatment. If there is no effective advance directive, then the test is whether the best interests of the patient require the treatment to be offered. It used to be thought that judicial permission had to be obtained before hydration and nutrition are withdrawn from a DoC patient.[198] The following decision appears to have removed that requirement.

KEY CASE *Re M (Withdrawal of Treatment: Need for Proceedings)* [2017] EWCOP 19

An application was made to Jackson J to authorize, if required, a withholding of clinically assisted nutrition and hydration (CANH) for M, even though without it she would die. The application was supported by M's family, her medical team, and an independent expert. M had developed Huntington's disease and was in a minimally conscious state (MCS). Applying the standard approach Jackson J started with the 'strong presumption' that it is in a person's best interests to stay alive. However, that was not an irrebuttable presumption and the court had to consider her best interests in a broad sense from her perspective and 'whether she would regard her future life as worthwhile.' After considering a range of evidence from relatives and doctors Jackson J concluded that the CANH was not providing her with a benefit and so it was not in her best interests for it to be continued. Interestingly, Jackson J accepted that the medical evidence was that the issue was finely balanced, but may have been tipped by the clear view of the family, but 'there was nothing wrong with that'. In a notable development, however, he went to hold that it was not necessary for the matter to be brought to court. Jackson J emphasized that a court declaration in these cases does not render the action lawful, but merely confirms that it would be lawful. He also noted that regularly doctors, families, and patients had to make decisions about withholding or withdrawing life support for many non-MCS patients and these are not subject to judicial oversight. He could not see why MCS cases had to be treated differently from other cases. He noted too the costs and time involved in having to bring applications to court. This might lead to patients being inappropriately given treatment to avoid litigation. If the decision to withdraw CANH was in line with the professional guidance from the GMC or BMA then it will be lawful. A second opinion should always be obtained. Where there is disagreement then the court could be involved.

[196] Kitzinger, Kitzinger, and Cowley (2107).   [197] See BMA (2009c).
[198] DCA (2007: paras 6.18, 8.18, and 8.19).

Supporters of this decision will welcome the fact that family members and doctors will now be able to make these decisions in line with professional guidance, without the stress and cost of litigation.[199] It might be thought extraordinary if a judge were to refuse an application where the family and medical team were in agreement. Indeed, there is no reported case of that happening, in which case the requirement for judicial approval looks like an expensive rubber-stamping exercise. Critics will be concerned that it is not impossible to imagine an agreement to end CANH being reached by doctors being worried about the costs of keeping MCS patients alive and relatives with an eye on an inheritance. The judicial oversight ensures the rights of patients are protected. However, there is no evidence that there have been cases where money has dominated the concerns.[200] It is hard to believe in such a case there would not be someone who would bring the matter to the attention of the court.

In *France v Lambert*[201] the ECtHR rejected an argument that the withdrawal of CANH from a DoC patient could amount to torture or inhuman or degrading treatment, and so infringe Article 3 ECHR.[202] In *Ms D v An NHS Trust Hospital*,[203] a declaration was made permitting doctors not to provide certain forms of life-saving treatment on a PVS patient. The declaration was made despite the objections of the patient's family. Colderidge J explained that it was in Ms D's best interests that she be allowed to die in a dignified way.

As *Re M* makes clear if there is a case of dispute then the matter can be brought to the court. In that case the key question will be best interests. That is, of course, the same test that will apply in any case where there is a question of withdrawal of treatment from a patient who lacks capacity. So we will consider these cases next.

3.3 Patients lacking capacity

Where an issue arises concerning life-saving treatment and a person lacking capacity, the general principles set in Chapter 4 apply. The first question now is whether the individual has issued an effective advance directive stating that he or she does not want to receive treatment. If the individual has done so, section 24 of the MCA 2005 requires a doctor to abide by that, even if so doing will lead to the death of the patient. An effective advance directive cannot, in this context, be overruled in the name of pursuing the patient's best interests. Where, however, the advance directive is ambiguous or there are doubts over its validity, it is likely that the courts will not give effect to it, where to do so would lead to death.[204] Where an effective advance directive states that the patient does want to receive treatment, then, following the decision in *R (Burke) v GMC*,[205] the life-saving treatment should be given, unless doing so would cause the patient real harm.

If an LPA has been made, then the donee can make the decision relating to life-saving treatment, but only if the appointment specifically states that he or she is to have the

[199] English and Sheater (2017); Baker (2017); Ruck-Keane (2017).
[200] Kitzinger, Kitzinger, and Cowley (2017); Kitzinger and Kitzinger (2016); Fritz (2017); Holland (2017); Wade (2017); Huxley and Birchley (2017).
[201] (Application 46043/14). See also *A Hospital v SW* [2007] EWHC 425 (Fam).
[202] See McLean (2006) for further discussion on the political issues associated with withdrawal of hydration.
[203] [2005] EWHC 2439 (Fam).   [204] Bartlett (2005).   [205] [2005] 3 FCR 169.

decision-making power over such treatment.[206] Court-appointed deputies are required to consent to life-sustaining treatment.[207]

If there is no advance directive, the law is governed by the MCA 2005. In section 62, the Act makes it clear that it is not intended to change the law on homicide or assisted suicide. Nothing in the Act will authorize a medical professional to do an act that intentionally causes death. The Act makes special provision to deal with 'life-sustaining treatment', defined as 'treatment which in the view of a person providing health care for the person concerned is necessary to sustain life'.[208] When considering such treatment, the key question is what is in the 'best interests' of the patient. This is defined in section 4. The normal approach to ascertaining best interests will be used. That is discussed in Chapter 4. When considering the best interests of the patient, section 4(5) makes an important point about what factors a doctor should consider: 'Where the determination relates to life-sustaining treatment he must not, in considering whether the treatment is in the best interests of the person concerned, be motivated by a desire to bring about his death.' This reflects the approach of the law that although it may be permissible for a doctor to do an act that he or she foresees may cause death, he or she must not do an act for the purpose of causing death.[209] In *Aintree University Hospital v James*,[210] Lady Hale said that this subsection should never mean that a patient is given treatment that is not in his or her best interests. That decision has become a key case on the best interests test as it applies in end-of-life cases.

KEY CASE   *Aintree University Hospital v James* [2013] UKSC 67

David James was seriously ill in hospital with cancer and a range of serious complications, which had led him to be placed on a ventilator and to receive ANH. He entered a state in which he had a very limited level of consciousness. He did not have capacity to make decisions for himself. The hospital sought a declaration that, 'in the event of a clinical deterioration', Mr James should have specified treatments withheld. There was no suggestion that ventilation or ANH would be withheld. The family disagreed. They felt that Mr James found enjoyment from his family and friends and that he had always been determined to fight the cancer. The judge at first instance had refused the declaration, but the Court of Appeal allowed an appeal by the hospital and the case went to the Supreme Court—although Mr James had died by the time the case came to that court.

Lady Hale gave some important observations on the application of the best interests test under the MCA 2005 to such cases. She emphasized that it is wrong to ask 'Is it in the best interests of the patient to die?' and likewise that it is wrong to ask whether 'it is in the best interests of a patient to withhold or withdraw treatment?'. Instead, the question was whether it was in the patient's best interests to *receive* treatment. If the treatment is not in the patient's best interests, it will not be lawful to give it.

Drawing on the MCA 2005 Code of Practice, Lady Hale explained that, in applying the best interests test, there would be a 'strong element of "substituted judgement", taking account of the past

[206] MCA 2005, s. 11(8).   [207] MCA 2005, s. 20(5).   [208] MCA 2005, s. 4(10).
[209] The provision is discussed in Coggon (2007).   [210] [2013] UKSC 67.

wishes and feelings of the patient. This could include 'altruistic sentiments and concern for others'. It was right to place weight on family life. Lady Hale agreed that the starting point is:

> . . . a strong presumption that it is in a person's best interests to stay alive . . . Nevertheless, they are also all agreed that this is not an absolute. There are cases where it will not be in a patient's best interests to receive life-sustaining treatment.[211]

She summed up her thinking as follows:

> The most that can be said, therefore, is that in considering the best interests of this particular patient at this particular time, decision-makers must look at his welfare in the widest sense, not just medical but social and psychological; they must consider the nature of the medical treatment in question, what it involves and its prospects of success; they must consider what the outcome of that treatment for the patient is likely to be; they must try and put themselves in the place of the individual patient and ask what his attitude to the treatment is or would be likely to be; and they must consult others who are looking after him or interested in his welfare, in particular for their view of what his attitude would be.[212]

Lady Hale accepted that it was relevant to consider whether treatment was futile, but by 'futile' the Court had to consider whether the proposed treatments would be ineffective in the sense of not being of benefit to the patient. In saying that, she noted that the treatment may not be designed to treat the underlying disease, but rather to make the dying as comfortable or dignified as possible.

The starting point in end-of-life cases is always the 'strong presumption in favour of life'.[213] However, that is subservient to an assessment of the best interests viewed from the perspective of the individual patients.[214] In *M v A NHS Trust*[215] Baker J looking at the case of a patient in MSC concluded:

> M does experience pain and discomfort, and her disability severely restricts what she can do. Having considered all the evidence, however, I find that she does have some positive experiences and importantly that there is a reasonable prospect that those experiences can be extended by a planned programme of increased stimulation.[216]

Notably in that case he had found it impossible to determine what M would have wanted had she had capacity to decide for herself. That case (and it was a controversial decision) may be seen as one where the presumption in favour of life prevailed because of a lack of evidence that she was, overall, suffering harm, or that she would not have wanted to continue living like that.

In most cases the focus on 'what decision he or she would have made if they now had capacity and so, in exercise of their right of self-determination was able to make the decision' dominates the discussion.[217] In *Briggs* it was held 'having his views and wishes

---

[211] At [35].   [212] At [39].

[213] *A NHS Foundation Trust v D and K* [2013] EWHC 2402 (COP), [23]; *Kirklees Council v RE* [2014] EWHC 3182 (Fam); *United Lincolnshire Hospitals NHS Trust v N* [2014] EWCOP 16.

[214] *Cumbria NHS Clinical Commissioning Group v Miss S and Ors* [2016] EWCOP 32.

[215] [2011] EWHC 2443 (Fam). See Heywood (2014) for an excellent analysis.

[216] At [8].   [217] Briggs v Briggs [2016] EWCOP 53.

taken into account and respected is a very significant aspect of P's best interests'.[218] In most cases this has led to the court approving the withdrawal or withholding of treatment. A good example is the judgment of Hayden J in *M v N*,[219] who, having heard from the friends and family, was able to conclude that withdrawal of life-sustaining treatment was in M's best interests because she would have found her circumstances profoundly humiliating and would have been alert to the distress caused to her family.

In *Wye Valley v B*[220] focusing on the values that P lived by meant that it was not in the best interests of a man who had lived his life following voices from the spirit world should not be given treatment against his wishes. He lacked capacity, but his life was marked by him following the voices of spirits and angels. The court held:

> the wishes and feelings, beliefs and values of people with a mental disability are as important to them as they are to anyone else, and may even be more important. It would therefore be wrong in principle to apply any automatic discount to their point of view. It is, I think, important to ensure that people with a disability are not—by the very fact of their disability—deprived of the range of reasonable outcomes that are available to others. For people with disabilities, the removal of such freedom of action as they have to control their own lives may be experienced as an even greater affront that it would be to others who are more fortunate.

What is particularly notable about this case is that it was not one where the view of P, when he had capacity which were followed, it was the views he had even when lacking capacity. The point being there never was a P who had capacity, whose values the courts would rely on.

Ascertaining what P would have wanted is not, of course, always straightforward. Hayden J in *M v N*[221] said that the view of families, friends, and those who knew the patient well was 'crucial'. The court would not only look at words spoken in the past, but also their lifestyle, codes, or beliefs by which a person used and their general personality. As the following case shows the court will be wary of putting too much weight on the views of relatives.

KEY CASE   *Abertawe Bro Morgannwg University Local Health Board v RY* [2017] EWCOP 2

RY was 81 and in a minimally conscious state. The issue arose whether he should receive deep suctioning via a tracheostomy, if it became necessary. His daughter, CP, was adamant her father was a 'devout Christian who prayed every day'. She said he believed any life was better than no life and that he would want everything done to be kept alive. Hayden J felt unable to rely on CP's account of her father's wishes. He noted CP herself had a strong religious faith, but there was little evidence about what RY's views were. He focused on a consideration of whether the proposed treatment would be 'overly burdensome'. The deep suctioning clearly caused RY pain, and it was not clear it produced medical benefits. He concluded the suctioning caused harm 'without purpose' and compromised the dignity of the patient. However, he ultimately declined to make an order as he hoped CP might, in light of the judgment, come to agreement with the medical team. Also there had been an improvement in RY's condition which meant the suctioning may not be necessary.

---

[218] Para. 56.   [219] [2015] EWCOP 76.   [220] [2015] EWCOP 60.   [221] [2015] EWCOP 76.

Sometimes the cooperation of the patient is key to the success of the treatment and so forcing the treatment on a non-consenting patient will be ineffective. This seemed to be the conclusion in *Re W (Medical Treatment: Anorexia)*[222] where a patient who lacked capacity as a result of anorexia had been forced to received treatment against her wishes. The forced treatment had not had any long-term benefits and the court held that the point had been reached where it was beyond the power of doctors or her family to improve her condition. It was better to stop and let her decide whether she wanted treatment, even though she would die without treatment.

3.4 The treatment of severely disabled children

Few areas of medical practice can be more distressing than cases involving severely disabled babies and young children.[223] The basic legal principles are those with which you will now be familiar: it is not permissible to do an act that intentionally causes the death of the patient, but a doctor may decline to provide treatment to a patient if that is in a patient's best interests and it is in accordance with established medical practice. The difficulty is that the approach taken in relation to adults, focusing on the values and beliefs of the individual, is not available in relation to children.

The overarching test is whether continuing treatment is in the child's best interests. This assessment must be made from the perspective of the individual and not from an assessment by an outsider. As Taylor LJ in *Re J (A Minor) (Wardship: Medical Treatment)*[224] emphasized: 'even severely handicapped people find a quality of life rewarding which to the unhandicapped may seem manifestly intolerable'. [225]

The hardest cases are those in which there is a disagreement between the medical teams and the parents. Such cases can be divided into two categories.

3.4.1 *The doctors wish to stop treatment, but the parents do not*

The court will make a determination of what is in the best interests of the child. The views of the parent are one factor, but do not determine that issue.[226] Where there is clear evidence that it is not in the best interests of the child to receive the treatment, it will not be given however much the parents want it. [227] Where the medical opinion is divided or unclear, it may well be that the views of the parents will tip the balance in favour of ordering treatment.[228] This approach is in line with the general principle of medical law, the courts are very reluctant to order doctors to give treatment to patients that the doctors do not believe to be appropriate for the patients.[229] It is, therefore, very

[222] [2016] EWCOP 13.
[223] See Nuffield Council (2007) for a helpful summary of the issues. An argument can be made that some disabilities are so severe that the sufferer should not even be regarded as a person. See, e.g., the discussion in McMahan (2002: 449) of anencephalic infants.
[224] [1990] 3 All ER 930, 935.
[225] See Ford (2005a) for a very helpful discussion on whether painful lives can have value.
[226] Weight should be attached the views of parents even if the parents lack mental capacity: *Re Jake (a child) (withholding of medical treatment)* [2015] EWHC 2442.
[227] *An NHS Trust v W* [2015] EWHC 2778 (Fam); *Great Ormond Street Hospital for Children NHS Foundation Trust v NO* [2017] EWHC 241 (Fam); *Re C* [1998] Lloyd's Rep Med 1.
[228] *Great Ormond Street Hospital for Children NHS Foundation Trust v NO* [2017] EWHC 241 (Fam).
[229] *Re J* [1990] 3 All ER 930; *R v Central Birmingham Health Authority, ex p Walker* (1987) 3 BMLR 32 *Re C* [1998] 1 FCR 1; *Royal Wolverhampton NHS Trust v B* [2000] 2 FCR 76; *NHS Trust v D* [2000] 2 FCR 577.

unlikely that doctors would be ordered by the court to give treatment they did not think would be appropriate.[230]

The courts are also clear that there is a strong presumption in favour of the course of action that will preserve life.[231] However, where the child's future is utterly bleak and the doctors conclude that there is no benefit in continuing treatment, then the treatment can be withheld, even if the consequence of doing so is that the child will die.[232] Moor J in *Kirklees Council v RE*[233] referred to the Royal College of Paediatrics and Child Health Guidelines 'Withholding or Withdrawing Life Sustaining Treatment in Children' which noted two kinds of cases where withholding treatment from sick children may be appropriate:

> 27. The 'no chance' situation is one where the child has 'such severe disease that life-sustaining treatment simply delays death without significant alleviation of suffering'. In such a situation where treatment delays death but neither improves life quality or potential, continued treatment is defined as being 'futile and burdensome and not in the best interests of the patient'.
>
> 28. The 'no purpose' situation is one where, although the patient 'may be able to survive with treatment, the degree of physical or mental impairment will be so great that it is unreasonable to expect them to bear it'. It adds that, in such cases, 'continuing treatment might leave the child in a worse condition than already exists with the likelihood of further deterioration leading to an impossibly poor life'.

The courts will play close attention to whether or not a child is receiving any benefit from life. In *An NHS Trust v MB*,[234] doctors wished to withdraw ventilation from a child suffering from spinal muscular atrophy (a severe degenerative condition, which meant that the child had virtually no movement and was expected to die within the year). The parents successfully argued that the child still had some benefits from life, in particular 'the single most important source of pleasure and emotion to a small child: his relationship with his parents and family'.[235] The judge placed much weight on the fact that, although he could communicate in a very limited way with them, the evidence suggested that MB had pleasure from being with his parents.

By contrast, in *NHS Trust v Baby X*,[236] the judge, in approving withdrawal of medical support, noted that the child seemed to have no awareness of those around him. Also, in a moving judgment in *An NHS Foundation Trust v R (Child)*[237] Jackson J concluded that treatment should be withdrawn in a case of a child who might have lived up to two more years, despite the parents' objections. He explained:

> I know that the family members believe that by surrounding Reyhan with infinite love and first-class care, they can protect him from many of the worst aspects of his condition, and I accept without question that they mean what they say. However, putting Reyhan first, I cannot in the end take the same view. The family members wish to continue on this journey, believing that they can carry Reyhan on their shoulders and put

[230] *Great Ormond Street Hospital for Children NHS Foundation Trust v NO* [2017] EWHC 241 (Fam).
[231] *Re C (baby: withdrawal of medical treatment)* [2015] EWHC 2920 (Fam).
[232] *The Charlotte Wyatt Litigation* [2005] EWHC 2293; [2005] EWCA 1181; [2005] EWHC 693; [2005] EWHC 117; [2004] EWHC 2247; [2006] EWHC 319 (Fam); see also *Re Winston-Jones (A Child)* [2004] All ER (D) 313; *Re K* [2006] EWHC 1007 (Fam).
[233] [2014] EWHC 3182 (Fam).   [234] [2006] EWHC 507 (Fam).
[235] At [28].   [236] [2012] EWHC 2188 (Fam).   [237] [2013] EWHC 2340 (Fam)

him down only when the time is right. This in my view overlooks the reality. If Reyhan is to continue on the journey of long-term ventilation, he will have to walk every step of the way himself. Others can surround and encourage him, but it is Reyhan, and Reyhan alone, who will have to bear the burdens while experiencing little if any pleasure. And the road that he would be asked to walk is one that would grow steeper with every passing week.

The following notorious case is a classic example of how the courts approach these cases.

KEY CASE   *Great Ormond Street Hospital v Yates and Gard* **[2017] EWHC 927(Fam); [2017] EWCA Civ 410; (2017) 65 EHRR SE9; [2017] EWHC 1909 (Fam)**

This extensive litigation, involving an 8-month-old baby, Charlie Gard, attracted worldwide publicity. Charlie was seriously ill, being severely affected by a genetic condition and developing a severe brain injury as a result. Everyone agreed his current quality of life was not worth sustaining. The Great Ormond Street Hospital sought a declaration to authorize the withdrawal of ventilation and provision of palliative care only. The parents disagreed and wanted Charlie to be given a novel form of treatment known as nucleoside therapy, which the hospital believed to be inappropriate. The hospital therefore also sought an order it was lawful that Charlie not receive that therapy. The case was first heard by Francis J who applied the standard approach. There was a strong, but not irrebuttable presumption in favour of prolonging life. However, the welfare of the child was paramount and involved a consideration of medical, emotional, and all welfare issues. Francis J made the order requested by the hospital, noting that all the doctors treating Charlie agreed the ventilation should be withdrawn and he should be allowed to die peacefully and with dignity. The treatment the parents wanted (and had raised funds for) was available in the USA, but was 'pioneering treatment' and it had never been used for a patient with Charlie's condition. Francis J heard evidence that the American doctors thought it would be very unlikely to succeed. However, they were willing to attempt the treatment if the parents could pay for it. Francis J determined that the travelling would cause him serious pain for a treatment which had little chance of success. That could not be said to be in his best interests.

There was an appeal to the Court of Appeal. There the entire medical team at the hospital confirmed that in their view there were no treatments which could improve Charlie's condition, which had worsened. However, the parents still wanted to attempt the nucleoside treatment. Evidence from an American doctor was that the English and medical teams agreed on the science, but there was a cultural difference. She was willing to try anything to save Charlie's life, even though the treatment had very little chance of success. The English team did not want Charlie to suffer the pain of travel, for a very remote chance of success. The Court of Appeal upheld Francis J's judgment, rejecting the argument that he had failed to attach sufficient attention to the presumption in favour of life. It was also argued that the court should respect the views of parents who wish to attempt a treatment unless it could be shown that significant harm would result from following doing so. However, that view was not adopted by the court, which concluded:

> When thoughtful, caring, and responsible parents are putting forward a viable option for the care of their child, the court will look keenly at that option . . . The court evaluates the nitty-gritty detail of each option from the child's perspective . . .The judge decides what is in the best interests of the child by looking at the case entirely through eyes focused on the

child's welfare and focused upon the merits and drawbacks of the particular options that are being presented to the court . . . Where, however, as in this case, the judge has made clear findings that going to America for treatment would be futile, would have no benefit and would simply prolong the awful existence that he found was the current state of young Charlie's life, he was fully entitled, on the basis of those findings to conclude as he did. The consequence of that conclusion is that the proposal for nucleoside therapy was not a viable option before the court.

The parents appealed to the Supreme Court, but it declined to give them leave to appeal. While the refusal to give leave to appeal focused primarily on procedural issues, it is notable that Lady Hale mentioned the 'significant harm' argument that was raised in the Court of Appeal, but stated the argument failed as the harm Charlie was suffering was significant. It would be dangerous to read too much into that statement made in a refusal to give leave to appeal judgment, but it might be considered by courts in the future.

The case was then taken to the European Court (*Gard v UK* (2017) 65 EHRR SE9). It rejected a claim that Charlie's right to life under Article 2 had been infringed:

the Court considers that in this sphere concerning the end of life, as in that concerning the beginning of life, states must be afforded a margin of appreciation, not just as to whether or not to permit the withdrawal of artificial life-sustaining treatment and the detailed arrangements governing such withdrawal, but also as regards the means of striking a balance between the protection of patients' right to life and the protection of their right to respect for their private life and their personal autonomy.

The English courts had considered the issue from the point of view of the child and heard the parents and doctors. They had struck a permissible balance between the rights of Charlie and his parents in this case.

The case returned a final time to Francis J, with the parents wishing to introduce evidence from a range of institutions and countries offering treatments for Charlie. Francis J confirmed his earlier judgment after hearing further evidence. Indeed, the latest MRI scans showed that Charlie was beyond help and future treatment had zero chance of success.

A careful reading of the facts of the case make it hard to see how the case raised such public outrage. The evidence was clear that the treatment had no chance of being effective, but transporting him to the treatment would cause pain. Yet, the outrage may reflect a bigger perception that doctors do not listen to parents and take over decision-making for them.

To critics of the courts' approach, asking whether life-saving treatment is in the best interests of a child is little more than an 'empty mantra'.[238] Margaret Brazier has complained that the courts took a 'medical' picture of what was best for the child and looked at through the eyes of the 'professionals'.[239] However, it should be noted that the courts have now made it clear that best interests should not be a consideration only of medical interests.[240] The courts do appear to place greater weight on the views of

---

[238] Brazier (2005b: 415).   [239] Brazier (2005b: 416).
[240] *The NHS Trust v A* [2007] EWHC 1696 (Fam).

parents where the professionals accept that they are reasonable views to hold, even if not consistent with the views of the doctors.[241] The difficulty is that if we were to move to a position in which parents' views always carry the day, it would be problematic in cases in which parents did *not* want their children to receive treatment that doctors wished to provide. Brazier also notes that although the judge gave careful consideration to the parents' views in recent cases, the views of the nurses who were actually providing the day-to-day care receive little judicial attention. Finally, there is the point to be made that, at least in the case of Charlotte Wyatt, the doctors' gloomy prognosis as to how long she had to live in the early cases proved to be wrong and this does nothing to reassure parents that 'doctors know best'.[242]

3.4.2 *The parents wish treatment to stop, but the doctors do not*

In *Re B*,[243] baby Alexandra had Down's syndrome and an intestinal blockage. The blockage could easily be removed in an operation and, had she not had Down's syndrome, there would have been no doubt that the doctors would have operated. The parents did not want the operation done and were happy for Alexandra to die. The Court of Appeal was willing to make the girl a ward of court. It would be in her best interests to receive the treatment. It could hardly be said that, after the operation, her prognosis was a life full of pain and suffering, and that she should die. A key point to remember in this case is that if the parents did not want to raise a child suffering from Down's syndrome, they could ask the local authority to find foster carers or adopters who would be willing to do so.

There are reported cases in which parents successfully objected to the proposed course of action of a medical team. In *Re T*,[244] a boy had suffered from liver failure and the medical team wanted him to have a liver transplant, without which he would die. The parents successfully applied for an order preventing the transplant without their consent. Three factors appear to have been crucial in this case. First, the parents were healthcare professionals and their views were clearly based on medical reasoning. Second, the parents had recently moved abroad to take up new jobs; the operation would require them to leave their new positions and return to the UK. Third, the Court of Appeal heard medical evidence that if the transplant was to be a success, it was essential that the parents were fully involved in the lengthy rehabilitation process that followed the treatment. Butler-Sloss P explained that the child and mother 'were one' for the purpose of the application when considering what order would promote the child's welfare. If the mother did not want to participate in the procedure, its chances of success were severely reduced.[245] However, it must be emphasized that this case was exceptional; normally, the views of medical experts will be preferred to those of parents, even if the parents' views are rational and understandable.[246]

So, in those difficult cases involving severely disabled children, the courts usually follow the doctors' opinions.

---

[241] Wilkinson (2013) supports this kind of approach.

[242] See Bridgeman (2009) for further discussion. See also Nuffield Council on Bioethics (2007).

[243] [1990] 3 All ER 927.   [244] [1997] 2 FCR 363.

[245] In fact, after the case, the mother changed her mind and consented to the treatment.

[246] *Re MM* [2000] 1 FLR 224; *Re A (Conjoined Twins)* [2000] 4 All ER 961; *The NHS Trust v A* [2007] EWHC 1696 (Fam).

A SHOCK TO THE SYSTEM

The *Shipman* case

In January 2000, Dr Harold Shipman was convicted of the murder of fifteen patients. A subsequent inquiry led by Dame Janet Smith found that, in fact, he had killed 215 between 1975 and 1998.[247] There were a further forty-five deaths about which a suspicion had arisen, but that could not be established as a fact, and thirty-eight cases about which there was so little information that the inquiry could not form a view. Most of Shipman's victims were healthy elderly women, whom he injected with a lethal combination of drugs during a routine consultation. It is far from clear why he acted in this way. In sentencing him for his murder convictions, Forbes J stated: '[N]one of your victims realized that yours was not a healing touch. None of them knew that in truth you had brought her death, death which was disguised as the caring attention of a good doctor.'[248]

Several things were striking about this case, not least that a man, thought by many in the town of Hyde where he practised to be the best doctor in town and widely respected, could in fact be one of Britain's most prolific mass murderers. The case can be regarded as sending all kinds of messages. Is it the ultimate example of medical arrogance? Only the position of high esteem in which Shipman was held and with which he must have regarded himself can explain why so many crimes could be committed. Does it show the dangers of the kinds of arguments used by some who support euthanasia: is this 'death with dignity' gone mad? Or is this simply one rogue doctor about whom no general lessons can be learned? Shipman killed himself on 13 January 2004 and so the answers will never be known.

Dame Janet Smith's inquiry called for changes in the registration of births and cremation certificates, tighter controls on drugs' provision to doctors, and improved training of coroners in an attempt to ensure that never again could one person kill so many people without suspicions being raised.[249]

4 Alleged inconsistency in the present law

The current law opposing euthanasia and assisted suicide is said, by some, to be illogical and unsupportable.[250] It is argued that it is based on two unsupportable distinctions: between intention and foresight; and between acts and omissions. We shall consider these separately.

4.1 Intention/foresight

As we have seen, for the law and for many commentators, there is an important distinction between 'intention' and 'foresight'.[251] The distinction has been justified on the basis that there is an important difference between aiming to produce a result and

---

[247] J. Smith (2002).   [248] Quoted in J. Smith (2002: 1).
[249] J. Smith (2002).   [250] See Williams (2007).
[251] See Somerville (2003: ch. 1), and Foster, Herring, Melham, and Hope (2011).

being aware that an outcome is a possible result of one's actions.[252] You may foresee that if you drink too much alcohol, you will get a hangover, but that does not mean that you intend it; a lecturer may foresee that his or her lecture will confuse his or her students, but this does not mean that he or she intends to confuse them. The reasons why a person acts tell us far more about that person's personality than they do about the results that the person foresees when he or she acts.[253] We would, for example, regard a dentist who drilled a tooth foreseeing pain in a quite different light from a dentist who drilled a tooth intending for there to be pain. Most supporters of the distinction between foresight and intention also approve of the doctrine of 'double effect', which sets out the circumstances in which, even though a result may be foreseen, it is not intended. There is some debate among supporters of double effect whether the doctrine can even be relied upon where a result is inevitable.[254] If a person knows that a consequence will inevitably result from his or her action, can it really be argued that it is not intended? Keown appears to believe that even if the effect is certain, if it is a side consequence, it is justifiable and not intended.[255] However, others say that the doctrine should be used only if the side consequence is highly probable or less.[256]

A further difficulty with the doctrine of double effect is that, in most of its sophisticated forms, there is more to it than simply drawing a distinction between foresight and intention. Under Keown's formulation, for example, it must be shown that there was a 'sufficiently serious reason for allowing the bad consequence to occur'.[257] But such a requirement does a lot of the work needed to ensure that the doctrine produces appropriate results (for example a lethal dose of pain relief being given to deal with a small amount of pain).[258] The need for the additional requirement shows it is not only a matter of what is foreseen or is intended that is important. It also might mean that, whatever its philosophical appeal, double effect is insufficiently clear or susceptible to proof to be useful as a legal doctrine.[259]

There are, however, plenty of people who reject the distinction between intent and foresight, and the doctrine of double effect.[260] Warnock sees the difference between intention and foresight as 'absurdly pedantic'.[261] Harris has criticized the doctrine for depending too much on how one expresses a problem.[262] He considers a scenario in which a group of potholers are trapped and the only way in which they can escape is to move a boulder; moving the boulder will crush one person to death. You could describe this as 'intending to make an escape route, foreseeing that this will kill someone', or 'intending to make an escape route by killing someone'. He suggests that the morality of an action depends on whether the action judged as a whole was right, not on how one is able to express what one is doing. One way of putting the argument is to say that we

[252] See, e.g., Keown (2002: ch. 2), Finnis (1991), and Garcia (1997).
[253] Maclean (1992: 90–4).
[254] Huxtable (2004) explores the ambiguities within the concept.
[255] Keown (2002).   [256] Cantor and Thomas III (2000).
[257] Keown (2002: 72). See later in the chapter, under the heading '5.2.3 Intention/foresight and the doctrine of double effect'.
[258] See Billings (2011) for further discussion.
[259] Foster, Herring, Melham, and Hope (2013).
[260] Price (1997b). For an interesting discussion on the concept, see Gurnham (2007).
[261] Warnock (2001: 39).   [262] Harris (1984: 44).

accept consequences in packages. If, for example, I need a filling and I go to the dentist, I can be said to intend to have the treatment. It is true that I do not want the pain, but the pain comes with the treatment: I accept the 'package' (the treatment *and* the consequent pain) because I decide that, even though there is pain, the treatment will, in the long term, be preferable for me.[263] I cannot say 'I intend to have the filling, but not to experience the pain', because life is not like that.

Harris, responding to the example of the person who drinks, foreseeing, but not intending, to have a hangover, suggests that even accepting that a person does not intend to have a hangover, he or she is responsible for it.[264] If, as a result of a hangover, that person were unable to work properly the next day, then we can justly blame that person. Harris argues, in deciding whether or not it is proper to administer a lethal quantity of pain-relieving drugs to a terminally ill person, that the crucial question should not be what the doctor's purpose was in administering the drugs, but whether the person should die.[265] Surely far more important than the doctor's intent are the questions 'Did the patient consent?',[266] or 'What was the doctor's motivation?'

One difficulty for those who wish to emphasize the difference between intent and foresight is its practicability. If a doctor is found to have injected a patient with a lethal amount of a pain-relieving drug, how are we to know what was his or her intent or foresight?[267] As the law stands, with its emphasis on intent, only a doctor foolish enough to admit that he or she intended to kill would face prosecution.[268] Further, if a doctor wishes to give a large dose of pain-relieving drugs to his or her patient, but seeks his or her lawyer's advice first, is it really sensible that the advice might be 'You can give the injection, but make sure that, at the time, you don't want the death and instead focus on wanting to relieve pain'? Such concerns have led some to suggest that, whatever its merits in terms of ethics, the doctrine of double effect does not provide a practical guide to medical practice.[269]

4.2 Acts/omissions

The second controversial distinction at the heart of the present law is a distinction between active and passive euthanasia (those cases in which an act of the doctor causes death and those cases in which the doctor's omission causes the death).[270] Lord Goff summarized the current law, in *Bland*:[271]

> It is not lawful for a doctor to administer a drug to his patient to bring about his death, even though that course is prompted by a humanitarian desire to end his suffering, however great that suffering may be . . . So to act is to cross the Rubicon which runs between—on the one hand the care of the living patient and on the other hand euthanasia—actively causing his death to avoid or to end his suffering. Euthanasia is not lawful at common law.

[263] Shaw (2002) summarizes the criticisms of the doctrine of double effect.
[264] Harris (1995b).   [265] Harris (1995b).
[266] Davies (1988) argues that the difference between murder and euthanasia is the same as the difference between raping and making love: it is the consent of the 'victim' that makes all the difference.
[267] Wilkinson (2000).   [268] Griffiths (2007).
[269] Foster, Herring, Melham, and Hope (2011).
[270] See the discussion in Miller, Truog, and Brock (2010), Coggon (2008) and McLachlan (2008; 2009).
[271] [1993] 1 All ER 821, 867.

This reflects the popular view that the duty not to harm others is stronger than the duty to assist.[272]

The distinction can be supported in terms of causation. An omission cannot cause death; death is caused by the underlying medical condition. An omission may be necessary for a death, while it cannot be sufficient. By contrast, an act can take over authorship and full responsibility for what happens.[273] Philippa Foot poses the question: are we as much to blame for allowing people in developing countries to starve to death as we would be if we were to kill them by sending poisoned food?[274] This 'common sense' intuition that there is an important distinction between acts and omissions appears to be one that is shared by many healthcare professionals working in the field. One survey of UK medical practitioners suggests that 75 per cent accept a moral distinction between active and passive euthanasia as of important moral significance.[275] However much the distinction has been considered to justify and explain at a practical level, it has been far less popular among philosophers.[276] Lord Mustill, likewise, was not convinced by the distinction drawn between acts and omissions, and he feared that, after *Bland*, the law had become 'morally and intellectually misshapen': 'Still, the law is there and we must take it as it stands.'[277] Two leading medical ethicists, Beauchamp and Childress, state:

> [T]he distinction between killing and letting die suffers from vagueness and moral confusion. The language of killing is so thoroughly confusing—causally, legally, and morally—that it can provide little if any help in discussion of assistance in dying.[278]

The specific concerns can be outlined as follows. First, the distinction can be said to lead to illogical results. As Lord Goff admitted in *Bland*:

> [I]t can be asked why, if the doctor, by discontinuing treatment, is entitled in consequence to let his patient die, it should not be lawful to put him out of his misery straight away, in a more humane manner, by a lethal injection, rather than let him linger on in pain until he dies. But the law does not feel able to authorise euthanasia, even in circumstances such as these, for, once euthanasia is recognised as lawful in these circumstances, it is difficult to see any logical basis for excluding it in others.[279]

Particularly topical is the practice of continuous deep sedation.[280] This involves sedating a patient by pain relief so that he or she is in a coma-like state. Then, food and hydration can be withdrawn and the person will die. This enables the medical team to claim that the death is as a result of an omission (the failure to feed or hydrate) rather than an act. Yet it might be argued that this is simply a way of manipulating the act/omission distinction to achieve death.[281]

[272] Foot (1976).
[273] Stauch (2000). See further Asscher (2008), who argues that the question of responsibilities is more important than the act/omission distinction in this context.
[274] Foot (1976).   [275] Coulson (1996).
[276] For arguments supporting the distinction between killing and letting die, see Callahan (1993) and Kamm (1998).
[277] [1993] 1 All ER 821, 885.   [278] Beauchamp and Childress (2009: 31).
[279] [1993] 1 All ER 821, 831.
[280] An excellent discussion can be found in Smith II (2013).
[281] For further discussion, see Raho and Miccinesi (2015); Raus (2011) and Bressington (2011).

Even some opponents of euthanasia are critical of the distinction between acts and omissions. To Keown, the focus on acts and omissions avoids the key question: did the doctor intend to produce death?[282] He argues that if a doctor intends to kill, this is wrong. Whether the doctor intended to produce death by an act or an omission is simply a detail about the method of killing, which should not carry moral weight[283]—although it might be asked whether a doctor withdrawing pain is intending death or relief from burdensome treatment.[284]

Second, it is difficult to know sometimes whether an aspect of one's behaviour is an act or an omission. Is switching off a life support machine an act or an omission?[285] Lord Neuberger in *R (on the application of Nicklinson) v Ministry of Justice*[286] seemed troubled by the distinction and referred to 'a certain and understandable discomfort with the notion that switching a machine off actually is an omission'. Williams makes the point in the following way:

> The question then arises whether stopping a respirator is an act of killing or a decision to let nature take its course? Common sense suggests it is the latter. Suppose that the respirator worked only as long as the doctor turned a handle. If he stopped turning, he would be regarded as merely commencing to omit to save the patient's life. Suppose, alternatively, that the respirator worked electrically but was made to shut itself off it would be an omission. It can make no moral difference that the respirator is constructed to run continuously and has to be stopped. Stopping the respirator is not a positive act of killing the patient, but a decision not to strive any longer to save him.

To some commentators, the difficulties in making the distinction between an act and an omission reveal that the moral principles governing a doctor's decision should not focus on the distinction between withholding or withdrawing treatment, but rather what duties a physician owes to his or her patient.[287] The issue comes to a head when a contrast is made between switching off a ventilator (which is seen as an omission) and switching off an internal device, such as a pacemaker (which is seen as an act). What, then, are we to make of a left ventricular assist device (LVAD)—that is, a mechanical heart pump—which is partly inside and partly outside the body?[288]

Third, it is argued by some that omissions cannot cause a result. Logically, the absence of an act cannot make something happen. In response, others claim that we regularly talk of an omission leading to an outcome: the student failed the exam because he or she failed to work hard enough, for example.[289] In the context of seriously ill patients, is there not a difference between letting nature take its course (that is, an omission) and doing an act that disrupts the course of events?[290] As Miller and Truog put it, withdrawing 'initiates the fatal sequence, as distinct from merely permitting it to continue without intervention to stop it'.[291] They therefore see a withdrawal of treatment as different from withholding treatment.[292] Holman J, however, was in clear disagreement:

> there is, and can be, no legal (nor indeed ethical) distinction between a decision to withhold artificial ventilation and a decision to withdraw or discontinue it once started. In

---

[282] Keown (2002: 14).   [283] Bennett (1966).   [284] McGee (2011).
[285] Leng (1982).   [286] [2014] UKSC 38 at [22].   [287] See the discussion in Merkel (2016).
[288] Kraemer (2011).   [289] Garrard and Wilkinson (2005: 66).   [290] McGee (2005).
[291] Miller and Truog (2012).   [292] See Wollard (2015) for a detailed discussion.

neither case does the decision involve killing the child. The child is not killed. He dies because of the natural result or effect of his underlying disorder or disease.[293]

Much of the philosophical discussion concerning the distinction between acts and omissions has centred on a hypothetical example put forward by James Rachels:

> Smith stands to gain a large inheritance if anything should happen to his six-year-old cousin. One evening while the child is taking his bath, Smith sneaks into the bathroom and drowns the child, and then arranges things so it will look like an accident. No one is any the wiser, and Smith gets his inheritance.
>
> Jones also stands to gain if anything should happen to his six-year-old cousin. Like Smith, Jones sneaks in to the bathroom planning to drown the child in his bath. However, just as he enters the bathroom Jones sees the child slip, hit his head, and fall face down in the water. Jones is delighted; he stands by, ready to push the child's head under if necessary, but it is not necessary. With only a little thrashing about, the child drowns all by himself, 'accidentally', as Jones watches and does nothing. No one is any the wiser and Jones gets his inheritance.[294]

Rachels argues that there is no difference between Smith and Jones in this scenario, and that this demonstrates that there is no moral difference between an act and omission. He accepts that, generally, omissions are not blameworthy, but this is because omissions are normally accidental or negligent, whereas actions rarely are.[295] A person rushing past a person drowning in a river is not normally intending that person to die, but a person who pushes another in is. He argues that the significance of his hypothetical example is that both Smith and Jones intend to kill. Where there is no difference in intention, he argues that there is no moral difference between what they have done. Rachels goes on to point out that killing a child by deliberately starving him or her would be one of the cruellest ways of killing, even though it would be an omission.

Nesbitt provides a powerful riposte to Rachels.[296] He argues that he would rather live in a world populated by people who would not rescue him if he were to get into trouble, but who would not try actively to kill him, than a world populated by people who would be willing to act to kill. He argues that if Rachels's scenario were modified so that Jones would not have been prepared to push the child's head under if necessary (that is, that he was willing to kill only by omission), there would be a clear difference between Jones and Smith. This, Nesbitt argues, suggests that the difference between acts and omissions is significant. Kuhse responds to this argument by saying that if she were in the process of a painful death, she would rather have people who were willing to act to kill her than those who would stand by.[297] The issue, she argues, is whether the killing is good or not—not whether there was an act or an omission. It is the outcome that matters, not how the outcome was produced. Another response to Rachels's scenario is that the two cases are different because the range of options open to Smith and Jones were

---

[293] *Central Manchester University Hospitals NHS Foundation Trust v A* [2015] EWHC 2828 (Fam).
[294] Rachels (1986: 112).
[295] Actions, it is said, are also more likely to result in a serious injury than omissions and are more likely to threaten society as a whole: Tooley (1980).
[296] Nesbitt (1995).   [297] Kuhse (1998); Kuhse and Singer (2001).

different, even if the end results of their behaviour were the same. They were different in that, for Jones, the only thing that he could do to avoid the end result was rescue the child; for Smith to avoid the end result, he could do anything he liked, except drown the child. Because the options open to them at the time in question differed, their acts have a different moral character.[298]

There are many problems with the sharp distinction between an act and an omission. Despite these philosophical problems, many argue that the distinction provides a useful guide.[299] It gives doctors who cease treating patients the comfort of saying that they did not kill their patients[300] and it also preserves the 'slippery slope' argument. Even if not logical, arguably the distinction is said to be in accordance with many people's intuition.[301] McCall Smith has suggested that, despite its theoretical difficulties, it provides a basis upon which many people think and act.[302] Leaving aside cases in which it is difficult to draw a distinction between an act and an omission, there are few cases in which a killing is justified (perhaps those in which the killing is in self-defence, for example), whereas generally 'letting die' is permissible (we are not responsible for failing to ensure that those starving in other countries do not die). So in broad terms the distinction has merits.[303]

5 Ethical issues: euthanasia

We will start with the ethical debates surrounding euthanasia, before turning to those relating to assisted suicide and terminating treatment. It is in the debate over euthanasia that many of the ethical issues are made most apparent.

5.1 The heart of the debate

Before getting into the detail of the debate over the issue, it is useful to summarize two extreme views on euthanasia.

(i) *Supporters of euthanasia* Those who support euthanasia say that there is nothing more horrific than a slow, pain-filled, undignified death. People faced with such a possibility should have the option of ending their life at a time and in a way of their choosing. We live in a society that emphasizes the right to autonomy—the right to make decisions over how we live our lives. To render illegal the killing of a person desperate to die is to deny that person the power to make one of the most important and intimate decisions of his or her life. Some people may have moral objections to euthanasia, but they should not impose their views on others. It is a matter of personal choice.

(ii) *Opponents of euthanasia* Those who oppose it argue that to permit one person to kill another is a profound violation of a crucial moral principle: the sanctity of life.

[298] Mohindra (2009: 293).   [299] Glover (1977: 186–8).
[300] Gillon (1999a).   [301] Gillett (1988).
[302] McCall Smith (1999). Kamisar (1998: 34) refers to the 'deep need' to distinguish between killing and letting die.
[303] McLachlan (2017).

To legalize euthanasia is to undermine the principle that all lives are of equal value. Support for euthanasia is premised on the assumption that there are some lives that are not worth living. That implies that there are some lives that are of greater value than others, and that is a repugnant idea. Further, any move to change the law will have a particularly harsh impact on vulnerable people, who will be easily manipulated into agreeing to euthanasia.

5.2 Definitions

Before considering some of the arguments for and against euthanasia, it is necessary to set out some definitions and distinctions. One of the difficulties facing anyone navigating the material in this area is that there is no agreement over many of the key terms. This can lead to arguments in which some of the disagreement is caused by alternative understandings of terms such as 'euthanasia' and 'sanctity of life'. Inevitably, not all of the following distinctions or definitions will be agreed upon by everyone, but an attempt has been made to use the most widely accepted understanding of these terms.

5.2.1 Voluntary/non-voluntary/involuntary euthanasia

To many writing on this topic, it is crucial to distinguish between the following:

(i)   *voluntary euthanasia*, as behaviour that causes the patient's death at the patient's request;

(ii) *non-voluntary euthanasia*, as behaviour that causes the patient's death without the consent *or objection* of the patient (that is, where the patient is unable to consent or object); and

(iii) *involuntary euthanasia*, which arises when the competent patient has not expressly consented to die, but is killed nonetheless.

There are few people who accept the justifiability of involuntary euthanasia. Indeed, some commentators argue that involuntary euthanasia should be simply described as murder, rather than dignified by being labelled 'euthanasia'.[304]

5.2.2 Active/passive voluntary euthanasia

English and Welsh law draws an important distinction between those cases in which the death of the patient is caused by an act and those in which it is caused by an omission.[305] To some, there is a clear distinction between a case in which a doctor deliberately injects a patient with a lethal dose of drugs and those in which the doctor decides not to perform an operation that would save the life of a patient or withdraws life-sustaining treatment from a patient. Indeed, some suggest that it is correct to describe as euthanasia only those cases in which a person has done an act.

---

[304] Biggs (2001: 12).   [305] Garrard and Wilkinson (2005) provide a useful discussion.

Many others, as we have seen, argue that there is no moral difference between an act and an omission intended to cause death; both should be treated in the same way.[306] They tend to argue that what matters is not how a person kills another (be it by act or omission), but the circumstances in which he or she acts or the intentions with which he or she acts.[307]

5.2.3 *Intention/foresight and the doctrine of double effect*

To some, euthanasia occurs only when the actor intends to kill the patient. If, for example, a doctor provides a pain-relieving drug to a patient in order to reduce a patient's suffering, although he or she knows that the drug will also cause the death of a patient, this will not be euthanasia because there is no intent.[308] Other commentators reject a distinction between intention and foresight, and argue that if a doctor foresees that his or her treatment will lead to a patient's death, this is equivalent to intention.

Many who support the idea that euthanasia occurs only where there is an intention to kill support the doctrine of double effect.[309] In essence, this doctrine holds that, in some circumstances, a person who is doing an act with the purpose of producing result A, but foreseeing that result B may well result from his or her actions, will be held to intend result A.[310] The exact meaning of the doctrine is disputed. Keown's version quotes four principles that render it permissible to do an act that produces a bad consequence:

(1) the act one is engaged in is not itself bad,

(2) the bad consequence is not a means to the good consequence,

(3) the bad consequence is foreseen but not intended, and

(4) there is sufficiently serious reason for allowing the bad consequence to occur.[311]

Relying on this doctrine, its supporters are able to say that a doctor who gives his or her patient pain-relieving drugs for the purpose of pain relief, but foreseeing that they will also have the effect of killing the patient, will not be said to have intended to kill the patient.

5.2.4 *Justified/excused euthanasia*

Another distinction is between those cases of euthanasia in which the act is justified and those in which it is excused. This distinction is, basically, as follows.[312]

(i) A *justification* is an argument that the killing was permissible, or even morally right.

(ii) An *excuse* admits that the killing was not permissible, but that the actor does not deserve blame.

---

[306] Miller, Truog, and Brock (2010).

[307] For a useful discussion of such arguments, see Dworkin, Frey, and Bok (1998), Kamm (1998), and Brock (1992).

[308] Keown (2002: ch. 2).

[309] See Foster, Herring, Melham, et al. (2011), who argue that there are a range of versions of the doctrine and that there are dangers in regarding it as a single doctrine.

[310] See McGee (2013a).   [311] Keown (2002: 20). See also Gormally (1995).

[312] The concepts are, in fact, more complex than appear from this outline: see Herring (2010c: ch. 12).

To most supporters of euthanasia, there is a strong case for claiming that killing was justified in some circumstances. Opponents reject an argument that euthanasia is justified. However, some opponents of euthanasia will accept that there may be cases in which the killing is excused, for example where a person, exhausted by the caring of an infirm spouse, kills his or her partner at the partner's request. Although opponents will argue that such a killing was wrong, they might accept that the killer has an excuse because of the mental strain that he or she was suffering.

5.2.5 Sanctity of life/vitalism/quality of life

At the heart of much of the debate on euthanasia is the principle of the 'sanctity of life'. Unfortunately, there has been considerable division over what exactly that principle means. It is clear that it has been used by judges and commentators to mean very different things.[313] It is perhaps helpful to distinguish the principles of 'vitalism', 'sanctity of life', and 'quality of life'.[314]

(i)   *Vitalism* This principle holds that human life has an absolute moral value. It is never justifiable to kill another person. Doctors should take all reasonable steps to keep humans alive. It is therefore impermissible for doctors to do an act that causes a patient to die or to fail to take reasonable steps to keep a person alive.

(ii) *Sanctity of life* This also holds that human life is a fundamental basic good. It states that a person should not be intentionally killed, be that through an act or an omission. Sanctity of life seeks to value the good of life itself. That good exists independent of any disability or incapacity. Craig Paterson argues: '[I]t is always and everywhere wrong to intentionally kill an innocent person regardless of any further appeal to consequences or motive.'[315] However, the theory of sanctity of life can be distinguished from vitalism in two regards.

(a)   The principle accepts that an act that shortens the life of a patient can be justifiable if it is not done with the intent to kill. It is the intentional killing that is outlawed by the principle and so the principle can be seen to support the doctrine of double effect.

(b)   It may be permissible to withdraw treatment if the reason for doing so is that the treatment offers no hope of benefit. The principle would not, however, justify withdrawal of treatment because the patient's life was not worth living.[316] It therefore does not agree with vitalism that life should be protected at all costs.

(iii) *Quality of life* The basic approach here is concerned with assessing whether the patient's life is worthwhile. It holds that certain lives are not worth living and that it is therefore right to end them. It rejects the argument put forward by supporters of the 'sanctity of life' approach that there is something good about life in and of itself. By contrast, it is claimed that what makes a life good are the experiences of the person and his or her interaction with others. A life that can no longer be experienced and in which relationships with others are impossible is a life that has

---

[313] Keown (1999: 253) sees a collapse of respect for the principle of sanctity of life around the world.
[314] Keown (2002: 43; 2006c: 109) stresses the importance of this distinction.
[315] Paterson (2008: 181).   [316] Keown (2002: 43).

lost its goodness. Some supporters of this approach would attach great weight to the assessment of the individual himself or herself as to whether his or her life still had value.

5.2.6 *The principle of autonomy*

The autonomy principle underlies much liberal political thought and was discussed in much greater detail in Chapters 1 and 4. To most supporters of euthanasia, the key ethical concept is the principle of autonomy. This is, in simple terms, the argument that people should be permitted to live their lives as they wish, as long as their choices do not harshly impact on others. The alternative, of the government or other people dictating to us how we should live our lives, is seen by many as unacceptable paternalism. [317]

5.2.7 *Ordinary/extraordinary treatment*

To some commentators, there is a fundamental distinction to be drawn between ordinary treatment, which doctors are obliged to provide to their patients, and extraordinary treatment, which they are not obliged to provide. Behind this debate is an argument over the lengths to which a doctor need go to delay the death, or prolong the life, of the patient. This can be said to be justified as part of the need to protect the dignity of the patient: it is undignified for a patient to have every attempt made in a desperate bid to save his or her life.

In *Ms D v An NHS Trust Hospital*,[318] Colderidge J made a declaration that doctors need not provide further life-saving treatments for a PVS patient. He held:

> In my judgement she should be allowed as dignified a passing as is achievable. Some might say that her dignity has already been severely compromised by the progress and incidence of this awful disease. To subject her body to further grossly invasive procedure can only further detract from her dignity.[319]

The distinction might also be justified as a reasonable allocation of resources. It would be foolish to expend substantial resources on treatment that has only a faint chance of saving the life of the patient.

To some commentators, although the distinction is a useful one, the words 'ordinary' or 'extraordinary' are not particularly helpful. It is not about whether the treatments are often used or not; rather, it is about whether the treatment is proportionate or beneficial to the patient. Gerald Kelly, in an oft-quoted statement, has suggested:

> Ordinary means are all medicine, treatments, and operations which offer a reasonable hope of benefit and which can be obtained and used without excessive expense, pain, or other inconvenience. Extraordinary means are all medicines, treatments, and operations, which cannot be obtained or used without excessive expense, pain, or other inconvenience, or which, if used, would not offer a reasonable hope of benefit.[320]

---

[317] See Stewart, Peisah, and Draper (2011) for a draft test for capacity in this context. It is lengthy, indicating the difficulty of the issue.
[318] [2005] EWHC 2439 (Fam).   [319] At [44].   [320] Kelly (1951: 551).

This interpretation suggests that the extraordinary/ordinary distinction is little more than a balancing of the benefits and disadvantages of the treatment, in which case it might be better to use different terminology.

5.2.8 *The difference between treatment and basic care*

Some commentators argue that there is a crucial distinction between medical treatment and basic care.[321] They take the view that although it may be legitimate to withdraw medical treatment from a patient, it is never permissible to withdraw basic care, such as feeding or cleaning. The argument is that to deny basic care is undignified and inhumane. So although a patient has the right to refuse medical treatment, he or she does not have the right to refuse basic care.

5.3 **Autonomy**

5.3.1 *The right to choose the time and manner of one's own death*

As already mentioned, the notion of autonomy is that people should be free to lead their lives as they wish and have control over their own bodies. People's decisions on how to live their lives deserve respect, even though other people might think them foolish.[322] A person's decision is respected not because it is a good choice, but because it is his or her own choice.[323] Denying a person respect for his or her views is the ultimate denial of respect for that person.[324]

Such respect is particularly important in relation to deeply personal or intimate issues, such as when to die. Dworkin has written: 'Making someone die in a way that others approve, but he believes a horrifying contradiction of his life, is a devastating, odious form of tyranny.'[325] Each person may have his or her own view of what is a good death—be it struggling to live for as long as possible, or dying before life becomes undignified or full of pain.[326] Each person should be free to select his or her mode of dying, and if that needs the involvement of others, they should be free to act as requested without fear of a criminal prosecution. Supporters of euthanasia sometimes claim that those opposing euthanasia are attempting to impose their own ethical or religious beliefs on others.[327] Joseph Raz has suggested that giving autonomy in death helps autonomy in life:

> [I]nevitably shaping one's dying contributes to giving shape, contributes to the form and meaning one's life has. Those who reflect, plan and decide on the manner of their dying make their dying part of their life. And if they do so well then by integrating their dying into their life they enrich their life.
>
> It can transform one's perspective on one's life; reduce the aspects of it from which one is alienated, or those that inspire a sense of helplessness or terror. It is a change that makes one whole in generating a perspective, a way of conceiving oneself and one's life free from some of those negative aspects.[328]

---

[321] Anscombe (1981).
[322] Seale and Addington-Hall (1994) consider the reasons why people wish to die in a particular way.
[323] Pedain (2003: 203).   [324] Harris (1995).   [325] Dworkin (1993: 217).
[326] Logue (1996) discusses the sociological understanding of a good death.
[327] See Williams (2005) and Dworkin, Nagel, Nozick, et al. (1998: 431).
[328] Raz (2012: 21). See also Davis (2013) for a claim that people commit suicide for fear they will not later be able to control their deaths.

Dworkin has argued that death is an area in which it is particularly important that a person's wishes be followed.[329] He distinguishes two kinds of choices: critical and experimental interests. Experimental interests are the interests that we have in things that we enjoy doing in and of themselves, such as eating certain kinds of food; critical interests are part of what we believe makes us who we are, such as a person's religious or ethical beliefs. It is especially important that critical interests are respected.[330] He argues that how a person dies is of critical interest to most people (their deaths should 'keep faith' with the way in which they lived their lives) and that it is therefore of fundamental importance that a person's wish is respected.[331] Not all supporters of autonomy are happy with Dworkin's analysis, however, because it appears to leave the door open for someone to say to a person requesting death: 'I know you are now saying that you want to die, but a better fit with your life story (your critical interests) would be for you to live longer.'[332] Kate Greasley has questioned whether, for most people, the manner of death is a critical interest.[333] The exact manner of his or her death is not normally regarded as a matter saying very much about a person's life.

5.3.2 Challenging the autonomy argument

Opponents of euthanasia tend to argue against an approach based on autonomy in one of four ways:

- by accepting that autonomy is an important principle, but arguing that there are other interests that need to be weighed against it;
- by saying that, in the context of euthanasia, it is not possible to be confident that the person has made a genuinely free and autonomous choice;
- by saying that autonomy cannot be used to justify an act that leads to death; or
- by saying that the argument proves too much, because it would justify euthanasia in circumstances which would be unacceptable.

These will be looked at separately.

5.3.3 Autonomy and the interests of others

First is the argument that other principles or values can be used to outweigh the principle of autonomy. But what might those be? The following are three possible contenders.

(i) *The right of the patient to choose to die must be counterbalanced against the interests of society as a whole* Dying is not an individual matter; it has an impact on others and society as a whole. It is, however, difficult to identify precisely the harm that relatives or society as a whole will suffer if we permit euthanasia. Clearly, there will be the grief that relatives suffer, but how does this compare with the pain of watching someone die in a slow painful way? But is there more? The House of Lords Select Committee held:

> We acknowledge that there are individual cases in which euthanasia may be seen by some to be appropriate. But individual cases cannot reasonably establish the foundation of a

[329] Dworkin (1998).
[330] Dworkin (1998) is therefore critical of the reasoning in *Bland*, focusing on Tony Bland's inability to experience anything, rather than considering how his death might fit in with his values (his critical interests).
[331] See Grubb (1997) for further discussion.
[332] Harris (1995).   [333] Greasley (2010).

policy which would have such serious and widespread repercussions. Moreover dying is not only a personal or individual affair. The death of a person affects the lives of others, often in ways and to an extent which cannot be foreseen. We believe that the issue of euthanasia is one in which the interests of the individual cannot be separated from the interest of society as a whole.[334]

(ii) *This right to die must be balanced against concerns that other patients who do not want to die will be pressurized into saying that they do*[335] In other words, it is better to have a legal system that denies some people the right to autonomy to die as they wish than to have a legal system under which some people might be killed under the label 'euthanasia' against their wishes. In essence, this argument is connected to the 'slippery slope' argument which we will look at later.[336] As we shall see, there is heated debate over whether, once voluntary euthanasia is permitted, it is possible to put in place mechanisms that ensure that involuntary euthanasia is not permitted. Even if that is possible, Lord Sumption in *Nicklinson* raised the problem of 'indirect social pressure':

> This refers to the problems arising from the low self-esteem of many old or severely ill and dependent people, combined with the spontaneous and negative perceptions of patients about the views of those around them. The great majority of people contemplating suicide for health-related reasons, are likely to be acutely conscious that their disabilities make them dependent on others. These disabilities may arise from illness or injury, or indeed (a much larger category) from the advancing infirmity of old age. People in this position are vulnerable. They are often afraid that their lives have become a burden to those around them. The fear may be the result of overt pressure, but may equally arise from a spontaneous tendency to place a low value on their own lives and assume that others do so too. Their feelings of uselessness are likely to be accentuated in those who were once highly active and engaged with those around them, for whom the contrast between now and then must be particularly painful. These assumptions may be mistaken but are none the less powerful for that. The legalisation of assisted suicide would be followed by its progressive normalisation, at any rate among the very old or very ill. In a world where suicide was regarded as just another optional end-of-life choice, the pressures which I have described are likely to become more powerful. It is one thing to assess some one's mental ability to form a judgment, but another to discover their true reasons for the decision which they have made and to assess the quality of those reasons. I very much doubt whether it is possible in the generality of cases to distinguish between those who have spontaneously formed the desire to kill themselves and those who have done so in response to real or imagined pressure arising from the impact of their disabilities on other people.

(iii) *There is a moral imperative or value that counterbalances the autonomy right*[337] The argument here is not that there are the interests of others or particular members of society that need to be protected, but that there are moral principles that the law should uphold, such as the sanctity of life, even if, in upholding them, the autonomy

---

[334] House of Lords Select Committee (1993: para. 237), discussed in Keown (2002: ch. 16).
[335] Mak, Elwyn, and Finlay (2003).
[336] See under the heading '5.10 Slippery slopes: where will it all end?'.
[337] Keown (2002: ch. 5).

rights of individual members of society are infringed. So the argument here is not that there are specifically identified harms, but that there is damage to the moral fibre of society, which justifies an infringement of people's autonomy.

Mary Neal[338] has argued that autonomy is not the only value that needs to be valued. She writes:

> To value respect for autonomy to the extent that we are prepared to sacrifice persons' lives for its sake is, in my opinion, to allow the principle of respect for autonomy to break loose from its ethical moorings—as one consideration within the overall scheme of valuing persons—and run amok. [P's] autonomy deserves to be respected only because we value [P] herself; its value is secondary to hers, and we must not fetishise it.

In her argument valuing a person may involve not following their autonomous decision. Is the person who desperately seeks to get medical help for their suicidal partner, valuing that partner for they are and could be; realizing there is more to value in them than their suicidal wishes?

5.3.4 *Autonomy and the possibility of choice*

Another kind of argument that can be made against autonomy in the euthanasia context is that it is not possible to make a fully informed, autonomous choice to die. Because the decision to die is of the utmost gravity and is irreversible, we should properly require the highest standards of competence. Some commentators suggest that no person suffering the pain and anguish of being close to death will be sufficiently competent to be able to consent to the treatment,[339] or that patients are often unaware of the effectiveness of pain relief or the availability of rehabilitative care for those with disabilities or with terminal illness, and therefore cannot make properly informed decisions.[340] Indeed, there is also some evidence that many of those seeking death are suffering depression[341] and that, once medication for depression is provided, the numbers of those seeking euthanasia falls—by 99 per cent, according to a report produced by the Royal College of Psychiatrists.[342] According to a leading research team at the University of Washington, 90 per cent of those who die from suicide have a diagnosable mental disorder.[343] We should not forget that, looking at suicide attempts generally, the cases that come to court are exceptional. Most suicide cases involve people plagued by mental illness and despair. These are not carefully thought-out, autonomous decisions.[344] Further evidence suggests that people with terminal illnesses keep changing their views on whether or not they want assistance in dying.[345] So to abide by a person's wish to die one day may be to work contrary to what his or her wishes will be the next day. The European

---

[338] Neal (2017).
[339] Gordijn, Crul, and Zylicz (2002).
[340] Coleman and Drake (2002); Woods (2002). Van der Maas, van Delden, and Pijnenborg (1991) found that, in their study, less than a third of patients who were seeking death retained a wish to die after alternative pain relief had been offered.
[341] Miller (2015).
[342] Royal College of Psychiatrists (2006: 3). See also Blank, Robison, Prigerson, et al. (2001).
[343] Mental Health Reporting (2013).
[344] Herring (2013d).
[345] Chochinov, Tataryn, Clinch, et al. (1999) state that the will to live is highly unstable among elderly terminal cancer patients.

Parliamentary Assembly Committee on Legal Affairs and Human Rights, considering such evidence, stated:

> Medical professionals working within the palliative care sector have emphasised the fragility of patients' desire for death and the rapid changes that, in their experience, may occur in response to good symptom control or psychological interventions. The dangers of acceding to rare requests for voluntary active euthanasia and physician assisted suicide should not be underestimated.[346]

The difficulty with this reasoning is that, even at its strongest, it may lead us to conclude that most people at the point of death lack competence, but it is difficult to believe that everyone will.[347]

5.3.5 *Can autonomy justify ending-life decisions?*

Some commentators argue that there is an irony in using the principle of autonomy in relation to death, which is the ultimate loss of the ability to make choices. In other words, we encourage autonomy to enable people to live the kind of lives that they wish—to flourish and develop as people.[348] Euthanasia, by contrast, is not promoting personality growth; it is the end of the person. It is therefore not possible to justify euthanasia on the basis of autonomy. Kate Greasley argues, having noted that even supporters of autonomy do not generally support a person agreeing to become a slave:

> Death spells the end of all good options because it spells the end of options, period. (In this way death seems even more inimical to autonomy than enslavement; we can imagine a slave having at least some options left open to him, albeit impoverished ones.) It is difficult to see, then, that helping someone to die can ever be compatible with the value of personal autonomy, even if in so doing we are acceding to his wishes.[349]

Alexander McCall Smith has warned against seeing autonomy as a good in and of itself.[350] He says that autonomy is a good because it enables us to develop our lives as we wish in connection with other people. Indeed, it is notable that we do not abide by the wishes of those who desire to sell themselves into slavery. In part, this is because such an exercise of autonomy undermines the values of autonomy that we treasure.[351] Critics might reply that this overlooks the fact that the way in which a person dies is regarded by many as an important part of their lives. A 'good death' is seen as a good conclusion to the end of someone's life, fitting in with the values that have determined their life to date. So seen, it is a reasonable aspect of a person's vision of a 'good life'.

5.3.6 *Autonomy and setting limits*

A fourth argument against the emphasis placed on autonomy is that most supporters of euthanasia do not believe that anyone who wants to be killed should be allowed to

---

[346] European Parliamentary Assembly Committee on Legal Affairs and Human Rights (2003: para. I).
[347] See Gorsuch (2000) for a further discussion of competence in this area.
[348] Gormally (1995).   [349] Greasley (2010: 303).   [350] McCall Smith (1997).
[351] But see Singer (2003), who argues that the reason for not enforcing slavery is the repugnant enforcement mechanisms that would have to be used.

do so. Dworkin, for example, has suggested that euthanasia should be available only for those who are predicted to die within six months.[352] Few supporters of euthanasia would agree that a young man whose girlfriend has just left him, who feels that life is no longer worth living, should be able to walk into a hospital and demand to be killed.[353] But if the principle of autonomy is the guiding light, why not? His choices should be respected whether we think them right or wrong.[354] Critics argue that, although it is said that the principle of autonomy is at the heart of the debate, the reality is that supporters of euthanasia respect the wishes of a person only if they think that his or her decision is a reasonable one. In other words, they will respect the wish to die only of those people whose lives are not worth living.[355] Dworkin has responded to such arguments that 'we might very well say as a community—we bet we might be wrong, but we bet—that if the teenage lover lives another two years, maybe even two weeks, he will be very glad not to have taken his own life'.[356] But such an argument might be thought to undermine the basis of autonomy, which is to let people make decisions of their own and not to permit others to assume that they know what someone really wants.[357]

There is no doubt that the hypothetical example of the lovesick teenager has caused some difficulties for some supporters of euthanasia. But there is a problem here for opponents of euthanasia too. Most opponents of euthanasia support the principle that, if a competent person refuses life-saving treatment, his or her wishes should be respected. But why does autonomy dominate when the wish is not to have treatment, yet not when the patient seeks active intervention to hasten death?[358] This issue raises the extent to which it is justifiable to distinguish an act and an omission. Yet, as we have already noted and shall see further, this is a distinction that many philosophers find difficult to maintain.[359]

5.3.7 *Autonomy and liberty at the end of life*

Kevin Yuill has argued that legalizing euthanasia or assisted suicide will undermine autonomy, because those seeking assistance will be interviewed by experts to assess their competence.[360] That will mean doctors can 'colonize our most intimate thoughts and influence what should be the most personal decision ever made'.[361] He is concerned that:

> Legalising assisted suicide reduces suicide to a medical choice. What should be profound and meaningful, the most human of human actions, loses its meaning. The question of whether 'to be or not to be' becomes a medical rather than a moral question.[362]

[352] Dworkin (1998: 1151).
[353] Frileux, Lelievre, Munoz Sastre, et al. (2003) found that the general public regards euthanasia as more appropriate the older, the more ill, and the greater the suffering of the person seeking death.
[354] This argument is developed in Ackernman (1998).
[355] Gormally (1997).   [356] Dworkin (1998: 1151).
[357] See Brassington (2008), who argues that assisted suicide should be available to people even if they are not terminally ill or suffering.
[358] For example, Keown (2002: ch. 5).
[359] See McGee (2011) for a bold attempt to justify the distinction.
[360] Yuill (2012).   [361] Yuill (2012: 9).   [362] Yuill (2012: 84).

Yuill's preferred response is to make lethal drugs more readily available so that people can commit suicide, having made their own decisions. Critics will see that as irresponsible, given the links between suicide and mental illness.

5.4 The sanctity of life: the key principle or religious mumbo jumbo?

For many opponents of euthanasia, at the heart of the issues surrounding euthanasia is the principle of the sanctity of life. The lives of every member of society should be valued so highly by our society that they should not be intentionally destroyed, even if that is what the particular individual wishes. Supporters argue that, once the principle is departed from, it inevitably becomes necessary to value some lives as less than others and not worth living. By contrast, the sanctity of life principle values all human lives equally and emphasizes that killing represents a unique wrong.[363] The House of Lords Select Committee on Medical Ethics concluded that the prohibition on intentional killing was 'the cornerstone of law and of social relationships'.[364]

Lord Wilson in *R (on the application of Nicklinson) v Ministry of Justice*[365] claimed that the principle 'is hard-wired into the minds of every living person. It lies at the heart of the common law and of international human rights and it is also an ethical principle of the first magnitude'.

The principle is supported particularly by those writing from a religious perspective, who often start from the principle that each person has been made in the image of God and is equally precious in God's sight.[366] However, the principle is also supported by those of no religious persuasion, but who are attracted by its insistence of the equal value of all human life. The argument that every person has a profound inherent value helps explain why we are all equally valuable. If we say that the value in life comes from a person's ability or possessions we lose the concept of equality. Somerville emphasizes the importance of the 'secular sacred', respecting the mysteries of life and death, which is of importance to the religious and non-religious.[367] She also emphasizes the 'deeply intuitive sense of relatedness or connectedness to other people and to the world and the universe in which we live', which means that each person's life has value for the whole of society.[368] Allowing death to occur when 'its time has come' is part of recognizing the mystery of life and death.[369] Somerville admits that this all sounds rather vague, but insists that this does not detract from the fact that it has been intuitively felt to be true by so many people for so long. Emily Jackson, by contrast, contends that it is impossible to have a secular understanding of the principle of sanctity of life.[370] She argues the principle makes sense only based on religious values. As a result, she argues that it should play no role in secular law.

---

[363] Linacre Centre (1994).
[364] House of Lords Select Committee on Medical Ethics (1993). See also Special Committee of the Canadian Senate (1995).
[365] [2014] UKSC 38 at [199].
[366] See Cohen, van Delden, Mortier, et al. (2008) for evidence that doctors with religious belief are more likely to oppose euthanasia than those without.
[367] Somerville (2001).   [368] Somerville (2002: 654).   [369] Somerville (2001: xiv).
[370] Jackson (2008b); cf. Wicks (2009), who states that a secular belief in the sanctity of life is coherent.

Opponents of the principle of sanctity of life generally accept that life is precious and valuable, but they reject the insistence that all life must be valued for its own sake.[371] In other words, supporters of euthanasia often take the view that there comes a point at which a person's life is so wracked with pain and indignity that its special value has been lost. Rachels, for example, argues that there is a difference between having a life and being alive.[372] To keep a person alive on a life support machine for years on end, even though there is no prospect of an improvement in his or her condition, is not to value the preciousness of life, but to demean it. Such commentators argue that the sacredness of life turns not on being alive, but on having a life worth living.[373] This is why we regard the death of a person in the full flush of health and youth as a tragedy, but the death of person who ceased to interact with the outside world months ago as almost a blessing.[374]

Ronald Dworkin, considering the position of a patient suffering from Alzheimer's disease, says that such a person:

> . . . is no longer capable of the acts or attachments that can give [life] value. Value cannot be poured into a life from the outside; it must be generated by the person whose life it is, and this is no longer possible for him.[375]

Dworkin sees value in life as about making something of one's life and living in earnest. Therefore, once someone is in great pain near the end of their life, then if, to them, their life has lost its value, then that person's life is no longer of special value and no longer protected by the sanctity of life principle.

We can now specify clearly the differences between supporters and opponents of the sanctity of life view.

(i)   Supporters of sanctity of life argue that life in and of itself is valuable. Even a person in a coma, with no awareness of the outside world and with no friends or relatives to be concerned about him or her, has value by virtue of being human. To reject such a view leads one to value the lives of disabled people less than those of others.[376] Finnis claims that:

> Human life is indeed the concrete reality of the human person. In sustaining human bodily life, in however impaired a condition, one is sustaining the person whose life it is. In refusing to choose to violate it, one respects the person in the most fundamental and indispensable way.[377]

In other words, life is valuable in itself. To value a person's life only for the experiences that he or she has is to adopt a dualist view of existence, which draws a sharp distinction between the mind and the body.[378] We cannot treat people like goods that have passed their 'sell by' date.[379]

(ii)   Opponents of sanctity of life emphasize that what makes life valuable are the things that people do with their lives. It is the experiences that people have, their relationships and activities, which give life meaning. A person with no experiences (or only

[371] Harris (1984); Glover (1977).   [372] Rachels (1986).   [373] Harris (1995a).
[374] Warnock (1992).   [375] Dworkin (1993: 230).   [376] Ramsay (1978).
[377] Finnis (1995b: 32).   [378] Finnis (1993).   [379] Sommerville (2001: xix).

pain-filled ones) and no capacity for relationships has lost the goodness of life.[380] Of a person suffering from PVS, Harris argues:

> It is a living human body (as in a sense it often is when brain death is diagnosed on a life-support system—it is warm, the blood circulates and so on) but it is not the living body of a person.[381]

The principle of sanctity of life has been approved by the judiciary. For example, Lord Goff of Chieveley said, in his speech in *Airedale NHS Trust v Bland*:[382]

> [T]he fundamental principle is the principle of the sanctity of human life—a principle long recognized not only in our own society but also in most, if not all, civilized societies throughout the modern world . . . But this principle, fundamental as it is, is not absolute.

But nowadays judges tend to emphasize that sanctity of life is not an absolute value. Typical are the comments of Baker J in *Gloucestershire Clinical Commissioning Group v AB*[383] who said of a patient in PVS:

> AB has no awareness. He merely exists. There is no prospect of recovery. This court accepts the fundamental importance of the sanctity of life . . . but that is not an absolute principle and does not impose an obligation to provide treatment where life is futile.

However, John Keown argues that the judiciary wrongly understood sanctity of life to be the same as vitalism.[384]

Supporters of the principle of sanctity of life face a number of difficulties.

(i)   Many supporters of sanctity of life support the current legal position that a patient is entitled to refuse life-sustaining treatment. However, this can involve the death of a person. The distinction that supporters make is between an act causing a death, which is said to infringe the sanctity of life principle, and an omission causing death, which does not. Whether the difference between an act and an omission is sufficiently strong to justify such a crucial distinction is a matter of debate.

(ii) Most supporters of the sanctity of life accept that a person can kill another in self-defence. So it is acknowledged that the principle of sanctity of life is not without exceptions: there are competing values that can justify the intentional killing of someone.[385] Why is it, then, that supporters of sanctity of life are not willing to consider any circumstances in which euthanasia is justified? Is it not, for example, possible to say that the life of someone dying in pain is a life that is valued by society, but that the ongoing pain justifies the end of the life?[386]

(iii) Supporters of the sanctity of life suggest that permitting euthanasia would involve having to accept that some people's lives are not worth living. This can be

---

[380] Glover (1977).   [381] Harris (1995b: 42). See also McMahan (2002).

[382] [1993] AC 789, [1993] 1 All ER 821, 864. See also *R (Amin) v Secretary of State for the Home Department* [2003] 3 WLR 1169, 1185, [30], *per* Lord Bingham of Cornhill; *Re J (A Minor) (Wardship: Medical Treatment)* [1990] 3 All ER 930, 938, *per* Lord Donaldson MR.

[383] [2014] EWCOP 49.   [384] Keown (2002).   [385] McMahan (2002).

[386] Stauch and Wheat (2004: 669).

challenged. McCormick argues that it is perfectly possible to say that every person is equally valued, but that not every life is, although to say to someone 'We value you, but not your life' will be seen as a contradiction to some.[387]

(iv) Harris points out that most supporters of the principle of sanctity of life believe that human life is precious and more valuable than the lives of other animals.[388] He argues that the one factor that might be said to distinguish humans from other animals is consciousness and interactive abilities; yet when these are lost, opponents of euthanasia are unable to explain why that is not the end of human life.

Ronald Dworkin has sought to develop an argument that both supporters and opponents of euthanasia in fact respect the sacredness of life; it is only that they are emphasizing different aspects of sacredness.[389] He argues that even supporters of sanctity of life do not treat the death of a seriously ill older person as so much of a tragedy as the death of a young person; likewise, opponents of sanctity of life are unwilling to support euthanasia where the person is in good health.

Dworkin explains this apparent contradiction in this way. He argues that life has value in three ways: subjectively (for the person themselves); instrumentally (it produces useful things for society and other people); and non-instrumentally or intrinsically (it is in and of itself valuable, just as a great painting is).[390] As to the intrinsic value of life, he suggests that this flows from 'two combined and intersecting bases of the sacred: natural and human creation'.[391] By the 'natural', he means that a person's life is the highest product of natural creation: the greatest achievement of God's, or evolution's, creationary process. A life is, as such, like a great work of art. By 'human creation', he sees the human effort that has been put into the person's life: by their parents, carers, and friends, but ultimately by the individual himself or herself. Hence, Dworkin argues, we see the death of a teenager as a waste of human investment and a tragedy, but death after a full life as less so. The difference between those who take a conservative or liberal view on euthanasia depends on the weight placed on the natural creation and the human investment. Those who emphasize natural creation are likely to oppose euthanasia, and those who emphasize the human investment are likely to support it. Dworkin's argument, however, is that most people recognize that life is sacred in both of these ways; the argument is over which understanding of sacred should take precedence.[392]

5.5 **Dignity**

Many commentators supporting euthanasia argue in terms of protecting the 'dignity' of the dying person.[393] In *Re O*,[394] Hayden said of a patient with minimal brain activity:

[387] McCormick (1998).
[388] Harris (1995b). The debate continues between Harris (1995) and Finnis (1995c).
[389] Dworkin (1993).
[390] The point is that people treasure a great painting in itself, not only because it gives people who see it pleasure.
[391] Dworkin (1993: 83).
[392] For challenges to Dworkin's argument, see Harris (1995a) and Holland (2003: 61–3).
[393] Biggs (2001). But see Foster (2011) for an argument the other way.
[394] [2016] EWCOP 24.

> The Courts must not pursue the principle of respect for life to the point where life has become empty of real content or to a degree where the principle eclipses or overwhelms other competing rights of the patient i.e. in this case simple respect for her dignity.

The argument based on dignity is that, when dying, a person gradually loses the control of physical and mental functions, and helplessness and dependence on others increases. In one survey, a majority of respondents stated that the one thing worse than death would be the distress of loved ones having to care for them over a lengthy period of physical deterioration.[395] It is not simply the inability to care for oneself that is demeaning, but also the inability to offer care and support to others. To enable a person to die with dignity—to die before he or she has reached the stage at which he or she is dependent on others for even the most basic of functions—is an option that people should have a right to take.

Critics of such arguments suggest that the notion of dignity has been barely defined.[396] Even if euthanasia is regarded as dignified for the person who dies, does it respect the dignity of those who have to do the killing, or of society as a whole?

Critics of the dignity argument also tend to emphasize the benefits of palliative care, which, it is claimed, enable a more dignified and good death than that offered through euthanasia.[397] However, supporters of euthanasia will claim that it should be for individuals to decide whether palliative care offers an acceptable alternative to death.[398] Others have characterized the notion of a 'dignified death' as an idealized social construct.[399] Death is nasty and painful normally; to try to pretend that it is not and to demand from medics a perfect, pain-free death represents the ultimate denial of the reality of death.

5.6 The cruelty argument: 'We put down animals; why not humans?'

In a similar vein to the argument about dignity is the argument concerning cruelty. It is argued that the legalization of euthanasia is all about the alleviation of pain and suffering. We do not let animals suffer painful deaths; we 'put them out of their misery'. Why not do the same in relation to humans?[400] Euthanasia is simply the expression of compassion.[401] Even if not used, the option of euthanasia can be regarded as a comfort to the dying, who can be reassured that if the pain becomes too much, they have the option of requesting euthanasia.[402] Singer argues that euthanasia can be supported on the basis of a simple utilitarian calculation:

> [I]f the goods that life holds are, in general, reasons against killing, those reasons lose all their force when it is clear that those killed will not have such goods, or that the goods they have will be outweighed by the bad things that will happen to them.[403]

---

[395] Pearlman, Cain, Patrick, et al. (1993).

[396] Holm (2016); Horn and Kerasidou (2016) and Sulmasy (2017); Schroeder (2008) discuss different meanings for the concept.

[397] Seale and Addington-Hall (1994) question such arguments.

[398] House of Lords Select Committee (2005: 7).

[399] Nuland (1993: xvi).

[400] Bachelard (2002) rejects this analogy on the basis that human fellowship and the impact of death on other people justifies distinguishing the deaths of humans and other animals.

[401] Zyl (2000).

[402] Quill (1993) sees the option of euthanasia as empowering for patients.

[403] Singer (2003: 527).

Critics of euthanasia might reply to such arguments in a number of ways. Many, of course, will simply reiterate the principle of the sanctity of life. Some will emphasize that arguments based on avoiding pain often show a failure to recognize the ability of palliative care to deal with pain—although some supporters of euthanasia reply that even if such pain relief is available in theory, it is often not made available in practice.[404] Some argue that our society has a problem with pain.[405] We have developed a growing intolerance to pain (or to the perception of it) and euthanasia is an easy way of avoiding it.[406] In other eras, pain was seen as an accepted part of life and perhaps even as having redemptive qualities.[407] We need to recapture that appreciation of pain. It should also be noted that research suggests that quality of life for those at the end of their lives is less dependent on the level of pain felt than on whether they are living with their caregivers, they have social support, and they have a sense of the spiritual.[408]

5.7 Public opinion: 'Let the people decide'

It is claimed that public opinion has reached the stage at which a clear majority of people accept that euthanasia should be permitted. However, such polls are difficult to interpret and subtle changes in the wording of the questions asked can produce startlingly different results.[409] Polls questioning members of the public and particular professional groups have yielded the following results.

PUBLIC OPINION

- In a 2002 National Opinion Poll, people were asked: 'Do you think that a person who is suffering unbearably from a terminal illness should be allowed by law to receive medical help to die, if that is what they want, or should the law not allow them medical help to die?' Eighty-one per cent thought that they should be allowed to receive it.[410] Remarkably, in a similarly worded question to doctors in 2009, only 8 per cent of doctors agreed.[411]

- In 2009, an opinion poll found that 74 per cent of people wanted doctors to be allowed to help terminally ill patients to end their lives.[412] A different poll in 2009 found that 78 per cent believed that relatives who help a terminally ill patient to commit suicide should not be prosecuted.[413] In 2011, a poll found that three-quarters of people supported a change in the law to allow assisted dying if people were terminally ill, but only a third supporting a change where there was no terminal illness.[414]

- A 2011 poll of disabled people found that 70 per cent were concerned that changing the law to allow assisted suicide would put pressure on vulnerable people to end their lives early.[415]

---

[404] Although the same point can be made to argue that allowing euthanasia will mean that less effort will be put into ensuring that proper pain relief is available to all: Marquis (1989).
[405] Lavi (2001).   [406] Lavi (2001).
[407] See Fernandes (2010) for development of this argument.
[408] Tang, Aarason, and Forbes (2003).
[409] House of Lords Select Committee on Medical Ethics (1994).
[410] Voluntary Euthanasia Society (2003).
[411] Seale (2009b).   [412] Bennett (2009).   [413] Dignity in Dying (2009b).
[414] *The Guardian* (2011).   [415] *Daily Telegraph* (2011).

- Seale, in a 2009 poll of doctors, found only 8 per cent definitely agreeing that a doctor should be allowed to end the life of a person with an incurable and painful illness, from which he or she will die.[416] Only 4 per cent thought that, in such a case, a doctor should definitely be permitted to give a lethal dose of medication for the patient to take himself or herself.

- The British Attitudes Survey found that 80 per cent say that the law should 'definitely' or 'probably' allow a doctor to end someone's life at their request if they have an incurable and painful illness from which they will die, but only 45 per cent still agreed if the illness was one from which the person would not die.[417] The survey found that those who attended religious services were far more likely to oppose euthanasia than those who did not.

- A 2015 Populus poll[418] found 82 per cent of the public support Lord Falconer's Assisted Dying Bill to give terminally ill, mentally competent people the legal option of assistance to die.

These surveys show that, among the general public, the legalization of euthanasia has the support of a majority, but there is notable opposition among some, but not all, professional groups. However, such surveys need to be treated with care. The way in which questions are put to people in surveys and the public's understanding of the terms used can affect the results obtained.[419]

5.8 The doctor–patient relationship

Some opponents of euthanasia claim that the possibility of euthanasia will undermine the relationship between doctor and patient, and disrupt a doctor's healing role.[420] It is noticeable that in Switzerland, where, under certain circumstances, assisted suicide is permitted, doctors play only a minimal role in the procedure, which is arranged by private clinics.[421] The Hippocratic Oath states: 'To please no one will I prescribe a deadly drug, nor give advice which may cause his death.'[422] The World Medical Association (WMA) reaffirmed its strong belief that euthanasia conflicts with basic principles of good medical practice.[423] The root of the concern has been vividly expressed by Capron:

> I never want to have to wonder whether the physician coming into my hospital room is wearing the white coat . . . of a healer—concerned only to relieve my pain and to restore me to health—or the black hood of the executioner.[424]

Hence it is argued that the knowledge that a doctor could kill the patient will undermine the trust that is at the heart of the doctor–patient relationship. Seeking advice

---

[416] Seale (2009).   [417] Park (2007).   [418] Dignity in Dying (2015).
[419] Hagelin, Nilstun, Hau, et al. (2004).   [420] BMA (2009c); Kass (1998).
[421] Zeigler (2009); Hurst and Mauron (2017).
[422] Reproduced in Mason and Laurie (2006).
[423] English, Gardner, Romano-Critchley, et al. (2001).   [424] Quoted in BMA (2004: 144).

from a physician who may be thinking 'It would be best if I were to give you a lethal injection and kill you' is a frightening prospect.[425]

Supporters argue that, on the contrary, it will create a more open and equal relationship between doctor and patient, with the patient being more able to discuss his or her true feelings.[426] The present law may discourage a patient from discussing his or her wish to die with his or her doctor for fear that it would put the doctor in a difficult position. On the other hand, if euthanasia were legal, would people be deterred from discussing their pain for fear that the doctor may pressurize them into considering euthanasia? We should also remember that, at present, doctors can give a lethal quantity of drugs as long as they are doing so with the intention of relieving pain, rather than killing. It appears that the fact that, under the present law, doctors are arguably permitted to kill does not appear to undermine the trust between patient and doctor.

5.9 A duty to die

In a highly controversial article, Hardwig has suggested that people may even be under a duty to die.[427] He argues that people must accept that, towards the end of their lives, when seriously ill, they will become a burden on their families and friends.[428] The burdens placed on relatives caring for the elderly can be intolerable. It can have a devastating impact on carers' family lives, job opportunities, and finances. Hardwig argues that: 'To think that my loved ones must bear whatever burdens my illness, debility or dying process might impose upon them is to reduce them to means to my well-being. And that would be immoral.'[429]

It should be emphasized that Hardwig is discussing a moral obligation, not a legal one. His arguments have received some support from Baroness Warnock, however, who has been reported as saying that those suffering from dementia have a duty to die, adding: 'If you're demented, you're wasting people's lives—your family's lives—and you're wasting the resources of the National Health Service.'[430] Others will see these as offensively disablist views.

What the arguments promoting a duty to die overlook is that this placing of burdens on families and on society is part of everyday life. The care of children, friends, and partners can place great burdens on people, but these burdens are not necessarily bad. The caring for others is part of the joy and fulfilment of life. Unfortunately, however, our society does far too little to support and enable such caring relationships to be valued.[431] Cholbi argues against Hardwig's view, suggesting that if there is a duty to die, then the relatives must be entitled to kill the individual.[432] Because we do not accept that those burdened with care are entitled to kill those whom they look after, we cannot accept that there is a duty to die.

---

[425] Kass (1998). See also Finnis (1998b).
[426] Baumrin (1998) argues that retaining the two-and-a-half-millennia-old tradition of respect for sanctity of life is crucial to retain public confidence in the medical profession.
[427] Hardwig (1997).   [428] Wilson, Curran, and McPherson (2005).
[429] Hardwig (1997: 35).   [430] Warnock (2001: 8).
[431] Warnock (2001) rejects any argument based on a duty to oneself to end the pain.
[432] Cholbi (2009).

A slightly different argument, but also controversial, has been put forward by Daniel Callahan.[433] He suggests that, once our life's work has been accomplished, then we should be willing to accept a natural death. His point is that the death of a young person is regarded as a terrible tragedy; the death of a person in his or her 80s may be sad, but does not have that element of waste. We need to accept that, once a person reaches a certain age, he or she has lived a 'fair innings' and extensive medical intervention to prolong his or her life should not take place. Callahan is not advocating euthanasia, but advocating non-intervention in later years.

5.10 Slippery slopes: where will it all end?

The 'slippery slope' argument is that even if it is morally acceptable to permit A, it should not be permitted, because it would lead to B, which is not morally acceptable.[434] In this context, the concern is that if voluntary euthanasia is permitted, it will inevitably lead to non-voluntary or involuntary euthanasia.[435] Of course, any jurisdiction that decided to permit voluntary euthanasia would be likely to put in place procedures that would be designed to ensure that euthanasia took place only if the patient consented. The question is whether these procedures would be effective.[436] As Penney Lewis points out, in order to succeed, a slippery slope argument would need to show that legalization of voluntary euthanasia or assisted suicide would lead to a slippery slope; so it would need to be shown that it was not other social forces that had caused the move to accept non-voluntary euthanasia.[437]

Keown argues that the slippery slope argument can be made in two ways, as follows.[438]

(i)   As a matter of logic, once voluntary euthanasia is permitted, there are no arguments that would justify opposing involuntary euthanasia, and so one will lead to the other.

(ii)   As a matter of practice, it is not possible to put in place procedures to ensure that there is no involuntary euthanasia. Indeed, in considering the position in countries in which voluntary euthanasia has been allowed, critics claim that there is evidence that involuntary euthanasia has occurred.

Looking first at the argument from a logical perspective, Keown argues that supporters of euthanasia are on the horns of a dilemma. If they accept that autonomy is key, then they should permit a perfectly healthy person who wants to die to receive euthanasia. However, Keown points out that few supporters of euthanasia would be happy to give euthanasia to a teenager who has been disappointed in love.[439] However,

---

[433] Callahan (1983).

[434] For detailed analysis of 'slippery slope' arguments generally, see Lamb (1988) and Walton (1992).

[435] Keown (2002) is a book-length consideration of the 'slippery slope' arguments against euthanasia. For a detailed response, see Smith (2005a; 2005b).

[436] Dworkin, Frey, and Bok (1998) and Dworkin (1998) argue that, when considering the 'slippery slope' argument, the burden is on those seeking to advance it, because they must justify denying respect of the autonomous decision of a patient wanting help to die.

[437] Lewis (2007a).   [438] Keown (2002).

[439] For an example of a commentator who does not think that suffering should be a requirement before euthanasia is permitted, see Varelius (2007).

if we allow euthanasia only where the person's decision is 'sensible' (for example when the person is in great pain, facing a terminal illness), then this means that we have to make a decision that a person is better off dead.[440] Once we are willing to make this kind of assessment when dealing with incompetent people, it follows that we must likewise accept that there are some cases in which it is desirable (that is, in the person's best interests) to die. Lillehammer rejects the logic of this argument, saying that it is perfectly coherent to hold that euthanasia is appropriate only where both the patient competently seeks euthanasia and such a patient is terminally ill.[441] These two requirements could be seen as 'individually necessary and jointly sufficient'.[442] As Gerald Dworkin puts it: 'This is why the view is called voluntary euthanasia—voluntary to indicate choice of the patient, euthanasia to indicate that the death is "good".'[443] But this leaves open the question of when the death is 'good'. Most supporters of euthanasia would accept this is so when a patient is suffering terrible pain and wants to die but what if he or she is merely tired of life?[444] And it is possible to imagine a case like Tony Nicklinson who is in a 'locked in condition', which is not terminal, but which he found profoundly distressing.[445]

Supporters of euthanasia state that euthanasia is appropriate not where a person's life is valueless, but rather where it has lost its value for that person.[446] Put this way, it is claimed it is possible to argue that a person who is not able to express a view should not be killed, because we do not know how he or she values his or her life, although that may still leave open the 'best interests' reasoning in *Bland*.[447]

Looking next at the slippery slope argument in the context of practice, the argument here is that whatever safeguards were put in place, they would not be effective in ensuring that there was only euthanasia where the patient voluntarily accepted. Battin suggests there are three kinds of abuse that could occur in the context of a legal system that approved of euthanasia.[448]

(i) *Interpersonal abuse* A person may be encouraged or pressurized into agreeing to be killed. This could be by overt pressure, or by indirect means.

(ii) *Professional abuse* Doctors may not want to waste time on expensive and time-consuming medical procedures, and may encourage patients to agree to euthanasia. Consciously or not, a doctor may exaggerate the pain that may arise in the future. There may even be concerns that physicians who have made medical mistakes may seek to cover them up by encouraging euthanasia. The concept of doctors trying to manipulate their patients into euthanasia may appear fanciful, but it is not difficult to find examples of doctors who have illegally killed quite a number of their patients.[449]

---

[440] See Yuill (2013), who sees this as a fatal objection to the autonomy-based argument.
[441] Lillehammer (2002).　　[442] Lillehammer (2002: 548).
[443] Dworkin (1998: 10).
[444] See for discussion of this, see Huxtable and Möller (2007).
[445] Varelius (2016).　　[446] Harris (1992).
[447] *Airedale NHS Trust v Bland* [1993] 1 All ER 821.
[448] Although Battin (1992) believes that it is possible to put in place safeguards to ensure that these concerns are met.
[449] Kinnell (2000) argues that it is wrong to see Shipman as a special case, and controversially claims that the medical profession attracts people who enjoy power over life and death.

(iii) *Institutional abuse* The medical and legal structures themselves may encourage the use of euthanasia, and manipulate patients into agreeing to be killed.

To consider whether such abuses are realistic concerns or scaremongering, it has become common to look to jurisdictions that have departed from the traditional approach of rendering illegal euthanasia and assisted suicide: the Netherlands; Belgium; and Oregon in the United States.[450] Perhaps predictably, supporters of euthanasia argue that these jurisdictions demonstrate that effective safeguards can be put in place, while opponents argue that evidence from these jurisdictions reinforces their concerns.[451] Lord Neuberger provided a thoughtful conclusion on the international evidence in *R (on the application of Nicklinson) v Ministry of Justice*:[452]

> It is true that the Falconer Report, supported by the reports of the two Canadian panels, states that in the Netherlands, Oregon and Switzerland there is no evidence of abuse of the law, which permits assisting a suicide in prescribed circumstances and subject to conditions. However, negative evidence is often hard to obtain, there is only a limited scope for information given the few jurisdictions where assisted suicide is lawful and the short time for which it has been lawful there, and different countries may have different potential problems. In other words, the evidence on that point plainly falls some way short of establishing that there is no risk. The most that can be said is that the Falconer commission and the Canadian panels could find no evidence of abuse.

A full investigation of the law and practice in these countries would take too long for this book, but some interesting factors emerge.[453]

There has been considerable debate over whether those countries which have liberalized their law have seen an increase in the number of people using assisted death, or whether those are now openly recorded, whereas previous they went unrecorded.[454] Indeed, supporters claim that as it has made assisted dying official patients are better protected because the area can be regulated.

Opponents of euthanasia who are concerned about the 'slippery slope' may point to the gradual liberalization of the law in Belgium.[455] In 2014, the Belgian law was extended to cover minors.[456] Unsurprisingly, this is permitted in only limited circumstances. The patient's condition must be physical, incurable, and caused by accident or illness; there must be no treatment which can alleviate the symptoms; death must be predicted in the near future; the parents (or authorized representative) must consent and the child must have the capacity to make the decision. This is the first country in the world to allow euthanasia of children.[457] To some this development is unproblematic. If children are suffering in terrible pain should they not be given access to euthanasia, in the same

[450] Although there are other countries that permit assisted suicide or euthanasia, for example the Northern Territory of Australia, under the Rights of the Terminally Ill Act 1995. See Lewis (2006) for a discussion of the position in France.
[451] See Gillon (1999b) for an example of a commentator who supports euthanasia in theory, but is deeply concerned about the difficulties that the Dutch have had in regulating the practice.
[452] [2014] UKSC 38 at [88].
[453] Lemmens and Kurz (2016) offer a negative assessment of the position in Belgium, while in *Carter v Canada* [2015] 1 SCR 331 it was concluded that the experience of jurisdictions which permitted euthanasia.
[454] Raus (2017); Keown (2006b); Devolder (2016); Materstvedt and Magelssen (2016); Cohen-Almagor (2015); Magnusson (2004).   [455] Cohen-Almagor (2015).
[456] Bovens (2015).   [457] Bovens (2015).

way an adult would be? Even if the child cannot consent, we could follow the normal approach in family law and allow a parent to consent on their behalf. However, many are concerned that children will be unable to make an autonomous decision to die. They may lack the intellectual capacity, emotional resilience, or societal support networks that adults have.[458]

There have been other controversial uses of the law in Belgium:

A SHOCK TO THE SYSTEM

In 2013, Nathan Verhelst, aged 44, was killed under the euthanasia laws. He was suffering unbearable pain following an unsuccessful gender reassignment surgery, which he felt left him 'a monster'.[459]

Also in 2013, twins were killed. They had been born deaf and had spent their whole life together. Now aged 45, they had been diagnosed with an eye condition that would render them blind. They felt unable to carry on living without being able to see or hear each other.[460]

In 2015, a 24-year-old woman who suffered with bouts of depression was permitted access to euthanasia.[461]

Third, the position in Oregon is interesting. There, a patient who satisfies the legislative safeguards can be given medication with which they can end their life. However, only around a half of those who acquire the medication take it. This suggests that what some people are seeking is the knowledge that they could end their life if they wish, rather than actually wanting to do so.

Before we leave the slippery slope argument, we should note that it should not be assumed that countries that outlaw euthanasia are immune from slippery slopes. As the Shipman case shows, even in the UK an enormous number of patients can be killed without the authorities being alerted.[462]

5.11 Concern over treatment of the vulnerable

Linked to the 'slippery slope' argument is the concern that permitting voluntary euthanasia would work against the interests of vulnerable people.[463] Those people suffering poverty, confusion, or general vulnerability may be pressurized into agreeing to euthanasia against their wishes.[464] Keown has claimed that many people who consent to euthanasia may, in fact, simply be suffering from severe pain, distress, depression, or 'demoralization',[465] and are therefore not in a position to make a rational decision.[466]

---

[458] See the differing views of Kaczor (2016); Keeling (2017); Bovans (2015).

[459] Gale (2013).   [460] Hall (2013).   [461] Buchanan (2015).

[462] Thunder (2003).   [463] Brogden (2001) has written of the 'geronticide'—that is, the mass killing of older people. Godiwala (2002) is critical of the way in which both sides of the debate have sought to use the 'vulnerable' to promote their cause.

[464] Street and Kissane (2000), Breitbart and Rosenfeld (1999), and Chochinov, Tataryn, Clinch, et al. (1999) discuss the psychological issues surrounding consent to euthanasia.

[465] The demoralization of terminally ill patients is recognized as a medical condition by some: Kissane, Clarke, and Street (2001).

[466] Keown (2002: ch. 5).

It should not be forgotten that people are often expected to take decisions over their medical treatment in the alien environment of hospital, without friends and support, and even their own clothes.[467] Indeed, for the less well-off, the alternatives to euthanasia or assisted suicide may well be less attractive than those easily able to afford high-quality nursing care.[468] There are concerns that euthanasia will work against the interests of women and those in ethnic minorities.[469] Katrina George lists as factors meaning that women's choices about euthanasia may not be voluntary 'structural inequalities and disparities in power—most evident in women's experience of violence—and social and economic disadvantage and oppressive cultural stereotypes that idealise feminine self-sacrifice and reinforce stereotyped gender roles of passivity and compliance'.[470] No doubt, the articulate, well-educated, and assertive will be in a position to take informed decisions about whether or not they wish to end their lives—but will the depressed, the despairing, and the poor?[471] Nor should it be forgotten that unscrupulous relatives, concerned that the medical and caring costs will decimate their inheritances, have an interest in encouraging euthanasia.[472] This is particularly so given evidence that many people nearing the end of their lives are desperate not to be a burden to their families.[473] It is noticeable that, in a survey of Swiss assisted suicide clinics, 65 per cent of those helped to die were women.[474]

Despite all of these points, there is a concern about the validity of consent from vulnerable groups in many kinds of medical treatment, but these do not normally mean that the treatment (if thought useful) is not made available.[475] The argument, to be convincing in and of itself, would also need to show that it would not be possible to protect vulnerable groups from improper manipulation by providing careful independent advice from trained counsellors, for example.

Lady Hale in *R (on the application of Nicklinson) v Ministry of Justice*[476] stated:

> It would not be beyond the wit of a legal system to devise a process for identifying those people, those few people, who should be allowed help to end their own lives. There would be four essential requirements. They would firstly have to have the capacity to make the decision for themselves. They would secondly have to have reached the decision freely without undue influence from any quarter. They would thirdly have had to reach it with full knowledge of their situation, the options available to them, and the consequences of their decision: that is not the same, as Dame Elizabeth pointed out in *Re B (Treatment)*, as having first-hand experience of those options. And they would fourthly have to be unable, because of physical incapacity or frailty, to put that decision into effect without some help from others. I do not pretend that such cases

---

[467] O'Neill (1984).   [468] Godiwala (2002); Kamisar (1998).

[469] King and Wolf (1998). Dieterle (2007) argues that the evidence from Oregon and the Netherlands does not bear out such concerns.

[470] George (2007: 2–3).

[471] Pacheco, Hershberger, Markert, et al. (2003) are concerned at the number of changes of mind among people seeking euthanasia.

[472] In *R v McShane* (1977) 66 CAR 97, the defendant wanted to persuade her 89-year-old mother to kill herself so that the defendant could get her inheritance. A secret camera installed by police showed the daughter giving her mother drugs in a bag of sweets and pinning on her dress a note saying, 'Don't bungle it'.

[473] Biggs (1998). Care not Killing (2006) argue that this is particularly a concern from the Oregon statistics.

[474] Fischer, Huber, Imhof, et al. (2008). See Zeigler (2009) for further discussion of the Swiss approach.

[475] Boonin (2000).   [476] [2014] UKSC 38, at [314].

would always be easy to decide, but the nature of the judgments involved would be no more difficult than those regularly required in the Court of Protection or the Family Division . . .

It should also be remembered that vulnerable groups should be an issue of concern under the current law, in that they can be left without treatment or can be provided pain-relieving (but lethal) drugs with little regulation or supervision.[477]

Perhaps the stronger case concerning the vulnerable is not that individuals might be pressured into committing suicide, but rather that we may create a culture in which that is expected. Kate Greasley has written of the dangers of the cultivation of a social environment in which controlled death is an accessible and normalized option, and in which both internal and external pressure to end one's life may consequently mount.[478] Will we create a society in which older people will feel that suicide is the appropriate thing to do, especially if they are becoming a burden to others? If there is to be a change in the law on euthanasia, we would need to do a lot more to improve the lot of older people in our society to counter that.[479] This fear was well captured by Lord Sumption in *R (on the application of Nicklinson) v Ministry of Justice*[480] in his discussion of 'indirect social pressure' (quoted at 5.3.3).

There have also been concerns about euthanasia from those writing from a disabilities perspective—in particular that legalizing euthanasia would send the message that the lives of disabled people were not worth living.[481] This is particularly likely if the law were reformed to allow only disabled people access to euthanasia. This might be seen to suggest that it was reasonable for disabled people to want to kill themselves.[482] Others have been concerned that opponents of euthanasia have been too quick to describe disabled people as 'vulnerable' and easily coerced or incompetent.[483] Biggs and Diesfeld, looking at the position of depressed people, are concerned that assisted suicide and euthanasia would only further isolate those suffering with depression, rather than force society to face up properly to the challenges of depression.[484] Although it has been argued that where people suffer from depression which cannot be treated that provides a further reason to comply with a request to die.[485] It is noticeable that a survey of Swiss assisted dying clinics found that, among older users, 'weariness of life' was commoner as an explanation for seeking to die than terminal illness.[486] A similar point can be made about those suffering from other forms of physical or mental disability.[487]

Some disabled commentators insist that the issue must be seen in the context of broader barriers disabled people face. Craig Wallace[488] writes:

> Until every person with disability has equal access to screening, prevention and treatment in our health system, suicide prevention resources, and meaningful alternatives to ending it all, offering us euthanasia isn't an act of generous equality. It's

[477] Jackson (2007).   [478] Greasely (2010).   [479] Herring (2013d).
[480] [2014] UKSC 38 at [228].   [481] Bickenbach (1998).
[482] Riddle (2016); Bickenbach (1998).   [483] Silvers (1998).
[484] Biggs and Diesfeld (1995: 34). See den Hartogh (2015) for a discussion of why the request of depressed people to die must be treated with caution.
[485] Schuklenk and van de Vathorst (2015).   [486] Fischer, Huber, Imhof, et al. (2008).
[487] Riddle (2017).   [488] Wallace (2017).

our Hobson's choice—a fake, cruel one-way exit for vulnerable people locked out of basic healthcare and other social and community infrastructure that others take for granted.

5.12 It happens

It can be argued that the reality is that euthanasia does occur and that it is widely accepted, even in countries, like the UK, that outlaw it. Rather than have a formal legal position that is consistently ignored, it is better to have legal regulation to ensure that there is no improper practice. We saw earlier in the chapter some of the surveys attempting to ascertain the level of euthanasia that takes place. The argument that can be made is that if euthanasia is going to take place—even if it is illegal—it would be better to permit euthanasia, but only if, for example, an ethical committee has approved the course of action.[489] Then at least we would have a system of checks and balances on a practice that, at present, goes ahead without any formal controls at all.

5.13 Unable to make up your mind?

You might find that, in considering all of these arguments, you are unable to make up your mind: you see the strength of the argument on both sides. Such a reaction has led some commentators to take the view that euthanasia should be regarded as not illegal, but neither as something to be encouraged. Boonin has emphasized that there is a difference between having a right to do something and it being right to do it.[490] He gives the example of there being a right to tell racist jokes, but that no virtuous person would choose to exercise that right.[491] Similarly, he argues that, in the context of euthanasia, a strong argument can be made for saying that a person has a right to engage in euthanasia, but that no virtuous person would do so. He argues that practising euthanasia can be said to amount to an agreement with the patient that the patient's life is not worth living. He therefore advocates that the law takes a neutral stance on euthanasia: not prohibiting it, but not promoting it either. Boonin backs this up by arguing that, otherwise, the state will be required to take a stance on the controversial issue of what gives life value—and on such questions the state should remain neutral. To opponents of euthanasia, permitting it, but not encouraging it, is not a 'neutral' stance, because it involves the law failing to respect the sanctity of life.

Another response for those who cannot make their minds up is that we should 'err on the side of life'.[492] The argument is that if we are not sure what the morally correct thing to do is, we cannot go too wrong if we prefer to keep a person alive. The point being made is that if we kill a person when we should not, that is a serious wrong; if we keep alive a person who should die, the wrong will be less serious. If we cannot decide which of the two wrongs will occur, it is preferable to select the less serious. This view, however, assumes that there is no serious wrong in keeping alive a person who might want to die.

---

[489] Magnusson (2002) examines the extent to which euthanasia is practised underground in the United States and Australia.
[490] Boonin (2000).   [491] Presumably, he has in mind the right to free speech.
[492] Merrell (2009).

A VIEW FROM ABOVE

Theological perspectives on euthanasia

As already indicated, many of those writing from a religious perspective oppose euthanasia. Interestingly the leaders of Britain's Christian, Jewish, Muslim, and Sikh communities wrote a joint letter to MPs in 2015, urging them not to pass a law permitting assisted dying.[493] In Judaism, Christianity, Buddhism, Hinduism, and Islam, respect is shown for the principle of sanctity of life. Every life is valuable and precious to God. It is easier for a religious person to see the life of a person suffering, say, PVS, as valuable and precious than it is for someone without faith. The person suffering PVS is still valued and loved by God, and hence is precious, even if no earthly person can relate to him or her. There might be thought to be a slight paradox here: for a non-religious person, it might be thought that death is a 'tragedy' and the end of everything; for many with a religious belief, there is hope of some kind of afterlife. It might therefore be thought that a religious view would be less concerned about causing death than a non-religious view. The answer to this conundrum appears to be that life, being created by God, is of value to God and so must not be taken.[494]

Most Jewish religious scholars draw a sharp distinction between accelerating the death of a dying person, which is prohibited, and removing an impediment to death, which is permitted.[495] At the heart of the Jewish approach, according to many scholars, is the notion that there is a 'time to die' and that death should not be inappropriately delayed nor life foreshortened. The difficulty is in defining what is an impediment to death, and this has led to some debate over whether and when, for example, life support machines can be switched off.[496]

Within Christianity, it is the Roman Catholic Church that has been most vociferous in its rejection of euthanasia, and support for sanctity of life and the principle of double effect.[497] Indeed, that doctrine has its origins in Roman Catholic theology. Many Christian writers from all denominations reject euthanasia and argue that life is a gift from God, which we are to treasure and steward, not destroy.[498] Notably, churches have played a significant role in the creation and support of hospices.[499]

Islam also tends to take a strong stance against euthanasia and assisted suicide. The prohibition on the intentional taking of life is emphasized in much Muslim writing. There is an emphasis on the idea of life being given on trust by Allah and therefore not being a person's to dispose of as he or she wishes.[500] Allah will and should control when a person will die.[501] However, the general Muslim view appears to be that this does not require doctors to provide futile treatment in a desperate bid to save someone's life.[502]

Key to Buddhist thinking on this issue is the precept not to take life and the virtue of compassion. The Dalai Lama has stated: 'From a Buddhist point of view, if a dying person has any chance of having positive virtuous thoughts, it is important—and there is a purpose—for them to live even just a few minutes longer.'[503] To Buddhist thought, the moment of death and its quality is important. This leads some Buddhist thinkers to support the hospice model of enabling a calm and controlled dying, without active intervention to hasten death. The idea of meeting death mindfully is seen as important. Others argue that Buddhist tradition is, in fact, tolerant of suicide and euthanasia, where doing so enables a person to have a conscious and dignified death.[504] However, the majority of Buddhist opinion appears to be that the high value placed on life by Buddhism cannot support euthanasia.[505]

There are two main views on euthanasia that can be found in Hindu thought. Perhaps the majority view is that disturbing the cycle of birth and rebirth by ending a life should be avoided. Indeed, this same point would argue against keeping a person on a life support machine for an unnecessary amount of time. Other Hindus regard ending a painful life as a fulfilment of a moral obligation and therefore not objectionable. Hinduism does, in some circumstances, allow suicide: *prayopavesa*. This is permissible only under strict conditions, including that non-violent means of suicide are used. Starvation would be permitted, but not shooting oneself.[506]

 FEMINIST PERSPECTIVES

Dying in relationship

Perhaps surprisingly, there has been relatively little written on end-of-life issues from an explicitly feminist perspective. There is, of course, no consistent feminist line opposing or supporting euthanasia, and feminists will adopt many of the arguments already mentioned. The distinctively feminist contributions to the debate include the following.

- Wolf has argued that those factors that are likely to result in requests for suicide (depression, poor pain relief, concern about being a burden on one's family) are more likely to fall on women than men.[507] She is concerned therefore that legalizing euthanasia would mean that women would be particularly likely to seek death.[508] Wolf is concerned also that physicians, in encouraging patients to consider euthanasia or suicide, may be affected by gendered perceptions. For example, a physician may regard a woman's concern that she will place an impossible burden on her husband as carrying more weight than a husband suggesting that he will be a burden on his wife, because caring is seen as a woman's role. Others have expressed concerns that women may find it particularly hard to persuade clinicians that they be permitted to utilize euthanasia.[509] There is some evidence that generally, in medical practice, women suffer higher levels of pain, but receive less effective treatment.[510]

- Feminist writers have been concerned with the emphasis placed on autonomy by those supporting euthanasia. Sidney Callahan[511] has argued that feminism has always recognized 'that human being must be born, nurtured, domestically maintained, and cared for when they are old and dying' and sees the pro-euthanasia argument as resting on 'the cult of the self-sufficient male independent rational agent, self-made and dominating', rather than valuing the relational contexts people live in. It has been argued that a woman's request to die must be considered in the context of her history, her intimate relationships, the resources available to her, and the level of care being

---

[504] Becker (1990; 1993).   [505] Hughes and Keown (1995); Keown (1999).
[506] Cromwell (2003).
[507] Wolf (1996: 283). See further Biggs (2003) and George (2007).
[508] See also Callahan (1995), although the evidence from Holland and Oregon does not show significantly higher numbers of women than men seeking death; cf. Carmel (2001), a study of Israeli women.
[509] Prado (1998).   [510] Hoffmann and Tarzian (2001).   [511] Callahan (2015).

offered. In the light of these, her choices may be profoundly constrained, and it cannot be assumed that a wish for death is a fully autonomous choice. Wolf talks of the danger that '[w]e construct a story that clothes the patient's terrible despair in the glorious mantle of "rights" '.[512] A call for euthanasia should lead, she suggests, to a redoubling of efforts to provide effective pain relief, not to acceding to the request. Others have promoted a relational autonomy, requiring decisions to be considered in the context of a society made up of interdependent people engaging in overlapping enterprises. This led Donchin to suggest that any death decisions should be made in the context of the family.[513]

- Feminists have also emphasized that much of the writing on legal responses to death have ignored deaths that can have a particularly powerful impact on women: abortion, miscarriage, and neonatal death are often downplayed, and there is little support for women affected in these ways.[514]

- Feminists also emphasize that much of the work for caring for the dying is undertaken by women.[515] In the heat of the euthanasia debate, the value and significance of this work is often overlooked.

6 Patients lacking capacity: ethical issues

As we saw earlier, where a patient lacks capacity, then, in the absence of an advance decision, an assessment on withdrawal of treatment will be made based on what is in the best interests of the patient.

Critics of the current law have made the following points.

(i) The law places too much weight on the distinction between an act and an omission. Under the present law, if the treatment or its withdrawal is classified as an act, then the *actus reus* of murder is made out, even if the doctors could have claimed to be acting in accordance with good medical practice. As we have seen, the distinction between acts and omissions is complex.

(ii) In *Bland*, their Lordships regarded artificial feeding and hydration as medical treatment, rather than basic personal care, and therefore that it could legitimately be withdrawn.[516] The BMA has issued guidance on withholding and withdrawing life-prolonging medical treatment.[517] The guidance takes the view that the artificial provision of food and water counts as medical treatment, which can therefore be withdrawn under the *Bland* ruling (if it no longer promotes the best interests of the patient).[518] Keown has argued that although the insertion of the gastrostomy tube would have involved a medical procedure, the pouring of the food down it did not require medical skill and would be analogous to spooning food into someone's mouth.[519] There is also

---

[512] Wolf (1996: 300).   [513] Donchin (2000).
[514] Field, Hockey, and Small (1997: 1–2).   [515] Biggs (1998: 284).
[516] Finnis (1993) is highly critical of this reasoning.
[517] BMA (2009). See also GMC (2010a).   [518] BMA (2009: 4).   [519] Keown (2002).

evidence that family members find it particularly distressing that their family member will die from thirst or starvation.[520]

The distinction between basic care and medical treatment is controversial. The argument that appeared to be accepted in *Bland* was that, even if it is appropriate to remove medication from a patient on the basis that that is in the patient's best interests, it is not appropriate to withdraw basic care, such as feeding or cleaning. The argument in favour of the distinction includes the suggestion that to permit death by starvation shows a serious lack of regard for the patient's comfort and dignity. Further, our society regards starvation as symbolically horrific. Even if there is no logical or moral basis for it, feeding the hungry is seen as a basic human obligation.[521] There are also dangers that permitting the withdrawal of sustenance will lead to a slippery slope, because it will permit the death of a person not from his or her illness, but from the lack of basic provision.[522] In other words, non-dying patients could be left to starve to death. This is a very different thing from letting a patient die from the disease from which he or she is suffering.

Critics of the distinction argue that the difference between treatment and basic care is impossible to draw.[523] Consider feeding, perhaps a classic example of basic care. If feeding is possible only through machinery or by the application of medical skill, does it become medical treatment?[524] Certainly, to the House of Lords in *Bland*, there was no distinction to be drawn between the provision of foods by artificial means and medical treatment.[525] Whatever the difficulties in drawing the distinction, for many people there is an intuitive feeling that letting a patient starve to death cannot be seen as proper medical treatment.[526] There is also a concern that the emotive phrase 'starve' is misleading. Beauchamp and Childress state that '[m]alnutrition is not identical with hunger; dehydration is not identical with thirst; and starvation is very different from acute dehydration in a medical setting'.[527] It should also be noted that, in a few cases, ANH can worsen a patient's medical condition.[528]

(iii) Some commentators have argued that the courts need to be more open, and accept that the legal treatment of DoC patients is about sensible use of resources and ending the strain on families and friends, which justified the decisions in *Bland*.[529] Morgan, perhaps a little brutally, states:

> [U]npalatable as it is, we must face the fact that Tony Bland is more expensive to maintain in PVS than he is to bury. Fiscally, at least, we save by deciding that Tony Bland has no interests worth further protection, that he is, to all intents and purposes, a wasting asset wasting assets.[530]

---

[520] Kitzinger and Kitzinger (2015).   [521] Carson (1986); Callahan (1983).
[522] Keown (2016).   [523] Beauchamp and Childress (2009).
[524] Keown (1997a) argues that his cannot be treatment: 'What is it treating?' he asks.
[525] BMA (2009c) suggests that artificial nutrition and ventilation can lawfully be withdrawn if they no longer benefit a patient.
[526] See *A Hospital v SW* [2007] EWHC 425 (Fam), in which the argument that withdrawal of hydration and nutrition breached a patient's Article 3 rights was rejected.
[527] Beauchamp and Childress (2009: 121).
[528] See the expert evidence given in *R (Burke) v GMC* [2005] 3 FCR 169.
[529] Alldridge and Morgan (1992); Biggs (2002: 42); Harris (1995a: 18).
[530] Morgan (2001: 220).

Indeed, a more general concern may be raised about spending vast resources keeping people alive, with only marginal quality of life.[531]

(iv) There is an argument that some DoC sufferers should be regarded as dead: they are unable to experience the things that make us human.[532] Without consciousness, they may be alive, but they have lost what makes them human.[533] McMahan suggests that a PVS patient should be treated in the same way as a corpse.[534] There are none of the goods of life for such a person in the future. Indeed, Sinnott-Armstrong and Miller suggest that what is wrong about killing someone is putting them in a state of universal and irreversible disability.[535] On that view, the person in MCS has already suffered the wrong of being killed.[536]

7 Refusal of treatment: ethical issues

English law makes it clear that a competent person can refuse treatment even if, without the treatment, he or she will die.[537] To force such treatment on someone could amount to a battery or a tort. Simply put, we do not have a duty to keep on living.[538] This is as true for pregnant women as it is for anyone else.[539]

What are the ethical issues surrounding the decision of a person to forgo medical treatment? A variety of views can be taken.

(i) A competent patient has an absolute right to refuse treatment. This appears to be the position taken by the law. In *St George's v S*,[540] the woman was entitled to refuse treatment even though, without it, she and her unborn child would die. Although the law respects the right of a patient to refuse treatment, it is notable in *Re B*[541] how carefully the court considered the issue of competence.[542] This could be supported on the basis that, given the gravity of the consequences, we have to ensure that the patient is competent. Especially in an emergency case, there is an argument for performing the necessary treatment and then, with the luxury of time, reconsidering the appropriate way of treating the patient.[543]

(ii) For some commentators, the key ethical issue is whether refusing necessary medical treatment can be regarded as suicide. If it is suicide, then there are ethical objections to it, but if it is not, then there are not. One view is that the intention of the patient provides the key. If the patient refuses treatment because he or she wants to die, then this is suicide, but if the patient does not act with the purpose of killing himself or herself (even

---

[531] Brierley, Linthicum, and Petros (2013) are concerned that doctors are too reverential of religious beliefs, and are spending resources on cases that are not cost-effective and which they would not otherwise give save to the patient, were it not for their (or their families') religions. See Foster (2013c) for further discussion.

[532] Although Wilkinson and Savulescu (2013) suggest that being in a minimally conscious state is even worse than suffering PVS.

[533] Veatch (1993).   [534] McMahan (2002).   [535] Sinnott-Armstrong and Miller (2013).

[536] Bevins (2013).

[537] *Re T (Adult: Refusal of Treatment)* [1992] 4 All ER 649, 652–3; *Airedale NHS Trust v Bland* [1993] 1 All ER 821, 860 *per* Lord Keith, 866 *per* Lord Goff, 881 *per* Lord Browne-Wilkinson, and 889 *per* Lord Mustill; *Re AK* [2001] 1 FLR 129.

[538] Hale (1996: 87).   [539] *St George's Healthcare NHS Trust v S* [1998] 3 All ER 673.

[540] [1998] 3 All ER 673.   [541] [2002] EWHC 429.

[542] Stauch (2002).   [543] Hale (2003: 7).

if death is foreseen), then the act is permissible.[544] A patient who refuses a blood transfusion for religious reasons may be said not to intend his or her death even though he or she may have foreseen it as an inevitable consequence of his or her actions.[545] Clearly, in this distinction, the doctrine of double effect is being relied upon.

(iii) Some commentators argue that the law should be more willing to override the refusal of a competent person to life-saving treatment. To follow the views of a competent patient blindly is to give too much heed to the 'cult of self-determination'.[546] Although to respect the refusal of the patient may be to recognize his or her autonomy, in so doing we ignore other important values, such as the importance attached to life. The courts' response to such arguments has been that the rights of the competent individual to self-determination will normally outweigh the interests of the state in promoting the sanctity of life.[547] In other words, the law does not ignore the other values in play in these questions; it simply attaches greater significance to autonomy than to the other values. Particular concerns arise where a person is borderline competent.[548] To return to the scenario of a teenager disappointed in love, if he had a septic cut, but refused treatment, should we really stand by and let him die? Indeed, it has been suggested that the courts do, in effect, carry out an assessment of the reasonableness of the patient's decision and that, where the decision is thought utterly unreasonable, then the patient is declared incompetent.[549]

(iv) David Shaw has argued that the current law is based on an illogical distinction: euthanasia is not permitted, but patients are entitled to reject life support.[550] He argues that the body should be seen as a life support machine for the brain. In the same way as a competent patient has the right to refuse life support from equipment and can demand that it be switched off, a patient should be permitted to refuse life support from his or her body and demand that it be 'switched off'. This view is based on a controversial understanding of the body, and requires a separation between brain and body that some commentators are unable to accept.[551]

8 Palliative care and hospices

It might be thought from some of the foregoing discussion that the dying can expect nothing but pain and discomfort. Opponents of euthanasia reject such a view and encourage the use of hospices or palliative care.[552] These emphasize the importance of dying well—of a peaceful, contented death—and reject attempts to induce an early death by euthanasia. Palliative care emphasizes pain relief, and psychological and emotional support, to assist in the last stages of life. There is evidence that even

---

[544] Price (1996) argues that, under this definition, there would be very few suicides.
[545] Gorsuch (2000).   [546] Mason and Laurie (2006: 552).
[547] *St George's Healthcare NHS Trust v S* [1998] 3 All ER 673. Wicks (2001) argues that this is reinforced by the HRA 1998.
[548] *Re JT* [1998] 1 FLR 48.   [549] Coleman and Drake (2002).
[550] Shaw (2007; 2011). For a rejection of these views, see McLachlan (2010).
[551] For example, Busch and Rodogno (2011).
[552] Have and Clark (2002) argue that the notions of euthanasia and palliative care are generally regarded as incompatible.

those who are suffering appalling disabilities or pain can enjoy life and do not wish to die by means of euthanasia.[553] Supporters of palliative care claim that, apart from in a very few cases, pain can be controlled to endurable levels.[554] While that may be true of physical pain, some commentators question whether it can deal with 'existential suffering'.[555] Where pain is utterly unbearable, there is always the option of sedation.

The aim of palliative care is to put the patient at the heart of care and to seek to treat the whole person: not only his or her physical needs, but also his or her emotional, spiritual, and psychological needs. The aim is to travel with the patient on the journey of the last few days of his or her life.[556] Palliative care focuses not only on the patient, but includes his or her family as well.[557] The World Health Organization (WHO) has described palliative care as:

> . . . the active, total care of patients whose disease is not responsive to curative treatment. Control of pain, other symptoms and psychological, social and spiritual problems is paramount. The goal of palliative care is the achievement of the best quality of life for patients and families.[558]

A group of European specialists have suggested four goals for palliative care: achieving the best quality of life for patients and relatives; the relief of suffering; enabling the patient to have a 'good death'; and preventing euthanasia.[559] However, as they admit, these goals may be in conflict and they are rather vague.[560] What is a 'good death', for example, is very much a matter of opinion and, for some, it requires the use of euthanasia.

The existence of hospice care is often emphasized by those seeking to oppose euthanasia. But to some, the provision of hospice care is all well and good, but is of little relevance to the debate over euthanasia. As the leading figure in Brian Clark's play *Whose Life is it Anyway?* states:

> I know that our hospitals are wonderful. I know that many people have succeeded in making good lives with appalling handicaps. I'm happy for them and respect and admire them. But each man must make his own decision. And mine is to die quietly and with as much dignity as I can muster.[561]

Similarly, Aneurin Bevan is reported to have stated that he would 'rather be kept alive in the efficient if cold altruism of a large hospital than expire in a gush of sympathy in a small one'.[562]

Hospices seek to emphasize that essential to being human are vulnerability, interdependence, and the need for care.[563] A high premium is placed on the importance of communicating with the patient.[564] As Dame Cecily Saunders, the founder of the hospice movement, has said:

[553] Gardner, Theocleous, Watt, et al. (1985). [554] Moreland and Rae (2000).
[555] Valerius (2013).
[556] Schotsmans (2002) discusses the importance of relational care in the context of palliative work.
[557] Gilley (2000) emphasizes the need to assist the partners, relatives, and friends of the dying.
[558] Cited in Biggs (2001: 38). [559] Clark, ten Have, and Janssens (2002b).
[560] Clark, ten Have, and Janssens (2002b). [561] Clark (1979: 76).
[562] Quoted in Saunders (2001: 430). [563] Hermsen and Have (2002).
[564] Blyth (1990).

To talk of accepting death when its approach has become inevitable is not mere resignation or feeble submission on the part of the patient, nor is it defeatism or neglect on the part of the doctor. For both of them it is the very opposite of doing nothing. Our work . . . is to alter the character of this inevitable process so that it is not seen as a defeat of living but as a positive achievement in dying; an intensely individual achievement for the patient.[565]

In the UK, much work is being done to expand the use of palliative care.[566] At present, it has been particularly used among cancer patients, although it is hoped to extend it to other patients soon.[567] There is also an increasing recognition that it is inappropriate to restrict palliative care work to 'hospices'; rather, palliative care should be a method of caring for those that are dying be they in a hospice, a hospital, a nursing home, or at home.[568] Indeed, many dying people wish to be at home, and therefore much effort is currently placed on providing community-based palliative care.[569] While such wishes are, of course, understandable, the immense strain that can thereby be placed on carers should not be forgotten.[570] There are also calls for palliative care—particularly with its focus on the person's psychological, spiritual, and emotional side—to be offered from the moment of diagnosis, not only when the person enters what may be the final stages of his or her life.[571]

The sad truth is that, when hospices are not available or used, the standard of care offered to the dying can be poor. In one leading study of elderly people being cared for in nursing homes, the overall standard of care was described as 'inadequate', and there was persistent overuse of unnecessary drugs and underuse of beneficial drugs.[572] Even those being cared for at home can suffer if their carers do not receive appropriate training.[573]

The government has accepted that much needs to be done to improve the standards of palliative care in the UK, even though there have been improvements over the years.[574]

It is, perhaps, too easy to have an idealistic view of the hospice.[575] It has been claimed that although hospices start out with the best of intentions and practice, all too easily they become dominated by routinization, bureaucracy, professional rivalry, and medicalization.[576] Others complain that the idealism of the founders of the palliative care movement has been replaced with bureaucratic battles and professional rivalries.[577]

---

[565] Saunders (1994: 174).

[566] National Council for Palliative Care (2009); NHS (2009d).

[567] Field and Addington-Hill (2000). For concern that there is still a lack of palliative care for non-cancer patients, see NHS Confederation (2005).

[568] Sindell, Katz, and Komaromy (2000).

[569] NICE (2004a: para. ES2); Thomas (2003); Clark, ten Have, and Janssens (2002a).

[570] Scambler (2003b).   [571] Finlay (2001).   [572] Fahey, Montgomery, Barnes, et al. (2003).

[573] NICE (2004b).   [574] DoH (2004m).

[575] Logue (1994) argues that although hospice care may be appropriate for some, it should not be regarded as the ideal solution for everyone.

[576] See James and Field (1992); McNamara (2004; 2001). Janssens, ten Have, Broeckaert, et al. (2002) report a survey of European palliative care workers, which found that 50 per cent were concerned about over-medicalization in palliative care.

[577] McNamara (2004).

It might be thought that no one could doubt the benefits of hospices and palliative care services. However, there is, in fact, only a little evidence that palliative care and hospices have better outcomes for patients than hospitals or are more cost-effective.[578] Indeed, some have suggested that the unique features claimed for hospice care are, in fact, found in ordinary hospital wards[579] and that some of the 'bad features' said to be found in hospitals can also be found in hospices.[580] One study suggested that there were only minor differences between hospital and hospice care, and that the differences that existed were made possible only by 'entrance policies' of hospices ensuring that 'difficult patients' were not admitted.[581] That said, few people are willing to suggest that hospices provide a less effective service than hospitals. A thorough survey of the literature on palliative care performed by the National Institute for Health and Care Excellence (NICE) found very slight benefits for patients from palliative care as opposed to traditional methods of caring, but that palliative care was greatly appreciated by patients and their families.[582]

It has also been argued that the attention paid to hospices has taken attention away from the care provided to dying people not able to find a place in a hospice. Hospices, it has been suggested, provide a high-cost service for a favoured minority of patients.[583] However, that can be taken as an argument for extending the work of hospices and palliative care units. A slightly different complaint is that the hospice movement offers a false vision of death: hope of a dignified death rarely matches reality. Lawton argues that, as the body disintegrates towards the end, common symptoms are delirium, urinary and faecal incontinence, sores, and discharges.[584] To offer 'death with dignity' may be to offer a false picture of what death is like. Despite all of these concerns, however, palliative care is now widely recognized as a better all-round treatment for the dying and their families, and its importance is likely to increase in the years ahead.

9 Reform of the law

There has been a trickle of private members' Bills that have been introduced to amend the law in this area, none of which have been passed.[585] The debates over reform of the law have continued to rage. If the law were to be reformed, the following would be some of the options.

9.1 The Assisted Dying Bill 2015

The report of the Commission on Assisted Dying has been influential in recent debates.[586] It called for a reform of the law to allow a person assistance to die. An Assisted

---

[578] NICE (2004a: ES13); Higginson, Finlay, Goodwin, et al. (2002). Fordham and Dowrick (1999) are critical of the little research that does suggest the effectiveness of palliative care.
[579] Seale and Kelly (1997), although that study found that relatives of dying patients preferred hospices.
[580] Johnston and Abraham (1995).
[581] Seale (1989).   [582] NICE (2004b).   [583] Douglas (1992).   [584] Lawton (2000).
[585] Any reform of the law will need to consider the complex issue of how life insurance will operate in cases of assisted suicide or euthanasia: see Davey and Coggon (2006).
[586] Commission on Assisted Dying (2012).

Dying Bill 2013 and 2015 was presented to Parliament, but neither were passed. The 2013 Bill allowed people access to assisted dying with the agreement of two medical professionals if a host of requirements were met. The 2015 Bill suggested an application to court. Clause 1 stated:

(1) Subject to the consent of the High Court (Family Division) pursuant to subsection (2), a person who is terminally ill may request and lawfully be provided with assistance to end his or her own life.

(2) Subsection (1) applies only if the High Court (Family Division), by order, confirms that it is satisfied that the person—

 (a) has a voluntary, clear, settled and informed wish to end his or her own life;
 (b) has made a declaration to that effect in accordance with section 3; and
 (c) on the day the declaration is made—

  (i) is aged 18 or over;
  (ii) has the capacity to make the decision to end his or her own life; and
  (iii) has been ordinarily resident in England and Wales for not less than one year.

Supporters of the Bill claimed it contained significant safeguards. It only applied to those with terminal illnesses and required the approval of a court and statements in support from medical professionals. It is worth noting that these criteria were so strict that it would not have applied to the parties in major litigation, for example, Diane Pretty, Debbie Purdy, and Tony Nicklinson, because none of them had terminal illnesses. Indeed one might think that those facing many years of pain or profound limitations have a stronger case for assisted dying than those who are due to die soon.

9.2 Prospective exemption from prosecution

Under the current law, someone helping a terminally ill relative to die must hope that the Director of Public Prosecutions (DPP) will decide not to prosecute. One possible reform is that a relative in such a case be able to obtain prospective confirmation that he or she will not be prosecuted. The advantages of this approach are that the relative (and the person wanting to die) can then act in confidence and without worry, and that a better assessment of whether the assistance is appropriate can be made while the person is alive than when he or she is dead.[587]

That proposal has attractions, but also problems. Even if a prospective decision were made, it would have to be subject to the caveat that the person killed wanted to die, at the time that he or she did die. So the promise of confidence will be mitigated by the fact that the relative could still face a prosecution if the deceased was not consenting at the time. Critics will also claim that there is a subtle difference in the message sent by the law when it says that someone has committed a crime, but that they will not be prosecuted, and that sent when it says in advance that they will not be acting illegally.

---

[587] Yeung (2012).

9.3 **Necessity**

The case for developing the defence of necessity is that we can keep the current law with its clear message 'Do not kill someone and do not help someone to die', which is the most appropriate message in the vast majority of cases when someone is approached by a suicidal friend or relative. However, the defence of necessity can allow us to acknowledge that, in exceptional cases (perhaps Tony Nicklinson was one), the normal law can be departed from.[588]

9.4 **Developing compassion defences**

Richard Huxtable sees the benefit of retaining the 'middle ground'—that is, of keeping the law as it is, with some amendments.[589] He justifies this on the basis that we need to recognize not only the value of life as determined by the individual, but also that life has intrinsic value.[590] The reform that he proposes is to develop a defence of mercy killing, or compassionate killing—that is, a defence for those who assist in killing relatives for compassionate reasons, while not offering judgement that what they did was the right thing to do.[591]

9.5 **Human rights reform**

The 2015 decision of the Canadian Supreme Court in *Carter v Canada (Attorney General)*[592] may offer some hope for those who believe the Supreme Court in England should rule the current prohibition on assisted dying as a breach of human rights. Emphasizing the importance of the right to autonomy, the court concluded that the criminal code prohibiting assisted dying violated the rights *to liberty and security of* 'competent adults who seek such assistance as a result of a grievous and irremediable medical condition that causes enduring and intolerable suffering'. While it noted that protection of the vulnerable was an important aim the blanket prohibition in Canadian law was overbroad because it impacted on those who had capacity as well as those under pressure or lacking capacity. The court concluded that the current prohibition was void when 'a competent adult person who (1) clearly consents to the termination of life; and (2) has a grievous and irremediable medical condition (including an illness, disease, or disability) that causes enduring suffering that is intolerable to the individual in the circumstances of his or her condition' seeks medical assistance to end life.[593] Whether, if the issue returns to the English Supreme Court, a similar line is taken remains to be seen.[594]

10 **Conclusion**

Our relationship with death is undergoing a remarkable change.[595] Some see an ever-increasing acceptance of the arguments in favour of assisted suicide and euthanasia, which will lead to a time when people expect to be in complete control of when and

---

[588] Herring (2013d).   [589] Huxtable (2013b).   [590] For further discussion see Watt (2015).
[591] Huxtable (2013c).   [592] 2015 SCC 5.   [593] Para. 127.
[594] Chan and Somerville (2016) offer some critical observations on *Carter*.
[595] Mann (1998).

where they die.[596] 'Make a diary date for death now!' may become a popular call, with assisted suicide being the normal preferred method of death.[597] The wish for a dignified death before we become 'unlovable' is a strong one for many.[598] But there are tensions in popular current attitudes towards death. While there appears to be a growing desire for people to be able to control the manner and time of their passing, there is also a growing wish for death to be 'natural'. There is much fear of over-medicalized death, and some would agree with Nietzsche that:

> In a certain state it is indecent to go on living. To vegetate on in cowardly dependence on physicians and medicaments after the meaning of life, the right to life, has been lost ought to entail the profound contempt of society.[599]

However, as has been pointed out, many relatives' image of a natural death is possible only with medical intervention.[600] Also, it should not be forgotten that medical advances have done much to improve the quality of people's lives and to enable them to live far longer than they would have done in the past.[601] How, in the future, our society will be meeting these potentially conflicting aims remains to be seen.

Age Concern organized *The Debate of the Age*, which set down the following principles for the care of all terminally ill patients:

(1) To know when death is coming, and to understand what can be expected.

(2) To be able to retain control of what happens.

(3) To be afforded dignity and privacy.

(4) To have control over pain relief and other symptom control.

(5) To have choice and control over where death occurs (at home or elsewhere).

(6) To have access to information and expertise of whatever kind is necessary.

(7) To have access to any spiritual or emotional support desired.

(8) To have access to hospice care in any location, not only in hospital.

(9) To have control over who else is present and shares in the end.

(10) To be able to issue advance directives which ensure wishes are respected.

(11) To have time to say goodbye, and control over other aspects of timing, and to be able to leave when it is time to go, and not to have life prolonged pointlessly.[602]

Many of these reflect the goals of palliative care and are principles on which people on all sides of the euthanasia debate can agree.

QUESTIONS

1. Consider the following argument:

   The ban on assisted suicide is ineffective (a regulated system would stifle more abuse), morally obtuse (it discriminates against the disabled and privileges the

[596] Batting (1998).   [597] Scambler (2003b).   [598] Sommerville (2002: 40).
[599] Nietzsche (1968: 88).   [600] McNamara (2001); Seale (2000).
[601] McLean (1999: 142).   [602] Age Concern (1999: 2).

incompetent over the competent) and though controversial, out of line with popular opinion. (Had Mr Pretty assisted his wife's suicide, would he have been prosecuted? Would a jury have convicted? Would he have been imprisoned?) We can regulate how we die very much better than we currently do.[603]

Do you agree?

2. BBC News reported that doctors had stood by after a woman had drunk anti-freeze in order to commit suicide.[604] She made it clear to the doctors that she did not want them to intervene. She also had an advance directive refusing treatment. The coroner held that not only were doctors permitted not to intervene, but also that it would have been unlawful if they had. Was that decision correct?

3. Consider the following.

> As long as we can dress the choice to take life in other clothes, such as refusing treatment or relieving pain, then we can acknowledge it. But naked decisions to take life as such are, to paraphrase T.S. Eliot, too much 'reality' to bear openly. We must hide the reality of how we made end of life decisions for fear of what we will find. Yet in doing so, society risks even greater harm. Many persons who need assisted suicide to relieve their suffering will not receive it. Some persons may still receive such assistance covertly, but without the advantages of openly following medical protocols that can assure efficacy and prevent arbitrary and abusive practices . . . If we practice and tolerate assisted suicide and euthanasia, we certainly need to do it openly to reassure the public and prevent abuse. At the same time, as T.S. Eliot reminds us, 'humankind cannot bear very much reality.' We also cannot tolerate the notion that doctors will openly take life, even with proper reporting and bureaucratic oversight. We are caught in the dilemma that we can permit assisted suicide only by not admitting it.[605]

Do you agree?

4. Minow asserts:

> I think the most honest statement of the issues presented in the physician-assisted suicide cases is this: the Court faced a choice of two lies to countenance. By lie I mean knowing misrepresentation; by countenance to extend approval or toleration. The first lie is that physicians do not already, and regularly, participate in assisting dying patients to end their lives. Every physician I have encountered acknowledges as much; many have written about it . . . The second lie is that permitting such assistance would not systematically and routinely be used to push dying people into death. The problem is not merely risks of abuse; the problem arises from the inauguration of a regime in which people would have to justify continuing to live . . . It is better to live with the lie that prohibition works so that, at the margin, those who engage in it do so with trembling.[606]

Do you agree that there are these two lies? If so, which is the better to live with?

[603] Freeman (2002: 270).   [604] BBC News online (1 October 2009).
[605] J. Robertson (1997: 342–3).   [606] Minow (1997: 20–2).

5. Some doctors are willing to deal with a terminally ill patient in the following way: sedate the patient, so that he or she has no awareness or feeling, and then withdraw food and hydration.[607] Within a few days, the patient will die. Is this a more or less acceptable way of treating such patients than giving them a lethal injection that immediately kills them?[608] If sedation is the best form of pain relief, should this be given, even if there is no intent to cause the patient's death?[609]

6. In this age of easy international travel, any attempt to prevent euthanasia or assisted suicide is unlikely to be effective. In England, it has become common to travel to the Swiss Dignitas Clinic.[610] Indeed it has been estimated that one in five users of the clinic is from Britain.[611] Is there something odd about a law that prohibits assisted suicide on its own shores, but allows people to make arrangements to travel overseas to access it?

7. Sheila McLean writes: 'To allow third parties to decide that life lacks quality for someone else, for example in the case of the PVS patient, yet at the same time to deny individuals the right to make that decision for themselves, is nothing short of bizarre.'[612] Do you agree?

8. Consider this scenario:

   A driver is trapped in a blazing lorry. There is no way in which he can be saved. He will soon burn to death. A friend of the driver is standing by the lorry. This friend has a gun and is a good shot. The driver asks the friend to shoot him dead. It will be less painful for him to be shot than to burn to death.[613]

   Should the friend shoot the driver? If you answer 'yes', does that mean that you must support active euthanasia?

9. One study of medical professionals working in the field found widespread support for the distinctions between acts and omissions, and intention and foresight, which many ethicists believe to be misguided.[614] Does this suggest that medical ethicists are 'out of touch', or that medical professionals are not thinking clearly about the issues?

10. As forms of computer-assisted and mechanically assisted forms of dying become more sophisticated, will it become harder to distinguish suicide and assisted suicide?[615]

11. Epstein argues that economic factors, in reality, play a major role in end-of-life decisions.[616] Have the ethical debates ignored the significance of monetary issues?

12. Weyers points to three sociological factors that she sees as particularly influencing attitudes in favour of euthanasia: increased individualism; a lessening of the taboos surrounding death; and a shift in power away from doctors and towards patients.[617] Do you agree? Do you see any social forces pushing against liberalizing the law on euthanasia?

---

[607] Savulescu (2014).

[608] This issue is discussed in Bressington (2011), Raus, Sterckx, and Mortier (2011), and Williams (2001).

[609] See Broeckaert and Olarte (2002). See also Koch (2005), who discusses the case of Teri Schiavo in the United States, where a sedated patient could be left to 'starve' to death, but could not be killed by a lethal injection.

[610] For a discussion of the work of Swiss assisted suicide clinics, see Fischer, Huber, Imhof, et al. (2008) and Zeigler (2009). For allegations concerning goings-on at the clinics, see M. Campbell (2009).

[611] Siddique (2014).   [612] McLean (1999: 158).   [613] Hope (2005: 15).

[614] Dickenson (2000).   [615] See Battin (2005: ch. 15).   [616] Epstein (2007).

[617] Weyers (2006).

13. Goodman describes a case in which a very sick baby was taken off a ventilator (with the parents' agreement) because the prognosis was very poor, with the understanding that the baby would die soon after.[618] Once off the ventilator, the baby started having spasms and gasping (as occasionally happens in such cases). The parents were very distressed and the doctor administered an injection, which killed the baby. Did the doctor commit murder? Did she act unethically?

14. Suzanne Ost suggests that we are seeing a de-medicalization of assisted dying, whereby assistance in death is done by relatives and others, rather than the medical profession.[619] Is this a good or a bad thing?

15. If the law on euthanasia were to be liberalized, should doctors be allowed to rely on conscientious objection not to be involved? If the law is not liberalized should doctors be allowed to rely on conscientious objection to use euthanasia?[620]

FURTHER READING

A comprehensive bibliography, including all references used throughout the book, is available online at www.oup.com/uk/herringmedical7e/.

There is so much that has been written on the issue that the following is only a small selection of the wealth of material.

Some general writings on end-of-life issues can be found in:

Battin, M. (2005) *Ending Life* (Oxford University Press).

Bhatia, N. (2015) *Critically Impaired Infants and End of Life Decision Making* (Routledge).

Bridgeman, J. (2017) ' "Leaving no stone unturned": contesting the medical care of a seriously ill child', *Child and Family Law Quarterly* 24: 63.

Chau, P.-L. and Herring, J. (2007) 'The meaning of death', in B. Brooks-Gordon, F. Ebtehaj, J. Herring, et al. (eds) *Death Rites and Rights* (Hart).

Coggon, J. (2010) 'Assisted dying and the context of debate: "medical law" versus "end-of-life law" ', *Medical Law Review* 18: 541.

Ford, M. (2005a) 'The personhood paradox and the "right to die" ', *Medical Law Review* 13: 80.

Griffiths, J., Weyers, H., and Adams, M. (2008) *Euthanasia and the Law in Europe* (Hart).

Harris, J. (2005e) 'The right to die lives! There is no personhood paradox', *Medical Law Review* 13: 386.

Herring, J. (2015b) 'The child must live: disability, parents and the law' in J. Herring and J. Wall (2015) *Landmark Cases in Medical Law* (Hart).

Huxtable, R. (2007) *Euthanasia, Ethics and the Law* (Routledge).

---

[618] Goodman (2010).   [619] Ost (2010).   [620] Adenitire (2016).

Jackson, E. and Keown, J. (2011) *Debating Euthanasia* (Hart).

Lewis, P. (2007) *Assisted Dying and Legal Change* (Oxford University Press).

McGee, A. (2005) 'Finding a way through the ethical and legal maze: withdrawal of medical treatment and euthanasia', *Medical Law Review* 3: 357.

McGee, A. (2015) 'Does withdrawing life-sustaining treatment cause death or allow the patient to die?' *Medical Law Review* 22: 26.

McMahan, J. (2002) *The Ethics of Killing* (Oxford University Press).

Ohnsorge, K. (2015) 'Intentions, motivations, and social interactions regarding a wish to die' in C. Rehmann Sutter, H. Gudat, and K. Ohnsorge (eds) *The Patient's Wish to Die* (Oxford University Press).

Otlowski, M. (1997) *Voluntary Euthanasia and the Common Law* (Oxford University Press).

Smith II, G. (2013) *Palliative Care and End of Life Decisions* (Palgrave Pivot).

Writing broadly opposing euthanasia includes:

Keown, J. (2002) *Euthanasia, Ethics and Public Policy* (Cambridge University Press).

Keown, J. (2006b) *Considering Physician-Assisted Suicide* (Care not Killing).

Paterson, C. (2008) *Assisted Suicide and Euthanasia* (Ashgate).

Sommerville, M. (2001) *Death Talk* (McGill-Queen's University Press).

Writing broadly in support of euthanasia includes:

Biggs, H. (2001) *Euthanasia* (Hart).

Commission on Assisted Dying (2012) *The Current Legal Status of Assisted Dying is Inadequate and Incoherent . . .* (Demos).

Dworkin, R. (1993) *Life's Dominion* (HarperCollins).

Ost, S. (2004) *An Analytical Study of the Legal, Moral, and Ethical Aspects of the Living Phenomenon of Euthanasia* (Edwin Mellen Press).

Smith, S. (2012) *End-of-Life Decisions in Medical Care: Principles and Policies for Regulating the Dying Process* (Cambridge University Press).

Van Zyl, L. (2000) *Death and Compassion: A Virtue-Based Approach to Euthanasia* (Ashgate).

Warnock, M. and MacDonald, E. (2008) *Easeful Death* (Oxford University Press).

For a discussion of the law, see:

Birchley, G. (2012) 'Angels of mercy? The legal and professional implications of withdrawal of life-sustaining treatment by nurses in England and Wales.', *Medical Law Review* 20: 337.

British Medical Association (2009) *End of Life Decisions* (BMA).

Coggon, J. (2006) 'Could the right to die with dignity represent a new right to die in English law?', *Medical Law Review* 14: 219.

Greasley, K. (2010) 'R (Purdy) v DPP and the case for wilful blindness', *Oxford Journal of Legal Studies* 30: 301.

Heywood, R. (2014) 'Moving on from *Bland*: the evolution of the law and minimally conscious patients', *Medical Law Review* 548.

Huxtable, R. (2013) *Law, Ethics and Compromise at the Limits of Life: To Treat or not to Treat?* (Routledge).

Keating, H. and Bridgeman, J. (2012) 'Compassionate killings: the case for a partial defence', *Modern Law Review* 79: 697.

McGee, A. (2011) 'Ending the life of the act/omission dispute: causation in withholding and withdrawing life-sustaining measures', *Legal Studies* 31: 467.

Michalowski, S. (2013) 'Relying on common law defences to legalise assisted dying: problems and possibilities', *Medical Law Review* 21: 337.

Mullock, A. (2011) 'Overlooking the criminally compassionate: what are the implications of prosecutorial policy on encouraging or assisting suicide?', *Medical Law Review* 18: 442.

Mullock, A. and Heywood, R. (2016) 'The Value of Life in English Law: Revered but not Sacred?', *Legal Studies* 36: 258.

Pattinson, S. (2015) 'Contemporaneous and advance requests: the fight for rights at the end of life' in J. Herring and J.Wall (eds) *Landmark Cases in Medical Law* (Hart).

Price, D. (2009) 'What shape to euthanasia after *Bland*? Historical, contemporary and futuristic paradigms', *Law Quarterly Review* 125: 142.

Riddle, C. (2017) 'Assisted dying and disability', *Bioethics* 31: 1467.

Williams, G. (2007) *Intention and Causation in Medical Non-Killing* (Routledge).

On the Dutch and Oregon experience, see:

Battin, M., van der Heide, A., Ganzini, L., et al. (2007) 'Legal physician-assisted dying in Oregon and the Netherlands: evidence concerning the impact on patients in "vulnerable" groups', *Journal of Medical Ethics* 33: 591.

Finlay, I. and George, R. (2011) 'Legal physician-assisted suicide in Oregon and the Netherlands: evidence concerning the impact on patients in vulnerable groups—another perspective on Oregon's data', *Journal of Medical Ethics* 37: 171.

Smith, S. (2005a) 'Evidence for the practical slippery slope in the debate on physician assisted suicide and euthanasia', *Medical Law Review* 13: 17.

On palliative care, see:

Randall, F. and Downie, R. (2006) *The Philosophy of Palliative Care* (Oxford University Press).

For feminist approaches, see:

Andrews, J. (2015) 'Keeping older women safe from harm', *Feminism & Psychology* 25(1): 105–8.

Biggs, H. (1998) 'I don't want to be a burden! A feminist reflects on women's experiences of death and dying', in S. Sheldon and M. Thomson (eds) *Feminist Perspectives on Health Care Law* (Cavendish).

Callahan, S. (2015) 'A feminist case against self-determined dying in assisted suicide and', *Feminism and Psychology* 25: 109.

Raymond, D. (1999) 'Fatal practices: a feminist analysis of physician assisted suicide and euthanasia', *Hypatia* 14: 1.

https://www.samaritans.org/ offer a safe place to talk.

Mental Health Law

INTRODUCTION

We should start by asking why there needs to be any special 'mental health law'. After all, we do not have 'broken leg law' or other law designed to deal with particular medical conditions. Indeed, as we shall see, there are those who believe that there should not be a special mental health law, but rather that the normal principles of medical law should be applied. Such a view gains support from the United Nations Convention on the Rights of Persons with Disabilities, Article 12(2) of which provides that people with disabilities should enjoy legal capacity 'on an equal basis with others in all aspects of life'.[1] There are even those who argue that there is no such thing as mental health, but that is something at which we will be looking much later.

The reason why mental health has its own special law is because the law permits the detention and treatment of people who are mentally ill, even if they are competent.[2] This goes against one of our most hallowed principles of medical law: that treatment may not be given to a competent person without his or her consent. The most common justification provided for infringing this principle is that to do so is necessary to protect the 'general public' from dangerous mentally ill people and/or for the protection of the individual himself or herself. Whether these are good enough reasons to infringe the fundamental principle is very much open to debate.[3] The end result of balancing the rights of the mentally ill and the protection of the general public is a law that is complex and, to many, unsatisfactory. But that may be inevitable. As Bartlett and Sandland indicate in the following quotation, the rationality of the law may not fit easily into the world of the 'irrational':

> The centrality of a medical model of insanity is asserted, imposing a scientific order onto the profoundly un-ordered world of the mad. While madness is displayed in the form of a disease, sanity is a constraint, both physical and moral, into which the insane person is confined through pressure of the group, the sane. All this is a construction of the reasoned, and reflects the world of the reasoned; to the insane person, it is an alien landscape.[4]

It is, however, unfortunate that the issue of the detention of the 'dangerously mentally ill' has come to dominate the law on mental health. It creates a skewed vision of mental illness in our society. As we shall see shortly, mental illness is widespread and very common. The vast majority of mental illness is treated voluntarily in the community,

---

[1] Bartlett (2012).
[2] It should not be assumed that those with mental illness lack capacity. One study found that 60 per cent of in-patients in a psychiatric ward had capacity to make decisions: Owen, Richardson, David, et al. (2008).
[3] Richardson (2015).
[4] Bartlett and Sandland (2007: 1).

with no special legal regulation. Indeed, an even larger amount may go unrecognized and untreated. Worries about the detention or rights of the 'dangerous' should not hide the needs of those suffering less dramatic, but still debilitating, mental illness.

The popular image of mental illness is a confused one. Images of the 'dangerous lunatic' sit alongside the image of the 'tortured genius'. There is still a strong negative attitude towards mental illness in our society. In a 2011 survey, only 6 per cent of people agreed with the statement 'People with mental illness are a burden on society'.[5] Of those questioned, 77 per cent agreed that 'People with mental illness have for too long been the subject of ridicule'. Only 62 per cent of people agreed that 'People with mental illness are far less of a danger than most people suppose'. Twenty-five per cent of respondents agreed that 'Most women who were once patients in a mental hospital can be trusted as babysitters'. Sixteen per cent agreed that one of the main causes of mental illness is a lack of self-discipline and willpower. Prejudicial attitudes were reflected when, in 2013, Asda and Tesco (and other suppliers) withdrew 'mental patient' fancy dress costumes, designed for use in celebrating Halloween.[6]

There is increasing awareness of the agonies of mental illness, but perhaps less of the positive benefits that it can bring. To many, the mentally ill are to be pitied, rather than valued. But one thing that will be clear as we turn to statistics on mental illness is that the idea that there is a sharp line between 'them' (the mentally ill) and 'us' (the sane) is misleading.[7] We may even be moving towards a time when mental illness is the norm.

1 Statistics on mental health

The level of mental illness is astonishing. Consider the following statistics.

REALITY CHECK

Mental health statistics

- In a recent survey 12.1 per cent of people report currently receiving mental health treatment, with 10.4 per cent receiving medication, and 3 per cent receiving psychological therapy.

- In a 2017 survey 17 per cent of people had a mental health problem in the previous week.

- 43.4 per cent of people say they have had a diagnosable mental illness at some point in their lives.

- Depression will affect half of women and a quarter of men before the age of 70. In any given year, between 8 per cent and 12 per cent of people will suffer depression.

- Depression was the second leading cause of years lived with disability worldwide, behind lower back pain. In 26 countries, depression was the primary driver of disability.

- Five per cent of those over the age of 65 and 20 per cent of those over 80 suffer dementia.[8]

---

[5] NHS Information Centre (2011f).   [6] BBC News online (26 September 2013).
[7] DoH (1999c: 10).   [8] All these statistics are from Mental Health Foundation (2017)

2 The Mental Health Act 1983

We will now look at the Mental Health Act (MHA) 1983, as amended by the Mental Health Act 2007. The 2007 reforms have attempted to bring the law more in line with human rights requirements and public expectations. Originally, the intention was that the new Act would produce a completely new scheme, but in the end the 2007 Act simply amended aspects of the law as set out in the 1983 Act.

Before looking at the Act, it is important to remember that there are two situations involving mentally ill patients in which there is normally no need to use the Act and other law can be relied upon:

- if the patient is competent and consents to treatment, it can be provided under the normal principles of medical law; and

- if the patient is incompetent, then treatment that is in his or her best interests can be given. This is done under the Mental Capacity Act (MCA) 2005, discussed in Chapter 4.

The Act is needed particularly where the patient is competent but does not consent to treatment for a mental disorder.

2.1 Involuntary admission to hospital

Most mentally ill patients consent to receiving treatment and there is therefore normally no need to use the MHA 1983. Indeed, the MHA 1983 Code of Practice makes it clear that involuntary admission should be used only where absolutely necessary:

> Before it is decided that admission to hospital is necessary, consideration must be given to whether there are alternative means of providing the care and treatment which the patient requires. This includes consideration of whether there might be other effective forms of care or treatment which the patient would be willing to accept, and of whether guardianship would be appropriate instead.[9]

However, where it is thought appropriate to provide mental health treatment against the wishes of the patient, then the Act becomes relevant.

There are three routes to involuntary admission to hospital, as follows.

2.1.1 *Admission for assessment (section 2)*

An application for an admission for assessment can be made by either the patient's nearest relative[10] or an approved social worker (ASW). Two registered medical practitioners

---

[9] DoH (2015e: para. 14.7).

[10] Under MHS 1983, s. 26, 'nearest relative' is defined as spouse or civil partner, cohabitants (who have lived together for at least six months), child, parent, sibling, grandparent, grandchild, uncle or aunt, nephew or niece. Where there are competing claims, those higher up the list have priority over those lower down the list. If within the same category, then those relatives of the full blood have priority over those of the half blood and older relatives take priority over their juniors. However, there is one way in which a relative can 'jump' to the front of the queue: if the patient is living with or being cared for by a relative, then that relative is the 'nearest relative' even if he or she is not at the top of the s. 26 list. Of course, a patient can object to an individual being appointed as 'nearest relative': *TW v London Borough of Enfield (Secretary of State for Health intervening)* [2013] EWHC 1180 (QB), in which there were allegations by the patient that her father had abused her.

must support the application.[11] If necessary, reasonable force can be used to transfer the patient to hospital. The MHA 1983, section 2(2), provides that:

> An application for admission for assessment may be made in respect of a patient on the grounds that—
>
> (a) he is suffering from mental disorder of a nature or degree which warrants the detention of the patient in a hospital for assessment (or for assessment followed by medical treatment) for at least a limited period; and
>
> (b) he ought to be so detained in the interests of his own health or safety or with a view to the protection of other persons.

Section 1(2) defines mental disorder as 'any disorder or disability of the mind'. The MHA 1983 Code of Practice lists the following as examples of a mental disorder:

- affective disorders, such as depression and bipolar disorder;
- schizophrenia and delusional disorders;
- neurotic, stress-related, and somatoform disorders, such as anxiety, phobic disorders, obsessive compulsive disorders, post-traumatic stress disorder (PTSD), and hypochondriacal disorders;
- organic mental disorders, such as dementia and delirium (however caused);
- personality and behavioural changes caused by brain injury or damage (however acquired);
- personality disorders;
- mental and behavioural disorders caused by psychoactive substance use;
- eating disorders, non-organic sleep disorders, and non-organic sexual disorders;
- learning disabilities;
- autistic spectrum disorders (including Asperger's syndrome); and
- behavioural and emotional disorders of children and adolescents.

The MHA 1983 specifically states that learning disability,[12] or alcohol or drug dependency, cannot be the sole basis for treating someone as having a mental disorder.[13] The reasoning behind this provision is the history of treating those showing what was regarded as 'immoral' or 'unusual' behaviour as suffering from some kind of mental illness. This does not prevent a person who suffers from a mental illness as well as, say, drug dependency from being classified as suffering from a mental disorder. However, if the learning disability 'is associated with abnormally aggressive or seriously irresponsible conduct on [the person's] part', then it can be regarded as a mental disorder.[14] The term 'irresponsible' is ambiguous. It is suggested that the best interpretation is that it means that someone is liable to cause injury to himself or herself or another, rather than being simply rowdy or disruptive. However, the courts may need to clarify the meaning of that term.

---

[11] At least one of the two must have a mental health qualification.
[12] MHA 1983, s. 1(3), defines learning disability as 'a state of arrested or incomplete development of the mind which includes significant impairment of intelligence and social functioning'.
[13] MHA 1983, s. 1(3).   [14] MHA 1983, s. 1(2A).

In *R v Mental Health Review Tribunal for South Thames Region, ex p Smith*,[15] it was held that the use of the phrase 'nature or degree' meant that a patient suffering from a serious mental condition could be detained under section 2 even though the present manifestations of it were not serious. In that case, a schizophrenic patient was not showing dangerous manifestations of his condition at present, but it was likely that he would do so in the near future.

The patient must be detained 'in the interests of his own health or safety or with a view to the protection of other persons'. It will be noted that this provision covers cases in which the patient poses a risk not only to other people, but also to him or herself.

Once admitted under section 2, patients can be kept in hospital for assessment for a maximum of twenty-eight days. If a patient is to be kept for longer, that must be under section 3 powers.[16] A patient can apply to have his or her case reviewed by a mental health review tribunal (MHRT) during the first fourteen days of detention. The nearest relative can discharge the patient on three days' notice, but the responsible medical officer can prevent this. Treatment can be given only for a patient being assessed with his or her consent, unless there is an immediate and serious danger.

As Peter Bartlett has pointed out, the criteria for admission under section 2:

> . . . provide little guidance to professionals as to who should, and who should not be admitted. In practice, standards have for some time been a function of professional culture rather than law, coupled with continued chronic under-funding. This latter has placed considerable restrictions on the number of persons confined at a given time, introducing standards indirectly by way of rationing.[17]

The House of Lords considered section 2 in the following case.[18]

KEY CASE   *MH v Secretary of State for Health* [2005] UKHL 60

M was severely mentally disabled and was detained in a hospital under section 2 of the MHA 1983. She had not applied to an MHRT within the first fourteen days. The hospital wished to arrange for her to be received into its guardianship. Her mother objected, as her nearest relative. The proceedings took longer than expected and so M was detained under section 2 for more than the normal twenty-eight days. M's mother asked that M's case be referred to an MHRT. This the Secretary of State did, but the tribunal decided that M's detention should continue. M sought judicial review. Her main complaints were that section 2 was incompatible with Article 5(4) of the European Convention on Human Rights (ECHR), because the burden was on the patient to make an application (to the MHRT) to review the detention; where the patient was incapable of exercising this right, there was inadequate protection of his or her rights, she argued. She also complained that section 29(4) of the 1983 Act was incompatible with Article 5(4) ECHR because it enabled the extension of the period of detention without a review of the lawfulness of the detention.

The House of Lords held that section 2 was not incompatible with the Convention. Every sensible effort should be made to enable a patient to apply to the tribunal if there were reason to think that

---

[15] (1998) 47 BMLR 104.
[16] See later in the chapter, under the heading '2.1.3 Admission for treatment (section 3)'.
[17] Bartlett (2003a: 331).   [18] See the discussion in Scott-Moncrieff (2006).

the patient wished to do so. Hospital managers had a statutory duty to take steps to ensure that patients understood their rights. Article 5(4) ECHR did not require every detention to be subject to judicial approval. The system tried hard to give patients and relatives easy access to MHRTs. It was true that a nearest relative did not have an independent right of application to the tribunal, but there were ways in which a nearest relative could get the case before a tribunal, as in this case, in which the assistance of the Secretary of State had been sought. Although it was important to ensure that the Convention rights of the mentally ill were 'practical and effective' rather than 'theoretical and illusionary', the protection in place surrounding section 2 was effective.

As to the section 29(4) issue, the patient could request that the Secretary of State refer the patient's case to an MHRT or challenge the lawfulness of the decision through judicial review in the courts. There was therefore an adequate way of ensuring that the detention was appropriate and this rendered the provision compatible with Article 5 ECHR. Their Lordships accepted that section 29(4) was capable of being operated in a way that was compatible with Article 5(4). However, the use of the power of the Secretary of State to refer a case to a tribunal could ensure that the power would not be used improperly. If the Secretary of State refused, there was always the option of judicial review.

If a patient is improperly detained under the MHA 1983, in theory he or she could claim for damages in the law of tort or under the Human Rights Act (HRA) 1998. However, it would be necessary to show not only that the detention was unlawful, but also that there was bad faith or negligence.[19] That would be difficult to prove.

2.1.2 *Emergency admission (section 4)*

If there is an emergency, a patient can be admitted under section 4 on the recommendation of one doctor. But that doctor must confirm that it is of 'urgent necessity' for the patient to be admitted and detained, *and* that waiting for a second doctor to confirm the need for an admission under section 2 would cause 'undesirable delay'. Remarkably, this doctor does not need to be a specialist in mental illness, although (if practical) it should be a doctor who knew the patient beforehand. The maximum length of time for which a person can be detained under section 4 is 72 hours. At the end of that time, the patient must be free to go, unless one of the other routes of admission has been invoked. Treatment cannot be provided to a patient detained under section 4 without his or her consent.

Other provisions in the Act can also be relied upon in emergencies. Under the MHA 1983, section 135, a justice of the peace (JP) may, upon the application of an ASW, require the detention in a place of safety for up to 72 hours of mentally disordered individuals who are being ill-treated, neglected, or not kept under proper control, or who are living alone and unable to care for themselves.[20] Section 136 of the MHA 1983 allows mentally disordered individuals found by police officers in public places to be removed to a place of safety (such as a hospital) for up to 72 hours if it appears to the police officer that they are in need of immediate care and control.[21]

[19] *TTM v Hackney LBC* [2010] EWHC 1349 (Admin).
[20] *Ward v Metropolitan Police Commissioner* [2005] UKHL 32 held that there is no power to insist that named individuals are present when the mentally ill person is detained.
[21] *Seal v Chief Constable of South Wales Police* [2007] UKHL 31.

2.1.3 *Admission for treatment (section 3)*

Unlike the other two grounds, the ground under section 3 of the 1983 Act is designed for longer-term detention. An application can be made by either the patient's nearest relative or an ASW.[22] Section 3(2) states:

An application for admission for treatment may be made in respect of a patient on the grounds that—

(a) he is suffering from mental disorder of a nature or degree which makes it appropriate for him to receive medical treatment in a hospital; and

(b) it is necessary for the health or safety of the patient or for the protection of other persons that he should receive such treatment and it cannot be provided unless he is detained under this section; and

(c) appropriate medical treatment is available to him.

Each of these three grounds for admission is subject to the opinion of a medically qualified officer.

(i) *The patient is suffering from a mental disorder of a nature that makes it appropriate for him or her to receive medical treatment in a hospital*[23] Section 1(2) defines mental disorder as 'any disorder or disability of the mind'. Notice that it is insufficient simply to show that a person has a mental disorder; the disorder must also be such that it cannot be treated in the community and that hospital treatment is required. The definition of a mental disorder is deliberately broad. There is no need to identify precisely from what disorder a person is suffering.

(ii) *It is 'necessary for the health or safety of the patient or for the protection of other persons that he should receive such treatment and it cannot be provided unless he is detained under section 3'* As with section 2, a person can be detained either if he or she is a danger to others or himself or herself. The reference to the requirement that the treatment cannot be provided unless the person is detained under section 3 means that if the patient is competent and able to consent to the treatment, there is no requirement for him or her to be detained under section 3.

(iii) *Appropriate treatment must be available to the patient*[24] The wording of this provision was debated at length in the House of Commons. The issue is how to deal with a patient suffering from a mental disorder where there is no treatment that can be offered to improve, or at least prevent a worsening of, his or her condition. Of course, this may be true of those with the most serious forms of mental illness. Section 145(4) is crucial here. It states that:

Any reference in this Act to medical treatment, in relation to mental disorder, shall be construed as a reference to medical treatment the purpose of which is to alleviate, or prevent a worsening of, the disorder or one or more of its symptoms or manifestations.

---

[22] Where a social worker makes the application, the next of kin must be consulted.
[23] According to *R (M) v South West London Mental Health NHS Trust* [2008] EWCA Civ 1112, a person can be assessed to determine whether these criteria are met without his or her consent.
[24] Rather unhelpfully, s. 3(4) states that 'references to appropriate medical treatment, in relation to a person suffering from mental disorder, are references to medical treatment which is appropriate in his case, taking into account the nature and degree of the mental disorder and all other circumstances of his case'.

This would appear to indicate that if no medical treatment is available to a patient, then he or she cannot be detained under the Act. The reasoning behind this is that if there is nothing that doctors can do to assist a patient, they should not be required simply to detain him or her, acting as a 'warehouse' for the untreatable. But that does mean that, in theory at least, a 'dangerous' person could be released because nothing can be done for him or her.

There is some ambiguity under the provisions, because the treatment can relate to a manifestation or symptom of the illness, rather than the condition itself. However, it is clear that simply feeding and generally caring for the patient will not amount to medical treatment. Section 145 defines treatment as including 'psychological intervention and specialist mental health habilitation, rehabilitation and care'. Much may depend on whether the courts give the word 'care' a broad or narrow meaning. The MHA 1983 Code of Practice emphasizes that a person can properly receive care even if he or she cannot be cured.[25] Further, it adds:

> Purpose is not the same as likelihood. Medical treatment may be for the purpose of alleviating, or preventing a worsening of, a mental disorder even though it cannot be shown in advance that any particular effect is likely to be achieved.[26]

In *MD v Nottinghamshire Health Care Trust*,[27] Jacobs J held that treatment under section 145 did not have to render the patient less dangerous. It was enough if it prevented the worsening of symptoms. This broad understanding of the treatability criterion may mean that it will be rare when it is not satisfied.

The Mental Health Alliance has serious concerns about the 'treatability criterion'. It argues that 'compulsory mental health treatment [should] be used only where there is no alternative; where it has therapeutic benefit; and when the person concerned is unable to decide for themselves about treatment'.[28] The Alliance fears that the legislation will lead to the system being clogged up with patients who cannot be treated and who should not be being detained. Whether these concerns are valid depends in part on how the 'treatability' criterion is interpreted.

The treatability test under the old law was discussed in *R v Canons Parke MHRT, ex p A*,[29] in which the issue was whether a patient could be detained if the proposed treatment was group therapy—the problem being that the patient had indicated that he did not wish to participate in the session. It was argued that the patient was therefore not treatable. Lord Justice Roch said:

> First, if a tribunal were to be satisfied that the patient's detention in hospital was simply an attempt to coerce the patient into participating in group therapy, then the tribunal would be under a duty to direct discharge. Second, 'treatment in hospital' will satisfy the 'treatability test' although it is unlikely to alleviate the patient's condition, provided that it is likely to prevent a deterioration. Third, 'treatment in hospital' will satisfy the 'treatability test' although it will not immediately alleviate or prevent deterioration in the patient's condition, provided that alleviation or stabilisation is likely in due course. Fourth, the 'treatability test' can still be met although initially there may be some deterioration in the patient's condition, due for example to the patient's initial anger at

---

[25] DoH (20015b).   [26] DoH (2015b: para. 23.4).   [27] [2010] UKUT 59 (AAC).
[28] Mental Health Alliance (2005: 1).   [29] [1994] 2 All ER 659.

being detained. Fifth, it must be remembered that medical treatment includes 'nursing and also includes care, habilitation and rehabilitation under medical supervision'. Sixth, the 'treatability test' is satisfied if nursing care etc., is likely to lead to an alleviation of the patient's condition in that the patient is likely to gain an insight into his problem or cease to be uncooperative in his attitude towards treatment which could potentially have a lasting benefit.[30]

Admission for treatment under section 3 is up to six months and can be extended for a second period of six months. It can then be extended a year at a time. It would therefore be possible for someone to be detained under section 3 for the rest of their life. Renewal simply requires the responsible medical officer to produce a report indicating that:

(i)   the patient suffers from one of the conditions required for section 3;

(ii)   that treatment is likely to alleviate or prevent deterioration of that condition *or* that, if the patient is suffering a mental illness or severe mental impairment, the patient if discharged is unlikely to be able to care for himself or herself, to obtain other care needed, or to guard him or herself against serious exploitation; and

(iii) continued treatment is necessary for the health and safety of the patient, or others, and detention is required.[31]

The possibilities of challenging detention under section 3 are limited. The main form of challenge will be by application to an MHRT. An application for civil proceedings can be brought to the High Court, but only if leave is obtained first.[32] The MHA 1983, section 139, states:

No person shall be liable . . . to any civil or criminal proceedings . . . in respect of any act purporting to be done in pursuance of this Act . . . unless the act was done in bad faith or without reasonable care.

This means that any criminal proceedings or claim in tort is unlikely to succeed if brought in respect of an act done in pursuance of the 1983 Act.

2.2 Detention of patients informally in hospital (section 5)

If a patient is in hospital informally (that is, he or she is competent and has consented to receive treatment), then a doctor in charge of the patient can detain the patient for up to 72 hours by reporting to hospital managers that an application for compulsory admission 'ought to be made'. Some nurses can detain an informal patient for up to six hours or until a doctor with authority to detain the patient arrives.

2.3 Treatment

A patient detained under the MHA 1983 can consent to treatment if competent. If not competent, he or she must be treated in the way that promotes his or her best interests.[33]

---

[30] At 679–80.   [31] MHA 1983, s. 20.
[32] Judicial review proceedings can be brought: *Ex p Waldron* [1986] QB 824. See further Allen (2007).
[33] MCA 2005, s. 4. See, e.g., *Trust A and Trust B v H* [2006] EWHC 1230 (Fam).

If competent and refusing treatment, then the patient cannot have treatment imposed upon him or her, except under Part IV of the Act. Section 63 permits treatment for mental disorder and does not authorize treatment for physical conditions unrelated to the mental disorder. This distinction between treatment for a mental disorder and for other matters has proved problematic.

As the following cases show, the courts have given a liberal interpretation to the notion of treatment of the mental condition.

- In *Re KB (Adult) (Mental Patient: Medical Treatment)*,[34] it was held that forced feeding could be regarded as medical treatment. The argument that this was not treatment of the patient's mental condition was rejected, because it was held that treating the symptoms was part of treating the disorder (anorexia nervosa).

- In *B v Croydon Health Authority*,[35] it was held permissible under section 63 to provide forced feeding for a patient suffering 'borderline personality disorder'. The Court of Appeal held that treatments designed to alleviate the consequences of the disorder could be regarded as treatment of the disorder.

- In *Tameside and Glossop Acute Services Trust v CH*,[36] a schizophrenic patient was thirty-eight weeks' pregnant. There were concerns that she would refuse to consent to a Caesarean section. The court found that the Caesarean section would be treatment and that, if necessary, restraint could be used to carry it out. The argument for this was that an ancillary aim of the Caesarean section was to prevent deterioration of the mother's mental health. This extends further the notion of treatment for a mental disorder to treatment designed to deal with physical matters that, if untreated, would worsen the mental condition of the patient.[37]

- In *Reid v Secretary of State*,[38] the House of Lords, considering the similarly worded Scottish mental health legislation, held that 'treatment for the condition' could include treatment that alleviated the symptoms and manifestation of the illness.

- In *R (B) v Ashworth Hospital Authority*,[39] the House of Lords held that it was permissible to provide treatment for any mental disorder from which the individual was suffering, even if it was not the one for which he had been originally detained under the MHA 1983.[40]

- Following *Norfolk and Norwich Healthcare (NHS) Trust v W*,[41] a reasonable degree of force can be used to require a patient to undergo treatment that is permitted under section 63.

- However, in a recent decision, *A NHS Trust v Dr A*,[42] a patient detained under the 1983 Act refused food, in large part as a protest against being deported. It was held that the forced treatment could not be seen as treatment under section 63 because the refusal to eat was not a symptom or manifestation of his condition. Any forced feeding would need to be justified under the MCA 2005 if there were a lack of capacity or (as in the case) under the inherent jurisdiction.

---

[34] (1994) 19 BMLR 144.   [35] [1995] Fam 133.   [36] [1996] 1 FCR 753.
[37] *Mental Health Trust and others v DD (No 2)* [2014] EWCOP 13 now provides detailed guidance on when a Caesarean section operation can be performed under the Mental Health Act 1983.
[38] [1999] 1 All ER 481.   [39] [2005] 2 All ER 289.
[40] See the discussion of this case in Bartlett (2006).
[41] [1996] 2 FLR 613.   [42] [2013] EWHC 2442 (COP).

• In *Nottinghamshire Healthcare NHS Trust v RC*[43] a Jehovah's Witness had a personality disorder, which caused her to self-harm. As a result she needed a blood transfusion. This could be justified under section 63 on the basis that although it was a not
a treatment of the personality disorder, it did treat the symptom or manifestation of
the disorder.

Article 3 ECHR would need to be considered here. It prohibits torture and inhuman and
degrading treatment. It might be thought that imposing treatment on a patient against
his or her wishes would be torture or inhuman or degrading treatment. Certainly, it
could be, but the courts have accepted that medical treatment of a mental condition will
not amount to inhuman or degrading treatment if it is a therapeutic necessity.[44] This
was the line taken by the European Court of Human Rights (ECtHR) in *Herczegfalvy
v Austria*,[45] and has been adopted by the English courts, for example in *R (B) v SS*.[46]
Indeed, it has been suggested that if the state acts in line with medically approved practice, it cannot contravene an individual's Article 3 rights.[47] However, what these human
rights cases emphasize is that if the patient is competent and does not consent to the
treatment, then forcing treatment upon him or her will infringe Article 3 unless it is
'convincingly' demonstrated that the treatment is medically necessary. As Collins J put
it in *R (JB) v Haddock*,[48] 'the more drastic the treatment, the more the doctor must
be satisfied of the need for it'. In *R (N) v M*,[49] the Court of Appeal held the following
factors to be relevant:

> The answer to that question [whether the treatment is justifiable in the light of Article 3]
> will depend on a number of factors, including (a) how certain is it that the patient does
> suffer from a treatable mental disorder, (b) how serious a disorder it is, (c) how serious a
> risk is presented to others, (d) how likely is it that, if the patient does suffer from such a
> disorder, the proposed treatment will alleviate the condition, (e) how much alleviation
> is there likely to be, (f) how likely is it that the treatment will have adverse consequences
> for the patient and (g) how severe may they be?

The Court of Appeal also held that as long as a respectable body of opinion held that the
treatment was necessary, this rendered it compliant with Article 3, even if other doctors
might disagree. Article 8 is also relevant, but it would not be infringed if the medical
treatment were necessary in the patient's best interests or for the protection of others.[50]
Similarly, in *R (B) v Dr SS*,[51] the Court of Appeal found that the detention of a man
suffering from bipolar disorder was justified as necessary for his own and others' protection, and therefore it was permissible to give him treatment without his consent. It was
not necessary to show that the treatment was required for his own or others' protection.
Lord Phillips CJ thought it illogical for it to be compatible with human rights to detain
a person suffering mental ill-health, but then not to be compatible to give him or her the
treatment needed. Because the patient in this case had been legitimately detained under
the 1983 Act, doctors were automatically authorized to provide treatment.[52]

[43] [2014] EWCOP 1317.   [44] *R (B) v Dr SS* [2006] EWCA Civ 28.
[45] Application no. 10533/83 (1993) 15 EHRR 437.   [46] [2005] EWHC 86.
[47] *R (P) v Secretary of State for Justice* [2009] EWCA Civ 701.
[48] [2006] EWCA Civ 961, [13].   [49] [2003] 1 WLR 562, [19].
[50] *R (PS) v G (Responsible Medical Officer)* [2003] EWHC 2335.
[51] [2006] EWCA Civ 28.   [52] See Fennell (2008) and Gurnham (2008) for discussion of the case law.

Where treatment is being given against the wishes of a competent patient, then a second opinion must be obtained from a registered medical practitioner appointed by the Secretary of State—known as a second opinion appointed doctor (SOAD)—who must consult two persons concerned with the patient's treatment who are not themselves doctors.[53] The patient has the option of taking the matter to a court if he or she disagrees with the decision reached by the doctor. As the Court of Appeal noted in *R (JB) v Haddock*,[54] it will be very rare for a judge to disagree with the opinion of the doctors.

The MHA 1983, in section 118, allows the Secretary of State to issue codes of practice governing how patients being detained under the Act should be treated.[55] The legal position of these codes was considered in the following decision.

KEY CASE *R (Munjaz) v Ashworth Hospital Authority* [2005] UKHL 58

Munjaz was being detained under the MHA 1983 in a high-security mental hospital. He had been placed in seclusion for periods of more than four days, which was in breach of the code of practice issued by the Secretary of State for Health. It was argued that the hospital's use of exclusion was unlawful under UK law and breached Articles 3, 5, and 8 ECHR.

Their Lordships divided three to two. The majority held that the code of practice amounted to guidance and not instruction. The code could be departed from, but only with great care and where the hospital had cogent reasons for doing so. Here, the trust, in departing from the code, had taken into account three key issues:

(i) the code had been written with mental hospitals generally in mind and not the special problems facing high-security hospitals;

(ii) the code had not recognized that there were patients for whom exclusion for longer than four days would be appropriate; and

(iii) the code had made it clear that the Secretary of State's code was guidance and that the final decision of the treatment of patients rested with those with practical care for them.

Lord Bingham, writing for the majority, accepted that the practice of the hospital was to use exclusion only as a last resort and where necessary to protect other patients. The hospital's policy included sufficient protections to ensure that a patient secluded for more than seven days would not have his or her Article 3 rights infringed. Munjaz was observed by a nurse every 15 minutes and his condition was regularly reviewed. The policy was an infringement of a patient's Article 8(1) rights, but the infringement was justified under Article 8(2) as necessary to prevent disorder or crime, for the protection of health or morals, or for the protection of the rights and freedoms of others. The policy was sufficiently precise and accessible to mean that the infringement of the Article 8(1) rights was in accordance with the law.

Lord Steyn, dissenting, regarded the code as setting down 'minimum centrally imposed safeguards' for vulnerable patients.[56] For him, the judgment of the majority:

. . . permits a lowering of the protection offered by the law to mentally disordered patients. If that is the law, so be it. How society treats mentally disordered people detained in high

---

[53] MHA 1983, s. 58(3)(b). If the patient wishes to challenge the treatment in court, both doctors can be required to attend: *R (Wilkinson) v Broadmoor Special Hospital* [2002] 1 WLR 419.
[54] [2006] EWCA Civ 961.   [55] DoH (2015b).   [56] At [46].

security hospitals is, however, a measure of how far we have come since the dreadful ways in which such persons were treated in earlier times. For my part, the decision today is a set-back for a modern and just mental health law.[57]

2.4 The Care Quality Commission

The Care Quality Commission's role is to visit hospitals where patients are detained and deal with any complaints that patients have. The Commission also raises issues that have not been specifically mentioned by patients. Its inspections will look generally at conditions in hospitals.[58] Their work was considered in more detail in Chapter 2.

2.5 The regulation of special procedures

The MHA 1983 provides that some kinds of treatment can be provided only if certain special procedures are undertaken. The first are surgical operations that destroy brain tissue or interfere with the brain's function, and hormone implants designed to reduce the male sex drive (section 57(1)). Such treatment can be given only when the patient consents and a second opinion is provided by a panel appointed by the Secretary of State (under section 57(2)). The panel can authorize the treatment only if the doctor on the panel certifies that the treatment should be given. That doctor should consult two people, one a nurse and the other neither a nurse nor a doctor, who have been concerned with the patient's treatment.

The second medical procedure for which there is special statutory regulation is electro-convulsive therapy (ECT), which is governed by sections 58 and 58A. The therapy can be given if either the patient consents or the patient is found to be incompetent. Where a second opinion is relied upon, it must be the opinion of a doctor appointed for the purpose; he or she must certify that the treatment is appropriate, bearing in mind the likelihood that it will alleviate or prevent the deterioration of the patient's condition. The fact that ECT can be given against the wishes of a competent patient is highly controversial, because the benefits and disadvantages of ECT are hotly debated amongst specialists in the field.

Third, psychiatric drugs can be given for three months. After that time, an independent doctor must consider whether the patient should continue to receive them or not (section 58), and reasons for the decision should be provided.[59]

2.6 Discharge under the MHA 1983

Detained patients can be discharged if the responsible medical officer believes that it is no longer necessary to detain the patient. Where appropriate, a community treatment order can be made (at which we will look next).[60]

---

[57] At [48].

[58] See Laing (2015) for concerns over how well it is performing its role.

[59] For all of the treatments covered by ss 57, 58, or 58A, urgent treatment may be authorized under s. 62.

[60] In *AK v Central and North West London Mental Health NHS Trust* [2008] EWHC 1217, it was confirmed that a patient who was improperly released into the community could sue the trust in the tort of negligence or under the HRA 1998.

A patient believing that he or she has been improperly detained can bring an action for *habeas corpus*; if this is established, then the court will order his or her release. The action is appropriate when there was no legal power to detain the patient. It is not appropriate where there was a legal power to detain the patient, but it is claimed that there was an improper exercise of discretion in deciding whether or not to detain the patient. In the latter type of claim, an application for judicial review could be brought.[61]

There is also the option of using informal procedures, which are to be heard by the 'managers' (that is, the non-executive directors, or NEDs) of the National Health Service (NHS) trust. A more formal process is the MHRT. Patients have the right to appeal to a tribunal once for each period of time during which their detention is authorized.

The following decision considers further the effect of being discharged by an MHRT.

KEY CASE   *R (von Brandenburg) v East London and the City Mental Health NHS Trust* **[2004] 2 AC 280**

The appellant had been detained in a hospital under the MHA 1983, section 2. He successfully applied to an MHRT for a review of his decision. The tribunal ordered his discharge within eight days, having concluded that he did not suffer from a mental illness. The eight days was to give time in which a care plan could be prepared. Before the eight days expired and before the appellant had been discharged, he was readmitted under section 3. The ASW argued that the appellant had failed to take his medication and so his mental condition had deteriorated. The appellant challenged his readmission under section 3. The key question for the House of Lords was whether it was lawful to readmit a patient under section 3 when an MHRT had ordered his discharge and there was no relevant change of circumstances.

The House of Lords held that:

> [A]n ASW [approved social worker] may not lawfully apply for the admission of a patient whose discharge has been ordered by the decision of a Mental Health Review Tribunal of which the ASW is aware unless the ASW has formed the reasonable and bona fide opinion that he has information not known to the tribunal which puts a significantly different complexion on the case as compared with that which was before the tribunal.[62]

Where a patient was readmitted, it would be helpful if the medical recommendation in support of that were to identify the new information upon which it was based. There was a limited duty on an ASW to give reasons why there should be readmission. The duty was limited because the disclosure of reasons could be harmful to the patient and so the reasons might have to be given in very general terms.

On the facts, their Lordships thought that the ASW had reasonably and in good faith concluded that there was further evidence that was not available to the tribunal. The readmission was therefore lawful.

---

[61] *R v Hallstrom, ex p W* [1985] 3 All ER 775.   [62] At [10], *per* Lord Bingham.

2.7 Community treatment orders

When a patient is discharged having been detained under the MHA 1983, the clinician can impose a community treatment order under section 17A of the Act.[63] This will mean that the release will be conditional. The order can be made if a clinician and a mental health professional agree that it is appropriate to make an order, and that the following conditions in section 17A(5) are made out:

(a) the patient is suffering from mental disorder of a nature or degree which makes it appropriate for him to receive medical treatment;

(b) it is necessary for his health or safety or for the protection of other persons that he should receive such treatment;

(c) subject to his being liable to be recalled as mentioned in paragraph (d) below, such treatment can be provided without his continuing to be detained in a hospital;

(d) it is necessary that the responsible clinician should be able to exercise the power under section 17E(1) below to recall the patient to hospital;[64] and

(e) appropriate medical treatment is available for him.

The conditions placed on the release must be for the following purposes:

(a) ensuring that the patient receives medical treatment;

(b) preventing risk of harm to the patient's health or safety;

(c) protecting other persons.[65]

The conditions can be suspended or varied by the responsible clinician.[66]

The responsible clinician can recall a patient subject to a community treatment order as set out under section 17E:

(1) The responsible clinician may recall a community patient to hospital if in his opinion—

(a) the patient requires medical treatment in hospital for his mental disorder; and

(b) there would be a risk of harm to the health or safety of the patient or to other persons if the patient were not recalled to hospital for that purpose.

(2) The responsible clinician may also recall a community patient to hospital if the patient fails to comply with a condition specified under section 17B(3) above.

2.8 Guardianship (sections 7–10)

An ASW or nearest relative can apply for guardianship.[67] This lasts for up to six months, but can be renewed. Two doctors must confirm that the patient is suffering from mental illness, severe mental impairment, psychotic disorder, or mental impairment of a degree that warrants guardianship, and that the guardianship is in

---

[63] This provision was added by the MHA 2007.

[64] In considering this factor, s. 17A(6) provides that 'the patient's history of mental disorder and any other relevant factors, what risk there would be of a deterioration of the patient's condition if he were not detained in a hospital' should be taken into account.

[65] MHA 1983, s. 17B(2).   [66] MHA 1983, s. 17B.   [67] Richardson (2002).

the interests of the patient's welfare or for the protection of others. The guardian must be a local social services authority or a person approved by that authority. Under section 8, the guardian can require the patient to live at a particular place, to attend places for the purposes of occupation, training, or medical treatment, or to permit a doctor, social worker, or other person specified by the guardian to see the patient. What a guardian cannot do is force the patient to undergo treatment. Guardianship can be discharged by the resident medical officer (RMO), the local social services authority, or the nearest relative. The patient can also apply to the MHRT for discharge.

3 Informal treatment

As has already been emphasized, if a patient is competent and consents to treatment, then there is no difficulty detaining and treating such a person.[68] However, in *R (H) v Home Office*,[69] it was held that the principle of necessity at common law permitted the detention of a person lacking capacity, provided that force was not required to detain a person. In *HL v UK*,[70] it was held by the ECtHR that this use of necessity was incompatible with the requirements of Article 5 ECHR.

It has been estimated that some 50,000 people in England and Wales were being detained under the principle of necessity in 2003,[71] so the European Court's decision required a change in the law. This was achieved by means of the MHA 2007 inserting a new section 64 into the MHA 1983. This new section deals with patients who are not being formally detained under the Act, but who are not resistant to receiving treatment for mental disorder. The treatment can certainly be given if the patient has capacity and consents. However, if the patient lacks capacity, then treatment can be provided only if the following five conditions in section 64(d) are met:

(1) The first condition is that, before giving the treatment, the person takes reasonable steps to establish whether the patient lacks capacity to consent to the treatment.

(2) The second condition is that, when giving the treatment, he reasonably believes that the patient lacks capacity to consent to it.

(3) The third condition is that—

(a) he has no reason to believe that the patient objects to being given the treatment; or

(b) he does have reason to believe that the patient so objects, but it is not necessary to use force against the patient in order to give the treatment.

(4) The fourth condition is that—

(a) he is the person in charge of the treatment and an approved clinician; or

(b) the treatment is given under the direction of that clinician.

---

68 BMA and Law Society (2004).   69 [2003] UKHL 59.
70 Application 45508/99 [2004] ECHR 471.   71 DoH (2005p).

(5) The fifth condition is that giving the treatment does not conflict with—

    (a) an advance decision which he is satisfied is valid and applicable; or

    (b) a decision made by a donee, deputy or the Court of Protection.

There are points to emphasize about this provision. First, the treatment cannot be given to a non-consenting patient if force is required to give the treatment. If force is required, then an application under section 4 should be made. Second, if the individual has made an advance directive or has appointed a donee under a lasting power of attorney (LPA), then these can, in effect, veto the use of section 64.

4 Codes of practice

The 1983 Act permits the Secretary of State to issue codes of practice on how the law is to operate.

The MHA 1983 Code of Practice produced in 2008 states the following guiding principles:

The five overarching principles are:

Least restrictive option and maximising independence

Where it is possible to treat a patient safely and lawfully without detaining them under the Act, the patient should not be detained. Wherever possible a patient's independence should be encouraged and supported with a focus on promoting recovery wherever possible.

Empowerment and involvement

Patients should be fully involved in decisions about care, support and treatment. The views of families, carers and others, if appropriate, should be fully considered when taking decisions. Where decisions are taken which are contradictory to views expressed, professionals should explain the reasons for this.

Respect and dignity

Patients, their families and carers should be treated with respect and dignity and listened to by professionals.

Purpose and effectiveness

Decisions about care and treatment should be appropriate to the patient, with clear therapeutic aims, promote recovery and should be performed to current national guidelines and/or current, available best practice guidelines.

Efficiency and equity

Providers, commissioners and other relevant organisations should work together to ensure that the quality of commissioning and provision of mental healthcare services are of high quality and are given equal priority to physical health and social care services. All relevant services should work together to facilitate timely, safe and supportive discharge from detention.[72]

---

[72] DoH (2015b: para 1.1).

5 The reforms to the law under the 2007 Act

5.1 Introduction

The journey to reform of the law on mental health has been a long one. In 1998, the government announced that it was going to reform the MHA 1983. In part, this was motivated by a growing acceptance that the current law was not compliant with the requirements of the ECHR. But there was also a perception that the Act was failing to protect the public adequately from 'dangerously ill' people. The resulting White Paper stated that:

> The 1983 Act . . . fails to address the challenge posed by a minority of people with mental disorder who pose a significant risk to others as a result of their disorder. It has failed properly to protect the public, patients, or staff. Severely mentally ill patients have been allowed to lose contact with services once they have been discharged into the community.[73]

One of the difficulties that bedevilled the debate over the reform was the conundrum 'How is it possible to protect the human rights of those with mental illness while adequately protecting the "general public"?' The fact that more than 2,000 comments were received on the government's draft legislation indicates the strength of feeling that the issue raises.

5.2 The key principles

The purpose of the 2007 Act was described as 'to protect patients and others from any harm that can arise from mental disorder'.[74] This, of course, neatly sidesteps the issue of what should happen when there is a conflict between what is the best treatment for the patient and what is most likely to protect the public. Critics, including the Parliamentary Joint Committee, complained that the Bill attached too great a weight to the need to protect the public. The government's response was as follows:

> We consider that the Committee's concerns about the balance of public safety and patient autonomy miss the point that our concern is about the balance between patient and public safety and patient autonomy. The great majority of people with a serious mental disorder are more likely to harm themselves than others, and it is wrong to paint a picture of a government or society obsessed with public safety. The Government's and society's concern is to protect very vulnerable people from harming themselves or, much more occasionally, others. And the concern to ensure that people can get the treatment they need to protect them from harming themselves or others is balanced by a concern to respect patients' rights to make decisions for themselves . . . We must stress that we see no conflict between protection from harm and ensuring that patient rights are fully and appropriately promoted. The Bill does both.[75]

We have already set out the law as it has been amended by the Act. However, some of the main changes that the 2007 Act made can be summarized as follows.

- There is a new definition of 'mental disorder'. The legislation no longer distinguishes between different kinds of mental disorder.

---

[73] DoH (2005d: 1).   [74] DoH (2004h: para. 1.2).   [75] DoH (2005d: 4).

- Section 3 is amended to mean that someone can be detained only if there is 'appropriate medical treatment for them'. Previously, treatment that would improve, alleviate, or prevent deterioration of their condition was required.

- The Act enables the making of codes of practice.[76]

- The Act creates a power to make community treatment orders.

- The Act provides for the Independent Mental Health Advocacy service, which can assist in applications being made to the tribunal.

- The circumstances in which the use of ECT can be used are tightened up.[77]

- The Act gives patients the right to make an application to replace their nearest relative if there are reasonable grounds for doing so.

- The Act gives greater powers to mental health professionals who are not psychiatrists by creating a category of 'approved clinician', who can carry out some of the roles that previously only psychiatrists could do.

The proposals created tensions between some of the professional bodies.[78]

5.3 Criticisms of the 2007 Act

The Bill, during its progress, was subject to a barrage of objections and it is possible here to mention only a few of the main complaints. The further reading provides ample additional material, if more is required.

(i)   There is no 'treatability' test or 'therapeutic benefit' test. Critics complained that the Act would require doctors to become 'jailors' by taking into hospitals individuals who are deemed to be dangerous, but for whom no medical treatment can be offered.[79] As seen earlier in the chapter, the Act does in fact require evidence that the individual can be offered treatment, but critics argued that the definition of 'treatment' is so wide (it includes 'care') that the restriction is meaningless. The Joint Committee warned that, without a 'treatability' test, the Act could be incompatible with the ECHR. However, the decision of the ECtHR in *Hutchison Reid v UK*[80] held that it is permissible under Article 5(1)(e) to detain a mentally disordered person for the purpose of protecting others, even if no treatment is provided.

(ii)   It was thought that the Act could lead to an increase in the use of compulsory powers in the community, through the use of the community treatment order.[81] The concern was that a larger section of the mentally ill community would face compulsory powers than did so under the existing law.[82] Further, the wider use of compulsory powers was considered a challenge to the relationship between patients and professionals, with patients likely to be unwilling to discuss the problems that they are experiencing with their treatment programme. Supporters of compulsory treatment suggested that it would mean that more patients would be able to leave

---

[76] MHA 1983, s. 118.   [77] MHA 1983, s. 58A.
[78] Butcher (2007).   [79] Richardson (2005).   [80] Application no. 50272/99 (2003) 37 EHRR 9.
[81] Moncrieff (2003). The arguments are well rehearsed in Pinfold and Bindman (2001), and Canvin, Bartlett, and Pinfold (2004).
[82] For some evidence that this is occurring, see Mental Health Act Commission (2009).

hospital, albeit under tightly supervised regimes. The government emphasized that there would be no forcible treatment of patients in the community.[83]

(iii) The over-emphasis on risk is a theme that united most critics of the Act: that there was too great an emphasis on risk to the 'public' and too little respect for the human rights of mentally ill people in the law. Notably, the risk to others in the 'relevant criteria' justifying compulsory detention was not required to be 'serious' or 'grave'.

(iv) The absence of provisions addressing problems experienced in getting access to services was also a problem. Some support groups argued that putting more money and effort into improving the quality of mental health services would be a better use of resources than amending the legislation.[84] The government, however, was adamant that it was improving services and would continue to do so. It was not the purpose of the Act to address directly all of the issues surrounding mental health, the government emphasized.

(v) A fundamental question was whether, if a patient is competent, he or she should be able to be treated against his or her wishes. It is, of course, contrary to general medical law principles that a person should be treated against his or her wishes. Does this apply to mentally disordered individuals? Some people believe that it does and that there should be a fundamental principle that, if competent, a person should not be given treatment against his or her wishes. Others believe that a narrow exception should be created in the case of mentally disordered people who pose a serious risk to others—and some would add 'or a risk to themselves'. Even among supporters of an exception to the principle, there was generally agreement that there should be narrowly defined circumstances.[85]

6 Protection from abuse

Much of the debate in relation to mental health is about protecting the public. However, it is important to appreciate that mentally ill people can be subject to abuse and mistreatment. It is notable how the law has been far more ready to protect the 'general public' from the mentally ill than it has been to protect the mentally ill from the 'general public'. The MCA 2005 has enabled orders to be made to protect people lacking capacity from others seeking to take advantage of them. That Act was discussed in Chapter 4.

7 Human rights

It is clear that the courts, in interpreting the MHA 1983 and the common law in cases involving the mentally ill, are paying increasing attention to the ECHR, as they are required to do under the HRA 1998.[86] The ECtHR has suggested that, owing to the vulnerability of mentally ill people and especially those detained in psychiatric hospitals, particular vigilance is required to protect their human rights.[87]

The European Convention contains a number of articles that are relevant to the issue.

---

[83] DoH (2005d: 19).   [84] Rethink (2005).   [85] Richardson (2005).
[86] *R (JB) v Haddock* [2006] EWCA Civ 961. For discussion of the impact of the HRA 1998 on mental health law, see Richardson (2005), Fennell (2005), Davidson (2002), and Gostin (2000).
[87] *Herczegfalvy v Austria* Application no. 10533/83 (1993) 15 EHRR 437.

EUROPEAN ANGLES

Article 5

Article 5 ECHR states that:

> Everyone has the right to liberty and security of person. No one shall be deprived of his liberty save in the following cases and in accordance with a procedure prescribed by law.

But this is subject to a number of exceptions. The relevant one for this chapter is Article 5(1)(e):

> the lawful detention of persons for the prevention of the spreading of infectious diseases, of persons of unsound mind, alcoholics or drug addicts or vagrants.

Winterwerp v The Netherlands[88] set down a number of criteria before the justification in Article 5(1)(e) could be satisfied, as follows.

(i)   The patient must be 'reliably shown' by 'objective medical expertise' to be of 'unsound mind'.[89]

(ii) The disorder must be such as to justify detention.

(iii) The patient can be detained only while he or she is suffering from the disorder.

The European Court has also emphasized that the detention must be proportionate to the mental condition of the individual.[90]

In *Aerts v Belgium*,[91] it was emphasized that the Convention permits the detention of a mentally ill person only for the treatment of that medical condition. If no treatment is available for his or her condition, then Article 5(1)(e) does not justify the person's detention. Detention in a prison in which no treatment was being offered was therefore unlawful. Release is required as soon as the person has recovered from the disorder to an extent such that his or her detention is not justified.[92] Any detention must be subject to regular review to ensure that the detention is still justified.[93]

Article 5(4) imposes important procedural safeguards in relation to detention:

> Everyone who is deprived of his liberty by arrest or detention shall be entitled to take pro-ceedings by which the lawfulness of his detention shall be decided speedily by a court and his release ordered if the detention is not lawful.

Under Article 5(4), there must be an effective and speedy means of challenging the compul-sory admission.[94] This led the Court of Appeal to find that the requirement that an MHRT could release a patient only if it was shown that the criteria for detention were not made out was incompatible with patients' rights under Article 5 ECHR.[95] It should be for the medical author-ities to show that the criteria existed rather than for the patient to show that they did not.[96]

---

[88] Application no. 6301/73 (1979) 2 EHRR 387.

[89] *Stanev v Bulgaria* (2012) 55 EHRR 22. In emergencies, the ECtHR made it clear that detention may be permissible without the evidence being provided.

[90] *Litwa v Poland* Application no. 26629/95 (2000) 63 BMLR 199.

[91] Application no. 25357/94 (1998) 29 EHRR 50.

[92] *Johnson v United Kingdom* Application no. 22520/93 (1999) 27 EHRR 440.

[93] *E v Norway* Application no. 11701/85 (1994) 17 EHRR 30.

[94] *R (on the application of Modaresi) v Secretary of State for Health* [2013] UKSC 53. See *R (C) v Mental Health Review Tribunal* [2002] 1 WLR 176 for a case in which the appeals process infringed an applicant's rights by being too slow.

[95] *R (H) v Mental Health Review Tribunal* [2001] 3 WLR 512; *Hutchison Reid v UK* (2003) 37 EHRR 9.

[96] This is now the law after the Mental Health Act 1983 (Remedial) Order 2001, SI 2001/3712.

Article 5 is also relevant in a case in which the patient's condition no longer justifies his or her detention. In *R v Secretary of State for the Home Department, ex p IH*,[97] the House of Lords confirmed that Article 5 required that if a patient is no longer suffering from a mental disorder, he or she should be released without unreasonable delay. However, their Lordships refused to take a more radical interpretation of Article 5 and require the release of a patient who could, with appropriate support, be released into the community where, despite all reasonable endeavours, that support could not be provided. This applicant took the case to the European Court,[98] where it was held that her mental condition had justified the continued detention. However, the difficulties and delays that she had faced in bringing the issue to a court following the failure before the MHRT (by releasing her conditionally) infringed her rights under Article 5(4).

Article 3

Article 3 ECHR is also relevant in that it prohibits torture or inhuman or degrading treatment. This could be relevant in two ways. First, it might be argued that any form of compulsory treatment is degrading. Given the widespread practice of non-consensual treatment for mental illness across Europe, a court may well hold that treatment is not inhuman or degrading simply by virtue of being non-consensual. Indeed, as we have seen, the courts have accepted that if the treatment is necessary for the therapeutic treatment of an incompetent person, it will not infringe his or her Article 3 rights.[99] However, if the treatment is not necessary for the person's treatment, it could infringe Article 3 if the circumstances in which the compulsory treatment is provided are such that it can be regarded as inhuman and degrading.[100] Unnecessary physical force used against a patient, where the force is not reasonable to give lawful treatment, may also breach Article 3.[101]

Second, it might be argued that not to treat someone suffering from a serious mental condition might infringe their Article 3 rights.[102] In *Keenan v UK*,[103] a suicidal patient who was not given the appropriate care was found to have had his Article 3 rights infringed.

Article 8

Article 8 ECHR, with its right to respect for private and family life, is also potentially relevant in the cases involving mentally disordered individuals. However, Article 8(2) permits an interference with that right if necessary in order, inter alia, to protect health or the interests of others. Forced treatment that does not amount to torture or inhuman or degrading treatment may still be unlawful under Article 8, if not justified under paragraph 2.[104] There is an argument that if the patient is competent and refusing treatment, it should only rarely be found justifiable under paragraph 2.[105] In *R (O'Reilly) v Blenheim Healthcare Ltd*,[106] it was held that passing on confidential information about a mentally disordered patient could infringe that patient's Article 8 rights, although on the facts of that case there was no such disclosure, and even if there had been, it could have been justified under paragraph 2 as necessary to protect the health of the patient and the safety of others.

---

[97] [2003] UKHL 59.   [98] *Kolanis v United Kingdom* [2005] All ER (D) 57.
[99] *R (B) v Dr SS* [2005] EWHC 86.
[100] *R (PS) v G (RMO) and W (SOAD)* [2003] EWHC 2335 (Fam).
[101] *Keenan v UK* Application no. 27229/95 (2001) EHRR 38.
[102] Wicks (2007).   [103] (2001) 33 EHRR 38.
[104] *R (Wilkinson) v Broadmoor Special Hospital* [2001] EWCA Civ 1545.
[105] Richardson (2005).   [106] [2005] EWHC 241.

8 Problems in mental health practice

So far, we have been looking at some of the difficulties in the legal regulation of mental health. It is time to look at some of the problems in the practical operation of mental health services.

8.1 Ethnic minority communities

There are serious concerns about the ethnicity of clients using mental health services.[107] Consider the following points.

- People from ethnic minority groups are up to six times more likely to be detained under the MHA 1983 than white people. However, it seems this is primarily linked to socio-economic disadvantage, rather than ethnicity.

- For men the prevalence of common mental health problems is fairly similar across different ethnic groups, although among women black women had a significantly higher prevalence rate (29.3 per cent for black British women as compared with 20.9 per cent for white British women).

- Poor mental health is particularly acute among refugees, two-thirds of whom have experienced anxiety or depression.[108]

The government has accepted that there are particular needs and issues relating to the use of mental health services by ethnic minorities, and claims to be seeking to address them.[109] One explanation is that we are seeing institutional racism, although Singh and colleagues found no evidence of that in their study.[110] An alternative explanation is that social deprivation and exclusion is linked to mental illness, and higher rates of this are found among ethnic minority communities.[111]

8.2 Sexuality

There have also been concerns about the treatment of gay and lesbian communities within mental health services.[112] Of course, there is historical baggage: it was not too long ago that 'non-orthodox sexuality' was itself regarded as a form of mental illness. Even today, it is claimed that gay, lesbian, and bisexual people can face discrimination when being open with mental health professionals about their sexuality. In one study, 36 per cent of gay men, 42 per cent of lesbians, and 61 per cent of bisexual women claimed to have faced negative or mixed reactions from mental health professionals.[113]

8.3 Sex and mental health

Feminists in particular have been concerned about the position of women within the mental health system.

---

[107] Sainsbury Centre for Mental Health (2005).
[108] All the statistics here are from Mental Health Foundation (2017).
[109] Mental Health Foundation (2017).   [110] Singh, Greenwood, White, et al. (2007).
[111] Mental Health Foundation (2017); Bartlett and Sandland (2007).
[112] Mind (1997); PACE (1998).   [113] Mind/University College London (2003).

FEMINIST PERSPECTIVES

Mental health

There are marked gender differences in mental health. When asked if they have had a diagnosable mental health condition 51.2 per cent of women say they have, as compared with 35.2 per cent of men. When asked if they have been diagnosed by a professional with a mental health condition, a third of women (33.7 per cent) but only a fifth of men (19.5 per cent) say they have.[114]

There have been regular complaints of sexism within the mental health system. The variety of claims made about the system demonstrates the complex interchange of preconceptions of women's behaviour. On the one hand, there are claims that women are too easily labelled as mentally ill.[115] Women are disproportionately represented among those voluntarily detained for psychiatric treatment.[116] There is a preconception that women are mentally fragile and therefore especially prone to mental illness.[117] Further, it is claimed that women whose sexual behaviour is regarded as abnormal are seen as exhibiting mental illness.

On the other hand, there are claims that mental health professionals do not take seriously the mental health problems women face. Unhappiness, self-deprecation, or unfulfilment are regarded by healthcare professionals as normal for women, some critics claim. This last point has led some to suggest that rather than examining more carefully the social and economic factors that cause women to suffer these feelings, the feelings are simply treated with drugs. We are, as one commentator has put it, seeing the 'medicalisation of female unhappiness'.[118] It is certainly true that one study has suggested that women are two-and-a-half times more likely to be treated for depression than men[119]—although whether that reflects the reluctance of men to seek help for mental health issues or the over-willingness of doctors to diagnose depression among women is a matter for debate.

There are certainly some mental conditions that it is possible to regard as a reaction to oppression faced by women within society: anorexia nervosa may be a good example. But some feminist commentators argue that it is dangerous to regard all conditions in this way, because it can inhibit proper research into women's mental health issues. For example, premenstrual tension (PMT) or syndrome (PMS) is little understood. Indeed, patients in hospital suffering manic depression find dramatic improvements in their condition on menstruation.[120]

A final point is that it may be suggested that the concept of mental health is gendered. At present, women are overrepresented as users of the mental health services, but this is because we do not regard violence, alcohol misuse, or child abuse as indicative of a mental illness. If we did so, the gender balance would shift. This raises the whole issue of how we define 'mental illness', a question to which we shall return shortly.

8.4 Shortfalls in provision on the ground

Users of mental health services and their carers or supporters have complained about shortfalls in the provision of mental health services.[121] The complaints were summarized by a former chief executive of the Sainsbury Centre for Mental Health thus:

> It would be surprising if a public service was tolerated when it was feared by its customers (whom it puts at risk), unable to show evidence of its effectiveness and paying its staff

---

[114] Mental Health Foundation (2017).   [115] Mosoff (1995).   [116] Fegan and Fennell (1998: 74).
[117] Goudsmit (1995).   [118] Scambler (2003d: 139).   [119] Scambler (2003d: 140).
[120] Fegan and Fennell (1998: 79).   [121] Dobson (2004).

uncompetitive rates. It would be astonishing if, nevertheless, such a service could not cope with demand. Yet this is a recognizable picture of acute mental health care in the NHS.[122]

A review by the Care Quality Commission paints a bleak view of mental health care.[123] Less than half of those who wanted talking therapies received them. Only 44 per cent of those with physical health problems reported that they were definitely taken care of. Of those questioned, 53 per cent said that they did not have trust and confidence in their psychiatrists, or that they did only sometimes. Of those with special dietary requirements, 18 per cent said that these were not met and 41 per cent said that they were only sometimes met.

A consistent complaint is that individuals with mental health issues, who are in need of assistance in the community, find it difficult to access the help that they need, and it is only when their condition reaches crisis point and they require detention that they receive it.[124] One study found that 28 per cent of those with mental disorders had been 'shunned' when they first sought help.[125] This leads to ever-increasing 'crisis management' costs, and to mental health services with decreasing funds and effort available for the care in the community of the less seriously ill. In other words, too little effort and funding is available for work designed to prevent people having to be taken into hospital for mental illness, and too much on dealing with them when they are there.

8.5 Coercion/consent

As already mentioned, a large number of patients are detained in mental hospitals not under the MHA 1983, but because they are voluntary patients or under the 'necessity' principle. However, there is reason to question whether consent to such detention is genuine. Studies of voluntary patients have shown that many of them are not aware of their status or to what they have consented. Also, 50 per cent were unclear of their legal status (that is, whether they were there voluntarily or whether they had been sectioned);[126] 67 per cent did not know the purpose of the medication that they were taking; and 90 per cent did not know the side effects of their medication. Few questioned realized that they had a choice about whether or not to take their medication.[127] It is perhaps inevitable that a person suffering mental health problems will consent to medical treatment and being admitted to hospital for fear of being 'sectioned' or of not being offered treatment.[128]

A SHOCK TO THE SYSTEM

In May 2011 the BBC television programme *Panorama* detailed abuse at the Winterbourne View private residential hospital of vulnerable adults, all of whom had mental health issues. The undercover report showed staff pinning residents to the floor, residents being forced to shower dressed and then taken outside in cold weather, and residents being slapped and taunted. The abuse was said by one expert to amount to torture. Arrests followed and the home was closed.

---

[122] Matt Muijen, quoted in Rethink (2005: 2).
[123] Care Quality Commission (2009).   [124] King's Fund (2003a).   [125] Rethink (2003).
[126] Bartlett and Sandland (2007).   [127] Billcliff, McCabe, and Brown (2001).
[128] Bonsack and Borgeat (2005).

8.6 **Prisons**

Up to 90 per cent of sentenced prisoners have identifiable mental health problems.[129] Sixty-six per cent of prisoners have a personality disorder, while the prevalence rate in the general population is 5.3 per cent. Forty-five per cent of prisoners have a neurotic disorder, while among the general population the rate is 13.8 per cent.[130] In 2016, there were 199 prison suicides.[131] Inevitably, there are concerns that people who should be receiving treatment for their mental disorders are instead being detained in prison for offences committed because they have not received the treatment that they should have.[132]

8.7 **Care in the community**

There is a concern about the level of support offered to patients in the community. If a patient has been discharged under the MHA 1983, then he or she has an entitlement to aftercare under section 117 of the Act.[133] This requires the health authority in the patient's area to provide him or her with aftercare services until they are no longer required.[134] However, in *R v Islington and Camden Health Authority*,[135] the Court of Appeal accepted that, in meeting that obligation, the authority would be required to consider competing claims on its resources.

Patients requiring support or supervision in the community should be given a care programme. This involves a system for cooperation between health and social services, to ensure that an assessment is made of patients' needs and any risk that they may present. A programme of care should be agreed between the health and social services, and a care coordinator should be appointed to oversee its implementation. The programme should be regularly reviewed. There is evidence, however, that the care programme approach is not working as it should, with patients either not having a plan or not knowing what it was.[136] Bartlett and Sandland, summarizing the reports into violent crimes committed by those being cared for in the community, write that 'the independent reports paint a depressing picture of overstretched, under-resourced and under-staffed community mental health teams, unable to maintain contact with patients who have little wish to cooperate with their "care plan" '.[137]

There has been an increased use of technology to provide support for care of those living in the community.[138] The use of computers, telephones, and 'smart microwaves'[139] can help a person to live effectively in the community. However, there is a concern that this use of technology will reduce the level of face-to-face support that a person with mental health issues may receive.[140]

There is relatively little that can be done to compel a patient in the community to act in a particular way, outside the powers of detention under the MHA 1983. One alternative is guardianship, which was discussed earlier in the chapter.[141]

---

[129] Sainsbury Centre for Mental Health (2009).   [130] Mental Health Foundation (2017).

[131] Mental Health Foundation (2017).

[132] Stephenson (2004); Sainsbury Centre for Mental Health (2007).

[133] The likelihood of a successful tort action if an authority fails to supply services appears remote. See Chapter 2.

[134] *R v Ealing District Health Authority, ex p Fox* [1993] 3 All ER 170.   [135] [2001] EWCA 240.

[136] Rethink (2003).   [137] Bartlett and Sandland (2007: 112).

[138] Perry, Beyer, and Holm (2009).

[139] These can tell from a bar code for how long food should be cooked.

[140] Perry, Beyer, and Holm (2009).   [141] See under the heading '2.8 Guardianship (sections 7–10)'.

9 Critics of mental health

So far, we have been discussing the concept of mental health without really getting to grips with defining it or challenging the very concept of mental health. The concept is, in fact, highly problematic. Society's understanding of mental illness is fluid. Tony Hope refers to a condition diagnosed by Dr Samuel Cartwright in 1851 called 'drapetomania', which was described as the tendency of black slaves to run away from their masters.[142] Until relatively recently, homosexuality was considered a psychological disorder.[143] As these examples show, today's mental illness may be tomorrow's normality.[144]

The definition of a mental disorder has always proved problematic. The American Psychiatric Association's *Diagnostic and Statistical Manual of Mental Disorders* have proved highly influential in professional circles in determining what does not count as a mental disorder. However, whenever a new edition is produced it provokes an outcry at what is included or what is left out. For example, the 2013 included depression resulting from grief, encouraging some to say that normal emotional responses were being included in the definition of a mental disorder. Similarly, for the first time 'premenstrual dysphoric disorder' was included, which some claim is no more than the common impact of menstruation. It is notable that the list of disorders appears to continually grow. Blumenthal-Barby[145] summarizes the concerns with the expansion of mental disorders:

There are at least five consequence-based ethical concerns about the expansion:

(i)   over-diagnosis/false positives in practice; risks and costs associated with pharmacological management of new conditions;

(ii)   medicalisation of phenomena that results in a shift to individual responsibility and neglect of larger structural issues;

(iii) trivialisation of the concept of mental disorder/decrediting of psychiatry; and

(iv)   treatment or eradication of phenomena that are desirable or valuable in some way.

Observations of this kind have led to a school of thought known as 'anti-psychiatry'. Although there are relatively few commentators who accept the extreme tendencies of its leading proponents, their arguments are important because, at the very least, they reveal how the concept of mental illness is contestable. The leading proponent of anti-psychiatry is Thomas Szasz.[146] He argues that psychiatric disorders are not illnesses, but rather a description of behaviour that offends or annoys people.[147] We have an image of how people 'ought' to behave, and if they do not adhere to our image, we label them as suffering from a mental illness.[148] As such, when our understanding of what kinds of behaviour are 'normal' changes, so does our concept of what constitutes mental illness. The example of homosexuality could be used to demonstrate this point. Seen in this way, psychiatry is a means of exercising social control over the 'different' and Szasz has even claimed that psychiatry is analogous to slavery.[149] He firmly rejects claims that mentally ill people are not responsible for their actions. A person does not, he claims,

---

[142] Hope (2005: 75).   [143] Kennedy (1981: ch. 1).   [144] Read, Mosher, and Bentall (2004).
[145] Blumenthal-Barby (2013).   [146] Szasz (1972; 2002; 2008).
[147] Szasz (2008: 3) accepts that there may be diseases of the brain, but these he regards as brain diseases, not mental disorders.
[148] Szasz (1972).   [149] Szasz (2002).

lose all control over every movement when he or she suffers a mental illness.[150] A person who hears voices and acts in response to them chooses to do so, says Szasz, and is therefore responsible for his or her actions.[151] In a moderate tone, Richard Bentall suggests that hallucinations and delusions are exaggerated forms of mental foibles, which we all experience.[152]

A rather different critique of psychiatry is to claim that mental health problems are (or nearly always are) the reaction of normal people to abnormal social pressures or oppressive family institutions.[153] For example, when a women who has suffered years of abuse kills her partner in desperation, some psychiatrists might claim that she suffered from 'battered women's syndrome', whilst others will classify her response as an understandable and reasonable reaction to an extreme situation, and not indicative of mental disorder.[154]

These issues can present problems for those diagnosed with mental conditions. Those who accept that they have a mental illness and are willing to receive treatment are seen as on the road to recovery. Those who dispute their diagnosis and deny any illness are regarded as problematic and in need of further treatment.[155]

Those who disagree with the anti-psychiatrists accept that, in the past, the concept of mental health has been misused, and argue that, while there may be conditions currently regarded as being a manifestation of mental ill-health that will not be so regarded in the future, we should not throw out the baby with the bathwater. There are people who are genuinely suffering and for whom mental health services offer real help, for which they are extremely grateful. To follow Szasz's line and not recognize their illness, leaving them without treatment, would be cruel. Szasz, in reply, would challenge any evidence that psychiatry does anyone any 'good', save by making their behaviour more acceptable by rendering them comatose. Critics of Szasz might accept that there is a danger of conflating 'abnormal behaviour' with 'mentally ill behaviour', but that to some extent this can be overcome by asking if the behaviour is normal for the particular individual. If it is, that might be regarded as indicative of a mental illness.[156] Indeed, one of the messages that must be taken seriously from Szasz's writing is the need to be clear, when a person is being detained under the MHA 1983, as to what the purpose for doing so is: is it to protect the public, to protect the patient's carers, or to protect the interests of the patient?[157]

At the heart of the debate may be the extent to which an individual diagnosed as mentally disordered can exercise autonomy. To Szasz, a person diagnosed as 'mentally ill' is, in fact, responsible and able to take decisions. To opponents, the person is not a fully autonomous agent; his or her 'manifestations' of intent do not reflect his or her 'true wishes'.[158] After all, if we accept that there is such a thing as the mind, must we not accept that the mind can become ill?[159]

If we accept that there is a concept of mental illness, there then comes the difficulty of defining and classifying it. Many now take the view that mental health is better regarded as a spectrum rather than two separate boxes. We are all more or less sane or insane,

---

[150] Szasz (2001). See the reply in Brassington (2002).
[151] Szasz (2001). Indeed, he suggests that the voices may be an expression of the person's true desires, which he or she does not want to accept.
[152] Bentall (2004).   [153] Laing (1959).   [154] Kaganas (2003).
[155] See discussion in Cavadino (1989: 30).   [156] Adshead (2003).   [157] McMillan (2003a).
[158] See McMillan (2003a); Sayers (2003).   [159] Brassington (2002).

depending on how you would rather see it. Certainly, it is difficult, if not impossible, to draw a sharp line between sanity and insanity.[160] Most definitions are based on the disturbance of mental functioning, which could involve disruption of thought processes, emotions, or motivations.[161] There is also a debate over whether it is possible to draw a sharp line between physical illness and mental illness. This becomes particularly relevant when the law seeks to prevent disability discrimination. In the medical profession, there tends to be a clear line between psychiatrists, who deal with mental illness, and physicians, who deal with physical illness. However, increasingly, the interaction of bodily and mental health indicates that the line is difficult to draw.

10 Dangerousness

As has been indicated, a key issue in the current law and debate over reform is over the 'dangerousness' of the mentally ill. This focus has been criticized by those who see a shift in government policy from a culture of welfare to a culture of control.[162]

10.1 Are the mentally ill dangerous?

The media sometimes portray the mentally disordered as a violent and dangerous group who could attack at any time. But, in fact, the majority of those with psychiatric problems are not dangerous.[163] When there is an attack by a mentally ill person, the media gives the case extensive coverage. This is not to belittle the occasions on which that occurs, but the danger must be put in perspective. As Eldergill states: 'People are more likely to win the National Lottery jackpot than they are to die at the hand of a stranger with a mental illness.'[164] He goes on to point out that 'people suffering from schizophrenia are one hundred times more likely to kill themselves than someone else, and those with a mood disorder are one thousand times more likely'.[165]

Indeed, there is evidence that people suffering from mental disorder are far more likely to be the victims of violence themselves than is an average member of the public.[166] Despite this, the government has pointed out that, of the 500 or so homicides each year, around 15 per cent are committed by those with a mental illness.[167] However, it should not be forgotten that the strongest link to homicides is not mental illness, but alcohol or drug misuse.[168]

10.2 Can we predict dangerousness?

The prediction of dangerousness is problematic.[169] For example, in one research survey, in only four out of sixteen research projects were 60 per cent or more of psychiatrists able to agree on whether an individual was dangerous.[170] Of the many attempts that have been made to develop an accurate way of assessing dangerousness, probably the most successful has been the MacArthur Violence Risk Assessment study, which used

---

[160] Kornll (2003).   [161] Kornll (2003).   [162] Farnham and James (2001).
[163] Hewitt (2008); Bowden (1996).   [164] Eldergill (2003: 333).
[165] Eldergill (2003: 333).   [166] Walsh, Moran, Scott, et al. (2003).
[167] DoH (2005p: para. 14).   [168] Shaw, Amos, Hunt, et al. (2004).
[169] Munro and Rumgay (2000).   [170] Montadon and Harding (1984).

106 variables to assess dangerousness.[171] Looking at 939 people, the researchers divided them into five risk bands, ranging from the most likely to be violent to the least. In the band of those labelled most likely to be violent, just over three-quarters were indeed violent. This is a significantly better outcome than most other studies. However, if all those in the highest risk band were detained, that would mean that nearly one in four of those detained would not, in fact, have been dangerous if not detained. Further, if only those in the higher band were detained, only 27 per cent of those in the sample who were violent would have been detained. To halve the number of violent incidents, it would be necessary to include the top two bands, which would mean that 36 per cent of those detained would not have been violent.[172] In another review, it has been suggested that twenty patients would need to be detained to prevent a single act of violence.[173]

10.3 If we can predict dangerousness, does it justify detention?

On the assumption that it is possible to identify a mentally ill individual as dangerous, does this justify detaining him or her? To some, it does: the state has an obligation to protect its citizens from death.[174] Indeed, this might be regarded as one of the primary duties of the state and as required under Article 2 ECHR. Any interference in the rights of the person detained is justified because the state is acting to protect the even greater rights of citizens not to suffer death or serious injury.

Opponents argue that we do not normally detain people who are not mentally ill, even if they have been classified as dangerous. Having a propensity to commit a crime is very different from committing it.[175] Until a person has committed a criminal act, predictions as to dangerousness do not normally justify detention. Why should we regard the mentally ill in any way differently from those with no mental disorder? To do so would be discriminatory.[176]

Supporters of preventative detention of the mentally ill could reply to such an argument in various ways. They may argue that we should detain all people predicted to be dangerous, whether they are mentally ill or not. They may alternatively seek to justify the discrimination by arguing, for example, that because the behaviour of mentally ill people is more difficult to predict, such people are more dangerous or that mentally ill people can be cured, and that this provides a distinction. However, there is little evidence to suggest that dangerous mentally ill people are any more unpredictable or curable than non-mentally ill dangerous people.

The argument in favour of detention based on the prevention of harm and saving lives could also justify the outlawing of the use of cars and the drinking of alcohol. Both of these measures would, no doubt, save far more lives than preventative detention, yet most people would baulk at these suggestions.[177] But is that because we are happy to see interference in the rights of 'them' (the mentally disabled), but not to see an interference in 'our' own rights? It has been estimated that approximately 10 per cent of people

---

[171] Monahan (2001). Bartlett (2003a) suggests that the test is too complex to use in a clinical setting.

[172] This summary is taken from Bartlett (2003a).

[173] Buchanan (2008).   [174] The government emphasized this in DoH (2005p: para. 14).

[175] Szasz (2003).

[176] Sjöstrand and Helgesson (2008); Hope (2004: 80); The Richardson Committee (1999).

[177] White (2002).

with a mental disorder show an increased risk of violence.[178] To put that in context, in a US study, it was found that 16 per cent of men aged 18–24 from low socio-economic classes were violent—a far higher percentage than those found suffering from mental disorder.[179] Arguably, then, a stronger case for preventative detention might be put up for locking up all poor young men, rather than those with mental illnesses. Would that be acceptable?

There is another issue here. If the dangerously mentally ill are to be detained for the purpose of prevention, then where, how, and by whom? Doctors are unlikely to be willing simply to oversee people who are not being detained for treatment, but prevention,[180] but non-medically qualified 'guards' may lack the experience and skills to care for those detained. Bartlett argues that hospitals are willing to care for the physically disabled even when nothing can be done for them and that the same attitude could be taken towards the mentally ill who have to be detained.[181]

11 Paternalism as the ground for detention?

If we do not accept dangerousness as a ground for detention on its own, what alternative justifications could there be? One is paternalism. We could simply say that treatment for mental illness is justified because that is best for the patient. This would especially be so where an effective treatment would be available.[182] However, this is generally regarded as a justification in cases in which the patient is incompetent; where the patient is competent and refuses treatment, it is not. We do not allow treatment for physical conditions to be given to competent patients on the basis of paternalism, so why should it be any different if the illness is mental?

One approach that has support in academic circles is that the test of treatment and detention should be based on capacity alone.[183] Compulsory treatment and detention is permissible under civil law only if the patient is competent and consents to treatment. If he or she is incompetent, then treatment and detention can be given if that is in the patient's best interests. To treat mentally ill competent people differently from non-mentally ill competent people is to discriminate on the grounds of mental illness. Bartlett emphasizes the wrong that is done to a competent person who receives mental health treatment against his or her wishes in this way:

> The violation of autonomy consequent on enforced treatment of a person with capacity is considerable. The introduction of psychiatric medication into an individual's body results in fundamental and substantial changes to the person's self. These changes are, of course, the objective of the treatment, and have social benefits. Many patients will also willingly consent to them, as they are perceived to have benefits to them too. That in no way alters the extraordinary nature of the intervention, however, and it is difficult to see that it should be provided to a patient with capacity who refuses it.[184]

[178] Walsh and Fahy (2002).   [179] Hawkins, Herrenkohl, Farrington, et al. (2000).
[180] Bartlett (2003); White (2002).   [181] Bartlett (2003).   [182] Stone (1975).
[183] See, e.g., Bellhouse, Holland, Clare, et al. (2003), Buchanan (2002), and Gunn (2000).
[184] Bartlett (2003: 142).

There is much to be said for this view. There are, however, problems.[185] The first is that it might be said to be politically unacceptable. It would, in theory, require a doctor to release into the community a dangerous, but competent, individual. Politicians would find it difficult to defend this before the general public.

The second and linked point has been already alluded to, and that is that the definition of 'capacity' is vague. It would arguably be inevitable that a person regarded as dangerous by a professional would be 'deemed' incompetent rather than be released. If this is so, the argument goes, we should adopt dangerousness as an open factor, with clear guidance as to how it should be assessed and the level of dangerousness required.

The third danger of the capacity approach is that the hurdle for capacity is set high so that only clearly rational people meet it. But that would restrict the rights of many who, at present, might be regarded as competent. Set the hurdle too low and it would mean that too many people who would be generally regarded as suitable for treatment would not receive it.[186]

A fourth argument may be that intervention may be justified in the name of autonomy. Craigie has argued that:

> When human agency is seriously compromised, preserving patient autonomy may sometimes require overriding a treatment decision to restore selfhood, on grounds that are not easily accounted for under the MCA without compromising the value-neutral aspirations of this area of law.[187]

A final point has been made by Peter Bartlett.[188] Many supporters of the capacity approach accept that, once a person has committed a criminal act, this justifies preventative detention; Bartlett argues that whether someone has committed a crime is a red herring. The crime may tell us nothing about the person's dangerousness and non-criminal acts may be far more indicative of dangerousness than criminal ones. There may be an argument that, having committed an offence, the person, to some extent, forfeits rights to liberty—but that would need some careful debate.

12 Conclusion

As this chapter demonstrates, there is difficulty in striking the correct balance between protecting the public from the perceived threat of mentally disordered people and protecting the rights of those who suffer mental illness. The debate over that balance has, however, meant that other issues have too easily been overlooked: abuse and violence in psychiatric in-patient facilities; the under-resourcing of community care; the lack of protection of mentally disordered people from abuse of various kinds; and the absence of an effective legal recognition of the position of those who care for the mentally ill.

---

[185] See also Prinsen and van Delden (2009).   [186] Bartlett (2003: 337 et seq.).
[187] Craigie (2013: 5).   [188] Bartlett (2003).

QUESTIONS

1. C. S. Lewis wrote:

    > To be cured against one's will and cured of states which we may not regard as disease is to be put on a level with those who have not yet reached the age of reason or those who never will; to be classed with infants, imbeciles and domestic animals.[189]

    Is it ever justifiable to treat a competent person for a mental disorder without his or her consent?

2. In early 2005, media attention focused on the case of a man weighing 33 stone, who suffered from Prader-Willi syndrome, an inherited condition that leads to over-eating.[190] He was detained for assessment by social services under the MHA 1983. It appeared that the major concern of the social services was that the patient's condition was not improving and that he had lost control over his eating. Was this a misuse of the Act? How would the press have reacted if the individual had died?

3. Often, the argument is made that we need to protect the general public from the mentally ill. Are not the mentally ill themselves members of the general public?

4. Are muttering to oneself and not responding to questions signs of a mental disorder? When does behaviour cease to be 'eccentric' and become the symptoms of an illness?

5. One mental health services user wrote that her medication delivered a 'nothingness which was dull and sweet'.[191] Is that a cure? Have we too easily forgotten the power of the drug industry?

FURTHER READING

A comprehensive bibliography, including all references used throughout the book, is available online at www.oup.com/uk/herringmedical7e/.

For useful general discussion on mental health law and policy, see:

Bartlett, P. (2012) 'The United Nations Convention on the Rights of Persons with Disabilities and mental health law', *Modern Law Review* 75: 724.

Bartlett, P. and Sandland, R. (2007) *Mental Health Law* (Oxford University Press).

Craigie, J. (2013) 'Capacity, value neutrality and the ability to consider the future', *International Journal of Law in Context* 9: 4.

Glover-Thomas, N. (2003) *Reconstructing Mental Health Laws and Policy* (Butterworths).

Large, M., Ryan, C., Nielssen, O., et al. (2008) 'The danger of dangerousness: why we must remove the dangerousness criterion from our mental health acts', *Journal of Medical Ethics* 34: 877.

---

[189] C. S. Lewis (1953: 228).   [190] Prader-Willi Syndrome Association (2005).
[191] Cardinal (1996: 108).

Laurance, J. (2003) *Pure Madness* (Routledge).

Peay, J. (2003) *Decisions and Dilemmas* (Hart).

Prinsen, E. and van Delden, J. (2009) 'Can we justify eliminating coercive measures in psychiatry?', *Journal of Medical Ethics* 35: 69.

Richardson, G. (1999) *Richardson Committee: Review of the Mental Health Act 1983* (DoH).

Richardson, G. (2002) 'Autonomy, guardianship and mental disorder: one problem, two solutions', *Modern Law Review* 65: 702.

Rogers, A. and Pilgrim, D. (2001) *Mental Health Policy in Britain: A Critical Introduction* (Palgrave).

Yates, V. (2007) 'Ambivalence, contradiction, and symbiosis: carers' and mental health users' rights', *Law and Policy* 29: 435.

For discussion of reforms to the law, see:

Dale, E. (2010) 'Is supervised community treatment ethically justifiable?', *Journal of Medical Ethics* 26: 271.

Fennell, P. (2005) 'Convention compliance, public safety, and the social inclusion of mentally disordered people', *Journal of Law and Society* 32: 90.

Fennell, P. (2008) 'Best interests and treatment for mental disorder', *Health Care Analysis* 16: 255.

Gurnham, D. (2008) ' "Reader, I detained him under the Mental Health Act" : a literary response to Professor Fennell's best interests and treatment for mental disorder', *Health Care Analysis* 16: 268.

McSherry, B. and Weller, P. (eds) (2010) *Rethinking Rights-Based Mental Health Laws* (Hart).

Richardson, G. (2002) ' "Autonomy, guardianship and mental disorder" : one problem, two solutions', *Modern Law Review* 65: 702.

Szmukler, G., Daw, R. and Dawson, J. (2010) 'A model law fusing incapacity and mental health legislation', *Journal of Mental Health Law* 11: 12.

On anti-psychiatry, see:

Adshead, G. (2003) 'Commentary on Szasz', *Journal of Medical Ethics* 29: 230.

Bentall, R. (2004) *Madness Explained* (Penguin).

Double, D. (2006) *Critical Psychiatry* (Palgrave).

Szasz, T. (2001) 'Mental illness: psychiatry's phlogiston', *Journal of Medical Ethics* 27: 297.

Szasz, T. (2002) *Liberation by Oppression: A Comparative Study of Slavery and Psychiatry* (Transaction).

Szasz, T. (2005) ' "Idiots, infants, and the insane" : mental illness and legal incompetence', *Journal of Medical Ethics* 31: 78.

Note on the Bibliography

A comprehensive bibliography, including all references used throughout the book, is now available free online. Readers can quickly and easily locate specific references by using the online, alphabetized bibliography.

In addition to this, all references are available in full in the footnotes throughout the text.

Go to www.oup.com/uk/herringmedical7e/

Index

Note: Because the entire work is about 'medical law and ethics' the use of these terms (and certain others which occur constantly throughout the book) as an entry point has been minimized. Information will be found under the corresponding detailed topics. References such as '178–80' indicate (not necessarily continuous) discussion of a topic across a range of pages.